P9-AQJ-969

DISCARDED

CROATIA
Land, People, Culture

Ivan Meštrović (Painting by Gustav Likan, 1961).

CROATIA

Land, People, Culture

VOLUME I

FRANCIS H. ETEROVICH
Editor
DE PAUL UNIVERSITY

CHRISTOPHER SPALATIN
Associate Editor
MARQUETTE UNIVERSITY

Foreword by Ivan Meštrović

Published for the Editorial Board by
UNIVERSITY OF TORONTO PRESS

In memory of
IVAN MEŠTROVIĆ,
sculptor and patriot, who
embodied the Croatian genius

Foreword

The publication of a reference book in English about Croatia and the Croatians is long overdue. The Croatians, although eager to learn about others, have, to a large extent, failed to acquaint the rest of the world with themselves and their culture. Much of the information about Croatia and the Croatians that appears in current foreign publications is unfortunately misleading or inaccurate. Therefore, when I was presented with the broad outline of the aims and content of the present work, I was eager to comply with the editors' request that I write a foreword to it.

Many readers, I fear, have not even heard of the Croatian nation. This can be partially explained by the fact that for centuries Croatia has not appeared on the world map as an internationally recognized independent unit. Those who have read extensively about the history of Europe are doubtless acquainted with the brave conduct of the Croatian soldiers in the armies of the Turkish and the Austrian Empires, but probably very few are familiar with Croatia's political and cultural history. Yet the history of the Croatians—not only as a people, but as a nation possessing its own parliament, one without whose consent no decisions affecting Croatia's fate could be made either in peace or in war—extends back at least to the ninth century. The nucleus of Croatia's statehood has never ceased to exist, and the consciousness of her national individuality has never been dimmed, no matter how mutilated her territory or how infringed upon her sovereignty.

How could this relatively small nation, geographically so vulnerable, from time immemorial the crossroads and battleground of imperialism both ideological and political, survive and preserve its national individuality? What has saved her from assimilation or obliteration by the numerically and culturally superior Latins and Germans from the

West and the overwhelming military power of the Ottoman Empire from the East? In this reference work, the answer becomes clear: Croatian religious, ethical, and cultural ideals have inspired the people with the courage to fight and even to die rather than give up their freedom and self-government.

A few observations, the fruit of my own meditation and reflection on the history and character of my people, are not amiss here. Recently a new theory has been advanced concerning the possible Iranian origin of the Croatians; be this as it may, it is certain that the Croatians first appeared on the European stage as a branch of the large Slavic family. When, in the seventh century, this particular group of Slavs left its homeland—somewhere north of the Carpathian Mountains—and finally settled in what is now Croatia, it found itself among peoples of mixed origin and diverse ethnic make-up: native Illyrians, scattered Celtic tribes, remnants of the earlier Roman population, and Greek colonists on some of the islands and part of the Adriatic coast. The Croatians imposed their language on these groups and through inter-marriage to a certain extent altered their own physical characteristics. Out of this amalgamation there emerged what is today known as the Croatian people.

It would seem that the Illyrian was the strongest influence on the Croatians, perhaps accounting for the martial spirit that they have always exhibited in their resistance to aggressors. This trait, combined with the Slavic inclination to cultivate the soil, became, down through time, the most typical characteristic of the Croatian personality. From the Greeks they probably derived their love for the sea and their appreciation of beauty. To the Celts might be attributed the more imaginative tendencies manifested by the Croatians.

Not long after the Croatians had settled in their new land, they organized their own state and freed themselves almost completely from the overlordship of Byzantium. Croatia's conversion to Christianity under the auspices of the Roman Catholic Church drew her into the orbit of Western civilization and enabled her to make rapid cultural strides and join the ranks of the other civilized nations of the Mediterranean basin. Gradually, in the course of centuries, the Croatians also formed close political and cultural ties with the Germans. Thus the Croatian mentality and cultural traits are basically Western.

The fact that they were beneficiaries of the Greek and Latin cultural heritage did not, however, mean that the Croatians lost their distinctive mental characteristics and creative genius. They have stubbornly

—almost instinctively—maintained and defended their national consciousness and their national ego. Catholicism did not transform the majority of the Croatians into Latins, as Islam did not make the minority Turks. Both Moslem and Catholic Croatians have looked upon their coreligionists as their brethren and have lived up to the high religious ideals that they hold in common. They have done so, however, under the condition that their national characteristics not be taken from them. Ever since their conversion to Christianity, the Croatians have insisted upon—and have obtained from the Holy See—the unique privilege of using Church Slavonic and their own Croatian language in the liturgy. A similar tenacity with regard to language was exhibited by those Croatians who, mainly because of the onslaught from the East, embraced Islam. In spite of Turkish domination, the Bosnian Croatians have maintained their Croatian language not only in their homes but also in the administration of their province, and to some extent in their literature. The authorities in Constantinople had to use the Croatian language to communicate with them; and when a number of Bosnian Croatians became important functionaries of the Ottoman Empire, they saw to it that the Croatian language was made a diplomatic language. The vigilance and determination which the Croatians have shown in retaining their language is typical of their unceasing struggle for the survival of their nation.

Despite their valor and military prowess, the Croatians have never been conquerors; they have never made claim to foreign territories. "Defend what is yours, and keep away from what belongs to others" is one of their mottoes. They do not consider fighting and warmongering to be their mission. Rather, throughout the centuries, many of their best citizens have devoted their talents to creative and artistic pursuits. It is significant that even the military leaders whom Croatia contributed so abundantly to both the Austrian and Ottoman Empires devoted their rare moments of leisure to study and to literary work. When almost all of Croatia was either subjugated by the Turks or under Venetian rule, the small free republic of Dubrovnik produced a veritable phalanx of outstanding poets. So also did several cities of Dalmatian Croatia which were not occupied by a foreign power. Thus, while two-thirds of the country was either under foreign yoke or defending itself against aggressors, one-third—Dalmatian Croatia—was producing eminent writers and humanists, building magnificent churches, and otherwise keeping pace with the other civilized nations. In those difficult times, a considerable number of Croatians, notably many priests, took refuge in Italy, where quite a few of them gained international fame as painters, sculptors, scientists, scholars, and churchmen.

Even when unceasing wars decimated the Croatian nation and reduced its inhabitants to illiterate peasants, the creative spirit of the people was kept alive. The peasants carried on the Croatian artistic tradition, and from the villages there poured forth poetry, heroic ballads, and lyric songs, many of them containing hundreds of verses. The peasants chanted and recited these verses at every gathering, keeping the spirit of the nation alive and the cultural thread unbroken. When, in the eighteenth century, this poetry came to the attention of Western poets and scholars, they were amazed at its richness and its fine artistic quality. To this same category of popular creativeness belong the colourful embroideries and the numerous sarcophagi and tombstones scattered throughout Bosnian Croatia. The tombs of the Bosnian noblemen and commoners who had embraced first Manicheism and later Islam are the most distinctive and original artistic creations of Croatia in the late Middle Ages.

The Croatians are a deeply religious people: Christian or Moslem, the Croatian takes his faith seriously. Religion forms the basis of his personality, and he cherishes it as a gift. There is no doubt that this deeply-anchored religious faith has been the source of the strength and spiritual inspiration which has enabled the Croatian people to survive individually and as a nation throughout centuries of struggle. The ethical motivation of the Croatians' long and bitter struggle has been the yearning to enjoy freedom in their homes and homeland. As a man's consciousness of himself as a person and as a part of a nation increases, so too does his striving for freedom. This striving becomes a prime need for him, as necessary as breathing. Only when this natural need has been satisfied can he, as an individual and a member of a nation, live a full human life, cooperating voluntarily with others and participating in the larger human community. Stated simply, the aim of the Croatian struggle for freedom is this: the Croatians desire the opportunity to express themselves freely and fully in every phase of human endeavor. They are strengthened in their desire by the conviction that their cause is just. A sense of justice and fair play has always animated and motivated the conduct of the Croatians, both individually and collectively. They have always been ready to suffer and even to die for justice. Their neighbors have often called them—sometimes sneeringly—the nation which never stops speaking of justice. Yet the Croatians refuse to embrace the philosophy that "might makes right" and they are convinced that justice, which can be effected only through understanding, is a basic law that governs all human relationships, whether between individuals or nations. They believe that justice and right are the means by which lasting peace and happiness for all men will be brought about.

It is the hope of all who have contributed to this book that it might help make Croatia and her people better known and understood in the light of truth and justice. May it find a sympathetic reception and fulfill its purpose of acquainting the reader with the historical background and cultural values of the Croatians, a people that has always been and ever wishes to remain a respected and worthy member of the great family of free nations.

IVAN MEŠTROVIĆ

South Bend, Indiana
1960

Editors' Note

The distinguished sculptor and author, Ivan Meštrović, died on January 16, 1962, before the completion of this volume. To the very last day of his life, he strove tirelessly after the fulfillment of the goals which he has set forth in the Foreword. It is our wish that these studies be presented to the public in his honor and memory.

FHE, *Editor*
CS, *Associate Editor*

Acknowledgments

THE PREPARATION of this volume required a great amount of effort on the part of many persons. It is not possible to list all of those who have contributed in one way or another to the completion of this volume, but the editors wish to express their gratitude to all of them.

For their valuable advice and assistance, the editors would especially like to thank the following: Clement S. Mihanovich, St. Louis University; D. A. Tomasic, Indiana University; Ante Kadić, Indiana University; Thomas F. Magner, Pennsylvania State University; Francis Dvornik, Harvard University; Dominik Mandić, Croatian Historical Institute (Chicago); Joseph Strmecki, University of Wisconsin; Kamil Avdić, John Crerar Library (Chicago); Michael Milkovich, Corning Museum of Glass (Corning, N.Y.); Joseph Batinica, Morgan State College; Pavao Tijan, Consejo Superior de Investigaciones Cientificas (Madrid); Ivo Vitezić, University of Vienna; Atanazije Matanić, University Antonianum (Rome); and Aleksandar Perc, Cologne.

The editors would also like to express their gratitude to the administrations of the Widener Library, Harvard University, and of the Harper Library, University of Chicago, for their kind cooperation, and to Professor Roman Smal-Stocki, Director of the Slavic Institute of Marquette University, for his advice and encouragement.

For permission to use illustrations, the editors are indebted to Ljubo Karaman (*Živa Starina*), H. Aschehoug and Company (*History of Salonitan Christianity*, by Ejnar Dyggve), and Elek Books Limited (*Yugoslav Life and Landscape*, by Alec Brown).

Contents

Illustrations

woman embroidering on a horizontal loom; enameled box for religious books; leader of the heroic game *alka*; eggs with various designs; lace from various regions.

Croatian authors: Stanko Vraz (1810–51); Petar Preradović (1818–72); Ante Tresić-Pavičić (1867–1949); Eugenij Kumičić (1850–1904).

Between pages 280 and 281

Croatian authors: Ante Kovačić (1854–89); Josip Kosarac (1858–1906); Silvije Strahimir Kranjčević (1865–1908); August Harambašić (1861–1911); Ljudevit Gaj (1809–1911); Ivan Mažuranić (1814–90); August Šenoa (1838–81); Luka Botić (1830–63); Franjo Marković (1845–1914); Vjenceslav Novak (1859–1905); Ksaver Šandor Gjalski (1854–1935); Janko Leskovar (1861–1949).

Croatian National Theater, Zagreb.

Vatroslav Lisinski (1819–54), composer of the first Croatian opera. Zinka Milanov (1906–), renowned Metropolitan Opera soprano. Gazi Husref bey Mosque (sixteenth century), Sarajevo. Zagreb Cathedral (thirteenth century). Cloister of the Franciscan Monastery, Dubrovnik (fourteenth century). Cloister of the Dominican Monastery, Dubrovnik (fifteenth century).

Between pages 312 and 313

The Cathedral in Šibenik (fifteenth century). Portal of the Cathedral of Trogir, sculpted by Radovan.

Ivan Meštrović, "Pietà"; "Croatian History." Jozo Kljaković, "The Oath of King Zvonimir." Maksimiljan Vanka, "Croatian Death in Pennsylvania."

Maps

Facing page

Introduction

With great satisfaction we note a considerable increase of activity in the field of Slavic Studies in North America today. The traditionally small group of students dedicated to Slavic Studies is currently being augmented by an ever-growing number of young and enthusiastic scholars. Although political and military grounds have played a major role in motivating this increased interest, the world at large will no doubt profit from the scholarly research into the extremely varied Slavic culture that is under way. If we in North America are to contribute to the fullest extent to the preservation and spread of liberty and peace in the world, it is essential that we come to know and understand the Slavic nations.

Yugoslavia is perhaps better known in the English-speaking world than any other Slavic nation, with the exception of Russia. It is true that the literature about Yugoslavia that has so far appeared in North America has been of a predominantly political and economic nature, concerned, for practical reasons of the moment, almost exclusively with events and circumstances in that country since World War II. The Communist experiment in Yugoslavia and the variations on it carried out by Tito after his official split with Moscow in 1948 are completely new trends in the history of the peoples of Yugoslavia; now more than ever before there exists the danger of a partial or distorted understanding of the history and culture of the country. An unbalanced and incomplete picture results when Yugoslavia is studied exclusively in the light of post-war political and economic data. We believe it essential that any thorough study of Yugoslavia must take into consideration the past cultural life of that country's many component parts. Political regimes come and go, but the culture of the people is passed on from one generation to the next, for it has its roots deep in the past and in the mind and heart of the people. There can be no real understanding of life and culture in modern Yugoslavia until this aspect has been duly considered.

Politically, Yugoslavia consists of a federation of six people's republics: Serbia, Croatia, Bosnia-Hercegovina, Slovenia, Montenegro, Macedonia, and two autonomous provinces ruled by the republic of Serbia, Vojvodina and Kosmet (this last term is an abbreviation for the names of the regions Kosovo and Metohija). From the standpoint of nationality, Yugoslavia is not a homogeneous unit. Five main nationalities are found in the country: the Macedonians, Montenegrins, Slovenes, Croatians, and Serbs. These five nationalities speak four main languages: Slovenian, Macedonian, Serbian, and Croatian. The latter two languages are regarded by many scholars today as linguistically identical, with considerable differences in syntax and vocabulary.

There are three principal religions in Yugoslavia: the Eastern Orthodox religion, by and large the religion of the Serbs, Macedonians, and Montenegrins; the Roman Catholic, the religion of the majority of Croatians and Slovenes; and the Moslem, the religion of a high percentage of the Bosnian and Hercegovinian population of Croatian stock. Following these religious divisions, there are four clearly recognizable cultures in Yugoslavia: the Byzantine in Serbia, Macedonia, and Montenegro; the Moslem (Turkish, Arabic, Persian) in Bosnia and Hercegovina; the German and Austrian in northern Croatia; and the Roman and Venetian in Istria, Croatian Littoral, and Dalmatia. All of these influences have, however, blended into the particular and distinct cultures of the five nationalities already mentioned, cultures whose origins are over two thousand years old. Finally, it should be added that there are in Yugoslavia today at least a dozen national minorities, most of them with their own particular language, religion, and cultural outlook. Albanians, Magyars, and Turks are but three important examples of these minorities.

The fact that many nationalities have been brought together to form one political unit adds to the difficulties facing one who wishes to arrive at an understanding of these peoples, of their cultures, histories, folklore, and languages. One can easily be misled by over-simplification—the only sure way toward a fuller grasp of the real cultural life, and consequently of the political, economic, and military life of the peoples in Yugoslavia is to study the constituent parts of this nation, so that a comprehensive, over-all view of the Yugoslav mosaic of cultures may eventually be obtained.

The overwhelming majority of Croatians live in two of the six people's republics, Croatia and Bosnia-Hercegovina. Croatian ethnic borders spread, however, far beyond these two republics. Croatians live in Vojvodina—more specifically in Bačka and Srijem, administered by the republic of Serbia—and in Kosmet, also incorporated in the republic of Serbia. There are Croatians in the parts of Medjimurje which are now incorporated in the republic of Slovenia, and still others live in the region of the Bay of Boka Kotorska, as well as in several towns located southeast of the bay, toward the Albanian border on the Adriatic coast. The section of the coast and the Bay of Boka Kotorska are now part of the republic of Montenegro. Smaller settlements of Croatians are found in neighboring countries, such as Hungary, Austria, and Italy, as well as in other European lands, and in the Near East, North Africa, South Africa, Australia, and New Zealand. By far the largest number of Croatian emigrants live in North and South America—in the case of the latter continent, especially in Chile and Argentina. The authors have endeavoured, wherever appropriate and possible, to take into consideration the Croatian settlements throughout the world in their articles.

The studies of Croatian national life and culture contained in this volume are but the first of a number of works that it is hoped will be undertaken in this field. The editors, and many other Croatian scholars throughout the world, feel that there is a real need for these articles and others like them, in view of the lack of sufficient available information on the topics with which they are concerned. The studies presented in this volume are intended to serve not only students of Slavic Studies but also all others who are interested in the life and culture of the Croatians, and it has been our aim to provide objective data in all the areas treated.

FHE, *Editor*

CROATIA
Land, People, Culture

Geographic and Demographic Statistics of Croatia and Bosnia-Hercegovina

FRANCIS H. ETEROVICH

Geographic Location

Yugoslavia

Croatia and Bosnia-Hercegovina are located within the borders of modern Yugoslavia, which is officially called the People's Federative Republic of Yugoslavia (PFRY). Yugoslavia is surrounded by the following countries: Italy and Austria on the northwest; Hungary on the north; Romania on the northeast; Bulgaria on the east; and Greece and Albania on the southeast. The Adriatic Sea separates Yugoslavia from Italy on the west.

Croatia and Bosnia-Hercegovina are surrounded by the following republics within Yugoslavia: Slovenia on the northwest; the autonomous province of Vojvodina on the northeast; Serbia on the east; and Montenegro on the southeast. The territory of Croatia and Bosnia-Hercegovina extends over that part of Europe which is composed of three very different geographic regions: the Pannonian Plains, the Balkan Peninsula, and the eastern shores of the Adriatic Sea.

Yugoslavia lies between 40° 51′ and 46° 53′ north latitude, and between 13° 23′ and 23° 02′ east longitude. Croatia lies between 42° 23′ and 46° 32′ north latitude, and between 13° 30′ and 19° 26′ east longitude. Bosnia-Hercegovina lies between 42° 26′ and 45° 15′ north latitude, and between 15° 44′ and 19° 41′ east longitude.

Administrative Division

People's Republics

SOURCE: *Statistički godišnjak FNRJ, 1961* / Statistical Yearbook of PFRY, 1961. Beograd, August, 1961, 22–23; 476–7. This source is referred to hereafter as *SGJ*, 1961.

The People's Federative Republic of Yugoslavia[1] is divided into six people's republics: Serbia, Croatia, Bosnia-Hercegovina, Slovenia, Montenegro, and Macedonia. There are also two autonomous territories, the province of Vojvodina, and the region of Kosovo-Metohija, both administered by the People's Republic of Serbia. The borders of the people's republics are determined mostly on the basis of nationality, with the exception of Bosnia-Hercegovina, in which Serbs, uncommitted Yugoslavs, and Croatians make up the bulk of population.

Each republic within Yugoslavia is divided into districts (counties), and each district into communes (towns). On March 15, 1961, the division according to districts and communes was as follows:

	Districts	*Communes*
Yugoslavia	75	774
Croatia	27	244
Bosnia-Hercegovina	12	122
Total for the two republics	39	366

Croatia: Districts[2]

District	*Population*	*District*	*Population*
Bjelovar	102,868	Osijek	218,687
Čakovec	112,551	Pula	175,094
Daruvar	80,897	Rijeka	221,303
Dubrovnik	72,590	Šibenik	158,682
Gospić	114,409	Sisak	171,449
Karlovac	226,873	Slavonska Požega	66,214
Koprivnica	99,920	Slavonski Brod	88,626
Krapina	185,764	Split	246,606
Križevci	80,716	Varaždin	176,352
Kutina	80,670	Vinkovci	164,138
Makarska	94,484	Virovitica	109,585
Našice	91,883	Zadar	142,900
Nova Gradiska	80,693	Zagreb	512,722
Ogulin	58,846		

[1]The new Yugoslavian constitution, adopted on April 7, 1963, has changed the official name of Yugoslavia to the "Socialist Federal Republic of Yugoslavia." This is the Communist way of saying that Yugoslavia has advanced as far as Russia on the road to Communism and has left the "people's democracies" of Eastern Europe behind. The new constitution divides Yugoslavia into six socialist republics and two autonomous provinces, Vojvodina and Kosovo-Metohija.

[2]A revision of the territorial division of districts was made on May 1, 1960. The population figures shown here for each district refer to the census made on March 31, 1953, but they have taken into consideration the latest territorial division. In 1962 a new territorial division was introduced in Yugoslavia, according to which the number of districts and communes was considerably reduced.

SWITZERLAND
AUSTRIA
SOVIET UNION
HUNGARY
ROMANIA
YUGOSLAVIA
BELGRADE
(Beograd)
ITALY
ADRIATIC SEA
BULGARIA
BLACK SEA
ALBANIA
GREECE
TURKEY
AEGEAN SEA
YUGOSLAVIA
AND NEIGHBORING
COUNTRIES

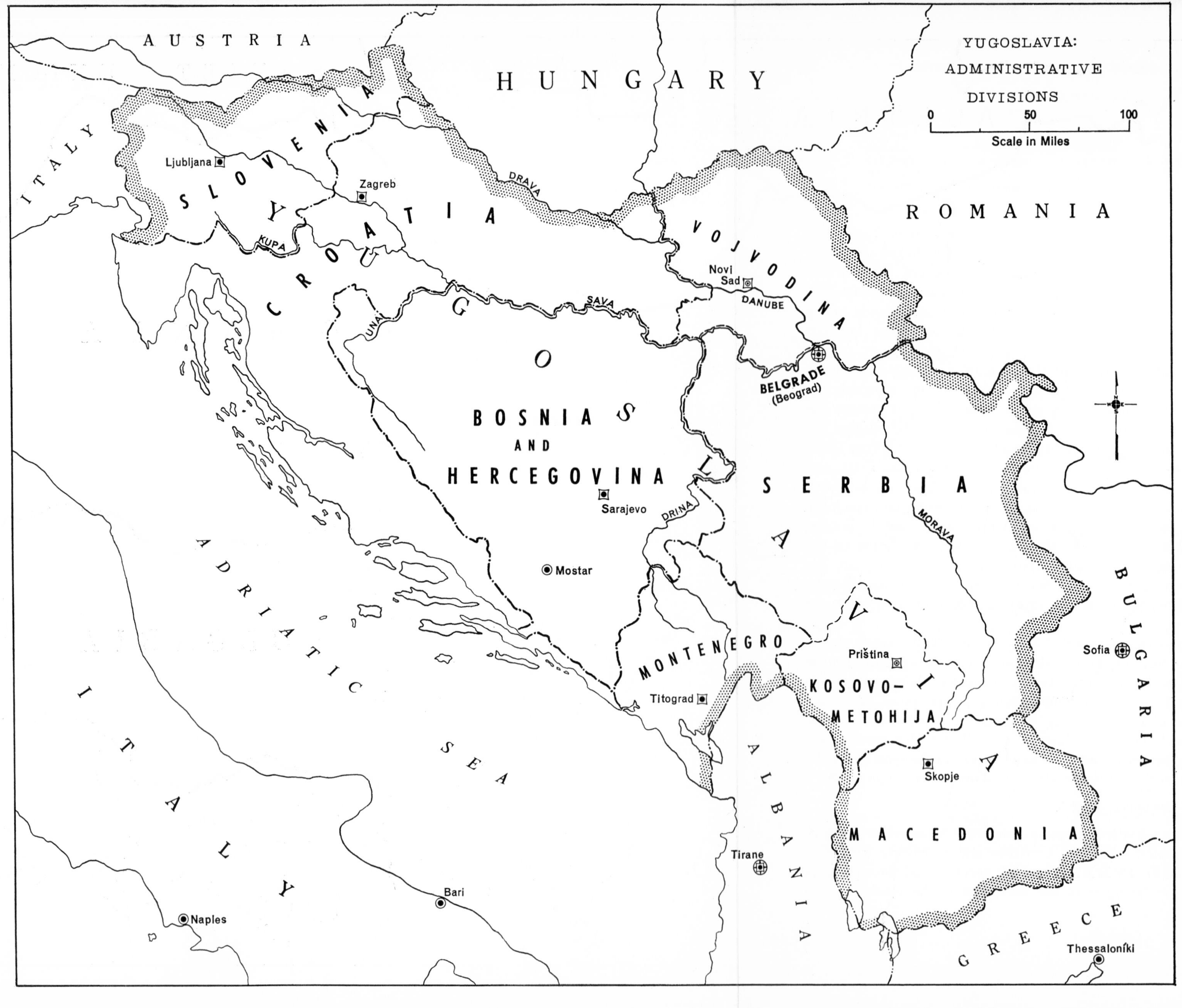
YUGOSLAVIA: ADMINISTRATIVE DIVISIONS
0
50
100
Scale in Miles
AUSTRIA
HUNGARY
ROMANIA
ITALY
SLOVENIA
Ljubljana
Zagreb
CROATIA
DRAVA
KUPA
VOJVODINA
Novi Sad
DANUBE
SAVA
UNA
BELGRADE (Beograd)
YUGOSLAVIA
BOSNIA AND HERCEGOVINA
Sarajevo
Mostar
DRINA
SERBIA
MORAVA
ADRIATIC SEA
MONTENEGRO
Titograd
Priština
KOSOVO-METOHIJA
Skopje
MACEDONIA
BULGARIA
Sofia
ALBANIA
Tirane
GREECE
Thessaloníki
ITALY
Bari
Naples

Bosnia-Hercegovina: Districts

District	*Population*	*District*	*Population*
Banja Luka	304,852	Livno	107,386
Bihać	177,599	Mostar	341,420
Brčko	244,426	Prijedor	221,528
Doboj	285,591	Sarajevo	335,242
Goražde	137,134	Tuzla	357,563
Jajce	127,185	Zenica	207,533

Boundaries

Croatia has the following boundaries within the PFR of Yugoslavia. On the *southeast*, the borderline starts at the entrance to Boka Kotorska and runs up to the northwest alongside the eastern Adriatic Sea coastline, ending at the mouth of the Dragonja River in Istria. This Adriatic borderline includes all the eastern Adriatic islands which extend along its coast. On the *northwest*, the borderline between Slovenia and Croatia follows the curve of the Dragonja River, crosses the Ćićarija mountain range and climbs northward again to Mount Snježnik (1,796 m.). From the city of Čabar, it runs alongside the Kupa River to its south-pointing curve; from there it crosses the Žumberačka Gora at Mount Sveta Gora (1,181 m.) and reaches the point where the Sutla River empties into the Sava River. From there, it follows the Sutla River to its source, crosses Maceljska Gora, and then joins the Drava River north of Vinica. Thence it follows the Drava eastward to Ormož, leaving it to cross Slovenske Gorice and reach the Mura River. On the *north*, the Mura and Drava Rivers, and the borderline between Donji Miholjac on the Drava River and Batina on the Danube River, separate Croatia from Hungary. On the *east*, the borderline between Croatia and Serbia runs alongside the Danube from Batina to Ilok, and from Ilok, crossing Srijem, to Lukavac on the Sava River.

Bosnia-Hercegovina is separated from Serbia by the small stretch of the Sava River from Lukavac to Rača and by the whole length of the Drina River. The borderline between them and Montenegro cuts across the Dinaric mountain range, ending at the point above the southeastern end of Konavli where Montenegro, Croatia, and Bosnia-Hercegovina meet. The borderline between Bosnia-Hercegovina and Croatia runs on the *north* along the Sava River, on the *west* along the Una River, and on the *southeast* along the Dinaric mountain range.

Area and Surface Configuration

Apart from the Adriatic Sea, there are three characteristic areas of Croatian and Bosnian relief: the Coastline and its islands; the Highlands, made up of the Dinaric Alps, which cover a good three-quarters of the territory stretching from the northwest to the southeast; and the Pannonian Plains in northern Croatia and Bosnia, with a few scattered low mountains.

Area in Square Kilometers[3]	
Yugoslavia	255,804
Croatia	56,538
Bosnia-Hercegovina	51,129
Total for the two republics	107,667

SOURCE: *SGJ*, 1961, 316. The table indicates the area of Croatia and Bosnia-Hercegovina in relation to that of Yugoslavia.

Regions and Provinces

A region is a section of a territory which has specific homogeneous physical features that make it different from other areas of the national territory. Some regions in Croatia have more than geographical significance, and reveal marked cultural differences as a result of prolonged foreign domination and its influences. We will call areas that have only geographical significance *regions*, and those that also have cultural significance *provinces*.

The Croatian regions and provinces are conveniently divided among three characteristic areas. In the *Pannonian Plains* there are the following provinces: Upper Croatia,[4] Slavonia, Srijem, Baranja, and Bačka; the regions to be found here are: Zagorje, Medjimurje, Podravina, Posavina, with Lonjsko Polje and Turopolje, and Žumberak. In the *Highlands* one finds these provinces: Lika and Krbava, Bosnia and Hercegovina; the regions here are: Gorski Kotar, Pokuplje, Kordun, Krajina, and Banija. On the *Adriatic coast* are found the provinces of Istria, Croatian Littoral, and Dalmatia; the regions of this area are: Ravni Kotari, Dalmatian Zagora, and Boka Kotorska. Among the islands of the eastern Adriatic coast are the following regions: Kvarner, the Mid-Dalmatian Islands, and the South-Dalmatian Islands. A regional geography of Croatia cannot draw the boundaries of each region and province exactly because of their many and various historical shiftings. However, any reliable geographical map of Croatia will

[3]In converting square kilometers to square miles, the following equivalence may be used:

1 square kilometer = 0.39 square mile
1 square mile = 2.59 square kilometers.

[4]Upper Croatia, the province extending west of Slavonia's small Ilova River, is referred to in this book by the following names: Civil or Ban's Croatia, in contrast to the former Military Frontier; Croatia Proper, in contrast to the rest of the Croatian provinces; and Northern Croatia, in contrast to Southern or Dalmatian Croatia.

Sarajevo, capital of Bosnia-Hercegovina.

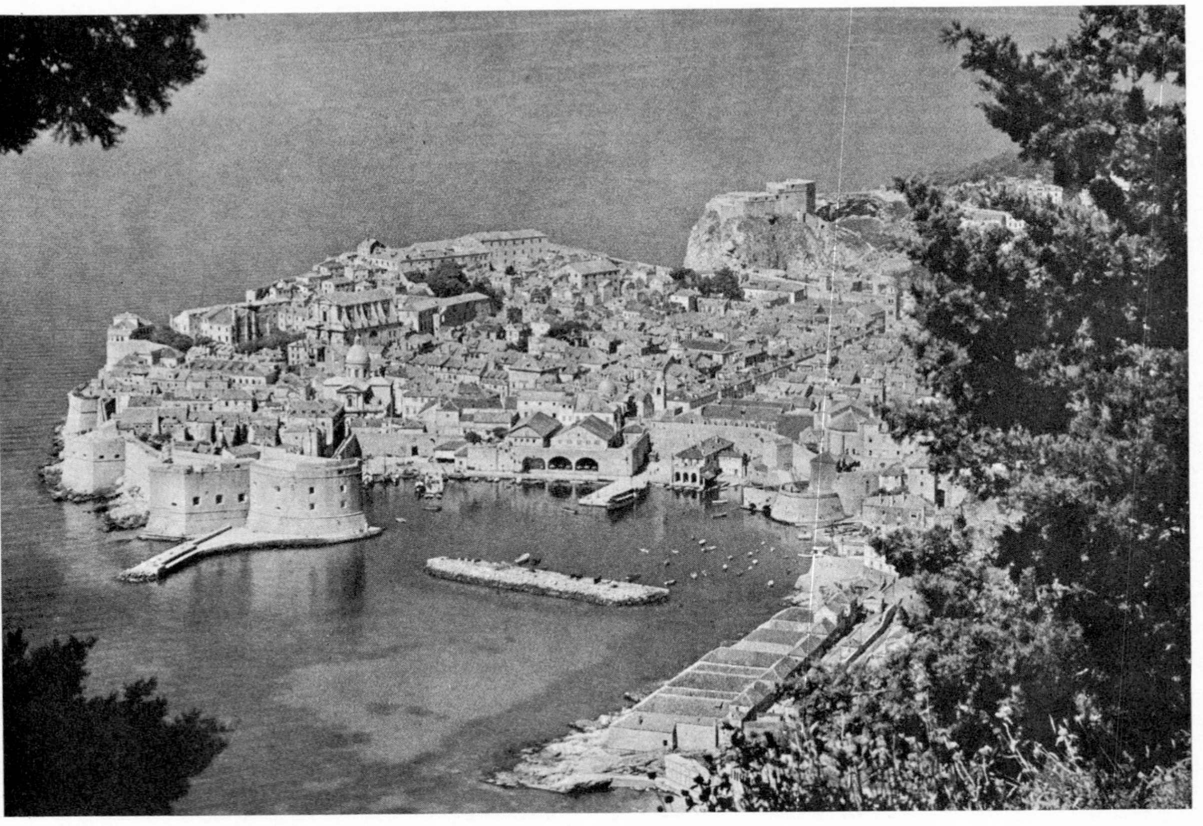

The seaport of Dubrovnik, Dalmatia.

register the names and boundaries of the Croatian regions and provinces.

Geographic Statistics

National Parks and Reservations

SOURCE: *SGJ*, 1961, 36. Only parks and reservations of more than 1,000 hectares are listed.

Croatia

	District	Area in Hectares	Height Above Sea Level in Meters
Paklenica	Zadar	2,797	100–1,700
Plitvice (Lakes)	Gospić	19,172	586–,1267
Risnjak	Rijeka	3,088	960–1,520
Zagrebačka Gora	Zagreb	21,700	260–1,035

Bosnia-Hercegovina

	District	Area in Hectares	Height Above Sea Level in Meters
Perućica	Goražde	1,400	700–2,000
Trebević	Sarajevo	1,000	900–1,600

Mountain Peaks

Croatia

SOURCE: *Geographic map of the People's Republic of Croatia.* Zagreb: Učila, 1960. Only peaks of more than 1,000 meters are listed.

Mountain	Peak	Altitude in Meters
Dinara	Troglav	1,913
Dinara	Kamešnica	1,849
Biokovo	Sveti Juraj	1,762
Velebit	Vaganski Vrh	1,758
Velebit	Mali Rajinac	1,699
Plješevica	Ozeblin	1,657
Plješevica	Plješevica	1,649
Velebit	Šatorina	1,624
Velebit	Visočica	1,619
Plješsevica	Kremen	1,591
Gorski Kotar	Risnjak	1,528
Velika Kapela	Bjelolasica	1,533
Svilaja	Svilaja	1,509
Velebit	Srnopas	1,404
Ćićarija	Učka	1,396
Mosor	Mosor	1,330
Mala Kapela	Seliški Vrh	1,280
Mala Kapela	Makovnik	1,164
Velika Kapela	Klek	1,182
Promina	Promina	1,148
Medvednica	Sljeme	1,035

BOSNIA-HERCEGOVINA

SOURCE: *SGJ*, 1961, 35. Only peaks of more than 2,000 meters are listed.

Mountain	Peak	Altitude in Meters
Maglić	Maglić	2,386
Volujak	Velika Vlasulja	2,337
Čvrsnica	Čvrsnica	2,228
Prenj	Prenj	2,155
Vranica	Nadkrstac	2,112
Čurkov Dol	Čurkov Dol	2,111
Prenj	Lupoglav	2,102
Treskavica	Barice	2,079
Vran-Planina	Vran	2,074
Bjelašnica	Vlahinja	2,057
Lelija	Lelija	2,032
Zelengora	Zelengora	2,015
Treskavica	Treskavica	2,008
Cincar	Cincar	2,006

Rivers

SOURCE: *Enciklopedija Jugoslavije*, Vol. 4. Zagreb, 1960, 578. Only rivers of more than 50 km. are listed. The numbers refer to the full course of rivers within Yugoslavia.

CROATIA

Drainage System	River	Length in Km.	Basin Area in Sq. Km.
Black Sea	Danube	588.5	177,666
	Drava	435.2	12,120
	Sava	945.5	95,551
	Kupa	291	9,800
Adriatic Sea	Zrmanja	69.2	780
	Krka	70.6	2,250
	Cetina	105	5,890

BOSNIA-HERCEGOVINA

Drainage System	River	Length in Km.	Basin Area in Sq. Km.
Black Sea	Drina	345.9	19,570
	Bosna	273	10,460
	Una	207	9,642
	Vrbas	227	5,570
Adriatic Sea	Neretva	213	11,798

The two republics have rivers disappearing into the subterranean passages of the karst formation:

River	Length in Km.	Basin Area in Sq. Km.
Lika	76.2	1,570
Trebišnjica	99.7	1,948
Gacka	47.8	830

Lakes

SOURCE: *SGJ*, 1961, 36. Only lakes of more than 3 sq. km. are listed.

CROATIA

Lake	Area in Sq. Km.	Height Above Sea Level in Meters	Greatest Depth in Meters
Vransko near Biograd	30.0	1.0	4
Ribnjak near Našice	11.0	103.0	—
Prokljansko near Šibenik	11.0	0.5	20
Ribnjak near Garešnica	6.2	107.0	—
Vrana on the island of Cres	5.6	14.0	84
Crna Mlaka	4.5	110.0	2.5
Ribnjak on Grubišno Polje	3.1	116.0	—
Lakes of Plitvice	1.9	522–632	49

Artificial Lakes

CROATIA

Lake	Area in Sq. Km.	Height Above Sea Level in Meters	Greatest Depth in Meters
Perućko on Cetina	13	—	64

BOSNIA-HERCEGOVINA

Lake	Area in Sq. Km.	Height Above Sea Level in Meters	Greatest Depth in Meters
Jablanica on Neretva	14	270.5	70

Types of Soil

SOURCES: Data are taken from the following articles in the *Enciklopedija Jugoslavije*: Bosnia-Hercegovina, Vol. 2, 9–11; Croatia, Vol. 4, 137–139; Yugoslavia, Vol. 4, 579–582.

The soils of Croatia and Bosnia-Hercegovina are variously constituted, according to climate, vegetation, and geological factors. The soils of the two republics are divided for the sake of convenience into the following groups. The principal regions in which the various types of soil are found are given in parenthesis.

ZONAL SOIL GROUPS

Podsols (everywhere in humid regions)
Degraded chernozems (Baranja and Srijem)
Terra Rossa (Adriatic coast and islands)
Coastlandic brown soils (along the Adriatic coast)
Mountain black soils (Dinaric Alps)
Coastlandic climatic salt soils (Kvarner Islands)

INTERZONAL SOIL GROUPS

Rendzins (Bosnia [Sarajevo] and Hercegovina [Mostar] regions)
Mineral grey: brown and yellow-brown carbonated soils (Croatian Zagorje)
Alkaline soils (easternmost parts of Croatia)
Marsh soils (eastern Slavonia and Baranja)
Anthropogenous soils (originated through man's cultivation)
All these soils are found intermixed with zonal soils.

AZONAL SOIL GROUPS

These are young soils to be developed into zonal or interzonal soil.
The main kinds are:
Alluvial and deluvial soils (along the Sava, Drava, and Danube Rivers)
Rough skeleton soils (on mountain tops)
Sand-dune soils (Podravina and Lika).

LOESS, FLYSCH, AND KARST

Loess is found everywhere, and flysh is found in karstic areas.
Karst is a bare limestone area found largely in the Dinaric Alps, along the Adriatic coast, and on islands. It has been formed as a result of the erosion of the soil due to the destruction of its vegetation and forests, and by the dissolution of limestone. However, one finds, even in these barren areas, considerably large formations of fertile soils closed in valleys between mountains. These stretches of soils are called in Croatian *Polja* (fields).

Polja (Fields)

SOURCE: *Naša Domovina* I. Zagreb, 1943, 11. Only fields of more than 8 sq. km. are listed.

Field	Area in Sq. Km.	Height Above Sea Level in Meters
Ličko	465.0	565–620
Livanjsko	380.0	700–740
Glamočko	133.5	888–950
Duvanjsko	122.0	860–890
Imotsko	101.5	285–350
Kupreško	93.0	1000–1124
Gacko	80.0	440–480
Sinjsko	68.2	350–440
Krbavsko	67.3	624–706
Gatačko	57.0	930–1000
Popovo	45.89	225–260
Petrovo	28.5	265–290
Ljubuško	23.0	70–100
Kninsko	18.0	230–270
Dabarsko	21.04	470–560
Nevesinjsko	17.5	830–890
Trebinjsko	18.0	270–285
Vrgoračko	17.1	1–57
Grahovo	16.0	770–800
Konavosko	11.62	69–90
Koreničko	10.92	637–665
Gračačko	8.44	544–547

The Adriatic Sea

The Adriatic Sea is a gulf of the Mediterranean Sea located between the Balkan and Apennine peninsulas. It has a surface of approximately 135,000 sq. km., and is about 770 km. long and 210 km. wide, with an average width of 160 km. It is only 72 km. wide at the Otranto-Valona gate, which separates the Adriatic from the rest of the Mediterranean Sea.

The more shallow North Adriatic, with the greatest depth of 266 m. near the island of Jabuka is separated from the deeper South Adriatic, which reaches its greatest depth at 1330 m. It is interesting to note that the eastern Adriatic coast (on the Croatian side) continues the depression process: the coast is still sinking into the sea. The result of this is the narrow coastline which dovetails between the sea level and the west-facing high, bare, and steep Dinaric slopes. Furthermore, this sinking has resulted in the formation of more than 900 islands along the coast, and a maze of gulfs, bays, and channels. Two peninsulas, Istria on the northwestern Adriatic Shore, and Pelješac in South Dalmatia, should also be mentioned here.

Islands

SOURCE: *SGJ*, 1961, 34. Only islands of more than 7 sq. km. are listed.

Island	Area in Sq. Km.	Highest Altitude
Krk	407.9	534
Brač	395.9	778
Cres	336.1	650
Hvar	289.0	626
Pag	287.0	348
Korčula	272.6	568
Dugi Otok	117.2	338
Mljet	97.9	514
Rab	86.1	404
Vis	85.8	587
Lošinj	74.5	588
Pašman	56.9	274
Lastovo	52.7	417
Šolta	51.9	237
Uljan	45.7	288
Kornat	33.1	236
Čiovo	28.6	218
Olib	25.6	72
Molat	22.7	142
Vir	22.3	116
Murter	18.6	127
Unije	18.0	138
Silba	16.8	80
Šipan	16.5	223
Iž	16.5	170
Žut	15.5	153
Žirje	15.4	131
Sestrunj	14.8	186
Prvić	13.6	356
Drvenik	12.0	177
Ist	9.6	164
Plavnik	9.2	194
Zlarin	8.6	170
Maun	8.5	64
Šćedro	7.5	113
Brijuni	7.4	42

Climate

SOURCE: *SGJ*, 1961, 42–50.

Because of their geographic location, in the southern part of the northern temperate zone, as well as their surface configuration and large mountainous area, Croatia and Bosnia-Hercegovina are lands with a diversified climate. There are two main climatic zones in these areas, the Mediterranean and the Continental.

The Mediterranean Climate

This climate, on the coastline and the islands of the Adriatic, is characterized by mild winters with moderate rain, and by dry, warm summers. July is the hottest month, and January the coldest.

Temperature. The average temperatures of the most important localities on the coast are given for the year 1960. Centigrade degrees are used. The maximum, minimum, and average temperatures are given for January and July.

Station	Month	High	Low	Average
Pazin	January	13.4	−12.8	3.1
	July	31.1	6.9	18.2
Rijeka	January	14.0	− 5.7	5.5
	July	29.5	12.0	20.6
Split-Marjan	January	17.0	− 3.5	7.8
	July	30.7	14.0	23.0
Herceg-Novi-Igalo	January	16.6	1.6	9.2
	July	34.0	13.3	23.1

Precipitation. The amount of precipitation is given in millimeters. The figures are for January and July, as well as the whole year, of 1960.

Station	January	July	Yearly Total
Pazin	68	154	1,569
Pula	70	115	1,121
Rijeka	128	201	2,338
Zadar	103	145	1,395
Split-Marjan	72	49	1,021
Hvar	108	22	824
Dubrovnik	102	69	1,520
Herceg-Novi-Igalo	156	48	2,353

Cloudiness. The average between 0 (completely clear sky) and 10 (completely cloudy sky) is given for January and July of 1960.

Station	January	July
Pazin	6.4	5.2
Pula	7.6	4.5
Rijecka	4.7	4.7
Zadar	6.3	3.0
Split-Marjan	6.9	3.2
Hvar	6.3	2.9
Dubrovnik	6.4	2.8
Herceg-Novi-Igalo	6.6	2.9

Humidity. The average humidity, expressed in percentages, is given for January and July of 1960.

Station	January	July
Pazin	80	75
Rijeka	68	66
Split-Marjan	65	58
Herceg-Novi-Igalo	75	62

Winds. The principal winds in the Adriatic climatic zone are the Jugo, the Bura, the Mistral, and the Burin. The Jugo (sirocco) blows from the south, bringing the African warmth up to the North Adriatic. It is moisture-laden, a fact which causes precipitation. The Bura is a dry, cold wind which blows from the Dinaric Mountains slopes out to the sea. Its speed can reach 50 meters per second and can bring death to both men and animals. It is especially strong and dangerous in the Kvarner region, near the city of Senj. *Senjska Bura* (The Bura of Senj) is well known in that region.

The Mistral is a cool breeze which carries with it some small moderation of the otherwise unbearable summer heat. While the continent becomes quite warm, the high sea remains comparatively cold and sends its refreshing, cool air from a northwestern direction to the warm shores along the east Adriatic coast. During the evening hours and the night, the Mistral is followed by the Burin, which blows in the opposite direction, from the land to the sea. It is a mild and fresh land wind.

The Continental Climate

This climate is found in the rest of Croatia and Bosnia-Hercegovina, and is subdivided into the Mountain and the Pannonian climates. The Mountain climate is found in Lika and Krbava, and mountainous regions of Bosnia-Hercegovina. The summers are hot, and the winters cold here. The most elevated areas have short, cool summers and also long winters, during which the mountain tops are covered by deep snow. Valleys, protected from cold winds, enjoy milder climate throughout the year.

The Pannonian climate zone stretches over the Pannonian Plains, bounded by the Mura, Drava, Danube, and Sava Rivers. It also spreads to lower Bosnia and Upper Croatia. Summers here are very warm, the temperature rising to 40° C. and over, while the winters are very cold, the temperature dropping to —20 C., and even lower. The land is covered with snow during the winter months.

The data which follow concerning the Continental climate are based on the statistics for the same year (1960) as those given for the Mediterranean.

Temperature. Centigrade degrees are used.

Station	Month	High	Low	Average
Osijek	January	7.7	−23.2	3.1
	July	34.3	5.2	19.5
Zagreb-Pleso	January	17.2	−21.7	1.7
	July	32.2	6.8	18.8
Sarajevo	January	15.0	−16.4	− 1.4
	July	31.4	5.9	16.9
Mostar	January	17.0	− 7.0	3.9
	July	34.4	13.6	23.0

Precipitation. The amount of precipitation is given in millimeters.

Station	January	July	Yearly Total
Osijek	84	90	827
Varaždin	28	119	863
Zagreb	42	112	951
Banja Luka	88	120	1040
Sarajevo	74	95	833
Mostar	114	69	1565

Cloudiness. The average between 0 (completely clear sky) and 10 (completely cloudy sky) is given.

Station	January	July
Osijek	6.9	4.8
Slavonski Brod	7.3	5.4
Zagreb-Pleso	7.4	5.1
Banja Luka	7.2	5.3
Tuzla	6.5	5.4
Sarajevo	8.1	5.3
Mostar	6.5	3.7

Humidity. The average humidity, expressed in percentages, is given.

Station	January	July
Osijek	89	74
Slavonski Brod	86	73
Varaždin	82	77
Zagreb-Pleso	87	74
Banja Luka	87	77
Tuzla	82	76
Sarajevo	84	73
Mostar	71	54

Winds. The table lists winds according to their direction in 1960. Numbers refer to their frequency, to the stillness, and to the days with strong winds. Observations were made three times daily, at 7:00 A.M., 2:00 P.M., and 9:00 P.M.

City	Month	Wind Direction								Stillness	Days with strong winds
		N	N–E	E	S-E	S	S-W	W	N-W		
Osijek	January	6	3	1	5	3	4	6	3	0	0
	July	5	8	5	16	8	10	24	17	0	0
Zagreb-Pleso	January	2	21	5	12	5	20	7	7	14	0
	July	6	19	5	4	12	23	6	7	11	0
Sarajevo	January	2	1	10	3	12	5	17	20	23	6
	July	5	2	13	15	4	3	12	17	22	5

Demographic Statistics

There follow some of the most important statistics on the demography of Croatia. The statistics are official, and are taken from the official statistical publications of modern Yugoslavia.[5] Population figures are given first according to nationality and religion, since these appear even today to be the most important characteristics in the study of Yugoslavian demography.

Population According to Nationality

SOURCE: *SGJ*, 1961, 325.

Since the population statistics of the 1961 census have not yet been published in their final form, the figures which follow are those obtained in the census of 1953. At that time, the total number of inhabitants was:

Yugoslavia	16,936,573
Croatia	3,818,817
Bosnia-Hercegovina	2,847,790
Total for the two republics	6,666,607

There are five principal nationalities in Yugoslavia: the Serbian, Croatian, Slovenian, Macedonian, and Montenegrin. Moreover, both the federal and local Bosnia-Hercegovinan governments are now attempting to create a sixth nationality, the Bosnian. The population of Croatia and Bosnia-Hercegovina is composed, in regard to nationality, of Croatians, Serbs, uncommitted Yugoslavs, and national minorities. Uncommitted Yugoslavs are found mostly among the Bosnia-Hercegovinian Moslems.

Croatian Population	
Yugoslavia	3,975,550
Croatia	3,117,513
Bosnia-Hercegovina	654,229
Total for the two republics	3,771,742

Serbian Population	
Yugoslavia	7,065,923
Croatia	588,411
Bosnia-Hercegovina	1,264,783
Total for the two republics	1,853,194

Uncommitted Yugoslav Population	
Yugoslavia	998,698
Croatia	16,185
Bosnia-Hercegovina	891,800
Total for the two republics	907,985

[5]It was the desire of the editors to present the final results of the latest Yugoslavian census in this volume. The results of this census, which took place in 1961, have, however, not yet been completely published. The figures used in this book are therefore based wherever possible on the partially published data of the 1961 census, and elsewhere on those of the previous census, taken in 1953 and published in 1959.

National Minorities

	Croatia	Bosnia-Hercegovina
Slovenes	43,010	6,300
Macedonians	2,385	1,884
Montenegrins	5,128	7,336
Albanians	1,001	1,578
Magyars	47,711	1,140
Turks	276	435
Slovaks	9,570	314
Gipsies	1,261	2,297
Bulgarians	464	108
Germans	11,242	1,111
Romanians	418	91
Ukrainians	5,980	7,473
Wallachs	2	2
Italians	33,316	909
Czechs	25,954	1,638
Russians	2,183	951
Others	4,401	2,460
Unknown	2,406	1,362
Total	196,508	36,489

Total Population of the Two Republics

Croatia	196,508
Bosnia-Hercegovina	36,489
Total	232,997

On March 31, 1953, nationality groups were present in Croatia and Bosnia-Hercegovina in the following percentages:

Croatians	55.7
Uncommitted Yugoslavs	13.4
Serbs	27.4
Minorities	3.4

Religious Affiliation of Population

SOURCE: *Popis stanovništva 1953. Konačni rezultati za FNRJ i Narodne Republike*: Knjiga I. Vitalna i etnička obeležja / Population Census, 1953. Final Results for PFRY and for the People's Republics: Book I. Vital and Ethnic Characteristics. Beograd: Savezni Zavod za Statistiku, 1959. Table II, 278–285.

The population of Yugoslavia, and of Croatia and Bosnia-Hercegovina, is composed, in regard to religion, of Roman Catholics, Eastern Orthodox Christians, Moslems, Protestants, Christians of other denominations, Jews, and non-Christians of other beliefs. Before the last war, Yugoslav religious statistics classified the religion of Christian citizens according to the religious affiliation shown on their baptismal certificates. Non-Christian citizens were classified according to rite of affiliation. (Moslems and Jews have a religious rite of acceptance for new members. For the Jews, this rite is circumcision. The Moslems have no official rite, but a child is given a name which is entered in a register by their religious registrar, called an imam.) The post-war Yugoslav statistics on religious affiliation are based on the individual citizen's declaration of religion. As a result of this latter method, the statistics include those without any religious affiliation as well as those who are undeclared, uncommitted, and indifferent as to religious affiliation. The numbers pertaining to those without any religious affiliation refer mostly to the members of the Communist Party and their families. In spite of the many pressures against religion, the overwhelming majority of Yugoslav citizens claim membership in one of the three major religious bodies. Eastern Orthodox Christianity is, by-and-large, the religion of the Serbs, Macedonians, and Montenegrins, and of a part of the citizens of Bosnia-Hercegovina and Croatia; Roman Catholicism is the religion of the majority of Croatians and Slovenes; and Islam is the religion of a sizable number of the Bosnian and Hercegovinan population of the Croatian stock.

RELIGIOUS AFFILIATION AS OF MARCH 31, 1953 (POPULATION)

	Total Population	Roman Catholics	Eastern Orthodox	Moslems	Other Religious Groups	Without Religion
Yugoslavia	16,936,573	5,370,760	6,984,686	2,090,380	362,872	2,127,875
Croatia	3,918,817	2,896,087	441,406	7,064	83,300	490,960
Bosnia-Hercegovina	2,847,790	601,489	1,002,737	917,720	15,375	310,469
Total for the two republics	6,766,607	3,497,576	1,444,143	924,784	98,675	801,429

RELIGIOUS AFFILIATION AS OF MARCH 31, 1953 (PERCENTAGES)

	Total Population	Roman Catholics	Eastern Orthodox	Moslems	Other Religious Groups	Without Religion
Yugoslavia	100	31.8	41.2	12.4	2.1	12.5
Croatia	100	73.9	11.3	0.2	2.1	12.5
Bosnia-Hercegovina	100	21.1	35.2	32.2	0.6	10.9
Total for the two republics	100	51.7	21.4	13.7	1.4	11.8

Cities of More Than 10,000 Population

SOURCE: *Statistički Bilten. Prvi rezultati popisa stanovništva od 31. marta 1961. godine* / Statistical Bulletin. First Results of the Census Conducted on March 31, 1961. No. 214. Beograd: FNRJ Savezni Zavod za Statistiku, October, 1961. Table VIII, 44–50.

The rapid industrialization of post-war Yugoslavia has attracted the youth of the country to the cities. This factor is mainly responsible for the considerable increase in the number of city dwellers and, at the same time, for the decrease in rural population. This increase in city population can be seen in the statistics of the census of 1961 as compared with those of the previous census of 1953.

Croatia. The capital city of Croatia is Zagreb. The Zagreb city limits include the following communes: Donji Grad, Gornji Grad, Dubrava, Maksimir, Medveščak, Črnomerec, Susedgrad, Remetinec, Trešnjevka, Trnje, and Peščenica.

Zagreb Within the City Limits

Population in 1961	427,319
Population in 1953	350,829
Increase	76,490 (21.8%)

The metropolitan area of Zagreb includes the following communes: Zaprešić, Samobor, Jastrebarsko, Velika Gorica, Dugo Selo, Sesvete, and Zelina. Jastrebarsko was not included in metropolitan Zagreb when the census of 1961 was taken.

Zagreb Within Its Metropolitan Limits

Population in 1961	597,142
Population in 1953	512,722
Increase	84,420 (16.5%)

Population of Cities in Croatia

The figures in the third column refer to the increase in population between the 1953 and the 1961 censuses.

City	Population	Percentage of Increase
Rijeka	100,339	33
Split	99,462	31
Osijek	71,843	25
Karlovac	39,803	25
Pula	36,838	29
Slavonski Brod	28,729	31
Sisak	26,466	38
Šibenik	26,253	46
Varaždin	26,239	36
Vukovar	25,826	38
Zadar	25,132	56
Vinkovci	23,113	21
Dubrovnik	22,961	20
Bjelovar	15,637	15
Virovitica	14,027	20
Slavonska Požega	13,112	30
Djakovo	12,069	26
Koprivnica	11,799	19

Bosnia-Hercegovina. The capital city of Bosnia-Hercegovina is Sarajevo. The figures in the third column refer to the increase in population between the 1953 and the 1961 censuses.

POPULATION OF CITIES IN BOSNIA-HERCEGOVINA

City	Population	Percentage of Increase
Sarajevo	142,423	27
Banja Luka	50,463	39
Tuzla	37,673	51
Mostar	35,242	36
Zenica	32,552	34
Brčko	17,834	45
Bijeljina	17,502	22
Bihać	15,552	42
Doboj	13,445	49
Prijedor	11,632	41

Central Railroad Stations

SOURCE: *Statistički Godišnjak FNRJ, 1962* / Statistical Yearbook of PFRY, 1962. Beograd, August, 1962, 626. Hereafter this source is referred to as *SGJ*, 1962. The railroad stations are listed in alphabetical order.

Croatia		*Bosnia-Hercegovina*	
Bjelovar	Sisak	Banja Luka	Prijedor
Dubrovnik	Slavonski Brod	Bihać	Sarajevo
Karlovac	Split	Bijeljina	Tuzla
Osijek	Varaždin	Brčko	Zenica
Pula	Vinkovci	Doboj	
Rijeka	Vukovar	Jajce	
Šibenik	Zagreb	Mostar	

Seaports

SOURCES: *SGJ*, 1962, 626; Dobrinčić, Martin. *Razvitak glavnijih luka u NR. Hrvatskoj* (Development of Principal Harbors in the People's Republic of Croatia). Zagreb: Yugoslav Academy, 1959, 8–29.

Croatia		*Bosnia-Hercegovina*	*Montenegro*
Pula	Šibenik	Ploče	Kotor
Rijeka	Split		
Bakar	Dugi Rat		
Kraljevica	Omiš		
Crikvenica	Makarska		
Senj	Metković		
Karlobag	Dubrovnik		
Zadar	Herceg-Novi		

Riverports

SOURCE: *SGJ*, 1962, 626.

Croatia	*Bosnia-Hercegovina*
Sisak on Sava	Brčko on Sava
Slavonski Brod on Sava	
Osijek on Drava	
Vukovar on Danube	

Airports

SOURCE: *SGJ*, 1962, 627.

Croatia	*Bosnia-Hercegovina*
Zagreb	Sarajevo
Split	Mostar
Dubrovnik	

2

Archaeology

VLADIMIR MARKOTIĆ

ARCHAEOLOGY, like history, aims at exploring and reconstructing the human past. The two disciplines differ, however, in that archaeology deals primarily with prehistory, the time before written documents, whereas history is principally concerned with the subsequent period. They also employ different methods: archaeologists excavate and historians use written documents. These two fields of research overlap when excavations are needed because written documents are inadequate or non-existent, as is the case, for example, of early Croatian history. In this article, we shall speak of archaeology in a broad sense and include both prehistory and historical archaeology, concluding our brief summary with the coming of the Turks in the fifteenth century.[1]

It is a relatively simple matter to determine the time when certain historical cultures existed and when certain events took place. The archaeologist may be able to find inscriptions that mention dates, or he may utilize historical documents. It is more difficult, however, to establish chronology in prehistory. The archaeologist is in a better position to speak with authority on the later part of prehistory than on the earlier part. Certain items, for example, were traded over a wide area, and by comparing these with the same or similar finds in Italy or Greece, where historical records already existed, we are able to

[1]Many scholars were kind enough to read the manuscript of this article in part or in full and to discuss it with me. A substantial number of their ideas and suggestions have been incorporated. It is a pleasure to mention, the assistance of Dr. Hugh Hencken of Harvard University, Dr. Robert W. Ehrich of Brooklyn College, and Mr. Robert Rodden of Cambridge University. For her editorial comments, the author is indebted to Mrs. Dody Giletti. All errors or omissions are, of course, my own. The article was written in 1959 and revised in 1961. Unfortunately, it was not possible to include all contributions published after 1961.

obtain an approximation of time. Of course, this method is of little help in early periods. Fortunately a physicist, W. F. Libby, has recently devised a method, called the "C-14 method" which is of much assistance in this area. The C-14 method is based on the radioactivity of excavated organic material, such as charcoal. Thanks to this method, at the moment of writing we are able to arrive at dates as far back as 60,000 years ago. Although this method is still not fully perfected, it gives an approximation of the dates of early cultures. However, the C-14 method has not yet been extensively used in Southeastern Europe.

The region which we shall consider here is composed of what are today the republics of Croatia and Bosnia-Hercegovina, which, in a sense, make up one geographical unit. This was the homeland of the Illyrian tribes, and even later, when these tribes no longer existed, the region was still occasionally called Illyria. Archaeology is assisted in this region, perhaps more than elsewhere, by place names that provide hints of certain activities in the past. Generally, names like *grad*, *gradac*, *gradina*, or *gradište*, meaning a town or a city, are an indication that a settlement is buried.

In the past, this region was divided administratively and politically into many provinces—Bosnia, Hercegovina, Dalmatia, Slavonia, and Croatia proper[2]—each province showing, mainly for political reasons, a different degree of accomplishment in archaeological work. Until 1918 the best and the greatest number of excavations were conducted in Bosnia and Hercegovina, while little work was done in Dalmatia, and even less in Croatia proper and Slavonia. Between the First and Second World Wars there was "a considerable stagnation,"[3] and during the latter war archaeological excavation almost ceased. Only the German archaeologist Robert R. Schmidt excavated in eastern Slavonia, and the Slovenian archaeologist Josip Korošec made a few test pits in Bosnia. Archaeological activities resumed after the Second World War, and large scale excavations have been carried out, primarily in Bosnia and Hercegovina, but also to a certain extent in Croatia.

I. Prehistory

The Palaeolithic or Old Stone Age

The earth's past is divided into geological ages. The last age, which may have started over a million years ago and which ended about

[2]The present federal republic of Croatia, which consists of Upper Croatia, Dalmatia, Istria, and Slavonia, is referred to in this article simply as Croatia.

[3]Alojz Benac, "Bosnia, Hercegovina and Montenegro," *Council for Old World Archaeology, Survey I*, Area 6–Balkans (Cambridge, 1959), 12.

10,000 years ago, is called the Pleistocene. The Pleistocene age is characterized by periodic advances of ice from the north to the south and down from the mountains. There were four major advances of ice, called glaciations. Interglacials occurred when the ice retreated, leaving a warm, sometimes subtropical climate. The cultures of this age are termed Palaeolithic[4] and are divided into the major divisions of Lower, Middle, and Upper. In our region only Middle and Upper Palaeolithic cultures have been discovered.

The most important discovery was that of Krapina Man and his implements in a cave near Krapina in northwestern Croatia by Dragutin Gorjanović-Kramberger.[5] He excavated from 1899 through 1905 at this site, which dates from the third interglacial period, perhaps some 100,000 years ago. Krapina Man belonged to the Neanderthal race, which can be described simply as being of medium size and having a sloping forehead and no chin. A great number of bones were found which Gorjanović-Kramberger estimated to have belonged to ten individuals, although another scholar has estimated that perhaps as many as twenty individuals were represented.[6] The American physical anthropologist Aleš Hrdlička[7] has stated that the most significant aspects of the skeletal finds were the presence among the remains of a fine series of teeth, the primitive character of some of these, the undoubted brachycephaly (round-headedness) of the skulls, the great range of variation of the jaws, and the relatively advanced characteristics of the long and other bones. Krapina Man was apparently a cannibal, for human bones which had been burned and split lengthwise, probably to extract the marrow, were discovered around the walls of the cave. The signs of industry found with Krapina Man are attributed to the Middle Palaeolithic Mousterian culture, which is characterized by certain points and "D"-shaped scrapers made of stone.

In 1911 the Bukovac cave[8] was discovered at Lokve, near Rijeka, some ten miles from the sea. The Upper Palaeolithic culture to which it belonged is later in time than the Krapina's Mousterian. The Upper Palaeolithic is characterized by greater diversity and a diminishing in size of the tools. Close to Krapina and near Varaždin is the Vindija

[4]For the Palaeolithic, see Srečko Brodar, "Das Paläolithikum in Jugoslawien," *Quartär* I (Berlin, 1938), 140–172.

[5]Dragutin Gorjanović-Kramberger, *Der diluviale Mensch von Krapina in Kroatien* (Wiesbaden: C. W. Kreidel, 1906).

[6]Aleš Hrdlička, "The Neanderthal Phase of Man," *Journal of the Royal Anthropological Institute*, LVII (1927), 249–274.

[7]Aleš Hrdlička, "The Krapina Man," *Xenia*, 510–511.

[8]Brodar, "Paläolithikum," 148–149. The industry is attributed to "Aurignatian," which occurred during the latter part of the fourth glaciation.

cave, where Stjepan Vuković has been excavating for some thirty years.[9] The site contains evidence of many cultures and is contemporary with those of both Krapina and Lokve. There are also two small sites nearby: one is Vuglovec and the other is Mačkova Špilja. Mirko Malez began to excavate in 1953 in the Veternica cave, six miles from Zagreb.[10] The industry found here is attributed to the Mousterian Culture. Cave bear bones were found lying in a way which suggests that bear-cult ceremonies had been performed. A human skull,[11] in some ways different from that of modern man, was also discovered. In a 1953 test excavation, conducted by Malez, one human bone and three bone artifacts were unearthed in the Cerovac cave near Gračac.[12]

All the discoveries mentioned were made in caves. The first two open sites were found only recently: one in Samobor, close to Zagreb, by Malez;[13] the other in Crkvina near the village of Makljenovac,[14] two miles south of Doboj in Bosnia, where a few hundred tools of Mousterian and Upper Palaeolithic cultures were excavated by Djuro Basler. Not far away is the Upper Palaeolithic site, Kulaši,[15] also discovered by Basler.

The Mesolithic or Middle Stone Age

When the Pleistocene Age ended, Palaeolithic Man had to adjust himself to the post-glacial environment, which saw the extinction or

[9]*Ibid.*, 144–145, 159–160. See also, Stjepan Vuković, "Prehistorijsko nalazište špilje Vindije," *Historijski Zbornik*, II (1949), 243–249, and Stjepan Vuković, "Paleolitska kamena industrija špilje Vindije," *Historijski Zbornik*, III (1950), 241–255.

[10]Mirko Malez, "Paleontološko istraživanje pećine Veternice u 1955 god," *Ljetopis* LXII (Zagreb: Jugoslavenska akademija znanosti i umjetnosti, 1957), 280–295; and Mirko Malez, "Novija istraživanja paćine u N. R. Hrvatskoj," *Acta geologica*, I (1956), 179–193.

[11]The skull, modern in type, was found in the Mousterian industry. Since other Mousterian tools were found always with Neanderthals or Neanderthaloid skeletons, this important find certainly needs clarification. See Mirko Malez, "Die Höhle Veternica, eine neue Palaeolithische Fundstelle in Kroatien," *Bulletin scientifique*, III (1956), 11–12. See also Carleton S. Coon, *The Origin of Races* (New York: Alfred A. Knopf, 1962), 554.

[12]Mirko Malez, "Erster Fund des oberdiluvialen Menschen im dinarischen Karst," *Bulletin scientifique* III, No. 2 (1956), 48.

[13]Mirko Malez, "Paläolithikum in Samobor bei Zagreb," *Bulletin scientifique* III, No. 3 (1956), 49. Only one artifact was discovered that seems to belong to the Mousterian Culture. It was probably the work of a mammoth hunter, for mammoth bones were found nearby.

[14]Djuro Basler, "Paleolitski nalaz na Usori," *Glasnik*, N.S., VIII (1953), 215–223; Srečko Brodar, "K odkritju kamenih industrij ob Usori," *ibid.*, 225–236; Djuro Basler, "Paleolitski nalaz na Crkvini u Makljemovcu," *Glasnik*, N.S., XII (1957), 93–108.

[15]Djuro Basler, "Paleolitsko nalazište u Kulašima," *Glasnik*, N.S., XV (1960–61), 27–38.

the northward migration of most of the Pleistocene animals. The cultures during this time are called Mesolithic. In our region no Mesolithic sites have been found yet. But since a Mesolithic site, Crvena Stijena (Red Cave),[16] located just a few miles inside Montenegro, has been discovered recently by Alojz Benac, it is likely that such sites will soon be found in the area under discussion here.

The Neolithic or New Stone Age

THE EARLY NEOLITHIC AGE

Neolithic cultures[17] spread from the Near East into Europe, and are commonly characterized by the presence of pottery and domesticated plants and animals. Neolithic innovations radically changed the socio-economic conditions of man. In Greece[18] and probably Rumania, early Neolithic sites containing the remains of domestic plants and animals, but no pottery, have been unearthed. In our region, however, no such discovery has yet been made.

THE MIDDLE NEOLITHIC AGE

The oldest culture discovered so far is Starčevo, which comprised a huge area including Bulgaria, Rumania, Serbia, eastern Hungary, western Ukraine, northeast Bosnia, and Slovakia. In Croatia it extended at least as far as Vučedol, near Vukovar, and Sarvaš, near Osijek, both in eastern Slavonia.[19] It was also found at Gornja Tuzla in northeastern Bosnia.[20]

Pottery in this culture was crudely made and was sometimes half an inch thick. It was pinched or impressed with the tops of the fingers or nails. Globular vessels had flat bases and sometimes small stand-rings. Only a small percentage of pottery was painted. Art found expression in idols and relief decorations on pots. At Sarvaš one such relief decoration, showing a woman, was found. The settlements were

[16]Mitja Brodar, "Crvena Stijena (Stratum V)," *Glasnik*, N.S., XII (1957), 51–55. See also Alojz Benac, "Crvena Stijena—1955 (I–IV Stratum)," *ibid.*, 19–50.

[17]For the Neolithic and Copper Ages of Bosnia, Hercegovina, Dalmatia, and the Littoral, see the excellent summary by Alojz Benac, "Studien zur Stein-und Kupferzeit im nordwestlichen Balkan," *42. Bericht der Römisch-Germanischen Kommission 1961* (Berlin, 1962), 1–171. Unfortunately, it was too late to incorporate this important monograph into this article.

[18]Vladimir Milojčić, "Die erste präkeramische bäuerliche Siedlung der Jungsteinzeit in Europa," *Germania*, XXXIV (1957), 208–210.

[19]R. R. Schmidt, *Die Burg Vučedol* (Zagreb: Das kroatische archäologische Staatsmuseum in Zagreb, 1945).

[20]Borivoj Čović, "Rezultati sondiranja na preistoriskom naselju u Gornjoj Tuzli," *Glasnik*, N.S., XVI (1960–1961), 79–139.

Upper: Mostar, Hercegovina. *Lower*: Velebit Mountain, Lika.

Motif from Slavonia.

Zagreb, capital of Croatia.

Left: Pula, Croatia: Temple of Roma and Augustus.
Right: Pula, Croatia: Roman Amphitheater from the second century.

Upper: Diocletian's Palace, reconstructed by Hébrard.
Lower: Diocletian's Palace as it stands today.

normally located near rivers. Fishing was probably the main occupation, but food was also obtained by hunting and agriculture. We have only two C-14 dates[21] for the Starčevo Culture, one 4915 B.C., the other 4440 B.C. Since these dates are probably not the earliest ones, we can estimate that this culture began in the sixth millennium. A more difficult task is the determination of its end, since it covered such a huge territory and may have survived much longer in the marginal than in the central areas. However, as there are C-14 data for the later cultures, such as the Danubian (about 4000 B.C.), and the beginning of Vinča (4010 B.C.),[22] we can estimate that it ended about 4200 B.C.

In the coastal region no early cultures have yet been discovered, but, by making comparisons with other Mediterranean sites, we may say that the early Neolithic was probably represented by cardial ware, so called because the surface of the pottery was impressed by cardium shells. However, farther inland in Hercegovina southeast of Mostar is the Zelena Pećina (Green Cave),[23] where excavations were conducted in 1955 by Benac. There, the lowest layer belonged to the oldest Neolithic culture discovered in Bosnia and Hercegovina. The pottery found was impressed by nails, fingers, and sharp tools. No cardium shell-impressed ware was unearthed, perhaps because the cave lies some distance from the sea. Some monochrome dark grey and brown pottery was also found there. The dark-grey color in the pottery points to connections with the Balkans, but certain pottery forms, especially handles, point to the western Mediterranean. According to Benac, the reason for this is that Zelena Pećina seems to lie on the border of the two cultural areas. There is no doubt that the site is closer to the coastal than the inland cultures. Benac believes that Zelena Pećina was partly parallel in time to, and continued even after, the Starčevo Culture. The main occupation of its inhabitants, judging from the bone remains, was hunting.

Another Neolithic locality is Kakanj in Bosnia. It lies on the left bank of the river Bosna, in Middle Bosnia, and was discovered in 1933 by Mihovil Mandić. A test excavation was conducted again in 1955 by Benac.[24] The site originally comprised 20,000 square meters, an enormous area for a Neolithic settlement. Stone implements included

[21]Vladimir Milojčić, "Zur Anwendbarkeit der C 14 Datierung in der Vorgeschichtsforschung," II Teil, *Germania* XXXVI (1958), 415.

[22]H. T. Waterbolk, "The 1959 Carbon-14 Symposium at Groningen," *Antiquity*, XXXIV (1960), 15.

[23]Alojz Benac, "Zelena pećina," *Glasnik*, N.S., XII (1957), 61–92.

[24]Alojz Benac, "Osnovna obilježja neolitske kulture u Kaknju," *Glasnik*, N.S., XI (1956), 167–182.

small knives, some having an archaic appearance. There were also polished axes, but no stone arrowheads. Bone was used for making awls and, as in Starčevo, for spatulae or spoons. Four-legged vases are very characteristics of the area. Similar ones were found in Danilo,[25] near Šibenik, and in a cave near Trieste. Only one impressed sherd and a few polychrome ones were found. The Arnautovići site near Visoko and the Danilo site belong to the same culture. The culture itself does not show any similarities with other cultures in Bosnia and Hercegovina. Benac believes that it started during Starčevo times and continued parallel to the early Vinča Culture in Serbia, but because of the Adriatic quadrupedal vessels it must have originated somewhere on the Adriatic coast. The older Vinča pottery, which is grey, brown, and sometimes red, extended from Serbia to Srijem and eastern Slavonia, and to northeastern Bosnia.

THE LATE NEOLITHIC AGE

In Slavonia and Srijem there was a local variation of the Lengyel Culture, originally from western Hungary, which checked and replaced the older phase of the Vinča Culture. Bi-conical and knob-like flat-bottomed jars are characteristic of this culture. It was of great importance for central Bosnia, for it was the primary origin of the famous Butmir Culture. A younger phase of the Vinča Culture made inroads into Srijem and into the vicinity of Tuzla in northeastern Bosnia.[26]

The Butmir site near Sarajevo, excavated by Vaclav Radimský,[27] created great interest among prehistorians because of the highly artistic sense expressed in the idols there. For a long time only one site was known, and the British archaeologist V. Gordon Childe[28] called it a quite eccentric station. In 1949, however, Benac discovered a new

[25]For the important excavations at Danilo, see Josip Korošec, *Neolitska naseobina u Danilu Bitinju. Rezultati istraživanja u 1953 godini I* (Zagreb: Jugoslavenska akademija znanosti i umjetnosti, 1958); Josip Korošec, *Neolitska naseobina u Danilu Bitinju. Rezultati istraživanja u 1953 godini II, Prilozi* / Supplements (Zagreb: Jugoslavenska akademija znanosti i umjetnosti, 1959).

[26]For the Vinča Culture at Donja Tuzla, see Ivan Puš, "Neolitsko naselje u Tuzli," *Članci i gradja za kulturnu istoriju istočne Bosne*, I (1957), 85–102; Alojz Benac, "Neke nove prethistorijske kulture u sjeveroistočnoj Bosni," *ibid.*, 209–213. For Gornja Tuzla, see Borivoj Čović, "Rezultati. . . ." For all Vinča sites in Bosnia, see Alojz Benac, "Neolitski telovi u sjeveroistočnoj Bosni i neki problemi bosanskog neolita," *Glasnik*, N. S., XV–XVI (1960–61), 39–78; Alojz Benac, "Grenzzone der Vinča-Kultur in Ostbosnien," *Archaeologia Iugoslavica* III (1959), 5–11.

[27]Vaclav Radimský and Moriz Hoernes, *Die neolitische Station von Butmir*, I (Vienna, 1895); Franz Fiala and Moriz Hoernes, *ibid.*, II (1898).

[28]Gordon V. Childe, *The Danube in Prehistory* (Oxford, 1929), 82.

site at Nebo;[29] another site at Kraljevica near Novi Šeher was found long ago. Though all three settlements belonged to the Butmir Culture, they were not occupied during the same period of time. Novi Šeher was older, and Nebo younger, than the Butmir site. The stone industry found in the Butmir Culture consisted of knives, arrowheads, and axes. Bone was used for awls and hoes. A few needles and one bone fishhook were discovered at Nebo. Ceramics were baked red, brown, and yellow. White paint was applied before firing and red paint afterwards. Some characteristic forms include vases on pedestals, amphorae, beakers, and knob-like or pear-like jars which are also known from the Lengyel Culture. As in Lengyel, the pots have few handles. Ornament consists of ribbons, triangles, rhomboids, and spirals made in the form of or a combination of *C*-shaped and S-shaped letters. Spirals appear in such great quantity, often as reliefs but also painted, that special studies have been devoted to them.[30] The Butmir people were agriculturists and raised two kinds of wheat as well as barley, lentils, and wild apples. They also had domesticated dogs, pigs, goats, sheep, and cattle, and hunted deer and bison. Seventy-two figurines were discovered at Butmir, but only three at Nebo. Some were so highly artistic, including such details as hair, that some archaeologists were at first reluctant to admit that their creators belonged to such an early period. A figurine at Nebo shows that its face had been painted with red paint. Such a custom is still in use today on certain occasions in Bosnia.

Late Neolithic sites belonging to the Mediterranean cultural sphere were excavated on the islands, on the coast, and also inland in Hercegovina. Best known among them is the Grabac Cave on Hvar Island, where Grga Novak excavated from 1936 to 1950.[31] Apart from a few stone and bone artifacts, almost all finds consist of pottery. Incised pottery is ornamented with thatched or pricked triangles and zig-zag ornaments. The painted pottery can be divided stratigraphically into three strata. Stratum A consists of three-color painting, such as red bands enclosed by grayish-blue stripes on a yellow background; the spiral was not yet known. The second, or Stratum B, consists of red painted pottery, some of it crusted where paint had been applied after firing. The next stratum, C, contains black and brown pottery,

[29]Alojz Benac, *Prehistorijsko naselje Nebo i problem butmirske kulture* (Ljubljana, 1952).

[30]Branko Gavela, "O pitanju originalnosti i datovanju butmirske kulture," *Glasnik*, N.S., IV–V (1949–50), 397–402; Benac, *Prehistorijsko*, 113–147.

[31]Grga Novak, *Prethistorijski Hvar. Grapčeva špilja* (Zagreb: Jugoslavenska akademija znanosti i umjetnosti, 1955).

and occasionally the rims and necks were painted with cinnabar-red paint which gave the pottery a lustrous appearance. The identification of the cinnabar paint was a surprise, for this paint, a mercury compound, is poisonous. This is, apparently, the only such discovery in the world. The pottery consists of bowls, plates, jars, and amphorae. Animal bones belonging to domesticated species have also been found. In the lowest stratum a sherd with incised lines, which Novak interprets as being a picture of a predynastic Egyptian ship with two deck cabins, was found. If Novak's interpretation is correct, this is the oldest known picture of a ship in Europe.

The painted pottery of Hvar is similar to that of Dimini, a late Neolithic culture in Greece. If this similarity connotes actual connections, then we can date the site as somewhat earlier than 3,000 B.C. The culture shows relationships with Sicily, Crete, and Macedonia as well. The use of poison for the painting of pottery is certainly very intriguing. Novak thinks that such pottery was used for religious rather than for everyday purposes. He also believes that the cave itself served for religious purposes only, and that the population lived in circular structures, built with a dry stone masonry technique, such as exist today to serve as shelters during bad weather. These structures are called *bunje* in Croatia. Some forty years ago their similarities with the megalithic structures of Malta and western Europe were noticed.[32] Certainly some were constructed during the Middle Ages. However, as no excavations took place, we do not know when they were built.

The Hvar Culture did not remain on the Adriatic Islands. It moved to the coast and in some instances even inland, as, for example, into the valley of Neretva. Here two sites are known to belong to the same culture. One is in Zelena Pećina,[33] and the other is Lisičići[34] near Konjic in Hercegovina. Both sites were excavated by Benac and are nearly identical in find material. The stone industry consisted of knives, scrapers, arrowheads, and axes. Bone was used for knives and needles. Plates, bowls, and one-foot-high vases were also found. Red paint had been applied on a black background on the vases, but handles had been rarely used. Lisičići has yielded only a few impressed sherds. Decorations consisted of triangles, rhomboids, spirals, and meanders. Solar and lunar ornaments are characteristic. The people

[32]Ćiril M. Iveković, "Bunje, ćemeri, poljarice," *Zbornik kralja Tomislava* (Zagreb: Jugoslavenska akademija znanosti i umjetnosti, 1925), 413–429.

[33]Alojz Benac, "Zelena pećina," *Glasnik*, N.S., XII (1957), 61–92.

[34]Alojz Benac, "Neolitsko naselje u Lisičićima kod Konjica," *Glasnik*, N.S., X (1955), 49–84.

were primarily farmers, but they also hunted deer and boar. The sites are at least partly contemporary with the site of Hvar. Close similarities with Mediterranean islands, such as Malta and Sardinia, give indications of the maritime origin of the culture. Though Lisičići lies near Butmir, it seems that there was no contact between the two localities. Mount Ivan, which divides Bosnia from Hercegovina, forms the borderline between the two cultural areas. To the north of this was the Bosnian-Danubian area and to the south the Hercegovinian-Mediterranean sphere.

THE INTRODUCTION OF METAL

Metal was first used in the Near East, and came to Europe first during the final phase of the Neolithic period. Since copper was the first metal worked, this phase is sometimes called the Copper Age. The time was one of crisis, great migrations, and cultural transitions. Life was becoming insecure and settlements were on the tops of hills, usually fortified. Agriculture continued, but stock raising became more prominent than before, especially the raising of sheep.

Belonging to this period was the Baden Culture, of which the best known site in Slavonia is Vučedol.[35] Its pottery has dark exteriors, is often channeled with alternating wide and narrow incisions, and has large handles which rise above the rim. Stone remained the major material for the manufacture of knives, axes and adzes, but metal was also used. Houses were relatively small and usually square in shape. Horse bones belonging to this culture have been found outside Croatia. The horses were probably domesticated and used for drawing wagons, the existence of which is indicated by a model found in Hungary. At Vučedol, men were buried on the right and women on the left side of the grave. The date usually suggested for the Baden Culture by comparison with Greece is 1900 B.C., but it is certainly much earlier. Some Italian archaeologists derive some features of the Early Bronze Age Rinaldone Culture in middle Italy from the Baden Culture, but no Baden settlements have been found between Slavonia and Italy. This Italian culture shows some similarities with the later Vučedol Culture.

It is not known what culture existed south of the Sava River during the Baden period, but numerous chance finds of copper tools, mostly axes, show that the knowledge of copper had spread to Dalmatia,

[35]For the Baden Culture at Vučedol, see R. R. Schmidt, *Die Burg Vučedol* (Zagreb: Das kroatische archäologische Staatsmuseum in Zagreb, 1945).

Hercegovina, and Bosnia. Perhaps the knowledge of metal came to these areas by sea.

The Bronze Age

Since copper is a very soft metal, smiths soon began to mix it with other metals. By trial and error it was discovered that the best alloy is made up of nine-tenths copper and one-tenth tin: this alloy is bronze.

THE EARLY BRONZE AGE

In this period we have the Vučedol Culture,[36] so called after the site in Slavonia. It was thought that Slavonia was the center of the culture. Other sites where Vučedol implements were found are, however, now known in Hungary, Austria, Czechoslovakia, East Germany, and Slovenia. In Slovenia the best-known site is Ljubljana. Vučedol pottery forms include bowls, pedestalled cups, jars, and amphorae. Some pots were cross-footed. Decorations were formed by cutting out the clay and, after firing, filling in the hollow with a white paste. Ornaments consisted of triangles, squares, circles, stars, crosses, and other geometrical designs. Some of these designs may have survived until today as tattoos in Bosnia and Albania. There were also clay model tables which probably served for cult purposes. In addition to bronze, horn and bone, as well as flint and other stones, were also used. In some sites, battle axes (hammer axes with knobbed heads) were found. Men and women were buried in the same grave, which may or may not indicate that the widow had to follow her husband to death. Graves were in cellars or cellar-like pits, and pots with food were laid beside the dead.

The Vučedol and Ljubljana Cultures moved southward. Elements of both subcultural groups, primarily Vučedol, have been found in Bosnia.[37] Furthermore, expansion is evident in the Sandžak region, which is east of Bosnia, and also in Montenegro, Zelena Pećina, the mainland of Dalmatia, and on the Island of Hvar.[38] Finally, it seems, the culture crossed the Adriatic and formed, at least partly, the base from which the fully developed Bronze Age Apennine Culture in Italy originated.

A Vučedol settlement near Tuzla in northeastern Bosnia has recently

[36]For the Vučedol Culture at Vučedol, see Schmidt, *Vučedol.*

[37]Alojz Benac, "Završna istraživanja u pećini Hrustovači," *Glasnik*, N.S., III (1958), 12.

[38]For the sites, see Josip Korošec, *Predzgodovinska naselbina na Ptujskem gradu* (Ljubljana, 1951), 180–185; Stojan Dimitrijević, "Prilog daljem upoznavanju vučedolske kulture," *Opuscula Archaeologica* I (1956), 5–56.

been identified.[39] It consists of a tell (a mound which in the course of time grows over a settlement) having a diameter of some 100 meters. As it was a swampy region, perhaps the Vučedol people had to defend themselves against the invading Tumulus people. The dates usually ascribed to the Slavonian Culture are 1800–1600 B.C., but some archaeologists surmise that it existed much earlier.

As stated above, the Vučedol and the Baden people were buried in cellars or cellar-like pits. Yet we find in the sites of the Early Bronze Age of Bosnia,[40] Hercegovina, Dalmatia, and Istria skeletons in a flexed position, surrounded and covered by stone slabs and with a stone hammer axe placed near the head. The grave inventory does not provide any clues as to which culture this people may have belonged. Since there are no stone slabs in the Vučedol Culture, the question arises whether or not other Early Bronze Age people existed contemporaneously with the Slavonian people. At any rate, flexed burials were discontinued after the Early Bronze Age, but stone cists were used throughout the Metal Ages, especially in Istria.

THE ORIGIN OF THE BADEN AND SLAVONIAN CULTURES

Most archaeologists believe that the Baden and Vučedol peoples were Indo-European speakers who made inroads on a non-Indo-European, probably Mediterranean speaking, area. The Indo-Europeanization started with the Baden people, and was probably completed by the Vučedol people. For this reason it is worthwhile to examine the possible origin of these cultures.[41] Some authors consider that the Baden Culture came from northern Europe or that it was, at least, a Nordicized Danubian culture. Other archaeologists point to the southeast, since, it seems, part of the pottery and certainly the metal originated there. Still other archaeologists point to similarities with some east Alpine and some western European cultures. Relations to local Danubian cultures, such as Lengyel, and similarities of ornaments to those on the Island of Cyprus have also been noticed. Most of these contradictions may, at least in part, be correct. From wherever these people came, they mixed with the local population and accepted some of the native traditions. This could explain, for example, the continuation of some Danubian traits during Baden and Vučedol times.

Since the Baden and Vučedol Cultures do not continue the older

[39]Benac, "Neke nove," 209–213. See footnote 26.

[40]See Borivoj Čović, "Nekoliko manjih preistoriskih nalaza iz Bosne i Hercegovine," *Glasnik*, N.S., XII (1957), 241.

[41]For various opinions, see Dimitrijević, "Prilog," 20–33.

traditions completely, their origin must be sought elsewhere. Close analogies to the Vučedol and East Alpine sites in Austria show that they were related. Among other things, designs point to a more northern part of Europe and there must have been some contacts with northern and western European groups. The ultimate origin must, however, be sought in eastern Europe, and perhaps even farther east. The Catacomb Grave Culture of the Ukraine and the Caucasus shows many similarities to Baden, Vučedol, and other related cultures. It had divided pots like Baden, and concentric circle motifs like Ljubljana. Cross-footed pots like the ones from Vučedol have also been found. Burials in cellar-like pits recall catacomb graves. Both areas had a similar economy in which stock breeding, including horses, played a major role. The burial of men and women in the same grave shows identical social customs. The wagon model points also to the steppes and an eastern origin of the the Baden and Vučedol Cultures. Thus archaeology suggests that perhaps the Indo-European speaking people may have originated somewhere around the Caucasus.[42]

THE MIDDLE BRONZE AGE

The Middle Bronze Age is usually dated from 1600–1250 B.C. Around 1600–1500 B.C. the Tumulus people entered Bosnia and Hercegovina. Their culture is called the Tumulus or Glasinac Culture,[43] and it existed in the area of Glasinac, east of Sarajevo, but it is also known from other mountainous areas in eastern and western Hercegovina and from western Bosnia. Tumuli or mounds were erected over graves, and each tumulus contains at least one burial. In the Glasinac region nine hundred tumuli have been opened. It is estimated that this number constitutes less than 5 per cent of the total number. Strangely, no weapons have been found in the graves of this period. We have learned a great deal about the burial customs of the Tumulus people, but we have not learned enough about their everyday life, since their settlements have been inadequately examined. Archaeological remains clearly show that these people were related to other Tumulus Cultures of Middle Europe.

Farther north in Slavonia were the Urnfield Cultures. Their people cremated their dead, buried the ashes in clay urns and covered these

[42]Marija Gimbutas, *The Prehistory of Eastern Europe* (Cambridge: American School of Prehistoric Research No. 20, 1956), 89; Gordon V. Childe, *The Dawn of European Civilization* (New York, 1958), 156–301.

[43]For the Glasinac Culture between Sarajevo and the Drina River during the Bronze Age, see Alojz Benac and Borivoj Čović, *Glasinac I. Bronzano doba* (Sarajevo, 1956).

with clay lids. The burials were not marked by mounds and were, therefore, more difficult to discover. The graveyards are called urnfields, and this name has come to stand for the culture as a whole.

In Hungary and adjacent areas there existed the closely related Pannonian Cultures. The great number of burials indicate that they had a considerable population. Stock breeding played a large part in their economy. Horses were not only domesticated, but were also used in farming. Battle axes of bronze were clearly derived from copper prototypes. Characteristic designs are similar throughout the whole area. Art found expression in idols, such as the ones found in Dalj and Bapska.

The westernmost site of a group which extended as far east as Rumania was Bijelo Brdo in eastern Slavonia.[44] This cultural group made the highly characteristic two-stage urns. These urns were, it seems, the prototypes of the Iron Age Villanovan urns in northern Italy. The Villanovans were, on the other hand, the predecessors of the Etruscans. Some archaeologists, like Hugh Hencken,[45] find even greater similarities between the Villanovan and the Pannonian cultures. The Bijelo Brdo Culture seems to have crossed the Sava River, for one such urn is said to have come from northeastern Bosnia.[46]

THE LATE BRONZE AGE

This period, usually dated from c. 1250 B.C. to perhaps 700 B.C., witnessed great ethnic movements. The most important of these was the spread of the Urnfield people. Urnfield migrations usually moved along flat land and rivers, probably because the Urnfield people came from a similar environment. Migrations often mean war and certainly an insecure life. Traveling merchants buried their most valuable possessions, bronze objects, and occasionally gold, hoping to unearth them after the time of trouble was over. These buried metal objects, or hoards, are extremely valuable for archaeological studies. The greatest hoard, consisting of 700 pieces, was found in the village of Varoš, near Brod in Slavonia. Recently Zdenko and Ksenija Vinski[47] made a

[44]Gordon V. Childe, *The Danube*, 284–285; M. V. Garašanin, "Datiranje dubovačko-žutobrdske grupe," *Zbornik Matice srpske*, No. 2 (1951), 83–88.

[45]Hugh Hencken, *Indo-European Languages and Archaeology* (Menasha: American Anthropologist, Memoir No. 84), 24.

[46]Alojz Benac, "Vaza bronzanog doba iz Bos. Rače," *Glasnik*, N.S., XI (1956), 183–186.

[47]Zdenko Vinski and Ksenija Vinski Gasparini, "Prolegomena k statistici i kronologiji prethistorijskih ostava u Hrvatskoj i u vojvodjanskom području Srijema," *Opuscula Archaeologica*, I (1956), 57–99.

detailed study of hoards in Croatia and Srijem. Only a few of the seventy finds belonged to the Middle Bronze Age. If we divide the Late Bronze Age into two phases, the first phase contained forty-eight, the second fifteen hoards. This would indicate that the greatest migrations took place during the first phase, and that in the second phase some stability had set in. Only a few hoards have been found belonging to the later periods.

The Bijelo Brdo people migrated, perhaps with some related groups, toward northern Italy. Other Urnfield groups from Central Europe, especially from Hungary, spread into Slavonia, northern and western Bosnia, Croatia, and Istria, and some went even farther west. The necropolises in Dalj, near Osijek on the Danube River, Vukovar, Velika Gorica and Horvati, both near Zagreb, and Ozalj on the Kupa River belong to the Urnfield cultures. One settlement was discovered in Novigrad, near Brod, in Slavonia. Zagreb-Horvati yielded pottery which shows similarities with the pottery of the Lausitz Culture which existed in East Germany. If this site really belongs to the Lausitz Culture, then it is the southernmost find of this culture. Another migration was to Greece. Greek tradition maintained that only the Dorians invaded Greece. Vladimir Milojčić,[48] however, thinks that there were at least three waves of invaders. The first invaders were people of uncertain origin from the inner Balkan and Danubian area who in the thirteenth century invaded Greece and destroyed the Mycenaean world. The second wave, in the eleventh century, consisted of Dorians and Thracians, from Albania and northeastern Serbia respectively. The third and last wave of invaders was the Illyrians from Bosnia and Macedonia who came in the ninth and eighth centuries.

At Donja Dolina[49] urn burials were earlier than inhumation. Thus the beginnings of Donja Dolina and, probably, Ripač fall into this period. In a newly discovered site near Gračanica[50] in northern Bosnia, ashes, burned bones, and other buried objects were covered with an inverted pot. Jewelry and weapons usually had been cremated with the body, but often they were placed in the urns after cremation. Pottery often had warts channeled with circles, especially in Donja Dolina.

In Glasinac, however, the old Tumulus Culture continued during

[48]Vladimir Milojčić, "Die dorische Wanderung im Lichte der vorgeschichtlichen Funde," *Archäologischer Anzeiger*, (1948–1949), 13–35.

[49]Ružica Bižić, "Grobovi u Donjoj Dolini," *Glasnik*, N.S., VII (1952), 222.

[50]Borivoj Čović, "Barice-nekropola kasnog bronzanog doba kod Gračanice," *Glasnik*, N.S., XIII (1958), 94.

this period. Connections with Middle Europe were still noticeable, less so with Hungary. Little contact existed, it seems, with Urnfield Cultures of northern Croatia. In Glasinac a few cremated remains without urns were found, dating back to near the end of the Bronze Age.[51] Such cremations were perhaps due to influences from the Urnfield Culture. In the Littoral, however, graves with skeletons were discovered. Fibulae, or safety pins, having the form of a violin bow, appeared now for the first time. By the end of this period, fibulae having an arch-like shape began to appear. The first iron objects, such as a ring and a small knife, also appeared.

The Iron Age

Iron was first used in northeastern Asia Minor, probably by the Hittites, who retained the secret of iron smelting until the breakdown of their empire after 1200 B.C. Iron has many advantages over bronze; it is harder, and deposits of iron ore are much more abundant than those of copper. Bosnia is especially rich in iron, and its numerous mines were active during the Iron Age and later periods. The Iron Age[52] lasted from the time of the first use of iron—in this region about 700 B.C.—until the coming of Roman civilization. It is divided into the Early and Late Iron Age, the former called Hallstatt and the latter La Tene.

THE EARLY IRON AGE OR HALLSTATT PERIOD

The Glasinac Culture[53] continued its development and reached its highest level during the Early Iron Age. In the beginning only weapons and tools were made of iron. The so-called "princely" burials, where the tribal chieftains were buried, began in the middle of this period. They were extremely rich, containing bronze vessels imported from Italy and perhaps from the Near East. In one such grave a greave was found with a picture of a stylized ship on it, thus indicating that the greave had been traded from the coast. These "princely" graves indicate that social stratification was highly developed and that political tribal units, as described later by classical writers, already existed. Swords found in graves had been broken, probably for ceremonial reasons,

[51]Taline, tumulus XIX, graves 4 and 5 (Alojz Benac and Borivoj Čović, *Glasinac I*, 22). Gučevo, tumulus IV, grave 2 (*ibid.*, 10).

[52]Alojz Benac, "Prehistorisko doba," *Kulturna istorija Bosne i Hercegovine*, ed. Alojz Benac *et al.* (Sarajevo, 1955); Ćiro Truhelka, "Bosna u prehistoričko doba, *Poviest hrvatskih zemalja Bosne i Hercegovine. Od najstarijih vremena do godine 1463*, ed. Krunoslav Draganović (Sarajevo: Napredak, 1942), 78–102.

[53]For the Glasinac Culture between Sarajevo and the Drina River, see Alojz Benac and Borivoj Čović, *Glasinac, II. Željezno doba* (Sarajevo, 1957).

and there were also spears and knives. Horse trappings were found in some chieftains' graves as well as in some of the graves of less important personages. Glass and amber were imported, the latter from northern Germany. Arc and spectacle fibulae are characteristic for this time. By the end of this period Greek imports began to make their appearance. Settlements were in the so-called *gradine*. These were dry-laid masonry fortresses with fortifications of earth, wood, stone, or a combination of these three materials. Most of them have only one trench, but as many as three or five trenches have been observed.

Donja Dolina and Ripač continued to develop during this period. Both were pile-dwelling settlements near rivers. At first urn burials were more common at Donja Dolina, but by the end of the period inhumation prevailed. The corpses were simply placed in the ground or into wooden coffins. Six burials in wooden coffins were found under houses. Women's graves were richer than those of the men. Although only one thirtieth of the known settlement has been excavated; seventeen houses have been unearthed, each containing from two to three rooms and an attic under the roof. Ripač, on the other hand, is more similar to some settlements in Istria than to Donja Dolina. Jezerine, in Bihać county, western Bosnia, was founded in the middle of the Hallstatt period, as was the nearby site of Ribići.

Cremation belongs to the last phase of the Early Iron Age in Sanski Most on the Sana River, which scarcely had any connection with the Glasinac Culture. Gorica, in Ljubuški County in western Hercegovina, began the practice of cremation about the same time. Here a regular crematorium was found, four meters wide by five meters long. The pits contained ashes, charcoal, burned bones, and bronze jewelry. Urnfield sites in Istria, where the urns were placed in cists made of stone slabs, probably also belonged to this period. Some sites, however, practiced inhumation as well. Urns placed in stone cists were found farther east in only one grave in Jezerine. The settlements in Istria, called Castellieri, had ditches of concentric rings made of earth, wood, or stone as at Glasinac.

The archaeological remains of nomadic horsemen groups stemming from the end of this period have been found in Dalj and Vukovar in Slavonia. It is thought that these remains belonged to the Cimmerians. Horse trappings similar to the Cimmerian ones have been found in Hungary and identical ones in Donja Dolina and Macedonia. Perhaps the ones from Glasinac can be attributed to the Cimmerians as well and were obtained by trade.

THE LATE IRON AGE OR LA TENE

This period dates from c. 450 B.C. to the coming of the Roman civilization. This was the period of Celtic expansion, but not all artifacts which appeared during this period have to be attributed to the Celts. The Celts actually occupied only Croatia proper, Slavonia, and parts of northern and western Bosnia. Especially in Slavonia there are many place names of Celtic origin. Glass and amber were imported in greater quantities than before, as were Greek helmets. Many objects from Italy were imported or imitated, and for the first time pottery was wheel-made.

The Glasinac Culture at first continued unchanged. "Princely" graves indicate political stability. Later, autochtonous forms started to disappear and foreign elements appeared. By the middle of the third century the Glasinac Culture ceased to exist—probably the people emigrated, but we do not know to what place. After that time, the Glasinac region was never as densely populated as before.

Donja Dolina was occupied until the middle of La Tene. Sanski Most, Gorica, and Jezerine, on the other hand, continued, and their greatest development took place in the middle of La Tene. Analysis of excavated material shows that Sanski Most was closer in time to Donja Dolina than to Jezerine and Ribići. Ribići was occupied even after the arrival of the Romans. Most of the pottery at Ribići was wheel-made. Jezerine is closely related to Prozor, Kompolje, Vrebac, and Vital, near Otočac in Croatia. These sites are attributed to the Japodes tribe. A warrior with a crested helmet and a spear in one hand, incised on a Jezerine stone plate, seems to have been a Japodian.

Cremation occurred some 25 per cent of the time at Donja Dolina, increased to almost 60 to 70 per cent at Sanski Most and Jezerine, and made up 98.8 per cent of all modes of burial at Ribići. This indicates that cremation was increasing again during the La Tene period.

Greek remains have been found mostly on the islands and on the coast, but little systematic excavation has been done yet.[54] Greek imports appeared early. A Corinthian helmet found in Glasinac is dated from the sixth century B.C. Greek vases on the coast have been traced back to the sixth or fifth century, and Greek coins as early. A silver coin tetradrahmus dates from the fifth century B.C. In addition, some thirty inscriptions in the Greek language have been found. Actual

[54]For the Greek remains, see Petar Lisičar, *Crna Korkira i kolonije antičkih Grka na Jadranu* (Skopje, 1951).

colonies, according to Roman writers, were founded in the fourth century B.C. The oldest colony is believed to have been Issa (Vis). Other colonies were, for example, Pharos (Hvar) and Tragurion (Trogir). However, since trade existed earlier, it has been postulated that there must have been an earlier Greek city. It is believed that this was the Dorian colony Korkyra Melaina (Korčula). It has been suggested that this city was founded c. 580 B.C. All three Greek cities mentioned minted their own coins.

THE ILLYRIAN LANGUAGE AND ARCHAEOLOGICAL REMAINS

In classical times Illyrian-speaking peoples lived in the region under discussion. Their language, which was Indo-European, is known from only a few names and brief inscriptions. The problem now confronting us is which of the cultures to connect with the Illyrian language. One school believes that the people of Vučedol and related cultures were Illyrians. This thesis can hardly be accepted, since the Italian Apennine Culture, which originated to some extent at least in the Vučedol Culture, occupied most of Italy, and yet the Illyrian language has been identified only on the eastern coast of Italy. Another school holds that the Illyrians came much later, in the beginning of the Iron Age. This is also difficult to accept, because the Glasinac Culture, according to Alojz Benac's and Borivoj Čović's detailed studies, does not show any break at this time. A third school, which seems to be in the majority, connects the Illyrians with Urnfield Cultures, such as the Pannonian and even the Lausitz Culture in eastern Germany. However, if the Glasinac people, who inhumed their dead, were Illyrians, one can hardly see how the Pannonians and even the distant Lausitz peoples, who cremated their dead, could also have been Illyrians. In addition to the style of burial, there were other sharp cultural differences between these two groups, which indicates that only one of them could have been Illyrian.

A fourth possibility remains, to connect the Illyrians and the Tumulus Cultures. Glasinac and, to a lesser degree, Castellieri in Istria had tumuli under which skeletons had been buried. The difference was that at Glasinac the bodies were extended while in Istria they were flexed. Ancient writers state that Illyrian was spoken on both the eastern and western coast of the Adriatic.[55] A few inscriptions were preserved at Picenum[56] in northern Italy, which show that the language

[55]Hencken, *Indo-European Languages*, 23.

[56]Friedrich Duhn and Franz Messerschmidt, *Italische Gräberkunde*, Zweiter Teil (Heidelberg, 1939), 164 ff.; Joshua Whatmouth, *The Foundation of Roman Italy* (London, 1937), 107–108, 257.

was related to Illyrian. The Roman writer Pliny[57] explicitly stated that the Picenes were of Illyrian origin. The tribes of Japyges, who occupied the area further south, in Apulia, are also thought to have been of Illyrian origin. They spoke Messapic. This language, of which some two hundred inscriptions have been found, is believed to have been related to Illyrian.[58] Both groups came from the eastern Adriatic after 1000 B.C., and both buried their dead in a flexed position under tumuli as in Istria. Other archaeological remains also show strong trans-Adriatic connections.[59] Therefore, the facts would indicate that the Illyrians should be connected with the Tumulus rather than the Urnfield Culture. The Veneti on the north Adriatic coast cremated their dead, and therefore could hardly be Illyrian speaking or of Illyrian origin as it is usually thought.

For all these reasons it does not seem possible to connect even the Urnfield sites in Croatia with the Illyrians. The archaeological remains show similarities to Urnfield cultures in northern Italy and Pannonia. It may be that, after the first invasion of the Urnfield people into Illyrian territory ended, the Illyrians began to expand back, and the increasing inhumation in such sites as Donja Dolina and in Istria would tend to substantiate this view. It is therefore possible that most of the sites with mixed burials were, by the time of the Celtic invasion, again populated by Illyrian-speaking people. The Celtic invasion, however, temporarily halted Illyrian expansion. The Illyrians later tried to occupy their lost territories. The Japudes, a mixture of Illyrians and Celts, according to classical writers, were probably Illyrian speaking, since the name Japodi, Japudes, and Japyges was found both in Illyrian speaking Picenum and in Apulia. This Illyrian expansion was permanently stopped by the Romans.

II. Historical Archaeology

The Roman Period

The tribes of Illyria were numerous, and we know, in general, their locations. The following tribes lived along the coast: the *Ardiaei*, who lived in the area from Albania up to the Neretva River; the *Dalmati*, west of the Neretva as far as the Krka River; the *Liburni*, west of them

[57]Karl Kromer, "Zum Picentenproblem," *Mitteilungen der prähistorischen Kommission der österreichischen Akademie der Wissenschaften*, V, No. 5 (1950), 131.

[58]Antun Mayer, "Bosna u ilirsko doba," *Poviest hrvatskih zemalja Bosne i Hercegovine*, ed. Krunoslav Draganović (Sarajevo: Napredak, 1942), 105.

[59]Duhn and Messerschmidt, *Gräberkunde*, 266 ff.; Whatmouth, *Foundation*, 111–112, 320–322.

as far as the Raša River in Istria. More inland in Lika, Carniola, and on the Kupa and Una Rivers dwelt the *Japudes*. The *Jasi* were located farther north in Slavonia as far as the Drava River. The *Breuci* were found in northern Bosnia, and the *Sardeati* along the Vrbas River. The *Daesitides* ranged from Sarajevo eastward up to the Drina River, and the lower Drina was the home of the *Maezei*. Around the source of the Krka, Una, and Unac Rivers lived the *Ditiones*, and south of them were the *Dindari*, who probably gave the name to the Dinaric mountain range. Both sides of the upper and middle Neretva River were inhabited by the *Naresii*, and the lower left bank by the *Daorsi*. All these tribes were Illyrian with the exception of the Japudes, who are mentioned above as an Illyrian-Celtic mixture. There was also a Celtic tribe, the *Scordisci*, who lived on the Danube and along the lower region of the Sava River.

With the formation of supra-tribal units, the Illyrians became strong enough to spread their dominance to the Adriatic Sea. The Ardiaei attacked the Greek colonies on the Adriatic coast and even made raids on the Greek mainland. This brought them to war with the Romans. The first clash took place in 229 B.C. The Romans won, and peace was restored. From this time on, Roman cultural influence became noticeable. The islands, the coast, and finally the interior were gradually occupied and came under Roman administration.[60]

Illyria was now divided into two provinces. One was called Dalmatia, which comprised the coast, eastern Istria, the southern part of Croatia proper, Hercegovina, and the greater part of Bosnia. The other province was called Pannonia, to which belonged part of northern Croatia proper, northern Bosnia, and Slavonia. Salona was the capital city of Dalmatia, and Siscia the capital city of Pannonia.

In order to prevent uprisings, the Roman military administrations built roads which connected their garrisons. The greatest construction period took place in the first century of our era, and the existence of the new roads was probably the main factor which discouraged revolts. The most important coastal roads went from northern Italy through Parentium (Poreč), Pola (Pula), Tarsatica (Rijeka), Senia (Senj), Salona (Solin), Narona (Vid), Epidaurum (Cavtat), and on to Albania. Another road, coming also from northern Italy, led through Siscia (Sisak), Servitium (Bosanska Gradiška), to Sirmium (Srijemska Mitrovica). A third one, coming from Petovia (Ptuj) in Slovenia, led

[60]For the Roman period, see Ferdo Šišić, *Povijest Hrvata u vrijeme narodnih vladara* (Zagreb, 1925), Chapters III and IV, 45–103. For Bosnia and Hercegovina in particular, see Dimitrije Sergejevski, "Doba rimske vladavine," *Kulturna istorija Bosne i Hercegovine,* ed. Alojz Benac *et al.* (Sarajevo, 1955).

through Aqua Viva (Varaždin), Mursa (Osijek), Teutoburgium (Dalj), to Belgrade. Both of the northern roads had many connections with each other and with the coastal road. One such connecting road led from Solin through Aequum (Čitluk near Sinj) to Bosanska Gradiška. Solin was also linked with Sirmium by a road through Delminium (Duvno).

The roads were about five to six meters wide and as straight as possible. They were often steeper than the highways of today, and the grade occasionally went as high as fifteen degrees. Such a construction is understandable, since the roads were built primarily for military purposes and not for the convenience of merchants and travelers. The network of roads was even more complex than it is today. Some modern roads have been built using the Roman roads for foundation; other Roman roads are still visible today. These roads are very important archaeologically, not only for knowledge about the Romans, but also about the peoples of later periods. They indicate the routes used by numerous ethnic groups during the Middle Ages.

At every 1,482 meters along the Roman roads there was a milestone, then called *marmor milliarium*, and today called *mramor* (marble) by the local population. They still stand in the less accessible mountainous areas. There were also sentry towers which overlooked the roads and stations, stations where horses were exchanged, called *mutationes*, *mansiones* where the travellers could sleep, and *posita statio* where the mail stopped. Along the roads were towns, called *municipia* or *coloniae*. The oldest *coloniae* in Dalmatia were Salona and Narona, and the oldest Roman town in Pannonia was Siscia. In the center of the municipia was a town hall or *curia*, a square or *forum*, a courthouse, and a temple. At Srebrnica the courthouse and the public bath have been excavated, at Duvno the forum, and at Pula and Srebrnica the temples have been unearthed. Statuettes of an emperor were placed in the forum. Stone-walled houses with brick floors surrounded the forum.

The Illyrians did not make bricks in pre-Roman times. Bricks were at first imported from Istria and northern Italy. Later they were made by the army, and finally they were produced locally. Some bricks had stamps showing in what factory they were made. Local factories have been found near Sarajevo, in Skelani on the Drina River, in Duvno, in Mogorjelo on the Neretva, and in Salona. Stamps were also put on some oil and wine amphorae. Private houses were made in imitation of Roman models, some houses having central heating and mosaic floors. Water was brought into the towns by means of aqueducts.

Salona originally consisted of three towns attached to one another, the middle town having originally been a Greek city.[61] Salona had high walls with four gates and numerous towers which were built in the latter part of the Roman period as a defense against the barbarians. Inside the city there was a theater, an amphitheater, and an arms factory. Salona was also the most important administrative, trading, and industrial center. The amphitheater had 15,400 seats, from which it has been estimated that the city had a population of approximately 60,000, although this figure is probably too low.

At the beginning of the Roman era the population of Illyria remained organized in tribal units called *civitates* by the Romans. These tribal units had some autonomy and were under a *praefectus* or *praepositus* who was assisted by his council, the *principes*. Tombstones of men with those titles have been unearthed. Later, these tribes obtained Roman citizenship. We know very little about villages in Roman times because only a few farmsteads have been excavated, and we do not know, for instance, whether their houses were built in a row or were scattered.

The military garrisons were built in square camps, at first surrounded by an enclosure of earth, later by stone walls. Smaller camps were about 120 to 150 meters on a side. Four such small camps have been found, but not yet excavated. The largest military camp, situated near Stolac, had three stone fortifications having a total length of over a mile and a half. Diocletian's Palace in Split, though built at the turn of the third century as a residence of the Emperor Diocletian and his court, was built following the rectangular form of a military camp, and it served for military purposes as well. The east and west sides are each 191 meters long, the northern is 151, and the southern is 157 meters long. The walls had sixteen towers with three main gates only, since the southern wall was built bordering the sea.

The workmen who built this palace were Greeks, for they left Greek letters on the walls. The palace was supplied with water by an aqueduct over five miles long which was repaired in the nineteenth century and which is still functioning. Inside the palace the most important buildings are the Mausoleum of Diocletian which today is the church of St. Domnius, and the temple to Jupiter, which today is the baptistry. Few excavations have been made in the palace itself. The most recent work revealed cellars with small rooms, and the removal of a Venetian wall brought to light the eastern or Silver Gate.

Of about the same date as Diocletian's Palace is Mogorjelo, on the

[61]Kruno Prijatelj, "Einige hellenistische Elemente in der Skulptur des antiken Salona," *Archaeologia Iugoslavica*, I (1954), 29–37.

Neretva. Originally it was a large country house, *villa rustica,* perhaps the emperor's estate, but later it was modified for defense purposes. It was rectangular in shape, 102 meters long and 86 meters wide, with towers at the corners of the walls. As in Diocletian's Palace, oriental and Hellenistic influences are noticeable in the architecture.

During the Roman period the dead were cremated or inhumed, cremation prevailing earlier and inhumation later. Coffins were of stone or lead, sometimes in houses of brick; ashes were deposited in stone or clay urns. At least one cemetery near Sarajevo contained graves in which the dead were placed in an east-west direction. The most interesting burial customs have been found among the Japudes,[62] at Ribići near Jezerine, where the dead were cremated and then placed in stone urns which were on the average half a meter high and engraved with various scenes from everyday life. On one urn a woman can be seen in a sitting position, turning to the right, a *cantharus* (a pot for drinking with two high, vertical handles) in her hand. In front of the woman stands a soldier with a spear in his hand. Another scene shows a row of women holding each other's hands, the first woman holding a *cantharus* in her left hand. Horsemen are shown singly and in a row. Animals depicted on the urns include fish, cattle, snakes, and boars, all probably used as religious symbols. The boar was, as is well known, a holy animal to the Celts. The urns seem to imitate houses. The stone urns were made between the first and third centuries A.D. Besides some similarity to ancient Greece, there is also a vague similarity to the archaic art of the Veneti. The survival of this art may have been caused by the isolation of the region.

Inscriptions on altars and tombs are almost all in Latin. Greek names have been found in Greek colonies on the islands and on the coast. Inland the Greek or Hellenized oriental names have been discovered in mining centers such as Srebrnica, and on the lower part of the Neretva River. Two inscriptions in Italic were unearthed in western Bosnia, and one inscription contains the name of the Germanic tribe, Bastarnae. No inscriptions in Illyrian have been found. Epitaphs in Latin give the name of the deceased, the year of his death, his status, and the name of the man who erected the tombstone. Family names are seldom found on the tombstones. The majority of the names are Illyrian, and only a few are Celtic. If the dead person had three personal names, the first two were those of a Roman emperor, showing under which emperor he or his family received Roman citizenship.

[62]Dimitrije Sergejevski, "Japodske urne," *Glasnik,* N.S., IV–V (1949/1950), 45–94.

Roman names appear at first only casually, mixed in with the Illyrian names, but later only Roman names are found. This gives a clue as to how fast Romanization spread in the area.

Mining continued during the Roman period, and exploration for ore was probably greater than ever before. In the valley of Japra, near Sanski Most, were iron mines and two foundries. Coins found there indicate that they were in operation in the second half of the third and in the fourth century A.D. Lead and silver were mined near Plumbum (Olovo) and Domavia (Srebrenica) respectively. The mining continued there into the Middle Ages, for *olovo* and *srebro* are in fact Croatian names for lead and silver. Dalmatia was famous for gold mining, and so was the upper area of the Vrbas River. Stone was quarried near Trogir, on the island of Brač, in Fruška Gora, in Srijem, and near Vrapče, which is located near Zagreb.

Coins were minted in two places; one mint was located in Siscia (Sisak), the other in Sirmium. Besides their usefulness for dating, the coin finds also show the intensity and direction of trade. For example, the coins of the fifth and sixth centuries are rarely found, thus indicating a lessening of trade due to a period of trouble.

The religion of the Illyrians in prehistoric times is totally unknown, but it must have been similar to that of the other Indo-European peoples. During the Roman period, inscriptions referring to their gods appeared. Unfortunately, the gods rarely retained their native names, but were mostly translated to fit the Roman cosmogony. According to numerous finds, the most popular god, especially in Pannonia, was Silvanus.[63] He was, in a way, genetically related to the Greek god Panus, and was portrayed like him as half man and half goat. Silvanus is often depicted in the company of three nymphs, holding their hands. His old Illyrian name was, it seems, Vidasus. The Illyrian goddess Thana was transformed, probably, into the Roman Diana, and Venus was known among the Illyrians as Iria. The Japudes' god Bindus was equated with the Roman Neptune. In Istria a god by the name of Boria was known. Apollo was locally known as Tadernus, and is considered by some scholars to have been originally a Thracian god. Medarus was the war god of the Illyrians. Later his cult spread and has been found even in North Africa. An unknown Illyrian god was known under the Roman name Terminus. A few inscriptions to him have been found, but no pictures. Reliefs found in the Japudes' territory, especially near Bihać, which show a survival of La Tene and

[63]Irma Čremošnik, "Reljef Silvana i nimfa iz Založja (Bihać)," *Glasnik*, N.S., XI (1956), 111–126.

Celtic art, may represent Celtic gods. The Roman gods were worshipped everywhere, primarily by Roman soldiers and officials. The most popular god was, it seems, Jupiter Capitolinus.

Place names like Crkvina, from *crkva* (church) show that a religious building is buried. Though some are from the Middle Ages, the majority, it seems, indicate Roman places of worship. In later centuries oriental religions came into being. The two most important religions were Mithraism and Christianity. Mithraism, originally Persian, was a dualistic religion that worshipped the sun. Like Christianity, it appealed to the people of the lower classes because of the social equality which it propagated. Other similarities to Christianity lay in the forms of worship, such as the blessing of the head, and the use of bread and wine in communion. The Mithra temples are called *spaelei*, and inside, opposite the entrance, there was usually a relief showing Mithra as a young man in Persian dress killing the sacred bull. Such religious centers have been found in more than two dozen places.[64] The most important was at Konjic, where a relief depicting the secret divine service was found.

EARLY CHRISTIANITY

Christianity, even after it had been proclaimed the official religion of the Empire, did not completely change the Roman civilization.[65] Nevertheless, many new traits appeared, especially in architecture. Christianity was introduced very early; missionaries had already appeared by the first half of the first century. The number of Christians must have become substantial, for the first bishops were mentioned in Sirmium toward the end of the first century, and in Siscia at the beginning of the second. The greatest spread of Christianity occurred, however, during the fourth and fifth centuries. Since in the oldest Christian cemetery in Salona over half of the inscriptions contained Greek names, it can be assumed that, at least there, the Christians were mainly Greek speaking, even though the first missionaries in Salona were from Syria.

After Christianity was proclaimed the state religion, pagan buildings were partly, and some completely, destroyed, whereas others were merely taken over and used by the Christians. An interesting example of this occurred in the mountains in the vicinity of Solin, where a cross

[64]Branimir Gabričević, "Iconographie de Mitra tauroctone dans la province romaine de Dalmatie," *Archaeologia Iugoslavica*, I, 37–53.

[65]For early Christian archaeology in general, and particularly for Bosnia and Hercegovina, see Ćiro Truhelka, *Starokršćanska arheologija* (Zagreb, 1931).

was placed above and at the bottom of a natural grotto-like niche which had served for pagan rites. Another instructive example is from Salona itself, where a Roman altar was symbolically turned upside down and made into a Christian font.

A great number of basilicas, or early churches, have been excavated, some twenty in Bosnia and Hercegovina alone. The churches differ in many ways from the basilicas of other parts of Europe, and the architecture shows classical, oriental, Gothic, and even Syrian influences. The dating of basilicas is not an easy matter, since few historical documents are available. Knowledge of the first invasion by the Goths and of their destruction of buildings and churches toward the close of the fourth century sometimes helps to determine if a basilica was built before or after that event. Two of the oldest churches were discovered in Hercegovina, and excavated by Ćiro Truhelka. One in Vidoštak, near Stolac, was an extremely small church, having dimensions of 7.80 by 3.80 meters. It was rectangular in shape with thick walls supported by pilasters on the south side. The presbyterium, the space before the altar, was already separated from the nave. Since this church was burned, and since the coins found there all date from the fourth century, it is postulated that the destruction took place during the first invasion of the Goths. Borasi, in the valley of Trebižat, is the other church, which is also of modest dimensions. The apse was semicircular on the inside and squared with three walls on the outside. The entrance door was on the right side; an unusual feature. Another interesting example of early Christian architecture is a basilica on Brijuni Island near Istria. It has two rows of seven columns, divided in three aisles. The apse is missing, and the sanctuary is inside. Similar basilicas have been found near Klis, in Dalmatia, and in a few other places in Istria.

A general pauperization followed the first invasion by the Goths. Coins from this period have been discovered only rarely. Most of the building material was taken from Roman ruins, some even from cemeteries. Larger churches were now built, and for the first time other buildings were attached to the church, in one of which lived the priest. In Skelani, in the valley of the Drina River, was a church which, although of modest size for this period, had three buildings connected to it. The church in Dabravine near Vareš was almost twice as large as the early basilicas. Ornaments show classical and oriental influence. The stone ornaments give the impression of having been copied from woodwork. Here were found representations of human beings which have not been discovered in other churches.

Buildings were attached to this church as well. It was, perhaps, a monastery, for it was found in a mountainous area. In a basilica at Breza near Visoko the ornaments also had the character of woodworking. Otherwise, this basilica has very little similarity to the church in Dabravine, which is nearby, although both were probably built at approximately the same time.

Perhaps the most important place in all of Christianity for the time following the Roman period, at least archaeologically speaking, is the Field of Solin.[66] Since no buildings were erected following the destruction of Salona, archaeologists thus have a unique opportunity to excavate and study the development of Christianity in great detail from antiquity to the coming of the Slavs. The southern parts of the walls that separated the towns were destroyed, and the unified city was called Salona. Its religious center was the episcopal church, a three-aisled basilica popularly called the Basilica Urbana. Attached to it on the southern side was another three-aisled church built in the form of a cross. Three doors led to the narthex, or lobby, which also served as the city church. Both churches were built in the first half of the fifth century and were connected with one another. Such double churches are also called twin churches, or *basilicae geminatae*, one of them being always congregational, the other a memorial church. Twin churches are known from other regions too, as, for example, the church of St. Michael and the churches of St. Mary and St. Thomas in Pula, the Basilica Eufrasiana in Poreč, St. Donatus and St. Peter's in Zadar, and a church on the island of Korčula. An unusual example is the twin church in Bistue Nova, or Zenica, which also consists of double basilicas, but whose two apses are connected with a third apse—a completely new form in early Christian architecture. North of the cathedral is the baptistry. The round baptistry, it seems, was modeled after the Mausoleum of Diocletian and built in the second half of the fifth century. The columns were imported from Byzantium. Similar examples are known from Poreč, Ravenna, and other cities. These and other features are collectively called Adrio-Byzantinism by Ejnar Dyggve.

An unexpected find was made in 1931 when Dyggve excavated a basilica with a baptistry. In his recently published important interpretation of his findings, he argues that during the early Christian period only a bishop had the right to baptize, and, therefore, that the newly discovered basilica was an episcopal cathedral, just as was the

[66]Ejnar Dyggve, *History of Salonitan Christianity* (Oslo: Instituttet for sammenlignende Kulturforskning, Serie A, XXI, 1951).

above mentioned Basilica Urbana. Since the churches were built about the same time and were thus contemporary, the other diocese must have been heretical, because there could only be one bishop in a city. The second basilica was, according to its style, built shortly before 500 A.D. Thus the heretical church must have been Arian, because the Arian Goths occupied Salona from 481–535.

Other churches in Salona were a basilica near the harbor, the Basilica Orientalis in the eastern city, and the Basilica Occidentalis, which was near the western gate of the town and the amphitheater. This latter church is extremely important because it had two small apses attached on the side of the main apse. This feature appears in other parts of Europe in the eighth century, but this church is two centuries earlier than that period. The basilica was, according to Dyggve, a precursor of the Romanesque church with a strong projecting apse and two chapels on the side. The last inscription in Salona is dated 612 A.D. The city was probably destroyed in 614 by the Avars and the Slavs, although the ethnical identity of the invaders has not yet been proven archaeologically.

Early churches were also built in the form of a cross, consisting of three semi-circular apses and a rectangular basis. Such churches are called *cella trichora*. Besides the one in Poreč in Istria, they are known in the Orient and North Africa, and were built during the earliest Christian period as well. Only two of the monasteries have been discovered, one in Rižinice and the other in Crkvine. Both monasteries were very small, and both were near Salona.

Very little church furniture has survived. An iconostasis which separates the nave from the apse has been discovered in the church in Dabravine, near Vareš. The altar excavated in the apse of the church of Borasi was a simple stone slab 0.90 meters long and 0.60 meters wide. The legs of the altar were also discerned in a basilica in Varošluk, near Travnik. The capitals were in unusual forms: the eagle, ox, and sheep. A plate discovered in Rušinac, near Split, shows a cross representing Christ symbolically with two sheep. Another relief from Zenica depicts a cross and Christ watching a flock, guarding against snakes and other animals. Other symbols discovered include plants such as the acanthus, as well as wine grapes, and palms, which had already been found on Diocletian's Palace. Perhaps the most common representation of animal, fish, or fowl was that of the peacock, usually located on the tympanum, which is the central and upper part of the iconostasis; others shown were fish and pigeons. Geometric decoration consisted of rosettes, meanders, circles, semicircles, triangles, rhomboids, monograms, and polygons, already known from prehistoric times. Crosses and monograms showed great variation.

A runic alphabet from the sixth century has been discovered inscribed on a column found near the church of Breza.[67] The alphabet belongs, according to Sergejevski,[68] to the Germanic tribe of Alans and not to the Goths, as is usually assumed. Gothic fibulae, however, have been discovered near Travnik and Mostar. According to the linguist Henrik Barić,[69] the Goths left their name in Gacko in Hercegovina, the Gacka River near Otočac, and the two villages named Gačani near Banjaluka. The name Brgud, which is encountered in three places—near Skradin, near Rijeka, and on the Krk Island—is perhaps of Germanic origin, although this is denied by the linguist Petar Skok. It is not impossible that some of the Goths stayed in Croatia, since the chronicles of the later Middle Ages confuse the Croats with the Goths.

While the majority of historians believe that the Roman towns were destroyed by the invading Slavs and that their inhabitants escaped to the coast, there are some indications that Roman civilization continued inland for a certain time.[70] However, it does not seem likely that the Illyrian language survived the Roman civilization. It probably disappeared before the Slavs invaded the country.

THE EARLY SLAVIC PERIOD

This period[71] includes the cultures of the Slavs and other peoples which existed after the first invasion of the Slavs in the second half of the sixth century.

Avaro-Kutrigur Culture[72] existed in the seventh century, and its center was located on the Pannonian Plains. This culture in many ways perpetuated Byzantine and Gothic art. The most important site in Croatia is Čadjavica, where earrings and decorative objects of silver and bronze have been found. Another site is near Knin, where decorated bronze objects have been found in graves. Stipe Gunjača believes

[67]Gregor Čremošnik and Dimitrije Sergejevski, "Gotisches und Römisches aus Breza bei Sarajevo," Vorläufiger Bericht, *Novitates Musei Sarajevoensis* (Sarajevo, 1930).

[68]Dimitrije Sergejevski, "Doba rimske vladavine," *Kulturna istorija Bosne i Hercegovine,* ed. Alojz Benac *et al.* (Sarajevo, 1955), 106.

[69]Henrik Barić, *Lingvističke studije* (Sarajevo, 1954), 76–77.

[70]Sergejevski, "Doba rimske," 109–111.

[71]For the problems of early Slavs in general, see Josip Korošec, *Uvod v materijalno kulturo Slovanov zgodnjega veka* (Ljubljana, 1952).

[72]For the Avaro-Kotrigur and Kesztehely cultures and the cultures of the early Slavs, see Ljubo Karaman, *Iz hrvatske prošlosti* (Zagreb: Matica Hrvatska, 1930). For illustrations, see Ljubo Karaman, *Živa starina* (Zagrab, 1942).

that an important center for the manufacture of jewelry existed near Knin. These graves probably belonged to the Avars, who, together with the Slavs, are believed to have been the destroyers of Roman Dalmatia. The Avars are called Obri in the Slavic languages, and many place names like Obrovac may show their former presence.

The Avaro-Kutrigur Culture developed into the Keszteheły Culture after the Kutrigurs left Pannonia, and lasted from the end of the seventh to the beginning of the ninth century. The center of the Keszteheły Culture was in western and middle Hungary. A great deal of metal has been found which had been worked in form of geometric decorations, often representing fighting animals. Such objects have also been found in Velika Gorica, Novi Banovci, near Stara Pazova in Srijem, and at Biskupija and Smrdelje near Skradin in Dalmatia. In Velika Gorica a great number of knives, axes, clay pottery, wooden dishes, and bronze buckles have also been found; the pottery was Slavic. Some scholars believe that this culture belonged to the Huns and Avars; others attribute it, probably correctly, to the Avars and Slavs. It is difficult to determine which necropolis was Avaric and which Slavic. Velika Gorica may have been Slavic. Krug near Zagreb, on the other hand, is believed to have been Avaric, for here the skeleton of a horse with trappings was found buried with a warrior.

Very little is known about the culture of the early Slavs, since archaeologists have been more interested in the Roman, early Christian, and Croatian periods, and have neglected the early Slavic remains. Furthermore, Slavic sites are not easily detected, because most of them are still inhabited. Thus we have learned about the early Slavs mostly from studying the contents of their graves. Their cultural remains do not exhibit any great wealth, perhaps because almost everything they had was made of wood and not much was preserved. At first the Slavic cultures in the region under discussion were practically identical to the other Slavic cultures, but gradually they changed, primarily due to outside influences.

Wood was widely used by the Slavs for houses, furniture, fortifications, tools, and containers.[73] Of metal were, for example, the two-edged daggers of Viking type, which were also used in western Europe during Carolingian times. Such daggers have been found in Biskupija, Koljane near Vrlika in Dalmatia, and in Mogorjelo. Pottery which is without a doubt Slavic has been found in many places.[74] The pots are

[73]Josip Korošec, "Sloveni i drvena kultura," *Glasnik*, N.S., VI (1951), 65–80.

[74]Irma Čremošnik, "Nalaz slovenske keramike u Rači 1947 god. i pregled nalaza slovenske keramike u Bosni do danas," *Glasnik*, N.S., IV–V (1950), 383–390.

large, without handles, made of clay and tempered with sand; they were wheel made. Decoration consisted of wavy and parallel lines, and the pots seemed to be imitations of the provincial Roman pottery. The earlier Slavic pottery might have been similar to the Roman, and this may account for the ready acceptance of Roman design by the Slavs. Some early hand-made pots of the so-called Prague type have been recently described by Z. Vinski.[75] Vinski has attributed this pottery to the Slavs. Karaman,[76] on the other hand, has pointed out that such pottery has been found in Bohemia, Moravia, and Slovakia as well, and that this territory did not comprise the original Slavic homeland. The pottery shows La Tene influence, and it is known that after the collapse of the Roman Empire native styles flourished anew.

Although the Slavs evidently cremated their dead, almost all the burials of the Kesztehely Culture were inhumations. One person only was placed in each grave. Rarely were man and woman or parent and child buried together, and all were laid in rows. Skeletons were found in an extended position, usually with an east-west orientation; the head was placed to the west and the arms were generally parallel to the body. At first they were simply laid in the earth, later a wooden board was placed under them, and still later the bodies were placed in wooden coffins. Pots of food and weapons were placed in the graves, and coins were put in the mouths of the deceased. The coins probably were intended to serve as payment for the transportation of the deceased into the other world, and the weapons for his future use, or perhaps so that he could fight his way into paradise. In six such graves near Biskupija, daggers, knives, spurs of the Carolingian type, flint, bronze frying pans, wooden pots, and gold coins of the Byzantine Emperor Constantine V (741–775) were discovered. The coins indicate that the graves date from the end of the eighth century.

The most significant find, however, was made in a woman's grave in Trilj, near Sinj. In a simple earthen grave in a village cemetery a gold treasure was found, consisting of a necklace, three pairs of earrings of the same type, but of different size, a ring, two buttons, and a Byzantine coin of Constantine V. The different sizes of earrings signify the three ages of a woman. The buttons are remarkably similar to the buttons used even today in Dalmatia. The jewelry may indicate that Byzantium was taking renewed interest in Dalmatia during the second half of the eighth century. The fact that the jewelry was made in

[75]Zdenko Vinski, "Gibt es frühslavische Keramik aus der Zeit der südslawischen Landnahme?," *Archaeologia Iugoslavica*, I, 71–96.

[76]Ljubo Karaman, "Glossen zu einigen Fragen der slawischen Archäologie, *ibid.*, II (1956), 100–109.

Byzantium also shows that the trade connections with Byzantium were strong.

There are, however, a few places where cremation is known. One is Smrdelje, near Skradin, where gold-plated bronze objects have been found. The objects, probably obtained through trade, belonged to the Kesztehely Culture, but the deceased are believed to have been Slavs. Another site is Gorica, near Knin. Recently a new cremation site has been discovered by Pavao Andjelić[77] under a tumulus near Konjic in Hercegovina. It is 4 meters long by 1.80 meters wide and is oriented in a northeast-southwest direction. The upper part of the tumulus is made of stone. Inside it, ashes, ceramics, egg shells, and animal bones have been found. Perhaps the animal bones came into the grave from the feast which the Slavs held after the funeral. Although tumuli are known from other Slavic countries, this was the first discovery of a tumulus in this region. The grave was from the eighth century, so perhaps cremation continued longer in the mountainous areas.

There are many place names connected with the old Slavic religion. Some examples are Svetigora or "Holy Mountain," Bogovica from *bog* or "god" in the Slavic language, and Trebište from *trebe* meaning "sacrifice," a word which does not exist any longer in the modern Croatian language. *Kapište* signifies a pagan temple or altar. The general names of the Slavic gods are preserved in the names of mountains or of their peaks, as in Djeva and Djevor. The names Triglav and Trojanci, "the three-headed one," are reminders of the fact that the Slavic gods had more than one head. The individual names of the gods, such as Svantovid, have been preserved, probably in Vidovica or Vidova Gora on Brač Island and other places. Most significant, however, are the place names of Perun,[78] the head of the Slavic pantheon and originally the deity of all Indo-Europeans: near Pazin, in Istria, are Perunčovac, and the localities Trebišća and Petrebišća. In Poljice, near Split, there is a hill called Perun at the base of which flows a brook called Žrnovnica, a name also connected with sacrifices. Other names are scattered in Lika and in Bosnia. One place named Perun is above the village of Slavin. The name Slavin may or may not signify that the Slavs moved into a region where the old Roman population still remained, since it is unlikely that the Slavs would give such a name to a place inhabited by themselves.

[77]Pavao Andjelić, "Dva srednjevjekovna nalaza iz Sultića kod Konjica," *Glasnik*, N.S., XIV (1959), 203–215.

[78]Miljenko Filipović, "Tragovi Perunova kulta kod južnih Slavena," *Glasnik*, N.S., III (1948), 63–80.

The old Roman civilization lingered on during the early Slavic period in a few Latin-speaking cities of the coast. The most important archaeological object of this period is the sarcophagus of John of Ravenna in the baptistry in Split. John was the first archbishop of Split following the destruction of Salona. It was he who transformed the Mausoleum of Diocletian into the church of St. Domnius, and Jupiter's temple into the baptistry. The dating of the sarcophagus is very controversial; the majority of archaeologists place it in the second half of the eighth century because of its decorative style. A few writers would date it earlier, mainly for historical reasons. Very similar in form and decoration is the sarcophagus of Prior Peter in the cathedral in Split, which is usually dated somewhat later than the aforementioned one. According to a medieval chronicle, Archbishop John brought the relics of St. Domnius from Salona to the Split cathedral. The oral tradition of the archdiocese of Split supported this view. The majority of archaeologists, however, accepted the thesis of Frane Bulić that the relics of the Saint are in the Lateran church in Rome. The occasionally bitter controversy ended only recently, when Cvito Fisković excavated in the apse of the Split cathedral and found a small box containing bones.[79] The inscription says that the bones were of St. Domnius and that they were brought to Split by Archbishop John.

In the Croatian territory in Sućurac, near Split, a tympanum in semicircular form has been found. This discovery shows that Christianity was introduced among the Croatians earlier than c. 800 A.D., the date usually assumed.

THE OLD CROATIAN CULTURE

After the last wave of Slavs and Avars had destroyed Roman Salona, the Croatians arrived about 626 A.D.[80] Until Christianity was introduced among them, their material culture was presumably similar to that of the other Slavs. A minority of historians believe that the Croatians were Christianized prior to the ninth century, some even placing the date in the seventh century. Whenever this may have happened, art historians are of the opinion that the architecture we are about to describe is post 800 A.D. This period is called the Old Croatian Culture, and is defined to include the churches and residences, the rich and very

[79]Dominik Mandić, "Sv. Venancij ili sv. Dujam prvi biskup i osnovatelj solinsko-splitske biskupije?" *Hrvatska Revija*, VIII (1958), 250–252.

[80]For the cultural remains of the Croats, see Ljubo Karaman, *Iz hrvatske prošlosti* (Zagreb: Matica Hrvatska, 1930). For illustrations see Ljubo Karaman, *Živa starina* (Zagreb, 1942).

characteristic decorations which adorned them, and the inscriptions which placed the whole period in historical light. Less often, other traits are considered. The culture is, on the whole, completely different from the previous one in the earlier Slavic period. It is the culture of the upper class, of the rulers, the aristocracy, the church, and the city people. It is therefore questionable whether one can call these remains a culture. Perhaps the term Early Croatian Art would be more suitable. The culture of the lower classes continued with little change, and the more distant places were from the cultural centers on the coast the stronger was the Slavic tradition.

The churches in Croatia were small, built from stone with a good deal of mortar, and had diverse and unusual ground plans. Characteristically, all of them were vaulted. The vaults were in the shape of a cross, barrel, cupola, or semi-cupola. Apses were at first semi-circular, and later rectangular. With buttresses and pilaster strips, these churches stand apart in European architecture. The remains of earlier buildings were used to a very small degree. A unique example is the monastery of Rižinice, near Solin, in the construction of which a Roman building and an Early Christian chapel were used.

Of the great number of churches that existed, only St. George's and St. Nicholas' in Nin, St. Peter's in Priko near Omiš, St. Nicholas' in Selca on the island of Brač, and St. Michael's in Ston remain standing completely. St. George's in Ravno, however, has been incorporated in a later church. The earliest churches were those whose apses were not yet separated, but were constructed so that the walls of the apses formed part of the side walls of the church. Such are, for example, the church in Rižinice near Split, which dates from the middle of the ninth century, and St. Luke's at Uzdolje near Knin, which dates from the end of the same century. These two churches each had one aisle. St. Peter's in Zadar, on the other hand, had three central columns with an aisle on each side. The essentially circular plan, from whose circumference niches open, is very common. St. Krševan's on Krk Island has three; the Holy Cross Church and St. Nicholas' in Nin have four niches. Some churches, such as those of the Holy Trinity in Poljud, near Split, St. Michael's in Pridraga, St. Ursula's in Zadar, St. Mary's in Trogir have six, and a church in Ošlje near Ston even has eight niches.

The church of the Holy Cross in Nin is nine meters long and nine meters wide and is in the form of a cross with a dome over the crossing. It was the See of a bishopric, and was once described as the smallest cathedral in the world. It is in many ways different from other circular churches. The various niches are not arranged in a clover-shaped pattern, but rather are in a straight line, one after the other. This characteristic is also found in a church in Bilice, near Šibenik, at St. Vitus' in Zadar, at St. Michael's near Pula, and in other churches in Istria as well. Another difference is that the middle apse of the Holy Cross Church is squared from the outside. The same thing has been observed in the church of the Holy Trinity near Split and in St. Ursula's in Zadar.

The church of St. Donatus, near Punat on the island of Krk, is unusual. It is built with the dry stone technique like a *bunje* structure and has a diversity of vaults. Uncommon also is the cupola in the church of St. George in Ravna, near Split, which is elliptical in shape. St. Nicholas', which is in a *cella trichora* form, is usually regarded as the oldest church with side niches, and that of the Holy Cross as the oldest of all churches. Ljubo Karaman, however, believes that both are relatively late, dating perhaps from the eleventh century. Ejnar Dyggve estimated that the circular churches dated from the tenth and eleventh centuries. If this reasoning is correct, then the oldest church is St. George's in Ravna, near Split, which dates from the beginning of the ninth century.

After the arrival of the Benedictine order in the middle of the ninth century, the style of the early churches changed. The Benedictines popularized the three-aisled form of church. Their period of greatest building activity was in the middle of the eleventh century; place names like Koludare and Koludrovica refer back to them. Three-aisled churches were built even earlier, however. The oldest is that of St. Mary in Bijaći, near Split, which dates from the middle of the ninth century. One of the two churches in Otok near Solin, built in the middle of the tenth century, was also three-aisled. The tombstone of Queen Helen was discovered inside one of the churches. Since Thomas of Split, a medieval chronicler, asserts that one was the mausoleum church of St. Stephen where "many kings and queens were buried," and that one was St. Mary's, the problem was to determine which was which. The excavator Frane Bulić believed that the larger church was St. Mary's and that the Sepulchral church had not yet been discovered. Later he hoped to unearth it at Šuplja Crkva (Hollow Church). However, the opinion of Karaman and Dyggve that the larger church was St. Stephen's and the smaller one St. Mary's prevailed. However, it is strange that not a single piece of tombstones other than that of Queen Helen has been discovered. Dyggve believes that the eleventh century church of St. Peter in Priko, which is one-aisled, but divided in three parts, copies the mausoleum church. Similar churches are St. Michael's near Ston, St. Nicholas' on Brač, and a great number of churches in Dubrovnik and on the nearby islands.

When the large basilicas were constructed in the eleventh century for the cathedrals and royal monasteries, the custom of building small churches was discontinued. The architecture of these basilicas did not imitate totally the style of basilicas of the Roman cities in Italy. Some forms and motifs of older churches in Croatia were still copied. Thus, one may speak of the Dalmatian-Croatian variant of early Romanesque architecture. An exception is St. Peter's on the island of Rab, which corresponds to other Benedictine buildings in southern Italy. Simplest in form is perhaps the Supetarska Draga church on the island of Rab, a basilica with three semi-circular niches. Others are the church in Biskupija, probably the cathedral of the Croatian bishop, *episcopus chroatensis*, a nearby church in Stupovi which was somewhat larger, and the bishop's cathedral, St. Moses', in Biograd. Furthermore, there are a great number of monasteries such as St. Peter's in Poljice, St. Lucy's in Baška on the island of Krk, St. Domnius' in Trogir, St. Thomas' in Biograd, St. Andrew's on the island of Rab, and St. Benedict's in Split.

An interesting problem arose concerning the identification of St. Peter's church, which was known from documents as the church where kings had been crowned. Bulić, and many other archaeologists after him, identified it as the ruin at Gradina, near Solin, which was a central church. However, as it was mentioned as a basilica, Dyggve identified it as a nearby three-aisled basilica popularly called Šuplja Crkva (Hollow Church). The church was much larger than any other in the vicinity of Solin, and therefore best suited for coronations.

In Roman towns on the coast, the church towers were built separately from the church, as, for example, in St. Mary's in Nin and in a church in Privlaka in Boka Kotorska. The towers of the Croatian churches are, on the other hand, part of the church. These are massive, not divided in floors, and become narrower at the top. One such early tower is still standing in the corridor of the western gate of Diocletian's Palace. St. Stephen's church in Otok is unusual because of its two towers. This is the oldest known example of two towers in Europe.

The origin of these churches has provoked many discussions, and there is still no agreement among the specialists. Earlier writers, such as R. Eitelberger, E. A. Freeman, T. G. Jackson, and W. Gerber, believed that they were a product of Byzantine influences. U. Villard de Monneret was essentially of the same opinion, although he believed that the ground plan and the decorations were the work of traveling

Holy Trinity Church, Split.

Upper: Tombstone of Queen Helen, from the tenth century.
Lower: The oldest inscription, about 1100 A.D., in Glagolithic Script, found at Baška, on the Island of Krk.

Left: Croatian King Zvonimir (?), from the eleventh century.
Right: An early Croatian tomb from Dalmatia.

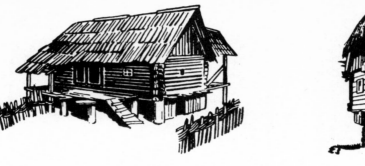

Dwellings. *Upper left*: *Sojenica* or *sošnica* in Gornja Dolina, near Bosanska Gradiška, Posavina. *Upper right*: *Brvnara* in Bosnia-Hercegovina. *Lower left*: *Brvnara* in Palanjek, near Sisak, Posavina. *Lower right*: *Bunja* or *cémer*.

Italian masters. C. M. Iveković at first believed that the Old Croatian Culture copied the Roman monuments, but he later emphasized the originality of the forms resulting from the geographical position of Dalmatia, where the influences of East and West met. Luka Jelić at first supported the Byzantine theory, but later believed that the churches were the product of a special Croatian-Iranian architectural school brought from the North by Croatians who, according to him, were descendants of the Iranian Alans. This opinion caught the attention of Josef Strzygowski,[81] who argued throughout his life for the influences from the East on European art in the Middle Ages. Originally he had believed that oriental influences reached Croatian architecture directly, but later he changed his theory. Near Eastern art, especially in Iran and Armenia, he asserted, was not brought directly to the cultural centers of Europe, but was first transplanted to the Germans and Slavs in northern Europe; since their buildings were made of wood, however, they did not survive. Later, Strzygowski maintained, the Croatians brought those forms to the shores of the Adriatic Sea. They continued to build with wood for a time, but since stone was available, they began to build with it. As a result, the early churches in Croatia contained features of the old Slavic architecture, especially the church of the Holy Cross in Nin.

Karaman, the best expert on Croatian art of the period, emphatically denies every aspect of this theory. According to him, all churches were made by local builders, although there might have been some imitation of the Roman and Early Christian buildings. The builders might have arrived independently at the idea of central churches. The churches do not imitate the monumental buildings either of the West or of the East. The diversity of the ground plans, the smallness, the primitive technique, and the irregularity of the arches show that the local builders had to solve their own problems, and each did so according to his own modest knowledge. There were no strong influences from the outside, as in similar cases in Spain during the Visigoth period and in England before William the Conqueror. This architecture was not especially Croatian in an ethnic sense, since it existed in the cities on the coast as well, which at this time were Roman speaking.

Dyggve, on the other hand, had a different view. He believed in the continuation of Early Christian art in Dalmatia, especially its Syrian component, and believed in the influences of the missionaries on Early Croatian architecture. He argued that, since the missionaries introduced Christianity, they must also have brought their building methods

[81] Joseph Strzygowski, *Die altslawische Kunst* (Augsburg, 1929).

and styles. This is not so conspicuous because the missionaries did not come from other countries, but from the nearby Roman cities on the coast. He insists on the similarity in ground plan between the earlier churches and the more recent ones. Examples of Byzantine influences on the other hand are, according to him, the two-storied barrel vaulted fore-hall of St. Stephen's in Otok and the church at Gradina.

The Croatian rulers had their early courts at various places. The courts consisted, at first, only of larger estates where the rulers stayed for a certain time in order to attend to state or jurisdictional business. Traces of one court, which consisted of six buildings, have been discovered in Bijaći near Split. Buildings were generally decorated in flat relief with crosses, lilies, stars, cords, palmates, arches, birds, and animals. The most characteristic decorations were the interwoven laces (*Geflechtsornamentik, scultura a intreccio*). These decorations are found along the coast from Istria to Kotor. Early forms had two, and later ones three, laces; in the early Romanesque period two, or more than three, laces were the fashion. The interweaving is often so complicated that a whole net is formed. The arcades were decorated in this way, as were the ciboria over the main altars, the surface of the iconostasis and fonts, sarcophagi, the doors, and the windows. On some parts of this decorative sculpture traces of blue, red, and gold paint have been discovered. The oldest decoration is perhaps the one on the outer surface of the font of the church of the Holy Cross in Nin. The plastic motifs of astragal were still continued. Inside the three interweaving laces which form a cross were the classical "eyes."

With the advent of the early Romanesque style in the eleventh century, this form of decoration began to disappear. It seems that it lasted longer in Dubrovnik and southern Dalmatia. Most twelfth century churches, such as St. Nicholas' in the Split suburb of Veli Varoš, do not have it. It survived, however, in the villages, as, for example, in the church of St. Martha in Bijaći which was rebuilt by the peasants toward the close of the twelfth century. Furthermore, it was found in the churches of Gradina in Solin, and Volarica in Lika. The last appearance of this type of decoration was probably in the thirteenth century on the wooden benches of the Split cathedral.

Little is known about the church furniture of the period. Only a few of the stone objects have remained, such as, for example, the iconostasis and tympanum, which often have inscriptions with the name of the ruler. The tympanum, which was earlier constructed in the form of a semiarch, was in this time built in a triangular form. Such an iconostasis still exists intact in the chapel of St. Martin, built around

800 in the corridor of the Porta Aurea (the golden or northern gate to Diocletian's Palace). A ciborium with four arcades was reconstructed from pieces found in the church of St. Martha in Bijaći. Pillars were either made from stones taken from ruins or else they were rustic imitations of classical columns. According to Truhelka, the more recent pillars clearly show degeneration in comparison with the Roman and Early Christian ones.

There is no agreement as to the origin of this mode of decoration. There are proponents of the theory of Langobard and Byzantine origin, and those who believe that it originated in the classical style of the decoration. Frane Radić traced this decoration to Byzantine art, but thought that it existed earlier in Croatia than in Italy. Strzygowski believed that the Croatians, like the Langobards, brought their style of decoration with them from northern to southern Europe. An example of this art in northern Europe was the "animal" style in which animal heads were interwoven in the laces. Truhelka disagreed with this theory and argued that the animal style was in reality nothing but the continuation of La Tene art and that it occurred too early to influence the Croatian decoration. He believed that the decoration was autochthonous in Croatia and already present in Early Christian art. The Croatians, however, developed it, and it spread from Dalmatia to northern Italy. Karaman, on the other hand, denies that it originated from the Langobard art. He points out that this kind of decoration is known apart from Italy, in France and in the regions of the Alps where the Langobards did not live. The Langobardic art was also different in technique, and came too early in history to be an influence. He believes that it originated in northern Italy and spread to Croatia toward the end of the eighth century. In both regions one can find identities of style and technique. Dyggve agreed with this theory.

After 1000 A.D. human figures appear again. One of the oldest is the representation of St. Mary on the tympanum in the church of St. Martha in Biskupija, not yet a relief, but rather an incised figure. Biblical figures were beautifully incised on plaques from the eleventh century in the church of St. Donatus in Zadar. Here we see the Flight into Egypt, the Massacre of the Innocents, the Nativity, and the Adoration of the Kings. In this last, the kings were not yet shown with crowns, but still as the three wise men. From the ruins of St. Stephen's "de pinis" near Split, a tympanum showing Christ and two angels has been unearthed. A more developed sculptured scene is preserved in the baptistry of the Split cathedral, where a marble plate shows three bearded men. One, with a crown on his head, is seated in a chair and holds a cross in his right hand and a scepter in his left. Another figure stands to the right of the crowned man, and a third lies prostrate before him. The controversy as to whether the sitting person represents Christ or a Croatian king was settled by Karaman, who proved that it pictured a Croatian king from the second half of the eleventh century, either Petar Krešimir or Zvonimir. Dyggve believes that Zvonimir is depicted, and that the relief was originally in Šuplja Crkva (Hollow Church), near Split, which he had identified as the crown church. The clothes worn by the monarch are of Frankish fashion, whereas the prostration shows Byzantine influence. Most interesting is the crown, which has pearls extending over the ears and three crosses on the top. Late in style is a stone relief from the island of Koločep, near Dubrovnik. The ornaments already show influences of the incoming Romanesque style. The relief shows a boy blowing a horn, a dog, and a winged horse.

During the Early Croatian period churches were painted on the inside. A recently discovered document states that the church of St. George near Split contained pictures of five kings. Only one fresco from this time, has, however, been preserved. It is in the church of St. Michael in Ston, and shows a bearded figure, the king-founder, holding a model of the same church in his hands and wearing the same type of crown as King Zvonimir in the Split baptistry. Karaman believes him to be Michael of Dioclea, which is the present Montenegro.

The only building not belonging to the early Croatian churches is the monumental church of St. Donatus in Zadar, which stands apart from other churches by virtue of its size and style. It is believed that it was built after 805, when Bishop Donatus visited western Europe. It is a central church, similar to the Carolingian round buildings, or rotundas, in Aachen and Fulda in Germany. Local masters are assumed to have built it. The oldest inscription is on the font in the church of the Holy Cross in Nin.[82] It gives the name of Duke Višeslav, who is

[82]The inscription in Latin is as follows: "Hec fons nempe sumit infirmos, ut reddat illuminatos. Hic expiant scelera sua, quod de primo sumpserunt parente, ut efficiantur Xristicole salubriter confitendo trinum perhenne. Hoc Iohannes presbiter sub tempore Vuissasclavo duci opus bene composuit devote, in honore videlicet sancti Iohannis Baptiste, ut intercedat pro eo clientuloque suo." Recently Mirko Šeper argued that the font, because of its style and inscription, was made in the eleventh century, but this position is rejected by Karaman. Since Duke Višeslav is not known from historical documents, the problem cannot be considered settled. See Mirko Šeper, "Der Taufstein des kroatischen Fürsten Višeslav aus dem frühen Mittelalter," *Nachrichten des Deutschen Instituts für merowingisch-karolingische Kunstforschung*, No. 14–16 (1957–58), 1–21; Ljubo Karaman, "O vremenu krstionice kneza Višeslava," *Peristil*, III (1960), 107–109.

not known from any historical documents. Above the door of the same church is another inscription, an extremely puzzling one,[83] which is thought to mean that a Godečav *župan* (tribal chieftain) constructed the church. The first inscription is believed to date from about 800 A.D., when Christianity was presumably introduced, and the second from the eleventh century.

Rižinice, given to the Benedictines by Duke Trpimir, whose name was preserved on a fragment, "pro Duce Trepimero," dates from the middle of the ninth century. The name of Duke Branimir has been found in at least three inscriptions. One from Šopot, near Benkovac, contains the oldest mention of the name *Hrvat*: "dux Crvatorum." Another was from Nin, and a third, found in the ruins of a circular, four-apsed church in Muć near Split, bears the date 888. There was possibly a fourth, but only a part of the name, "animer," was preserved. In the church of St. Luke, at Uzdolje, near Knin, an inscription has been discovered bearing the name of Duke Muncimir and the date 895. There are at Knin two stone plates with inscriptions, one of which mentions the Great Duke Držislav. The title, Great Duke, otherwise unknown, is highly intriguing, for Držislav is known from historical documents as a king.

The most important archaeological discovery in Croatian history was made by Bulić, who in 1898 excavated the tombstone of Queen Helen. The inscription states that the Queen's husband was King Michael and her son King Stephen. The historian Ferdo Šišić identified the kings Krešimir and Držislav from these Christian names. This discovery settled the controversy as to whether the Croatian rulers were kings in this time. The English translation of the inscription reads as follows:

> In this grave rests Helen, servant of God, the famous wife of Michael the King and mother of Stephen the King, who for a time held the reins of state herself. She renounced royal splendor on the eighth day after the Ides of October. She was laid here in the nine-hundred and seventy-sixth year after the Incarnation, in the fourth indiction, in the fifth lunar cycle, in the seventeenth "epacta," in the fifth solar cycle, at the sixth day. This is she, who during her life was mother of the realm, whereupon she became mother of the poor and patroness of widows. Thus, oh ye brother, as ye do look here, pray, saying: Oh, Lord, be merciful to her soul.[84]

In the archaeological museum in Split a column is preserved with an inscription which was correctly interpreted only a few years ago by the historian Miho Barada.[85] The inscription records the victory of the

[83]This inscription reads as follows: "Godesavo iuppano qui isto domo co[struxit]."

[84]The English translation is after Ferdo Šišić's reading. See his *Povijest,* III (1960), 107–109.

[85]Miho Barada, "Episcopus chroatensis," *Croatia sacra,* I (1931), 161–215.

archbishop of Split over the apostate Sedeha. Sedeha, a self-styled bishop and leader of the religious opposition, lived, according to Thomas of Split, a medieval writer, in the second half of the eleventh century, but the deciphering shows that he lived earlier. The medieval writer, it seems, confused two periods of religious struggles. Other inscriptions mention the names of *župans*, abbots, and other persons of less important rank. The most significant of these inscriptions was found in the church of St. Peter in Poljice, on the sarcophagus of Peter Crni, known from documents as the richest businessman of his time. All of these inscriptions are in Latin, but there are also inscriptions in the Croatian language written in Glagolitic script. The oldest inscription on stone is from Baška on the island of Krk and mentions King Zvonimir, and for the first time in the Croatian language the name *Hrvat* appears. The document is usually dated as c. 1100 A.D., but recently Josip Hamm[86] argued that the beginning of the inscription was made when King Zvonimir lived, and he dates it as 1077 A.D. Glagolitic script did not exist only on the coast. Recently Marko Vego[87] analyzed a Cyrillic inscription in Hercegovina that also contained a few Glagolitic letters. The forms of the Glagolitic letters point to the tenth or eleventh century. This indicates that in Bosnia and Hercegovina the Glagolitic script existed earlier than the Cyrillic.

It was formerly believed that the Early Croatian churches and their characteristic decoration existed only on the coast. However, the first *crkvina* in Bosnia excavated by Irma Čremošnik[88] in Rogači, near Blažuj in the Sarajevo field, brought to light a circular church with six symmetrical niches, similar to the church of the Holy Trinity in Poljud. The excavator estimates that it was built toward the end of the twelfth, or at the beginning of the thirteenth, century. Another, a one-aisled church wih a semicircular apse, was unearthed at Lisičići[89] in Hercegovina, also by Čremošnik, and shows a similarity to a church in Biskupija. A third church, St. Peter's in Zavala, excavated by Marko Vego,[90] was one-aisled and believed to be from the twelfth century. In the first and third churches, interweaving laces have been discovered;

[86]Josip Hamm, "Datiranje glagoljskih spomenika," *Radovi*, I (Zagreb: Staroslavenski Institut, 1952), 5–72.

[87]Marko Vego, "Humačka ploča—najstariji ćirilski pisani spomenik u Bosni i Hercegovini (X ili XI stoljeće)" *Glasnik*, N.S., XI (1956), 41–61.

[88]Irma Čremošnik, "Izvještaj o iskopinama u Rogačima kod Blažuja," *Glasnik*, N.S., VIII (1953), 303–315.

[89]Irma Čremošnik, "Izvještaj o iskopavanjima na crkvini kod Konjica," *Glasnik*, N.S., IX (1954), 211–226.

[90]Marko Vego, "Arheološko iskopavanje u Zavali," *Glasnik*, N.S., XIV (1959), 179–201.

they have been found in Livno and at Glamoč in Bosnia as well. Farther north, they were known previously only in Sisak. After the Second World War, however, such decorations were discovered in Marija Gorska, near Lobor, in Hrvatsko Zagorje.[91] Similar decorations in Rakovac and Banoštor, in Srijem,[92] according to Karaman, belong to Byzantine rather than to Croatian art.

In the village of Biskupija, a number of human figures made of stone have been discovered. One of them is of a bearded man[93] with a moustache, whose clothes are fastened by a belt from which hangs a Carolingian dagger. Round plates, probably of bronze, were sewn along the lower edges of this clothing, which, according to Karaman, may have preserved the form of the ancient Slavic clothing style.

The placing of graves in rows continued in Dalmatia until about 1000 A.D., but under the influence of Christianity the graves were made of stone and covered by a stone slab. Gradually, in the ninth century, the custom of placing pots with food, coins, and weapons in the graves began to disappear. In Glavičine,[94] near Mravinci around Split, a necropolis from the ninth and tenth centuries consisting of 130 graves has been unearthed. The skeletons, extended as before, were placed in an east-west direction. A large number of objects were found with them, among them 78 earrings, 28 rings, 8 copper plates and shells of a chicken egg. The burial of the last of these objects with the bodies indicates that the old pagan customs had not yet died out completely in Dalmatia. In a grave near Mogorjelo in Hercegovina, even a bear's tooth has been found. The clothes of the deceased were often embroidered and interwoven with gold. In one male grave, the remains of a silk garment have been found. Also discovered have been rare examples of stone sarcophagi in which important people were probably buried. In one such grave the skeleton was surrounded neither by weapons nor pots of food, but rather by spurs, a cross, and a golden coin of the Emperor Basilius (867–886).[95] Some graves contained daggers and spurs, and others only bows, arrows, and axes. As these latter two groups of objects were always found separately, the separation may indicate a special, or at least military distinction.

The Carolingian types of daggers[96] continued to be made during this period, but after the year 1000 their upper parts were made longer. In the eleventh century, the daggers became more pointed. Such a dagger

[91]Ljubo Karaman, "Umjetnost srednjeg vijeka u Hrvatskoj i Slavoniji," *Historijski Zbornik*, I (1948), 110.

[92]*Ibid.*, 117–119.

[93]Karaman, *Živa starina*, 74.

[94]*Ibid.*, 110–116.

[95]Karaman, *Iz Kolijevke*, 215.

[96]Karaman, *Živa starina*, 124–126.

depicted on a stone plate found near Split, shows a warrior wearing a helmet, a dagger, a spear, and a shield. In the next century the handle of the dagger became flat. Such types of daggers have been found in Dalmatia, and were also reproduced on the medieval tombstones in Bosnia and Hercegovina. The Slavs apparently did not have helmets originally, but the Croatians adopted them in the eighth and ninth centuries. Since shields have never been discovered, one may assume that they were made of wood and hide, and were, therefore, not preserved. The one shown on the above-mentioned stone plate was small and round. Spurs,[97] which have been found in great number, were made very artistically in the form of an arc with a short, sharp point. Usually they were made of bronze and silver, but some were gold plated.

Metal was also used for jewelry, especially for earrings. Some 900 earrings have been discovered, most of them dating from the ninth and tenth centuries. They were made of bronze or of gold-plated silver, and were either smooth or filigreed. Ornaments of from one to three berries were often attached to the lower part. Usually the earrings were discovered in the graves of women, but some male graves contained them too. The custom of men wearing earrings did not disappear, and even today men still wear one earring in remote villages in Dalmatia. Some of the earrings were worn in the ears, while others hung over the temples from another ring. This last type was also found among the other Slavs, and this showed Byzantine influence, although they were made by native jewelers who gave them their individual characteristics. After the first millennium the number of earrings placed in graves diminished. Very few fibulae have been discovered, and this may indicate that the people used belts to hold their clothing in place. The clothes, even of the common people, were perhaps also of Frankish origin.

Farther north, in Slavonia, especially along the Drava River, a great number of cemeteries belonging to the Bijelo Brdo Culture[98] have been discovered. The best known localities are Bijelo Brdo itself, which is near Osijek, from which the culture is named, Kloštar near Djurdjevac, Veliki Bulovac near Ludbreg, and Svinjarevci near Vukovar. This culture succeeded the Kesztehely Culture, and is dated by the coins of the Hungarian kings as having existed about 950–1150. Its center was in the Danubian regions and continued the early Slavic traditions to which new traits were added. The earthen graves were placed in rows oriented in an east-west direction. Beside the extended skeletons,

[97]*Ibid.*, 126–128. [98]*Ibid.*, 122–124.

which had gold coins in their mouths, there were pots with food, a custom that indicates a cultural lag of at least two hundred years between Dalmatia and Slavonia. Other objects found in the graves were necklaces of interwoven bronze wires, necklaces of glass, bracelets, earrings, pendants on the earrings, and S-shaped earrings. Although the S-shaped type of earring has been found among all Slavs, the center from which they spread was probably in Hungary. Many of these implements were unknown in Dalmatia. Other metal objects found were sickles, knives, scissors, and spoons.

Slavic pottery, poorly fired and decorated with the characteristic weaving and parallel lines, has been found in all sites. Franjo Ivaniček,[99] who recently conducted an excavation in Bijelo Brdo, found two kinds of pottery above a Roman layer. The first is attributed to the Langobards of the seventh and eighth centuries, and the second he considered to be Slavic from the tenth and eleventh centuries. Vinski,[100] on the other hand, believes that both were Slavic, and dates the first type from the eighth and ninth centuries. Karaman[101] agrees with Vinski, and states that such pottery was made from the eighth to the ninth centuries, and that the same type was also found in Frankish pottery from Carolingian to Ottonian times.

A new necropolis has been recently excavated by Vinski[102] in Lijeva Bara, near Vukovar. Although some 430 graves have been unearthed, it is estimated that this number comprises less than half the total. This indicates that a considerable population lived in large settlements in northern Croatia. A fortification in Mrsunjski Lug, near Brod, was built in an irregularly circular form and had a diameter of seventy-seven meters. The construction was of pressed clay, and no traces of wood or stone were found. Vinski,[103] who conducted the excavation, believes that it was one of the fortifications built against the Hungarians on the Dilj Mountain.

[99]Franjo Ivaniček, "Istraživanje nekropole ranog srednjeg vijeka u Bijelom Brdu," *Ljetopis*, LV (Jugoslavenska akademija znanosti i umjetnosti, 1949), 111–144.

[100]Zdenko Vinski, "K izvještaju o iskapanju nekropole u Bijelom Brdu," *Historijski Zbornik*, IV (1951), 304–311.

[101]Ljubo Karaman, "O potrebi povezivanja arheologa, historičara umjetnosti i historičara u proučavanju ranosrednjovjekovne Slavonije," *Historijski Zbornik*, V (1952), 62, n. 15.

[102]Zdenko Vinski, "Prethodni izvještaj o iskapanju nekropole na Lijevoj bari u Vukovaru 1951., 1952. i 1953. godine," *Ljetopis*, LX (Jugoslavenska akademija znanosti i umjetnosti, 1955), 231–255. See also Zdenko Vinski, "Ausgrabungen in Vukovar," *Archaeologia Iugoslavica*, III (1959), 99–109.

[103]Zdenko Vinski and Ksenija Vinski Gasparini, *Gradište u Mrsunjskom Lugu* (Zagreb, 1950).

In the late Middle Ages the Romanesque and Gothic styles spread to Croatia. Architecture and ornaments do not show great difference from those in other countries. However, at the same time, huge stones were made into tombstones in Bosnia and Hercegovina and some border areas of the neighboring countries in a way not known anywhere else.

MEDIEVAL TOMBSTONES IN BOSNIA AND HERCEGOVINA

Usually on hills overlooking valleys a great number of necropolises were built of large stones. They are locally called *stećak, biljeg, mramor,* or *mašet.* (*Stećak* comes from *stati,* "to stand," *biljeg* means "mark," and *mašet* is derived from the Italian *masseto,* "big stone.") Folk tradition attributes them to the Greeks, Christians, Hungarians, giants, and the like.

In order to understand the many and complicated problems of the tombstones, we shall have to say a few words about Manichaeism.[104] Manichaeism was an heretical religious movement that combined Christian concepts with the old Iranian dualism. From the Bogomils in Bulgaria the religion spread through Albania and across the Adriatic to Italy and France, where the adherents were called Patarenes and Albigenses respectively. Dominik Mandić believes that it appeared in Dalmatia and Bosnia in the eleventh century. Soon the ruler, the court, and the majority of the aristocracy and of the people accepted this creed. The Manichaeans existed in Bosnia until the coming of the Turks in 1463. Thereafter they were gradually converted to the Moslem religion.

A census taken in Bosnia and Hercegovina in 1887–1888 showed that the number of tombstones was 26,067.[105] Another census made some ten years later revealed 59,500 tombstones.[106] More were discovered later.[107] They have been found even in counties which were supposed to have none. About 900 gravestones exist at the source of the Krka River,[108] and about 800 on the Pelješac Peninsula and other localities in

[104]For the best treatment of the Manichaean problems as well as the latest findings, see Dominik Mandić, *Bogomilska crkva bosanskih krstjana* (Chicago: The Croatian Historical Institute, 1962).

[105]Ćiro Truhelka, "Sredovječni stećci Bosne i Hercegovine," *Poviest hrvatskih zemalja Bosne i Hercegovine,* ed. Krunoslav Draganović (Sarajevo: Napredak, 1942), 633.

[106]Aleksander V. Solovjev, "Broj grobnih spomenika u Bosni i Hercegovini," *Glasnik,* N.S., X (1955), 217–218.

[107]Cvetko Popović, "Manji prilozi za pitanje bogumila u Bosni," *Glasnik,* N.S., XII (1957), 235–240.

[108]R. S. Šilović, "Stećci u okolici Trogira," *Bulićev Zbornik* (Split, 1924), 689–693.

Dalmatia.[109] Furthermore, they have been found in Montenegro, in western Serbia, a few in central Serbia, and some allegedly also in Albania. Recently some tombstones in Croatia have been recognized as belonging to the same category. These are in Lika, and three hundred of them have been found in a site in Slavonia.[110] Therefore the original number of tombstones in all the regions must have been about 75,000.

Although from the sixteenth century on a great deal has been written about these tombstones, a systematic survey and description was started only some ten years ago. Separate monographs have been published about Radimlja, near Stolac in eastern Hercegovina, and Široki Brijeg and Ljubuški in western Hercegovina, Kupres in western Bosnia, and Olovo and Ludmer, near Srebrenica in eastern Bosnia.[111] Some 1,500 tombstones have been described, and their basic forms defined. Most common are flat-lying slabs and box-shaped blocks of stone. To differentiate between these two kinds of tombstones an arbitrary size was taken; those stones under 40 centimeters in height were considered flat-lying and those above 40 centimeters box-shaped. The slabs make up a third, the box-shaped blocks a fifth, and sarcophagi on slabs make up one-seventh of their total number. Other forms are plates on slabs, box-shaped locks of stone slabs, sarcophagi, and obelisks. In less than a dozen instances grave stones had the form of a cross. Double sarcophagi have been discovered in a few places. Stele (an upright placed stone) from ancient buildings and amorphous stones were used in Ludmer only. This latter custom is known from Bosanski Petrovac, in western Bosnia, where amorphous stones were used instead of tombstones until quite recently. In Ludmer, three-quarters of the hewn stones are of a "standing" form, such as stele or obelisks. In Olovo only one stone in 263 was thus. The largest tomb-

[109]Luka Katić, "Stećci u Imotskoj Krajini," *Starohrvatska Prosvjeta,* III (1954), 131–167.

[110]Andjela Horvat, "O stećcima na području Hrvatske," *Historijski Zbornik,* IV (1951), 157–165.

[111]The summary was written using primarily the following monographs: Alojz Benac, *Radimlja* (*Srednjevjekovni spomenici Bosne i Hercegovine,* I) (Sarajevo, 1950); Alojz Benac, *Olovo* (*Srednjovjekovni nadgrobni spomenici,* II) (Beograd, 1951); Alojz Benac, *Široki Brijeg* (*Srednjovjekovni spomenici Bosne i Hercegovine,* III) (Sarajevo, 1952); Dimitrije Sergejevski, *Ludmer* (*Srednjovjekovni nadgrobni spomenici,* IV) (Sarajevo, 1952); Šefik Bešlagić, *Kupres* (*Srednjovjekovni spomenici Bosne i Hercegovine*) (Sarajevo, 1954); Marko Vego, *Ljubuški* (*Srednjovjekovni nadgrobni spomenici,* VI) (Sarajevo, 1954). The two latest works by Bešlagić were published too late for consideration in this article. These are *Stećci na Blidinju* (Zagreb: Jugoslavenska akademija znanosti i umjetnosti, 1959) and "Boljuni. Sreknjovjekovni nadgrobni spomenici," *Starinar,* XII (1961), 175–205.

stone is the one near Sarajevo, which is estimated to weigh about 70,000 pounds. On the whole, the tombstones in Hercegovina are larger, probably because huge stones were more easily available there.

The origin of the different forms is still being discussed. One school thinks that the Slavs brought the custom of building a wooden house over the grave from the north, changing it later from wood to stone. Some tombstones show clearly the form of a house, including the roof. In fact, one inscription begins: "Se kuća . . ." (This house . . .). Another school sees close similarities with the Roman sarcophagi and assumes that they were copied from them. A third school finds similarities to the medieval architecture in Dalmatia, especially in Dubrovnik and in Italy. Such similarities are seen, for example, in arcades and colonnades, mainly in Hercegovina. It seems that these three opinions are not necessarily contradictory, and that they may all be correct.

Most of the tombstones are without ornament. According to Aleksandar Solovjev,[112] the outstanding historian of the Bosnian Manichaeans, in Radimlja County 48 per cent of the gravestones are decorated, in Široki Brijeg, 41 per cent, in Olovo 23 per cent, in Ludmer 16 per cent, in Kupres 11$\frac{5}{10}$ per cent, and in Travnik only 4 per cent. The ornaments consist of half-moons, stars, circles, rosettes, and twisted cords; features which have been known since Neolithic and Roman times. Some of them, like the rosette, are carved in wood even today. There are also spirals, flowers (for example, lilies), plants, trees, swastikas, and crosses. We know little about the meaning of these signs. It is thought, following Georg Wilke,[113] that they were all death symbols. The moon and stars are well known signs of the night, and therefore of death. The lily is a symbol of the moon. The swastika is also a death symbol. The circle and the rosette are thought to represent the sun, and are symbols of hope and resurrection. Solovjev,[114] on the other hand, thinks that sun and moon are works of the good god, and are the sky ships that bring the good souls to paradise.

Towers are shown on a few stones. Many tombstones were decorated with weapons, such as a dagger or a spear; some are decorated with a flag, a bow, an arrow, or a mace. In Ludmer, daggers are depicted without a shield. Bows and arrows are characteristic of Hercegovina. Generally, a dagger signifies a free man, but it may also signify a professional warrior. The great diversity of weapons and shields, and

[112]Aleksandar Solovjev, "Bogumilska umjetnost," *Enciklopedija Jugoslavije,* I (Zagreb, 1955), 644.

[113]Georg Wilke, "Ueber die Bedeutung einiger Symbole an den Bogumilendenkmälern," *Glasnik,* XXXVI (1924), 27–38.

[114]Solovjev, "Bogumilska," 644.

their relationships to each other may be due to different military ranks. The heraldic signs differ even among Široki Brijeg, Ljubuški, and Radimlja—all located in Hercegovina. On the stones in Hercegovina the deceased is often depicted standing erect with one unnaturally enlarged open hand. The meaning of this is unknown.

Human figures are depicted engaged in dancing, hunting, and in tournament. The dance is the South Slavic *kolo.* It is an old Slavic custom to hold a feast at which dances are performed after the burial. It is believed that the dance in relief on the tombstones is a funeral dance, for the *kolo* was danced in reverse order. Such examples of reversed dancing which signified mourning can be found in folklore and poetry,[115] and this custom was also known in Croatia proper in the nineteenth century. The figures shown in the dance are men or women only, but men and women are also shown together occasionally. There are a few hunting scenes that depict a bear or stag hunt. The last stone bearing an inscription was unearthed at Visoko near Sarajevo a few years ago and shows a hunting scene. A man with pointed shoes, a moustache, and a beard is depicted holding a spear with two left hands and hunting a bear with three dogs.

In a few instances other human figures are shown standing alone. Some knowledge of the hierarchy of the Manichaean Church may help to understand these. The bishop of the church was called *djed,* which in Croatian also means "grandfather." The *djed* was also known among the Bulgarian Manichaeans; he was assisted by a *gost* (guest) and a *starac* (old man). This last title is known among the Manichaeans in Italy as *ancianus.* On two stones the inscription states that the deceased was a *gost.* On one of them a figure is shown in a short dress holding a book in one hand and a cane in the other. About a dozen stones without inscriptions show such a cane, which is believed to signify a high church official. Some of these stones are called locally *djedov stećak* (grandfather's tomb). It has been accepted only recently that a bishop may be buried under such a stone.[116]

From the twelfth to the sixteenth century there were only a few churches and a few crosses in Bosnia, for the Manichaeans despised them. However, archaeologists have discovered a few tombstones in the form of a cross. Some of them may possibly be those of Christians, but others belong without doubt to the Manichaeans. In the latter

115Drago Vidović, "Pretstave kola na stećcima i njihovo značenje," *Glasnik,* N.S., IX (1954), 275–278.

116Jovo Vuković and Ante Kučan, "Jedan stari bosanski nadgrobni spomenik i natpis," *Glasnik,* N.S., II (1947), 51–68.

instance, however, these are not real crosses, but rather stylized human figures,[117] since the Manichaeans showed Christ with horizontal arms and this, superficially, may look like a cross. In fact, on some cross-like stones one can clearly recognize a head, eyes, a moustache, and a beard.

Although the majority of the people seem to have belonged to the heretical church, it would be wrong to assume that under every tombstone there lies a Manichaean. We find, for example, a tombstone in the form of a cross where the deceased was very anxious not to be confused with heretics, since the inscription states that he was of the true Roman religion. In Široki Brijeg,[118] a man is depicted on a tombstone leaning with one hand against a tree holding a child with a cross in the other hand. Both the man and the child have aureolas, or halos, over their heads. It is believed that the man was St. Christopher, because almost the same representation of him has been found on the coat-of-arms in the city of Rab, which is Catholic. Furthermore, Catholicism is confirmed by two crossed keys—a Catholic symbol—on the upper face of a stone. It is possible that all the necropolises in Široki Brijeg belonged to the Catholics. Perhaps this has also been the case in Ljubuški, farther south, where one-third of the stones are ornamented with crosses. Near Trebinje, in eastern Hercegovina, an inscription says that the deceased was called Nikolavus, a name derived from the Catholic Nikolaus. Furthermore, some tombstones in eastern Hercegovina may have belonged to members of the Eastern Orthodox Church.

Only a few of the graves have been examined by archaeologists, who for the most part have opened the ones located under spectacular stones with the assumption that they belonged to important people. Grave robbers, it seems, already had the same idea, for the majority of these graves were empty; others, not robbed, contained few objects. Fortunately an undisturbed grave of an important statesman has recently been discovered.[119] In addition to many contemporary objects, a glass was found near the skull, and the corpse had a gold coin in its mouth, suggesting that the old pagan customs had not died out even among the highest aristocracy. Stones with inscriptions have been found in only some hundred instances, most of them saying, "Here lies . . . on his land," or "his inherited," or "his noble and inherited

[117]Aleksander Solovjev, "Jesu li bogomili poštovali krst," *Glasnik*, N.S., III (1948), 81–102.

[118]Benac, *Široki Brijeg*, 47.

[119]Marko Vego, "Nadgrobni spomenici porodice Sanković u selu Biskupu kod Konjica," *Glasnik*, N.S., X (1955), 164.

property," and so on. Very common is an inscription which has also been found quite recently in the United States: "I was as you are, you will be as am I." The inscriptions are in *bosančica,* the Bosnian variant of the Cyrillic script.

In a few instances it is possible to date the tombstones by the form of the monument, but inscriptions are preferable, since names that are also known from historical documents sometimes appear. These point to the second half of the fourteenth, the fifteenth, and the sixteenth centuries, as do the forms of the daggers. Since obelisks are customarily made by Moslems, they point to the second half of the fifteenth century and later. Sabers are of oriental origin, and are found only on the obelisks. However, as inscriptions represent the cultural climax, simple tombstones, especially those without decorations, may well go back to the thirteenth century, or even earlier.

Bibliography

Andjelić, Pavao. "Dva srednjevjekovna nalaza iz Sultića kod Konjica," *Glasnik,* XIV (1959), 203–215.

Barić, Henrik. *Lingvističke studije.* Sarajevo, 1954.

Benac, Alojz. "Završna istraživanja u pećini Hrustovači" *Glasnik,* N.S., III (1948), 3–42.

———. *Radimlja* (*Srednjevjekovni spomenici Bosne i Hercegovine,* I). Sarajevo, 1950.

———. *Olovo* (*Srednjevjekovni nadgrobni spomenici,* II). Belgrade, 1951.

———. *Prehistorijsko naselje Nebo i problem butmirske kulture.* Ljubljana, 1952.

———. *Široki Brijeg* (*Srednjevjekovni spomenici Bosne i Hercegovine,* III). Sarajevo, 1952.

———. "Neolitsko naselje u Lisičićima kod Konjica," *Glasnik,* N.S., X (1955), 49–84.

———. "Preistorisko doba," *Kulturna istorija Bosne i Hercegovine,* ed. Alojz Benac *et al.* Sarajevo, 1955.

———. "Osnova obilježja neolitske kulture u Kaknju," *Glasnik,* N.S., XI (1956), 167–182.

———. "Vaza bronzanog doba iz Bos. Rače," *Glasnik,* N.S., X (1956), 183–186.

———. "Crvena Stijena—1955" (I–IV Stratum), *Glasnik,* N.S., XII (1957), 19–50.

———. "Neke nove prethistorijske kulture u sjeveroistočnoj Bosni," *Članci i gradja za kulturnu istoriju istočne Bosne,* I (1957), 209–213.

———. "Zelena pećina," *Glasnik,* N.S., XII (1957), 61–92.

———. "Bosnia, Hercegovina and Montenegro," Area 6—Balkans, I, COWA Survey. Cambridge: Council for Old World Archaeology, 1959, 12–13.

———. "Grenzzone der Vinča-Kultur in Ostbosnien," *Archaeologia Iugoslavica,* III (1959), 5–11.

——. "Neolitski telovi u sjeveroistočnoj Bosni i neki problemi bosanskog neolita," *Glasnik*, N.S., XV–XVI (1960–1961), 39–78.

——. "Studien zur Stein- und Kupferzeit im nordwestlichen Balkan," *42. Bericht der Römisch-Germanischen Kommission 1961*. Berlin, 1962, 1–171.

Benac, Alojz, and Čović, Borivoj. *Glasinac, I. Bronzano doba*. Sarajevo, 1956.

——. *Glasinac, II. Željezno doba*. Sarajevo, 1957.

Bešlagić, Šefik. *Kupres* (*Srednjevjekovni spomenici Bosne i Hercegovine*, V). Sarajevo, 1954.

——. *Stećci na Blidinju*. Zagreb, 1959.

——. "Boljuni. Srednjovjekovni nadgrobni spomenici," *Starinar*, XII (1961), 175–205.

Bižic, Ružica. "Grobovi u Donjoj Dolini," *Glasnik*, N.S., VII (1952), 201–229.

Brodar, Mitja. "Crvena Stijena (Stratum V)," *Glasnik*, N.S., XII (1957), 51–55.

Brodar, Srečko. "Das Paläolithikum in Jugoslawien," *Quartär*, I (Berlin, 1938).

Childe, Gordon V. *The Danube in Prehistory*. Oxford. 1929.

——. *The Dawn of European Civilization*. New York, 1958.

Coon, Carleton S. *The Origin of Races*. New York: Alfred A. Knopf, 1962.

Čović, Borivoj. "Barice—nekropola kasnog bronzanog doba kod Gračanice," *Glasnik*, N.S., XIII (1958), 77–96.

——. "Ilirska nekropola u Čarakovu," *Glasnik*, N.S., XI (1956), 187–204.

——. "Nekoliko manjih preistoriskih nalaza iz Bosne i Hercegovine," *Glasnik*, N.S., XII (1957), 241–255.

Čremošnik, Grga, and Sergejevski, Dimitrije. "Gotisches und Römisches aus Breza bei Sarajevo." Vorläufiger Bericht. Sarajevo: *Novitates Musei Sarajevoensis*, 1930.

Čremošnik, Irma. "Nalaz slovenske keramike u Rači 1947 god. i pregled nalaza slovenske keramike u Bosni do danas," *Glasnik*, N.S., IV–V, (1949–1950), 383–396.

——. "Izvještaj o iskopinama u Rogačima kod Blažuja," *Glasnik*, VIII, (1953), 303–315.

——. "Izvještaj o iskopavanjima na crkvini kod Konjica," *Glasnik*, IX (1954), 211–226.

——. "Reljef Silvana i nimfa iz Založja (Bihać)," *Glasnik*, N.S., XI (1956), 111–126.

Dimitrijević, Stojan. "Prilog daljem upoznavaju vučedolske kulture," *Opuscula Archaeologica*, I (1956), 5–56.

Duhn, Friedrich, and Messerschmidt, Franz. *Italische Gräberkunde*, Zweiter Teil. Heidelberg, 1935.

Dyggve, Ejnar. *History of Salonitan Christianity*. Oslo: Istituttet for Sammenlignende kulturforskning, Serie A., XXI, 1951.

Fiala, Franz, and Hoernes, Moriz. *Die neolitische Station von Butmir*, II. Vienna, 1898.

Filipović, Miljenko. "Tragovi Perunova kulta kod južnih Slavena," *Glasnik*, III (1948), 63–80.

Gabričević, Branko. "Iconographie de Mitra tauroctone dans la province romaine de Dalmatie," *Archaeologia Iugoslavica*, I (1954), 37–63.

Garašanin, Milutin V. "Datiranje dubovačko-žutobrdske grupe," *Zbornik Matice srpske*, No. 2 (1951), 83–88.

Gorjanović-Kramberger, Karl. *Der diluviale Mensch von Krapina in Kroatien*. Wiesbaden: C. V. Kreidel, 1906.

Hamm, Josip. "Datiranje glagoljskih spomenika," *Radovi* I. Zagreb: Staroslavenski Institut, 1952, 5–72.

Hencken, Hugh. *Indo-European Languages and Archaeology*. American Anthropologist, Memoir No. 84. (Menasha, 1955).

Horvat, Andjela. "O stećcima na području Hrvatske," *Historijski Zbornik*, IV (1951), 157–165.

Hrdličha, Aleš. "The Krapina Man," *Xenia Honoribus Illustrissimi Domini Professoris Doctoris Caroli Gorjanović-Kramberger*. Zagreb, 1925–26, 510–511.

——. "The Neanderthal Phase of Man," *Journal of the Royal Anthropological Institute*, LVII (1927), 249–274.

Ivaniček, Franjo. "Istraživanje nekropole ranog srednjeg vijeka u Bijelom Brdu," *Ljetopis*, LV (Jugoslavenska akademija znanosti i umjetnosti, 1949), 111–114.

Iveković, Ćiril M. "Bunje, ćemeri i poljarice," *Zbornik kralja Tomislava*. Zagreb: Jugoslavenska akademija znanosti i umjetnosti, 1925, 413–429.

Karaman, Ljubo. "Crkvica sv. Mihajla kod Stona," *Vjesnik hrvatskog arheološkog društva*, N.S., XV (1928).

——. *Iz hrvatske prošlosti*. Zagreb: Matica Hrvatska, 1930.

——. *Živa starina*. Zagreb, 1942.

——. "O umjetnosti srednjeg vijeka u Hrvatskoj i Slavoniji," *Historijski Zbornik*, I (1948), 103–127.

——. "O potrebi povezivanja rada arheologa, historičara umjetnosti i historičara u proučavanju ranosrednjovjekovne Slavonije," *Historijski Zbornik*, V (1952), 57–62.

——. "O bosanskim srednjovjekovnim stećcima," *Starohrvatska Prosvjeta*, III (1954), 171–182.

——. "Glossen zu einigen Fragen der slawischen Archäologie," *Archaeologia Iugoslavica*, II (1956), 100–109.

Katić, Luka. "Stećci u Imotskoj Krajini," *Starohrvatska Prosvjeta*, III (1954), 131–167.

Korošec, Josip. *Predzgodovinska naselbina na Ptujskem gradu*. Ljubljana, 1951.

——. "Sloveni i drvena kultura," *Glasnik*, N.S., VI (1951), 65–80.

——. *Uvod v materijalno kulturo Slovanov zgodnjega veka*. Ljubljana, 1952.

——. *Neolitska naseobina u Danilu Bitinju. Rezultati istraživanja u 1953 godini*, I. Zagreb: Jugoslavenska akademija znanosti i umjetnosti, 1958.

——. *Ibid.*, II, *Prilozi* (Supplements) 1959.

Kromer, Karl. "Zum Picentenproblem," *Mitteilungen der prähistorischen Kommission der Oesterreichischen Akademie der Wissenschaften*, V, No. 5 (Vienna, 1950).

Malez, Mirko. "Die Höhle Veternica, eine neue Paläolithische Fundstelle in Kroatien," *Bulletin scientifique*, III (1956), 11–12.

——. "Erster Fund des oberdiluvialen Menschen im dinarischen Karst," *Bulletin scientifique*, III (1956), 47–48.

———. "Novija istraživanja pećina u N. R. Hrvatskoj," *Acta geologica*, I (1956), 179–193.

———. "Paläolithikum in Samobor bei Zagreb," *Bulletin scientifique*, III (1956), 49–50.

———. "Paleontološko istraživanje pećine Veternice u 1955 god.," *Ljetopis*, LXII (Zagreb: Jugoslavenska akademija znanosti i umjetnosti, 1957), 280–295.

Mandić, Dominik. *Bogomilska crkva bosanskih krstjana.* Chicago: The Croatian Historical Institute, 1962.

Mayer, Antun. "Bosna u ilirsko doba," *Poviest hrvatskih zemalja Bosne i Hercegovine*, ed. Krunoslav Draganović. Sarajevo: Napredak, 1942, 103–120.

Milojčić, Vladimir. "Die dorische Wanderung im Lichte der vorgeschichtlichen Funde," *Archaeologischer Anzeiger*, 1948–1949, 13–35.

———. *Chronologie der jüngeren Steinzeit Mittel- und Südost- Europas.* Berlin, 1949.

———. "Die erste präkeramische bäuerliche Siedlung der Jungsteinzeit in Europa," *Germania*, XXXIV (1957), 208–210.

Novak, Grga. *Prethistorijski Hvar. Grapčeva špilja.* Zagreb: Jugoslavenska akademija znanosti i umjetnosti, 1955.

Popović, Cvetko. "Manji prilozi za pitanje bogumila u Bosni," *Glasnik*, N.S., XII (1957), 235–240.

Prijatelj, Kruno. "Einige hellenistische Elemente in der Skulptur des antiken Salone," *Archaeologia Iugoslavica*, I, 29–37.

Puš, Ivan. "Neolitsko naselje u Tuzli," *Članci i gradja za kulturnu istoriju Bosne*, I, 85–192.

Radimský, Vaclav, and Hoernes, Moriz. *Die neolitische Station von Butmir*, I. Vienna, 1895.

Schmidt, R. R. *Die Burg Vučedol.* Zagreb: Das kroatische archäologische Staatsmuseum in Zagreb, 1945.

Šeper, Mirko: "Der Taufstein des kroatischen Fürsten Višeslav aus dem frühen Mittelalter," *Nachrichten des Deutschen Instituts für merowingisch-karolingische Kunstforschung* (Erlangen), No. 14–15 (1957–1958), 1–21.

Sergejevski, Dimitrije. "Japodske urne," *Glasnik*, N.S., IV–V (1950), 45–94.

———. *Ludmer.* (*Srednjevjekovni nadgrobni spomenici*, IV). Sarajevo, 1952.

———. "Doba rimske vladavine," *Kulturna istorija Bosne i Hercegovine*, ed. Alojz Benac *et al.* Sarajevo, 1955.

Šilović, R. S. "Stećci u okolici Trogira," *Bulićev Zbornik* (Split, 1924), 689–693.

Šišić, Ferdo. *Povijest Hrvata u vrijeme narodnih vladara.* Zagreb, 1925.

Solovjev, Aleksander. "Bogumilska umjetnost," *Enciklopedija Jugoslavije*, I (Zagreb, 1955), 644–645.

———. "Broj grobnih spomenika u Bosni i Hercegovini," *Glasnik*, N.S., X (1956), 217–218.

———. "Jesu li bogomili poštovali krst," *Glasnik*, N.S., III (1948), 81–102.

Truhelka, Ćiro. "Bosna u prehistoričko doba," *Poviest hrvatskih zemalja Bosne i Hercegovine*, ed. Krunoslav Draganović. Sarajevo: Napredak, 1942, 78–102.

———. "Sredovječni stećci Bosne i Hercegovine," *Poviest hrvatskih zemalja*

Bosne i Hercegovine, ed. Krunoslav Draganović. Sarajevo: Napredak, 1942.

Vego, Marko. "Arheološko iskopavanje u Zavali," *Glasnik*, XIV (1959), 179–201.

——. "Humačka ploča najstariji ćirilski pisani spomenik u Bosni i Hercegovini (X ili XI stoljeće)," *Glasnik*, XI (1956), 41–61.

——. *Ljubuški* (*Srednjevjekovni nadgrobni spomenici*, VI). Sarajevo, 1954.

——. "Nadgrobni spomenici porodice Sanković u selu Biskupu kod Konjica," *Glasnik*, N.S., X (1955), 157–167.

Vidović, Drago. "Pretstave kola na stećcima i njihovo značenje," *Glasnik*, N.S., IX, 275–278.

Vinski, Zdenko. "Ausgrabungen in Vukovar," *Archaeologia Iugoslavica*, III, (1959), 99–109.

——. "Zur Anwendbarkeit der C14 Datierung in der Vorgeschichtsforschung. II Teil," *Germania*, XXXVI (1958), 409–417.

——. "Gibt es frühslavische Keramik aus der südslawischen Landnahme?" *Archaeologia Iugoslavica*, I (1954), 71–96.

——. "Prethodni izvještaj o iskapanju nekropole na Lijevoj bari u Vukovaru 1951, 1952 i 1953 godine," *Ljetopis*, LX (Zagreb: Jugoslavenska akademija znanosti i umjetnosti, 1955), 231–255.

Vinski, Zdenko and Vinski Gasparini, Ksenija. *Gradište u Mrsunjskom lugu*. Zagreb, 1950.

——. "Prolegomena k statistici i kronologiji prethistorijskih ostava u Hrvatskoj i u vojvodjanskom području Srijema," *Opuscula Archaeologica*, I (1956), 57–99.

Vuković, Jovo and Kučan, Ante. "Jedan stari bosanski nadgrobni spomenik i natpis," *Glasnik*, N.S., II (1947), 51–68.

Vuković, Stjepan. "Paleolitska kamena industrija špilje Vindije," *Historijski Zbornik*, III (1950), 241–255.

——. "Prehistorijsko nalazište špilje Vindije," *ibid.*, II, 243–294.

Waterbolk, H. T. "The 1959 Carbon-14 Symposium at Groningen," *Antiquity*, XXXIV (1960), 14–18.

Whatmouth, Joshua. *The Foundation of Roman Italy*. London, 1937.

Wilke, Georg. "Ueber die Bedeutung einiger Symbole an den Bogumilendenkmälern," *Glasnik*, XXXVI (1924), 27–38.

3

Political History to 1526

STANKO GULDESCU

Theories of the Croatian Origins

No contemporary accounts of the coming of the Croatian people to the lands occupied by their present-day descendants have survived to our time. In the absence of verifiable records, diverse theories have been advanced to explain who the original Croatians were and why and how they came to settle along the Adriatic littoral and in the northern Balkans. Since these several theories are discussed in some detail in my *History of Medieval Croatia*, it will suffice to allude to them very briefly in this essay.[1]

When the concepts of modern nationalism penetrated into the Croatian lands in the first part of the nineteenth century, they were pervaded by romanticist influences stemming from the literary and artistic vogue that had swept Europe after the Napoleonic wars. A group of Croatian and foreign intellectuals conceived the idea that the Croatians, Serbs, and Slovenes were descended from the Illyrian tribes who had inhabited the Adriatic and Balkan areas in ancient times. Later on wide credence was given to the notion that the Croatians were a purely Slavic stock and originally identical with the Serbian and Slovene tribes. This assumption was and continues to be based upon the fact that the Croatian language belongs to the Slavic linguistic family and resembles the speech of the Serbians and Slovenes. But we know that the Finno-Ugrian Bulgars, whose name is perpetuated in that of the modern Bulgarian state, were absorbed and Slavicized by their mass of Slavonic subjects, so that today they are considered to be

[1]Stanko Guldescu-Juldanić, *History of Medieval Croatia to 1526* (The Hague: Mouton & Co., 1964), Chapters 2–3.

an indisputably Slavic people. There is an increasing amount of evidence accumulating to suggest that the primitive Croatian tribes experienced the same fate. As late as the thirteenth century, however, the Croatian nobility seems to have been conscious of its non-Slavic origin.[2] Unfortunately the surviving records of this caste provide no clues to the solution of the mystery of the Croatian ethnic identity.

The earliest evidence of the presence of Croatians in Europe is the mention of their name in the Greek form *Choroathos* in inscriptions carved on tombstones near the site of the Greek colony of Tanaïs in southern Russia. These sepulchral inscriptions date from the second or third century A.D. Most scholars ascribe them to Iranian (Persian) elements who for many centuries dominated the steppes of southern Russia. Undoubtedly the Scythians and Sarmatians, who succeeded one another as masters of the steppe land, both included in their ranks a mélange of Iranian frontier elements.[3] Inevitably the Sarmatians in particular must have exerted great influence over the Slavic peoples who lived between the Don and Danube Rivers, for they achieved political dominance over them.[4] Even genuinely Slavic tribes were subjected to Iranian ruling castes. The late Rumanian historian, Dr. Nicolae Iorga, is only one of a number of competent scholars who believe that the Slavs made their first appearance in history as members of the Sarmatian confederation. Professors Francis Dvornik and Nikola Županċić think that the original Croatians were an Iranian Sarmatian rather than a Slavic people.[5] On the other hand, there is an increasing tendency to credit the Tanaïs inscriptions to still another Iranian-Caucasian group, the Alans. This tribe appeared on the Black Sea

[2]V. Klaić, "Hrvatska plemena od XII do XVI stoljeća," *Rad Jugosl. akad. znanosti i umjetnosti*, CXXX (1897), 15ff. See also L. Hauptmann, "Die Herkunft der Kärntner Edlinge," *Vierteljahrschrift für Sozial-und Wirtschaftsgeschichte*, XXI (1928), 263–274, and his "Podrijetlo hrvatskoga plemstva," *Rad*, CCLXXIII (1942); Thomas Archidiaconus, *Historia Salonitana*, Vol. XXVI of *Mon. spect. hist. Slav. meridionalium* (Zagreb, 1894), 25.

[3]M. Rostovtseff, *Iranians and Greeks in South Russia* (Oxford, 1922), 38–39; E. Minns, *Scythians and Greeks* (London and New York, 1923), 41–43. The findings of these scholars should be compared with those of Max Wasmer, *Untersuchungen über den ältesten Wohnsitz der Slaven: 1. Die Iranier in Südrussland* (Leipzig, 1923).

[4]Rostovtseff, *Iranians*, 135–146, *passim*; M. Ebert, *Südrussland im Altertum* (Bonn and Leipzig, 1921), 106.

[5]N. Županċić, "Prvobitni Hrvati," *Zbornik kralja Tomislava u spomen tisućugodišnjice hrvatskoga kraljevstva* (Zagreb, 1925), 291–296; F. Dvornik, *The Slavs. Their Early History and Civilization* (Boston, 1956), 22–24, 47–53. See also B. Antonoff, *Skythien und der Bosporus* (Berlin, 1931), *passim*; Minns, *Scythians*, 35–129, *passim*; L. V. Südland (Pilar), *Južnoslavensko pitanje* (Zagreb, 1943), viii–x, 6–9, 11–12.

littoral in the first century of the Christian era, settled around Tanaïs, and remained in this area for three full centuries.

In their own language the Croatians call themselves *Hrvati.* There seems to be an etymological connection between this term and the Alan word for "friend," *hu-urvatha.*[6] On the shores of the Black Sea the Alans absorbed two Sarmatian peoples, the Siraci and Aorsi. Many Alans, too, affiliated themselves with the Gothic nation which, in the third century A.D., replaced the Sarmatians as the masters of southern Russia. The names "Safrac" and "Andag," which appear in the Gothic annals, are clearly Alanic. Also, the Goths undoubtedly absorbed both Sarmatian and Slavic groups during their two centuries of rule over the steppe land. Often the Romans themselves did not know whether the peoples living west of the Vistula were Gothic or Sarmatian.[7]

To the east of the Goths and Alans, in the basins of the Don and Donetz Rivers, there lived a confederation of tribes which bore the name Antes.[8] They were a ruling warrior caste of Iranian-Caucasian origin who had subjugated a larger mass of Slavic farmers. Hence they were usually thought to be Slavs themselves. Antes, Goths, and Alans all yielded to the advance of the Huns about 375 A.D. For some time the Antes, along with the Ostrogoths (East Goths) and Alanic elements associated with the latter, remained subject to the Huns. In the fifth century, the Ante empire was revived, and Croatian tribes were known to the west of the Ante confederacy. There is reason to believe that these Croatians represented an amalgam of Iranian stocks who were or had been ruled by the Ostrogoths, but who had become Slavicized through association and intermarriage with Slavic elements which had survived the Hunnish holocaust.[9] There must also have been intermarriage between the Croatians and the Antes.

Meanwhile the Visigoths, or West Goths, accompanied by a large

[6]Roman St. Kaulfuss, *Die Slawen in den Ältesten Zeiten bis Samo* (623) (Berlin, 1842), 6–9. Hauptmann accepts this identity.

[7]Caspar Zeuss, *Die Deutschen und ihre Nachbarstämme* (Munich, 1837), 275–312, 691–694; P. J. Safarik, *Slavische Alterthümer* (Prague, 1837), I, 16.

[8]Both the Byzantine historian, Procopius, and the Goth, Jornandes, seem to have been aware of the non-Slavic origin of the Antes. On this people, see L. Niederle, *Manuel de l'antiquité slave* (2 vols.; Paris, 1923), I, 189–193; Schord Bekmursin Nogmov, *Geschichten und Lieder der circass. Völker* (Leipzig 1866); and Jornandes' account in Theodor Mommsen (ed.), *De origine actibusque Getarum,* Vol. V of *Mon. Germaniae historica* (Berlin, 1882), 62–63.

[9]This thesis has been advanced with particular reference to the Goths rather than to the Iranians by Professor Rus of the University of Ljubljana, in *Kralji dinastije Svevladičev* (Ljubljana, 1932). As indicated elsewhere in this study, however, the Iranian and the Gothic theories of Croatian origins are dependent upon one another.

Alanic contingent, had fled across the Danube to escape the Huns between 376 and 378 A.D.[10] At the beginning of the fifth century a mixed Visigothic-Alanic horde, under Radagas and Alaric, descended upon Italy and those territories that are today known as Croatian. Other such inroads occurred in 406, 459, 471, and 489. This last-indicated invasion resulted in the establishment of an Ostrogothic kingdom that included Italy, Dalmatia, Bosnia, Slavonia, Istria, and what is today known as Upper Croatia. In fact, from about 454 A.D. until the middle of the following century, the Ostrogoths claimed rule over all lands south of the Danube and eastward of the confluence of that river with the Sava. The bulk of their Visigothic kinsmen had moved westward by this time into Gaul and Iberia (modern France and Spain). The Iranian and Gothic theories of the Croatian origins depend upon the assumption that considerable numbers of Goths, Alans, and other Iranian stocks included in the Gothic horde, remained in the lands that were destined to become Croatian. In a war that lasted from 534 to 553 the Byzantines (Eastern Roman Empire) overthrew the Ostrogothic kingdom, and the Ostrogoths "went over the mountains," as contemporary chroniclers put it, and disappeared from the pages of history. Were these mountains the Julian Alps at the head of the Adriatic Sea? Their fathers and grandfathers had crossed these ranges in 489, when Theodoric the Younger led them out of the latter-day Croatian territories into Italy. Some authorities think that groups of Alans, and possibly other Iranian elements as well, stayed in the backlands of Dalmatia, Upper Croatia, and Bosnia when Theodoric took the bulk of his people on to Italy.[11] Professor Ljudmil Hauptmann, who does not put much faith in the identification of the Croatians with the Ostrogoths, nevertheless has acknowledged that there is no reason to suppose that the Gothic or Iranian settlements established by Theodoric in Upper Croatia, Bosnia, and other regions of modern Croatia disappeared when the Italian kingdom of the Ostrogoths col-

[10]E. Benenger, "Der westgotisch-alanische Zug nach Mitteleuropa, *Manus Bibliothek*, LI (1931), 118 ff.

[11]On the Alanic element in Croatian ancestry, see Luka Jelić, *Hrvatski spomenici ninskoga područja iz dobe hrvatskih vladara* (Zagreb, 1911), 2–32, *passim.* See also Hauptmann, "Die Herkunft der Kärntner Edlinge"; Dvornik, *The Slavs*, 64; Z. Vinski, *Uz problematiku starog Irana i Kavkaza* (Zagreb, 1940), 20–21; P. Lesiak, "Edling-Kazage," *Carinthia* (Klagenfurt), I (1913), 84. The word "Kaseg" crops up in many Croatian settlement areas. It seems to have designated the members of a ruling Iranian caste that dominated Slavic agriculturists. Professor Hauptmann thinks that over a period of many centuries, beginning in the pre-Christian era, an Iranian tribe known as the Harahvati emigrated from old Iran into the Caucasus where they intermarried with a Caucasian tribe, the Kasegs. The Alans may represent an offshoot of this union.

lapsed.[12] There certainly was available to the Ostrogothic fugitives from Italy a ready-made "hideout" in the modern Croatian uplands, whether they made use of it or not. Although the Byzantines drove the Goths from the Dalmatian coast, the power of the Greeks did not extend far inland. And while most scholars still tend to discount or to explain away their testimony, the fact cannot be overlooked that three of the four oldest surviving accounts that deal with the settlement of the Croatians on the Adriatic positively identify this people with the Goths.[13] The composers of these chronicles do not seem to have been

[12]Dr. Rus has contended that there was a Gothic group in the latter-day Croatian lands that survived the collapse of the Ostrogothic Italian kingdom. See *Kralji dinastije Svevladičev*, 131ff. Professor Hauptmann's statement appeared in an issue of *Germano-slavica* (Prague, 1935), 98. The late Professor Francis Preveden also acknowledged, in his *History of the Croatian People* (New York, 1955), that the Croatians probably absorbed "rather small" groups of Goths.

[13]In 1509 there was found near Omiš what is usually referred to as the "Old Croatian Chronicle" or *Kraljevstvo Hrvata* (Kingdom of the Croatians). A Latin and later an Italian translation of this work were made. The translation came to be known as the *Libellum Gothorum* or "Book of the Goths" because it stated that the Goths were the people from whom the latter-day Croatians derived. Dr. Dominik Mandić has recently advanced evidence to prove that this chronicle was originally written between 1074 and 1081. See his *Nenapisano poglavlje hrvatske pismenosti* (Buenos Aires, 1961), 377–379. This is a special reprint of an article that appeared in *Hrvatska Revija* (Buenos Aires), XI, No. 4 (44). Mandić thinks that the unknown compiler confused the Goths with the Croatians because the Latins used to call Croatians "Goths," that is, "barbarians," as a derogatory form of reference, and therefore simply lumped the two together. See, however, his *Bosna i Hercegovina* (Chicago, 1960), 36–37, 39, in which he notes the early association of the sub-Carpathian Kajkavci-speaking Slavs—whom he believes to be the ancestors of the people of modern northwestern Croatia—with the Goths. See also, for a more detailed treatment of the *Kraljevstvo Hrvata*, his *Crvena Hrvatska* (Chicago, 1957), Chapter II.

A Latin priest who knew Croatian seems to have translated the *Kraljevstvo Hrvata* into Latin between 1143 and 1163. He joined to it additional materials pertaining to his native Duklja (Dioclea), together with a description of events of which he himself had been an eyewitness, or which he had heard about from people who were old when he was still a young man. His chronicle became known as the "Chronicle of the Priest of Dioclea." Available editions include Ivan Crnčić (ed.), *Popa Dukljanina Ljetopis* (Kraljevica, 1874); Ferdo Šišić (ed.), *Letopis Popa Dukljanina* (Beograd-Zagreb, 1928); and V. Mošin (ed.), *Ljetopis popa Dukljanina* (Zagreb, 1950). See also "Kraljevstvo Hrvata," in "Presbyteri Diocleani, De regno Sclavorum," ed. J. Lucius (Lučić), *De regno Dalmatiae et Croatiae* (Amsterdam, 1666), 287–302; G. Schwandtner (ed.), *Scriptores rerum Hungaricarum* III (Vienna, 1748), 474–509; Ivan Kukuljević-Sakcinski, "Kronika hrvatska iz XII vieka," *Arkiv za povjestnicu jugoslavensku*, I (Zagreb, 1851), 1–37. Archdeacon Thomas of Split, who probably finished his *Historia Salonitana* (Vol. XXVI of *Mon. spect. hist. Slav. merid.*) shortly before his death in 1268, also described the Croatians as Goths, but said they were also known as Slavs because they came from Poland. See chapter 7 of his work, and the defense of its accuracy by Father Kerubin Šegvić, *Toma Splićanin* (Zagreb, 1927), and "Tommaso l'arcidiacono e la sua opera," a supplement to *Bollettino d'archeologia*

aware, however, of the large Iranian element that was included in the Gothic nation. Nor do the supporters of the Iranian theory of the Croatian origins seem to realize that the validity of this hypothesis depends upon the intimate association of Iranians and Goths over a period of three centuries.

In any case, it appears evident that the ancestors of the modern Croatians were a mixed ethnic group. Iranian-Gothic blood must have thinned out progressively with the passage of time. There were no neighboring Gothic or Iranian groups from which the Croatians could draw accretions of strength, possibly excepting the Iranian Iasyges, who, until well into the fourth century, dominated various Slavic tribes along the left bank of the Danube. About 334 A.D. a Slav revolt drove them across the river into Roman territory, and subsequently they came under the rule of the Ostrogoths. Probably they were the last non-Slavic group to contribute a strain of blood to the nascent Croatian nation before or during the time that it effected its settlement on the Adriatic.[14]

When this settlement on the Adriatic Sea occurred is a matter of speculation. The earliest known commentator on Croatian affairs, the

---

e storia Dalmata (Split, 1914). See also Šegvić, *I Croati e la loro missione storica durante tredici secoli* (Rome, 1941).

On the Gothic-Croatian relationship, see also G. Ruggeri, *Contributo all' antropología física delle regioni dinariche e danubiane e dell' Asia anteriore* (Firenze, 1906); Ludwig Gumplowicz, "Die politische Geschichte der Serben und Kroaten," *Politische Anthropologische Revue*, anno 1 (Lipsin, 1913), 780; Johann Valvasor, *Die Ehre des Herzogthums Krain* (Laybach-Ljubljana, 1689), II, 157–159; Tadija Smičiklas, *Poviest hrvatska* (2 vols.; Zagreb, 1879 and 1882), I, 79; Ferdo Šišić (ed.), *Enchiridion fontium historiae Croatiae* (Zagreb, 1914), 139–148 (documents). Of course, the Ostrogoths were subjected to Iranian cultural influences from the first days of their arrival in southern Russia, as their art shows very clearly.

[14]According to their own account, the Iasyges were of Median descent. Their customs, mores, and administrative organization closely resembled those of the Parthians. In 471 they accompanied the Ostrogoths and Alans in their invasion of Dalmatia and upper Croatia. On this people, see Karl Freiherr v. Czoernig, *Ethnographie der Österr. Monarchie* (3 vols.; Vienna, 1857), II, 16ff. and Mandić, *Bosna i Hercegovina*, I, 31–32. A popular account of the Iranian theory in general is given in Fra Oton Knezović, *Poviest Hrvata* (Madrid, 1961), 16–17. Dr. Mandić summarizes this theory in *Crvena Hrvatska*, 198–199, and his footnotes on page 198 contain a reference list on this subject. See also S. Sakač, "Iranische Herkunft des kroatischen Volksnamens," *Orientalia Christiana periodica*, XV (1949), 313–340; H. Gregoire, "L'origine et le nom des Croates et leur prétendue patrie caucasienne," *La nouvelle Clio*, IV (1952), 323, and V (1953), 3, 466; George Vernadsky, "Great Moravia and White Chorvatia," *Journal of the American Oriental Soc.*, LXV (1945), 257–259; L. Hauptmann, "Kroaten, Goten, und Sarmaten," *Germanoslavica* (Prague), III (1935), 347; Südland (Pilar), *Južnoslavensko pitanje*, viii–ix.

Byzantine emperor, Constantine Porphyrogenitus, composed his *De administrando imperio* between 948 and 952 A.D. He asserted in this volume that his predecessor, Emperor Heraclios (610–641), invited the Croatians to take possession of the eastern shore of the Adriatic for the purpose of driving out a neo-Hunnic tribe known as the Avars, who were giving Byzantium trouble at the time.[15] Most scholars accept Constantine's account of the Croatian settlement and assume that it took place between 626 and 641 A.D. From the coast the Croatian clans fanned out to take possession of old Roman Illyria and Pannonia, that is, of modern Upper Croatia, Bosnia, and the territory between the Drava and Sava Rivers[16] that later was to become known as Slavonia. It can be inferred that the Croatians extended their sway southward as far as present-day Albania and inland up to the Drina River.

Despite the widespread credence given to Porphyrogenitus' relation, there are obvious discrepancies in it. He said that the Croatians came to the Adriatic from White Croatia, which lay north of the Carpathian Mountains. Alfred the Great of England (871–901), the compiler of the eleventh-century *Russian Primary Chronicle*, or *Book of Annals*, and various ninth- and tenth-century Arab commentators, all mention this state, whose seat apparently was in the vicinity of the modern Polish city of Cracow.

Now, if the Croatians came from this area to Dalmatia for the express purpose of expelling the Avars, or more probably the Slavic subjects of the Avars, from this Byzantine-claimed land, they must have set some kind of record for celerity of movement. Population migrations in ancient and medieval times were slow affairs, unless some aggressive group such as the Huns was driving another mobile element in wild flight ahead of it. There is no indication that the Croatians left their trans-Carpathian homeland because of hostile pressure—unless, indeed, it was to escape the domination of the lowland Slavs of modern Poland, who were beginning to organize a state and to impose their rule upon their neighbors.

In 626 the Avars and the Slavic tribes subject to them were besieging Byzantium itself. Since the center of the Avar power was between the Danube and the Tisza, there could hardly have been a corporal's

[15]The eminent Russian historian, George Vernadsky, identifies the Avars with the Iranian Sarmatians and the Antes. He believes that they entered Europe from Turkestan. See his *Ancient Russia* (New Haven, 1943), 82, 90. The Byzantine Theophanes described the Avars as an "insolent people of unknown origin." See also Otto Maenchen-Helfen, "The Yüeh-Chih problem reexamined," *Journal of the Amer. Oriental Soc.*, LXV (1945), 71–81; Czoernig, *Ethnographie*, II, 16, 27–32, *passim*; Valvasor, *Die Ehre*, II, 214–225.

[16]Porphyr., *De adm. imperio*, ed. Moravcsik-Jenkins (Budapest, 1949), chapter 30, 142, and chapter 31, 146, 148.

guard of Avars left in Dalmatia. Doubtless there were Slavic subjects of the Avars in Dalmatia, but why would an emperor as astute as Heraclios have depended upon pseudo-Slavs to fight other Slavic tribes that were giving him so much opposition? And how could he have gotten into touch with people living north of the Carpathians on such short notice and then have wafted them to Dalmatia on some sort of magic carpet in time for them to have rendered him any service against the Avars? When these considerations are taken into account, it is hard to escape the conviction that Porphyrogenitus erred either purposefully or through ignorance in recording this story of the Croatian settlement.[17]

It has to be remembered that the Byzantine ruler was not interested in writing history as such. He wanted to compile a guide or instruction sheet for his son and successor to orient him in ways of dealing with Byzantium's neighbors. Constantine VII may have wanted to establish a tradition of Croatian cooperation with Byzantium. Or he may only have repeated an account of the Croatian settlement that had popular credence at Byzantium in his day. He undoubtedly drew some of his information from the Byzantine archives, but he relied chiefly upon reports received from imperial agents in the Dalmatian towns of Split (Spalato), Zadar (Zara), and Dubrovnik (Ragusa). Neither these individuals, nor any tenth-century Croatians who may have visited the imperial court, can be assumed to have possessed much knowledge about events that had occurred in the Croatian lands three or four centuries previous.

It might be noted, however, that Constantine stated that the meaning of the word "Croatian" was "those who hold much land." In 1948, Abbé Tadin, at a congress on Byzantine studies held in Brussels, expressed his opinion that the suffix *mir*, which appears in so many Croatian names, originally meant "lord," as did *mihr* in ancient Iranian. Some of the names mentioned in the Byzantine ruler's account would also seem to be Iranian rather than Slavic.

To sum up, the literal accuracy of this Byzantine account seems to be fully as suspect as those of the Croatian settlement found in other

[17]For criticisms of Constantine's relation, see F. Rački (ed.), *Ocjena starijih izvora za hrvatsku i serbsku poviest* (Zagreb, 1884), 1–42; and Armin Pavić, *De administrando imperio* (Zagreb, 1906). I have not yet had an opportunity to examine the recent critical study offered by B. Grafenauer, "Prilog kritici izvještaja K. Porfirogeneta o doselenju Hrvata," *Historijski zbornik*, V (Zagreb, 1952), 1–56. The emperor's work gives two contradictory accounts of the Croatian settlement. Chapter 30 seems to have been written by a different author than chapters 31–36. Probably Porphyrogenitus used different secretaries to write up his notes. Chapters 29–30 should be compared with chapters 1–3 of the Dioclean chronicle.

early sources such as the *Kraljevstvo Hrvata* (Kingdom of the Croatians), which probably was composed between 1074 and 1081, the *Ljetopis Popa Dukljanina* (Chronicle of the Priest of Dioclea), apparently written between 1143 and 1163, and the thirteenth-century *Historia Salonitana*. If anything, these three later versions of the settlement might be considered more reliable than Constantine's story because local materials, both written and oral, were available to the compilers of these works, while the imperial commentator did not have access to such sources.

A comparison of all four of these tales of the Croatian settlement suggests that this nation took possession of its new homeland in several waves rather than in one sudden push-button mass movement.[18] If there is anything to the story that Heraclios imported the Croatians to fight the Avars, or the Slavic henchmen of the Avars, there must have been Croatian groups closer at hand than in the trans-Carpathian area to serve his purpose. A number of historians, sociologists, and archaeologists believe that, while there may have been a Croatian invasion of Dalmatia between 626 and 641, this eruption did not mark the first appearance of Croatians in this province. In other words, there probably already were Croatian elements living in the Croatian and Bosnian back country, and it is from them that the residents of White or Great Croatia north of the Carpathians learned about the attractions of the new settlement area. It might be remembered that the Byzantine historian Procopius noted that the Germanic Vandals, even after they had established a kingdom in northern Africa, continued to keep in touch with their kinsmen who had remained in middle Europe. There is nothing more likely than that Croatian bands who had established themselves in the northern Balkans at an earlier date still managed to keep in contact with that part of their nation which remained in trans-Carpathian White Croatia.

The Seventh and Eighth Centuries—A Period of Historical Darkness

There is no positive information as to the religion of the Croatians when they arrived in their new habitat in the Balkans.[19] Porphyrogeni-

[18]See Mandić, *Bosna i Hercegovina*, I, 28–45; Südland (Pilar) *Južnoslavensko pitanje*, 4–10; Rus, *Kralji dinastije Svevladičev*, 131 ff. On old White Croatia north of the Carpathians, see F. Rački, "Biela Hrvatska i Biela Srbija," *Rad Jugoslavenske akademije znanosti i umjetnosti*, LII (1880), 141–164.

[19]Nadko Nodilo published a series of articles, entitled "Religija Srba i Hrvata na glavnoj osnovi pjesama, priča, i govora narodnog," in *Rad* between 1885 and

tus' history indicates that they may have been baptized as Catholic Christians soon after their arrival in Dalmatia. There is some question as to whether the emperor meant that a regularly organized Croatian church was set up at this time or whether he was only talking about a clerical reorganization of the already established Dalmatian church. Dr. Mandić has recently drawn new evidence from ecclesiastical records to strengthen the supposition that in Dalmatia a number of Croatian groups may have been baptized in the time of Heraclios.[20] It is not certain, however, that the Croatians were pagans in the first part of the seventh century. Professor Miho Barada believes that they were Arian Christians, since they were ruled by or associated with the Arian Ostrogoths and Visigoths for so long a period of time.[21] Proponents of the Gothic theory of Croatian origins also have argued that the baptism reported by Constantine was one designed to purge them of heresy rather than to convert them from paganism.[22]

It seems certain that for some time the Croatians fought against and persecuted the Latin and Slavic elements that they found living in Dalmatia and adjacent regions. About 678, however, they seem to have been involved in a peace that the Byzantine emperor, Constantine II Pogonatus, concluded with the Avars. Two years later, the Croatians are supposed to have promised Rome that they would not molest the Latin inhabitants of Dalmatia any longer.[23] Probably they agreed to refrain from attacking the Slavs who had preceded them into the coastal lands as well.[24]

1890. That curious medieval compilation, *L'Abrégé des merveilles,* which contains some references to "Slavs" who "follow the religion of the Magians (Zoroastrians) and adore the sun," and who also were fire worshippers, should be compared with the account of the Arab Ibn Rusta, who wrote an account of the Croatians in Galicia, basing it on a ninth-century sourse. See J. Markwart, "*Osteuropaeische und ostasiatische Streifzuege* (Leipzig, 1903), 466–469. Some Moslem sources say that the early Croatians worshipped cattle, which may indicate a carry-over among some Croatian elements of the veneration for cattle prescribed by Zoroaster in old Iran. On the old Slavic religion, see also Valvasor, *Die Ehre*, 373ff.

[20]Dominik Mandić, *Rasprave i prilozi* / Studies and Contributions (Rome, 1963), 109–144.

[21]The *Historia Salonitana* declared that they were "very rude Christians of Arian belief." Professor Barada believes that the Croatians accepted the Arian heresy during their period of association with the Ostrogoths. "Nadvratnik VII stoljeća," *Serta Hoffilleriana* (Zagreb, 1940), 415, n. 56.

[22]Father Šegvić has expounded this theory in various writings.

[23]S. Sakač, "Ugovor pape Agatona i Hrvata," *Croatia Sacra* I (Zagreb, 1931), 1–32; *Historia Salonitana*, chapter 10.

[24]It seems to me that there is no evidence to support the assumption shared by Professors Mandić and Preveden that the Croatians mixed peacefully with the Slavs who had preceded them into Dalmatia and other areas. As indicated above,

There is much evidence to indicate that by the end of the seventh century the Croatian ethnographic boundaries reached along the coast from the Raša River in Istria to deep into what is now Albania. Inland, the Croatian tribesmen occupied what we know in our own time as Upper Croatia, the land between the Sava and Drava Rivers, and part of what later became southern Hungary, most or all of Bosnia and Hercegovina, and sections of eastern Slovenia and Carinthia.[25]

Three Croatian principalities grew up within this framework of settlement. Northwest of the Cetina River lay the new White or Dalmatian Croatia. It encompassed modern Upper Croatia, western Bosnia, northern Dalmatia, and eastern Istria. Pannonian Croatia included the Sava lands of modern Slavonia and, at least for a time, Srijem and northern Bosnia. South of the Cetina, extending as far as the lake of Scutari in Albania, was what came to be known as Red Croatia.

It seems likely that throughout the seventh and eighth centuries the Croatians acknowledged Byzantine sovereignty, although the Greeks were not able to make their power felt outside of the militarily organized Dalmatian Theme (province) which clung to the coast, where it included such cities as Split, Trogir, and Zadar. Dr. Mandić has recently endeavored to prove that in the autumn of 753 the Croatian "king" or chieftain, Budimir, convened a great meeting of the Croatian clans on the field of Duvno (Delmno) high up in the Bosnian mountains.[26] This meeting is mentioned in the *Kraljevstvo Hrvata*, and in the Chronicle of the Priest of Dioclea, but there is no indication of the date.[27] Other authorities believe that it took place in the ninth or tenth centuries.[28] Although Mandić has constructed a series of in-

---

there is reason to suppose that it was the Slavic subjects of the Avars rather than the Avars themselves whom the Croatian conquerors expelled from Dalmatia. The documents offered in F. Rački (ed.), *Documenta historiae chroaticae periodum antiquam illustrantia, Mon. spect. hist. Slav. merid.*, VII (Zagreb, 1877), 271–272, should be compared with pages 26–33 of the *Historia Salonitana.* See also J. Mikoczi, *Otiorum Croatiae liber unus* (Buda, 1806), 89–112; and Mandić, *Bosna i Hercegovina*, I, 45, 387–389.

25V. Klaić, *Povijest Hrvata* (5 vols.; Zagreb, 1899–1911), I, 32–33; N. Z. Bjelovučić, *Etnografske granice Hrvata i Slovenaca* (Dubrovnik, 1934), 11; Niederle, *Manuel*, I, 90; J. Horvat, *La formation de la Croatie d'aujourd'hui* (Zagreb, 1943), 75–79.

26D. Mandić, *Hrvatski Sabor na Duvanjskom Polju g. 753* (Buenos Aires, 1957).

27Chapter 9 of the *Kraljevstvo Hrvata* and also of the *Ljetopis Popa Dukljanina* contain mention of a work called the "Methodos," which Dr. Mandić presumes to be a sort of record or protocol of the proceedings on the Duvno Field. See Šišić, *Letopis*, 302–308; Mošin, *Ljetopis*, 50–56; Mandić, *Crvena Hrvatska*, 18–38.

28The "Nestor of Croatian historians," Ivan Kukuljević-Sakcinski, found a corre-

genious hypotheses to prove his case, the question of the date of this Sabor or assembly will doubtless remain a subject of argument for a long time to come.

There is no historically verified mention of the Croatians as such until the time of the Frankish monarch, Charlemagne (769–814). In 791 Charlemagne attacked the Avars, who still ruled much of Danubian Europe. Some Croatians were subjected to their authority and there may have been a blending of the two groups. But in 795 Vojnomir, prince of Pannonian Croatia, aided the Franks in capturing the main Avar *hring*, or fortified circular camp. It was located in the old territory of the Iranian Iasyges between the Danube and Tisza Rivers.[29] By 796 the overthrow of the Avar power was complete, and at this point the Avars disappear from the pages of history as completely as the Sarmatians and Ostrogoths before them. Most of the survivors seem to have been settled under Croatian chieftains in Lower Pannonia, the district extending from Orljava to Zemun, which included the latter-day Bosnian Posavina and the Mačva section of modern Serbia. Some Avar remnants may have been left in north Dalmatia and in the Lika and Krbava areas.[30]

Vojnomir had ruled the tribes between the Danube and the Drava, probably as a vassal of the Avars. There were various non-Croatian Slavic groups under his authority. After the overthrow of the Avar state, he had to accept Frankish overlordship. The Franks had seized the Byzantine ports in Istria on their march eastward to do battle with the Avars; this action brought them into touch with the Istrian and Dalmatian Croatians. They penetrated into Dalmatia as far as the Zrmanja River. Thus they were able to impose their rule upon Dalmatian as well as upon Pannonian Croatia. Between 812 and 817 they seem to have effected agreements with Byzantium whereby the latter acknowledged their control of the two northern Croatian principalities while most of Red Croatia remained within the Greek sphere of influence.[31]

---

spondence between the Sabor that the *Kraljevstvo* and *Ljetopis* reported as being held for the purpose of settling religious and administrative matters, and the recorded acts of the ecclesiastical Synod of Split of 925. On this point see below. Šišić thought that the Sabor took place about 884. Other historians have dated it as late as 1059.

[29] Rački, *Documenta* (M.S.H.S.M., VII), 295–297; Valvasor, *Die Ehre*, IV, 247–249; Hans Pirchegger, "Karantanien und Unterpannonien zur Karolingerzeit," *Mitteilungen des Inst. f. Oesterr. Geschichte*, XXXIII (1912), 274.

[30] On Avarian survivals among Croatian family names, see Czoernig, *Ethnographie*, II, 16. See also Klaić, *Povijest*, I, 42–43.

[31] Mandić, *Hrvatski Sabor*, 18–19.

The Formation of the National Monarchy

Both White or Dalmatian Croatia and the Pannonian Croatian principality had as their political overlord the Count of the Friulian March. The Friulian March was one of the border territories set up by Charlemagne on the frontiers of his extensive empire. Both Croatias were subordinated to the spiritual jurisdiction of the Frankish patriarch of Rome. Parenthetically, it is important to note that the Franks did not have to employ among the Croatians the tactic of forcible conversion to Catholic Christianity that highlighted their relations with so many other contemporary peoples. This circumstance in itself tends to buttress the thesis that the conversion of the Croatians must have occurred in the seventh century.

Frankish rule apparently weighed more heavily upon the Pannonian Croatians than it did upon their Dalmatian kinsmen. Prince Ljudevit, who ruled the Pannonian element from his capital of Sisak on the Sava, protested against the exactions imposed upon his people by the Count of the Friulian March. When he failed to receive satisfaction, he resorted to armed rebellion. From 819 to 822 he put up a successful resistance to the Frankish armies, although the Dalmatian Croatian ruler Prince Borna sided with his Germanic overlords in this struggle. Evidently there was little solidarity of feeling among the Croatians of this era, for even after Borna died (821) his soldiers continued to fight for the Franks. Finally Ljudevit was defeated, and a relative of Borna assassinated him.

From this time until the last quarter of the ninth century, the Dalmatian Croatians served the Italian Carolingians faithfully enough. For a time, too, the Pannonian Croatians vigorously defended the Frankish frontiers against the Bulgars, who between 827 and 845 exerted themselves to take over Ljudevit's Pannonian legacy. It might be noted that there is no mention in the surviving sources of any involvement of the Serbian tribes in this struggle. In the absence of such mention, it is difficult to comprehend how the Serbians could have occupied the territory between the Croatian and Bulgarian settlement areas, as their modern descendants claim that they did. There should be taken into account, too, the circumstance that the Frankish chronicler and biographer of Charlemagne, Einhard, noted in 822. He referred to the Serbians, in his *Annals*, as a nation known to the Franks by hearsay only. These facts make it evident that the contention advanced by Ljudmil Hauptmann and other writers that the Serbians must have been neighbors of the Croatians in ancient times, and must have come to the Balkans with them, lacks any kind of historical substantiation. In any case, the Bulgars took possession of eastern Pannonian Croatia or Srijem about 845.

The last period of the three-cornered Frankish-Croatian-Bulgar war coincided with the reign of Prince Mislav in Dalmatian Croatia. The principal achievement of this ruler was the creation of a navy, which in 839 is reported to have defeated a Venetian fleet that sailed into Croatian waters. Mislav is also thought to have signed a treaty with the representatives of the Republic on the island of Korčula following this encounter. He organized his court on the Frankish model but took advantage of the weakening of Frankish authority under the less capable successors of Charlemagne to concentrate in his own hands the administration of justice, the protection of the church, and command of the armed forces.[32]

Apart from the references contained in the Frankish annals, the Croatian name appears, for the first time since the Tanaïs inscriptions, in a charter issued by Mislav's successor, Trpimir, under date of March 4, 852. There has also been preserved a broken stone inscription which designates Trpimir as "dux Chroatorum." Although Trpimir gave his name to the national dynasty, which, in the following century, transformed the Croatian lands into a kingdom, his own offspring were passed over on his death in 864 in favor of a certain Domagoj. This latter ruler seems to have favored the Latin church party over the pro-Byzantine ecclesiastical element that existed among the Croatians. He also had to fight another war against the Venetians. Then, following the death in 875 of the Frankish emperor and Italian king, Louis II, Domagoj revolted against Frankish authority. Although this uprising was carried through to a successful conclusion, Domagoj did not live to see the triumph of the national cause.

His death in 876 initiated a period of internecine warfare that capped the struggle against the Franks. Prince Branimir, the son of Domagoj, and a relative of Trpimir, emerged from this civil strife as the Croatian "strong man." Branimir acknowledged neither Frankish nor Byzantine suzerainty, and he may be regarded as the real founder of Croatian independence. He provoked the Venetians by imposing a new tax levy on their shipping, and then in 887 he inflicted a severe defeat upon the Republic's navy. The Serenissima had to agree to pay an annual tribute to the Croatian rulers in return for the right of free navigation in the Adriatic. For his part, Branimir undertook to restrain the piratical inclinations of his seafaring subjects, as well as those of the Neretvan corsairs, who sometimes acknowledged the authority of

[32]For a popular account of Croatian history in this part of the century, see Tadija Smičiklas, *Poviest hrvatska* (2 vols.; Zagreb, 1879–1882), I, 171–178.

the Croatian rulers. Branimir also involved himself in Pannonian affairs.

Branimir's contemporary in Pannonian Croatia was Prince Braslav. Braslav aided Svatopluk, ruler of the Moravian Slavic state, against the Franks in 873. Soon thereafter he returned to his Frankish allegiance, however, and in 884 he received from his Germanic overlords title to the lands between the Drava and Sava. He then did homage to the Byzantine emperor for these territories. Thereupon the Greek ruler entrusted him with the defense of "all Pannonia" against the latest wave of neo-Hunnic invaders to override eastern Europe, the Magyars. Braslav found himself unable to hold back the Magyar menace without outside assistance. He appealed for help to Branimir, who dispatched Trpimir's son, Muncimir, to oppose the Magyar inroads. In 891, Muncimir repulsed a Magyar assault upon the Pannonian Croatian land.[33] He seems to have succeeded Branimir in the following year as ruler of the Dalmatian Croatians. When Braslav died, sometime between 893 and 896, the way was clear for the union of Pannonian Croatia—which included the modern Posavina and Podravina regions—with Dalmatian Croatia. The boundary between the two Croatias at this epoch appears to have extended from the Kupa River to Kozara in Bosnia and then through the mountains of the Bosnian Posavina to the Drinjača River at its confluence with the Drina. Beyond the Drina there lay the Serbian country.

At Bijaći, near Trogir (Traù), Muncimir maintained a barbarically brilliant court. Documents surviving from his reign mention the names and offices of various *župani* (counts) and court officials.[34] Muncimir asserted that he reigned by hereditary right and he dispensed justice from the same stone seat that his father, Trpimir, had used for this purpose. He sent his son, Tomislav, to Pannonian Croatia to establish the authority of his house over that land as soon as he heard of the death of Braslav.

Tomislav had to fight off the renewed assaults of the Magyars, who swam their horses across the Drava to attack Pannonian Croatia from all sides. The oldest Hungarian chronicle, that of the Anonymous Notary of Bela IV (1236–1273), says that in the year 900 the Magyars actually conquered all of the Croatias. They rode victoriously through the Bosnian and Dalmatian mountains to the Adriatic to capture

[33]On this war and Braslav's reign, see the documents in Rački, *Documenta* (M.S.H.S.M., VII), 379–382.

[34]Daniel Farlati, *Illyricum sacrum* (7 vols.; Venice, 1751–1819), III, 82. Muncimir himself bore the title of "Divino munere iuvatus Chroatorum dux." See *Documenta* (M.S.H.S.M., VII), 14–17; Šišić (ed.), *Enchiridion*, 124.

Split.[35] But there is no historical confirmation of such an event, and Zagreb, Požega, and Vukovar, which the Notary says the Magyars captured on their way back to Hungary, did not exist at this time. The consensus of historical opinion is that the Notary confused the happenings at the end of the ninth century with the events that accompanied the Hungarian-Croatian union that was effected between 1091 and 1107. Undoubtedly the Magyars laid waste the Upper Pannonian countryside far and wide, for Bavarian sources for the year 900 say that not a church remained standing in this region, and that the inhabitants fled to the Croatians and Bulgarians for shelter.[36] This statement indicates that it was Slovakian western Pannonia rather than Croatian Pannonia that the Magyars conquered. The oldest Croatian chronicles, which antedate the Notary's account by a considerable margin, declare flatly that Tomislav repelled all Magyar onslaughts.[37] This version of the Croatian-Magyar conflicts seems more credible than the Hungarian source, for just a few years after 900 Croatia reached the pinnacle of its power. So complete a recovery from the subjection reported by the Notary would indeed be remarkable.

There is no doubt that the Magyar attacks upon Pannonian Croatia did accelerate the union of the two Croatias, however. Tomislav himself is reported to have taken over the government of Pannonian Croatia in a formal ceremony held at Sisak, where Ljudevit and Braslav had once reigned. Whether this event occurred before or after Tomislav succeeded Muncimir as ruler of Dalmatian Croatia is not known definitely. In an entry that refers to the year 914, the thirteenth-century *Historia Salonitana* accords to Tomislav the title "Duke of the Croatians." Other sources indicate that he may have assumed the dignity of kingship by this time.[38] By 923 the pope evidently recognized his royal status, although many authorities believe that the Croatian ruler was crowned (or perhaps crowned himself) only in 925.

[35]S. Endlicher (ed.), "Anonymi Belae regis notarii de gestis Hungarorum liber," *Rerum Hung. Mon. Arpadiana* (St. Gallen, 1849), 118.

[36]*Documenta* (M.S.H.S.M., VII), 387.

[37]Crnčić (ed.), *Popa Dukljanina Ljetopis*, 22. Crnčić believes that principal Hungarian-Croatian conflicts occurred in 919 and 924 when the Hungarians rode through Istria to attack Italy. Croatian cavalry strength explains why Tomislav was able to defeat these nomads who consistently defeated the Franks and other Germanic tribes until 955. See Smičiklas, *Poviest hrvatska*, I, 217, 222.

[38]F. Rački, "Kada i kako se preobrazi hrvatska kneževina u kraljevinu," *Rad*, XVII (1871), 70–89. See also *Documenta* (M.S.H.S.M., VII), 189, and the text of the letter written by Pope John X (914–928) to Tomislav, given in Ivan Kukuljević-Sakcinski (ed.), *Jura regni Croatiae, Dalmatiae, et Slavoniae* (3 vols.; Zagreb, 1861–1862), I, 8–11; *Documenta* (M.S.H.S.M., VII), 189; Šišić, *Enchiridion*, 216 ff.

Two years earlier, the Byzantine emperor, Romanus Lecapenus, had ceded to Tomislav the control of Split, Zadar, and Trogir on the Dalmatian mainland, and of Krk and Rab among the Adriatic islands. Thus the Croatian coastland became politically independent of Byzantium, and soon Tomislav was able to bring under his scepter the islands of Vis, Brač, and Hvar. Only Dubrovnik and Kotor now stood outside the power of the Croatian king. Byzantium had to make these concessions to the rising Croatian power because the Bulgars, under one of their greatest tsars, Simeon I, had initiated what is referred to sometimes as the Bulgar-Byzantine "Hundred Years War." It was to end only in 1018 with the total collapse of the First Bulgarian Empire. This denouement might never have come about had the Bulgars succeeded in inducing Tomislav to make common cause with them against the Greeks. It is at least doubtful that Byzantium, plagued as it was by Asiatic and other foes, could have withstood a combined Bulgar-Croatian assault in the day of Simeon and Tomislav. But, as indicated above, the Byzantines outbid their rivals, and the Croatians defeated an attempted Bulgarian invasion of the newly constituted kingdom.[39]

The last years of the reign of this first of the Croatian kings were signalized by the convening of important church synods or councils, which were held at Split between 925 and 928. An important issue that required settlement was the use of the national language in the services of the Croatian churches. Early in the Middle Ages the Croatians had developed a form of script based on an alphabet known as the Glagolitic, rather than upon Latin letters. This Glagolitic alphabet and script is not related to the Cyrillic alphabet and writing devised by the Byzantine missionaries, Cyril and Methodius, for the use of the Moravian Slavs, whom they were endeavoring to convert to Christianity. Unless, indeed, as Professor Mandić has lately asserted, Cyril and Methodius became acquainted with the Glagolitic and used it as the basis for their construction of the Cyrillic letters.[40] In any

[39]*Documenta* (M.S.H.S.M., VII), 116, 391–393, 425. See also D. Mandić, "Croatian king Tomislav defeated Bulgarian emperor Symeon the Great on May 27, 927," *Journal of Croatian Studies*, I (1960), 32–43. Recently material has been discovered on the Croatian-Bulgar peace concluded after this battle. See Vinko Foretić, "Korčulanski kodeks 12 stoljeća," *Starine*, XLVI (1956), 30.

[40]See Mandić *Nenapisano poglavlje hrvatske pismenosti*, 364–367. See also his *Hrvatski Sabor*, 35–38, and *Crvena Hrvatska*, 208–211. Mandić's findings, which are buttressed by references to ecclesiastical and other records, should be compared with the explanation offered by M. Hocy, "Die westlichen Grundlagen der glagolitischen Alphabets," *Südostdeutsche Forschungen*, IV (Leipzig, 1939), 509–600. See also F. Dvornik, *Les Slaves, Byzance, et Rome au IX siècle* (Paris,

case, the Split synod of 925 either dealt with political as well as ecclesiastical affairs, or Tomislav convened a special Sabor which took up both state affairs and church matters soon after the Split deliberations ended. As already mentioned, Professor Mandić is convinced that the great Sabor that is described without definite indication of date in chapter 9 of the "Old Croatian Chronicle," or *Kraljevstvo Hrvata,* and of the "Chronicle of the Priest of Dioclea," took place in 753. He believes that chapter 9 of these volumes are both based upon an eighth-century Croatian source, the "Methodos," which contained the record or protocol of the proceedings of the Sabor on the Duvno field. This work is mentioned in chapter 9 of each of the two later Croatian chronicles, but no copy of it has survived the ages. Hence many scholars have reached different conclusions concerning the date of this Sabor, and many of them feel that it must have been held soon after the Split synod of 925, possibly for the express purpose of controverting some of the decisions reached by this great church council. This dispute over the date of the Sabor promises to be one of the most hotly disputed points in Croatian historiography. Since it is not possible in an abbreviated treatment of this kind to examine the several theses advanced with the care that they merit, it seems best to leave the matter open for further investigation and to merely refer the interested reader to the sources of fuller information.[41]

Nothing more is heard of Tomislav after the Synod of Split, unless he was indeed the ruler who presided over the Sabor on the Duvno field. He is supposed to have died on March 10 or 11, presumably in 928, but the history of the period 928–935 is extremely unclear and has given rise to much controversy among historians.[42] As a matter of fact, from this time until the end of the twelfth century, the Papal Register

1926), 319–320. The best general treatment of the use of the Glagolitic and of the Slavonic liturgy in the services of the Croatian churches is probably still I. Tkalčić, *Slavensko bogoslužje u Hrvatskoj* (Zagreb, 1904).

[41]Kukuljević came to the conclusion that the Split synod must have been connected with the crowning of a Croatian king on the Duvno Field, as reported in chapter 9 of the old chronicles (*Kraljevstvo* and *Ljetopis*). See his series of articles, "Prvovjenčani vladaoci Bugara, Hrvata i Srba, i njihove krune, "*Rad,* LVII (1881), 188–233, LVIII (1881), 1–52, and LIX (1881), 103–157. See also *Documenta* (M.S.H.S.M., VII), 187–197; Farlati, *Illyricum Sacrum,* III, 84–102; Tomislav Maretić, "Prvi spljetski sabor i glagolica," *Zbornik Kralja Tomislava,* 385–390. For a popular Croatian conception of the Split proceedings, see Klaić, *Povijest Hrvata,* I, 83. See also the documents in Šišić, *Enchiridion,* 211–224.

[42]Some historians believe that he died in 928 and was succeeded, presumably by a brother, who reigned as Trpimir II from 928–935. Others believe that there was no Trpimir II, but that Tomislav continued to rule for some years after 928. On this point, compare Mandić, *Crvena Hrvatska,* 171–182, with S. Runciman, *History of the First Bulgarian Empire* (London, 1930), 211.

contains only three references to Croatian affairs. Nor do Byzantine, Venetian, or French chroniclers have much to say about events in Croatia. We do know that the Croatian rulers had brought into being a national state, which reached the apogee of its development under Tomislav. His kingdom included some 100,000 square kilometers, and its population must have exceeded 2,000,000 persons. These figures are truly impressive for tenth-century Europe. Writing in the middle of this century, Porphyrogenitus stated that Croatia took in the entire coastal stretch from Istria to the Cetina. But the imperial annalist said, too, that parts of old Red Croatia, notably Zahumlje, which lay between the Neretva River and Dubrovnik—and thus included what today is central Hercegovina, and Trebinje or Travunja, which occupied the region between Dubrovnik and Kotor—were Serbian rather than Croatian territories. In Tomislav's time these areas were included within the framework of the Croatian kingdom.

The explanation of the change in the political nationality of these districts is to be found in the circumstance that, upon the conclusion of the short reign of Tomislav's son, Krešimir I (The Old), civil war broke out between his sons or their respective partisans.[43] In 948 the Venetians took advantage of this internal dissension to attack the Croatian coast. The Serbians, too, were able to seize Zahumlje, Trebinje, part of Bosnia, and several Croatian *župe* (districts that corresponded on a small scale to the counties of Hungary and western Europe).[44] It is evident that the emperor identified Zahumlje and Trebinje, as well as Duklja (Dioclea), which lay south of Kotor, in terms of political rather than ethnic nationality. Ecclesiastical records prove that all of these territories were Roman Catholic, used the Latin liturgy, and were subordinated to the archbishopric of Split, the metropolitanate of the entire Croatian kingdom.[45]

Between 949 and 969 the legitimate Croatian king appears to have been Krešimir II, although this younger son of the first Krešimir had some difficulty in quenching the fires of civil war that had cost the life of his elder brother Miroslav (945–949). Gradually Krešimir was able to re-establish his control over the Primorje—the coast between the

[43]Mandić believes that Krešimir I reigned only from 938 to 944. See *Bosna i Hercegovina*, I, 185, 286.

[44]Mandić, *Bosna i Hercegovina*, I, 186.

[45]Mandić, *Crvena Hrvatska*, 107. On these lands, see also N. Z. Bjelovučić, *Crvena Hrvatska i Dubrovnik* (Zagreb, 1929), 5–24; F. Šišić, *Povijest Hrvata u vrijeme narodnih vladara* (Zagreb, 1925), I, 456–457; Knezović, *Poviest Hrvata* 58–100; Šišić (ed.), *Letopis*, 305–307. For the ethnic details, see Mandić, *Crvena Hrvatska*, 107–123 and 184–186.

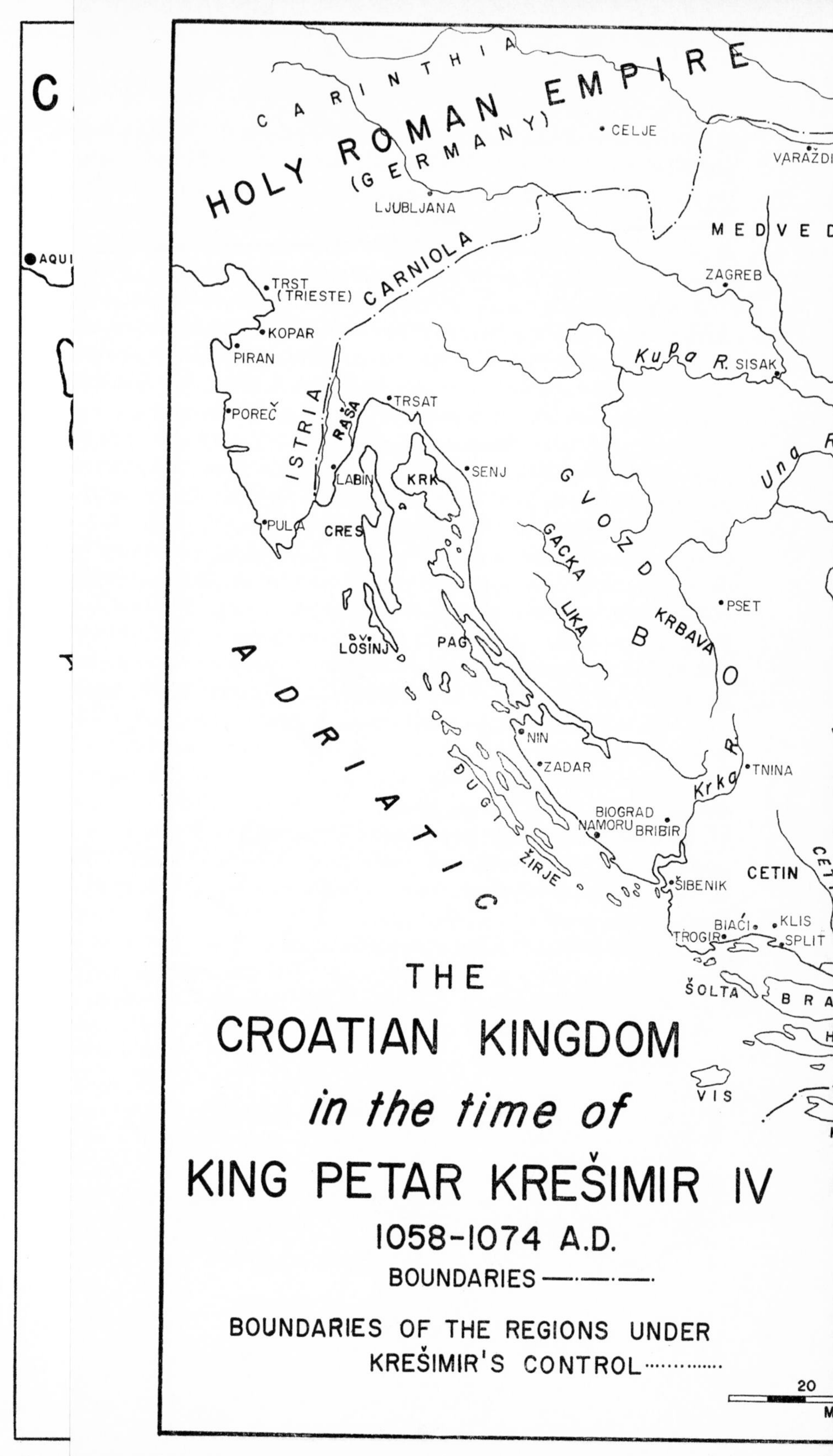
HOLY ROMAN EMPIRE
(GERMANY)
CARINTHIA
CELJE
VARAŽDIN
LJUBLJANA
CARNIOLA
MEDVED
ZAGREB
TRST
(TRIESTE)
KOPAR
PIRAN
Kupa R.
SISAK
ISTRIA
RAŠA
TRSAT
POREČ
Una R.
LABIN
KRK
SENJ
GVOZD
PULA
CRES
GACKA
LIKA
PSET
KRBAVA
SV. LOŠINJ
PAG
B
O
ADRIATIC
NIN
ZADAR
Krka R.
TNINA
DUGI
BIOGRAD NAMORU
BRIBIR
ŽIRJE
ŠIBENIK
CETIN
BIAĆI
KLIS
TROGIR
SPLIT
ŠOLTA
VIS
THE
CROATIAN KINGDOM
in the time of
KING PETAR KREŠIMIR IV
1058-1074 A.D.
BOUNDARIES
BOUNDARIES OF THE REGIONS UNDER
KREŠIMIR'S CONTROL
20

HUNGARY
PEĆUH
Drava R.
ICAVA
VILJEVO
Danube R.
VUKOVAR
Tisza R.
Sava R.
Vrbas R.
SIRMIJ
BEOGRAD
BYZANTINE
PLIVA
ZVORNIK
Drina R.
N
I
A
LIJEVNO
RAMA
R.
Morava
Neretva R.
SERBIA
MOSTAR
Tara R.
Piva R.
Lim R.
VAR
ZAHUMLJE
ORČULA
STON
MLJET
TRAVUNJA
DUBROVNIK (RAGUSA)
S
E
A
ZETA
EMPIRE
BAR
ULCINJ
40
60
LES
jrh

Cetina and Neretva. About 960 he drove the Serbians from that part of Bosnia which had fallen under their control. Krešimir utilized the services of a number of Jewish counselors and he maintained diplomatic and commercial relations with the Khazar Jewish state in southern Russia, which shortly was to succumb to the pressure of the Muscovites. Krešimir II used Jewish emissaries, too, to establish contact with Abderrhamen III, the Caliph of Spanish Cordoba, who maintained a Croatian body of guards at his court.

In 969 Krešimir's son, Stipan Držislav, succeeded to an inheritance that was still divided. Stipan was an able diplomat and he set to work to repair the damage sustained by the kingdom during the period of internecine struggle. Through the cultivation of friendly relations with Byzantium he was successful in extending Croatian sovereignty southward once more. Perhaps his sway extended as far as northern Albania, where Croatian linguistic elements still linger in the speech of the population as an evidence of a very long period of Croatian occupation in past times. Sometime between 986 and 989 the Greek emperor granted Držislav a gold crown and other regalia symbolic of royalty. It is this circumstance which explains the reference made in the *Historia Salonitana* to Držislav as the first of the Croatian kings. The father of Croatian historiography, Franjo Rački, seems to have proved, however, that Tomislav was the first Croatian king, although it is true that this powerful ruler may simply have crowned himself without bothering to secure international recognition of his status. Whereas Tomislav bore the title "Rex Chroatorum," Držislav styled himself "Rex Dalmatiae et Croatiae." Probably this was the designation that the Byzantines conceded to him. The long "Hundred Years War" now was nearing its climax, and the Bulgar tsar Samuel was seeking Croatian support, just as his predecessor Simeon had done in Tomislav's time. Once again the Byzantines outbid the Bulgars, however, through the grant of the regalia and approval of the extension of Croatian control southward along the Dalmatian shore. Samuel promptly attacked Duklja, Kotor, and other places, and for a time his forces were able to take possession of part of Srijem and Bosnia.[46] But the Bulgars could not wage war on two fronts and soon had to abandon their Croatian conquests.

Chapter 13 of the *Historia Salonitana* notes that the boundaries of Držislav's kingdom reached northward to the Danube, while chapter 15 affirms that the jurisdiction of the Bishop of Knin, who bore the

[46]Šišić, *Povijest Hrvata u vrijeme narodnih vladara*, I, 468–469; Mandić, *Bosna i Hercegovina*, I, 113, 287, 372, 392.

title "*episcopus chroatensis*" extended to the Drava. Historically these statements are important because they do much to invalidate the claim later advanced by the Magyars that they took possession of the Drava-Sava land at the beginning of the tenth century. Certainly Držislav's power must have reached to the Drava, or the spiritual jurisdiction of a bishop who was his vassal would scarcely have been acknowledged in that region.

Tradition attributes the adoption of the Croatian coat-of-arms, a red and white chess or checker board, to Stipan Držislav. This monarch's diplomatic skill did not enable him to stave off the trouble with Venice that developed toward the end of his reign. Doge Peter Orseolo concluded a commercial agreement with Byzantium, whereby Venice received the right to trade in all parts of the Eastern Roman Empire. Orseolo then refused to pay the tribute that Venice had owed to the Croatian rulers from the ninth century. In 994 the Republic attempted to seize the Croatian island of Vis. When Držislav died in 997, war broke out between his sons over his inheritance. His younger offspring, Krešimir and Gojslav, joined forces to fight their elder brother, Svetoslav, and they accepted Venetian assistance to win the day, and so to take over their father's state.

Krešimir and Gojslav then exercised a kind of joint dominion over the Croatian kingdom. Stipan, the son of Krešimir, married Hicela, the daughter of Doge Peter Orseolo.[47] Following the death of the latter, the Republic exiled the Orseolo family. Krešimir and Gojslav took advantage of this development to reimpose Croatian control over the Dalmatian cities, which Orseolo had temporarily won for Venice after Držislav's death. But by 1018 Basil II of Byzantium had ended the long "Hundred Years War" with the Bulgars and had extinguished Bulgarian independence altogether. Krešimir, too, had to acknowledge Greek suzerainty. During his last years of rule, he took care to cultivate friendly relations with Byzantium, but he also allied himself with the Hungarian kingdom which he aided in a war that it fought against Conrad II of Germany. The contention later advanced by the Hungarians—that they gave Slavonia, the land between the Drava and Sava Rivers, to the Croatians as a reward for the assistance rendered by the latter in the struggle with the Germans—is certainly erroneous. It is nonetheless not altogether clear who controlled Slavonia in the eleventh century. The oldest surviving sources refer to it as a masterless land. At least Krešimir III, on his deathbed, had the satisfaction of knowing that the accession of his son Stipan would be unopposed.

[47]On this period see *Documenta* (M.S.H.S.M., VII), 425–29.

Stipan had been educated in Venice and had traveled widely in various parts of the then known world. Despite his Venetian upbringing and kinship with the Orseolos, he pursued anti-Venetian policies after his coronation. He worked vigorously to combat Venetian influences in the Dalmatian towns, but the exact status of these places vis-à-vis Venice and the Croatian kingdom during Stipan's reign is not known.[48] He is reported to have bestowed a twenty-five-mile stretch of territory, including the valley of the Ombla River, upon the Croatian city state of Dubrovnik. He is also said to have founded churches in this town and in others in its vicinity.[49] Stipan died in 1058, leaving two sons, Petar Krešimir, and a younger offspring whose name has not been preserved for posterity, although the son of this anonymous prince was evidently named Stipan after his grandfather.

Petar Krešimir, who ruled as Krešimir IV, was a shrewd diplomat: he knew how to take advantage of every fluctuation in the international situation. Byzantium still retained a shadowy legal sovereignty over Split, Trogir, and Zadar, but the validity of her rights depended upon the strength of her military power. In 1071 the fatal disaster of Manzikert lost to her forever her most important province, Anatolia, which henceforth was to be a recruiting ground for the Seljuk and Ottoman Turks rather than for Byzantium, as it had been in the past. The Dalmatian towns hastened to recognize the sovereignty of Petar Krešimir after this event. The Croatian monarch now was able to establish undisputed Croatian control over the entire littoral, including the Neretvan territory.

Even before Manzikert, the definitive incorporation of the Dalmatian towns in the Croatian kingdom had virtually been a foregone conclusion. The papacy supported Croatian territorial aspirations as a counterpoise to the power of Byzantium. Yet, up to the latter years of the reign of Petar Krešimir, the Latin coastal cities had maintained a lukewarm attitude toward acceptance of Croatian sovereignty over them, and they had flirted with Venice as well as with Byzantium. Papal recognition of Petar Krešimir's title of "King of Croatia and Dalmatia" confirmed his assumption of authority along the entire coast. It is only from his time on that Dalmatia came to be fully integrated

[48]Farlati, *Illyricum sacrum*, I, 223. The Latin towns and islands were becoming Croatianized, however. See Šišić, *Povijest Hrvata u vrijeme narodnih vladara*, I, 297 ff., 408–411 *passim*, 436, 483, 522ff., 612; Mandić, *Postanak Vlaha prema novim poviestnim iztraživanjima* (Buenos Aires, 1956), 18–19; Knezović, *Poviest Hrvata*, 117. Šibenik, Biograd-na-Moru and other places were ethnically Croatian.

[49]F. Appendini, *Notizie istorico-critiche sulle antichità, storia e letteratura di Ragusei* (2 vols.; Dubrovnik, 1849), I, 163.

with Croatia proper, and that the term Triple or Triune Kingdom could be legitimately used to describe the union of Croatia, Slavonia, and Dalmatia. Red Croatia and Bosnia were included in the Croatian state, which now appeared stronger than it had been in the day of Tomislav and Držislav.

But religious dissension was tearing apart from within the imposing edifice built up by the Croatian monarchs. In all likelihood the Mass had been celebrated in the national language in many Croatian churches since the time of Branimir.[50] The idea of a national church, in communion with Rome, but following Byzantine rather than Latin practices, was popular in tenth- and eleventh-century Croatia. Except for the hierarchy, which often included non-Croatians, few Croatian priests knew much, if any, Latin. Church synods held at Split in 1059 and 1060 prescribed the use of Latin and the Roman rite in all of the Croatian churches.[51] Petar Krešimir ceded supreme ecclesiastical authority to the Latin bishops. Hence they had ready access to the court and were able to exert much influence upon the political policies of the state. A serious schism then developed between the adherents of the national church idea and the advocates of the Latin party. The bishop of Knin, who is supposed to have favored the national church group, functioned as Petar Krešimir's chancellor. His office issued laws, decrees, charters, and other documents. In one of these, that dates from 1066, there occurs the first officially recorded use of the Croatian name that has come down to us, although there is no doubt that it was employed often enough long before this time.[52]

In the days of the national rulers, "Croatia" meant all the land from the Adriatic inland as far as the Drava and the Drina. Mostly it included the territory as far east as the Drina, which marked the westernmost extension of Serbian sovereignty. Often the Byzantine historians noted that west of this river there lived a nation that differed from the Serbian with respect to government, religion, national life, and customs.[53] It is probable that dialectical differences in the speeches used by the two peoples were more pronounced than they are today.[54]

[50]*Documenta* (M.S.H.S.M., VII), 192.

[51]*Enchiridion*, 232–238. See also Farlati, *Illyricum Sacrum*, III, 127–130.

[52]*Documenta* (M.S.H.S.M., VII), 511–512. The use of Croatian terms for court dignitaries indicates that Croatian as well as Latin must have been spoken in court circles.

[53]Mandić, *Crvena Hrvatska*, 184–186.

[54]Since the middle of the nineteenth century, the Croatians have used the *ijekavski* speech of the *što* dialect as the common literary language. The Serbs use the *ekavski* speech of the same dialect. Hence the idea has arisen that the Croatian and Serbian literary languages are identical, and the term "Serbo-Croatian" has

"Dalmatia" usually meant only the Latin cities and islands of the old Byzantine Theme, although sometimes the term seems to have been employed to designate the whole coastal stretch as far as the Cetina, and even southward of that river. The name "Slavonia" was still not used by the Croatians themselves to describe the territory between the Drava and Sava. Early medieval sources distinguished between this area, which was known as "Pannonian Croatia," or "Croatia of the Sava," and the "lands of the Vindes," that is, of the Serbians, Slovenes, and Slovaks. But the Italians referred to all Croatian districts as "Slavonian," and in time this term came to be synonymous with "Croatian." Venice was a slave-trading entrepôt, and the Venetians did not differentiate between the Croatian and Serbian, Slovene, or other Slavic prisoners that they took.[55] The insistence of many Croatians on the maintenance of Greek practices in the Croatian churches, and on the use of the Glagolitic rather than the Latin script, unquestionably helped identify this people of mixed origin as a purely Slavic group.[56]

On Petar Krešimir's death in 1073 or 1074, his nephew Stipan, the legitimate heir to the throne, was set aside in favor of Slavac, who probably was the head of the great Snačić—or, possibly, the Kačić—clan, which controlled the Neretvan and adjacent territories. Michael Dukljanski, of Duklja or Dioclea in old Red Croatia, took advantage of this dynastic alteration to declare the independence of the Red Croatian or Dioclean state. Owing to the Manzikert catastrophe, which had so weakened the power of Byzantium, and to dynastic strife in the Greek empire, Michael was able to set himself up as a sovereign in his own right, and henceforth the paths of the two northern Croatias were to diverge, perhaps forever, from their old southern associate. Today the Serbian ethnic strain has replaced the Croatian in large parts of this old Croatian territory.[57]

Slavac seems to have been ban of the Neretvan province at the

been coined to describe them. Dr. Christopher Spalatin of Marquette University, a linguistic expert, treats this problem in his article "Do Croats and Serbs speak the same language?," *Osoba i Duh* (Madrid, 1951). Until the last century, the Croatians habitually used *čakavski* or *kajkavski* dialects in their writing more than they do today.

[55]See R. Heynen, *Zur Entstehung des Kapitalismus in Venedig* (Stuttgart, 1905), 32–35.

[56]On the effect of the persistence of Byzantine practices in the Croatian churches, see F. Šišić, *Pregled povijesti hrvatskoga naroda* (Zagreb, 1911), 1–72.

[57]For the ethnic details, see Mandić, *Crvena Hrvatska*, 107–123, 184–186. Mandić believes that the *Kraljevstvo Hrvata* was written between 1074 and 1081 to justify the secession of the Red Croatian territory from the Croatian kingdom: *Bosna i Hercegovina*, I, 189–190, 290, 334, 339; *Nenapisano poglavlje hrvatske pismenosti*, 397; *Crvena Hrvatska*, 18–38.

time of Petar Krešimir's demise. The title "ban" is a peculiarly Croatian designation, and is generally taken to be indicative of the Iranian origin of the Croatian nation. The bans of the national dynasty were great territorial lords whose status resembled that of the old Marzbans of the Iranian kings.[58] There seems to have been three of them in Petar Krešimir's time. According to an Austrian source, the *Chronicon pictum Vindobonense* (*Wiener Bilderchronik*), a certain Dimitar Zvonimir had functioned as ban of a territory "which lay near Hungary and Carinthia." This region is generally assumed to be the land between the Drava and Sava, or Slavonia, although, as indicated above, no really definite data about eleventh-century Slavonia has survived the vicissitudes of the ages. Zvonimir's clan affiliation is unknown, but he must have belonged to one of the twelve great houses that ruled south of the Gvozd Mountains in old White or Dalmatian Croatia, because he married the sister of the Hungarian king, who certainly was unlikely to bestow her hand upon just anybody. Zvonimir seems to have been absent from Croatia at the time of Krešimir IV's death; he was aiding his Hungarian kinsmen in a war that they were fighting with the Serbians.[59] Probably this is why Slavac was able to make himself king, since Petar Krešimir had associated Zvonimir with himself in details of government during the last years of his reign, and surviving documents mention this brother-in-law of the king of Hungary in such a way as to suggest that he was being groomed for the royal dignity. Slavac was able to function as king for only about one year (1074–1075), for the Normans of Apulia invaded Dalmatia, captured him, and carried him off to Italy. With this ephemeral ruler out of the way, Zvonimir's accession to the throne was assured. Pope Gregory VII sent a papal legate to crown him, and Zvonimir acknowledged the Croatian crown to be a fief of the papacy.[60]

The immediate consequence of this action was that Byzantium transferred to Venice all of the ancient legal jurisdictions and rights that she once had exercised over the cities and islands of her Dalmatian Theme. For the moment this was only an empty gesture, since Zvonimir had a firm grip on the entire coastal territory once the Normans had withdrawn. Both Croatia and Norman Sicily now were

[58]See M. Ehtéchan, *L'Iran sous les Achéménides* (Fribourg, 1946), 40.

[59]Ladislas V. Szalay, *Geschichte Ungarns*, trans. H. Wögerer (Pest, 1866), 189–190; *Documenta* (M.S.H.S.M., VII), 453.

[60]On this "time of troubles," see Mandić, *Bosna i Hercegovina* I, 188–190; Šišić, *Povijest Hrvata u vrijeme narodnih vladara*, 538–566, *passim*; *Documenta*, (M.S.H.S.M., VII), 103–146; *Jura regni*, I, 16–29; Matija Mesić, "Dimitar Zvonimir Kralj hrvatski," *Rad* XXXIX (1877), 115–141.

papal vassals, so Zvonimir allied himself with the Byzantine bête noire, Robert Guiscard, the ruler of Sicily. Their combined squadrons won a great victory over the Byzantine and Venetian squadrons, off Corfu in 1084. After this event, the Greek emperor Alexius Comnenus made his peace with the papacy and asked Rome to aid him in his perennial war with the Seljuk Turks who held Anatolia, the old reservoir of Byzantine military power and agricultural prosperity. The answer to this appeal was the launching of the First Crusade a decade later. First, however, the papacy wanted Zvonimir to lead a kind of Croatian crusade against the Bogomil heretics in Bulgaria and a nomadic people, the Patzinaks or Pechenegs, who were threatening Byzantium in this same area.

The Croatian kings were not absolute or arbitrary rulers. They had to secure the consent of Sabor, the parliamentary assembly of high nobles and prelates, before they could send an army outside the borders of the kingdom. It is a singular fact that after their conquest of their present-day homeland, the wars fought by the Croatians in the course of their subsequent history have almost always been defensive ones. But Zvonimir was faithful to his obligations to the papacy, and he is popularly supposed to have convened a great Sabor on the field of Knin. There is some indication that freemen in general, as well as the nobles and prelates, may have attended this meeting, for peasants and mountaineers seem to have been present. They may have come only as attendants or bodyguards of the lords, however. Ban Petar Snačić assumed the leadership of the faction which did not want to execute the papal commission against the heretics and nomads. The feud between the national (Byzantine practices) and the Latin church parties seems to have flamed up again too. The northern Croatians are said to have backed Zvonimir, but the argument culminated in a general melee, in which Zvonimir was fatally wounded. Popular tradition still designates a little hill, the *rotna gomila* (Conspirator's Mound), as the place where he met his end. But the whole story of this Sabor may be an invention of later writers, for there is no positive mention of Zvonimir after 1087 in the most authentic extant sources.[61]

As time passed, a golden haze came to surround the memory of

[61]Dr. Stjepan Gunjača, the director of the Museum of Croatian Antiquities in Split, has written the latest word on this question and has adduced much evidence to prove that Zvonimir died a violent death, as tradition has it. See his "Kako i gdje je svršio hrvatski kralj Dimitrije Zvonimir," *Rad*, CCLXXXVIII (1952); see also Crnčić (ed.), *Popa Dukljanina Ljetopis*, 32–36; F. Rački, "Dopunjci i izpravci za stariju povjest hrvatsku. 3. O smrti hrvatskoga kralja Dimitrija Svinimira," *Rad*, XIX (1872), 62–104; I. Kršnjavi, *Zur historia Salonitana des Thomas Archidiacon in Spalato* (Zagreb, 1900), 146–169.

Zvonimir's reign. Typical of the nostalgic tributes to the last great national king is this one:

Also in the time of the great king there was joy in the whole land, because there was a superfluity of goods of all kinds and the fine cities possessed great wealth in gold and silver. And the poor did not fear that they would be exploited by the rich nor the weak that they would be exposed to the violence of the strong, nor the servant that his master would do him an injustice. For the king held his protecting hand over all, and as he himself possessed nothing unlawfully, so he did not permit others to do so. And the land was full of goods of every kind, and the adornments which the women and young people wore had greater value than the worth of an entire estate in other countries.[62]

Certainly the kingdom seems to have prospered economically in Zvonimir's time, for Croatian maritime commerce, since the early days of Petar Krešimir's rule, overshadowed that of Venice in the Adriatic, and was well known in the Mediterranean as well. In the fall of 1888, when the Austrians were laying a railroad line from Siverić to Knin, they found it necessary to cut through a hillock known popularly as the *Kapitul*, which was located about one kilometer east of the present site of Knin. They uncovered the remains of church buildings, and further investigations undertaken by the noted Croatian archaeologist Frane Bulić revealed adequate evidence that Knin was a principal seat of old Croatian royalty and the center of its administration of justice. Stone sculptures and marble slabs, ornamented with a variety of interlaced patterns that are typically Croatian, were recovered. Zvonimir himself is supposed to have been buried near Knin, where the Croatian crown and other royal regalia probably were kept for a time after his death. The mystery that surrounds the ultimate fate of these symbols of Croatian royalty remains unsolved.

Stipan II, the last of the House of Trpimir, now was retrieved from a monastery in which he had spent twelve years of his life (1077–1089). He seems to have reigned only until 1090. In 1090 Ladislas of Hungary took possession of all territory up to the Gvozd mountains, that is, of present day Slavonia. Apparently the Hungarian monarch did not enter this Croatian district as a conqueror, but in response to the pleas of at least some elements in the Croatian population and in accordance with the wishes of his own sister, Zvonimir's widow. Anarchy seems to have threatened during the years of Stipan II's weak

[62]Lucius (Lučić), *De regno Dalmatiae et Croatiae*, 308. See also Milan Šufflay, "Zu den ältesten kroatisch-ungarischen Beziehungen," *Ungarische Rundschau*, IV (1915), 888. But there are evidences of internal dissension in Zvonimir's Croatia, too: see *Documenta* (M.S.H.S.M. VII), 117, 124, 140.

rule, and many people probably wanted to see the restoration of peace and order, whoever would restore it.[63]

Petar Snačić is then supposed to have been put on the throne by the national church party, which was also anti-Hungarian. According to the fourteenth-century Venetian chronicler, Dandolo, Petar reigned until 1097, when he was defeated and killed by Koloman, the new king of Hungary. There is no other historical record of "King" Petar Snačić. Dr. I. Kršnjavi constructed a chain of evidence at the beginning of the present century to prove that Zvonimir actually was killed on the field of Knin in 1089, but that popular tradition managed to confuse his demise with the fate of a legendary "counter-king" who opposed the Hungarian claims.[64] The lack of agreement concerning the careers and destinies of these two individuals is indicative of the fact that the factual framework of Croatian medieval history is pervaded by lacunae which have given rise to much controversy and speculation. Hence the early period of the Croatian story does not possess the clarity that is to be found in the national records of many other peoples.

The Hungarian Period

For more than four centuries Croatia and Slavonia were now destined to share the fate of Hungary. The Venetians tried hard to take possession of Dalmatia, but Koloman made good for the moment the Hungarian claim to this part of the Trpimirović legacy. For a long time Croatian historians have endeavored to prove that in 1102 Koloman concluded, with the twelve great clans south of the Gvozd, an instrument known as the *Pacta Conventa,* which recognized the legitimacy of his succession to the inheritance of the House of Trpimir. In return he guaranteed the integrity of the existing property possession of all freemen and agreed to respect and maintain Croatian laws and customs. There probably was some kind of agreement effected between Koloman and the Croatians, but about a decade ago Dr. Ljudmil Hauptmann proved that the charter supposedly issued by Koloman to the town of Trogir—which supplies the foundation for the knowledge of the provisions of the supposed *Pacta Conventa*—seems to be a falsification dating from the fourteenth rather than from the beginning of the twelfth century. It is interesting to note, however,

[63]*Historia Salonitana,* chapter 17.

[64]Kršnjavi, *Zur historia Salonitana,* 34–41. The authority for the reign of Petar Snačić is the fourteenth-century Venetian chronicler Dandolo. See A. Dandolo, *Chronicon Venetum,* ed. Muratori, XII.

that until almost the middle of the nineteenth century the Magyars themselves never denied the Croatian thesis of a peaceful arrangement made between their ancestors and the Hungarian ruler. Then a nationally chauvinistic element, called into life by Louis Kossuth, began to claim that Koloman had made no agreement with the Croatians—he had simply conquered them.[65]

What really happened was that a kind of federal relationship was established between the two countries. Until 1301 the Magyar royal line of the Arpads ruled Croatia as well as Hungary. But these Hungarian kings did not have the power to legislate at their own pleasure in so far as Croatia and Dalmatia were concerned. Without a formal invitation from Sabor, the medieval Croatian parliament, the sovereigns were not even supposed to enter Croatia-Dalmatia with a military force. The actual rulers of Croatia and Dalmatia were the Croatian bans. There is a popular saying, "Tko sudi, onaj vlada" (He who judges, rules), that expresses the traditional Croatian concept of the Hungarian-Croatian relationship under the Arpads.

Srijem, however, probably was taken over by the Magyars as early as 1071, and the Arpads seem to have felt that Slavonia was Hungarian rather than Croatian territory. The twelve great clans had no properties between the Gvozd and the Drava, so they were not interested in the fate of the Drava-Sava lands. They did see to it, however, that foreigners received no holdings south of the Gvozd. Until the last quarter of the thirteenth century, the Arpads usually were crowned separately as Hungarian and Croatian kings. They swore on the cross and Bible to respect Croatian laws and to maintain Croatian rights and privileges.[66] It is only in 1451 that we find the first instance of a Hungarian statute being applied to the Croatian country. Hungarian rather than Croatian laws apparently prevailed in Slavonia.[67]

[65]Stephan Horvath, *Ueber Kroatien als eines durch Unterjochung erworbene ungarische Provinz und des Königreichs Ungarn wirklichen Teiles* (Leipzig, 1844). Šišić has summed up the evidence on both the Croatian and Hungarian sides of this argument in his *Enchiridion*, 409–423; see also pages 462–464 and 561–562. The Croatian interpretation of the dual relationship is presented in J. Pliverić, *Beiträge zur Ung.-Kroatische Bundesrechte* (Zagreb, 1886), 204–228. See also Šufflay, "Zu den ältesten k.-u. Beziehungen," 889; Kršnjavi, *Zur historia Salonitana*, 146–169.

[66]*Jura regni*, I, 22, 23, 26, 29, 31, 35, 36.

[67]In the nineteenth century, the Kossuthist element in Hungary advanced the claim that the Magyars owned the land between the Drava and Sava as early as the tenth century. According to this school of thought, it was only in the thirteenth century that the territory containing the modern counties of Zagreb, Varaždin, and Križevci came to be called Slavonia. They were not known as Croatian until the last decades of the eighteenth century. See F. Pesty, *Die Entstehung Kroatiens* (Budapest, 1882), 71–72. Dr. Miho Barada has advanced the suggestion that Dimitar Zvonimir was a member of a junior branch of the Trpimirović line of kings

As heirs of the national rulers, the Arpads ruled all of Dalmatia north of the Makarska littoral. A long-drawn-out struggle for the control of the coastland began with Venice after the death of Koloman, who had known how to restrain the ambitions of the Italian "Queen of the Adriatic." Both the Arpads and their successors, the Angevins, who reigned from 1301 to 1382, expected themselves to preserve Croatian commercial and national interests vis-à-vis the rising power of Venice. But in 1163 the last great emperor of Byzantium, Manuel Comnenos, inflicted a severe defeat upon the Hungarian-Croatian dual kingdom. He invaded Dalmatia in person, and we are told that the Croatian *župani* (local noble administrators) had to appear before him barefooted and with ropes around their necks. From 1168 to 1180, Dalmatia, Bosnia, Srijem, and all Croatia from the Velebit Mountains to the Neretva acknowledged Greek sovereignty. Manuel's death ended this renaissance of Byzantine dominance in the Balkans, and it was Venice which profited ultimately from the interlude.

The particular object of Venetian aspirations was the town of Zadar. In 1202 the doge, Henry Dandolo, induced the host that had assembled at Venice for the purpose of launching a fourth crusade against the Mohammedan powers which dominated Egypt and the Holy Land, to divert its efforts to the capture of Zadar. The success of this endeavor enabled the Venetians to plant their feet firmly in Dalmatia for the first time since Roman days. In these tempestuous years of war with Byzantium and Venice, the Arpads were in no position to combine the administration of their Hungarian and Croatian-Dalmatian kingdoms. Even when the later Arpads had the intention of effecting a closer union of the two countries, dynastic quarrels and external pressures, such as the Mongol invasion of 1241–1242, permitted the continuation of Croatian autonomy. The Šubić clan emerged as masters of the lands south of the Gvozd, and when the Arpad line became extinct in 1301, the "kingmaker," Mladen Šubić, engineered the accession to the Croatian-Dalmatian throne of Charles Robert of the Neapolitan branch of the French house of Anjou. The Magyars chose another ruler, and only in 1307 was Charles Robert able to make good his claims in Hungary. This episode has been cited as evidence of the fact that the Croatians did not consider that their kingdom was part of the Hungarian state. They merely recognized the suzerainty of the Hungarian reigning house over Croatia-Dalmatia.

Charles Robert allowed the Croatians to go their own way for almost

---

which governed Slavonia during the eleventh century. See his study "Dinastičko pitanje u Hrvatskoj XI. stoljeća," *Vjesnik za arheologiju i historiju dalmatinsku* (Split, 1932), 159–174.

twenty years. Finally he intervened in Croatian affairs to curtail the power of Mladen II Šubić who had aroused the ire of other Croatian noble houses. Once the king had removed Mladen from the Croatian scene,[68] a noble "Fronde" developed, when the Nelipić family invoked Venetian assistance against the royal power. Charles Robert's successor, Louis I (1340–1382), fought several wars with Venice over the possession of Dalmatia. Although the Serbians made common cause with the Venetians against the Hungarian-Croatian state, Louis succeeded in reuniting all the Croatian territory between Istria and Kotor. Even Dubrovnik recognized his nominal sovereignty. Parenthetically, it should be noted that Dubrovnik represented a synthesis of the Latin and Croatian cultures. It was never a Serbian town, although most Western writers of the modern era designate it as such.[69] It was referred to in earlier times as the "jewel of the Croatian crown" although it maintained its independence from any outside political authority by astute diplomacy during a great part of its history.

Because of the treatment meted out to Mladen II Šubić, his family cherished a burning hatred against the Angevin rulers. They accepted assistance from both the Serbians and the Venetians and did not scruple to betray Croatian territory into the hands of these peoples. Finally, Louis I induced the pope to persuade them to exchange their fortress of Ostrovica, key to the defenses of Zadar and Šibenik, for the territory of Zrinj on the Una River. Thus, in later times the house of Šubić became known as the Zrinski.

Medieval Bosnia

Louis I married Elizabeth Kotromanić, the daughter of the Ban of Bosnia. Bosnia doubtless was an early Croatian settlement area[70] and seems to have existed as a little principality along the upper course

[68]There appears to be no basis for the popularly held conception that Charles Robert did away with Mladen. See Miho Barada, "Vrijeme smrti i obiteljski odnošaji bana Mladena II," *Zbornik naučnih Radova Ferdi Šišiću*, ed. G. Novak (Zagreb, 1929), 167–171.

[69]The Croatian dialect was used in this city-state at least from the eleventh century, and probably long before that. Until late in the Middle Ages Serbian was not spoken here, and Serbians were not allowed to remain overnight within the town walls. On the question of the introduction of the Serbian dialect into Dubrovnik, see M. Rešetar, "Die ragusanischen Urkunden des XIII–XV Jahrhunderts," *Archiv für Slavische Philologie*, XVI (1894), 321–368, XVII (1895), 47–87.

[70]E. Dümmler, "Ueber die älteste Geschichte der Slaven in Dalmatien," *Sitzungsberichte der philosophisch-histor. Klasse d. Wissenschaften in Wien*, XX (1856), 373–374, 397–398; Sava Štedimlija, *Crvena Hrvatska* (Zagreb, 1937), *passim*; *Poviest hrv. zemalja Bosne i Hercegovine* (Sarajevo, 1942), *passim*; D. Mandić,

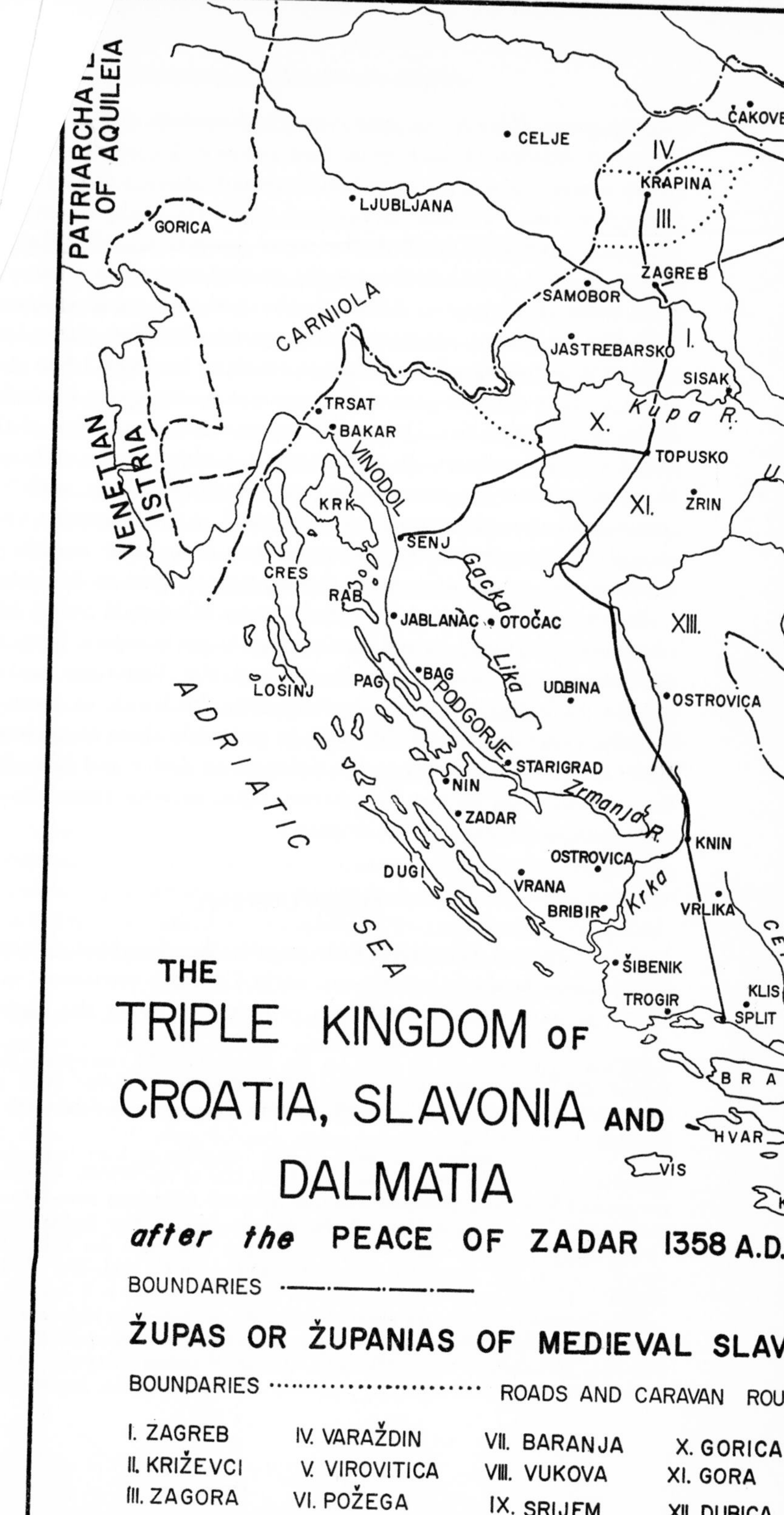
THE
TRIPLE KINGDOM OF
CROATIA, SLAVONIA AND
DALMATIA
after the PEACE OF ZADAR 1358 A.D.
BOUNDARIES
ŽUPAS OR ŽUPANIAS OF MEDIEVAL SLAV
BOUNDARIES
ROADS AND CARAVAN ROUT
I. ZAGREB
II. KRIŽEVCI
III. ZAGORA
IV. VARAŽDIN
V. VIROVITICA
VI. POŽEGA
VII. BARANJA
VIII. VUKOVA
IX. SRIJEM
X. GORICA
XI. GORA
XII. DUBICA
PATRIARCHATE OF AQUILEIA
GORICA
LJUBLJANA
CELJE
ČAKOVEC
KRAPINA
ZAGREB
SAMOBOR
JASTREBARSKO
SISAK
CARNIOLA
VENETIAN ISTRIA
TRSAT
BAKAR
VINODOL
Kupa R.
TOPUSKO
ZRIN
KRK
SENJ
CRES
RAB
Gacka
JABLANAC
OTOČAC
LOŠINJ
PAG
BAG
PODGORJE
Lika
UDBINA
OSTROVICA
ADRIATIC SEA
STARIGRAD
NIN
ZADAR
Zrmanja R.
KNIN
OSTROVICA
DUGI
VRANA
BRIBIR
Krka
VRLIKA
ŠIBENIK
TROGIR
KLIS
SPLIT
BRAČ
HVAR
VIS

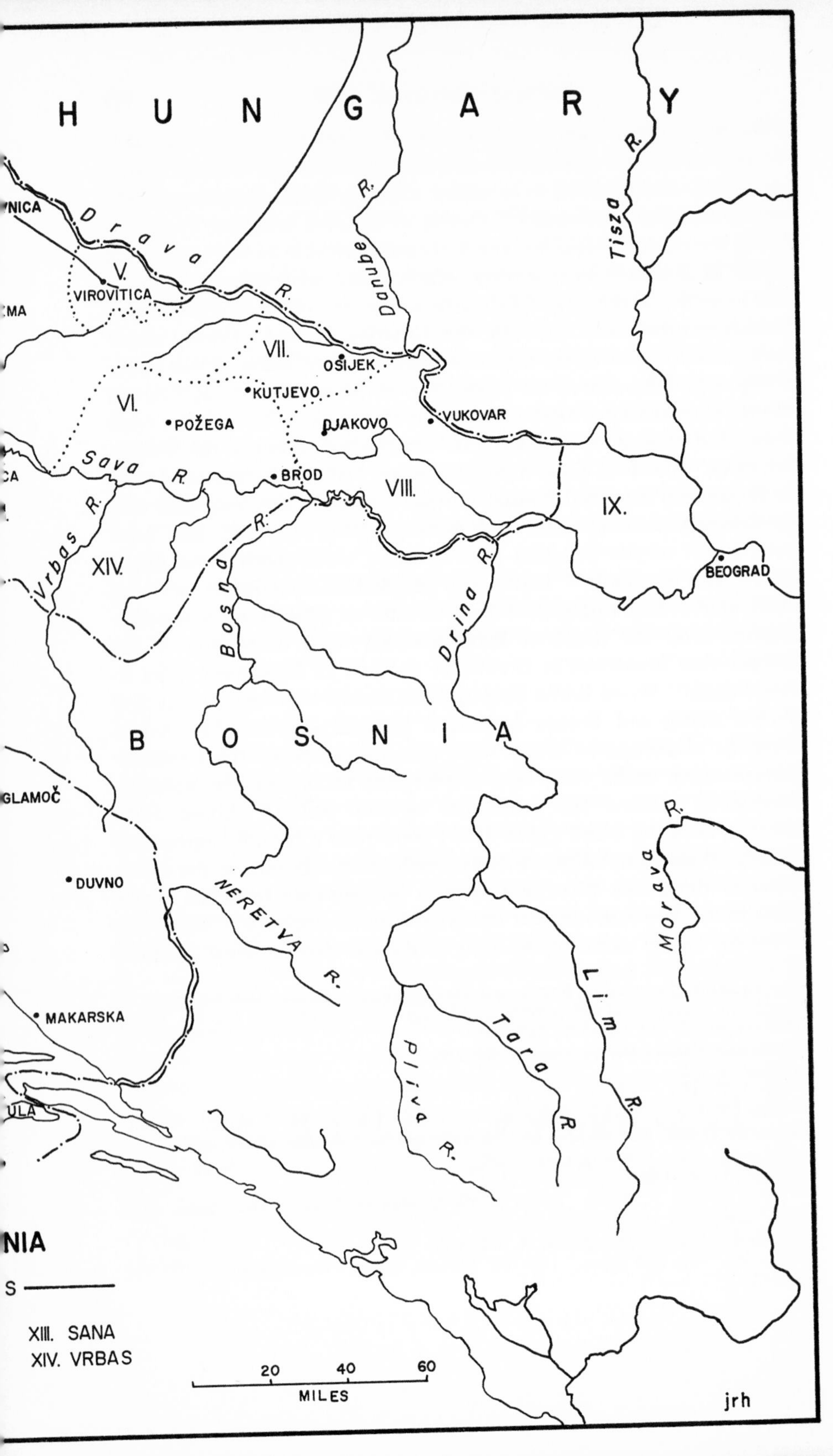
H U N G A R Y
Drava R.
Danube R.
Tisza R.
V.
VIROVITICA
VII.
OSIJEK
KUTJEVO
VI.
POŽEGA
DJAKOVO
VUKOVAR
Sava R.
BROD
VIII.
IX.
BEOGRAD
Vrbas R.
XIV.
Bosna R.
Drina R.
B O S N I A
GLAMOČ
DUVNO
NERETVA R.
Morava R.
Lim R.
Tara R.
Pliva R.
MAKARSKA
NIA
XIII. SANA
XIV. VRBAS
20
40
60
MILES
jrh

of the Bosna River in the early period of Croatian history. The territory that in modern times has constituted northern and western Bosnia was usually closely allied to or united with the Croatian state up to the time of Miroslav (945–949).[71] Owing to the civil war that broke out during the reign of Miroslav, the Serbians were able to take possession of part of Bosnia.[72] Hercegovina, which today takes in parts of what used to be the Trebinje and Zahumlje states, described by Constantine Porphyrogenitus, was ruled by the Croatian Hranić princes, whose sway extended also along the coast from Omiš to Kotor. Their castle of Stipangrad dominated the chief town of the region, Blagaj.[73] About 960 the Croatian king Michael Krešimir II expelled the Serbians from Bosnia and reunited it with Croatia.[74] In the last stages of the Bulgar-Byzantine "Hundred Years War," however, first the Bulgars and then the Byzantines mastered Bosnia.[75] Stipan I brought this land back into the Croatian political framework between 1040 and 1042, and it remained part of the Croatian state complex under both Petar Krešimir IV and Zvonimir.[76] Bodin, son of Michael Dukljanski, who—as noted above—had established Red Croatia or Duklja as a separate kingdom after the death of Petar Krešimir, took advantage of the disorder that broke out in Croatia at the end of Zvonimir's reign to seize Bosnia.[77] When Bodin died in 1102, Duklja experienced a period of civil strife, and Bosnia became a political derelict. The Arpad monarchs of Hungary-Croatia were anxious to restore the Croatian-Bosnian union under their own scepter, but for a time the Bosnians successfully resisted the fulfillment of this policy.[78] About 1137, however, Bela the Blind (1131–1141) concluded a friendly agreement with the Bosnian nobility, whereby northwestern Bosnia to the lower course of the Bosna River and along a line running from the upper Vrbas to the Makarska littoral recognized his sovereignty.[79] When the Kotroman family came to the fore in Bosnia, despite some conflicts

---

"The Croatian character of Bosnia and Hercegovina," *The Croatian nation in its struggle for freedom and independence* (Chicago, 1953), 108–113; Mandić, *Bosna i Hercegovina*, I, 182, 184–185, 347–358.

[71]Mandić, *Bosna i Hercegovina*, I, 186, 286.

[72]*Ibid.*, I, 185.

[73]*Ibid.*, I, 118.

[74]*Ibid.*, I, 186; J. Pauler, "Wie und wann kam Bosnien an Ungarn?," *Wissenschaftliche Mitteil. aus Bosnien und Hercegovina*, II (Vienna, 1894), 160.

[75]Mandić, *Bosna i Hercegovina*, I, 187.

[76]*Ibid.*, I, 187–188.

[77]*Ibid.*, I, 290; F. Rački. "Borba južnih Slovena za državnu neodvisnost u XI vieku," *Rad*, XXX (1875), 93.

[78]Mandić, *Bosna i Hercegovina*, I, 341–342.

[79]Pauler, "Wie und wann," 158–163; Mandić, *Bosna i Hercegovina*, I, 190–191 and 342.

with the Hungarians, they found it expedient to acknowledge Arpad suzerainty.[80]

The Kotromans functioned as hereditary bans of Bosnia under the Arpad as well as the Angevin kings. The status of Bosnia vis-à-vis Hungary was analogous to that of Croatia. Hungarian laws did not apply in either of these Croatian lands, and the union was in each case a purely personal one, the sole tie with Hungary being through the person of the king. The Hungarians interfered in Bosnian internal affairs only in connection with the several "crusades" launched against the heretical Bogomil sect, which was very strong in medieval Bosnia.[81] The Bosnians, however, did have to supply military aid to the Magyars in the wars fought by the latter against the Venetians, Bohemians (Czechs), and Serbians.[82] On the other hand, when Serbia, under her most powerful ruler Stephan Dushan (1330–1356) attacked Bosnia in 1350, Hungary left the Bosnians to work out their own salvation. Stipan II Kotromanić succeeded in defeating the Serbian attempts to annex this old Croatian territory.[83]

His successor, Stipan Tvrdko Kotromanić, continued to acknowledge the overlordship of Louis I of Hungary-Croatia for a time. The Kotromanić family originally had taken a favorable attitude towards the Bogomil heretics, but from the middle of the thirteenth century it had become strongly Catholic, and hence was hated by a large part of the population. A major rebellion on the part of the Bogomil nobility drove Tvrdko out of Bosnia between 1365 and 1367, and he recovered his authority there only by virtue of the military assistance that he received from his sovereign, Louis.[84]

The rapid decay of the Serbian state, especially after the disastrous defeat sustained at the hands of the Ottoman Turks on the Maritsa River in 1371, created a situation in the Balkans that made it possible for Tvrdko to set himself up as an independent sovereign. Louis I's involvement in Polish and Neapolitan affairs reduced his interest in Bosnia, and, as already pointed out, he himself was married to a member of Tvrdko's family. Apparently he had no opposition to, and perhaps even favored, Tvrdko's regal ambitions. Tvrdko first strengthened his state by adding to it a part of old Rascia (Serbia), called

[80]Mandić, *Bosna i Hercegovina*, I, 195–197, 201, 203, 206, 233–239, *passim*, 278–279, and footnotes 557, 342–346, 349, 355–358.

[81]Professor Mandić has contributed the latest study of the Bogomils, *Bogomilska Crkva Bosanskih Krstjana* (Chicago, 1962).

[82]Mandić, *Bosna i Hercegovina*, I, 191, 195, 342, 343, 346.

[83]*Ibid.*, I, 228.

[84]*Ibid.*, I, 238–240.

Podrinje, because the annexation of this territory gave him a strong natural frontier in the belt of mountains between the tributaries of the Drina and the Morava. Then, in 1377, he proclaimed himself king of Bosnia and took possession of Trebinje.[85] But, in this period of the Middle Ages, the idea prevailed that only the pope or the Holy Roman (German) Emperor had the legitimate right to create new kingdoms. Thus Tvrdko could not secure international recognition of his new royal status, especially since the Holy Roman Emperor, Charles IV of Luxemburg, was grooming his son, Sigismund, to succeed Louis I in Hungary-Croatia. Charles and Sigismund both considered Bosnia to be an integral part of the Croatian state and were unlikely to yield their claim to it. Therefore Tvrdko decided to claim the Serbian crown, which was an old and legitimate one. Although he was related to the Nemanya dynasty, which ruled Serbia, he had no actual right to call himself "King of Serbia, Bosnia, and the littoral," as he commenced to do. As a matter of fact, Tvrdko had no interest in Serbian affairs and did not even devote the attention that might have been expected of him to the newly acquired Podrinje.[86]

After the death of Louis I in 1382, Tvrdko effected a friendly agreement with his relative and Louis' widow, Elizabeth Kotromanić, whereby he was able to take possession of Kotor (1385). Elizabeth acted as regent of the Hungarian-Croatian kingdom during these years. Since Louis left no male heirs, the queen-regent married off her daughter Mary to Sigismund of Bohemia. The latter wanted to establish the hereditary right of his family to the newly created Bosnian crown, as well as to the Hungarian-Croatian thrones. Therefore he proposed that the Kotromanići, at least after Tvrdko's time, should content themselves with their old hereditary ban status. Tvrdko was unwilling to see his state swallowed up in Hungary-Croatia, and the Croatians themselves preferred to have as their ruler one of the Neapolitan Angevins rather than Sigismund. In 1387 and in the succeeding years, Tvrdko encouraged the pro-Angevin party in Croatia-Dalmatia, and in 1389–90 he even succeeded in taking possession of the western part of the old Zahumlje state and the territory between the Neretva and the Cetina. The civil war raging in the Croatian kingdom between the partisans of the Angevins and the followers of Sigismund allowed him to extend his authority even further—all the way from the Cetina to the Zrmanja. He had already asserted his own claim to the Croatian throne and he now proclaimed himself "Stipan

[85] *Ibid.*, I, 246.
[86] *Ibid.*, I, 245–246.

Tvrdko, by the Grace of God King of Rascia (Serbia), Bosnia, Dalmatia, Croatia, and the littoral."[87] But before he could consolidate his holdings, he died—early in 1391.

Tvrdko's passing cleared the way for the assertion of Sigismund's ascendancy in all of the Croatian lands. Stipan Dabiša, who succeeded to the Bosnian inheritance, needed Sigismund's assistance against the mighty power of the Ottoman Turks, who had crushed the Serbs on the Kosovo Polje (Field of the Blackbirds) in 1389, and who in 1393 extinguished Bulgarian independence more effectively than Basil II of Byzantium had been able to do almost four centuries before. Accordingly, Dabiša seems to have made an agreement with Sigismund, whereby he recognized the overlordship of the latter.[88] In 1394, however, Sigismund carried the war against the Angevin party into Bosnia and accused Dabiša of supporting the insurgents. The Bosnian ruler had to cede back to the Hungarian-Croatian kingdom the lands taken from it by Tvrdko.[89]

Civil war broke out in Bosnia as well as in the Croatian lands proper, after Dabiša's death in 1395.[90] A combined Turkish-Serbian attack upon Bosnia in 1398 failed, despite the confused situation that prevailed in the kingdom.[91] A new "kingmaker," Hrvoje Vukčić Hrvatinić, now began to dominate Bosnian politics. He also led the party in Croatia that favored the candidacy of the Angevin claimant to the Croatian throne, Ladislas of Naples. The Croatians actually crowned Ladislas as their king at Zadar in 1403. But he entrusted Vukčić with the defense of his interests and returned to Naples for safety. Six years later, Ladislas sold the rights to Dalmatia that he had inherited through the Hungarian Angevins—Venice paid him 100,000 ducats for the cession of his claims.

This transaction virtually brought to an end the three-century-long struggle for the possession of the eastern Adriatic shore. Sigismund was too much preoccupied by the wars that he had to fight with the Turks, as well as with the Hussite revolts in his own Bohemia, to resist the Venetians in Dalmatia. Only through the violation of a safe conduct given to the partisans of Ladislas was he able to make his authority recognized in Croatia itself. Nor did he succeed in ending Bosnian independence, although he put intermittent pressure on that state, which needed his help against the Turks. It was the Turks who, for the next three centuries, were to challenge the power of Venice in the old Croatian heartland, Dalmatia.

[87] *Ibid.*, I, 247.
[88] *Ibid.*, I, 249–250.
[89] *Ibid.*, I, 251.
[90] *Ibid.*, I, 254.
[91] *Ibid.*

In the fifteenth century the succession to the Hungarian-Croatian throne came to be governed by the elective rather than by the hereditary principle. Sigismund died in 1437 without male issue. After the abandonment of his claims by the king of their own choice, Ladislas of Naples, the Croatians preferred to stand aloof from the competition that developed between the Jagellons of Poland-Lithuania, the Austrian Hapsburgs, and other claimants. They even refused to send representatives to the assemblies held by the Hungarians to decide between George Podiebrad of Bohemia, Alfonso V of Aragon-Naples, and the Hapsburg, Emperor Frederick III. Perhaps just because of this abstention of the Croatians from the deliberations, the Magyars passed over all of these candidates and elected as Hungarian-Croatian king Matthias Corvinus, the son of the Magyar-Wallach military paladin, John Hunyady, the Sibinjanin Janko of Croatian popular legend. Owing to the fact that he was not of royal descent, the Croatians had no special feeling for Corvinus.[92] With his illigitimate son Ivan Corvinus they enjoyed excellent relations, however. Ivan married a Frankopan and functioned for some years as ban and duke of Croatia even after his father's death in 1490.[93]

The Turkish Wars

By this time, Croatia had become the main bulwark of European defense against the Ottomans. In 1391 the Turks raided Slavonia and carried off sixteen thousand captives. However, Petar Morović intercepted and destroyed the Moslem column near Požega on its way back to Turkish territory. Then Hrvoje Vukčić, in the course of his perennial feud with Sigismund, introduced the Turks as auxiliaries into the Croatian lands. Another Croatian noble house, the Kosača, emulated this example, after it separated Hercegovina from the Bosnian state. This division of course facilitated the swallowing of both entities by the Turkish empire which engulfed Bosnia in 1463 and Hercegovina in 1482.[94] Many Bogomils accepted Islam, as did the noble landowners who were anxious to save their properties. The bulk of the other Croatian inhabitants emigrated in the course of the following century,

[92]Klaić *Povijest Hrvata*, III, 83–93.

[93]On the relations of Ivan Corvinus with the Croatians, see F. Šišić, "Rukovet spomenika o hercegu Ivanišu Korvinu i o borbama Hrvata s Turcima (1473–1496)," *Starine*, XXXVIII (1937), 1–180.

[94]A. Knežević *Kratka povijest kralja bosanskih*, Vol. I, *Pad Bosne* (Dubrovnik, 1884); J. W. Zinkeisen, *Geschichte des osmanischen Reiches in Europa* (Gotha, 1854), II, 148–149.

especially after the fall of the great border fortresses, which long continued to protect Croatia proper and Hungary from large-scale Moslem invasions, even when the Bosnian kingdom itself had ceased to exist. The Ottomans brought in Serbians, Kutzo-Vlachs or Macedo-Rumanians, Albanians, and other Orthodox elements. By the latter part of the nineteenth century, most of these peoples had become Serbianized. Hence the Serbians were able to advance and to have accepted by Western authorities the claim that Bosnia and Hercegovina were ethnically Serbian, since the Catholic Croatian group now constituted a minority.[95]

The collapse of Bosnia naturally facilitated Turkish penetration of the remaining Croatian lands. In 1478 the ban army cut off and destroyed an Ottoman raiding column some 21,000 strong. Juraj Vitovec and the Zrinskis (Šubići) inflicted two more severe defeats upon Moslem armies in the years immediately following. Once again, in 1491, the ban forces smashed a Turkish array, killing 9000 of them and liberating 18,000 captives taken by the Ottomans in the Hapsburg lands.[96] Then, in the early summer of 1493, another strong Moslem column swept out of Bosnia to execute the Asiatic tactic, learned from the Mongols, of leaving "only earth and water" behind it.[97]

Hastily, Ban Mirko Derenčin called up the feudal levies of the nobles south of the Gvozd. These hurriedly assembled and indifferently mounted units arrived in time to intercept the raiders as they returned from Austrian territory. Near Udbina the Croatian leaders held a grim war council. Members of the Frankopan family, veterans of the incessant border fighting, warned Derenčin to delay his attack until the raiders reached mountainous terrain, where the speed of their horses would count for little. Derenčin insisted that Croatian honor

[95]Proof of the Croatian character of Bosnia up to the time of the Turkish conquest is afforded by (1) the identity existing between Croatian and Bosnian documentary forms, (2) the use of the Croatian system of dating rather than the Byzantine calendar followed by the Serbians, (3) the distinctively Croatian terminology and ecclesiastical names employed in the medieval Bosnian churches—Bosnian lay names, too, were distinctively Croatian, (4) the essentially Croatian characteristics of Bosnian architecture, both with regard to general design and specific ornamentation—for instance, the peculiarly Croatian ornamental *troplet*, which consists of three woven strips, and (5) the use of the Bosančica script (which represents a development of the Croatian Glagolitic writing) in all Bosnian literary remnants including those of the heretical Bogomil sect. See *Poviest hrvatskih zemalja Bosne i Hercegovine*, I, 698–705, 823–829; Mandić, *Bosna i Hercegovina*, I, 450–458.

[96]Aleksije Olesnicki, "Bezimeni turski ljetopisac o bojevima Turaka sa Hrvatima godina 1491 i 1493," *Rad*, CCXLV (1933), 210–219.

[97]On the effect of the Turkish cavalry raids into Croatia, see J. Predavec, *Selo i seljaci* (Zagreb, 1934), 69.

demanded that he give battle on the open plain. To this the Frankopans answered bitterly: "O Ban, this is not a cavalry parade from one village to another to play a Hungarian card game. On this day you are initiating the ruin of the Croatian nation. Today you will see how the Turks can fight."

Three generations of the oldest nobility of the land fell almost to a man in this battle, for even after the field was obviously lost, the lords fought on stubbornly rather than seek safety in flight. At the last, many of them turned their horses loose "that the good steeds might live," and waited dourly on foot for the final assault. The old aristocracy south of the Gvozd never recovered from this disaster on the Krbavsko Polje, which ever afterward has continued to bear the name "Field of Blood."[98] Now the way was open for foreigners to acquire lands in Croatia, and ultimately for non-noble elements of alien origin to take over the national leadership. Despite the failings of the old ruling class, it can hardly be said that either middle-class intellectuals or political chiefs of peasant origin have been able to give a more fortunate direction to Croatian energies since the eclipse of the nobility than did the aristocracy during its period of ascendancy.

The surviving lords put up a better fight against the Turks in the years that followed the Krbavsko Polje than have the modern leaders of the nation in the struggle with the Communists. Every inch of the blood-soaked ground that remained to the ancient Triple Kingdom was grimly contested. In 1513 Ban Petar Berislavić, the "father of the peasants," completely crushed a huge Ottoman force. Eight years later, he won another brilliant victory but was ambushed by sixty Turks near Korenica. Though unattended, he refused to surrender, and he literally died on his feet with his sword in his hand. It seemed that his death released the flood waters that he had kept dammed up for a time, for by 1523 the horsetail standards waved over Ostrovica, the old stronghold of the Šubić princes of Bribir.

Now the hour of Jajce had struck. On August 29, 1526, Louis II Jagellon of Hungary and Croatia led the Hungarian part of his army to disaster on the field of Mohacs. Although few Croatians were involved in this debacle, the contest for the vacant throne that ensued between the Austrian Hapsburgs and John Zápolya, *voyvoda* of Transylvania, paralyzed the forces of resistance. Srijem, and all of Slavonia

[98]On this battle, see Olesnicki, "Bezimeni turski"; Valvasor, *Die Ehre*, IV, 390–392. Valvasor offers a version of the altercation between the Frankopans and the Derenčin different from the one given here, which is based upon a Glagolitic manuscript preserved in a Dalmatian monastery.

as far as Osijek and Djakovo, fell to the star and crescent, and the Bosnian pashas ravaged Venetian-claimed Dalmatia. Soon the exposed Lika and Krbava districts shuddered beneath the hoofs of the Turkish horses. Ottoman military tactics anticipated the later Nazi, Fascist, and Marxist methods of devastation and extermination. The Venetian Marino Sanudo, declared that by the end of 1533 the Turks had carried off 600,000 people from the Croatian territories to sell in the slave markets of the East. To replace this population loss, the Ottomans imported Orthodox groups. It should be remembered that the sultans long continued to use Serbians, Albanians, Greeks, Bulgars, various categories of "Vlachs," and other Orthodox stocks as auxiliary troops. They gave to these elements land in Bosnia, Slavonia, and those parts of Croatia proper that they were able to master.

The Accession of the Hapsburgs

The Austrian Hapsburg house had won considerable popularity among the Croatians, owing partly to the character of Maximilian I (1493–1519) and partly to the circumstance that this family was practically the only source from which the Croatians had been able to secure military and financial aid in their unending struggle with the Turks. The Berislavić and Keglević families in particular were Hapsburg partisans. And even before the death of the last Jagellon king at Mohacs, Sabor had seriously considered the advisability of seceding from Hungary and accepting the suzerainty of Archduke Ferdinand, the brother of the Holy Roman Emperor, Charles V, who also was the king of Spain and the ruler of many other territories.[99]

On January 1, 1527, the Croatian Sabor accepted the claims advanced by Ferdinand to the Jagellon inheritance.[100] Unfortunately, Count Krsto Frankopan, who earlier had concluded an agreement with the Hapsburg ruler, decided to repudiate his bargain. He induced the Slavonian Sabor to declare for Zapolya, and the result was civil war. Frankopan himself fell in the first encounter, and the Slavonian Sabor promptly acclaimed Ferdinand, who seems to have enjoyed general support among the Croatians, although only a minority of the Magyars espoused his cause. Finding himself unable to resist the Hapsburg power with his own resources, Zapolya invoked Turkish assistance. The consequence of his action was that for a century and a half much

[99]Südland (Pilar), *Južnoslavensko pitanje*, 24.

[100]I deal extensively with this episode in the first chapter of my *Hapsburg Croatia-Slavonia from 1526 to 1814*, which is now being prepared for publication.

of Croatia and Dalmatia, as well as Slavonia, Srijem, and central Hungary, suffered the blighting effects of Turkish misrule. During this period these territories were cut off altogether from anything except hostile military contact with the forces of Western culture. The Orthodox elements mentioned above likewise gained a firm foothold in the Croatian lands. Even that part of Croatia which lived under Hapsburg rule was little more than a military frontier province, a gigantic armed camp where the farmer could only go out to work his fields armed to the teeth and with a saddled horse standing close beside him ready for instant flight if, as so often happened, an Ottoman raiding party appeared.

The Croatians had entered upon a new and painful period of their national history. It would have been no consolation to the generations of those times to know that their twentieth-century descendants were to experience an even harsher destiny.

Croatian Political Chronology to 1527

700 B.C.–100 A.D.	Iranian Scythians, Sarmatians, Alans, and Antes settle and dominate large areas of southern Russia. Subjugate and influence Slavs, but are eventually absorbed by them.
2nd–3rd centuries	Greek equivalents of "Croatian" (*Khoroathos* and *Khorouatos*) carved on tombstones near Greek colony of Tanäis on Black Sea.
3rd–4th centuries	Goths control steppe lands of southern Russia. Fuse with Iranian elements and dominate many Slavic groups. Defeat Antes.
375–376 A.D.	Huns overthrow Gothic empire. Goths, Iranians, and Slavs under Hunnic domination or flee southward across Danube.
5th century	Ostrogothic–Alanic invasions of present-day Croatian territory. Ostrogoths rule Dalmatia, Istria, Bosnia, Lower Pannonia (Slavonia), Srijem, Upper Croatia. A Croatian state north of the Carpathians known as White or Great Croatia seems to have come into being at some undisclosed time.
527	First recorded Byzantine notice of entrance of Slavs in considerable numbers into the Balkans.
534	Beginning of Byzantine-Ostrogothic war. Fighting in Dalmatia and Bosnia, as well as Italy.
547–548	Ostrogothic expedition to Dalmatia, modern Upper Croatia, and Bosnia to enlist "local barbarians" (Slavs, Alans, or other Iranians?) as allies against Byzantines. Some Slavs brought into Dalmatia by Goths.
551–553	Other Slavic invasions reported.
553	Ostrogoths north of the Po allowed to leave Italy by their Byzantine conquerors. Contemporary chroniclers note only that they "went over the mountains" (Julian Alps at head of Adriatic Sea?). No further trace of the Ostrogoths in history.
592	Avar-Slavic invasion of Dalmatia.
597–598, 600	New Avar-Slav inroads.
601	Byzantines defeat Avars and Slavs.
602	Slavs settle in Istria and Venetia.
614	Salona captured by Avars and Slavs.
626–641	Croatians invade Avar territory and defeat Avars and their Slavic vassals. Croatians take possession of Dalmatia and spread out from here over Slavonia, Upper Croatia, Istria, Bosnia, and Illyricum (Dioclea and Coastal Albania). Writing three centuries afterward, Emperor Constantine Porphyrogenitus VII of Byzantium states that this Croatian invasion came from White Croatia or Trans-Carpathian Croatia.
641–671	Reported baptisms of Croatians.

680	Croatian tribes reputed to have concluded agreement with Papacy, whereby they agree to refrain from attacking Latins in Dalmatia and Istria.
8th century	Formation of the three Croatian principalities of White (west or Dalmatian), Red (southern), and Pannonian (northern) Croatia.
753	According to calculations of Professor Dominik Mandić, "King" Budimir convenes a great Sabor (meeting) on the field of Duvno in western Bosnia to settle administrative and ecclesiastical details of the nascent Croatian state.
795–796	Prince Vojnomir of Pannonian Croatia aids Franks to overthrow the Avar empire. Avar remnants settled under Croatian chiefs in Lower Pannonia.
796–803	White (Dalmatian or western) Croatia and Pannonian (northern) Croatia become Frankish vassal states. Croatians reported attending Frankish court at Aachen, where their linen garments arouse Frankish envy.
812–817	Franks and Byzantines conclude agreements whereby the Dalmatian cities and islands remain under Byzantine sovereignty, while the rest of the Croatian lands remain subject to the Franks.
819–822	Revolt of Pannonian Croatians (Prince Ljudevit) against Franks. Prince Borna and Dalmatian Croatians aid Franks against Ljudevit. Einhard, Frankish chronicler, identifies Serbians as a nation known to the Franks by hearsay only.
823	Franks form new political unit from White (Dalmatian) Croatia, Friulia, Istria. Becomes part of Frankish kingdom of Italy.
839	Croatian fleet (Prince Mislav) reported to have defeated Venetian navy (Doge Peter Tradenico). Peace treaty follows. Venetians may have agreed to pay tribute for navigation privileges in Adriatic waters.
845–864	Reign of Prince Trpimir.
871	Croatian fleet aids Franks to capture Bari from Arabs. Byzantines attack Dalmatian coast.
876	Unsuccessful Croatian attack on Grado (Italy, near Aquilea). Prince Domagoj initiates Dalmatian revolt against Frankish rule.
878–879	Civil strife in Croatia. Prince Branimir emerges as Croatian "strong man."
880–890	Prince Braslav reigns at Sisak, capital of Pannonian Croatia. Maneuvers between Franks, Bavarians, Byzantines, and Magyars. Requests Dalmatian aid against Magyars.
891	Muncimir, son of Trpimir, sent by Branimir to aid Braslav. Repulses Magyar attacks.
899–900	Magyars ride through western Pannonia to attack Italy. On return lay waste Upper Pannonia (Slovakia). Inhabitants flee to "Croatians and Bulgars" for protection. No historical confirmation of the claim advanced by the Hungarian

	chronicler, the "Anonymous Notary of Bela IV" (1236–1273), that the Magyars overran Croatia in the year 900.
910–914	Tomislav becomes duke of the Croatians.
923	Tomislav becomes first Croatian king.
927	Croatian-Bulgarian war (Simeon I).
925–928	Ecclesiastical Synod of Split.
945–949	Civil strife in Croatia. Serbians move into Zahumlje, Trebinje, Bosnia, and several Croatian *župe* (counties).
948–952	Emperor Constantine VII Porphyrogenitus of Byzantium composes *De administrando imperio*. Chapters 29–36 of this work constitute earliest surviving detailed historical account of the Croatians.
960–968	Michael Krešimir II recovers Bosnia and other Croatian territories from the Serbians.
986–989	Stipan Držislav receives golden crown and other regalia symbolic of royalty from Byzantium. Assumes title Rex Dalmatiae et Chroatiae.
989–992	Stipan Držislav brings Latin cities and islands (Split, Trogir, Zadar, etc.) under Croatian control.
993	War between Galician Croatians and Russians. Outcome unreported, but evidently involved disappearance in Russia of the Croatian name, which is mentioned often in accounts of tenth-century Arab writers (Ibn Rusta, Gardizi, etc.).
994–999	Venetians attack Vis and Neretvan corsair state.
997–1000 A.D.	Civil war between the sons of Stipan Držislav. Venetians seize Dalmatian cities and islands. Prince Stipan sent to Venice as hostage and marries (later) Hicela, daughter of Doge Peter Orseolo.
1007–1018	Krešimir III restores Croatian control over the Latin towns of Dalmatia.
1024	Byzantines take Krešimir's wife and younger son to Constantinople as hostages. Krešimir cultivates friendly relations with both Byzantines and Magyars. Status of Latin towns unclear.
1027	Magyars help Krešimir to rewin Trogir and Split.
1029	Hungarian-Croatian army defeats Germans (Aug. 29?).
1031	According to nineteenth-century Hungarian historians, Hungary in this year cedes Slavonia to Croatia for the assistance against the Germans mentioned above.
11th century	Russian Primary Chronicle (Book of Annals) mentions Galician and Adriatic Croatians (Ch. X, XXI, XLV).
1059–1060	Church Synods at Split prohibit use of Glagolitic and Slavonic liturgy in Croatian churches.
1061–1064	Rebellion of national church party (Byzantine customs, Glagolitic alphabet—Vuk and Zdeda).
1074–1075	Slavac, probably head of the great Kačić clan, succeeds Petar Krešimir IV (1058–1074) as king. Normans and Venetians

	invade Dalmatia. Normans carry off Slavac to Italy. Composition of oldest surviving Croatian chronicle, *Kraljevstvo Hrvata* (Kingdom of the Croatians).
1076	Dimitar Zvonimir is crowned by papal legate. Acknowledges that the Triple (Triune) Kingdom of Croatia, Slavonia, and Dalmatia is a papal fief. (Zvonimir's tribal origin unknown, but Professor Mandić believes that he belonged to a junior branch of the Croatian royal house which reigned over Slavonia).
1089	Reported assassination of Dimitar Zvonimir at a Sabor held on the field of Knin. Stipan II ascends throne.
1089–1091	Anarchical conditions prevail in Croatia, Slavonia, and Dalmatia.
1091	King Ladislas of Hungary invades Slavonia and annexes Croatian territory up to Gvozd mountains. Normans again invade Dalmatia.
1094	Ladislas reported to have founded bishopric of Zagreb.
1091–1097	Reported reign of Petar Snačić as king of the anti-Hungarian element.
1095	Provincial Synod at Zadar.
1096	Crusading armies traverse Croatia and Dalmatia.
1097	Hungarians invade Croatian territory south of Gvozd. Reported battle of Petrova Gora and death of Petar Snačić.
1102	King Koloman of Hungary probably concludes some kind of agreement with the Croatian clans south of the Gvozd. Croatia-Dalmatia becomes associated or autonomous kingdom under suzerainty of Hungarian royal house.
1107	Croatian troops sent to Apulia to fight against the Normans on behalf of Byzantium. Byzantium acquiesces to extension of Hungarian control along Dalmatian coast.
1116	Beginning of Hungarian-Croatian wars against Venice for possession of Dalmatia.
1138	Bosnia acknowledges sovereignty of Hungarian-Croatian king.
1168–1180	Byzantines establish control over Croatian lands.
1180	Ban Kulin establishes virtual independence of Bosnia.
1181–1191	Venetians unsuccessfully besiege Zadar.
1202	Venetians divert Fourth Crusade from Egypt to Zadar.
1241	Mongols overrun Hungary after victory on Sajó River.
1242	Mongols devastate Slavonia and Croatia. Fail to take Knin and Trogir. Reported destruction of large Mongol army on Grobničko (Graveyard) Polje. (Smaller Mongol force probably trapped and destroyed here.) Bela IV grants far reaching autonomy to Grič—the upper town of Zagreb.
1266	New privileges to Grič and Zagreb. Burghers freed from military service, certain taxes, and other obligations. Archdeacon Thomas of Split composes *Historia Salonitana*.

1270 Croatians refuse to recognize accession of Stephen V of Hungary.

1272 Sabor appoints Pavle Šubić ban. Serfs allowed right of appeal from seigneurial to banal court.

13th century Bogomil heresy strong in Bosnia. Papacy incites crusades against it.

1301 Arpad line of Hungarian-Croatian kings dies out. Mladen I Šubić ("the kingmaker") has Charles Robert of the Neapolitan Anjous crowned as Croatian king. Magyars choose other candidates but finally recognize Charles Robert's claim in 1307.

1322 Šubić and Nelipić families quarrel. Charles Robert breaks power of Mladen II Šubić.

1346–1348 Hungarian-Croatian war against Venice. Zadar revolts against Venetian rule but Louis I fails to remove it.

1353 Stipan Tvrdko succeeds Stipan Kotromanić as ban of Bosnia. Vassal of Louis I of Hungary-Croatia.

1358 Louis I forces Venice to relinquish her claims to Dalmatia.

1372 Tvrdko takes advantage of decay of Serbian power to seize districts along the upper Drina, Trebinje, the Pelješac peninsula, and the Dalmatian coast down to Kotor. Maintains good relations with Louis, who is involved in Poland and elsewhere.

1377 Tvrdko proclaims himself "King of Bosnia and Serbia."

1378 Venetians capture Šibenik and destroy town archives.

1380 Louis I again defeats Venetians. Forces reaffirmation of provisions of peace of 1358. The Adriatic virtually a Hungarian-Croatian Sea.

1383 Tvrdko encourages Croatians to support claim of Neapolitan Anjous to Croatian throne against pretensions of Louis' widow and daughter (Elizabeth Kotromanić and Mary, her daughter).

1383–1385 Civil war in Croatia.

1388–1390 Tvrdko extends control over parts of Dalmatia and Croatia. Claims Croatian crown himself, but is defeated by Mary's husband, Sigismund of Luxemburg.

1391 Death of Tvrdko. Recession to Hungary-Croatia of the Croatian territory acquired by Bosnia. Turks invade Slavonia and are beaten by forces of Petar Morović.

1401 All Dalmatia except Dubrovnik acknowledges Ladislas of Naples.

1403 Ladislas crowned king at Zadar. Entrusts protection of his interests in Croatia-Dalmatia to Hrvoje Vukčić, who also dominates Bosnian political life.

1408 Sigismund makes his authority recognized in Croatia-Dalmatia and in Bosnia.

1409 Ladislas of Naples sells his hereditary claim to Dalmatia to Venice for 100,000 ducats.

1412	Venetians take Šibenik again.
1421	Trogir, Split, Brač, Hvar, Korčula fall to Venice.
1435	Pressburg diet sets up Croatian and Slavonian defensive districts against Turkish attacks.
1448	Hercegovina splits off from Bosnia (Duke Stipan Kosača).
1463	Turks conquer Bosnia. Part of Croatian population accepts Islam. Other Croatian elements emigrate. Turks import Orthodox settlers (Serbs, Greeks, Bulgars, Albanians, Macedo-Rumanians (Vlachs) into Bosnia.
1464	Recapture and heroic defense of Bosnian stronghold of Jajce. In revenge, Turks ravage Dalmatia and Croatia.
1468	Major Turkish inroad into Croatian lands.
1478	Croatians destroy Turkish raiding force.
1479	Juraj Vitovec defeats large Turkish army.
1480	Count Ivan Frankopan cedes Krk to Venice.
1481	Sons of Stipan Kosača cede Makarska district to Venice.
1482	Hercegovina falls to Turks. Same process of religious conversion, emigration, and importation of Orthodox elements as in Bosnia.
1483	Zrinskis defeat Turkish invasion force.
1491	Croatians recognize Maximilian I of Austria as their king. He takes possession of Istria and northern Dalmatia. Maximilian concludes Treaty of Pressburg with Jagellon kings of Poland-Lithuania. Hungarian-Croatian thrones to Jagellons, but Hapsburgs to succeed to this inheritance if Jagellon line becomes extinct. Croatians defeat Turkish raiding army.
1493	Defeat of Croatians by Turks on Krbava Polje. Fatal blow to old nobility south of Gvozd.
1513	Ban Petar Berislavić crushes Turkish army.
1514	Turks ravage Lika and Krbava.
1521	Berislavić again defeats Turks, but is separated from his men and killed.
1522	Berislavić and Keglević families press Louis II Jagellon to entrust defense of Croatian Kvarner coast with Senj and other Croatian fortresses to Archduke Ferdinand Hapsburg of Austria (grandson of Maximilian I). Knin and Klis repulse Moslem attacks.
1526	Hungarian army defeated by Turks at Mohacs. Louis II, last of the Jagellons, falls. Frankopani and Karlovići organize defense of Slavonia and Croatia. Srijem and much of Slavonia overrun by Moslems. Ilok, Vukovar, Osijek, Djakovo taken.
1527 (Jan.-Sept.)	Croatian Sabor accepts claim to throne advanced by Ferdinand. Slavonian Sabor decides (Jan. 6) in favor of John Zapolya, Magyar Voyvoda of Transylvania. Civil war results. Slavonian Sabor declares for Ferdinand after death in battle of Count Krsto Frankopan, Zapolya's chief advocate in Slavonia.

Bibliography of Medieval Croatia

The oldest known source for the study of Croatian history is the *De administrando imperio*, composed by, under the direction of, or by order of Emperor Constantine VII Porphyrogenitus between the years 948 and 952. It is the general consensus of opinion among modern scholars that the second-oldest source, *Kraljevstvo Hrvata* (Kingdom of the Croatians), was written during the years 1074–1081. It consists of twenty-three short chapters and was penned originally in the Croatian western or *čakavština* dialect and in the Glagolitic script used in medieval Croatia. A Latin cleric, known in history as the Priest of Dioclea, translated this Croatian work into Latin and added another twenty-four chapters to it. His literary activity seems to have covered the years 1148–1163. In later times his work came to bear the title of *De regno Sclavorum.* Still another ancient source is the *Historia Salonitana*, which probably was completed by Archdeacon Thomas of Split shortly before his death in 1268. There are a number of editions of these older works and as many interpretations of their content.

The first attempt that was made to elaborate a recital of Croatian history on the basis of these sources was that of Ivan Lučić (Lucius), in his well known study, *De regno Dalmatiae et Croatiae libri sex* (Amsterdam, 1666). A second writer, worthy of consideration even today, was the Jesuit Daniel Farlati, who dealt extensively with political as well as ecclesiastical materials in his great work, *Illyricum sacrum*, published in eight volumes in Venice between 1751 and 1819.

The father of modern Croatian critical historiography was Dr. Franjo Rački (1828–1894), who long functioned as president of the Yugoslav Academy of Sciences and Arts in Zagreb. He contributed to the publications of this Academy a vast amount of source materials and critical discussions. Other nineteenth-century Croatian historians of stature were: Ivan Kukuljević-Sakcinski (1816–1889), often referred to as the Nestor of Croatian historiographers; Šime Ljubić (1822–1896), who is known principally because of his compilation of materials dealing with Croatian-Venetian relations in the Middle Ages, and also for a similar work on Ragusan history; and Radoslav Lopašić (1835–1893), who concerned himself chiefly with the history of the Croatian Military Frontiers.

Modern Croatian historians include Ivan Kr. Tkalčić (d. 1905), Vatroslav Jagić (d. 1923), Tade Smičiklas (d. 1914), Vjekoslav Klaić (d. 1928), the archaeologist Frane Bulić (d. 1934), Ferdo Šišić (d.

1940)—who was perhaps the most prolific of modern Croatian writers, Ćiro Truhelka (d. 1942), Miho Barada (d. 1957), Grga Novak, Jaroslav Šidak, Dominik Mandić, and Stjepan K. Sakač. The life and work of Šišić is described by Jaroslav Šidak, in the third edition of Šišić's *Pregled povijesti hrvatskoga naroda* (Zagreb: Matica Hrvatska, 1962), 491–507.

A few words should be said about Bosnian historiography, since Bosnian history has been divorced for such long periods of time from the history of the other Croatian lands. Attention was first drawn to Bosnian history by the abbot Mavro Orbini, in his *Il regno degli Slavi* (Pesaro, 1601). Farlati, in the following century, devoted pages 37–39 in the fourth volume of his *Illyricum sacrum* to a study of the history of the Catholic bishopric of Bosnia, and gave this land much incidental mention in the other volumes of this monumental work as well. In 1776, Farlati's collaborator, Filip Laštrić, published his *Epitome vetustatum Bosnensis provinciae* at Ancona. A few years later, Maximilian Schimek brought out his *Politische Geschichte des Königreiches Bosnien und Rama* in Vienna. After a lapse of over half a century there appeared, in 1851 at Zagreb, *Zemljopis i poviesnica Bosne* (Geography and History of Bosnia). The author of this work was Slavoljub Bošnjak (Ivan Franjo Jukić). The first critical documented study of Bosnian history was made by Vjekoslav Klaić, whose *Poviest Bosne do propasti kraljevstva* (History of Bosnia to the Fall of the Kingdom) was published at Zagreb in 1882. Dr. Ivan Bojničić translated this work into German under the title of *Geschichte Bosniens* (Leipzig, 1885). In 1888, the Hungarian, J. V. Asboth, published another worthwhile study, *Bosnien und Hercegovina* (Vienna), and this was subsequently translated into English. Another Magyar, Dr. L. Thallóczy, finished his *Studien zur Geschichte Bosniens und Serbiens im Mittelalter* at Munich in 1914. Several of the works of Dr. Ćiro Truhelka and of Dr. Dominik Mandić have been cited in the general bibliography given below. It might also be noted that Truhelka contributed studies of a great number of documents and inscriptions copied from medieval tombstones in Bosnia to such publications as *Glasnik zemaljskoga muzeja u Sarajevu* (Bulletin of the Provincial Museum in Sarajevo) and *Wissenschaftliche Mitteilungen* (Vienna).

Apart from an enormous quantity of periodical materials—such as Rački's "Bogomili i Patareni," which he brought out in volumes seven, eight, and ten (1869, 1870) of *Rad*, published by the Academy—and special treatises of various kinds, systematic histories of Bosnia and

Hercegovina have been prepared in recent years by the following: Dr. Vladimir Ćorović, *Historija Bosne*, Part I (Belgrade, 1940); Professor Krunoslav Draganović (ed.), *Poviest hrvatskih zemalja Bosne i Hercegovine*, I (Sarajevo, 1942); and Dr. Mandić (Studies as listed in the following bibliography).

I. SOURCES

Acta Bosnae potissimum ecclesiastica cum insertis editorum documentorum regestis. Ab anno 924 usque ad annum 1752, ed. Eusebius Fermendžin (*Monumenta spectantia historiam Slavorum Meridionalium*, Vol. XXIII). Zagreb: Yugoslav Academy, 1892.

Acta Croatica, Vol. I., ed. Djuro Šurmin (*Mon. Historico-iuridica Slavorum Meridionalium*). Zagreb, 1898.

Codex diplomaticus regni Croatiae, Dalmatiae et Slavoniae, Vols. II–XV, ed. Tade Smičiklas and Marko Kostrenčić. Zagreb, 1904–1934.

Danduli Andreae Chronicon Venetum (*Scriptores rerum Italicarum*, Vol. XII, ed. G. Muratori). Milano, 1728. Second edition, Bologna: E. Pastorello, 1938–1958.

Diplomatarium relationum reipublicae Ragusinae cum regno Hungariae, ed. J. Gelcich and L. Thalloczy. Budapest, 1887.

Einhardi Annales, ed. G. H. Pertz (*Scriptores Rerum Germanicarum*, Vol. I, 1895).

Johannis Diaconi Chronicon Venetianum, ed. G. H. Pertz (*Monumenta Germaniae historica*, Vol. VII; G. Monticolo, *Cronache Veneziane antichissime*, Vol. I). Rome, 1890, 59–171.

Jornandes, "De origine actibusque Getarum," ed. Theodor Mommsen (*Monumenta Germaniae historica*, Vol. V). Berlin, 1882.

"Kraljevstvo Hrvata" / The Kingdom of the Croatians, "Presbyteri Diocleani," *De regno Sclavorum*, ed. J. Lucius (Lučić) (*De regno Dalmatiae et Croatiae*). Amsterdam, 1666, 287–302. See G. Schwandtner's edition of same in *Scriptores rerum Hungaricarum*, Vol. III, Vienna, 1748, 474–509. See also Kukuljević-Sakcinski, Ivan, ed. "Kronika hrvatska iz XII vieka" / A Croatian chronicle of the Twelfth century, *Arhiv za povj. Jugoslavensku* I. Zagreb, 1851, 1–37; Šišić, Ferdo. *Letopis Popa Dukljanina*. Beograd-Zagreb, 1928, 383–416; Mošin, Vladimir. *Ljetopis popa Dukljanina*. Zagreb, 1950, 39–68.

Kukuljević-Sakcinski, Ivan, ed. *Jura regni Croatiae, Dalmatiae et Slavoniae*. 3 vols. Zagreb, 1861–1862.

———. *Monumenta historica Slavorum Meridionalium* (*Acta Croatica*, Vol. I). Zagreb, 1863.

———. *Codex diplomaticus regni Croatiae, Dalmatiae et Slavoniae*. 2 vols. Zagreb, 1874–1875.

———. "Regesta documentorum regni Croatiae, Dalmatiae, et Slavoniae, saeculi XIII," *Starine*. Vols. XXI, XXII, XXIII, XXIV, XXVI, XXVII, XXVIII. Zagreb: Yugoslav Academy.

Ljubić, Šime. *Listine o odnošajih izmedju Južnoga Slavenstva i mletačke republike*. Vols. I–X. Zagreb: Yugoslav Academy, M.S.H.S.M.

Monumenta spectantia historiam Slavorum Meridionalium. Vols. I–XLIV. Zagreb: Yugoslav Academy, 1868–1948.

Monumenta historico-juridica Slavorum Meridionalium. Vols. I–XIII. Zagreb: Yugoslav Academy, 1877–1938.

Monumenta Croatiae Vaticana. Vol. I, ed. Dominik Mandić. Chicago-Rome, 1962.

Porphyrogenitus, Emperor Constantine VII. *De administrando imperio,* ed. Moravcsik-Jenkins. Budapest, 1949. (Chapters 29–36.)

Presbyteri Diocleani, *De regno Sclavorum.* (*De regno Dalmatiae et Croatiae,* ed. J. Lucius [Lučić]. Amsterdam, 1666, *Popa Dukljanina Ljetopis,* ed. Ivan Crnčić. Kraljevica, 1874; *Letopis Popa Dukljanina,* ed. Ferdo Sišić. Beograd–Zagreb, 1928; *Ljetopis popa Dukljanina,* ed. Vladimir Mošin. Zagreb, 1950.)

Rački, Franjo, ed. *Documenta historiae chroaticae periodum antiquam illustrantia* (Vol. VII, M.S.H.S.M.). Zagreb, 1877.

Šišić, Ferdo. *Priručnik izvora hrvatske historije* (Enchiridion fontium historiae Croatiae). Vol. I (to 1107). Zagreb, 1914.

Strohal, Ivan, ed. *Statuti primorskih gradova i općina* / Statutes of the Coastal Towns and Municipalities. Zagreb, 1911.

Supetarski kartular, ed. Viktor Novak and Petar Skok. Zagreb, 1952.

Thalloczy, Lajos, and Hodinka, Antal. *Codex diplomaticus partium regni Hungariae adnexarum* (*A horvat veghelyek okleveltara* / Archives of the Croatian Frontier Fortresses, 1490–1527). Budapest, 1903.

Theiner, Augustinus, ed. *Vetera monumenta historica Hungariam sacram illustrantia.* Vols. I–II. Rome, 1859–1862.

——, ed. *Vetera monumenta Slavorum meridionalium historiam illustrantia maxima parte nondum edita, ex tabulariis Vaticanis deprompta et collecta.* Vol. I. Rome, 1863; Vol. II. Zagreb, 1875.

Thomas Archidiaconus. *Historia Salonitana,* ed. F. Rački (Vol. XXVI, M.S.H.S.M.). Zagreb, 1894.

Tkalčić, Ivan K., ed. *Monumenta historica episcopatus Zagrabiensis saec. XII et XIII.* 2 vols. Zagreb, 1873–1874.

——. *Monumenta historica liberae et regiae civitatis Zagrabiae.* Vols. I–XI. Zagreb, 1889–1905; Vols. XII–XVIII, 1929–1953, edited by Emilije Laszowski.

II. HISTORICAL AND SCIENTIFIC REVIEWS

The following periodicals contain a great many relatively short treatments or discussion of historical questions, sources, and other materials relating to Croatian history.

Anali Historijskog Instituta u Dubrovniku / Annals of the Historical Institute in Dubrovnik, 1952– .

Arhivski Vjesnik / Bulletin of Archives. Zagreb, 1958– .

Bolletino di archeologia e storia dalmata. Vols. I–XLII. Split, 1878–1920.

Bulletin international de l'Académie Yougoslave des sciences et des beaux-arts. Classe d'histoire et de philologie. Zagreb, 1932– .

Časopis za hrvatsku povijest / Journal of Croatian History. Zagreb, 1943–4.

Croatia Sacra. Vols. I–XIV. Zagreb, 1931–1944.

Glasnik zemaljskoga muzeja u Sarajevu / Bulletin of the Provincial Museum in Sarajevo. Sarajevo, 1889–1945. New Series. Vols. I–XVIII. Sarajevo, 1945–1962.

Godišnjak Istorijskog društva Bosne i Hercegovine / Yearbook of the Historical Society of Bosnia and Hercegovina. Vols. I–XIV. Sarajevo, 1949–1962.

Historijski Zbornik / Historical Studies. Vols. I–XIV. Zagreb, 1948– .

Hrvatska prošlost / Croatian Past. Zagreb, 1940–1944.

Jadranski Zbornik / Adriatic Studies. Split, 1956– .

Ljetopis Jugoslavenske Akademije Znanosti i Umjetnosti / Chronicle of the Yugoslav Academy of Sciences and Arts. Vols. I–LXIII. Zagreb, 1867–1962.

Narodna Starina / National Antiquities. Vols. I–XII. Zagreb, 1922–1933.

Rad Jugoslavenske Akademije Znanosti i Umjetnosti / Acta, Yugoslav Academy of Sciences and Arts. Vols. I–CCCXXII. Zagreb, 1867–1962.

Radovi Instituta Jugoslavenske Akademije u Zadru / Acta, Institute of the Yugoslav Academy in Zadar. Zadar, 1954– .

Slovo. Časopis Staroslavenskog Instituta. / The Word. Review of the Old Slavic Institute. Vols. I–X. Zagreb, 1952–1960.

Starine / Antiquities. Yugoslav Academy. Vols. I–L. Zagreb, 1869–1960.

Stari pisci hrvatski / Old Croatian Writers. Yugoslav Academy. Vols. I–XXXV. Zagreb, 1869–1962.

Starohrvatska prosvjeta / Old Croatian Civilization. Old series, 1895–1903. New series, 1927–1928. 3rd Series, 1949– . Yugoslav Academy.

Vjesnik Državnog Arhiva u Rijeci / Bulletin of the State Archives in Rijeka. Rijeka, 1953–1956.

Vjesnik Historijskog Arhiva u Rijeci / Bulletin of the Historical Archives in Rijeka. Rijeka, 1957– .

Vjesnik Hrvatskog Arheološkog Društva / Bulletin of the Croatian Archeological Association. Zagreb, 1879–1891. New Series, 1895–1943.

Vjesnik Hrvatskog Državnog Arhiva / Bulletin of the Croatian State Archives. Old Series, 1899–1918. New Series, 1925–1945.

Vjesnik za arheologiju i historiju dalmatinsku / Bulletin of Dalmatian Archeology and History. Split, 1920–1962. (This journal is a continuation of the *Bolletino di archeologia e storia dalmata*, listed above.)

Vrela i prinosi / Sources and Studies. Zagreb, 1932–1941.

Wissenschaftliche Mitteilungen aus Bosnien und der Hercegovina. Vols. I–XIII. Vienna, 1893–1916.

Zbornik Historijskog Instituta Jugoslavenske Akademije u Zagrebu / Bulletin of the Historical Institute of the Yugoslav Academy in Zagreb. Zagreb, 1954– .

Zbornik radova. Sveučilište u Zagrebu. Filozofski Fakultet / Yearbook of Studies. University of Zagreb. Department of Philosophy. Zagreb, 1953– .

III. SPECIAL OR REGIONAL STUDIES

Appendini, Fr. M. *Notizie istorico-critiche sulle antichità, storia e letteratura de' Ragusei.* Ragusa (Dubrovnik), 1802–3.

Barada, Miho. "Episcopus chroatensis," *Croatia Sacra* I. Zagreb, 1931, 161–215.

———. "Dinastičko pitanje u Hrvatskoj XI stoljeća," *Vjesnik za arheologiju i historiju dalmatinsku*. Vol. 50, 1928–29. Split, 1932, 157–199.

Bjelovučić, N. Z. *Crvena Hrvatska i Dubrovnik* / Red Croatia and Dubrovnik. Zagreb, 1929.

Bogišić, V. *Pisani zakoni na slovenskom jugu* / Written Laws in the Slavic South. Zagreb, 1872.

Buć, S. *Naši službeni povjesničari i pitanje podrietla Hrvata* / Our Official Historians and the Question of the Origin of Croatians. Zagreb, 1941.

Bulić, Frane. "Dolazak Hrvata i pohrvaćivanje Dalmacije" / The Coming of the Croatians and the Croatization of Dalmatia, *Sveslavenski Zbornik*. Zagreb, 1930.

Bulić, F., and Bervaldi, J., "Kronotaksa spljetskih nadbiskupa" / Chronology of the Archbishops of Split, *Bogoslovska Smotra*. Zagreb, 1913.

Cessi, Roberto. *Venezia e i Croati*. Rome, 1942.

Chalandon, Ferdinand. *Les Comnènes. Etudes sur l'empire byzantin au XI et XII siècles. Jean II Comnène (1118–1143) et Manuel I Comnène (1143–1180)*. Paris, 1912.

Czoernig von Czernhausen, Karl. *Ethnographie der Oesterr. Monarchie*. 3 vols. Vienna, 1857.

Dabinović, Antun. *Hrvatska državna i pravna poviest* / Croatian Constitutional and Legal History, Part I. Zagreb, 1940.

———. "Les Angevins en Croatie et en Hongrie," *Annales de l'Institut Français de Zagreb*, nos. 5, 6, 7, 9, 12. Zagreb, 1938, 1939, 1940.

Digović, P. *Dalmatie*. Lausanne, 1944, 1–69.

Dvornik, Francis F. *Les Slaves, Byzance et Rome au IX siècle*. Paris, 1926.

———. *The Slavs: Their Early History and Civilization*. Boston, 1956.

Engel, Johann Christian von. *Staatskunde von Dalmatien, Kroatien, und Slavonien*. Halle, 1798.

———. *Geschichte des Ungarischen Reichs und seiner Nebenländer*. 3 vols. Halle, 1798–1801.

Farlati, Daniel. *Illyricum Sacrum*. 8 vols. Venice, 1751–1819.

Gebhardi, L. *Geschichte der Königreiche Dalmatien, Kroatien, Slavonien, Rascien, Bosnien, Rama, und Ragusa*. Pest, 1805.

Godra, Barth. *Monographie von Syrmien*. Zemun, 1873, 1–84.

Gruber, Dane. *Nelipić, knez cetinski i kninski* / Nelipić, Count of Cetin and Knin. Zagreb, 1886.

———, and Spinčić, Vjekoslav. *Poviest Istre* / History of Istria. Zagreb, 1924.

Gumplowicz, L. *Politička poviest Srba i Hrvata*. / Political History of the Serbians and Croatians. (Special reprint and translation of the article written in German by Gumplowicz for the *Politische Anthropologische Revue* of the same year.) Zagreb, 1913.

Hammer-Purgstall, J. von. *Geschichte des osmanischen Reiches*. 10 vols. Vienna, 1836.

Heynen, R. *Zur Entstehung des Kapitalismus in Venedig*. Stuttgart, 1905, 32–35.

Horvat, Josip. *Politička povijest Hrvatske*. Vol. I. Zagreb, 1936.

———. *Kultura Hrvata kroz 1000 godina* / A Thousand Years of Croatian Culture. 2 vols. Zagreb, 1939, 1942.

———. *La formation de la Croatie d'aujourd'hui*. Zagreb, 1943.

Horvat, Rudolf. *Povjest Hrvatske*. Zagreb, 1904. Second ed. 1924.

———. *Povjest Medjumurja*. Zagreb, 1907. Second ed. 1944.

Jelić, Luka. *Hrvatski spomenici ninskoga područja iz dobe hrvatskih narodnih vladara.* / Croatian Remains From the Vicinity of Nin Dating From the Time of the National Rulers. Zagreb, 1911.

Klaić, Vjekoslav. *Slavonien vom X bis zum XIII Jahrhundert*. Zagreb, 1882.

———. *Povjest Hrvata*. 5 vols. Zagreb, 1899–1911.

———. "Hrvatski sabori do god. 1790" / The Croatian Diets to 1790, *Zbornik Matice Hrvatske*. Zagreb, 1925, 247–311.

Knezović, Fra Oton. *Hrvatska povijest*. Madrid, 1962.

Koharić, Janko. *Das Ende des kroatischen Nationalkönigtums*. Zagreb, 1904.

Kovačić, Josip. *Hrvatska prije hiljadu godina pa do danas.* / Croatia From a Thousand Years Ago Until Today. Zagreb, 1926.

Krišković, Vinko. *Hrvatsko pravo kućnih zadruga* / Croatian Law of the Communal Family. Zagreb, 1923.

Krmpotić, M. D. *Croatia, Bosnia, and Hercegovina and the Serbian Claims*. Kansas City, 1916.

Kršnjavi, Isidor. *Zur historia Salonitana des Thomas Archidiacon in Spalato*. Zagreb, 1900.

Kukuljević-Sakcinski, Ivan. *Borba Hrvatah s Mongoli i Tatari* / The Struggle of the Croatians with the Mongols and Tartars. Zagreb, 1863.

Lenel, W. *Die Entstehung der Vorherrschafts Venedig an der Adria*. Leipzig, 1897.

Mandić, Dominik. *Postanak Vlaha prema novim poviestnim iztraživanjima* / The Origin of the Vlachs According to New Historical Investigations. Buenos Aires, 1956.

———. *Crvena Hrvatska*. Chicago, 1957.

———. "Hrvatski Sabor na Duvanjskom polju god. 753" / The Croatian Sabor on the Field of Duvno in the Year 753, *Hrvatska Revija*, VII. Buenos Aires, 1957, 5–40.

———. *Bosna i Hercegovina*. I. *Državna i vjerska pripadnost sredovječne Bosne i Hercegovine* / The State and Religious Affiliation of Medieval Bosnia and Hercegovina. Chicago, 1960.

———. "Nenapisano poglavlje hrvatske pismenosti" / An Unwritten Chapter of Croatian Literature, *Hrvatska Revija*, XI, 1961.

———. *Bosna i Hercegovina. II. Bogomilska crkva basanskih krstjana* / The Bogomil Church of the Bosnian Christians. Chicago, 1962.

———. *Chroati Catholici Bosnae et Hercegovinae in descriptionibus annis 1743 et 1768 ex*. Chicago-Rome, 1962.

Marczali, Henry. *Les relations de la Dalmatie et de la Hongrie du XI au XIII siècle*. Paris, 1899.

———. *Ungarisches Verfassungsrecht*. Tübingen, 1911.

Marković, Ivan. *Dukljansko–barska metropolija* / The Metropolitan See of Dioclea–Bar. Zagreb, 1902.

Markwart, J. *Osteuropaeische und ostasiatische Streifzuege*. Leipzig, 1903, 466–469.

Mayer, E. *Die dalmatisch-istrische Munizipalverfassung im Mittelalter und ihre römischen Grundlagen*. Split, 1903.

Mikoczy, J. *Otiorum Croatiae liber unus*. Buda, 1806.

Minns, E. H. *Scythians and Greeks*. Cambridge, 1932.
Niederle, Lubor. *Manuel de l'antiquité slave*. 2 vols. Paris, 1923, 1926.
Novak, Grga. *Prošlost Dalmacije* / The Dalmatian Past. Vol. I. Zagreb, 1944.
Orbini, Mavro. *Il regno degli Slavi*. Pesaro, 1601.
Pilar, Ivo. "O dualizmu u vjeri starih Slovjena i o njegovu podrijetlu i značenju" / Dualism in the Belief of the South Slavs and Its Origin and Meaning, *Zbornik za nar. život i običaje Južnih Slavena*, XXVIII (1931).
———. *Južnoslavensko pitanje* / The Yugoslav Question. 2nd ed. Zagreb, 1943. v–31.
Pliverić, Josip. *Beiträge zur Ung.-kroatische Bundesrechte*. Zagreb, 1886. (Especially 204–228).
Preveden, Francis. *A History of the Croatian People*. Vol. I. New York, 1956; Vol. II. New York, 1962.
Prodan, Don Ivo. *Je li glagolica pravo svih Hrvata?* / Was the Use of the Glagolitic Script the Right of All Croatians? Zadar, 1904.
Rački, Franjo. *Odlomci iz državnoga prava hrvatskoga za narodne dinastije* / Fragments of Croatian State Law in the Time of the National Dynasty. Vienna, 1861.
———. *Ocjena starijih izvora za hrvatsku i serbsku poviest* / Criticism of the Oldest Sources of Croatian and Serbian History. Zagreb, 1884.
Rostovtseff, M. *Iranians and Greeks in South Russia*. Oxford, 1922.
Ruggeri, G. *Contributo all' antropologia física delle regioni dinariche e danubiane e dell' Asia anteriore*. Firenze, 1908.
Rus, Jože. *Kralji dinastije Svevladičev* / Kings of the Svevlad Dynasty. Ljubljana, 1931.
———. *Krst prvih Hrvatov in Srbov*. Ljubljana, 1932.
Šafarik, Jos. *Slavishe Alterthumer*. 2 vols. Prague, 1837. St. Kaulfuss, Roman. *Die Slaven in den ältesten Zeiten bis Samo (623)*. Berlin, 1842.
Sakač, S. *Historijski razvoj imena "Hrvat" od Darija I do Konstantina Porfirogeneta* / Historical Development of the Name "Croatian" from the Time of Darius I to that of Constantine Porphyrogenitus. Zagreb, 1943.
———. "Ugovor pape Agatona i Hrvata proti navalnom ratu" / A Pact between Pope Agathon and the Croatians against an Aggressive War, *Croatia Sacra* I. Zagreb, 1931, 1–84.
Schimek, Maximilian. *Politische Geschichte des Königreiches Bosnien und Rama*. Vienna, 1787.
Šegvić, Kerubin. *Toma Splićanin* / Thomas of Split. Zagreb, 1927.
———. *Borba za hrvatsko bogoslužje i Grgur Ninski* / The Struggle for the Croatian Liturgy and Gregory of Nin. Zagreb, 1930.
———. *Die Kroaten und ihre Mission während 13 Jahrhunderte der Geschichte*. Zagreb, 1941.
———. *Die gotische Abstammung der Kroaten*. Berlin, n.d. (An Italian edition of this work appeared in 1941–1942.)
Sermage, Count C. J. P. *Die ursprüngliche Vereinigung der Königreiche Croatien, Dalmatien und Slavonien mit der Krone Ungarns*. Vienna, 1836.
Šidak, Jaroslav. *"Crkva bosanska" i problem bogumilstva u Bosni* / The Bosnian Church and the Problem of Bogomilism in Bosnia. Zagreb, 1940.
Šišić, Ferdo. *Vojvoda Hrvoje Vukčić Hrvatinić i njegovo doba* (1350–1416) / Duke Hrvoje Vukčić Hrvatinić and His Times. Zagreb, 1902.

———. *Hrvatska povijest.* 3 Vols. Zagreb: Matica Hrvatska, 1906–13.

———. *Pregled povijesti hrvatskoga naroda.* Zagreb: Matica Hrvatska. First ed., 1916; Third ed., 1962.

———. *Die Wahl Ferdinands I von Oesterreich zum König von Kroatien.* Zagreb, 1917.

———. *Geschichte der Kroaten.* Vol. I. Zagreb: Matica Hrvatska, 1917.

———. *Povijest Hrvata u vrijeme narodnih vladara* / History of the Croatians in the Time of the National Rulers. Zagreb, 1925.

———, ed. *Letopis popa Dukljanina.* Beograd-Zagreb, 1928.

———, ed. *Priručnik izvora hrvatske historije. 1. Do god. 1107* (Enchiridion fontium hist. Croatiae). Zagreb, 1914.

———. *Poviest Hrvata za kraljeva iz doma Arpadovića.* Zagreb, 1944.

Smičiklas, Tade. *Poviest Hrvatske.* 2 vols. Zagreb, 1879, 1882.

Štedimlija, Sava M. *Crvena Hrvatska.* Zagreb, 1937.

———. *Tragom popa Dukljanina* / On the Trail of the Priest of Dioclea. Zagreb, 1941.

Sticotti, P. *Die römische Dioclea in Montenegro.* Vienna, 1913.

Strohal, Ivan. *Pravna povijest dalmatinskih gradova. 1. Osnove razvitku pravne povijesti dalmatinskih gradova* / Legal History of the Dalmatian Towns. 1. Bases for the Development of the Legal History of the Dalmatian Towns. Zagreb, 1913.

Strzygowski, J. *Starohrvatska umjetnost* / Old Croatian Art. Zagreb, 1927.

Šufflay, Milan. *Hrvatska i zadnja pregnuća istočne imperije pod žezlom triju Komnena (1075–1180).* Zagreb, 1901.

Szallay, Ladislas von. *Geschichte Ungarns.* Trans. H. Wögerer. Pest, 1866.

Thalloczy, Lajos. *Studien zur Geschichte Bosniens und Serbiens im Mittelalter.* Munich and Leipzig, 1913.

Tkalčić, Ivan K. *Slavensko bogoslužje u Hrvatskoj* / The Slavonic Liturgy in Croatia. Zagreb, 1904.

Tresić-Pavičić, A. *Izgon Mongola iz Hrvatske* / The Expulsion of the Mongols from Croatia. Zagreb, 1942.

Truhelka, Ćiro. *Naši gradovi* / Our Towns. Sarajevo, 1904.

———. *Kraljevski grad Jajce* / The Royal Town of Jajce. Sarajevo, 1904.

Urica, Nikola. *Kako je postala "unija" izmedju Hrvatske i Ugarske?* / How Did the "Union" Between Croatia and Hungary Come About? Zagreb, 1905.

Valvasor, Johann von. *Die Ehre des Herzogthums Krain.* 4 vols. Laybach (Ljubljana), 1689.

Vernadsky, George. *Ancient Russia.* New Haven, 1943.

Vinski, Z. *Uz problematiku starog Irana i Kavkaza* / The Problem of the Old Iranians and Caucasians. Zagreb, 1940.

Wasmer, Max. *Untersuchungen über den ältesten Wohnsitz der Slaven. 1. Die Iranier in Südrussland.* Leipzig, 1923.

Weigand, Gustav, *Die Sprache der Olympo-Wallachen.* Leipzig, 1888.

———. *Vlacho-Meglen.* Leipzig, 1892.

Zbornik kralja Tomislava u spomen tisućugodišnjice hrvatskoga kraljevstva / The King Tomislav Anthology in memory of the Millennial Anniversary of the Croatian Kingdom. Zagreb, 1925.

Zeiller, J. *Les origines chrétiennes dans la province de Dalmatie.* Paris, 1906.

Zinkeisen, Baron Johann. *Geschichte des osmanischen Reiches.* 7 vols. Hamburg, 1840–1863.

4

Military History

IVAN BABIĆ

The Conquest of the Present Homeland

According to Constantine Porphyrogenitus, the Byzantine Emperor and historian, the Croatians had, in the sixth century A.D. in present-day Poland, an organized and militarily powerful state called Great Croatia or White Croatia. They moved to the south, enlisted by the Byzantine Emperor Heraclios (610–645) to subdue and pacify the Avars, a warlike Asiatic people, who, from their stronghold in the Carpathians, constantly plundered the northwestern part of the empire between the Adriatic Sea and the Drina River. In bitterly fought battles, the Croatians succeeded in routing the Avars completely, and in subsequently settling the conquered lands. Because of a lack of fertile soil, a part of them moved northward to the area between the Sava, Una, Drava and Mura Rivers and settled there. These events did not occur as a single happening, but rather took place over a period of decades. As a rule, the Croatian warriors were the first to enter new territory. After they had driven away the enemy and pacified the area, the rest of the population followed and took possession of the conquered lands. Eventually they absorbed the remnants of the Avars, Celts, Goths, and some Slavic tribes already found there, and began to build their nation on the conquered soil.

The basic unit of the Croatian state, whose main feature—as everywhere in that epoch—was its military organization, was the large family (*zadruga*). Many closely related *zadrugas* formed a brotherhood (*bratstvo*). These in turn united into districts (*županas*). The head of a *župa* was the *župan*, in whose hands supreme power—primarily military, but also judiciary and tributary—was held. In time of war, the *župan* had to lead the armed forces of the *župa*, which were composed of a fixed number of fully armed and equipped men placed at his disposal by each *zadruga* and *bratstvo*. These forces were made up mainly of highly mobile light cavalry, armed with lances, bows, and arrows. Their tactics consisted in swift movements, violent attacks by surprise if possible, and steady pursuit of the defeated enemy until it was destroyed. This was a new type of army, one whose tactics were superior to the old-fashioned ones of the Roman legion. Such were the forces which defeated the Avars, and which conquered and pacified the area which from that time until this has been the homeland of the Croatian people.[1]

In the higher structuration of the Croatian state's political and military organization, many *župas* were grouped into provinces (*banovinas*) each with a *ban* as its head. Nominally, the *ban* was to be elected by the *župans*; in point of fact, in most cases he rose to power by his own merits and capacities. During important wars, he was the supreme commander of the united forces of all *župas*.

Strategic Characteristics of the New Homeland

The lands which the Croatians conquered and settled have undergone changes of name throughout history. These lands include the territory that is at present known under the regional names of Croatia, Slavonia, Dalmatia, Bosnia, Hercegovina, and Istria. Except on the northern and northwestern sides, where they lie open to Central Europe, these lands have good natural boundaries and form a closed strategic area. On the west, the boundary is the Adriatic Sea; on the southern and eastern sides, the boundary is a line starting near Budva on the Adriatic and going through the Montenegrin mountains to the upper Drina River, following it to its confluence with the Sava River, and then following the Sava to the Danube.[2] This is the line which the Emperor Theodosius drew as the division between the Western and Eastern Roman Empire. It is based upon geographical facts and not upon any casual or compulsory circumstances. The lands which lie on the east side of this boundary represent a separate geographic and strategic entity—the heart of the Balkan area—through which the principal strategic ways lead from Asia and the Aegean Sea to Central Europe.

Whereas these lands are the bridge between Asia and Europe, the Croatian homeland should not be considered a bridge at all. It is

[1] Ljudmil Hauptmann, *Die Kroaten im Wandel der Jahrhunderte* (Berlin: Wiking Verlag, 1943), 56ff.

[2] Vidal de la Blanche, *Geografía Universal* (Barcelona, 1928).

rather an integral part of Central Europe, with its flank open to attack from the east, and its economic route to the outside world leading through the Adriatic. In any historical period when these lands, or a part of them, were dominated by a power whose center of force lay to the east of their natural boundaries—in the Balkans or in Asia—political and strategical equilibrium was broken to the detriment of all of Europe.[3] For this reason, during the historic epoch of the Turkish invasions, these lands were the battlefield of many nations and the bulwark for the defense of Europe from the danger originating in the neighboring important area, the heart of the Balkans. Historical continuity has strengthened this natural division, making the Drina River a boundary between the Eastern and Western churches, between the Croatian and Serbian states during the Middle Ages, and eventually between two civilizations, the Occidental and the Byzantine.

The National State in the Middle Ages

The geographical configuration within this area did not help to promote the formation of a unified state organization. Chains of mountains divided the area into separate geographical entities. At first, then, several independent states (*banovinas*) were formed. Pannonian Croatia sprang up between the Una, Sava, and Drava Rivers; in northern Dalmatia and Bosnia, White Croatia was formed; and in southern Dalmatia, Hercegovina, and parts of present Montenegro and Albania, Red Croatia arose.

Pannonian Croatia had to endure heavy fighting with the Franks, at that time the most powerful state in Europe. The Croatians, under Ban Ljudevit Posavski, during struggles which lasted for more than twenty years, defeated ten Frankish armies. Finally, however, Ljudevit fell in a battle near Sisak (822), and his state was subjected to Frankish sovereignty for almost a century. White Croatia had similar problems with Venice, which tried its utmost to secure political and commercial domination on the eastern coast of the Adriatic. There were many fluctuations in this struggle, until the Croatian Prince Domagoj destroyed the Venetian fleet (877) and forced Venice to pay a yearly tribute for the privilege of free navigation. This privilege lasted until the year 1000, when Venice defeated the Croatian fleet and conquered some islands on the Croatian coast. Red Croatia soon disappeared. Its northern regions were united with White Croatia, while those areas

[3]Ivan Babić, "Yugoslavia in Western Strategy," *The Croatian Nation in Its Struggle for Freedom and Independence* (Chicago, 1955), 311ff.

which lay beyond the aforementioned natural geographic boundaries were lost for the Croatian nation.[4]

Croatia rose to her zenith under Prince Tomislav, who united all the Croatian lands and proclaimed himself king (925) in the town of Duvno, in western Bosnia. The Croatian army at that time, according to Constantine Porphyrogenitus, was made up of "as many as 60,000 horsemen and 100,000 foot-soldiers, up to eighty galleys, and up to one hundred cutters. . . ."[5] The structure of this army corresponded roughly to the social structure of the nation of that time. The horsemen belonged mostly to the ruling class, that is, to the Croatian tribes who conquered and ruled the land. They represented the elite and the shock-force of the army. The footmen came mostly from the Croatianized remnants of other peoples; they formed the force which supplied garrisons in the land and kept order there.

Tomislav was succeeded by various kings, the most notable of whom was Petar Krešimir (1058–1074), under whose rule Croatia reached the peak of her strength. It should be stressed that, in spite of such extraordinary power, the Croatians never engaged in offensive and imperialistic wars. They protected their land successfully in defensive wars, defeating the Bulgarian King Simeon, the greatest of all Bulgarian rulers, throwing him back over the Drina River, and repelling Hungarian attacks coming from the north.[6]

The Croatian-Hungarian Union

When King Zvonimir, one of the Croatian rulers, died childless (1089), the Hungarian King Ladislaus laid claim to the Croatian throne, since Zvonimir's widow was his sister. The Croatians elected Petar Svačić as their king, who resisted the Hungarians for a short time, but who was eventually defeated in battle in the Gvozd Mountains (1097) in Upper Croatia. Feeling that the Croatian resistance had nevertheless not been completely broken, the new Hungarian King, Koloman, wisely preferred to negotiate with the Croatians. In 1102 a Hungarian-Croatian treaty called the *Pacta Conventa* was concluded. This treaty was to be the cornerstone of the Croatian nation until 1918. Through it the Croatians entered into a personal union with Hungary—the Hungarian-Croatian king pledged himself to respect the constitutional

[4]Ferdo Šišić, *Povijest Hrvata u doba narodnih vladara* / History of Croatians in Times of National Rulers (Zagreb, 1925).

[5]Babić, *The Croatian Nation*, 7.

[6]Francis R. Preveden, *A History of the Croatian People*, I (New York: Philosophical Library, 1955).

rights of Croatia. In the military provisions of the treaty, the Croatians pledged themselves to put at the disposal of the king, should a foreign enemy cross the frontiers of the kingdom, a force of at least ten fully armed cavalrymen from each *zadruga.* These forces would be maintained by the Croatians until they crossed the Croatian boundary on the Drava River; from that point their maintenance and pay would be the responsibility of the king for the duration of the war.[7]

The adoption of the Christian faith of the Western Church (in the seventh century), and of a common life with the Hungarians, gradually changed the whole social structure of the Croatian nation. The old, *zadruga* type of society was replaced by a feudal system of the Western pattern. Many noblemen lost their wealth, became peasants, or emigrated to cities. Others accumulated wealth and power and became feudal lords who turned their own tribesmen into serfs. Some held power as hereditary rulers, challenging even the power of kings. The most notable of these rulers were Paul and Mladen Šubić (1298–1322), who ruled as hereditary bans of Croatia-Dalmatia, as well as of Bosnia.[8]

This social transformation in its turn influenced the military organization of the nation. During the early years of the Hungarian-Croatian union, the old *zadruga* system prevailed. To every *župa* a sector was assigned for defense; the *župas* established their own armies by a levy which could be partial or general. If great danger were in sight, many *župas* would unite their armies under the command of the ban or king.[9] One of the most important military events of the period occurred in 1242. A huge Mongolian army, under Genghis Khan's commander, Batu Khan, penetrated into Croatia after it had defeated everyone who opposed it, including the Hungarians on the Sajó River. In Croatia, this army experienced its first losses on the way from Peking to the Adriatic. In spite of a long siege, Batu Khan was not able to break the defense of the fortress of Kalnik (northern Croatia), where King Bela had taken refuge. When his troops suffered heavy losses at Grobničko Polje, Trogir, and Klis, Batu Khan began to withdraw. At about the same time, news of Genghis Khan's death reached the army, whereupon it turned back to Russia. Thus Europe was freed from one of the greatest dangers in its history.[10]

[7]Šišić, *Povijest Hrvata,* 318ff.

[8]Rudolf Kiszling, *Die Kroaten. Der Schicksalsweg eines Südslawenvolkes* (Graz-Köln, 1956), 13.

[9]Slavko Pavičić and Franjo Perše, "Hrvatska vojna povijest," / Croatian Military History, *Naša Domovina* / Our Country, I (Zagreb, 1943), 187 ff.

[10]Šišić, *Povijest Hrvata,* 412.

In the twelfth century, the traditional *župa* military organization had already disappeared and had been replaced by the feudal pattern common to Western Europe. Each nobleman had his own army, corresponding in strength to his wealth and ambitions. In the fourteenth century, the feudal armies in Croatia were organized according to the *banderia* system. Every *banderia* had 400 men and was divided into units consisting of one-half, one-quarter, or one-eighth of the total strength of the *banderia.* There were normally both king's-own and ban's-own *banderias* in Croatia. All powerful warlords had their own *banderias*; the most notable were those of the princes Frankopan and Šubić-Zrinski, the princes Nelipić, Kurjaković of Krbava, and Babonić of Blagaj, the bishop of Zagreb, and the prior of the monastery of Vrana in Dalmatia. Many minor noblemen had their own troops, as did every *župa* and some important cities. While some of the forces were composed of mercenaries, most of them were militia-type troops based on levy. Taken as a whole, Croatia possessed an impressive armed force; but, as often happened in feudal times, it was not always used for the benefit of the king and the country. Frequently it was used for the settlement of differences between the noblemen themselves, or even against the king, especially in the dynastic feuds which plagued Hungary and Croatia after the extinction of the Arpad dynasty (1301).[11] Such was the military picture of Croatia before the time of the Turkish invasion.

Croatians as the Bulwark for the Defense of Western Europe

After defeating the Bulgarians on the Maritsa River (1371), and the Serbs at Kosovo Polje (1389), the Turks turned to the Balkans (especially to the Serbian lands with their important strategic routes of Nišava-Morava and Vardar-Morava) as a means of penetrating into the heart of Europe. The Croatians, of necessity, were their first victim. In defending their homeland, the Croatians at the same time defended Europe—sometimes helped by her, sometimes abandoned by her—in a series of bloody wars lasting over a period of more than four centuries.

The Turks first entered Bosnia. This Croatian land led, during the Hungarian-Croatian union, a more or less independent life. Nominally, all Bosnian rulers were vassals of Croatian kings; how far this was enforced in practice depended upon the situation of the moment.[12] The

[11]Kiszling, *Die Kroaten*, 16.

[12]L. V. Suedland, *Južnoslavensko pitanje* / The Problem of South Slavic Peoples (Zagreb, 1943), 79 ff.; Savfet Bašagić, *Kratka uputa u prošlost Bosne i Hercegovine* / A Brief Introduction Into the Past of Bosnia and Hercegovina (Zagreb, 1886).

unfortunate fact is that the Turks came into Bosnia at the invitation of the Bosnian ruler Hrvoje Vukčić Hrvatinić, to help him in his feud with the Hungarian-Croatian king (1415). In the years that followed, they penetrated into Croatia, devastating the land as far as the Austrian border. By 1435 they were already in possession of Sarajevo, and in 1437 the Bosnian king, Stephen Tomašević, acknowledged their supreme authority. In 1463, however, under pressure from his Hungarian-Croatian suzerain, he refused to pay the yearly tribute to the Turks. Emir Mohammed II (1430–1481) then entered his territory with a strong army and defeated and beheaded him at Jajce. The Bosnian-Croatian independent state thus disappeared, and Bosnia remained under Turkish domination until 1878.[13] Mohammed II received the title of *Fatik* (Conqueror), and soon became sultan. A wise statesman, he promised not to interfere with the feudal structure of the country, and held out hopes of power and glory to its nobility by making accessible to them the highest places of authority in the empire. The whole of the nobility and a large section of the rest of the population—mostly those of the Bogomil faith (an heretical Christian sect)—peacefully passed over to the Islamic religion. Because of this peaceful conversion, Bosnia remained the only country in the whole Turkish Empire with a Western feudal-type social structure, and during the following centuries it became practically autonomous. The Turkish authorities interfered little in local affairs; the real power was in the hands of the local Croatian nobility—the only hereditary nobility in the empire. Many of the nobles rose to the highest positions and made history as rulers and military leaders.[14] In that era of religious intolerance, this conversion made the Catholic and the Islamic Croatians enemies. Thus, while these two groups fought for the glory of their respective religions, Croatian blood was shed on both sides.

In subsequent years, the Turks began a series of incursions deep into Upper Croatia. To face this grave menace, the Croatians created the rank of "captain-general" (1477). The military leader who held this title had to be nominated by the Croatian parliament (Sabor), and was subordinated to the ban. He was responsible for the country's defense, and led the armed forces in war.[15] The Croatians assumed the offensive in 1478. Between the Una and Glina Rivers they routed a Turkish army of 20,000 cavalrymen, and pursued and destroyed it near Jajce (Bosnia). By 1479 the Turks were again defeated by Ban George

[13]Hauptmann, *Die Kroaten*, 29 ff.

[14]Joseph Matl, *Das kulturelle und politische Werden der Suedslaven* (Berlin, 1929), 158; Ivan Kukuljević, *Znameniti Hrvati* / Famous Croatians (Zagreb, 1886).

[15]Hauptmann, *Die Kroaten*, 36 ff. Kiszling, *Die Kroaten*, 26 ff.

Vidovec; and in 1491 Ban Ladislaus Eggervary defeated a Turkish army of 11,000 men.

In 1493 the Turkish commander Jakub Kadun Pasha broke into Croatia. Ban Mirko Derenčin, having raised 15,000 men, met him at Krbavsko Polje, near Udbina. The Turks, with their swift horsemen, won a sweeping victory. In this battle, one of the most fateful in Croatian history, Croatian losses totaled 12,500 men, among them the cream of the Croatian youth and the bulk of the country's nobility. Their properties gradually came into the hands of new noblemen, mostly of German and Hungarian origin, and thus began the tendency toward denationalization of the Croatian lands. Moreover, for a long time Croatia was too weak to furnish an effective defense–its land was continually exposed to invasions and devastation, and the population either perished, was taken into Turkish slavery, or fled to the north. To the Croatian regions the Turks brought their subjects from Asia and the Balkans: Vlachs, Bulgarians, Greeks, Serbs, Armenians, Czinczars, and others. Being mostly of the Orthodox faith, the sultans favored their subjection to the Serbian Orthodox Church, which was obedient to and subordinated to the Turks, in contrast to the Roman Catholic Church, which was independent and hostile. These peoples, then, became Serbs, although they were not of Serbian blood.[16]

Sultan Soliman the Great, in his drive to Vienna in 1521, conquered Belgrade and Šabac in Serbia, but he was not able to conquer the fortress of Petrovaradin, in eastern Croatia. Eventually he withdrew the bulk of his army, but eastern Slavonia and Srijem remained under Turkish occupation. In the spring of 1526, Soliman returned, completely routing the army of the Hungarian-Croatian king Louis, who drowned in the swamps near Mohacs (Hungary). Very few Croatians took part in this battle, yet it had an important influence upon the future of Croatia. Since they were now in great danger, the Croatians looked for some way of strengthening the defense of their lands. To this end, they elected Ferdinand of Hapsburg as their king in 1527. In this way they affirmed their sovereign rights as a kingdom independent of the Hungarians, and at the same time they linked their fate with the Hapsburg dynasty for some centuries to come.[17]

It is an historical fact that the decline of the Turkish offensive power was connected with the names of two Croatian military leaders. The first of these was Ban Nicholas Jurišić. When Soliman the Great and his Grand Vizier Mehmed Pasha Sokolović (the most successful Grand Vizier in Turkish history, and, ironically, an Islamized Croatian from

[16]Suedland, *Južnoslavensko pitanje*, 79 ff. [17]Šišić, *Povijest Hrvata*, 197 ff.

Bosnia) marched against Vienna in 1532, they were met at the fortress of Kiszeg (south Hungary) by Jurišić. A long, unsuccessful siege of the fortress made Soliman lose too much time and forced him to turn back. In 1566 he returned once more against Vienna. This time the Croatian Count and Ban Nikola Šubić Zrinski blocked his way at the fortress of Szigetvár, Hungary (formerly Sziget). The Turkish army of 100,000 men and 300 guns was not able to break the resistance, in spite of a siege that lasted for several months. When the defenders were left without food and ammunition, they made a last heroic suicidal attack, in which most of them fell. History has awarded Ban Nikola Šubić Zrinski the honorary title of "the Croatian Leonidas." This episode inspired the German poet Karl Theodor Körner to write a famous tragedy (*Zriny*), and the Croatian composer Ivan Zajc to create the most popular Croatian opera, *Nikola Šubić Zrinski.* Soliman died during the siege of Vienna, and his whole army, demoralized, withdrew. Vienna was thus saved, and an armistice which was signed at Constantinople was later repeatedly renewed, so that peace followed for a long period.[18]

The Organization of the Military Frontier

Owing to the continuing Turkish menace, the Croatians decided to establish a permanent defense organization. Thus a military organization of a new and original type, called Vojna Krajina (Military Frontier Zone) was born. Most of the Croatian people lived under it until 1881, and it has left deep traces on the Croatian people and their way of living.

The initial organization laid down by the Croatian Sabor in Križevci (1537–38) stipulated the creation of a militia-type army based on levy, which was to be subordinated to the ban. The captain-general was to lead it in the field. The land was divided into a Vendian Military Zone between the Drava and Kupa Rivers, and a Croatian Military Zone between the Kupa and the Adriatic. As impoverished Croatia was not able to bear all the expenses, the Austrian provinces of the Hapsburgs agreed to a yearly contribution. Initially there was no continuous defense line, but simply a network of castles, strongholds, fortresses, and fortified cities. Some of these had permanent garrisons which could be reinforced by hastily mobilized militia.[19] This organization

[18]Kiszling, *Die Kroaten*, 25. Ferdinand Strobl, "Tuerkenkrieg 1541–45," *Altens Handbuch*, 304 ff.

[19]J. H. Schwicker, *Geschichte der Oesterreichischen Grenze* (Vienna, 1883), 112.

was strengthened in the Bruck Edict (1578), by which a permanent war council was formed in Graz, the rank of "Administrator of Vojna Krajina" was created, the strength of the permanent army was fixed at 4,000 men, and a yearly contribution by the Austrian provinces of 500,000 Kronen was established. The first administrator to be appointed was Archduke Charles of Hapsburg, a very able man. His first act was the construction of a fortress (named Karlovac in his honor) on the confluence of the Kupa and Korana Rivers. This was to be the stronghold of the whole defensive system.[20]

In 1593 the long period of peace came to an end, when the Turks penetrated into Hungary and Croatia. They were defeated at Sisak by Count Egenburg, but in the following year, with the help of a new army, they succeeded in conquering Sisak. Subsequently, the main Turkish war operations were, for a time, transferred to Hungary. In Croatia, bloody and devastating guerrilla warfare then took place, but this did not substantially change the general situation. The only event worth mentioning was the conquest of the fortress of Petrinja by Captain-General George Lenković, which permitted the advance of the Military Frontier limit to the Una River, thus forming a separate district named Banska (Ban's-own) Krajina, subordinated directly to the Ban.[21]

In 1630 the Military Frontier was withdrawn from the authority of the ban and the Sabor, and placed under that of the emperor. The whole male population of the Military Frontier was subject to lifelong military service, but thereby obtained the advantage of being free men, subject directly to the emperor, rather than being serfs to noblemen. The entire zone was divided into two regions, each one under a Colonel-General. A system of alarm was perfected which permitted the gathering, in fixed places, of between six and seven thousand men within a few hours.[22] All of these measures strengthened the military capabilities of the Frontier in a certain sense, but also created deep discontent among the Croatian nobility, because they infringed upon Croatian constitutional rights.

After the Turks suffered a decisive defeat at Vienna (1683), desperate efforts were made to drive them out of Hungary and Croatia. In the latter, Colonel-General Count Leslie, from Varaždin, conquered Virovitica and some other Slavonian fortresses, including Gradiška (1684). The following year, Ban Nicholas Erdödy cleared the Turks

[20]Franz Vanicek, *Spezialgeschichte der Militaergrenze*, I (Vienna, 1875), 62 ff.
[21]*Ibid.*, 76 ff.
[22]*Ibid.*, 86 ff.

from Croatia as far as the Una River, while other Croatian forces, under Markgrave Louis von Baden, penetrated into Bosnia and won an important victory near Derventa. The Franciscan priest Luka Mesić freed Lika, and another priest, Luka Imbrišinović, freed Požega. The war received new impetus when the famous Prince Eugene of Savoy assumed leadership. He won a decisive battle at Senta, Vojvodina, and conquered Belgrade, and even Sarajevo. Eventually the Turks signed a peace treaty at Srijemski Karlovci (1699), whereby they had to abandon all of Croatia and Slavonia except for a part of Srijem. In this way a large part of the Croatian lands again became free, although Bosnia remained under Turkish and Dalmatia under Venetian rule. The limits of the Military Frontier were now advanced to the Una and Sava Rivers. On the negative side, the repopulation of the newly conquered areas produced the exodus of a part of the Croatian Catholic population from Bosnia. To their homes the Turks brought people from the Balkans and from Asia. The newcomers—as had happened before—adopted both the Orthodox religion favored by the Turks and Serbian nationality; later they formed the Serbian minority in Bosnia, which has remained one of the causes of tension between Croatians and Serbs right down to the present time.[23]

After a short period of peace, the Turks again attacked, but were defeated in Hungary and Croatia. By a new peace treaty in Požarevac (Serbia) in 1718, they lost a part of Bosnia. But in a new war they were victorious, and after 1739 the frontiers of Croatia again ran along the Una-Sava line. During this period, Croatian territory amounted to some 15,500 square miles: 3,700 in Civil Croatia under the ban, and 11,800 in the Military Frontier.[24] The latter had about 36,000 men fit for military service.[25] In spite of all reforms, these men were not satisfactorily organized into closed and well-disciplined tactical units. Constant contact with the Turks and with cruel methods of warfare had left their traces upon the souls and habits of these warriors, and upon the whole population as well. The area, in short, was not populated with peace-loving people. Acts of brigandry and plundering were rather common. This fact, and even more the wish to use in a rational way the extraordinary capacities and excellent military performances of these fighters, hardened as they were by physical strain and a frugal life, led to the decision for one more thorough reform of the status of the Military Frontier. A series of extraordinary measures against brigandry

[23]Suedland, *Južnoslavensko pitanje*, 79 ff.; Kiszling, *Die Kroaten*, 34 ff.
[24]Babić, *The Croatian Nation*, 16.
[25]Kiszling, *Die Kroaten*, 39.

followed, which eventually ended when a figure who has since become a legend, the Croatian Baron Franjo Trenk, enlisted fighters from the Frontier (by granting them amnesty) in a military unit, "Trenk's Pandurs." He brought them to the European battlefields, where they covered themselves with glory because of their extraordinary military exploits, and at the same time gave rise to tales and legends of hardship and cruelty.[26]

The organization of the Military Frontier underwent various changes. Its final form, taken in 1752, was the following:[27]

	Infantry Regiment	*Name of Regiment*	*Headquarters*
Ban's-Varaždin-Karlovac: General Command in Zagreb	1	Karlovac-Lika	Gospić
	2	Karlovac-Otočac	Otočac
	3	Karlovac-Ogulin	Ogulin
	4	Karlovac-Slunj	Karlovac
	5	Varaždin-Križevci	Bjelovar
	6	Varaždin-Djurdjevac	Bjelovar
	10	1st Ban's-Own	Glina
	11	2nd Ban's-Own	Petrinja
Slavonia-Srijem: General Command in Petrovaradin	7	Brod	Vinkovci
	8	Gradiška	Nova Gradiška
	9	Petrovaradin	Mitrovica

At the head of the whole organization was a commanding general with headquarters in Zagreb. He had, as his immediate collaborators, two field marshals and four generals. The head of every regiment was a colonel, and the regiments were divided into battalions, companies, and platoons. The high-ranking officers were mostly German, although a small number of them were Croatian. Lower-ranking officers were predominantly Croatian. On every echelon, right down to battalion, there was an officer (with a corresponding staff) for each of the following duties: military affairs, justice, technical services, forest service, schools and education, and general administrative services. The commanding officer was entrusted with and responsible for all military, judiciary, and administrative activities, and other duties as well. Each branch of service was governed by well-conceived written statutes.

Practically the whole population lived in a constant state of war, and every able man from age eighteen to sixty was subject to military service. The men always had to have their weapons with them, even while working the fields, ready at any moment to leave their daily

[26]Vanicek, *Spezialgeschichte*, I, 531 ff.
[27]Pavičić-Perše, "Hrvatska vojna povijest," 194.

occupations and move to their gathering places. Within two to six hours the units could be assembled at their places ready to move to battle. In recompense for this imposed military service, no man was a serf; all the inhabitants of the Frontier were free men. Besides military service, the whole population was subject to public works service, so that under military discipline roads, bridges, public edifices, schools, irrigation systems, and the like could be built. The school system was, for that epoch, quite advanced; there were almost no illiterates, and the major part of the men spoke fairly good German. The military capabilities of the Military Frontier were extraordinary. In 1815, for instance, of the 940,548 persons who lived in the Frontier, 473,000 were men. Of these, 135,924 were suitable for military service, that is, 47.4 per cent of the entire male population.

The peasants were the cornerstone of this whole organization. In 1815 they made up 94.1 per cent of the population. Wisely planned succession laws were promulgated, which prohibited the splitting-up of rural properties so that an economically powerful entity, based upon the traditional type of *zadruga*, was preserved as the basic unit of the whole economic and social structure. It was able to subsist even when all the men fit for military service were on the battlefield.

The Military Frontier, moreover, served as a sanitary cordon for the whole of Europe against the plague and other diseases from the Asiatic region. In 1710 a "Plague Edict" was promulgated, which was later reinforced. When pestilence was known to be present in Turkey, all travelers and merchandise coming from there were subject to twenty-one, twenty-eight, or forty-two-day quarantine delay before being allowed to enter Croatia and to move farther into Western Europe.[28]

On Foreign Battlefields

When the Turkish peril lessened, the Hapsburgs became involved in a series of conflicts with various European powers, and they used Croatian troops in all their major wars of that time. These troops consisted mostly of light cavalry armed with lances and arquebuses, and excelled in reconnaissance missions, swift attacks, and pursuits. The heavy cavalry (cuirassiers) was armed with heavy swords and pistols, and was used to pierce the enemy's battle formation. The infantry (muskateers) was armed with light fusils (muskets); arquebusiers used heavy fusils; and lancers were mostly armed with lances. There were also some artillery units.

[28]Hugo Kerchnawe, *Die alte Militaergrenze* (Vienna, 1943), 35 ff.

The Croatians took part in the Thirty Years' War on all the battlefields in Europe. In 1619–1620 they fought in Bohemia. In 1622 they were the first to enter Heidelberg, after swimming across the Neckar River under circumstances which became legendary. They defeated the Hungarian leader Gabor Betlen, an ally of Gustavus Adolphus (1594–1632) of Sweden, in 1626. The Croatians penetrated deep into Germany, as far as Rostock, and took the fortress of Stralsund and Rügen Island. In the decisive battle of Lützen (1632), where Gustavus Adolphus fell, the Croatians played a decisive part with their twenty cavalry squadrons. Their actions in the battle of Nordlingen (1634) were a major factor in that victory. They fought under the command of the most renowned military leaders of that epoch: Count Wallenstein, Count Tilly, Croatian Count George Zrinski, General Isolany, General Johann von Werth, Ban Nicholas Zrinski, his brother Peter, General Piccolomini, and others.[29] Whenever these leaders had Croatian troops under their command, they had to assume the title "General of the Croatians." The leaders, and the Croatians with them, often passed as mercenaries from one side to the other—a rather common occurrence in those times. Everywhere the Croatians distinguished themselves with extraordinary military exploits. Their capabilities were well known, as was their faithfulness to their leaders; thus they were sought after for the most responsible missions and duties. The French king, Louis XIII (1610–1643), formed a body-guard of Croatians, which was part of the French royal guard until the French Revolution. At the court of Saxony's Prince-Elector John George, a Guard unit called the *Kurfürstliche Kroaten Leibcompagnie zu Ross* (Prince-Elector's Croatian Cavalry Body-Guard Company) was formed in 1656.[30]

After the Thirty Years War, the Croatians were used in the War of Spanish Succession. They distinguished themselves in battles at Mantua and Milan in Italy, Hochstadt in Germany, and in the Netherlands and France. In many of these battles they were led by the famous Prince Eugene of Savoy.[31] In the Seven Years War between Maria Theresa and the Prussian King Frederick, the Croatians took important parts in decisive battles at Rosbach and Leytjen (1757), Kunnersdorf (1759), Thorgau (1760), Budjejovice, and others. They covered themselves with military glory, and won esteem from all military leaders, even from their enemies, as the best of soldiers. Yet, at the same time, having brought with them the cruel methods of their traditional warfare

[29]Pavičić-Perše, "Hrvatska vojna povijest," 196.
[30]*Ibid.*
[31]Vanicek, *Spezialgeschichte*, II, 112 ff.

against the Turks, they so excelled in brutality that it became common to say: "Deliver us, O Lord, from the plague, war, and the Croatians."[32]

During the same epoch, other Croatian units continued to fight the Turks at home. A Croatian corps some 30,000 men strong, under Prince Lichtenstein, defeated the Turks at Dubica in 1788. Another corps of 12,000 men, under Count Mitrowski, conquered Šabac (Serbia) and Novi (Croatia).[33]

The Napoleonic Wars

In 1796 and 1797, Croatians made up part of the Austrian army which fought against Napoleon in Italy under General Davidović (also a Croatian). By the peace treaty of Campoformio (1797), the Venetian Republic was suppressed, and the Hapsburgs obtained control of all of its possessions east of the Adige River, including Dalmatia. After many centuries, all the Croatian provinces, except Bosnia and Hercegovina, were thus united under the same power. In the new war against Napoleon, some 48,000 Croatians fought in Germany and Italy. Having lost the battle of Austerlitz (1805), the Hapsburgs had to cede all former Venetian possessions to Napoleon, who united them in the newly formed Kingdom of Italy.[34]

In 1809 the Croatians had approximately 100,000 men, fighting in Italy, Germany, and Poland. Furthermore, a Croatian Karlovac-Corps of about 10,000 men under the Croatian General Stojčević, fought at home against some 12,000 men of Marshal Marmont, with the aim of driving the French from Dalmatia. This war, in which guerrilla tactics were sometimes used, was a very bitter one. Eventually the Croatians, reinforced by a corps from Upper Croatia under General Knežević, forced Marmont to withdraw to Zadar, where he tried to embark. The war was nevertheless lost in the battle at Wagram, and the Hapsburgs had to hand over to Napoleon the territory of four Military Frontier regiments, and a part of Civil Croatia up to the Sava. This area, together with Dalmatia and some other provinces, was united in the "Province of Illyria" under the rule of Marmont.[35]

Of all his conquests, Napoleon was most favorably impressed by the military organization of the Military Frontier and the value of its soldiers. He kept the whole organization intact, forming three regiments called the *Régiments de Chasseurs d'Illyrie* (later called the *Régiments Croates*), which took part in the victory parade in Paris

[32]Rupert Schumacher, *Des Reiches Hofzaun* (Darmstadt, 1942), 17 ff.
[33]Kiszling, *Die Kroaten*, 49 ff.
[34]Schumacher, *Hofzaun*, 37 ff.
[35]Vanicek, *Spezialgeschichte*, IV, 249 ff.

(1811). He formed a special military school for Croatians in Karlovac and sent some two hundred Croatian youths to French military schools. In 1813, *Le Premier Régiment des Hussards Croates*, composed of six squadrons, was formed in Karlovac. On the whole, about 11 per cent of the Croatian population of Illyria was drafted for French military service.[36]

Under French command, the Croatians fought in the army of General Carré (1809); in 1811, in the division of General Baron Delzons; in the division of General Pourrailly in 1812; and in the divisions of Generals Junin and Oudinot in 1813. After the Napoleonic defeat at Moscow, the First and Third Regiments of Croatians under Field Marshal Šljivarić (also a Croatian) formed the rearguard which saved the remnants of the *Grande Armée* from final annihilation in the retreat over the Berezina River. On that occasion, Napoleon himself addressed the Croatians with the words: "Croatians, yesterday I personally witnessed your heroic deeds. You have won glory and immortal honor." In his memoirs, Marshal Marmont quotes these words of Napoleon when referring to the Croatians: "I never had better and more valiant soldiers."[37] Even now, in the homes of many peasants in Croatia, the French military award of the "Légion d'honneur" can be found in a place of honor.

At the same time, those Croatians who remained under Austrian rule fought on the side of Austria. In the Battle of the Nations at Leipzig, Croatians had the misfortune of having to fight against each other. After Napoleon's defeat at Leipzig, the Croatians, under General Radivojević, attacked Karlovac, which was defended by French-Croatians. These latter changed their allegiance and passed over to their brothers without fighting. Other Croatian troops, under General Tomašić, conquered northern Dalmatia, fighting on occasion in collaboration with the British fleet. Finally, a Croatian army, under General Milutinović, conquered southern Dalmatia, the former Republic of Dubrovnik, and Boka Kotorska, where they had to fight against the Montenegrins, who, instigated by Russia, claimed Boka Kotorska for themselves.[38]

From Napoleon to the First World War

After Napoleon's fall, relative peace reigned in the Croatian lands, interrupted occasionally by Turkish incursions from Bosnia, which

[36]Kiszling, *Die Kroaten*, 48 ff.

[37]Pavičić-Perše, "Hrvatska vojna povijest," 197.

[38]Kiszling, *Die Kroaten*, 49 ff.

sometimes provoked bloody punitive expeditions of Croatian troops deep into Bosnia. The Karlovac regiment attacked Kulen Vakuf in 1835, for example, and four regiments were sent against Turkish fortress of Izačić in 1836.[39]

In 1848, the Hungarians raised the banner of national freedom against the Hapsburgs. Unfortunately, the Hungarian concept of freedom meant the subjugation of other nationalities in the Hungarian part of the empire to their hegemony. In defense of their national interests, the Croatians aligned themselves against the Hungarians. Ban Baron Joseph Jelačić was appointed by the emperor "Ban of Croatia and Slavonia, Governor of Dalmatia and Rijeka, and Supreme Commander of all Croatian troops." When, because of certain political intrigues at the Viennese court, this appointment was withdrawn, Jelačić refused obedience and, solemnly confirmed by the Sabor, mobilized all Croatian troops of the second and third levy (the elite fighting troops of the first levy were in Italy under Marshal Radetzky). On September 7, 1848, he declared war on Hungary "in the name of the Kingdom of Croatia, Slavonia, and Dalmatia," and on September 14 he crossed the Drava River with some 45,000 troops. He defeated the Hungarians at Schwechat.[40] Defeated also by the Austrians and Prussians, the Hungarians capitulated at Vilagosz. Later political developments turned these victories more against Croatian than Hungarian independence. The Croatians made up the bulk of the Austrian army which, in 1859, defeated the Italians at Custozza. In the war against Prussia in 1866, the Croatian light cavalry won significant initial successes in the battle at Koeniggraetz, although these initial victories were nullified by the later course of the battle on other parts of the battlefield.

A Hungarian-Croatian agreement settled the relations between these two nations in 1867, the year after general obligatory military service had been introduced in Croatia.[41] The military provisions of the agreement provided for separate Croatian armed forces, called *Hrvatsko Domobranstvo* (Croatian Home-Defenders). These forces were subordinated to the common Hungarian-Croatian War Ministry in Budapest, and a separate department for *Domobranstvo* was established there. The *Domobranstvo* consisted of four infantry regiments (the 25th in Zagreb, the 26th in Karlovac, the 27th in Sisak, and the 28th in Osijek), the 10th Cavalry Regiment in Varaždin, and the 6th Artillery Regiment in Zagreb. Administratively, they formed a separate Croatian Military

[39]Vanicek, *Spezialgeschichte*, IV, 174 ff.
[40]Hauptmann, *Die Kroaten*, 65 ff.
[41]Kiszling, *Die Kroaten*, 55 ff.

Region in Zagreb, and in war the 42nd Division. Their official language was Croatian.

A gradual suppression of the Military Frontier began in 1871, and the Frontier was definitely incorporated into the civil administration of Croatia in 1881. A thorough military reorganization was the result. From the old Frontier regiments, a new division (the 36th) was formed. It consisted of four infantry regiments (the 16th in Bjelovar, the 53rd in Zagreb, the 78th in Osijek, and the 79th in Gospić), the 6th Cavalry Regiment in Varaždin and the 13th Artillery Regiment in Zagreb. The official language in these units was German, and they were a part of the common Imperial Army. Together with the 42nd Division they formed the 13th Army Corps, with headquarters in Zagreb.[42] At the head of this corps, and of both Croatian divisions, were such Croatian generals as Grba, Borojević, Sarkotić, Šnjarić, Lipovčak, Ljubičić, Uzelac (later supreme commander of the Imperial Air Force), and Mihaljević.

In 1878, Austria received the mandate from the Berlin Congress to occupy Bosnia and Hercegovina. Two Croatian generals were entrusted with this task. The main force, composed mostly of the Croatian 13th Corps, under General Filipović, crossed the Sava River at Slavonski Brod and, after rather heavy fighting, conquered Sarajevo. Another force, under General Jovanović, penetrated from Dalmatia into Hercegovina, and, after minor skirmishes, entered Mostar. These were the last military events involving Croatian participation before the First World War.

The First World War

In the First World War, the Croatian people made up about 13 to 14 per cent of the monarchy's entire mobilized manpower. Bosnia and Hercegovina, taken alone, where even men sixty years of age were drafted, gave an incredible 30 per cent of its population to the war effort.[43] At the outbreak of the war, there were in the Imperial Army 375 generals and admirals; of these, 55 generals and 2 admirals were Croatians.[44] The Croatians from Upper Croatia and Slavonia were incorporated mostly into the 13th Army Corps; those from Dalmatia and Istria into the units of the 15th and 16th Army Corps and into the Imperial Navy; while those from Bosnia and Hercegovina were taken into eight Bosnia-Hercegovina regiments and eight Bosnia-Hercegovina light battalions.

[42]Alphons Wrede, *Geschichte der k. u. k. Wehrmacht* (Vienna, 1903), 35 ff.
[43]Pavičić-Perše, "Hrvatska vojna povijest," 199.
[44]Kiszling, *Die Kroaten*, 97.

During the initial war period, the 13th Army Corps was employed against Serbia on the Sava and lower Drina Rivers; the Dalmatian units were used on the upper Drina and Lim Rivers; and the Bosnians fought mostly on the Russian front and partly on the Serbian. The two offensives against Serbia in 1914 were unsuccessful, due in part to the excellent fighting qualities of the Serbs and their experience from the Balkan wars, and in part to the poor leadership of the Austrian commander, General Potiorek. The experience of this period demonstrated that not only the Croatians but also the members of the Serbian minority from all Croatian lands—in whose willingness to fight against the Serbs there were some doubts—fought in a distinguished manner in Serbia and elsewhere, and could be considered among the best of the monarchy's troops. The feeling of belonging to the Croatian homeland that prevailed among the Croatian Serbs, was, at that time, stronger than their Serbian national consciousness. Later on in the war, the spirits of everyone—Croatians and others—ebbed because of the course of political events in the monarchy.

At the end of 1914, the bulk of the Croatian troops was transferred to the Russian front, where they took part in the winter offensive as the main shock-force which pushed the Russians back from the Tatar and Jablanica passes in the eastern Carpathians, and conquered Stanislav and Nizniow in Galicia. In the Gorlitze offensive (May, 1915), they fought in Bukovina, where they drove the Russians back to the Bessarabian frontier, and held their positions against repeated and bloody counter-attacks during the whole year of 1915 and the beginning of 1916.[45]

When Italy entered the war (May, 1915), all Dalmatian troops were hastily brought from the quiet Serbian front to the Italian front, and were merged into the 58th Division. A little later, almost all the Bosnian troops, and for a time some units from Upper Croatia, fought against Italy under Marshal Borojević. The fighting spirit of the Croatians on the Russian front fell lower and lower. Parts of the 36th and the whole 42nd Division were badly routed in 1916 between Dnjeper and Prut, and desertion was widespread because of the stubborn refusal of the Hungarians to accede to Croatian claims for the political reorganization of the monarchy. Later, in 1917, Wilson's Fourteen Points, containing the right to self-determination of peoples, looked very attractive to the Croatians on the Russian front. The Croatians on the Italian front fought until the very end in an examplary way. Their struggle was not for the king and emperor; it was rather for the defense of

[45]Pavičić-Perše, "Hrvatska vojna povijest," 199; Kiszling, *Die Kroaten*, 97 ff.

Croatian soil against Italian imperialism, expressed in the provisions of the famous London Treaty, already widely known among them. The flagrant failure of the Italian thirteen offensives, and the near breakdown of Italy, were mostly the result of the extraordinary and stubborn resistance of the Croatians.[46] Even when the Sabor formally broke ties with the monarchy on October 29, 1918, and proclaimed the independent "State of Slovenes, Croatians, and Serbs," and even when the armistice was signed, Croatian troops kept on resisting the Italians. They separated the non-Croatian leaders from their ranks, elected their own Croatian officers, and, in relative order, under very light Italian pressure, gradually withdrew (by foot and by rail) to their homeland, where they disbanded. Some Croatian units in the Austrian army in Albania withdrew in perfect order to Boka Kotorska, where they were demobilized in the most orderly manner and sent back to their homes. The Croatians on the Russian front were less fortunate. They became involved in the disordered circumstances of the general collapse and revolution, and a great number of them never reached home.[47]

The Yugoslav Legion

The idea of a Yugoslav Legion,[48] composed exclusively of Croatians, Serbs, and Slovenes from the monarchy, many of whom were prisoners of war in Russia or emigrants in America, originated with the Yugoslav Committee, which, on the Entente's side, acted for the liberation of the southern Slavs from Austria-Hungary. The purpose was to contribute to the Entente's military victory and to obtain in this way better understanding for the Yugoslav cause. This idea was, from the very beginning, opposed by the Serbian government, especially by Prime Minister Pašić. He was willing to accept volunteers, but only if they joined the ranks of the Serbian army, which, after its expulsion from the homeland in 1915, was reforming on Corfù and Bizerta. This was, in fact, the clash between basic concepts which later destroyed Yugoslavia: the concept of Yugoslav unity with equal rights for all her peoples, as opposed to that of Serbian hegemony.

When the Serbian government, with the agreement of the Allies, obtained permission from the Russian authorities for voluntary drafting among the prisoners in the Russian camps—mostly Croatians—the response was poor. This was chiefly owing to the principles involved, but

46Kiszling, *Die Kroaten*, 101, 121–122.

47*Ibid.*, 118 ff.

48Pavlova Milada, *Jugoslavenski Odbor* / Yugoslav Committee (Zagreb, 1924); Pavle Ostović, *The Truth About Yugoslavia* (New York, 1952), 62 ff.

also partly to the Balkan methods (insults, beatings, physical tortures, and so on) used by members of the Serbian mission, to which the Austrian Slavs were not accustomed. A little later, when the Serbian emissaries passed from voluntary to compulsory drafting, a series of disturbances broke out among the prisoners, mainly in Odessa. These were suppressed with the utmost cruelty; a mass murdering of prisoners took place, and their corpses were thrown into the Black Sea. This lasted until the whole affair was stopped by the Russian authorities. While the exact number of those murdered was never known, it has been estimated at between ten and thirty thousand.

Eventually a unit under the name of the "Serbian Volunteer Corps" was formed. When Romania collapsed in 1916, the 1st Division of this corps was hastily sent to Dobrudja to stop the Bulgarian advance. These men fought magnificently; of some 18,000 soldiers, this division lost almost 60 per cent—2,162 dead and 7,370 wounded. Even after this exploit the dissension within the Corps continued, and in 1917, 12,740 enlisted men (7,352 Serbs, 3,787 Croatians, 1,241 Slovenes, and 360 others) and 151 officers (4 Serbs, 98 Croatians, 42 Slovenes, and 7 others) left the corps. There remained only 19,472 enlisted men and 779 officers. This force was transferred from Russia to the Salonika front, reinforced by volunteers from America, and at last changed its name to the "Yugoslav Division." About 28,000 men strong (almost equal to the strength of the entire Serbian army),[49] this force took a decisive part in the break-through of the Bulgarian and German lines at Salonika in 1918. These events, widely known throughout Yugoslavia, contributed much to the weakness and low morale of the future Yugoslav army.

The Yugoslav Army (1918–1941)

When Yugoslavia was created (1918), the Serbs took the reins of the army, as well as of the whole state. They adopted the viewpoint that the new army was a simple continuation of the old Serbian army under another name. They, in consequence, ignored and suppressed the whole military past—traditions, customs, forms of organization, and so on—of all non-Serbian peoples in Yugoslavia. The old Serbian army was an excellent fighting instrument. The Serbs are generally first class soldiers: valiant, self-confident, intelligent, capable of acting independently, and faithful to their companions and their units. Of extraordinary physical resistence, they represent a type of warrior as good as one

[49]Svetozar Pribičević, *La dictature du Roi Alexandre* (Paris, 1933), 62.

could wish for. Their ranks did not possess a high standard of military knowledge, yet they compensated for this by common sense, a spirit of initiative, and a willingness to do their best, even to die in fulfillment of their duty. Above all, the whole army was imbued by a fanatical Serbian patriotism. In the old Serbia—nationally homogeneous—this represented a great moral force. In the new multinational state, it was anachronistic and acted against all non-Serbian nationalities, primarily against the Croatians, who were the most numerous and most nationalistic. Moreover, by tradition, the Serbian army always became involved in politics. It was Serbian army officers who (1903) murdered King Alexander Obrenović and his wife Draga, and brought the Karadjordjević dynasty to the throne. For decades, Serbian army officers (Chetniks) organized and conducted illegal guerrilla warfare in Macedonia against the Turks, Bulgarians, Greeks, and Albanians in order to further Serbian imperialistic aims. Serbian army officers likewise organized the murder of Archduke Franz Ferdinand and his wife in Sarajevo (1914), which event was the immediate cause of the First World War.

The new army was numerically strong, with 200,000 men in peacetime and almost 2,000,000 men in war. From sixteen peacetime divisions, twenty-eight war divisions and two mountain brigades were established. Of these, thirteen infantry divisions, one cavalry division, and one mountain brigade were to be formed on Croatian soil. Yet, because of a complicated mobilization system (imposed by considerations of Serbian political interests to the detriment of military efficiency and principles), only six of the infantry divisions had a Croatian majority among the rank and file, all under Serbian leadership.[50]

The new army's basic principles of military organization (the same which were in effect in 1912) were outmoded, yet no substantial reforms were made until 1941. The military leaders were neither willing nor able to reorganize the army according to the standard necessary for modern warfare. Instruction was rudimentary and inadequate. Financial means (25 to 30 per cent or more of the yearly national budget) were wasted in a sea of incompetence and corruption. The traditional Serbian and Croatian custom of forming army units from men of a single region, who are bound to close spiritual ties, was deliberately broken and substituted for by the so-called "extra-territorial military service." This consisted of bringing Serbian soldiers to Croatian garrisons (in order to have occupational forces there) and dispersing non-Serbs in small groups far from their homes (thus avoiding the danger

[50]Author's private archive.

of possible rebellions). This was one of the main causes of the break in the spiritual cohesion which had distinguished the units of the old Serbian army, as well as that of the Croatian.

In promotions and appointments to important positions, nepotism and political reliability (exclusively from the Serbian viewpoint) were the main criteria—not aptitude. The officers of the former Austro-Hungarian army were accepted only after a long and humiliating screening. Many did not want to be subjected to this procedure, and many others resigned shortly after admission. The non-Serbs, especially the Croatians, were rarely admitted to military schools. They were held back in promotions and posted in garrisons far from Croatian lands. The whole life of the army was subordinated to the aim of making it the backbone of Serbian hegemony over the non-Serbian nationalities, and not the instrument for the defence of the country against foreign enemies.

The national composition of the Yugoslav army at the beginning of 1941, by percentage, was roughly as follows (The military law, based on the Serbian family pattern, favored the exemption of Serbs from military service, and thus the figure 35.5% in the third column.):[51]

Nationality	*Population*	*Rank and file*	*Non-coms*	*Officers*	*Generals*
Serbs	41.0	38.0	84	79	97
Croatians	30.0	32.5	8	10	2
Slovenes	9.0	9.0	5	9	1
Macedonians	6.0	6.5	1		
Albanians	5.0	5.5			
Hungarians	3.5	3.5			
Germans	1.5	1.5			
Others	4.0	3.5	2	2	

Not one non-Serb became an army commander, or was appointed to any high position in the War Ministry, in the General Staff, or in military schools, or other leading positions. Only two Croatians and one Slovene were, for a short time, division commanders. The army interfered continually in politics, provocatively promoting Serbian national interests, traditions, and values, and suppressing all others. It organized Chetnik units within the army, and Chetnik political militia-bands for terrorizing the non-Serbian population. In 1936, the Croatian Peasant Party (which contained the overwhelming majority of Croatians) was compelled in self-defense to form "Croatian Peasant and Citizens' Protection-Troops" (*Hrvatska Seljačka i Gradjanska Zaštita*). This militia had small value as a fighting force in a regular war, yet its very existence contributed to limiting the excesses of Chetnik bands

[51]*Ibid.*

and the National Police (*gendarmerie*). The moral standards of the army fell lower and lower. In the critical years after 1938, when a large number of reservists were called to arms, many signs of deep moral crisis were visible. Mutinies occurred, for example, in the 42nd Regiment in Bjelovar, the 106th Regiment in Karlovac, in units in Banjaluka and Mostar, and in other units as well. The only answer of the military authorities, however, was oppression, never reform.

After the coup d'état (a conspiracy of army officers) of March 27, 1941, general mobilization was ordered. The response of the population was poor: less than 50 per cent of the people in non-Serbian areas, and a poor 60 per cent in Serbian areas, responded. When, on April 6, the Germans and Italians attacked, the army collapsed within a few days. The Germans, coming from Bulgaria, completely routed the best of the Serbian divisions in Serbia and Macedonia between April 6 and April 9, without any serious fighting. They entered Belgrade without opposition on April 13.[52] On the Croatian front, the Croatian Sava Division offered weak resistance south of the Drava River, and then yielded. The Germans entered Zagreb on April 10, some hours after the Croatian nationalist circles had proclaimed the "Independent State of Croatia," severing all ties with Yugoslavia. The Slovenian divisions quietly dispersed and disappeared between April 6 and April 9. The Hungarians occupied Bačka and Baranja, and the Italians, taking advantage of German victories, simply marched into part of Slovenia, the western part of Croatia, Dalmatia, and Montenegro, and encountered no serious resistance. During all this time, the Chetnik army units and Chetnik militia bands followed in the rear of the fleeing armies, spreading terror and committing atrocities against the non-Serbian population until the time when they fused with the defeated army. On April 17, the Serbian General Kalafatović signed the surrender.[53]

The Croatian Army and its Enemies in the Second World War (1941–1945)

Authority in the Independent State of Croatia (*Nezavisna Država Hrvatska: N.D.H.*) was taken over by Dr. Ante Pavelić, the head of an ultranationalistic pro-fascist Croatian political group, Ustasha. Pavelić ruled in a dictatorial way; even after a kind of Croatian Sabor was constituted, he was the only and omnipotent ruler of the country. The state, in fact, was never really free and independent. It was divided

[52]Kurt Tippelskirch, *Geschichte des zweiten Weltkrieges* (Bonn, 1951), 171.
[53]Tippelskirch, *Ibid.*, 171 ff.

into a German and an Italian occupational zone. The relation of the new Croatian army to the occupational Italian 2nd Army was regulated by the Pact of Rome and by other arrangements made later as the need arose. All Croatian troops in their zone were operationally subordinated to the Italians. Theoretically, the Italians also had the rights of control over the instruction and organization of the whole Croatian army; but, in practice, they were never in a position to use these rights, because the Croatians, and even the Germans, did everything to avoid this. The relation of the new army to the Germans was settled according to the practical local situation. All Croatian armed forces—including those in the Italian zone—depended on the Germans for organization, arms, and equipment. Training was left mostly to the Croatians, although some units were instructed in German training centers in Austria, in order to avoid Italian interference.

From the very first, the Croatian armed forces began to develop into two separate parts: the Regular Army (*Hrvatsko Domobranstvo*—Croatian Domobrans), and the Ustasha Militia (*Ustaška Vojnica*). This arrangement was later regularized by law (1942). In establishing the Croatian armed forces, numerous obstacles had to be overcome. While the Croatian people greeted the fall of Yugoslavia with joy and, in a certain sense, were grateful to the Germans for contributing to the destruction of this "jail of the Croatian nation," the greater part of the Croatians distrusted Hitler's policy and were fearful of the possibility of his victory. They also distrusted Pavelić and the Ustasha government, on the one hand for being exponents of the Nazi-Fascists, and on the other for not being able to bring order and organization to the country. The resentment against the Ustasha government grew deeper after it forcibly disbanded the *Hrvatska Seljačka i Gradjanska Zaštita*, and still deeper after the signing of the Pact of Rome (1942), by which almost the whole Croatian coast was ceded to Italian imperialism. Discriminatory measures on the part of the government in favor of the Ustasha Militia shook the morale in all the ranks of the Croatian Domobrans, which had to bear the heaviest part of the fighting.

The lack of professional officers and of non-commissioned officers was a severe handicap for both the Croatian Domobrans and the Ustasha Militia. This lack of officers was due partly to the fact that the Serbs, during the twenty-three years of the existence of Yugoslavia, did everything in their power to restrict the admittance of the Croatians to military schools. The number of officers, who were trained in allegiance to the Yugoslav unity to which the new Croatian state was opposed, were not considered trustworthy for the new army. The anger and hate accumulated in the recent past by the Serbs and Croatians, as well as the anti-Croatian propaganda from the Communists and Serbians—mostly among the Serbian minority in Croatia—together with the Allied propaganda against the Nazi-Fascists, caused a part of the population to rebel against the newly created Croatian state. Lack of experience in ruling, a narrow political outlook, and errors and grave misdeeds of the Ustasha authorities in suppressing the rebellion helped swell the ranks of the rebels and aggravate the task of the Croatian armed forces.

The Italians sabotaged every effort of the Croatians in the political, economic, and military fields. They never permitted an orderly conscription of recruits in their zone, hindered the operations and movements of Croatian troops, and openly helped the rebels. The Germans did not trust the Croatians entirely, and they held very tight control over the organization of the Croatian armed forces. They permitted the forming of new units, and supplied arms and equipment only at moments and in measures which suited their necessities and interests. They used the Croatian troops chiefly in field operations that were necessary for the protection of their communication links with the Balkans and of areas important to their war economy, making it scarcely possible for the Croatians to defend the objectives and areas vital to their national life. Because of these facts, and many other difficulties of lesser importance, the growth of the Croatian armed forces never was able to proceed in an orderly and systematic way—improvisations, half measures, and almost daily changes in purpose and plans were forced by circumstances.

The Croatian army, as well as the whole Croatian nation, was, in fact, engaged in two wars simultaneously. First there was the great war in which their real rulers—the Nazi-Fascists—exploited them for their own (Nazi-Fascist) interests (conversely, the Croatians, in so far as they were able with their limited opportunities, tried to exploit the Germans for the organization and equipment of the Croatian armed forces). The second war was the limited Croatian private war, imposed upon them by the Communist and Serbian rebels. The main goal of this war was the preservation of the Croatian state, and the avoidance of the restoration of Yugoslavia either under the rule of the Serbian hegemonists or under Communist dictatorship. Though this latter war was of primary and vital interest and importance for the future life of the nation, the Croatians could carry it on only sporadically, in areas, and with the limited forces allowed them by the occupying armies.

They considered the Germans to be their natural allies, for the moment, in their struggle against the Communists and partly against the Chetniks, yet at the same time as their oppressors—in Hitler's future New Europe. They looked to the Allied victory as a means of saving themselves from Hitler and Mussolini, and at the same time distrusted the Allies for helping the Communists and for their view of the possible restoration of Yugoslavia.

In such a complicated political situation, the whole nation, its armed forces as well as its individuals, could not fix upon a logical and consistent line of conduct. In this fact lies the explanation of the ever-changing behaviour of the army units in the fighting—revealing a strong fighting spirit for some time, then suffering inexplicable defeats, later winning sweeping victories again, and so on. The forces of the Croatian Domobrans consisted of an army, a navy, and an air force. The whole territory was divided into three Corps Regions (Zagreb, Brod, and Sarajevo.)[54] Initially five divisions were formed. A Volunteer Legion (filled partly by compulsorily drafted personnel), consisting of one infantry regiment and one artillery group, was sent to the Russian front. This Volunteer Legion was eventually destroyed at Stalingrad. The commander of the 6th Germany Army, Field Marshal von Paulus, under whose command the Croatians had fought, once stated that of all the auxiliary troops on the Russian front the Croatians were the best fighters; then he listed the Slovaks, Romanians, Hungarians, and Italians, in that order.[55] The air force sent a combat and a bomber group to Russia, and the navy a small detachment to the Black Sea. Later on, for reasons of prestige, the Italians forced the incorporation of one Croatian battalion into the Italian army on the Russian front.

The Croatian Domobrans were a true "people's army." Their officers and rank and file were overwhelmingly democratic in outlook. The greater part of them were not partisans of the Ustasha; rather they leaned mostly on the Croatian Peasant Party, which was considered to be in favor of the Allies. Some attempts were made by the high-ranking officers of the Croatian Domobrans to establish contacts with the Allies for the dual purpose of fighting against the Nazi-Fascists and of avoiding domination of the country by the Communists after the war, but on the Allied side no understanding was encountered.

[54]"Zakonska odredba o oružanoj sili NDH" / Laws Concerning the Organization of the Armed Forces in the Independent State of Croatia, *Vojni Vjesnik* (March, 1942).

[55]Kiszling, *Die Kroaten,* 188.

Thus the Croatian Domobrans fought to the bitter end, trying vainly to preserve Croatian lives and homes from destruction, and the Croatian state from extinction. In all the fighting it refrained from any form of violence against the civilian population. But while the Domobrans fought the bloody war as humanely as possible, many others did just the contrary. The negative attitude toward the Ustasha regime and toward the Axis policy sometimes resulted in passivity and a lack of fighting spirit.[56]

According to law, the Ustasha Militia (a rough equivalent of the Fascist Militia and the SS) had to be filled by volunteers. Owing to a lack of enthusiasm among the Croatian youth for the Ustashas, it was partly filled by a compulsory draft. At first ten battalions, and one battalion for the protection of railways, were formed; a little later ten additional battalions were added. An overwhelming number of the officers, and a part of the rank and file, were partisans of the Ustashas; they were mostly idealists and fanatic Croatian nationalists. Resentment against the Serbs—a consequence of the Serbian misdeeds in former Yugoslavia—was another characteristic trait which dominated their feelings. They fought bravely with fanaticism and passion, but also sometimes cruelly, neither asking nor giving mercy.

The enemies of the Croatians, besides the Germans and Italians, were the Chetniks and the Partisans. The Chetnik movement began in Serbia, immediately after the capitulation, under the leadership of the former colonel of the Yugoslav army, Draža Mihajlović. The rebels took the name "Yugoslav Army in the Homeland," although they were exclusively Serbian Chetniks. When the Germans forcibly suppressed the rebellion, the remainder of the Chetniks fled to Montenegro and eastern Bosnia. Centers of rebellion sprang up in Hercegovina and in other places where the Ustashas had begun to take cruel vengeance for Chetnik misdeeds committed during the war days. The Communists remained quiet as long as the Soviets were bound by the Soviet-German Pact. They rose, under the leadership of an old-time Communist, Joseph Broz, called Tito, only after Molotov's appeal (June 22, 1941) to all Communist parties of the world to act according to the decisions of the Seventh Congress of the Comintern. At first the Chetniks and the Communists (commonly called Partisans) worked together. Their leaders even met on two occasions to draw up a common plan for action, but could not agree.

[56]On the Domobrans, see: Stephen Clissold, *The Whirlwind: An Account of Marshal Tito's Rise to Power* (London: Cresset Press, 1949); Kiszling, *Die Kroaten.*

Very soon they fell out with each other, their disagreement stemming from the clash between the two basic concepts concerning the future of the peoples of Yugoslavia.

The Chetniks represented the old imperialistic idea of a Great Serbia which would absorb the whole of Macedonia and Montenegro and most of the Croatian lands. Based on his legal authority, Mihajlović (who was promoted to the rank of general and appointed War Minister by the exiled Yugoslav government in London) intended to form an organization, Yugoslav in name and Serbian in fact, able to assume power in the country after the Allied victory. Taking advantage of the fact that the Croatians had fought on the Axis side, he hoped to subjugate them and impose upon them the hegemony of the Serbs—the only co-participants in the Allied victory. Due to the movement's narrow ideological basis and the low moral standards of its leaders, it attracted only the ultrachauvinistic element of the Serbs and those people who had no other escape from the terror of the occupying armies and the Ustashas.

These circumstances, together with a lack of ability to organize, prevented the Chetniks from forming an efficient political and military system. They lost ground everywhere, even in Serbia, and very soon ceased to be an important factor in the struggle against the occupying armies. From October, 1941, onward, they practically abandoned all fighting against the invaders, except for some minor clashes and the helping of downed Allied airmen. In order to survive, the Chetnik commanders, with the consent of General Mihajlović, concluded formal pacts of collaboration with the Italians, who used them partly for fighting against the Partisans and even more for the persecution of the Croatian population. In Serbia they collaborated from the very beginning with, and received financial and material help from, the head of the pro-German puppet government of General Nedić. Within Croatian territory, with the help of the Italians, whose imperialistic aims coincided with those of the Chetniks, they dedicated themselves to the physical extermination of the Moslem and Catholic population, with the purpose of clearing certain areas which the Serbian imperialists claimed for themselves. Occasionally they fought against the Partisans, their most dangerous contenders for future power. When, in 1943, the Italians surrendered to the Allies—even earlier in some areas—the Chetniks concluded formal pacts of collaboration with the Germans and with their arch-enemies the Ustashas. Thus, paid, armed, equipped and fed by Italians, Germans, and Ustashas, some Chetnik units survived the war and, together with the German and Croatian armies withdrew to Austria and Italy, where they surrendered to the Allies. General Mihajlović was later caught by the Communists, tried, and shot. The whole history of the Chetnik activities during the war is a notorious example of Byzantine duplicity and treachery.[57]

The Partisans (whose official name was "The Yugoslav National Movement for Liberation") nominally represented all Yugoslav political parties and ideologies. Their official claims were the creation of a new Yugoslavia, federative and democratic, with equal rights for all her peoples and with a normal social structure according to liberalistic principles. Attracted by such a broad ideological basis and by skillful propaganda, many truly democratic elements sided with them. They were, moreover, joined by those forced to flee from their homes because of Chetnik and Ustasha atrocities, German repressions, Italian intrigues, and Partisan provocations. Thus their ranks swelled continually in spite of great losses suffered by them in various phases of the war. The real power inside the movement was in the hands of a small number of hard-core Communist revolutionaries, who held all important and key positions of a political and military nature. Their real aims were the taking over of power in the new Yugoslavia (federative in exterior form, but ruled by a highly centralized Communist dictatorship with a social structure along a strict Marxist line), previous destruction of the old political order and social structure, and the elimination of all real or potential enemies of Communism, even of their former partners in the struggle.[58]

It is not the object of this study to deal in detail with the vicissitudes of all the military operations on Croatian soil. The war raged all over the country—it was typical and destructive guerrilla warfare. Because the three domestic protagonists—the Ustashas, Chetniks, and Partisans —were extremists, this warfare assumed the most bloody and brutal forms. The atrocities of the Chetniks and Ustashas were mostly the product of passion, mutual hate, and nationalistic hysteria; but they were nevertheless the work of amateurs. The atrocities of the Partisans were, however, the work of experienced professional terrorists, and were planned with a double purpose: the extermination of all actual or potential contenders for future power, and the deliberate and

[57]On the Chetniks, see: Clissold, *The Whirlwind*; Winston Churchill, *The Second World War* (London: Cassell, 1948–54); Mladen Lorković, *Kroatiens Kampf gegan Bolschevismus*; Vjekoslav Vrančić, *Hochverrat—II Ital. Armee*; *Enciklopedija Jugoslavije* / Encyclopedia of Yugoslavia, II (Zagreb, 1956), 572 ff.

[58]On the Partisans, see: Clissold, *The Whirlwind*; Kiszling, *Die Kroaten*, 179 ff.; Fedor Dragojlov, "Partisanenkrieg," *Wehrkunde* (Munich, 1956); Milovan Djilas, *The New Class* (New York, 1957).

cunning provocations of German and Ustasha repression of the helpless population, which then was forced to take refuge in the Partisan ranks. Thus every instance of destruction and terror, from whichever part it came, worked to the advantage of the Partisans and helped them in their drive to power.

The first Partisan action began in Serbia. Later the Partisans organized small groups all over the country, which committed a series of acts of sabotage, attacks on communications, and the like. The most important of these acts was the rebellion around Drvar in Bosnia. There, some 3,000 industrial workers, led by Communist leaders and aided by the deliberate passivity of the Italians, drove out the existing Croatian authorities, conquered a wide area in western Bosnia, and there organized the first territory under Communist power. During the course of the war, it became the main stronghold for all further operations on Croatian soil. From time to time the Communists were driven out of this area, but they always managed to regain it. In the middle of 1942 all Partisan forces from eastern Bosnia joined this area, enlarged it, and, in November of that year, formed the "Antifascist Council for the National Liberation of Yugoslavia" in Bihać. About this same time their armed forces were thoroughly reorganized. From small, mostly improvised Partisan detachments, they organized their forces on a real military basis. Their forces consisted of 2 army corps with a total of 9 divisions, 36 independent brigades, 70 battalions, 15 companies, and 79 Partisan detachments—a total of some 150,000 men.[59]

The growing menace to German communications, as well as to economically important areas within Croatian territory, and the evidence that the Italians were systematically sabotaging every action directed against the Partisans (and even helping them secretly), forced the Germans to enlarge the Croatian army. At the beginning of 1942, four new mountain brigades, a mobile police brigade, and two volunteer regiments were established. Out of the rearmost parts of the Croatian Legion on the Russian front, reinforced by men from Croatia, the 369th Legion Division, *Vražja Divizija* ("Devil's Division") was formed in Austria; its rank and file were mainly Croatians, while most of its officers were Germans. It was formally stipulated that this division (as well as two other Legion divisions set up later) should be used exclusively for fighting on Croatian soil. The 369th Legion Division was 12,000 men strong and arrived on the Croatian battlefields at the end of 1942. The Croatian Domobrans then consisted of about 125,000 men. The Ustasha Militia increased its 25 battalions to

[59]Kiszling, *Die Kroaten,* 184 ff.

35 and a defensive brigade, totaling 23,000 men. From this force of about 148,500 men (without the 369th Division), some 90,700 men were ready for service at the front.[60]

From the end of 1942, the Croatian armed forces grew steadily as the general German military situation worsened and the ever-present menace in southeastern Europe compelled the Germans to increase the strength of the auxiliary forces under their command. In the second half of 1942, they decided to create a second Legion Division (the 373rd "Tiger Division"). This division was combat-ready in 1943. Here, also, all of the officers and most of the ranks were German.

After the German defeat at Stalingrad, the intensified SS predominance in Germany was also felt in Croatia. In spite of opposition in high Croatian military circles—and even of the leading circles of the *Wehrmacht* in Croatia—Himmler sent SS Group Leader Kammerhofer to Croatia. He established his headquarters in Osijek and, with the consent of Pavelić, put under his power all Croatian police forces, forming a police division for the protection of railways. This division had some 10,000 men, half of them Croatians and the other half made up of Germans and the members of the German minority group from Croatia. Moreover, he formed an SS division (*Handžar*) of Croatian Moslems from Bosnia. All of these forces were directly subordinated to Himmler.[61]

With the capitulation of Italy (September, 1943), a series of events was initiated, all of which were of capital importance for the political and military situation in Croatia in the years to come. On the positive side for the Croatians were the facts that they were freed from the hated Italian occupational forces and that they recovered the territories which they were forced to cede to Italy according to the stipulation of the Pact of Rome. They also disarmed many Italian units and captured large amounts of arms and equipment. On the negative side, the Partisans captured even larger quantities of Italian arms and equipment. At the conference at Teheran (November, 1943), they were accepted by the Allies as a military ally. On November 29, Tito created the "National Committee for Liberation," which was recognized by the Allies as a *de facto* government for Yugoslavia. Mihajlović was definitely abandoned; the exiled government in London enjoyed Allied hospitality but held no real power. A little later, the Allies sent

[60]Vjekoslav Vrančić, "Postrojenje i brojčano stanje hrvatskih oružanih snaga" / Organization and Numbers of the Croatian Armed Forces, *Godišnjak Hrvatskog Domobrana* (Buenos Aires, 1953), 152.

[61]Kiszling, *Die Kroaten*, 188.

to Yugoslavia a British military mission, headed by General MacLean; another member of the mission was Mr. Randolph Churchill. The supply of arms, ammunition, and equipment for the Partisan army was organized by sea and air, and the support of their operations by the Allied air force was assured. All this gave the Partisan political movement and their army new impetus, and made possible for them military operations on a large scale as never before. Defeated and decimated in combined German and Croatian offensives earlier in 1943, they now recuperated and grew even stronger than before.[62]

In order to meet the new situation brought about by the defection of Italy, the Germans promised the Croatians modern arms and equipment for four mountain and four light brigades, and one motorized brigade, as well as similar arms for Pavelić's Ustasha Body-Guard Brigade. Yet, partly because of a lack of new recruits (only 17,000 were available), and partly because of changes in the general situation, these reinforcements were never received. Instead, a more thorough reorganization of the Croatian army was effected. Most of the Domobran and Ustasha units were combined: from 3 mountain, 4 light and 23 Ustasha brigades, 15 infantry divisions were formed. A new Legion Division, the 392nd or *Plava* (Blue), started its training in Austria. A shock brigade and a defensive Ustasha brigade were formed. All training centers were placed under an Instruction Division. The total strength of the Croatian army at that time was 258,000 men.[63]

The last reorganization of the Croatian and of the Partisan armies took place at the end of 1944 and the beginning of 1945. All Croatian Domobran units were incorporated into the Ustasha formations; five Ustasha corps were formed, consisting of from three to four divisions each. The 1st, 2nd, and parts of the 3rd Corps were stationed in Slavonia, the remainder of the 3rd and the 4th in northern Bosnia, and the 5th in southwestern Croatia.[64] The Partisan forces, which, between August and October of 1944—with the support of Russian armor and some Bulgarian units—conquered all of Serbia and Belgrade, consisted at the same time of 50 divisions, grouped into 4 armies. The 3rd Army (7 divisions) was stationed in eastern Slavonia and Bačka; the 2nd (12 divisions) in the area of Tuzla in Bosnia; the 1st (10 divisions) in Srijem; and the 4th (14 divisions) in central Dalmatia. Seven divisions were held as Tito's reserve. He had, moreover, the support of Russian tanks and of the Bulgarians. It must be noted that the size

[62]Clissold, *The Whirlwind*; Churchill, *The Second World War*.
[63]Vrančić, "Postrojenje," 156 ff.
[64]Kiszling, *Die Kroaten*, 214.

of the Partisan divisions was much smaller than that of those in any regular army.[65]

During the same period (1944–1945), the German withdrawal from the Balkans was in full swing. A front in eastern Slavonia (mostly on the Bosut River), eastern Bosnia, and Hercegovina was temporarily held. A series of violent and bloody Partisan attacks followed (especially on the Bosut River), yet the front held until the spring of 1945, when, in the framework of the general withdrawal, the Germans, as well as the Croatian troops, withdrew on all fronts. Gradually, mostly under heavy fighting, they abandoned the whole of the Croatian territory. It must be stressed that, in spite of the desperate political and military situation (it was evident to everyone that the Germans had lost the war and that the Croatians were on the losing side), the Croatian army maintained a high fighting spirit. Strict military discipline, a sense of duty, and a determination to fight to the last moment prevailed everywhere. The men fought the last battles for their homes, hoping for some change in the general situation, one which never came. They continued to withdraw in a most orderly manner, and fought on bitterly in spite of a lack of ammunition, which the Germans (already short of all kinds of war materials) kept mostly for themselves.

The End of the War

On May 4, 1945, a meeting of the Ustasha government was held in Zagreb. It was decided that the entire government would withdraw the following day to Klagenfurt, Austria, in the hope of establishing contact (which was never made) with the Allied military authorities. Pavelić would follow a day later.

On the night of May 6 General von Loehr (under whose command the Croatian troops had fought during the last phase of the war) informed Pavelić in Rogaška Slatina (Slovenia) that the Germans had signed the surrender. He passed on to Pavelić all rights and responsibilities of command over the Croatian troops.[66] The next morning, Pavelić ordered an acceleration of the withdrawal of the Croatian army (which was already in Slovenia). He ordered the army to cross the Austrian border and to surrender to the English instead of to the Partisans. Then he left the army to its fate, fled with a small escort to

[65]Dušan Kveder, "Der jugoslavische Partisanenkrieg," *Algemeine Schweizerische Milizschrift*, VII–IX.

[66]Fedor Dragojlov, "Der Krieg 1941–1945," *Algemeine Schweizerische Milizschrift*, VII.

Austria, and avoided personal participation in the fateful events of the following days.

The Croatian troops continued their withdrawal in an orderly manner, partially repelling Partisan attacks, near Donji Dravograd and Prevalje. The last battle was fought on May 13 against the 51st Partisan Division[67] for the possession of the bridges over the Drava River at Dravograd. On May 14 the Croatians reached the area of Bleiburg, which was already in English hands. The commanders of the various units, lacking orders from their superiors, established contact with the English for the purpose of surrendering to them. The English at first acceded to their wishes and ordered the mustering of troops for an alleged inspection, but the next day they changed their minds. English tanks, together with Partisan units, surrounded the Croatians; Spitfires flew over them, and an order was issued to lay down their arms immediately. The Croatians were formally assured both by the English and by the Partisans that they would be treated according to the rules of the Geneva Convention regarding prisoners of war. About 100,000 men laid down their arms; some 20,000, realizing the danger of being handed over to the Partisans, fought their way out and escaped. Another column of some 100,000 men—partly army units and partly civilian refugees—which had not yet reached Bleiburg, surrendered in various places.

The English crowded this human mass into the area of Bleiburg, and then handed them over to the Partisans. The latter immediately began to transport the men by foot in several columns to Maribor. As soon as they were out of the sight and control of the English, the mass murder began; some 5,000 men were shot before reaching Maribor. There the rest were enclosed in barracks and depots at Tezno, and during the following days, in a systematic way, all members of former Ustasha units, as well as almost all regular officers of the Croatian Domobrans, were murdered and their corpses thrown into the tank defence trenches of the old Yugoslav fortifications. Here, and in some other places in Slovenia, some 40,000 Croatian soldiers were murdered. The rest were led by foot to several prison camps in Croatia, the largest of which was at Prečko (a suburb of Zagreb).

At the end of May, so-called "death columns" were organized; by foot, without food and water, the men were marched hundreds of miles, through Croatian villages, by way of Bjelovar and Osijek to

[67]Milan Basta (Com. Gen., 51st Partisan Division), "Šest dana rata nakon rata"/ Six Days of War After the War, *Nedeljne Informativne Novine* (September 4, 1960).

Petrovaradin and then to Vršac (Banat). Anyone who was not able to march because of hunger or weakness was shot, and his corpse left on the road. The villagers were strictly prohibited from offering food or drink to the prisoners, and sometimes men and women were shot for helping the weakened men. In Vršac and in Kovin a series of mock trials was set up, in which many of the remaining prisoners were sentenced to death. Only a few returned to their homes. It is estimated that about 100,000 men (the exact number will never be known) lost their lives on their way from Bleiburg to Vršac.

5

Economic Development

DRAGO MATKOVIĆ

Croatian economic history has its origins in the unexplored past of the Croatian tribes who pursued animal husbandry, hunting, apiculture, and agriculture in their earliest settlements in White Croatia. It is known today that even in their original native land the Croatians were engaged in blacksmithing, metallurgy, and trade. The territory between the Drava, Danube, and Drina Rivers and the Adriatic Sea, where the Croatians had settled in the sixth and seventh centuries A.D., afforded such a variety of climate and soil that prerequisites for various types of economic activity were present. Old trade routes and military roads, which bound Europe and Asia, crisscrossed this territory. This area was composed of zones of different economic systems which complemented one another. Soil and climatic conditions in most areas were favorable to agriculture. The Adriatic Sea provided a basis for a free and intensive development of interregional trade. Even in the earliest times, urban life flourished along the coast. Strong commercial intercourse insured a market for home products. Shipping, trade, and various crafts developed in the Dalmatian coastal cities in the Roman days; later, these were of utmost importance to the economic development of Croatia. The Croatians learned much about seafaring and deep-sea fishing, as well as about viticulture, from the Roman population of the coastal cities, as the latter was gradually assimilated by the Croatian people.

Social Structure

The Croatians, at the time of their settlement, were made up of several tribes which were subdivided into *bratstva* (brotherhoods). These in turn consisted of close-knit kinship groups called *zadrugas*, which conducted and held property in common and stood under the direction of an elected elder. Large-scale private land ownership by an individual person or family was originally unknown. A Croatian tribe was ruled by a *župan* (head of the tribe) whose territory was called the *župa*, and later the *županija*. As a rule, the *župa* had a centrally-located fortified place, which was originally used as a place of refuge, and later also as the seat from which the territory was ruled. When several *župas* united to form a larger unit, their common ruler was called a *ban*. In the course of time, the most successful *ban* imposed his supremacy upon the others. Later the *bans* and other tribal leaders gradually became vassals of the Croatian king and received fiefs from him. Ruling families gradually emerged, which endeavored to appropriate tribal property and to subjugate the free peasantry.

The use of woodlands, pastures, and water resources was regulated at first according to the needs of the original settlers, and then, after the development of the village, by the village community. However, in those regions where cattle-raising prevailed, settlement unions lasted longer, as did the holding of property in common. Even after the distribution of arable land and the creation of individual peasant economies, woodland and pasture lands remained undivided as common property. From the eleventh century on, individual property ownership became more common. In the thirteenth century, the tribal system experienced its most significant decline. In the process of feudalization the majority of the farmers became serfs (*kmeti*). Very few peasants and craftsmen remained free. Until the fifteenth century there were even some genuine slaves on the Croatian lands. The serfs were bound to the soil and were allowed to leave their land only by permission of the landlord. The rights of the landlord were constantly expanded, and the duties of the serfs increased proportionately. Under the common crown of Croatia and Hungary, Croatia developed a nobility, whose well-known families acquired the position of mighty landlords. Thus the agricultural system of Croatia became similar to that of Western European feudalism.

Changes Due to Christianity

The medieval influence of Christianity in Croatia was reflected not only in the worship and outlook of the people, but also in their manners, customs, and needs, in their material and intellectual culture, and, last but not least, in their economic way of life. The needs of a great number of monasteries and churches called for more elaborate equipment and great building projects, which resulted in the development of architecture, handicrafts, and arts of all kinds. The fine arts and ornament, mural, and church painting likewise developed. The Croatians of that time were proficient in metal work. The art of the goldsmith also blossomed, but was centered exclusively in the cities. The fact that, little by little, some churches or churchmen became landowners, meant that they assumed an increasing importance in the economic development of the country. With their conversion to Christianity in the seventh century, the economic relations of the Croatians with Western nations considerably increased.

In the fourteenth century, the *zadruga*—the typical Slavic clan organization—was almost in the process of dissolution, owing to Croatia's long contact with Western Christian nations, where the *zadruga* did not exist. However, when the power of the state weakened during the Turkish wars, the *zadruga* blossomed to new life. This organization was a community based upon blood relationship and collective ownership of land, in which one family, or several families, tilled the soil as a unit, and in which there was only a limited amount of division of labor. When a *zadruga* split up, every head of the family founded a new smaller *zadruga* with his children and grandchildren.[1] The *zadruga* became particularly important on the so-called Military Frontier (in Croatian, *Vojna Krajina*; in German, *Militärgrenze*) where it survived until the nineteenth century.

Production

The basis of the Croatian economy consisted of cattle-raising, hunting, and farming of a primitive and extensive character. The reason for this lay in the constant wars, invasions, and destruction to which the population was exposed for many centuries, which afforded little opportunity for peaceful activity. In agriculture the farming methods of the original settlers, brought from White Croatia, had hardly changed up to the beginning of the eighteenth century. The use of manure was virtually unknown until that time. Grain production played a decisive part in agriculture. Viticulture was also of great importance. Dalmatia produced and exported olive oil. Horticulture and fruit-growing, how-

[1]Milan Ivšić, *Temelji seljačkog zakonika* / Foundations of the Agricultural Code (Zagreb, 1933), 20.

ever, developed relatively late. Potatoes were not raised until the eighteenth century. The most advantageous conditions for agriculture prevailed in the large-scale economies of the nobility, since these had at their disposal not only a large number of workmen—which was of decisive importance in the Middle Ages—but also because they had better farming equipment and better organization of production. Cattle-raising was also well developed. The monasteries owned extensive pasture lands and raised cattle. The horse was of great importance as a means of transportation. The most common domestic animals were hogs, goats, and beef cattle. However, sheep were also important, owing to the fact that their raising required relatively little effort, and that their production of milk and wool was considerable. Poultry was raised on every large and small farm. Water-driven mills were used in many places. Fishing was successfully carried on, especially in the regions on the Adriatic Coast.

Economic Changes

With Croatia's rapid adaptation to the economic standard of the neighboring middle European countries, agricultural laws also changed in favor of the great domains. This process of development, along with the prevalence of various social and economic abuses, resulted in an impoverished peasantry. The increased economic and social power of the nobility led not only to weakening of central government, but also to some forms of exploitation in social life. As a result of wars and foreign invasions, the original Croatian nobility was decimated and their lands given to foreign nobles, who felt themselves bound solely to the land and not to its inhabitants. The numerous and steadily growing privileges, and the social power of the nobility, as well as of some of the upper clergy, worked very much to the detriment of the independence and personal freedom of the peasant population. The history of the Croatian people, which for centuries had staunchly defended its national independence, records a tragic lot for the peasantry. Wars often destroyed at one fell swoop what the peaceful labor of centuries had achieved. In these wars, as well as in economic and natural disasters, the political and economic strength of the Croatian people steadily declined. The dissatisfaction of the oppressed peasantry repeatedly caused unfortunate uprisings. The most famous of these insurrections was in the year 1573, when the Croatian peasantry revolted, under the leadership of Matija Gubec. But the peasants soon suffered defeat at the hands of the nobles and were horribly punished.

The Emancipation of the Peasants

After several vain attempts, the freeing of the peasants in Croatia was achieved in the year 1848. Thus was ended the administrative and judicial power of the landlords, and the personal services of the serfs to them.

Another aspect of the peasant emancipation was the agricultural organization of a strip of land along the border of the Ottoman Empire known as the Military Frontier, which was organized in 1553, and whose boundaries were finally determined in 1746. This organization was formed to safeguard not only the Hapsburg Empire but also all of Western Europe against Turkish attacks. In this territory, which was subdivided into several military regions, every man between the ages of eighteen and sixty was constantly in military service. These "border people" (in Croatian, *Graničari*; in German, *Grenzer*) remained free, that is, they never became serfs, although the soil they tilled belonged to the emperor. The military authority in this region was responsible not only for all economic matters, but also for all other issues dealing with agriculture. The regime of the Military Frontier was abolished in the year 1881, and this strip of territory was annexed to the Croatian motherland.

In Dalmatia and Istria there existed a special type of feudal tenancy called the *colonatus*, according to which the *colonus* (tenant farmer) tilled land that was not his own and was obligated to turn over a previously determined portion of the harvest to the landowner. Although the *colonatus* was similar to the serf system, it nevertheless differed decidedly from it. The distinguishing characteristic of the *colonatus* was its private juridical contract between tenant and landowner. This practice had its origin in Roman law, and had not yet disappeared at the time of the Second World War.

Agrarian Conditions in Bosnia-Hercegovina

In Bosnia-Hercegovina, legal conditions of rural society developed in a manner different from those of other Croatian regions. Here, too, a serf system existed. The Bosnian serf, however, was originally obliged to turn over to the lord only one-third of the harvest, and was not obliged to render any other services. He was free and even able to leave his place of residence, so that his position was better than that of his contemporaries in northern Croatia. In addition to serfs, there were free farmers and also slaves.

The conquest of Bosnia-Hercegovina by the Turks effected no essential changes. At first the agrarian order, despite some changes, remained basically as it had been. Since the nobles became converted to Islam, they were able to retain their possessions, and their relations with their serfs also continued to follow the same pattern as before. In principle, only Moslems could be manorial lords, and Christians could be only serfs, or, in a very few cases, free farmers. Gradually there developed in Bosnia-Hercegovina a system of municipalities with a predominantly Moslem population. This social and economic structure was common to Bosnia-Hercegovina until the beginning of the nineteenth century. In the course of time, however, the agrarian situation was changed by various measures predominantly advantageous only to the feudal lords. This made the position of the peasantry unbearable and led to unrest, and eventually proved to be one of the causes of the occupation of Bosnia-Hercegovina by the Austro-Hungarian Monarchy. This occupation introduced and furthered the economic development of Bosnia-Hercegovina. Serfdom was not, however, entirely abolished until after World War I.

Changes in Agricultural Economy during the Capitalistic Period

The spread of money and the credit economy shook the foundations of the *zadrugas*. A law of 1880 facilitated the break-up of the *zadrugas*, and their rapid disintegration and a partitioning of their estates followed. The result of this was the division of the land into small sections. Numerous miniature farms came into existence, and a farm proletariat developed. It was only forty years later that further subdivision of the land was partially arrested. In order to build homes and farm buildings, and to purchase cattle and implements, the new owners were forced to borrow considerable amounts of money. This led to heavy indebtedness on the part of the new farmers.

The rapid and inorganic break-up of the *zadrugas*, and the gradual transition from the natural, and later feudal, economy to a market and money economy completely changed the structure of the agricultural system in Croatia. The position of Croatian agriculture was considerably weakened by overseas competition in the European markets. Owing to a great demand for credit, many inexperienced and unskilled peasants fell into the hands of usurious money lenders, who in many cases completely ruined the peasants' status as independent farmers. These dispossessed farmers now sought a living either by hiring themselves out as farm laborers, or by moving into the cities, while many even decided to emigrate to the United States. A flight from the land began, one which could not be stemmed in the following decades.

As a result of these conditions, the Croatian farmers began to build up the cooperative system as the only effective instrument for self-help. In Pannonian Croatia, cooperative credit associations were first organized in the year 1900, and purchasing and selling cooperatives in 1907.[2] In Istria the first cooperative was founded at Kopar in 1884, and was followed by a credit union in Pula in 1892. In Dalmatia the first credit cooperative was begun in 1896, and in Bosnia in 1904. In Zagreb the "Croatian Agricultural Bank" was established in 1902 as a federation of all Croatian credit unions. Little by little, other types of cooperatives were founded, which later were merged into a larger federation. In the year 1919 the "Central Association of Croatian Farmers' Cooperatives" came into being. One year later the Catholic-oriented "Cooperative Association" followed. The large cooperative organization, "Economic Union" (*Gospodarska Sloga*), founded in 1935, was of considerable importance, not only economically but also politically.

The agrarian reforms effected after World War I benefited only a limited number of small farms. They brought neither economic strength to the peasantry as a whole, nor any tangible alleviation to the population pressures on the land. The outdated agrarian constitutions of the individual Croatian regions were not altered to keep pace with the changing needs of the peasantry. The agrarian reforms did not solve the economic problems of agriculture, and after the tapering-off of the post-war boom period, there came in 1927 a rapid increase in peasant indebtedness. In order to prevent the complete financial-political breakdown of the agricultural system, the government was forced, on April 19, 1932, to issue a general moratorium of farmers' debts. The general credit shortage which soon arose weakened the entire economic process to such an extent that the moratorium, originally intended as a provisional solution, developed into a permanent condition. Nor was it possible to re-establish the financial solvency of the farmers.

The Development of Urban Life

In Croatia, during the Middle Ages, urban life and culture were relatively well developed. The town was not only the center of economic life, but also the focus of spiritual and material culture, which

[2]The information on the cooperative system is taken from: Vilko Rieger, *Das landwirtschaftliche Genossenschaftswesen in den kroatischen Ländern* / The Agricultural Cooperative System in the Croatian Lands (Berlin, 1939).

fostered economic welfare too. It was especially in regard to its wealth that the town contrasted sharply with the village, where poverty and a very modest material culture reigned. During the entire Middle Ages, the urban economy of the Croatian countries showed a development that was to a large extent independent and markedly different from that of the villages. Some of the earliest Croatian cities developed around pivotal military points, not as centers for barter and trade for the surrounding population, but rather as places of refuge during times of war.

The periodic visits of foreign merchants to the villages and important market places awakened in the Croatians the initiative for the exchange of goods. The medieval Croatian cities required frequent visits by the traveling merchants who could satisfy the economic needs of their population. These merchants settled where a demand for goods had been formed and where they found customers. They established permanent market places, where the farmers would meet once a week to exchange their produce for manufactured goods. This weekly market-day usually took place in the busiest part of the city, where the shops and workshops of merchants and craftsmen were to be found.

Town Economy and the Guild System

In time the city achieved a solid economic and legal order, which also insured the existence of various craftsmen by providing certain legal protection for them. The work of the craftsman belonged to a long tradition in the Croatian lands. Its earliest form was the domestic craft, which was carried on chiefly by women. The organization of the handicraft economy was very primitive in the beginning. For a long period of time, the person producing handiwork at home worked long hours for a set clientele, using the latter's material. The craftsman's product went directly to the consumer—there was no middleman. During the Middle Ages, the craftsman held a respected position in the Croatian social order. Through the organization of guilds and brotherhoods, his efficiency was increased. Strict regulations governing training and admission into the guilds contributed to this new efficiency. In Croatia, royal privileges were granted the guilds about the middle of the fifteenth century. The crafts and the cities became important sources of culture in Croatia. In the course of time, however, the craft guilds became monopolistic and used their power to limit competition. From the end of the seventeenth century, and especially in the nineteenth century, the guilds showed signs of decline, and finally, in 1859, they were dissolved and replaced by free trade.[3]

The city, in its organization, represented a much more perfect entity than the village. Over a period of several centuries, the cities developed into centers of trade and business as well as of consumption. These cities were endowed with municipal charters, with a number of economic and legal privileges, and with relatively great economic independence. They had their own administrations, and their own finances and tariff regulations. In Pannonian Croatia, the following cities were given privileged status as "free royal cities": Varaždin (1209), Zagreb (1242), Križevci (1252), Koprivnica (1356), Senj (1483), and Karlovac (1777).[4]

The Spectacular Growth of the City-Republic of Dubrovnik

The city-republic of Dubrovnik was particularly known throughout the entire Mediterranean because of its extensive trade. From the year 1358, Dubrovnik was under the protection of the Hungarian-Croatian kings, and thus experienced a rapid rise.[5] Almost the entire trade on the Balkan Peninsula was for centuries in the hands of the merchants from Dubrovnik, with whom even the Venetians and Genovese could not keep pace.[6] Dubrovnik established its own trading posts, one after another, in all of the larger cities of the Balkan Peninsula, and in all the significant cities of the Near East. Dubrovnik did not assert itself as an independent city-republic by force, but rather by its excellent system of government and its skillful diplomats.

This city-republic was the only medieval city south of the Danube which was never occupied by the Turks. In order to promote trade and simultaneously to advance and insure shipping, Dubrovnik began, at a very early date, to make commercial and political agreements with other cities and states. The most flourishing period of Dubrovnik's trade was between the thirteenth and fifteenth centuries.[7] Trade with the interior was carried on by caravan. It was not until the time of the Turkish supremacy in the Balkans that the trade of Dubrovnik

[3]Rudolf Bičanić, *Doba manufakture u Hrvatskoj i Slavoniji* / Epoch of Manufacturing in Croatia and Slavonia (Zagreb, 1951), 77.

[4]Josip Horvat, *Kultura Hrvata kroz 1.000 godina* / 1000 Years of Croatian Culture (Zagreb, 1942), 23, 79.

[5]Franjo Lepel, *Geschichte der Stadt und Republik Ragusa* / History of the City and Republic of Dubrovnik (Dresden, 1931), 10.

[6]*Ibid.*, 21.

[7]*Ibid.*, 22.

gradually began to show signs of decline, despite the privileges received from the sultans. Nevertheless, Dubrovnik was able to retain, until the time of Napoleon, its aristocratic and republican form of government. In the fourteenth century, a constantly used trade route led from Dubrovnik to Prizren, a flourishing commercial city, and still farther to the significant mining city of Novo Brdo, near Priština in Serbia.[8] From Priština yet another trade route led to Bulgaria. Among the exported goods of that period, an important role was played by textiles, which Dubrovnik had begun to produce.[9] Dubrovnik also carried on a busy trade in salt and certain other articles of general consumption. In the sea trade, the insurance business was of great importance.[10] The coins minted in Dubrovnik itself boasted a wide circulation. However, other larger cities of Dalmatia, such as Zadar and Split, also had their own mints. Many types of money were found in the various territories of Croatia. Not only money minted in the Croatian lands was circulated, but also that of many foreign cities and states. Money was used primarily as a means of payment, but also as a measure of value. It almost completely replaced barter, and slowly but surely accelerated the trading of goods in the medieval urban economy of Croatia. Of all the Croatian mints, that of Dubrovnik was in operation for the longest time, from the twelfth to the nineteenth century.

Mercantile Political Economy

Charles VI (1711–1740), Maria Theresa (1740–1780), and Joseph II (1780–1790) fostered economic development in the Croatian regions through such measures as the founding of manufacturing concerns and trade companies and the building of roads and harbors. With the abolition of inland tariffs in 1715, the obstacles to inland trade were removed. Mail service, which until then was anything but uniform, and lay even partly in private hands, was completely reorganized. In the year 1717 free shipping was proclaimed for the Adriatic Sea, and in 1719 Rijeka was declared a free port.[11] In the same year, the Orient Company, the main exponent of the daring economic-political ideas of

[8] *Ibid.*, 26.

[9] Grga Novak, "Vunena industrija u Dubrovniku" / Wool Industry in Dubrovnik, *Rešetarov Zbornik* (Dubrovnik, 1931), 99–107; D. Roller, *Dubrovački zanati u XV i XVI stoljeću* / Dubrovnik's Skills in the 15th and 16th Centuries (Zagreb, 1951), 5.

[10] J. Tadić, "Pomorsko osiguranje u Dubrovniku u XVI stoljeću" / Maritime Insurance in Sixteenth Century Dubrovnik, *Rešetarov Zbornik* (Dubrovnik, 1931), 109–112.

[11] K. Berger, *Der Hafen von Fiume* / The Harbor of Rijeka (Köln, 1936), 16.

Charles VI, was founded in Trieste. This company also extended its activity to the Croatian ports and territories. Mercantile policies led to an increase in national wealth through the promotion of shipping and wider trade with foreign countries. These enterprises were further supported by trade agreements. However, the protective tariffs, introduced in the year 1754 by the Hapsburg monarchy to the advantage of the economic development of the Austrian lands, badly hampered the further development of the manufacturing industry in Croatia.[12]

The building and upkeep of roads in Croatia had been neglected for centuries; thus, in order to further commerce, many new roads were built during the eighteenth century. In 1726 the first road which connected the port of Rijeka with Karlovac and the interior was built, and at the end of the eighteenth century the road connecting the harbor of Senj and the interior was completed.[13] At this same time the work of regulating the most important Croatian river, the Sava, began. Until the middle of the eighteenth century, shipping and ship-building on the Croatian rivers had developed only spasmodically. By the end of the eighteenth century, shipping on the Sava and Danube had become considerably more lively, and ship-building increased, if only slowly. In the eighteenth and nineteenth centuries, the most important wharfs on the Sava were located in Sisak and Jasenovac, and those of the Drava River in Vukovar and Petrovaradin, as well as in Osijek.[14] Of prominent economic importance was the Luise Road, built between Rijeka and Karlovac in the year 1811, and counted among the most beautiful and modern of European highways at that time.[15] During these years, a considerable transit trade flourished between the Danube valley and the Adriatic harbors. This trade went through the Croatian lands, bringing them great economic advantages. Croatia soon became an independent customs district with its own customs boundaries.

Characteristic of the development of Croatian manufacturing at the end of the eighteenth and the beginning of the nineteenth centuries was the fact that handicraft production in smaller or larger establishments still prevailed, while in Western Europe industrial capitalism had already started to develop. During the middle of the eighteenth century, mining, which had already been actively pursued in the sixteenth and seventeenth centuries, was reactivated. By the middle of the nineteenth century a number of smaller mining centers and smelting works, a copper foundry, a sulphur factory, as well as several small

[12]Bičanić, *Doba manufakture*, 15.
[13]Horvat, *Kultura*, 73, 128.
[14]Bičanić, *Doba manufakture*, 139.
[15]Horvat, *Kultura*, 177.

coal mines, were in operation in northern Croatia.[16] During the same period silk culture developed significantly, and Croatian silk enjoyed a good reputation on the international market.

Forest and Land Exploitation

In the second half of the eighteenth century and at the beginning of the nineteenth, the forests, which were for the most part of prime quality and represented Croatia's greatest natural resource, covered more than half of the surface of the land. The most extensive forests were once those of beech and oak trees. There were also considerable woods of elm, ash, maple, linden, and alder trees. Pine forests were represented mainly by fir, juniper, and pine trees. Although sawmills, such as the one in Čabar, for example, had already existed in the seventeenth century, extensive exploitation of the Croatian forest wealth really did not begin until the eighteenth century, and during the first half of the nineteenth century it represented the most important branch of manufacturing in the land.[17] Of great significance was the production of oak barrel staves, which were exported in large quantities to England, France, and Germany. However, in the course of time, the best oak forests of Croatia were destroyed by reckless exploitation. The production of potash, which was also based on exploitation of the forests, had long been common in Croatia, but only from around 1750 until about 1850 was there a sudden growth in this branch of production.[18] At the same time, the production of charcoal was significant, and customers were found not only in the native foundries, but also abroad, where it was exported in great quantities, as was potash. During this period, Croatia had only a few small textile enterprises, whereas the leather industry, with its most important centers in Rijeka, Osijek, Karlovac, and Zagreb, was better developed.[19]

In the production of food, the efficient sugar refinery erected in the year 1750 at Rijeka had special importance; during the eighteenth century and the beginning of the nineteenth, this refinery was the largest manufacturing concern in the entire Austrian Empire, as well as one of the largest in Europe.[20] Rijeka was also the most important center for grain mills and the production of noodles. It had numerous oil works, brandy and liquor distilleries, and a considerable number of breweries. This city was the most important center of production in the

[16] Bičanić, *Doba manufakture*, 89.
[17] *Ibid.*, 106.
[18] *Ibid.*, 122.
[19] *Ibid.*, 145.
[20] *Ibid.*, 155.

Croatian lands during the pre-capitalistic period, and in the year 1842 it possessed as many as sixty-two different production plants.[21]

From the second half of the seventeenth century, tobacco was raised in Croatia, and tobacco factories came into being in all of the cities; in the year 1809, thirty such plants operated in Rijeka alone.[22] The production of glass and bricks had also begun to show considerable progress by the end of the eighteenth century.

Industrial Development

Industrial development gained momentum in Croatia in the 1840's, partly in connection with the technical development in Western Europe. The Croatian economy, patterned on the example of Western Europe, was gradually built up on a capitalistic foundation. In the year 1835 the first steam engine was put into operation in the paper mill of Rijeka. This factory, founded in 1828, was Croatia's first industrial enterprise. The first spinning machines were introduced in 1847 at Varaždin, and mechanical looms at Rijeka in 1851. The first steam-operated sawmill was erected in Prezid (1849); the first sugar factory in Čepin (1836); and the first steam mill in Varaždin (1846). A factory for machine construction was opened in Rijeka in 1854. The year 1856 saw the first Croatian match factory built in Osijek; this was one of the first factories of its kind in Europe. In the same year a factory for farm machinery was erected, also in Osijek. In 1860 steam-driven plows were put into operation on Croatian farms.[23]

Of great significance for the Croatian economy was the founding of the First Croatian Savings Bank in the year 1846. It was not only the first bank of its kind, but also numbered itself among the first banking establishments of southeastern Europe.[24] This banking institute soon developed into the most powerful bank in all the Balkan countries.

New means of communications were opened up by the invention of the electric telegraph. Soon thereafter, in 1851, the first Croatian telegraph line was constructed, connecting Zagreb with Vienna. In the year 1862 the first railroad line, Sisak-Zagreb-Zidani Most-Trieste was completed.[25] With this line, Austria hoped to divert Croatian trade from Rijeka. The first railroad line in Bosnia, Dobrljin-Banja Luka, was

[21]Horvat, *Kultura*, 333.
[22]Bičanić, *Doba manufakture*, 160.
[23]*Ibid.*, 215.
[24]Horvat, *Kultura*, 331.
[25]J. Gorničić-Brdovački, *Razvitak željeznica u Hrvatskoj do 1918 godine* / Railroad Development in Croatia Until 1918 (Zagreb, 1952), v.

put into operation in 1872, and in the following year the railroad line Budapest-Zagreb-Rijeka came into being.[26] In the year 1891 the most important narrow-gauge stretch was opened: Brod-Sarajevo-Metković.[27] During the following decades, until 1918, several railroad systems were built in the various Croatian territories—not, however, according to the needs of the Croatian economy, but rather according to those of Austria and Hungary. As a result, the railroads in the Croatian lands represented a most inorganic network, as far as the Croatians themselves were concerned.

The Capitalistic Development of Croatia

Characteristic of the Croatian economy of the 1860's and 1870's was the development, with ever-increasing strength, of industrial production. A second important factor in these times was the rapid expansion of the railroads and steamers. With the new industrial development, in which English, French, and German capital also participated, there arose a tendency toward a concentration on dwellings and business, which initiated a movement of the population from the country to the city. Since the importance of handiwork declined in favor of mechanization, the craftsmen felt themselves threatened by the upsurge of industry and they demanded restrictions on free trade. The principle of free trade was, however, retained as a basis of economic life.

The transition period in the economic development of Croatia was accompanied by considerable difficulty. Competition with foreign products set in, which caused great and irreparable harm to handicrafts in Croatia. A number of handiwork establishments were adversely affected and gradually disappeared entirely. In connection with this development, certain villages and cities declined economically. In spite of this, the more enterprising craftsmen adapted themselves to the newly-created situation. New branches of handicrafts sprang up, such as the mechanical, electrical, and chemical ones, and at the beginning of the nineteenth century one could count 70, and by 1862, more than 120 different branches of handiwork in Croatia.[28]

Though certain conditions favorable to trade and to the industrial economy did exist in the Croatian lands, the economic development of Croatia was very much hampered by the fact that it was economically

[26] *Ibid.*, vi.

[27] F. Martin, *Eisenbahngeographie Jugoslaviens* / Railroad Geography of Yugoslavia (Würzburg, 1937), 10.

[28] Bičanić, *Doba manufakture*, 47.

dependent on Austria and Hungary. These latter nations pursued the policy of developing industry only in their own countries. In spite of this, Croatia was able to develop until the beginning of World War I its own, though humble, industry in various parts of the country, usually involving the factory-type processing of domestic products.

Of special significance in this regard were grain mills, oil refineries, canneries, and sugar refineries. Alcohol, textiles, wood, furniture, and paper were manufactured. Also of importance were iron foundries and blast furnaces in Vareš, Topusko, and Bešlinac, a steel-rolling mill in Zenica, rich soft coal mines in Kreka, Banovići, Zenica, Vareš, Mostar, Siverić, Golubovac, Krapina, Budinšćina, and Raša (Podlabin), and iron ore mines in Vareš, Ljubija, Petrova Gora, and Trgovska Gora. At this time the utilization of the rich water-power of the Croatian rivers also began, which resulted in the erection of a series of power plants.

After World War I, a renewed expansion of industrial activity was evident, particularly in its effect upon the textile, mining, and foundry industries. Especially worthy of mention are the erection of a new, larger steel-rolling mill in Zenica and the beginning of operations in the aluminum factory in Šibenik. The textile industry enjoyed rapid development as the basis of the production of consumer goods. The shoe industry also flourished, especially at the shoe factory in Borovo, the largest in the Balkan countries. The wood, furniture, aluminum, and cement industries, which operated on native raw materials, were likewise able to make significant progress. The machine industry succeeded in expanding, particularly in the manufacture of railroad cars, in railroad repair workshops, in ship-building, and in the production of agricultural implements and machines. Not until shortly before World War II did the systematic utilization of the significant Croatian oil wells begin, with the aid of the American Vacuum Oil Company. The building up of a machine industry was prevented by a shortage of capital, since the surplus of domestic capital, as a result of the inimical economic policy of the Belgrade government toward Croatia, remained very small. Foreign capital was thus greatly needed, and before long the investment of foreign capital increased considerably.

The Development of Merchant Fleets

The Adriatic Sea has always been a decisive factor in the Croatian economy, and the source of several important economic branches with which the Croatians have concerned themselves ever since settling on the coast. In addition to providing industries of minor importance, such as the sponge and coral fisheries, the sea has been important for shipping, fishing, ship-building, and salt production. More recently, the tourist trade has lent additional economic significance to the sea.

The Croatians have had a noteworthy shipping industry ever since they settled along the Adriatic, although the earliest instances of shipping can hardly be counted, since there was no clearly defined difference between the warships and the trade ships of the period. Dubrovnik, at a very early time, established an international reputation for its shipping, and its flag was encountered on all seas. Its warship fleet was small, and this accounted for its larger commercial fleet. Even in the sixteenth century the ships from Dubrovnik sailed all the seas of Europe.[29] In those times the city had at its disposal over 300 large ships.[30] In 1654 approximately 160 large trading vessels were in its possession—several of which had a capacity of over 27,000 hectoliters—in addition to a large number of smaller ships.[31] However, the horrible earthquake of 1667 was a great blow to Dubrovnik, and the city recovered very slowly, never regaining its former size and significance. The coastal cities of Split, Zadar, Trogir, Hvar, Korčula, Kotor, and Šibenik were also of importance to maritime trade. Their fleets, however, in no way compared with the fleet of Dubrovnik. Nevertheless, for a long time Split was the most important harbor on the Adriatic coast.

In order to counteract piracy, which caused much difficulty for the Croatian coastal cities, and in order to safeguard shipping on the Adriatic, the cities united, and thereby they were able to count on the support of Venice. When, in 1420, Venice spread its power over the Croatian coastal cities, she eliminated their former city autonomy. Since this affected trade, Dalmatian shipping therefore diminished in importance. In the year 1422, Venice issued a decree that all Dalmatian ships were required to land in Venice first, and later on even stronger measures were taken, which considerably hampered shipping on the Croatian seacoast.[32] When Venice recognized the independent city of Dubrovnik as a dangerous competitor, it enlarged the harbor of Split and erected there a storage place for its Balkan trade. Merchants from

[29] Around 1500, Palladius Fuscus (of Padua) wrote, in his *De situ orae Illyricae*: "Nulla Europae pars adeo abdita est . . . ut in ea Ragusinos non invenias negotiantes." ("No part of Europe is so hidden . . . that one would not find in it Ragusan merchants.") Quoted in the Oxford Dictionary under the entry "Argosy."

[30] Grga Novak, *Naše more* / Our Sea (Zagreb, 1932).

[31] *Ibid.*, 160.

[32] Vladislav Brajković, *Etude historique sur le droit maritime privé du Littoral Yougoslave* (Marseille, 1933), 63.

the great Turkish Empire, as well as from India and Persia, visited the city of Split. Thus shipping and trade in the Croatian coastal cities was saved from certain downfall.

After the discovery of America and of the sea route to India, the importance of trade in the Mediterranean, and with it that of trade in the Adriatic Sea, diminished considerably. European trade took to other routes. It was the beginning of the gradual but certain decrease in trade and shipping for Venice, and also for the Dalmatian cities. At the end of the eighteenth century, the Croatian city of Kotor in Boka Kotorska came to the fore with its fleet of trading vessels. Over 300 ships for heavy shipping and more than 300 smaller vessels were at its disposal.[33] However, these fleets were mostly destroyed during the Napoleonic Wars.

During the French occupation of Dalmatia from 1805 until 1814, trade and shipping again blossomed. During this period, it is reported that the important harbor of Trieste served the major part of the Croatian trading vessels.[34] The pirate raids of 1808 were again a bitter blow to shipping. England conquered the island of Vis in 1811 (losing it the next year), which consequently became the center for smuggling goods from England to Dalmatia, Italy, and Austria.

After the overthrow of Napoleon, Dalmatia was annexed by Austria in 1814—Venice no longer existed as a city-republic—and more peaceful times began at last for the Croatian seacoast. It was able to renew successful efforts to reconstruct what an epoch of wars and unrest had destroyed in trade relations and economic wealth. In the year 1869 the Suez Canal was opened, and, as a consequence, the importance of the Adriatic Sea, particularly for trade with India and East Asia, grew considerably. Despite the fact that steamships were gradually becoming common at that time, the period between 1850 and 1871 represented the rise and the climax of Croatian shipping. At that time the harbors of Boka Kotorska, especially Perast, and the peninsula of Pelješac were most important because of the numbers of their ships. During the middle of the nineteenth century, the shipping of Boka Kotorska recuperated from the losses suffered during the Napoleonic Wars, and in the year 1852 more than 60 ships were at its disposal. In 1865 the Pelješac Shipping Company Incorporated (Pelješko Brodarsko Dioničko Društvo) was founded, with 33 vessels for shipping on the high seas.

The maritime prosperity brought about by sailing vessels did not last

[33]Novak, *Naše more*, 253.
[34]A. Premužić, *Privreda* (October, 1933), 176.

long, however. By the 1890's, steamships had come to the fore and brought with them an upheaval in ship-building and shipping methods which caused a serious crisis. The first steamships docked in the harbor of Rijeka in 1840, and 1870 saw the first steamer located there. Steamers pushed sailing vessels more and more into the background, and the reduction of Croatian sail-shipping ensued in rapid order, so that sailing companies were discontinued. In the year 1888 even the once mighty Pelješac Shipping Company shut down. Croatian shippers were too conservative; furthermore, a lack of necessary capital did not enable them to meet the danger that the rise of the steamer represented. The former centers of sail-shipping were unable to recuperate from their loss of capital. Austria and Hungary took advantage of the situation and developed shipping in Trieste and Rijeka respectively. Trieste became the main harbor for the Austrian half of the monarchy, and Rijeka for the Hungarian half of it. Only these two harbors were connected with the interior via good railroad connections, whereas the other harbors remained isolated and had only local importance.

The first Croatian coastal steamship company, Krajač and Company, was founded in the year 1871, merged with the M. Švrljuga and Company freight concern in 1891; thus came into being the Hungarian-Croatian Steamship Company, with headquarters in Rijeka. This soon developed into the mightiest coastal freight company in the Austro-Hungarian Monarchy. At the same time, five other steamship companies existed in Dalmatia, but these maintained only coastal shipping. In spite of this fact, Dubrovnik enjoyed greater advancement both in coastal and ocean shipping, and in 1910 was the home of the following companies: Račić, Marinović, Dubrovačka Plovidba, Krunajević and Jeličić, Obalna Plovidba, and Gračić. Thus Dubrovnik once again became the focal point of Croatian shipping.

With the aid of generous government subsidies, Austro-Hungarian shipping developed favorably, and in 1914 it had at its disposal over a million gross tons. Not only the captains and officers, but also the crews, were almost exclusively Croatian. After the fall of Austria-Hungary (1918), the major part of the fleet was assigned to Italy and France. Yugoslavia received only those ships whose owners were Croatian. The assignment to Italy of the harbors of Trieste and Rijeka, which were economically so closely connected with the Croatian coastal territories, represented a great obstacle for the reorganization of shipping, which was only made worse by a lack of understanding on the part of the Yugoslav government.

During the years between 1924 and 1930, Croatian shipping made notable advancements. The increase in tonnage, caused almost exclusively by the rise in tramp steamer tonnage, can be traced to both the constant enlarging of the established fleet and the founding of new companies. The world-wide economic crisis which began in 1929 affected Croatian shipping most unfavorably. After the stagnation and shrinking of tonnage, the year 1937 again brought a notable boom, and the Dubrovnik Shipping Company, Incorporated (Dubrovačka Parobrodarska Plovidba A.D.) remarked in its business report for the year 1937 "that [1937] should be remembered as a brilliant period of free shipping." The total Croatian fleet tonnage in 1938 was 416,630 gross tons. In addition to passenger and freight service to Italian, Albanian, Greek, Turkish, Bulgarian, and Rumanian harbors, Croatia also carried on freight services with the harbors of the Near East, North Africa, Spain, France, England, the North Sea, the Baltic Sea, and South America. During the Second World War, with the sinking of a major portion of Croatian tonnage, the eventful history of Croatian shipping received a further mighty blow.

Salt-Water Fishing

Deep-sea fishing was for centuries of vital importance to the Croatian coastal population, since the extensive coastline has little arable surface which could provide sufficient sustenance for the inhabitants. Fishing was and is still the most important branch of economy for the numerous towns along the coast. Sea food represents an essential part of the nutrition of the people who live there. A large portion of the population which was active in agriculture also participated in the fishing industry. Large fish runs have always been common in the Adriatic, and generally consist of sardines, mackerel, and tuna—the so-called "blue-fish."

There is a distinction between winter and summer fishing, and the latter is of decisive economic importance. The summer fishing season was apparently already well developed in the fourteenth century, and there are documents from the middle of the fifteenth century which refer to its development and organization.[35] Since time immemorial, the bluefish caught in the summer season have been salted, and in more recent times they have been canned for export. Lately the results of the catch have become poorer, and earlier times prove much better by comparison. In the year 1553, for example, the fishermen of Vis alone caught over 200,000 pounds of sardines in a single night. The fishing

[35] Grga Novak, *Dokumenti za povijest ribarstva* / Documents for the History of Fishing, I (Zagreb, 1952), 21.

vessels were also much more numerous in earlier times—for example, in 1848 the fishermen of the island of Vis owned 142 different fishing vessels.[36]

Ship-Building

Ship-building, especially at the seacoast, has always been one of the oldest and most important branches of the Croatian economy. A tradition many centuries old, together with favorable climatic conditions, which enable work to continue throughout the entire year, has proved favorable to the development of ship-building. Building materials were available in the interior—the rich Croatian forests provided wood, and the mines iron.

From the end of the eighteenth century, ship-building showed favorable advancement, and after the 1830's rapid development. However, the greatest peak was reached in the year 1855.[37] The Croatian shipbuilders developed such skill that they became famous far and wide, and their ships were esteemed and sought after because of their seaworthiness. The most significant shipyards were found in Rovinj, Cres, Krk, Volosko, Lošinj Mali, Rijeka, Martinšćica, Bakar, Kraljevica, Senj, Trogir, Zadar, Šibenik, Split, Milna, Korčula, and Gruž.

Later, with the decline of sailing vessels, these shipyards lost their importance. In more recent times, however, the shipbuilding industry has again developed along the Croatian coast. The most important shipyards at the present time are located at Pula, Rijeka, Kraljevica, Trogir, Split, and Korčula.

Tourism

Croatia, situated as it is between East and West, is by its nature an ideal tourist land. With a variety of landscapes, a position geographically favorable to transportation, good climatic conditions, historical and cultural monuments, and picturesque cities and towns—especially those on the coast—Croatia fulfills every natural requirement for a tourist country. The most remarkable and wonderful contrasts are found along the Adriatic coast with its many islands; an inexhaustible variety of landscape surprises and bewitches the foreign guest. For these and other reasons, the tourist trade began to develop along the Croatian coast in relatively early times, and by the end of the nineteenth century, several cities and towns—above all Dubrovnik and

[36]Novak, *Naše more*, 19.
[37]Bičanić, *Doba manufakture*, 129.

Opatija—were counted among the best-known centers of the tourist trade in all Europe.

Even though a rapid development of tourism would have been very important to the Croatian economy before the Second World War, possibilities were not sufficiently utilized. Thus tourism, because of the neglectful attitude of the Belgrade government, could not be fully developed at the time. At the height of the tourist season, transportation and accommodation were inadequate, even for the demand from within the country itself, so that private homes had to assist in taking care of foreigners. German tourists were the most numerous group provided for by Croatian hotels and rooming houses. Other tourists came mainly from Austria, Switzerland, and Czechoslovakia. The number of tourists during the months of June, July, August, and September comprised three-fourths of all the tourists during a given year, and because of the lack of proper accommodation at that time, the economic aspects of Croatian tourism suffered extensively. Foreign tourism was concentrated on the coast areas, where lodging possibilities were best.

During the last year of peace, 1938, the tourist trade in Croatia brought in foreign currency amounting to some seven million dollars. This amount without a doubt shows the success of tourism in Croatia, and proves the great attraction which the Croatian sights along the Adriatic coast have for foreigners. With the outbreak of the Second World War, tourism in Croatia was disastrously curtailed at the very moment when it was ready to come into its own.

Bibliography

Barada, Miho. *Starohrvatska seoska zajednica* / Old Croatian Village Community. Zagreb, 1957.

Berger, K. H., *Der Hafen von Fiume* / The Harbor of Rijeka. Köln, 1936.

Beritić, L. *Utvrdjivanje grada Dubrovnika* / Fortification of the City of Dubrovnik. Zagreb, 1956.

Bersa, J. *Dubrovačke slike i prilike* / Dubrovnik's Images and Conditions. Zagreb, 1941.

Bičanić, R. *Ekonomska podloga hrvatskog pitanja* / Economic Basis of the Croatian Problem. Zagreb, 1938.

———. *Doba manufakture u Hrvatskoj i Slavoniji* / Manufacturing Era in Croatia and Slavonia. Zagreb, 1951.

Bösendorfer, Josip. *Agrarni odnosi u Slavoniji* / Agrarian Relations in Slavonia. Zagreb, 1950.

Brajković, V. *Etude historique sur le droit maritime privé du Littoral Yougoslave.* Marseille, 1933.

Bratanić, B. *Oraće sprave u Hrvata* / Arable Implements in Croatia. Zagreb, 1939.

Decaris, A. *Die Agrarfrage Dalmatiens* / The Agrarian Problem in Dalmatia. Split, 1928.

Despot, M. *Privreda Hrvatske XVII–XX stoljeća* / Croatian Economy from the Seventeenth to the Twentieth Century. Zagreb, 1957.

Drašković, J. *Disertacija ili razgovor darovan gospodi poklisarom zakonskim i budućem zakonotvorcem kraljevinah naših*. Zagreb, 1832.

Fellner, A. *Die wirtschaftliche Entwicklung der Muehlenindustrie Kroatien-Slavoniens* / The Economic Development of the Mill Industry in Croatia-Slavonia. Vienna, 1921.

Fisković, C. *Naši graditelji i kipari XV i XVI stoljeća u Dubrovniku* / Our Architects and Sculptors of the Fifteenth and Sixteenth Centuries in Dubrovnik. Zagreb, 1947.

Fortunić, V. *Crtice o ribarstvu uopće, a nadasve na području bivše Republike Dubrovačke* / Short History of Fishing in General, and Especially of the Fishing in the Territory of the Former Republic of Dubrovnik. Dubrovnik, 1930.

Gorničić-Brdovački, J. *Razvitak željeznica u Hrvatskoj do 1918 godine* / Development of Railroads in Croatia to 1918. Zagreb, 1952.

Hefele, F. *Naši domaći obrti* / Our Home Crafts. Zagreb, 1896.

Herkov, Z. *Gradja za financijsko-pravni rječnik feudalne epohe Hrvatske* / Materials for the Financial and Legal Dictionary of the Feudal Epoch in Croatia. Zagreb, 1956.

Herkov, Z. *Statut grada Rijeke iz g. 1530* / Statute of the City of Fiume in the year 1530. Zagreb, 1948.

Horvat, J. *Kultura Hrvata Kroz 1.000 godina* / 1000 Years of Croatian Culture. 2 vols. Zagreb, 1939, 1942.

Horvat, R. *Kako su nekada živjeli hrvatski obrtnici* / How the Croatian Craftsmen Once Lived. Zagreb, 1929.

Hribar, A. *Kolonat ili težaština* / Kmetski odnosi u Primorju. Zagreb, 1923.

Ivšić, M. *Les problèmes agraires de Yougoslavie* / The Agrarian Problems of Yugoslavia. Paris, 1926.

———. *Temelji seljačkog zakonika* / Foundations of the Agrarian Code. Zagreb, 1933.

———. *Društveni život na selu* / Village Social Life. Zagreb, 1937.

———. *Problemi suvremenog života* / Problems of Contemporary Life. Zagreb, 1937.

Jelinović, Z. *Borba za jadranske pruge i njeni ekonomski ciljevi* / Struggle for the Adriatic Railroads and its Economic Aims. Zagreb, 1957.

Jireček, K., and Cvjetković, B. *Važnost Dubrovnika u trgovačkoj povijesti srednjeg vijeka* / Dubrovnik's Importance in the Commercial History of the Middle Ages. Dubrovnik, 1915.

Kesterčanek, F. *Kratka povijest šuma i šumskog gospodarstva u Hrvatskoj* / Brief History of Forests and Forest Economy in Croatia. Zagreb, 1883.

Krišković, V. *Hrvatsko pravo kućnih zadruga* / Croatian Law of Domestic Communities. Zagreb, 1925.

Lakatoš, J. *Industrija Hrvatske* / The Industry of Croatia. Zagreb, 1924.

Laszowski, E. *Gradja za gospodarsku povijest Hrvatske u XVI i XVII stoljeću* / Materials for the Economic History of Croatia in the Sixteenth and Seventeenth Centuries. Zagreb, 1951.

Laszowski, E. *Rudarstvo u Hrvatskoj* / Mining in Croatia. Vols. I and II. Zagreb, 1942, 1944.

Lepel, F. *Geschichte der Stadt und Republik Ragusa* / History of the City and Republic of Ragusa. Dresden, 1931.

Mayer, E. *Die dalmatinisch-istrische Munizipalverfassung im Mittelalter und ihre römischen Grundlagen* / The Dalmatian-Istrian Municipal Constitution and its Roman Foundations. Weimar, 1903.

Mayer, H. *Das dalmatinische Kolonat* / The Dalmatian Colonate. Vienna, 1911.

Matasović, J. *Iz ekonomske historije 175–1758* / Some Facts of the Economic History from 175–1758. Zagreb, 1929.

Matković, D. *Die Seeschiffahrt und Seeschiffahrtspolitik Jugoslawiens* / Maritime Navigation and Yugoslavia's Maritime Policy. Cologne, 1939.

Medini, M. *O postanku i razvitku kmetskih i težačkih odnosa u Dalmaciji* / About the Origin and Development of Manorial Relations in Dalmatia. Zadar, 1920.

Mirković, Mijo. *Ekonomska historija Jugoslavije* / Economic History of Yugoslavia. Zagreb, 1958.

Milobar, F. *Izabrana poglavlja iz narodnoga gospodarstva* / Selected Parts of the National Economy. Zagreb, 1902.

Muderizović, R. "Bosanski majdani za turske uprave" / Bosnian Mines Under Turkish Administration, *Glasnik Zemaljskog Muzeja* XXX (1918), 21–28.

Novak, G. "Vunena industrija u Dubrovniku do sredine XVI stoljeća" / The Wool Industry in Dubrovnik until the middle of the Sixteenth Century, *Rešetarov zbornik* (Dubrovnik, 1931).

———. *Naše more* / Our Sea. Zagreb, 1932.

———. *Prošlost Dalmacije* / The Past of Dalmatia. 2 vols. Zagreb, 1944.

———. *Dokumenti za povijest ribarstva na istočnoj obali Jadranskog mora*, sv. I: *Otoci Vis i Hvar* / Documents for the History of Fishing on the Eastern Shore of the Adriatic Sea, vol. I: Islands of Vis and Hvar. Zagreb: Yugoslav Academy of Sciences and Arts, 1952.

Omrčanin, I. "La Zadruga Croata ossia la comunità di famiglia in Croazia" / Croatian Zadruga or Domestic Community, *Annuario di Diritto Comparato e di studi Legislativi*, vol. XXVII, fasc. 10, 1952.

Pivec-Stelè, M. *La vie économique des provinces illyriennes 1809–1813*. Paris, 1930.

Poparić, B. *Povijest pomorstva* I, II. / History of Seafaring. 2 vols. Zagreb, 1932, 1933.

Rieger, V. *Das landwirtschaftliche Genossenschaftswesen in den kroatischen Ländern* / The Agricultural Cooperative System in the Croatian Lands. Berlin, 1939.

Rijeka / Fiume. Zbornik / Symposium. Zagreb, 1953.

Roller, D. *Dubrovački zanati u XV i XVI stoljeću* / Dubrovnik's Crafts in the Fifteenth and Sixteenth Centuries. Zagreb, 1951.

———. *Agrarno-proizvodni odnosi na području Dubrovačke republike od*

XIII do XV stoljeća / Agrarian-Productive Relations in the Territory of the Republic of Dubrovnik from the Thirteenth to the Fifteenth Century. Zagreb, 1955.

Steiner, V. *Die Volkswirtschaft der Königreiche Kroatien und Slavonien vom Standpunkte der Landwirtschaft* / The Economic System of the Kingdoms of Croatia and Slavonia from the Agricultural Viewpoint. Zagreb, 1917.

Tadić, J. "Pomorsko osiguranje u Dubrovniku XVI stoljeća" / Maritime Insurance in 16th Century Dubrovnik, *Rešetarov zbornik* (Dubrovnik, 1931), 109–112.

Tomasevich, J. *Peasants, Politics, and Economics in Yugoslavia.* Stanford & London, 1955.

Utišenović, M. *Die Hauskommunionen der Südslaven* / The Domestic Community of the Southern Slavs. Vienna, 1859.

Vrbanić, F. *Prilozi gospodarskom razvoju hrvatsko-slavonske Krajine u 19. vijeku* / Contribution to Economic Development of the Military Frontier in the Nineteenth Century. Zagreb, 1900.

6

Ethical Heritage

FRANCIS H. ETEROVICH

Ethical tenets have the power to guide any national life to its explicit goals. The ancient and accumulated wisdom of life directs a people in determining its truest relationship to its own material and spiritual resources, to its neighbors in the world, and to God. Ethical values help to mould a balanced, honest, self-controlled people which will respect, love, cultivate, and, if necessary, die for the same cherished values. These intangible values may themselves become the nation's highest goals: it is a sign of high morality and culture in a people when it steadily sacrifices visible and immediate goods for those which are invisible and ultimate. An examination of the national culture of a nation would be incomplete without a study of that country's ethical heritage.

There is a basic ethical unity in mankind. Common principles of ethics and orderly life are the heritage of all nations—both civilized and primitive. It would seem to follow then that a study of ethical values among the Croatians could not especially help one reach an understanding of their cultural personality. Yet each nation has incorporated and practiced universal principles of ethics in its own unique way. Each nation cherishes some values more than others to the extent that a number of well-defined values become characteristic components of its particular way of life. The Croatians too have emphasized and cherished certain values. The quality of "cherishing," of cultivating an emotional attachment, requires that we take into account not only values but also attitudes toward those values.

Religion and ethics, although they are two distinct spheres, have been closely united in the long history of mankind. Ethics has made religion a practical way of life; religion has given morality its foundation, aim, and sanction. Within Croatia and Bosnia-Hercegovina there are three main religious groups, the Roman Catholics, the Orthodox Eastern Christians, and the Moslems. Each of these groups follows its own system of ethics. This study is primarily devoted to a consideration of the ethical heritage of the Roman Catholic Croatians.

It is important, in order to avoid any misunderstanding, to point out that a great part of the Croatian Catholic ethical heritage dates from the pre-Christian era. Among the virtues, that stem from this period, one may mention hospitality, honor, fidelity, tightly-knit familial bonds, and a deep love for the native land. Among the perennial vices that can be traced back to this era are revenge, envy, and a destructive hatred of the enemy. Christianity has strengthened these virtues and, to lesser degree, subdued many of these vices; it has also added its own individual contribution to the Croatian ethical heritage: an emphasis on love of God and neighbor, and the salvation of the individual through the workings of grace.

We shall attempt to present the basic traits of the Croatian moral personality by analyzing the salient ethical principles, the chief virtues and corresponding shortcomings, as well as the morality of the social relations of this people. The area considered in this article is rather an extensive one; each value and its contrary could be an interesting subject for an individual study. Our intention, however, is to give the reader a comprehensive, over-all view of general Croatian ethical values and attitudes. There has been to this point too little research in the collection, classification, and interpretation of the moral facts and values among the Croatians. In our study we have drawn on folk songs and proverbs, beliefs, customs, and laws, passages from literature and poetry, and examples from political, military, legal, and social history. To these sources we have added our own observations, reflections, and conclusions, as well and have made use of the few articles and books that have been written on the subject.

A vast task still lies ahead in this area of study, however. Much more research needs to be carried out in this field. Insufficient statistical information pertinent to the topic is as yet available. It is our earnest desire that this study serve as a beginning—however modest—and a stimulus to students to engage in scientific research on the Christian moral heritage[1] among Croatians.

[1]In the course of this study, we have assumed that the reader is familiar with the nature of Christian morality, which derives from both the Old and the New Testaments. The Ten Commandments (Exodus 20: 1–8) condenses the morality of

Basic Moral Principles

Divine Justice

The Catholic Croatians are, as a rule, a God-fearing people. They believe that God is the zealous guardian of the moral order. He is often depicted in Croatian folk songs and stories as intervening in human affairs in order to protect the innocent, reward the good, encourage moral actions, give testimony to truth and justice, and even foretell the victory of those who are persecuted because of their honesty and integrity.[2]

Above all, God is, in Croatian folklore, the judge and avenger of the wicked. In folk literature, an "enraged divine justice" often persecutes the criminal: the reprobate cannot find peace of mind, lives haunted by his conscience, and dies in terrible agony; his soul is then thrown into hell, and his body, not permitted even the rest of the grave, is taken by evil spirits and goes about disturbing people. This terrible punishment is vividly described, for instance, in the poem "Prokleti Duka Šetković" (Damned Duka Šetković), about a man who killed his mother in the most cruel way.[3] It is not merely coincidence that the great literary works of the Croatians have so often expressed the central idea of their general moral code: that divine justice punishes evil men.

Marko Marulić (Marcus Marulus, 1450–1524), a great Christian humanist and the father of Croatian Renaissance literature, dedicated his life to the restoration of the moral values which he believed were on the decline in his day. His epic poem—the first Croatian printed work—"Istorija svete udovice Judit" (The History of the Holy Widow Judith), written in 1501 and published in 1521, applies the biblical narrative of the Book of Judith to the Croatian people, who were

---

the Old Testament, and the Sermon on the Mount (Matthew, chapters 5, 6, and 7) gives the principal points of the morality of the New Testament. The central theme of the Old Testament is justice, while that of the New Testament is love—love of God and neighbor. In the Christian view, the spirit of the Old Testament existed chiefly in the zealous observance of the Law, while that of the New Testament consists in inner sanctification by means of participation by the faithful in the divine life of wisdom and love, a participation usually termed "the life of grace."

[2]Petar Bakotić, "Pojav čuda i zakon reda u narodnoj književnosti" / The Appearance of Miracles and the Law of Moral Order in Folk Literature, *Zbornik za narodni život i običaje Južnih Slavena* / Scientific Papers On the Life and Customs of South Slav People. Vol. 31 (Zagreb: Yugoslav Academy of Sciences and Arts, 1937), 47.

[3]Number 39 in *Hrvatske narodne pjesme* / Croatian Folk Songs. Vol. I. *Junačke Pjesme* / Heroic Songs (Zagreb: Matica Hrvatska, 1896), 113–122.

fighting the Turks at the very walls of his native city of Split in Dalmatia. The poet seeks to instill courage in his hard-pressed people by giving them a message of hope: just as divine justice once punished Holofernes and his army, who threatened to destroy the Jewish people, so the same divine justice will now punish the Turks and save the Croatian people from captivity.[4]

Ivan Gundulić (Joannes Gondola, 1588–1638) of Dubrovnik wrote *Osman*, an epic poem in twenty cantos (two of them, the fourteenth and the fifteenth, are missing, but substitutes were masterfully composed by Ivan Mažuranić in the nineteenth century), in which he describes the victory of Ladislaus, the Polish king, over the Turkish Sultan Osman in 1621, and the death of the latter at the hands of his janissaries during the rebellion which took place in Constantinople the next year. The poet, profoundly Christian in his attitude toward faith and morals, sees in these two events a great sign of the liberation of the Slavic peoples from the Turks. The basic idea of his poem is found at the beginning and at the end: the might of tyrants and their empires will pass away, and the proud will be humiliated and the humble exalted by divine justice.[5]

Ivan Mažuranić (1814–1890), a modern Croatian poet of humanist and Christian tradition, has shown in his epic poem "Smrt Smail-Age Čengića" (Death of Smail-Aga Čengić) that divine justice inexorably punishes all despots and tyrants. A handful of Montenegrin fighters, the instruments of divine justice, fortified on a night trip to the headquarters of Smail-Aga by the mysteries of the Christian faith and the sacraments of penance and the Eucharist, arrive at dawn and surprise the cruel party of Smail-Aga and his dignitaries, who enjoy torturing the Christians. Montenegrins kill Smail-Aga and his henchmen.

> Mažuranić composed his poem with a firm conviction and with an unflinching faith that in the eternal order of things every just and every evil man will be rewarded in due time according to their merits. This is the idea which permeated the whole intellectual and emotional life of the poet . . . this is the philosophical and moral thought which pervades his whole literary activity, and this is the central idea of his poem *Death of Smail-Aga Čengić*. . . . This is the reason why his poem—though full of blood, revenge, the suffering of the innocent, and of craftiness and the worst passions of the depraved human soul—leaves a feeling of serenity and optimism. The poet is consoling the just with the conviction that human injustice is

[4]Milorad Medini, *Povijest hrvatske književnosti u Dalmaciji i Dubrovniku* / History of Croatian Literature in Dalmatia and Dubrovnik. Book I: Sixteenth Century (Zagreb: Matica Hrvatska, 1902), 85.

[5]Franjo Trogrančić, *Storia della letteratura croata. Dall' Umanesimo alla Rinascita Nazionale* (Secolo XV–XIX) (Studium. Rome, 1953), 163–165.

transitory and divine justice inexorable, and with faith in the ultimate victory of moral values over the momentary triumph of evil.[6]

Idealized View of Morality

The folk songs, stories, and proverbs of Croatia mainly describe two types of human beings: the one kind is aggressive and violent and has no moral standards; the other is innocent and God-fearing but unfit to fight, and hence often a victim of the more aggressive type of individual. The former lives according to the standards of the animal world, in which the supreme law is the preservation of biological life. The violent man is compared to a beast and is called a man "without a soul." He is lawless and homeless and at war with society and its institutions. In contrast, the innocent man lives according to ethical human standards and God's commandments. He believes that the soul is the better part of the human being and that it is destined to live eternally. This man does good and avoids evil, regardless of suffering and trials at the hands of the godless and aggressive man, and regardless of the loss of goods which he might incur in obeying the law of God and of his conscience.

This idealized view of morality is very common among the Croatians. To them the world is a stage on which evil men fight with good men. The good, in spite of all adversities, are bound to win. This will happen either by long-suffering and passive resistance to the evil men, as the folk-literature theme just mentioned indicates, or by honorable battle against their enemy, as folk-poetry abundantly illustrates. By and large, Croatians have been more intent on the latter course, on fighting their enemies than on suffering at their hands. The fighting spirit is particularly strong among the Dinara Mountain dwellers in Bosnia, Hercegovina, Lika, and Dalmatian Zagora. On the other hand, there are others—living on the northern plains and along the southern coastal areas and islands—who believe that an enemy can be defeated by more peaceful means. Both groups have to endure long struggles and suffering. The struggle is unequal, because the evil men, or the enemies of the nation, use every means, regardless of morality, and fight not only openly, but secretly, using all manners of ambush, deceit, fraud, and concealed murder, while the good men must fight honorably and relentlessly for victory. In fact, the suffering of a small

[6]Ivan Mažuranić, *La morte di Smail-Aga Čengijić. Poema.* Introduction, translation, and footnotes by Franjo Trogrančić. (Genova: Briano, 1949), xxii. See also J. W. Wiles, *The Death of Smail-Aga Čengić* (London, 1925). Trogrančić presents some worthwhile reflections on the moral content of this epic poem in his introduction.

nation like Croatia has often reached the most tragic dimensions in time and intensity.[7]

Perfection of Humanity

In Croatia, what might almost be termed a cult of humanity (*čovještvo*) has developed down through the centuries. True humanity is understood as a synthesis of the best and noblest qualities of the human being. It consists in a harmonious blending of biological and moral qualities in the same person. The greatest achievement of one's life is to be the perfect man.

The knight (*vitez*), whose deeds are related in folk songs, typifies ideal humanity. His physical and spiritual virtues are developed to the utmost degree. The health, strength, and beauty of his body find an excellent and a superior counterpart in the qualities of his soul. Together, a perfect body and a perfect soul make him a perfect, integral man. The knight has no vices. He commands admiration and respect. He protects the innocent and fights their oppressors. He nobly defends his honor in battle—a battle which is fought openly, on the field of honor, and according to rules. This vivid image of knightly humanity is still very much alive among the Croatian people, especially among those in Bosnia-Hercegovina. There, chivalry is more a moral concept than a feudal title.

Besides the knight, there is another magnificent figure in Croatian

[7]It is interesting to note here that two books have recently been written by outstanding Croatian political leaders, both living in exile. The titles of these two books are almost identical, but the content of each is written in a different spirit.

Dr. Vladko Maček (d. 1964), the president of the Croatian Peasant Party, while in Washington, D.C., has written *In the Struggle for Freedom* (New York: Robert Speller and Sons, 1957). Pp. 280. Pacifism, the main trait in the personality of Dr. Maček, pervades the pages of his account of the last sixty years of Croatian history, viewed in the perspective of the birth, growth, triumph, and present survival of the émigrés of his political party. This leader of a once mighty political party among the Croatians was the decided opponent of tyranny, and yet he firmly believed that it is better to suffer injustice than to inflict it upon others. He dismissed violence as a means of political gain.

Dr. Ante Pavelić (d. 1960), the founder and leader of the Ustasha Movement among the Croatians, was of the view that the injustice and violence that the Croatians suffered at the hands of the Serbs should be retaliated against by force. He founded the Croatian Liberation Movement among the Croatian émigrés after the last war. The purpose of this organization is the same as was that of the Ustasha Movement, with the difference that its members consider the enemies from whom the Croatian people must be liberated to be the Communists who took over in Yugoslavia after World War II. Dr. Pavelić's successor is Dr. Stjepan Hefer, a rather moderate and well educated man. Hefer's book, which reflects current ideas and attitudes among the members of the C.L.M., is entitled *Croatian Struggle for Freedom and Statehood* (Buenos Aires, 1959). Pp. 238.

folk literature and song. This man is simply called "hero" (*junak*), and, as a rule, he is noted for his moral integrity, although, contrary to the knight, he may have vices. Hero may have either an earthly or a heavenly origin; in any case, his mission is to do the will of God and of other heavenly beings. He often shows consideration and humanity toward his enemies. Real persons—such as the tragic hero of the battle on Krbavsko Polje (1493), Ban Mirko Derenčin; Ban Petar Berislavić (1513–1520); Ban Nikola Šubić Zrinski (1542–1566); and Ban Petar Zrinski (1665–1670) and Count Franjo Krsto Frankopan, both beheaded in Wiener Neustadt, near Vienna, in 1671—have remained in the memory of the people as heroic figures to be admired forever.

Principal Virtues and Vices

Love of God and Neighbor

The central virtue in the Christian moral scheme to which the Croatians adhere is love of God and of one's neighbor. To Christians, God is a loving Father, who has created all good things. The world in its beauty and majesty, and human nature, with its capacity for strength and beauty, wisdom and intuition, joy and happiness, are the gifts of divine love. In His greatest gift, God sent His son, Jesus Christ, to redeem men from the slavery of original sin and personal sins and to make all men children of God through grace and heirs of heavenly glory—provided that they cooperate with the workings of grace in their souls. This cooperation proves itself principally by love of God. But those who love God must also love all men; all men are brethren, one of another. This spirit of universal brotherhood has inspired many Croatians throughout their history.

Christian love of neighbor urges, in the first place, the practice of almsgiving (*milostinja*) and the feeding of the poor. The destitute, the needy, the poor, the prisoner—all are considered brethren in Christ. They should not be discriminated against on account of religion or ethnic origin. A good deed done for them equals the same deed done for Christ Himself. Moreover, the Church preaches the Gospel, which relates works of charity to the salvation of one's soul, and since charitable deeds help the souls of the dead to reach heaven more easily and more speedily, many a good Croatian feudal lord or pious and rich commoner would leave his possessions to churches for charitable purposes.

Churches and monasteries had a great share in caring for the needy. In our own time, before the end of World War II, when the government and private agencies took over the task of social welfare and relief, many religious groups, particularly of women—like the Sisters of Mercy of St. Vincent De Paul and the Sisters of the Holy Cross—operated hospitals, homes for the aged, orphanages, and kitchens for the poor. City governments were also active in taking care of the poor and sick, even in the distant past. The city-republic of Dubrovnik, to mention only one example here, had, in the eighteenth century, beside the foundations sponsored by churches and monasteries, city foundations for lepers, for helping various artisans, such as carpenters and shoemakers, for providing dowries for poor girls, for hospitals, for distributing food and clothes to the poor, and for the ransom of those Ragusans who, while sailing and trading on the seas, had fallen into captivity. There were no fewer than twenty-four foundations for this latter purpose alone.[8]

Love for one's neighbor is perhaps best represented among the Croatians in friendly relationship. Friendship (*prijateljstvo*) is highly valued and sought after eagerly. It is built upon the principle that human qualities attract mutual admiration and esteem. Friendship develops in a mutual communication of the inner content of friendly feelings and thoughts. There is no need, however, that friends share their inner life completely. The innermost part of this life is never exposed, even between the closest friends. Friends are few and carefully selected, and the loyalty of friends is tested by mutual help and sacrifice. It is interesting to note here that differences of opinion in religious, political, and even cultural matters will break friendships very easily among the Croatian people. A disagreement in such vital matters is never purely academic or marginal; it immediately affects one's social relations, and particularly friendship, the most delicate of them all.

The spirit of love of neighbor can be easily detected in the hospitality (*gostoprimstvo*) that is traditional among the Croatians. Hospitality is one of the most conspicuous social virtues among the Croatians, and it is encouraged by Christian brotherly love, although its roots go deeply into pre-Christian Croatian history. It carries a strict duty to lodge a stranger caught in bad weather or in the darkness of night. A guest, whether he be a fellow countryman or a foreigner, is welcomed as though he were God's personal messenger.

[8]Kosta Vojnovic ed. *Bratovštine i obrtne korporacije u republici dubrovačkoj od XIII. do konca XVIII. vijeka*, 2 vols. *Monumenta historico–iuridica Slavorum Meridionalium* (Zagreb: Yugoslav Academy, 1899–1900) I, 173.

Guests are traditionally well fed and sheltered, and even presented with gifts to take home.

For centuries, Catholic Croatians accepted refugees and immigrants from various parts of the Balkan Peninsula, people who had fled before the Turks or who were, during the periods of Turkish dominion, settled by the Turks themselves in the Croatian lands. The Croatians had often been required to flee from the Turks and thus they understood the fate of the banished. The newcomers belonged to many races, but were chiefly of one religion—the Orthodox. Other groups that have come to Croatia, though in smaller numbers than the Orthodox, have found an amicable reception in their new country. Germans, Slovenes, Czechs, and Slovaks have felt so much at home in Croatia that in spite of having their own schools and press many have been assimilated and have become full-fledged Croatians without coercion. These groups have given the nation a long series of outstanding contributors to culture. In recent generations alone, one might mention bishops like Josip J. Strossmayer, Antun Bauer, Josip Stadler, and Antun Mahnić; university professors such as Milan Šufflay, Aleksandar Gahs, and Ljudmil Hauptmann; musicians such as Vatroslav Lisinski, Fran Lhotka, and Boris Papandopulo; and writers like Stanko Vraz and August Šenoa.

The spirit of brotherhood (*bratstvo*) has led Croatians to the idea of uniting the South Slavic nations. The German national awakening of the nineteenth century found a receptive spirit in Croatia. The native nobility, learned clergy, and other literate men were the first to conceive and advocate the union of all South Slavic nations into one single commonwealth. The leading apostle of this idea was the Roman Catholic priest and later bishop, Josip J. Strossmayer (1815–1905). His notion of such a union was to make Croatia a cultural center of the Balkan Peninsula from which the radiation of the Christian civilization and the union of two Christian Churches, the Roman Catholic and Eastern Orthodox, could be effected. This highly idealistic conception of a Yugoslav commonwealth did not spread, however, among the other South Slavic nations.

In spite of a lack of understanding on the part of the Croatian Orthodox, who sided more and more with the Serbs, the idea of a Yugoslav commonwealth encompassing Croatia, Serbia, Slovenia, and other South Slavic peoples continued to grip the imagination of the best Croatian minds. On the eve of the First World War, and during that war, some prominent Croatians, such as the politicians Ante

Trumbić[9] and Frano Supilo, the artist Ivan Meštrović,[10] and intellectuals like Hinko Hinković and Josip Jedlovski managed to emigrate from Austria-Hungary and to reach Britain, France, and America. In 1915 these men founded the Yugoslav Committee in London, an organization which advocated the union of all South Slavic peoples after the war. They found support in all of the Allied and associated countries (except Italy), but they were financed exclusively by the Croatian emigrants of the American hemisphere, particularly by those of the Republic of Chile. Because of two different conceptions of the Yugoslav Commonwealth—the Croatian conception of a federation of free and equal peoples, and the Serbian view of a political and economic expansion that would make Yugoslavia into an enlarged Serbia—the Yugoslav Commonwealth never really worked in practice.[11] Yugoslavia collapsed like a house of cards in 1941 under the attack of Hitler's armies.

During the last war the most outstanding Croatian advocate of universal brotherhood—through his sermons in Zagreb's cathedral and his action of giving protection to Jews, Orthodox, and politically persecuted Catholics—was late Aloysius Cardinal Stepinac (1898–1960). During the war, when the German soldiers were patrolling the streets of Zagreb, Archbishop Stepinac preached many famous sermons condemning the racial politics promoted by Nazism. Radio London and American and Russian stations diffused these sermons on many occasions. Typical of the content of these important talks are the following inspiring words, delivered on October 25, 1942, the Feast of Christ the King, in the Cathedral of Zagreb:

. . . All nations and all races, as reflected in the world today, have the right to lead a life worthy of men and to be treated with the dignity with which

[9]Ante Smith Pavelić, *Dr. Ante Trumbić—Problemi hrvatsko-srpskih odnosa* / Dr. Ante Trumbić—Problems of Croatian-Serbian Relations (München, 1959). Pp. xvi + 337. The author expertly describes the leading role of Dr. Trumbić in the Yugoslav Committee during World War I.

[10]Ivan Meštrović, *Uspomene na političke ljude i dogodjaje* / Memoirs of Political Men and Events (Buenos Aires, 1961). Pp. 417. Chapter 2 of this book treats the part Meštrović had in the Yugoslav Committee.

[11]P. D. Ostović, *The Truth About Yugoslavia* (New York: Roy Publishers, 1952), 54, 76. It is interesting to note that while most of the Croatian founders of Yugoslavia, through the Yugoslav Committee and otherwise, have been disappointed in both the Royal and Communist Yugoslavias, and have given up the idea of the Yugoslav commonwealth, Mr. Ostović, himself a Croatian and a participant in the Yugoslav Committee, has kept his political faith in Yugoslavism against all odds. But he honestly points out in his work the difficulties stemming from the political men, non-Croatians, who were responsible for the failure of both Yugoslavias to bring about a just solution to the problem of the five main and three minor nationalities which make up the nation.

one treats a man. All of them without exception, whether they belong to the race of Gypsies or to another, whether they are Negroes or civilized Europeans, whether they are detested Jews or proud Aryans, have the same right to say, "Our Father, who art in heaven" (Matt. 6:9). . . . That is why the Catholic Church has always condemned, and condemns today as well, every injustice and every violence committed in the name of the theories of class, race, or nationality. . . . One cannot extinguish from the face of the earth Gypsies or Jews because one considers them inferior races.[12]

Shortcomings

The noblest form of love of neighbor is that of behaving toward an enemy as one would toward one's own brother. This is charity in the highest degree, and it is not easily achieved by individuals, and seldom by nations. Croatians have the usual shortcomings with respect to this form of charity. They look upon an enemy not as a brother, but simply as an evildoer, an aggressor, a man "without a soul." They possess not only a spirit of self-defense, which is justifiable and understandable, but they also have a conviction that the enemy must be destroyed.

The law of vengeance (*osveta*) is an ancient custom: in the distant past in Croatia, it often happened that when a member of a joint family (*zadruga*) or clan was killed by an enemy, the surviving relatives swore revenge upon the killer and his family. Blood vengeance was a sacred duty of all the members of closely united families and clans. Christianity has overcome this custom, but the spirit of vengeance has not, however, disappeared altogether.

One of the reasons why many gifted and resourceful Croatians have not found recognition among their people is the existence of a prevalent and deep-seated envy, often referred to as "Croatian envy" (*jal*). What is the motivation of this collective vice? Is it pride, or vainglory, which induces people to be afraid of being overshadowed by others' good qualities? Or perhaps discomfort in the presence of persons who are different from others? Or is it a feeling of inferiority caused by encountering superior individuals? Each of these factors may play an influential part in the creation of envious feelings. All of them together, however, do not yield a satisfactory answer to the question of the cause of "Croatian envy."

[12]Richard Pattee, *The Case of Cardinal Aloysius Stepinac* (Milwaukee: The Bruce Publishing Company, 1953), 279. This is by far the best work on the trial of Archbishop Stepinac held from September 30 to October 11, 1946. The book contains abundant documentary material supporting the innocence of the accused prelate. We have reviewed this book in the *Journal of Croatian Studies*, II (1961). Acknowledgment is made here to the Bruce Publishing Company for their kind permission to quote from Professor Pattee's book.

It seems that an explanation of this trait can be found in a national psychology that has resulted from long centuries of hard fighting against many aggressors. The Croatian people are strongly self-protective and tenacious, and to some extent nationally suspicious and sensitive to political dangers. Croatian envy seems to be a hidden fear of potential enemies. Superior individuals appear to the Croatians to be especially susceptible—because of their greater powers and gifts—of wanting to dominate others; such people are, then, potential enemies. The destruction of such "enemies" follows the regular patterns of envy in action: gossip, defamation, hatred of the enemy's success, joy in his failure, abandonment in his misery.

It is often thought that another fault, discord (*nesloga*), is the typical vice among Croatians. Self-conscious and self-reliant, a gifted observer and thinker, critical of others, and often dissatisfied with himself, the Croatian is too rugged an individualist to join any kind of organized activity. He is unprepared and undisciplined to agree upon the basic aims and principles of a particular organization, and yet he is very imaginative and inventive concerning ends, ideals, and distant goals, regardless of any organized practical working toward them. One may say that the Croatian is too attached to distant and lofty goals to be busy about the particular means leading to them. He often lacks a realistic approach to life; he does not know how to plan to reach a particular goal by using the means available here and now.

The emphasis on individual self-sufficiency that characterizes the Croatian has far-reaching social consequences. Conflicts within the family, village, and town are very frequent. The nation is not yet blended into one frame of mind; there are as many regional types as there are major provinces of Croatia. A few of these might be mentioned, together with their general characteristics. The Dalmatian is an extrovert, quick to react, quick to understand people and problems. The Bosnian tends to be proud, manly, choleric, and dignified. The Slavonian is often a diligent worker who reacts slowly and judges slowly.[13] It is true that some unity exists in language, national consciousness, patriotism, a strong demand for political independence, and the attachment to the Western civilization—but this unity is less secure in matters of concrete cooperation for the attainment of political, economic, and cultural goals. As a rule, one may say that the achieve-

[13]Vladimir Dvorniković, *Karakterologija Jugoslovena* / Characterology of the Yugoslavs (Belgrade, 1939). This work contains useful material on the psychological and ethical personalities of the various nationalities in Yugoslavia.

ment of unity and cooperation between different regions, political parties, and cultural organizations is ordinarily very difficult, unless all are equally threatened by some common danger, and this is indeed the situation with regard to the Croatian people.

Dominated by foreign powers for too many centuries, the Croatians have developed a rather negative attitude toward any political authority. This does not mean that they reject leaders in the political or any other sphere; on the contrary, they experience a real need to be led. But instead of giving to their leaders organized support, they give them their love and faith. Leaders are accepted on emotional grounds, because of their personal charm, their selfless service to national ideals and to their identification with the people's dreams. They are expected to perform wonderful deeds and to achieve goals literally by themselves; they are looked upon by their neighbors as heroes who possess extraordinary or even superhuman powers.

Another vice opposed to brotherly love is religious intolerance (*nesnošljivost*). Interfaith conflicts are likely to arise in a pluralistic society. Since it is not possible for all religions to be true, and since every man thinks his own religion is the true one, it is an easy step to the conclusion that other faiths, being wrong, have no right to exist. Besides, every religion is expansive in its nature and seeks new adherents in order to show them the way of salvation. As long as this is done peacefully, using persuasion and good example, religious intolerance is not likely to be aroused; but quarreling, fighting, and the use of power and coercion in inter-religious relations represent the type of religious intolerance to which we refer.

Catholics, Moslems, and Orthodox in Croatia have held firmly to their own religions and have become extremely sensitive about any interference from the religions of their countrymen; they have often refused to have any connections with the members of another faith, even in civic life. True, all agree that the use of force is an unsuitable method of spreading religion and that faith cannot and must not be forced upon anyone, that it is a gift from God which must be freely accepted. Yet in spite of this, history reveals us many examples of misdirected zeal, by which the believers of one faith forced their religion on others.

The struggles between Croatians of the Catholic faith and those of the Moslem faith lasted for four centuries. Both groups have remained faithful and firm in their religions. Bosnian Moslems, as an elite vanguard of the Turkish Empire, invaded the last remnants of the Croatian Catholic territory from the fifteenth to the nineteenth century in an attempt to include all of Croatia in the Moslem world. Such zeal and missionary fervor, such fidelity to Islam, has not been seen since medieval times. Nonetheless, Croatians of the Catholic belief defended every inch of their land staunchly, fought and died "for the honorable cross and their precious freedom." No wonder that the many memories of the past are still vivid enough to foment distrust and mutual suspicions among the Croatian people.

The Orthodox who fled from the Turks, or who were brought into Croatia by the Turks, lived in peace with the older native inhabitants until the last century. Then active propaganda from Belgrade was started among them, and it was said that they were Serbs because they shared the same religion as the residents of Serbia; their loyalty, therefore, was not to their native land of Croatia, but to Serbia (where religion and nation have been identified, to the detriment of the former). The propaganda was successful. The Orthodox sided first with Khuen Hedervary, the ban in Zagreb who was forced on the Croatians by the Hungarians in the years 1883–1903. First the Hungarians and then the Austrians heaped privileges on the Orthodox. When the new state of Serbs, Croatians, and Slovenes came into existence in 1918, and the Serbs began to make out of it an enlarged or Greater Serbia, they found, amid growing Croatian opposition, loyal helpers among the Orthodox. During the years of the last war, when the Croatians established their own state on the ruins of Yugoslavia, the Orthodox professed their loyalty to the exiled Yugoslav government in London. Thus they joined the ranks of Serbian Chetniks, under the leadership of General Draža Mihajlović, and fought Catholics and Moslems enlisted in the ranks of the armed forces of their new state, in the Domobran army and the Ustasha Militia.

The time for bloody revenge seemed to both sides to have arrived then and there. The civil war, inspired by political and religious differences, broke out in all its brutality. Hate blinded both sides. Atrocities were perpetrated daily by each side; the Chetniks specialized in exterminating the Moslem and Catholic population, and the Ustashas retaliated against the Orthodox population. In addition, the Communist Tito, the leader of a small group of Partisans, advanced quickly when the Allies endorsed his cause, late in 1943. Tito ably exploited the bloody conflicts among the three religions and between the two political plans (the Croatian and the Yugoslavian) in order to insure a full post-war victory for his Communist Party. Meanwhile, German and Italian troops sided with one or another of the three contenders, in the hope that the mutual bleeding would help their cause in the

Balkans. Hell broke loose over Croatia; death and the destruction of property, roads, and railroads spread across the mountains, plains, and coastal areas. The victory of Tito in 1945 imposed silence on all other Yugoslavian groups and raised the Communist cause above all other interests and struggles. Since then, religion has been forced to limit itself to ritual observance, and the desire for political independence has been ruthlessly suppressed.

A few words on the Reformation in Croatia are perhaps appropriate here. When the teachings of John Calvin spread through Hungary and started to gain a foothold in Croatia, the Croatians soon girded themselves to stop any penetration by these new doctrines. The Croatian Diet formulated a law in 1567 that "everyone who leaves the Catholic religion be proscribed, and that he should not be allowed to possess any personal or real estates, to occupy any position, or to have any decoration in the kingdom of Croatia and Slavonia."[14] When the Hungarians tried to spread Calvinism in Croatia by passing a law at the Diet in Pressburg (Bratislava) in 1597, the Croatian Ban Ivan Drašković (1596–1608) stood adamant against such an intrusion. He declared that he would rather separate the whole of his realm (Croatia and Slavonia) from the union with the Hungarian crown than let into Croatia, while he was its ban, that plague, deadly to souls, and most fatal to the country.[15] In 1609, Ban Toma Erdedi Bakač unsheathed his sword before the Hungarian and Croatian representatives in the Diet at Pressburg, and said about Calvinism: "With this sword—if it cannot be done otherwise—we shall defend ourselves against that plague. We have three rivers the Drava, Sava and Kupa. We shall have our new guests drink one of them."[16]

The Croatian Diet, in an effort to keep out the Calvinist brand of Christianity—already legally accepted in Hungary—repeatedly stated in subsequent decrees at the beginning of the seventeenth century that it recognized only the Roman Catholic religion in Croatia and Slavonia, and ordered heretics (Calvinists) expelled from its lands.

[14]Kocijanić, *Pape i hrvatski narod*, 56.

[15]Georgius Rattkay, *Memoria regum et banorum regnorum Dalmatiae, Croatiae et Sclavoniae inchoata ab origine sua, et usque ad presentem annum MDCLII deducta.* Vienna, 1652. We have used the Viennese edition of 1772. The text is found on page 169: ". . . se malle cum universo Regno ab unione Hungaricae Coronae separari, quam mortiferam illam animarum pestem, ac funestissimam Reipublicae labem sub Banatu suo admissam aut concessam videre."

[16]Rattkay, *Memoria regum*, 148–9. The text reads as follows: "hoc, inquit, ferro, si aliter fieri non poterit, pestem istam a nobis eliminabimus, tresque nobis adsunt fluvii Dravus, Savus, et Colapis, e quibus unum novis hospitibus sorbendum dabimus."

This special law of the Croatian Diet, different from and opposed to that of the Pressburg Diet, was ratified by King Rudolph of Hapsburg (1576–1608) on January 16, 1608, and by his successor Matthias II (1608–1619) on December 6, 1608.[17] Those times, however, are gone and forgotten. Once the Protestants finally came to Croatia they lived there undisturbed. The Croatians saw clearly that their country had become a land of many creeds and that a spirit of love is the most suitable one to inspire good mutual relations among Croatians of different faiths.

Sense of Justice

Another deep-seated ethical characteristic of the Croatian people is its sense of justice (*pravda*). This small nation, so often endangered by great and powerful neighbors desirous of satisfying their imperialistic longings in Croatia, whetted its sense of justice. The Croatians themselves have not claimed neighboring territories, but they have fiercely defended their own land against aggressive neighbors. Throughout their history they have faithfully followed the simple and basic law of justice: to each, his own.

This same sense of justice is found among the people with regard to their dealings in internal affairs. They have often made laws to secure and promote justice. Croatian laws were first proposed in assemblies, where clergy, noblemen, and commoners would meet and decide on particular legal principles and measures. Examples of collections of laws made in this way are the *Methodos* in the ninth century, ratified at Duvno Polje in Bosnia in 753;[18] the *Vinodol Code* (*Zakon Vinodolski*, 1280)[19]; and the *Poljica Statute* (1460).[20] These, and

[17]Ferdo Šišić (ed.), *Monumenta spectantia historiam Slavorum meridionalium.* Vol. XLI (*Acta comitialia regni Croatiae Dalmatiae Slavoniae.* Vol. IV: 1578 to 1608). The supplement for the years 1573–1605 is also found in this volume (Zagreb: Yugoslav Academy, 1917). Pp. xxii + 603. The text of the law of the Croatian Diet of July 5, 1604, stating its wish to uphold the Roman Catholic religion to the exclusion of Calvinist infiltration, is found on pages 449–450. The ratification by King Rudolph of Hapsburg is found on page 496. The ratification of the same law by King Matthias II is contained in vol. V, 9–10 of *Acta comitialia.*

[18]Dominik Mandić, "Hrvatski Sabor na Duvanjskom Polju godine 753" / Croatian Diet on Duvno Polje in the Year 753, *Hrvatska Revija* I (Buenos Aires, 1957), 5–40. See the discussion on *Methodos*, p. 34. See also pages 367–369 in Mandić, "Nenapisano poglavlje hrvatske pismenosti" / Unwritten Chapter on Croatian Letters, *Hrvatska Revija* IV (1961).

[19]The text of the *Vinodol Code* has been critically edited by R. Strohal, in *Mjesečnik Pravničkog Društva u Zagrebu*, 1912. We have used a reprint from this monthly, entitled "Zakon Vinodolski–Uvod, Tekst i Tumač" / The Vinodol Code–Introduction, Text, and Commentary.

[20]The text of the *Poljica Statute* was published in *Monumenta Historico-iuridica*

many other codes which have been preserved, point to the high legal consciousness of their composers. The code of Vinodol, for instance, expresses in its fifth, sixth, and seventh sections a deep understanding of humanity in the way it solves questions concerning public order and the security of property; there are well-established fines for stealing another's property, but there is no capital punishment attached to any crime. Only crimes against the prince and his court were punishable by death if the prince so deemed. Feudal law in feudal times!

After the fourteenth century, the Croatian people made their laws through their representatives, the clergy, nobility, and guild delegates in the Diet. Once a law had been made and promulgated in their Diet, it had a binding force on all—lawmakers and common people alike. The ruling group of citizens had to fulfill their well-defined duties toward the people, just as the people had to perform their duties towards the government. When the king, the emperor, or the nobility did not act in accordance with justice, the people became restless and ready to revolt.

From the end of the fifteenth century, the Croatian peasants continually revolted against the feudal impositions of their landlords and sought the justice and liberty established in pre-feudal days. This demand for the "Old Justice" (*Stare pravice*) went on for many centuries and culminated in 1753, when a northern Croatian peasant from Stubica, Matija Gubec, led the most famous of these revolts. Although the revolt did not succeed and its leader was killed, Gubec remains in Croatian history as a symbol of the struggle against injustice.

Dr. Ante Starčević felt this deep sense of justice in his people when, in the nineteenth century, he founded the Party of Right; its main purpose was the vindication of the right of the Croatian people to be an autonomous political entity in the Austro-Hungarian Empire. Similarly, in the twentieth century, the largest political party among Croatians between the two world wars, the "Croatian Peasant Party," took as the motto of its legal struggle: "For Justice and Humanity." This party was founded in 1904 by the brothers Ante and Stjepan Radić.

Slavorum meridionalium, Vol. IV: *Statuta lingua croatica conscripta* (Zagreb: Yugoslav Academy, 1890). Pp. lxxxii + 265. In this volume are found the statutes of Vinodol, Poljica, Vrban, the island of Krk, and the towns of Kastav, Veprinac, and Trsat. The material has been edited by Dr. Franjo Rački, Dr. Vatroslav Jagić, and Dr. Ivo Crnčić.

Harmony, Order, Peace

Perhaps the most significant ethical trait among Croatians is their striving for harmony (*sklad*), order (*red*), and peace (*mir*). Throughout the long centuries of their history, the Croatians have shown reverence for the blessings of order and peace. This should be credited to the fact that they entered the circle of western European nations very early in their history through their christening in the seventh and eighth centuries; this cultural and religious affiliation has deeply embedded into their minds Greek harmony, Roman order, and Christian peace. Christianity tamed the Croatians from the dawn of their history on the shores of the Adriatic Sea. Not only did Christianity start their cultural history, but also it laid the foundation for their ethical civilization and their assimilation to the West.

The tragedy of Croatia's longing for peace is written in many bloody wars imposed on the nation throughout its history. The Croatians' own fighting has been defensive; to them, war is a great disaster and causes only a loss of material and spiritual values. It should be avoided at all cost and may be resorted to only when necessary to repel aggression. Although small in area, the republics of Dubrovnik and Poljica were prototypes of a harmonious, an orderly, and a peaceful world. The *Statute of Poljica*, already mentioned, is a legal document showing a democratic functioning of the ruling group in their relations with commoners, serfs, foreigners, and slaves. Ivan Gundulić (1589–1638) presented Dubrovnik's view of the world in his drama *Dubravka*, in which Dubrovnik's ideal was revealed in its social and spiritual harmony,[21] order, and peace.

Freedom

Another ethical value treasured by the Croatians is freedom (*sloboda*), which they have always sought, though never at the expense of the freedom of other nations. The Croatians have constantly tried to harmonize their desire and struggle for liberty with ethical principles. Freedom to them is simply the necessary atmosphere in which both national and individual personalities can be fully and freely developed. The Croatians have also wanted freedom for other nations and never have become oppressors; they have sympathized with all nations in

[21]It is interesting to note that the Croatian word *skladan* (courteous) has a richer meaning in the usage of Dubrovnik than elsewhere. In Dubrovnik it means not only "courteous," but also "the whole harmonious and balanced personality." *Rječnik hrvatskoga ili srpskoga jezika* / Dictionary of the Croatian or Serbian Language (Zagreb: Yugoslav Academy, 1880–1958). See the entry *skladan*, under *D*.

their struggle for freedom and independence. Ukrainian, Polish, Slovak, and Macedonian patriots are able to count many friends among the Croatians.

Croatian repugnance to foreign domination is well known. For many centuries all the political powers of Byzantium, Venice, Vienna, Budapest, and Belgrade found the subduing of the Croatians an exceptionally difficult task. The Croatians have spent much of their history offering stubborn resistance to foreign powers who attempted to take away their national culture and to impose an alien language, even an alien national consciousness upon them. The Italianization, Germanization, Magyarization, and Serbization of Croatia has succeeded to a very minor extent; the Croatians have survived all of the trials and ordeals received at the hands of foreign powers. For this they have paid a high price in blood and sorrow, however.

Freedom is apt to be fully appreciated only when it is once or even often lost, and then won back with difficulty. This is the history of the Croatians, a history of tears in Croatian homes and on battlefields—all for freedom. "Better to drop into the grave than to become a slave" is a popular folk saying of theirs.[22] To the Croatians freedom is second only to their religion. Thus this motto in their centuries-long struggle with the Turks: "For the venerable cross and precious freedom."[23]

The free Republic of Dubrovnik possessed a full appreciation of its freedom. On the white flag of this republic, which sailed on many seas from the sixteenth to the nineteenth centuries, the Latin word for freedom, *libertas*, was inscribed. Above the entrance to the fortress Lovrijenac, which was used to defend the city of Dubrovnik from the sea, there is still a Latin inscription which reads: *Non bene pro toto libertas venditur auro* (Freedom should not be sold for all the gold [in the world]). The first hymn to liberty in European literature was composed in Dubrovnik.[24] Ivan Gundulić, at the end of his *Dubravka*, enthusiastically praises freedom in these terms:

> O beautiful, O precious, O sweet liberty;
> Gift in which the Lord gave us all riches;
> You are the true cause of all our glory;
> You are the splendor of this Dubrava.[25]

[22]In Croatian: *Bolje pasti u grob, nego biti rob!*

[23]In Croatian: *Za krst časni i slobodu zlatnu!*

[24]Josip Horvat, *Kultura Hrvata kroz 1.000 godina* / A Thousand Years of Croatian Culture (Zagreb, 1939), 363.

[25]*Dubrava* is the poetic name for the then city-republic of Dubrovnik (Ragusa).

All silver, all gold, all human lives
Cannot pay for your pure beauty![26]

Work and Recreation

The Croatian feels that all honest work (*rad*) is worthy of respect. He develops justifiable pride, strength, and self-confidence in working for his family and regards laziness as a dishonorable way of life. As a rule, he has to work hard to gain the necessities of life. Nevertheless, with the exception of the population in Slavonia and Upper Croatia, work is not generally looked upon as an all-obliging duty, but often rather as something of a necessary evil. It is too hard in the fields, too distasteful in the factory, and too monotonous in the office. Many Croatians do not seem to realize that the raising of economic standards in their own lives depends primarily upon the rational division of tasks among the people who must do their part of the work effectively. The Croatians are, however, rightly resentful when forced labor is imposed upon them in order to achieve common goals.

It is interesting to point here to an attitude manifested by many of the Croatian intelligentsia toward manual work. In a recent book on Poland this attitude was described with regard to the Polish intelligentsia. Because of the similar line of thought of these two groups on this point, the following excerpt from this volume, *Poland: Its People, Its Society, Its Culture*, is relevant. One might justifiably substitute the phrase "old Croatian nobility" for "old Polish nobility":

> Among the intelligentsia there is a tendency to look down on any kind of physical labor. The type of work which is most valued is that which involves intellectual activity. A sharp distinction is made between the "life of the spirit" and the "gray life" of everyday existence. Having absorbed many of the traits and attitudes of the old Polish nobility, the *szhlachta*, the intelligentsia tend to view themselves as the "aristocrats of thought and spirit". Learning and education are viewed as ends in themselves. To have broad intellectual interests is a mark of "culture" and sophistication, but little emphasis is placed on the practical use of one's knowledge, despite the government's effort to popularize vocational training.[27]

[26]In Croatian: O lijepa, o draga, o slatka slobodo, / dar u kom sva blaga višnji nam Bog je do, / uzroče istini od naše sve slave, / uresu jedini od ove Dubrave, / sva srebra, sva zlata, svi ljucki životi / ne mogu bit plata tvoj čistoj ljepoti! *Stari pisci hrvatski* / Ancient Croatian Writers (*Djela Gjiva Frana Gundulića* / Works of Gjivo Franjo Gundulić, Book 9). Third edition. Edited by Djuro Körbler and revised by Milan Rešetar. (Zagreb: Yugoslav Academy, 1938), 318.

[27]Clifford R. Barnett, *Poland: Its People, Its Society, Its Culture* (New York: Grove Press, Inc., 1958), 406. Acknowledgment is made to the author and to the original publisher of this book, Human Relations Area Files, Inc., for granting permission to quote from this book.

This trend of high esteem for the intellectual at the expense of vocational work has resulted from a type of education which was highly valued in Croatia between the world wars. The humanities have been decidedly more valued than vocational training by the small fragment of population geared to higher education. The humanities—law, philosophy, the communication arts, science, history, and geography—train students first to think and judge critically, then to plan an action, but do not particularly teach students how to carry out this plan. Ideas —original or common, great or small—are held in much more esteem than their application to life.

The Croatians enjoy life in general and recreation in particular. The folksong accompanies the work of the peasant and is sung in praise of plowing, sowing, harvesting, weaving, and housework; all of these agrarian and domestic activities have been idealized in poetry and song. Weddings, baptisms, feast-days, and religious holydays are occasions for the hard-working peasant to celebrate. Even funerals provide opportunities to meet friends and to invite them to an abundant table. Dancing, singing, and playing are inseparable from these celebrations. Drinking and toasting, usually with a home-made wine, have very elaborate rules, and the Statutes of Križevci (*Križevački Statuti*) are noteworthy in this connection. Besides all of this, the people living in cities find their entertainment in sports, movies, the drama, and opera.

One of the most cherished Croatian recreational activities is a conversation (*razgovor*) in friendly circles. Radio and television began to interfere only recently with the long and ardent hours spent in the enjoyment of the art of conversation. Nor do the Croatians converse only about business outlooks and about present or contemporary problems; their favorite topics are those related to the national past and to future political interests and the effect of international affairs on national politics.

Fighting for Values

An understanding of the true meaning of life and of the special mission of an individual and of a nation is the most powerful stimulus in the struggle (*borba*) to attain the goals of life. Such a struggle is not a simple discharge of surplus energy; rather, it is a positive activity in the service of higher ideals. The goals of the Croatians throughout the centuries of their struggles have been their indestructible values: freedom, justice, and the security of home and country. Once these ethical values are placed above material goals, they demand sacrifice and heroism. This is the reason behind the heroic struggles of the Croatians. They have very often had to exchange the plowshare for the sword or gun in order to preserve their country and their own lives. Ethical values become stronger when adhered to through many struggles; in striving for higher goals, the moral personality is built up to unsuspected heights. In fateful moments, in wars, in the midst of ruin, in the face of persecution and death, individuals and groups may suddenly reveal a moral power which they could never have imagined in peacetime. "Hardship reveals heroes" is a common saying of the Croatian people.[28]

Croatian heroism has been acclaimed in modern times throughout all of Europe. There were few wars in Europe in which the Croatians did not participate and in which they did not behave heroically. But those far-flung struggles were in the service of foreign commanders and their particular aims. The main struggle, of course, was at home, in the defense of the homeland against the Turkish invasion. The Croatian military leaders—the Šubićs, the Berislavićs, the Nelipićs, the Zrinskis, and the Frankopans—were real heroes, and they were recognized as such by the great military figures of Europe, Napoleon I, Frederick II, Peter the Great, and the Ottoman sultan, Suleiman I, the Magnificent.

We shall cite only two examples of heroic Croatian resistance to the Turkish invasions. In 1566, with only a small troop of selected soldiers, Nikola Zrinski dared to resist a huge Turkish army from the fortress of Sziget in Hungary. Before the decisive battle, he spurred his fighters on by swearing that he would live and die together with them, and his soldiers all swore the same oath. The next day, he and almost all of his followers were killed in battle. A second example of Croatian courage occurred in 1595, when the Turks threw their tremendous armed might against the stronghold of Petrinja near Sisak, and were repelled by the Croatians at the walls of the city. The commanders and fighters in the besieged town urged each other to fight until death ". . . for the Christian faith, for the Catholic religion, for their homes, for their wives and children, for their most valued possessions, for the welfare and preservation of their beloved Fatherland. . . ."[29]

28In Croatian: *Na muci se poznaju junaci.*

29Rattkay, *Memoria regum*, 157–8. The full text in Latin reads as follows (italicized parts are those quoted above in English): "Eia boni socii! masculo pectore nunc est opus, quando extremam fati nostri videmus imminere horam, et ideo antequam aut turpiter occumbamus, aut certe in immanissimam abducamur servitutem, pugnemus fortiter imprimis *pro fide Christiana, pro Religione Catholica, pro aris, pro focis, pro coniugibus, liberis, charissimisque pignoribus, pro salute*

In the sixteenth, seventeenth, and eighteenth centuries, the Turks devastated and dissected Croatia, reducing her to a state of *reliquiae reliquiarum* of the once famous Croatian kingdom. However, they were never quite able to subdue her military might and consequently never succeeded in occupying all of Croatia. Struggle and suffering have only led the Croatians to love their faith and freedom, their homes and homeland with greater intensity.

The Dignity of Man

Croatians, bearing the influence of Christianity, honor the dignity of the human person. They consider the greatest of all goods to be man himself; man is an intelligent and free individual worthy of respect. The Croatian is not a gregarious person and dislikes being looked upon as one of a mass. He thinks with his own mind, feels with his own heart, and is proud of his thoughts and his freedom. It is said that three Croatians in a group will always represent three political parties—a fact which emphasizes their independent thinking about common issues. The civic and, to some extent, religious conformity imposed on modern man finds an unsympathetic reception among the Croatians.

Slavery, as a condition completely contrary to the dignity of the human person, has not been favored by the Croatians in their history. In the Middle Ages, the Croatian king, Zvonimir (1074–1089), pledged himself under oath to "oppose the slave trade"[30] in his lands, which lay

denique, atque conservatione Patriae dulcissimae; nam nulla iam superest nobis futura via, praeter dextras et virtutem, victi nullam speremus salutem."

[30]Prince Zvonimir took this oath in the Church of St. Peter in Salona in 1076, when he was crowned Croatian king by Gebizo, a legate of Pope Gregory VII. The content of the oath has a special significance, in that it contains very advanced moral and social reforms for those times. Here is the complete Latin text of the oath of King Zvonimir; the italicized parts indicate the reforms to which Zvonimir pledged himself: "In nomine sancte et individue Trinitatis. Anno dominice incarnationis millesimo LXXVI, indictione XIV, mense octobris. Ego Demetrius, qui et Suinimir nuncupor, dei gratia Croatie Dalmatieque dux, a te Domino Gebizo, ex apostolice sedis legatione Domini nostri pape Gregorii potestatem obtinente, in salonitana basilica sancti Petri synodali et concordi totius cleri et populi electione de Chroatorum Dalmatinorumque regni regimine per uexillum, ensem, sceptrum et coronam inuestitus atque constitutus rex, tibi deuoueo, spondeo et polliceor, me incommutabiliter completurum omnia, que mihi sua reuerenda iniungit sanctitas, uidelicet ut in omnibus et per omnia apostolice sedi fidem obseruem; et quidquid hoc in regno tam apostolica sedes quam sui legati sanxerunt aut sanxerint, irreuocabiliter custodiam; *iustitiam excolam, ecclesias defendam; primitie, decime, omniumque ad ecclesiam pertinentium procurator existam; uite episcoporum, presbyterorum, diaconorum, subdiaconorumque, ut caste et regulariter uiuant, prouideam; pauperes, uiduas atque pupillos protegam; parentelle illicitam copulam destruens legitimam dotem annulo sacerdotisque benedictione constituam et constitutam corrumpi non permittam; hominum uenditioni contradicam; atque in omnibus que*

on the crossroads between Byzantium and Western Europe. The *Statute of Poljica* contained humane laws for the treatment of slaves. The Republic of Dubrovnik abolished the slave trade in the year 1416, at a time when slavery flourished all over the Balkan Peninsula (and would continue to flourish until the nineteenth century). The Ragusans justified their act in the following significant words, found in the decree of their Greater Council: "We consider such trade to be base, evil, and abominable, against all humanity, and to bring a great burden and disgrace to our city, that human beings, made in the image and likeness of our Creator are treated as merchandise and sold, as it were, like animals."[31]

Epic folk poetry often mentions honor (*čast*), face (*obraz*), and honesty (*poštenje*), three of the values treasured by the Croatians, all of which are connected with personal dignity.[32] In the patriarchal joint family of peasants and shepherds, honor was regarded as the highest value. Such a value is an extremely personal one: every adult male acquires or loses it on account of his good or bad conduct. A heroic moral code from pre-Christian times determines what is honorable and what is dishonorable in one's conduct. In Croatian feudal society, honor and dignity were class privileges. However, an individual could lose it if he did not live up to class standards. The National Awakening in the nineteenth century introduced a collective type of honor for the whole

---

ad rectitudinis statum congruunt, deo auctore, me equum exhibeam. . . ." See Franjo Rački, *Documenta historiae croaticae periodum antiquam illustrantia* (Zagreb, 1877), 103–4.

King Zvonimir undertook to carry out the following social and moral reforms in his kingdom: to practice justice for all, to defend the churches, and see that they received their rightful share of contributions from the faithful; to see to it that the clergy lived chaste and orderly lives; to protect the poor, the widows, and the orphans; to end the practice of marriage between close relatives, and to provide a dowry so that marriages could be celebrated in churches with a ring and the benediction of a priest; to oppose the slave trade; and to do, with the help of God, all that honesty and integrity required.

[31]"Considerantes talem mercantiam esse turpem, nefariam et abominabilem et contra omnem humanitatem et cedere ad non paruum onus et infamiam ciuitatis nostre, videlicet quod humana species, facta ad imaginem et similitudinem creatoris nostri, conuerti debeat in usus mercimoniales et vendatur, tamquam si essent animalia bruta." See Constantin Jireček, "Die Bedeutung von Ragusa in der Handelsgeschichte des Mittelalters," *Die Feierliche Sitzung der Kaiserlichen Akademie der Wissenschaften* (Vienna, May 31, 1899), 193, n. 58.

[32]Jovan Brkić, *Moral Concepts in Traditional Serbian Epic Poetry* ('s-Gravenhage, The Netherlands: Mouton and Co., 1961). Pp. 177. The author analyzes the concepts of honor, faith, and treason (ch. 4 pp. 99–110), examining the epic folk poetry of the Dinaric tribes in Montenegro and Eastern Hercegovina. The same values can be noted among the Croatian people in Bosnia and western Hercegovina, as well as in other Croatian regions.

nation. Personal, class, and national honor could be achieved only by complying with the moral code of the particular society, be it patriarchal, feudal, or national. Dishonor (*sramota*), bad reputation (*crn obraz*), and the charge of dishonesty (*nepoštenje*), attributed to a person who commits immoral deeds, are the greatest disgraces a Croatian can suffer.[33]

Croatians feel that human dignity and honor demand their faithfulness (*vjera, vjernost*) to an oath or a pledge, contract, or pact, and more especially to a person. They regard the breach of a pledge, or unfaithfulness (*nevjera*), as shame or disgrace (*sramota*), and, in military life, as treason (*izdaja*), to be punished exemplarily. However, conflict between two loyalties could arise. Two examples might be taken from early Croatian history to illustrate this point. Ljudevit Posavski (*c.* 810–823), a ruler of Pannonian Croatia, tried to throw off the Frankish yoke and succeeded in challenging the Franks for two years. However, Duke Borna (*c.* 810–821), a ruler of Dalmatian Croatia, and a Frankish vassal, allied himself with the Franks and fought against Ljudevit, the unfaithful Frankish vassal. The people, faced with this conflict of loyalties, looked upon Ljudevit as a hero and Borna as a traitor.[34]

A second example of this kind of dilemma involves King Zvonimir, who kept until death the emphatic and solemn formula of the oath used in medieval treaties, "I do firmly pledge" (*Deuoueo, spondeo et polliceor*), which he made to Pope Gregory VII on the occasion of his coronation on October 9, 1076.[35] His mysterious death (1089) in the field near Knin has often been attributed to overzealous loyalty to his oath, by which he tried to provide men and arms for the Crusades organized by Pope Urban II (1088–1099). The people saw in Zvonimir's foreign policies a danger to their own existence.[36]

In heroic folksongs, the word of honor (*časna riječ* or *besjeda*) is the

[33]Valtasar Bogišić, *Zbornik Sadašnjih Pravnih Običaja u Južnih Slovena: Gragja u odgovorima iz različitih krajeva Slovenskoga Juga* (Zagreb: Yugoslav Academy, 1874), 576. Bogišić has collected opinions of people in different Croatian regions on the topics of honor and dishonor. He used the following questions in his inquiry: What is the view of the people concerning honor and dishonor? Do they prefer severe penalties to disgrace? The answers which he obtained are listed according to the different regions in which they were collected. The great majority of those questioned answered that they held honor in high esteem and would prefer even a severe penalty to loss of honor.

[34]Francis R. Preveden, *A History of the Croatian People*, I (New York, 1955), 52–53.

[35]Rački, *Documenta*, 104, n. 30.

[36]Preveden, *History*, 85–86.

highest pledge a knight or hero may give. If he breaks his word, a hero, or any other violator, loses his honor and falls into disgrace (*sramota*). High esteem for the word of honor is shown, for instance, in the folksong *Banović Strahinja*,[37] in which Ban Strahinić, a Croatian hero, meets an old dervish, his former prisoner. Here, as in many other cases, the breach of a pledge is regarded not only as a social dishonor and shame but as a moral offense as well.[38]

As a rule, the Croatians have shown, throughout their history, great fidelity to their collective treaties and pledges. The Catholic Croatians have often been singled out for their loyalty to the Roman Church. Pope John X (914–928) called them "very special sons of the Holy Roman Church" (*specialissimi filii sanctae Romanae Ecclesiae*);[39] Pope Leo X (1513–1521) honored them with the title "bulwark of Christianity" (*antemurale Christianitatis*);[40] and the late Pope John XXIII, in a eulogy on the late Cardinal Stepinac referred to "fervent and pious Croatia."[41] However, historic pressures, as well as today's political conditions, have estranged a good number of Croatians from their ancestral faith.

Croatian soldiers, fighting in foreign armies on many European battlegrounds in the past, have distinguished themselves by fidelity to their military oaths. Napoleon employed Croatian regiments in his Russian campaign (1812), and he valued their military virtues and their faithfulness.[42] The Austrian emperors looked on the Croatians as their trustworthy and loyal subjects. The Military Frontier (*Vojna Krajina*) in Croatia was for centuries the best defense of the Austro-Hungarian Empire. Loyalty to their country has cost the Croatians immense material and spiritual sacrifice. The conquerors of their country have perceived the unshaken faith of the Croatians and have tried to minimize this moral force by calling it "stubbornness" or "irrational idealism" at various times. The fact is that Croatian history consists in the struggle of the people for their freedom—religious, political, economic, and social.

[37]*Serbocroatian Heroic Songs: Novi Pazar, Serbocroatian Texts.* Collected by Milman Parry, and edited by Albert Bates Lord (Belgrade-Cambridge, 1953) II, 2, p. 34.

[38]Bogišić, *Zbornik*, 452 f.

[39]Ferdo Šišić, *Priručnik izvora hrvatske historije* / Handbook of Sources of Croatian History, Vol. I, Part 1: To the year 1107 (Zagreb, 1914), 215.

[40]*Croazia Sacra* (Rome, 1943), 20–21. This is a symposium of monographs on the personality of the Catholic Croatians.

[41]*L'Osservatore Romano*, Vatican City, February 18, 1960.

[42]*Naša Domovina* (Zagreb, 1943), 197.

Vices Opposed to Human Dignity

A number of vices pose real threats to the self-respect and dignity of the Croatians. Alcoholism, not only as an individual, but also as a social vice, is all too prevalent among the people. Unfortunately, no statistics are available to picture more specifically the evil caused to both body and spirit by the immoderate use of such alcoholic beverages as brandy, wine, and beer in Croatia. Nonetheless, it is certain that this vice has spread throughout the country, and that it is especially prevalent in Srijem, Slavonia, and Bosnia, and less widespread, but nevertheless existing, in Croatian Zagorje, Northern Croatia, Dalmatia, Lika, and Hercegovina.

A vice almost unknown in Croatia before this century, which has spread throughout the country between the world wars, is that of the use of vulgar expressions. These originated in, and continue to come from, the neighboring countries to the east of Croatia. This vice is definitely a degrading one with respect to the cultural level of the nation and to the dignity of its citizens.

Finally, another vice should be mentioned, which is of a more anti-religious nature, that of blasphemy and cursing: blasphemy (*hula* or *bogo-hulenje*) dishonors God, and cursing (*kletva*), is an utterance by which one wishes that evil befall one's fellow man. These two habits contribute to the lowering of the moral and religious level of the Croatian nation. Blasphemy is especially prevalent in Dalmatia and Dalmatian Zagora, and cursing in Croatian Zagorje and Northern Croatia. The Croatian Diet has formulated several decisions against blasphemy and cursing,[43] and during the last war a law was passed concerning these two vices, and the Church has also often used its parish missions to fight them.

The Morality of Social Relations

The Family and Kinship

For the Croatians, a physically and morally healthy family life is the foundation of the national life. Owing to the custom, once common, of a large joint family (*zadruga*) living under the same head—usually the

[43]For example, the law against blasphemy formulated at the Hungarian-Croatian Diet at Pressburg in 1563, repeated and reinforced by the Croatian Diet in 1756. Fraknoj, Vilmos, *Monumenta comitalia Regni Hungariae.* Magyar Ország-gyülési Emlékek 1557–1563. (Budapest, 1876), 596.

oldest male—the Croatians have developed a sort of cult of the family and the nearest of kin.[44]

In modern times, the foundations of the patriarchal type of family all over the world have been shaken. The Croatian family has not escaped the influence of the modern age, but most of the older familial habits and values have remained.

Croatian parents have the final decision in the choice of the spouse for their sons and daughters. The parents take into consideration the family backgrounds and the individual qualities of the young man and woman involved. A young man contemplating marriage, they feel, should like work and be thrifty; a young lady ought to be skilled in the ways of housekeeping, and should have a humble and submissive nature. The requisite virtues of a marriageable young lady, Croatian parents believe, include modesty, innocence, patience, and a capacity for enduring work. She is expected, in short, to be able to look after her household.

The customs surrounding a Croatian wedding ceremony, in both home and church, create a dramatic effect upon the newly-weds, one which remains in their memory for the rest of their lives. The family hearth is considered sacred among the rural people, who still make up at least one-half of the Croatian people. Strict discipline is practised in the education of children, and they are taught to respect and obey their parents and their grandparents. As a rule, a child is looked on as a blessing from God. A large family is felt to be a foundation of economic strength in the rural areas, since technological advances have been

[44]This may be illustrated by the rich variety of kinship terms in Croatian. The family circle is widely extended to include relatives on both sides. In addition, the best man (*vjenčani kum*) and the bridesmaid (*djeveruša*), the godfather (*kum*) and the godmother (*kuma*) are very close to the family members. God-parenthood (*kumstvo*) is an ancient institution that entails the lifelong obligation of godparents to their godchildren. In Dalmatia, every married woman in a village is an aunt, and every married man an uncle, to all the children there. Moreover, two persons may become very closely related to each other by mutual consent as brothers-by-friendship (*pobratimi*), or sisters-by-friendship (*posestrime*) or brother-sister-by-friendship. Their families must agree and recognize this relationship.

It is obvious that this practice of creating a large circle of family relations has its origin in the joint type of family (*zadruga*), once very common among Croatians. For kinship terms in Croatian among the people in Bosnia and Hercegovina, see Ivan Zovko, "Rodbinski nazivi u Herceg-Bosni," *Zbornik za narodni život i običaje Južnih Slavena*. Vol. 7, No. 2 (Zagreb: Yugoslav Academy, 1902), 369–381. The above entries, *kum, kuma*, *pobratim*, and *posestrima*, are explained in *Rječnik hrvatskoga ili srpskoga jezika* (Zagreb: Yugoslav Academy, 1880–1958). See also Vladimir Mažuranić, *Prinosi za hrvatski pravno-povijesni rječnik* (Zagreb: Yugoslav Academy, 1908–1922).

applied to farming only in a minor way as yet in Croatia. The virtues of family life are also praised in Croatian folksongs and poems. The most moving among these describe the love which unites the family members: the love of a mother for her children, of a sister for her brother, or the love shared by a young couple. The love of family members prescribes that one is always ready to put forth the greatest sacrifices and even to suffer death for the sacredness and honor of the family.

Although the birth-rate in Croatia is high in comparison with that of some European nations, birth control—keeping the family down to perhaps one or two children—is common in some parts of the country, especially in Slavonia, Srijem, and Northern Croatia. Other areas remained almost untouched by this practice between the world wars, but it would be hard to find any particular district where birth control is not in use today. Abortion has been practiced for some years in Slavonia, Bosnia, and Hercegovina, to some extent in Dalmatian Zagora, and in all of the cities of Croatia. After the last war, instances of abortion were widespread in Dalmatia, although no statistics as to its prevalence there are as yet available.[45]

The reasons why these methods of limiting births are used in Croatia are various, and it is interesting to note that economic grounds do not seem to be the most common ones. Slavonia and Srijem are the richest areas of the country, and yet the poorest districts—Lika, Hercegovina, and Dalmatia—have the most children. Slavonians often justify the limitation of the number of children in a family by their desire to have their property remain in the possession of one family and not to have it divided. But moral reasons are also very important here, and lack of instruction, moral sloth, and lack of faith often play large roles in this matter. The divorce rate in Croatia has expanded in the post-war years. Younger people tend to grow up without strong religious and moral education and often look upon divorce as the ever-present "out" for marriages which are not working well.

Patriotism

Croatians are known throughout the world for their patriotism. Next to his mother and his wife and family, the Croatian man loves his homeland (*domovina*) the most. For an explanation of such a deep patriotic love, one needs to turn to the sacrifices made and the tears and blood spilled for the homeland; everyone holds dearest that for which he has

[45]See Tomo Habdija, "Raširenost pobačaja u svijetu i kod nas i njegovi uzroci" / The Extent of Abortions throughout the World and Among Us, and Its Reasons, *Život* / Life, I (Zagreb, 1939), 39.

sacrificed the most. Another reason for the Croatians' strong patriotic love lies in the fact that fully one-half of them are rural people. The love which the man of the soil has for his land, and for his forests, rivers, and mountains, is universally known.

There is beauty in Croatia, and there is wealth; but there are also wastelands and poor farming areas. Many a Croatian peasant has to scrape together sufficient food for himself and his family from a small portion of poor land. Strangely enough, however, such frugality and intimate dependence on the land only causes the men to love their land even more. They look on it not primarily as a source of wealth, but as a source of food for sustaining life.

Croatian folk poems have been written in praise of many geographical features of the country, including rivers such as the Sava, Drava, Danube, Drina, Neretva, Cetina, and Kupa. Mountains that are frequently referred to are the Dinara, Velebit, Trebević, Plješevica, Jahorina, Vlašić, and Romanija. Among towns often cited we find Rijeka, Bakar, Senj, Zadar, Dubrovnik, Kotor, Kladuša, Klis, Mostar, Sarajevo, Banjaluka, Travnik, Bihać, Sisak, and Osijek. Also referred to in folk songs are whole regions of Croatia, for example, "flat" Srijem (*ravni Srijem*), "rich" Slavonia (*bogata Slavonija*), "wide" Posavina (*široka Posavina*), "little" Medjimurje (*malo Medjimurje*), "poor" Lika (*siromašna Lika*), Istria, "the orphan" (*sirotica Istra*), "proud" Bosnia (*Bosna ponosna*), "heroic" Hercegovina (*junačka Hercegovina*), and "small" Dalmatia (*malena Dalmacija*). The Croatian national anthem[46] immortalizes this intense love for the homeland, especially in its first two and its last two stanzas:

O beautiful, our homeland,
O valiant and beloved country.
Ancestral land of ancient glory,
May thou always live honorably!

We love thee, since thou are glorious to us,
We love thee, since thou art unique to us.
We love thee, where thou art a plain,
We love thee, where thou art a moutain!

[46]Composed by Antun Mihanović (1796–1861) in 1835, under the title *Horvatska Domovina* / Croatian Homeland. It was set to music by Josip Runjanin (1821–1878) in 1846, and was declared the national anthem in 1891. For the history and content of the Croatian national anthem, see the article "*Hrvatska himna*," by Vinko Nikolić, *Hrvatska Revija*, IV (Buenos Aires, 1955), 393–398. The same author has written in Spanish on this subject, in *Studia Croatica* I, 1 (Buenos Aires, 1960), 7–9. The Croatian national anthem is similar—in both inspiration and content—to the song that Americans consider their "second" national anthem, *America the Beautiful*, by Catherine Lee Bates and Samuel August Ward.

Flow, speedy Sava, flow,
Let not the Danube lose thy strength.
Wherever thou art murmuring, tell the world
That the Croatian shall love his home
While the sun warms his fields,
While the storm bends his oak trees,
While the grave hides his dead,
While his living heart beats![47]

The Nation

The Croatian people have striven for centuries to attain self-government and the independence of a national state. Before they came into the country along the Adriatic in the seventh century, they had their own state near Kraków, in present-day Poland. Soon after their arrival in their new homeland, they organized a state with national rulers, which lasted from the seventh century until the beginning of the twelfth century. Though in some degree combined with and under the rule of the Hungarians (since 1102) and the Austrians (since 1527), the Croatian people retained some attributes of statehood until the end of the First World War.

Croatia's struggle for political independence could very easily be compared with the American struggle for independence, for both efforts had a similar ethical background. It may be said, in the final analysis, that the Declaration of Independence amounts to this: that governments are not absolute but exist for the security of certain inalienable rights of their people, and that when a government fails in this task, it loses its authority and may be replaced. The government of the British Crown—the reasoning of the Declaration states—failed to perform its task in the United Colonies; on the contrary, it acted against its legitimate duties. Therefore, the British Crown lost its authority over its American subjects, who were as a consequence not merely free, but also had the duty to set up their own government. America threw off English mastery primarily because that ruling power did not fulfill the duties which a government has toward its citizens, the duties of protecting them and improving their prosperity. Thus, it was only ethical for a people to elect their own government, one which would better satisfy the demands of justice and the common good.

[47]In Croatian: Lijepa naša domovino, / Oj junačka zemljo mila. / Stare slave djedovino, / Da bi vazda časna bila! / Mila, kano si nam slavna, / Mila si nam ti jedina. / Mila, kuda si nam ravna, / Mila, kuda si planina! / Teci, Savo hitra, teci, / Nit' ti Dunav silu gubi. / Kud li šumiš, svijetu reci: / Da svog doma Hrvat ljubi / Dok mu njive sunce grije, / Dok mu hrašće bura vije. / Dok mu mrtve grob sakrije, / Dok mu živo srce bije!

The Croatian case is a similar one, in that the Croatians have borne much injustice from foreign governments. The list of injuries and injustices committed against them by regimes with headquarters in Vienna, Budapest, and Belgrade is too long to be recounted in detail here. The Croatians were halted in their material and spiritual development by foreigners who could not or would not sympathize with their needs. Therefore, although they possess the desire to remain good neighbors to everyone and to understand fully the ever-growing need for world union (but not merger!), they believe that a free democratic republic of their own is the best guarantee that they will be able to peacefully develop their own abilities, culture, and material resources.

The classical and Christian interpretation of the state is that it must make secure the common well-being of the people; the state is not established for the purpose of acquiring, preserving, and broadening the power of the governing group. In their Diet (Sabor), the Croatians themselves conducted their nation's business and decided whether to go into battle in order to defend their homeland; long ago they organized their own judicial system and elected their own ruling bodies. For these people, the state was a moral association with a moral goal: the common good of its citizens. Above the door of the Lower House (Malo Vijeće) in Dubrovnik, this inscription can still be found: *Obliti privatorum; publica curate*, that is, "Forget your private interests and see to the republic's interests." The rural republics of Poljica and Vinodol are two examples of widespread democratic government. A democratic interpretation of government is innate in the Croatians. They want their own government in order to make their own decisions concerning themselves and to develop themselves freely. They despise the idea of any form of tyranny, whether of their own or of foreign making.

This consciousness of a national state has remained alive among the Croatians through the course of many centuries. The folk poem, "Marina Kruna" (The Crown of Mary)[48] is generally interpreted symbolically as an expression of the deep sorrow of the Croatians for their lost kingdom, which fell to the Hungarians in 1102, and the longing of the nation to renew its independent state of the Middle Ages (before 1102). The poem begins with these moving lines:

A cold wind blew,
—O, darling mine—
A cold wind frowned.

[48]Petar Grgec, *Hrvatske narodne pjesme* / Croatian Folk Songs (Zagreb, 1943), 134.

It blew from the East,
To carry away Mary's crown.[49]

State and Church

In the Byzantine East, especially in the centuries closely preceding the Great Schism of 1054, there was no clear division between temporal (state) and spiritual (church) powers. Rather, there prevailed a system whereby an emperor held supreme control over the Church, even in those matters of faith and morals normally reserved for the Church authorities.

In Western Europe, when the Western Roman Empire crumbled in the fifth century, the Church remained the only moral and often the only political power during the barbarian invasions from Asia and northern Europe. The Church continued to be faithful to her spiritual mission of the sanctification and salvation of souls, but her bishops and priests were often forced to carry the sword in order to defend cathedrals and convents from the barbarians' attacks. Under these conditions, the authority of the Church grew steadily until it reached its highest point in the Middle Ages under Pope Gregory VII (1073–1085). The Church in Christian Europe regarded herself as being above the state, adhering to the principle that spiritual power is above temporal. While this principle is in itself perfectly right it was too often applied incorrectly, with the result that undue clerical influence was frequently found in political matters. A similar state of affairs prevailed in the centuries of Humanism and the Renaissance, and even later, until in the last century the basic tenet of secularism, the total separation of Church and state, was proclaimed.

The Croatians generally oppose both caesaropapism and clericalism with regard to relations between Church and state. On the whole, the Church and the state in Croatia have worked together but have not united. Only in time of war and other calamities has the situation been otherwise. For example, when the governing group disintegrated in the struggle with the Turks, the Archbishop of Zagreb assumed the state's government. However, he returned this power to the civil authorities as soon as the latter were reorganized. The Croatian Diet respected the Church, and vice versa, but each authority was sovereign in its own field—the Church in the sphere of Croatian spiritual life, in the realm of the sanctification and salvation of her followers; the state in the field of the worldly and temporal prosperity of Croatian citizens. Christ

[49]In Croatian: Popuhnul je hladan vetar, / Aj ni nena, zlato moje, / Popuhnul je hladan vetar, / Hladan vetar od Levanta / I odnesal Mari krunu.

Himself designated this division of powers, when He said: "Render to Caesar the things that are Caesar's and to God the things that are God's" (Luke 20:25). Both spiritual and civil powers are autonomous in their own realms, although their cooperation is necessary and natural, for they both work for the benefit of the people. This is particularly true where matters such as the education of youth, public morals, and interfaith relations are concerned—areas in which both powers have vital interests.

The history of the relationship of the Croatian Diet and the Archbishop of Zagreb, coupled with the tragic experience of the people of Yugoslavia between the two recent wars, when the Serbian Orthodox Church was the state Church—to the detriment of all other churches—shows clearly the justification of the Croatian ideal: a free state and a free Church.

International Relations

In international relations, the political life of the Croatians has always remained on the level of fair play: the Croatian ideal of international relations has never been based on deception, power, or aggression. The contract of the Croatians with Pope Agathon in the seventh century (at the very beginning of life in their new country) stated that they would never lead aggressive wars against other nations, but that if others should invade them, they would defend themselves and be defended by St. Peter, that is, by the Church. The context of that pact has been preserved for us by the Byzantine Emperor, Constantine Porphyrogenitus. The Emperor stated:

> After their baptism, the Croatians made a pact signed with their own hand and made under strict and solemn oath to St. Peter the Apostle, to the effect that they would never violate the territory of others to wage wars on them, but rather that they would live in peace with all those who wished it. The Pope of Rome himself had promised them that if other people should invade the territory of the Croatians and force them to war, God would fight for the Croatians and would aid them; and [that] Peter, the disciple of Christ, would procure victory for them.[50]

The Christian concept of a just war has dominated Croatian thinking—and hence Croatian history—for more than thirteen hundred years. History bears no record of any Croatian desire, much less of any attempt, to conquer foreign lands. Their wars have been defensive wars.

Small nations, such as Croatia, cannot afford to use unfair methods

[50]Constantine Porphyrogenitus, *De Administrando Imperio*, ch. 31, quoted in Rački, *Documenta*, 291–292.

in international relations, even if they should wish to employ them. For, if ethics in international relations be denied, only one rule remains: might makes right, a vicious principle which places the small nations, economically and militarily weaker, on the losing side. On the other hand, by preserving their own borders, by stressing the basic rights of all nations to equality and freedom, and by pointing to their own cultural values, small nations may exercise reasonable hope for the final victory of justice over injustice, freedom over tyranny, and culture over barbarism.

The Post-War State of Morals

The traditional way of life among the Croatian Catholic people has been gravely disturbed as a result of the Communist take-over of political power in Yugoslavia (May 1945). Tito's regime claimed the whole man right from the beginning. It imposed a Marxist world outlook, dialectical materialism, and a Marxist ethic, in which the destiny and happiness of the individual is secondary to that of collective Marxist goals. In principle, the new regime excludes any other creed and code. In practice, it proceeds slowly, since the end of religious "superstition" and "capitalist" morality cannot be achieved overnight. To that end, the Communists have concentrated their efforts on the youth of the country. In many instances the youth have been taught secularized Christian ideals of self-sacrifice, brotherly love, hard work, and discipline—all for the victory of Communist cause.

We have no ready answer to the important question of what is left of Christian morality and patriarchal values among the Croatian people after almost two decades of Communist indoctrination. Has the regime succeeded in molding a new, Marxist type of young man and young woman? Judging from the young (twenty to thirty year-old) refugees from Yugoslavia in recent years, one might observe that the youth resent everything connected with Communism, and hence the Communist ethics as well. However, no other system of morality is known to many of them, and therefore, they regard economic values as being on the top of the value scale. In Croatia today, Christian morals are still strong in small but vigorous groups in the towns and cities, as well as among the peasants at large. In spite of the apparent truce between the Communist regime and the Church, there is nevertheless a constant struggle carried on beneath the surface between these two rivals for human minds and hearts. No one can predict with certainty the outcome of this conflict.

7

Folk Arts and Handicrafts

TOMO MARKOVIĆ

THE FOLK ARTS of the Croatians are distinctive, and their handicraft work is especially noteworthy for its richness of form and ornament. Even today the Croatian people take great pride in making with their own hands many articles of fine craftsmanship for use in their daily life and to enhance their homes on special occasions, such as feast days. The elaboration and ornamentation of the handicraft items in which the Croatians specialize clearly express the fine aesthetic sense which these people possess.

The origins of folk carving, pottery, building, metalcraft, weaving, design, and tattooing are to be sought in the many lands where the Croatians lived throughout their long history. Some of these cultural activities may have originated in the Croatians' former homelands—the country around the modern Kraków, and, some scholars argue, the region of Iran (Persia). Others were begun and adapted in the Croatians' present country; ethnologists term the products of these cultural activities "protobalkanic."[1] Other cultural products, the origins of which have been traced back to the Mediterranean shores, are called Preroman and Roman. Through the ages, many cultural influences have come to the Croatians from other areas too—from the Pannonian Zone and the Alpine Zone,[2] from the Germanic north, the

[1]Milovan Gavazzi, "Etnografska struktura Balkana" / The Ethnographic Structure of the Balkans (Zagreb: Mimeographed lecture series), 31. In the writing of this article, the author has made use of notes taken at the University of Zagreb in the years 1928–1932, during the regular lectures offered by Dr. Milovan Gavazzi, professor of anthropology; his own research materials collected in Bosnia-Hercegovina, 1932–1945; and interviews held in refugee camps at Fermo and Bagnoli in Italy, 1945–1948.

[2]The Pannonian Zone includes the area on both sides of the Danube River, which was settled by the North Croatians, Hungarians, and Rumanians. The Alpine

Christian and Moslem east, the Appenine west, and particularly from Venice. In this way, significant differentiations appeared among the Croatian provinces, and these are continued in their folk arts, especially in those of Bosnia and Hercegovina, but also in those of Dalmatia. These differences were further strengthened by historical events, but in spite of all differences, a common national consciousness and one language have remained. These latter two elements have bound the many and varied cultural influences in Croatia into one cultural whole.

Our division of the Croatian folk arts follows the one customarily used in ethnology: work is classified under the categories of wood, clay, stone, metal, and cloth. In order to give a more comprehensive picture of the folk arts in Croatia, we shall include in this discussion the activity of gourd and egg coloring, as well as that of tattooing, which is still of much significance in some regions. Color will be treated throughout as a medium of ornamentation.

Wood

Buildings

Wood is used in constructing many of the homes typical of Croatia. *Sojenice* or *sošnice* are very ancient palafitte houses (dwellings built on piles fixed in the beds of lakes or rivers) and are found today on the Bosna and Pliva Rivers, as well as in Posavina, near Slavonski Brod, in Jasenovac, and in Stara Gradiška. This type of dwelling belongs to the Protobalkanic Cultural Period and dates from the Iron Age. This is evident from the discoveries of the palafitte settlements of that period found in the village of Donja Dolina on the Sava River, near Bosanska Gradiška.[3]

Dwellings called *brvnare*, made from ordinary logs, are the typical homes found in mountainous regions that are covered with timber. In the western part of Posavina, where there are large oak forests, this type is the most common of wooden peasant dwellings. The *brvnare* once had several wings and were richly decorated with wood carvings. Even churches were built exclusively from wooden materials, and in

---

Zone includes peoples settled in the Alps and belonging to the following countries: a small part of northwestern Croatia, Slovenia, Austria, northern Italy, Switzerland, and southern France.

[3]Gavazzi, "Etnografska struktura," 8, 31; Čiro Truhelka, "Bosna u doba prehističko" / Bosnia in the Prehistoric Age, in the symposium *Povijest hrvatskih zemalja Bosne i Hercegovine* / History of the Croatian Lands of Bosnia and Hercegovina, published by the learned society *Napredak* and edited by Krunoslav Draganović (Sarajevo, 1942), 90–93.

Turopolje one can still see some twelve small wooden churches which date from the era of the Baroque architectural style.[4]

Furnishing and Decorating

In making pieces of furniture for the home, wood is the most common material used by the Croatian craftsmen. It is used in making balconies, stairway railings, shelves, wall cabinets, and chests—all of which are decoratively carved. Many articles for daily use are also beautifully carved by hand, such as scythe-handles, grindstone boxes, distaffs, spindles, spools, wooden cups and other vessels, needle cases, mirrors, flutes, and stools. The technique of decorating is varied and includes gouging,[5] chip-carving,[6] line-carving,[7] perforating,[8] wood-burning,[9] dotting,[10] inlaying of wire in wood, and sealing with wax.[11] Decorative motifs popular among these artisans are dots, straight and wavy lines, vegetal configurations, and geometrical figures, especially triangles and circles, which are often filled in with a six-pointed star. Animal and human motifs are used less frequently; they are usually found on two objects, canteens and fiddles (*gusle*). Among the very ancient decorative motifs of the Croatians is the cross with small hooked ends, the swastika, that is still seen on old distaffs and colored eggs, and in embroidery work. The Moslems of Central Bosnia call such crosses *žabice*, that is to say, "little frogs."

Outstanding centers of ornamental hand work in wood are found in

[4]Ljerka Topali, "Drvene crkvice i seljačko drveno graditeljstvo u Turopolju" / Little Wooden Churches and Peasant Wooden Architecture in Turopolje, a special reprint from *Etnografska istraživanja i gradja* / Ethnographic Research and Materials, Book III (Zagreb, 1941).

[5]Gouging (*dubenje*) is done with a special tool twisted and adapted to the kind of object to be worked on, such as a grindstone box, a trough (for the watering and feeding of animals), or a canoe. See Milovan Gavazzi, "Obradba drveta" / Woodwork, in the series under the general title "Etnografija Južnih Slavena" / Ethnography of the Southern Slavs (Zagreb: Mimeographed lecture series).

[6]Chip-carving (*rovašenje*) involves the cutting and simultaneous carving of individual designs (lines) or other elements, such as small triangles, so that the profile of the carving is in the form of a wedge.

[7]Line-carving (wood-carving: *crtkanje drva*) is the making of common designs on cases and chests with the aid of sharp tools. This technique is a very ancient one. Gavazzi, "Etnografska struktura."

[8]Perforating (piercing: *rad no proboj*) consists in the cutting of decorative motifs through thin wooden surfaces. Gavazzi, "Etnografska struktura."

[9]Wood-burning (etching: *žeženje*) is done with a red-hot stylus; the design is burned into the wooden surface. Gavazzi, "Etnografska struktura."

[10]Dotting (punching: *punciranje*) is done with a small iron punch, which prints small decorative dots on cases and flutes. This is a very ancient decorative motif. Gavazzi, "Etnografska struktura."

[11]Sealing wax is laid in cut-out motifs in wood. Gavazzi, "Etnografska struktura."

western Bosnia, particularly in the area surrounding the towns of Livno, Duvno, Kupres, and Prozor; in neighboring Hercegovina, in the town of Konjic; and in the Dalmatian Zagora. The people of the Coastal Zone make chests that are similar in ornamentation to those made in the Appenines. The woodwork of the town of Konjic is notable for its Oriental names and characteristics. We should also mention the famous woodwork of the town of Livno, in which silver wire is inlaid in wooden objects such as tobacco cases, cigar holders, canes, inkstands, and blotters.

Pottery

Types

Two kinds of pottery-making[12] are prevalent among the Croatians. The one type is found in the Dinaric Alpine Region, stretching westward to the Adriatic coast, and eastward to the Drina River. In this method, the pottery is made from clay that is mixed with fine limestone (the mixture is called *vrsta*), and they are worked in a spiral technique that involves the use of a potter's wheel operated with one hand, while the other hand models the clay. The objects are baked in the open, without any kiln. These simple, indeed almost primitive, products are not glazed, but are merely sprinkled (the verb is *kaliti* in Croatian) or spattered with a liquid barley paste.

The second method of pottery-making involves clay which has not been mixed with lime, so that it produces a smooth surface, which can be easily polished. The modeling is done with the aid of a potter's wheel that is operated by foot, and both hands are thus free to do the molding. The finished objects are works of finer craftsmanship than those typical of the Dinaric Region, and quite creative ornaments are produced in one or more colors. This method is employed in the Pannonian Zone and in the territory bordering on the Alpine Region.

Dinaric Pottery

Among the significant objects of the Dinaric pottery group are *pekve* sometimes called *crijepnje* or *pokljuke*. These are low, cone-shaped covers used for baking bread on the open hearth. In using these, hot embers are poured around the little upturned clay ledges, which encircle the outside of the *pekva*, and which keep the embers from

[12]Milovan Gavazzi, "Keramika ili lončarstvo" / Ceramics or Pottery, "Etnografija Južnih Slavena" / Ethnography of the Southern Slavs (Zagreb: Mimeographed lecture series).

falling upon the fireplace. The *pekve* originated in the Ancient Protobalkanic Period. This was indicated in the discovery of a *pekva* dating back to the Bronze Age. The discovery was made in excavations near Ripač[13] and the *pekva* which was uncovered there is identical with those in use today.

The so-called *pijure* are large clay vessels shaped somewhat like a deep dish, and are used to separate cream. Keeping in mind the ancient pastoral traditions of the Croatian lands, it is not unlikely that the *pijure* also belong to the Ancient Protobalkanic Cultural Period. *Mangale* are large round pans and look like inverted hats rising from round pedestals. Hot embers are placed in these vessels, and they are used for warming hands and for roasting coffee beans. The word *mangale* is of Turkish derivation and signifies a glowing ember. A clay vessel that is identical with the present-day *mangale* of baked clay was discovered in Mrsunjski Lug,[14] near Brodski Stupnik in the district of Slavonski Brod, where Slavic strongholds dating from the early Middle Ages have been found. Today the *mangale* are popular throughout Bosnia-Hercegovina and in the Moslem east. In open workshops and in the Oriental type of open market place, they are considered indispensable for heating.

Another article of Dinaric pottery is the *ćup*, which is very useful for conserving butter and for preserving jam. The *ćup* has a small circular base, is wide in the middle, and has a rolled-edge top which is somewhat broader than its base. The size of the *ćup* varies considerably. This container is similar to the Roman amphora, except that it has no handles. Professor Milovan Gavazzi is inclined to believe that the word *ćup* originated in the Illyrian language,[15] although this term is common among the Turks. *Bakre* are a more shallow type of bowl, with a lip-edge, and are used for cooking cornmeal, cabbage, dry meat, and other similar foods. In Bosnia, the *bardaci* and *testije* are jugs in frequent use. The *bardak* has a beak or spout, while the *testija* does not. The Moslems use these wares for ritual washings, as well as for many other purposes.

The pottery which we have described in this section is plain and only occasionally contains incised or molded ornamentation. The decorative motifs are strokes, dots, and rectilinear and curvilinear patterns, which are pressed in with the fingertips around the border

[13]Milovan Gavazzi, "Etnografska struktura," 32.

[14]Zdenko Vinski, *Gradište u Mrsunjskom Lugu* / Ruins in Mrsunjski Lug (Zagreb: Archaeological Museum, 1950), 19. An exposition of the first excavation of a Slavic stronghold from the early Middle Ages in Croatia.

[15]Gavazzi, "Keramika."

or, in the case of jars and jugs, in the convex area at the middle of the container.

Bosnian Pottery

In Bosnia one finds pitchers and various other types of pottery of fantastic shapes with names and forms similar to those of the Moslem East. The town of Kiseljak,[16] near Visoko, is a noted center for work with incised ornamental motifs and for decorations executed in a light chestnut-brown color. Haberland links the work of Kiseljak with that of the Mycenaean products. Gavazzi is more inclined to think that these objects are influenced by the Levantine-Arabic ceramics.[17]

The primitive ceramic productions that we have mentioned are in direct contrast to the pottery of the Northern Zone. Some of the forms of the latter—glazure, variegated floral motifs, and plastic decorations in plant and animal patterns—indicate that they originated at a later time in history than the more primitive objects.

STONE

Buildings

Stone is the chief material used in building houses in the Adriatic Zone and in the karst regions of Bosnia and Hercegovina. Among the very old structures of this type are the *poljarice*, *ćemeri*, and *bunje*.[18] These are round little houses constructed from blocks of ordinary stone, and they resemble a low tower with an irregular cupola. They have several rows of circular rings stretching around their girth, and at the top of the cupola is an opening on which a disc is placed. These structures are used for shelter as well as for storage, and they can be seen throughout Dalmatia. From a comparison with objects discovered in southern Italy, Sardinia, and on the northern border of Africa, it is evident that these stone constructions belong to the Ancient Mediterranean Cultural Period.

In passing, it might be well to touch upon the old stone structures,

[16] *Ibid.* See also Arthur Haberland, "Die volkstümliche Kultur Europas in ihrer geschichtlichen Entwicklung," in Georg Buschan, *Illustrierte Völkerkunde*, Book II (Stuttgart: Strecker und Schröder, 1922–26).

[17] Gavazzi, "Keramika."

[18] Gavazzi, "Etnografska struktura," 36. See also his "Primitivne nastambe" / Primitive Dwellings, in the lecture series "Etnografija Južnih Slavena"; and Ćiro Iveković, "Bunje, ćemeri, poljarice," in the symposium dedicated to the first Croatian King Tomislav *Zbornik kralja Tomislava* (Zagreb: Yugoslav Academy, 1925).

which the Croatians erected upon their arrival on the Adriatic coast. The churches and oratories found here are predominantly small.[19] Some of these are still standing today; in a great many cases, however, only the foundations have been preserved. A great deal of decoratively interwoven ornamentation characterizes these churches and oratories. Dr. Ljubo Karaman, one of the best cultural historians in the field of Croatian art, points out that in the construction of these churches art was introduced by the Slavs.[20] Josip Strzygowsky finds remarkable resemblances between the structure of the small old Croatian churches and that of the Sassanids in Sarvistan and the Persepolis in Persia. These resemblances are emphasized by those who adhere to the theory of the Iranian origin of the Croatians.[21]

Tombstones and Other Stonework

Among Croatian artistic works in stone, the tombstones from the Middle Ages which are found in Bosnia and Hercegovina are outstanding. These are called *stećci* or *mramorovi* and are ascribed to "Bosnian Christians." According to Alexander Solovjev[22] some 59,500 of these stone markers have been found. Only a few are inscribed with the *bosančica* script and decorated in relief. The best-known monument is that erected in memory of Prijezda, a nobleman who later became ban of Bosnia. It is found in Zgošća,[23] near Vareš in Bosnia, and dates from the thirteenth century. Today it is to be found in the National Museum in Sarajevo. This monument is shaped like a house, with the following dimensions: the double-eaved roof has a length of 8′8″; the height at the corners is 4′9″, and to the peak of the roof, 5′6″; the width at the base is 4′6″, and at the edge of the eaves, 4′9″. The stone rests on a large flat supporting base. It is decorated with a chiseled relief which displays scenes from the daily life of the aristocracy of the time: hunting scenes, richly adorned horses, and gay public festivals—among which is the famous national *kolo*, a dance. A significant number of these tombstones are found in the neighboring Dalmatian Region. Notable also are the tombstones of the

[19]Ljubo Karaman, *Pregled umjetnosti u Dalmaciji* / A Survey of Art in Dalmatia (Zagreb: Matica Hrvatska, 1952), 16–19.

[20]*Ibid.*, 16.

[21]Stjepan Sakač, "Intorno all' etnogenesi slava. Nuove opinioni sull' origine e la formazione dei popoli slavi," *La Civiltà Cattolica* 2383, 2385 (Rome, Oct. 1 and Nov. 5, 1949).

[22]Maja Miletić, "I'Krstjani' di Bosnia alla luce dei loro monumenti di pietra," *Orientalia Christiana Analecta* (Rome, 1957), 25.

[23]Ćiro Truhelka, *Studije o porijeklu* / Studies of Origins (Zagreb: Matica Hrvatska, 1941), 44–57.

Handicrafts. *Upper*: Grindstone boxes. *Center left*: Wooden cups. *Center right*: Distaffs. *Lower left*: Needle cases. *Lower right*: Spools.

Dinaric pottery. Water vessels from Kiseljak, near Kreševo, Bosnia.

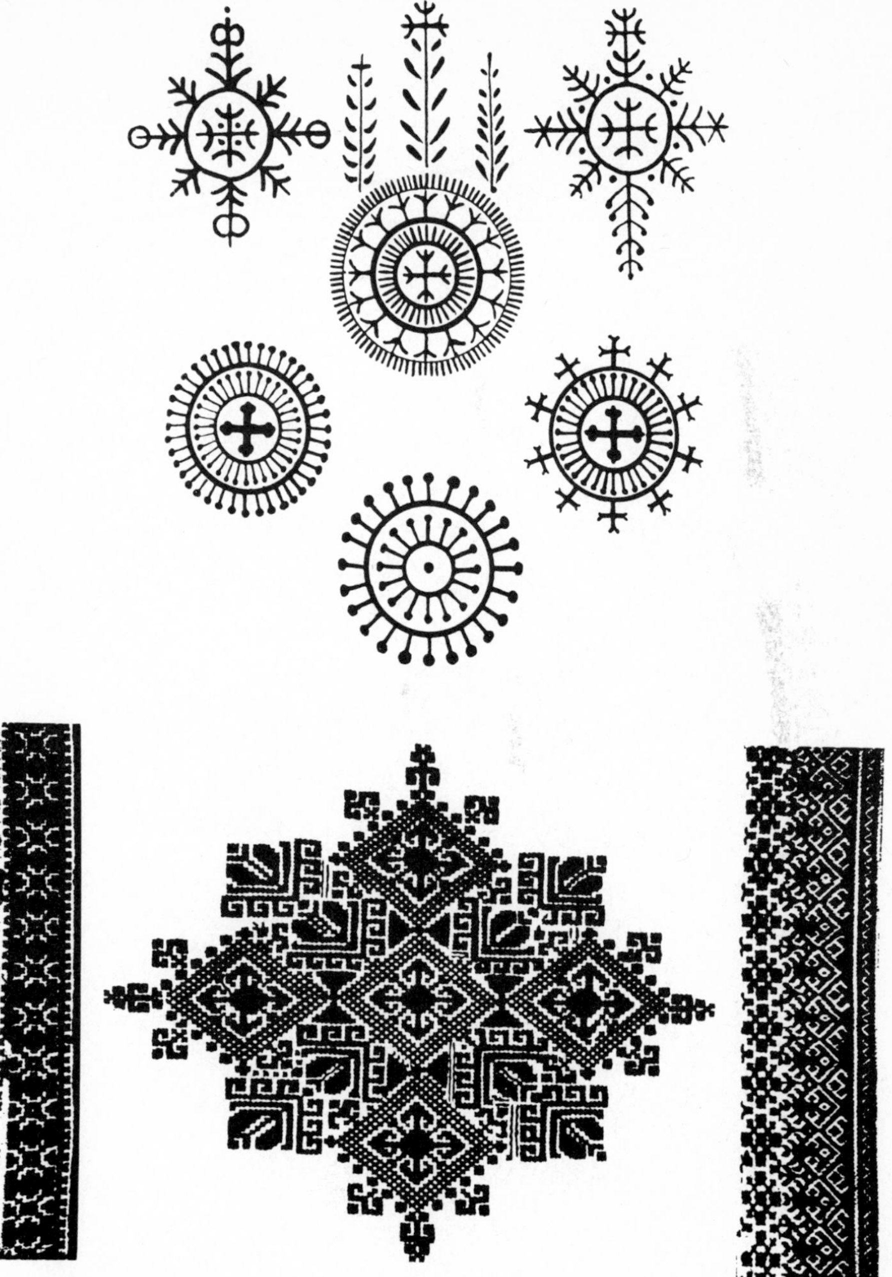

Upper: Tattooing design. *Lower*: Embroidery design from North-Western Bosnia.

Upper: Costumes from the Žepče countryside in Bosnia.
Lower: Woman embroidering on a horizontal loom.

Left: Enameled box for religious books. *Right*: Leader of the heroic game *alka*. His right hand rests on the yataghan, a long Turkish knife.

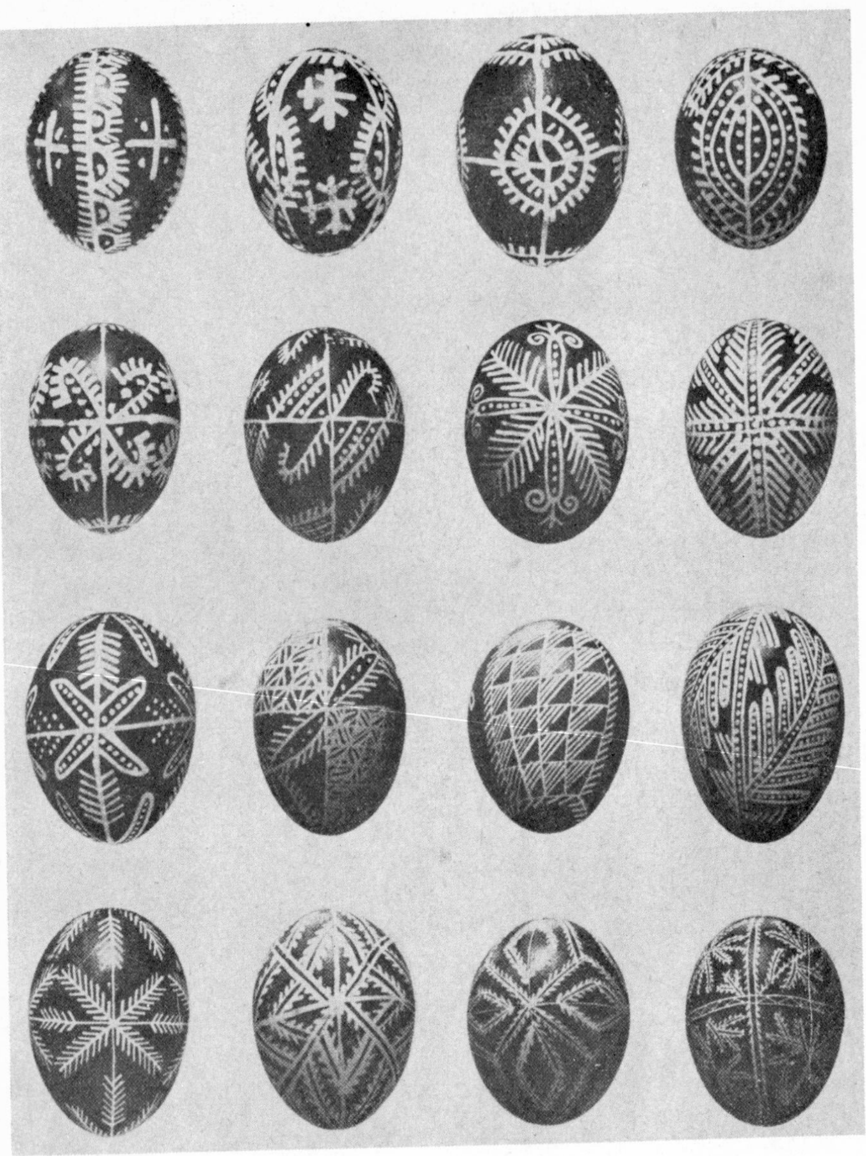

Croatian folk art: eggs with various designs.

Croatian lace from various regions.

Croatian authors. *Upper left*: Stanko Vraz (1810–51). *Upper right*: Petar Preradović (1818–72). *Lower left*: Ante Tresić-Pavičić (1867–1949). *Lower right*: Eugenij Kumičić (1850–1904).

Moslem aristocrats, especially in Sarajevo, Travnik, and Livno, among other places in Bosnia and Hercegovina. The tombstones in some of the older Catholic cemeteries are also outstanding and are distinguished by their beautifully elaborated symbolic decorations and inscriptions in *bosančica.*

To these works in stone one might also add the numerous Croatian stone bridges, especially that on the Neretva River in Mostar, and the ones in Višegrad and in Trebinje. Throughout Croatia there are also many different fortifications, castles, and forts of stone worthy of note; and in both Bosnia and Hercegovina there are numerous mosques with slender minarets and watch towers.

Metal

Ancient Heritage

For a proper appraisal of the accomplishments of the Croatians in the field of handicrafts in which metal is used, it is well to keep in mind that the knowledge of metalcraft was probably very scanty in the ancient homeland of the Croatians. It was only in their new country that they came on a rather highly developed art of metal production. We can assume this from the prehistoric metal artifacts discovered in Croatia. As a tangible example of the influence which the peoples who preceded the Croatians exerted on the future inhabitants of their lands one might mention the well-known headgear of the inhabitants of Lika. These are little round caps that have a decorative ornamental tassel which hangs over one temple. A replica in brass of such a cap was found in the excavations of objects dating from the Bronze Age, in Kompolje, near Gospić, in the province of Lika.[24] The ancient manner of forming this replica was the same as the modern technique of hammering brass.[25] Brass is used in modern times in Croatia for making many popular accoutrements, such as earrings, and, among the people in Bosnia and Dalmatia, as a fringe for head coverings.

The Croatian technique of working with metal wire originated in some distant age. The artisan twists and winds wire in spiral motifs and thereby produces lovely fringes and loops. These artistic wire fringes are very common in parts of the Dinaric Alps. They are really no more than an imitation of similar decorative objects from some prehistoric period.

[24]Gavazzi, "Etnografska struktura," 33, and Muška nošnja / Male Costumes, "Etnografija Južnih Slavena."

[25]Milovan Gavazzi, "Obradba Kovina" / Metal Work, in the lecture series "Etnografija Južnih Slavena."

Byzantine Influence

New methods of working with metal were acquired from Byzantium, by way of the neighboring Latin coastal cities which were under Byzantine political jurisdiction. In recent times historians have accentuated the influence on the Croatians of their Pannonian neighbors,[26] for along Lake Balaton there existed a center of combined metal and leather production, which the Hungarian archaeologists ascribe to the Kutrigurian Avars. To this area belong also the discoveries in the cemetery of Biskupija, near Knin.[27] The Byzantine influence is revealed in the findings at the Women's Cemetery in Trilj near Split. From available historical data, we learn that in the time of Peter Krešimir IV (1058–1074) mention was made of a native goldsmith by the name of Grubiša.[28] Later a contemporary of King Zvonimir (1076–1089), Bishop Lawrence of Split,[29] sent his own master craftsman to Syria to learn the goldsmith's trade, in order that he might make various articles from precious metals for use in churches.

In the following centuries (from the twelfth to the eighteenth), stronger ties with Byzantium and Italy advanced the Croatian technique of working with metal still further. This is evident from the crosses, candlesticks, relic containers, and other sacred vessels that have come down to us. The outstanding centers of this craft were Zadar, Rab, Nin, Biograd-on-the-Sea, Trogir, Split, Dubrovnik, and Boka Kotorska.

Bosnian Metalwork

In the second half of the fifteenth century, Bosnia came under the influence of the Turkish east, and even today it manifests a number of distinctly Turkish characteristics. We find in Bosnia the rich cultural inventory and inspiration of the Orient. In the field of excellent workmanship in metal we should mention especially swords,[30] knives, pistols, enameled boxes for religious books, cases, containers, and cartridge holders. This type of metalwork is done by hammering perforations and indentations on the reverse side of the object with a

[26]Karaman, *Pregled,* 13–14.

[27]*Ibid.,* 14.

[28]Josip Horvat, *Kultura Hrvata kroz hiljadu godina* / The Culture of the Croatians Through a Thousand Years (Zagreb, 1939), 120.

[29]*Ibid.*

[30]Vejsil Ćurčić, "Starinsko oružje u Bosni i Hercegovini" / Ancient Weapons in Bosnia and Hercegovina, *Glasnik Zemaljskog Muzeja u Sarajevu* (1926), 109ff. See also Milan Praunsberger, *Oružje starih Hrvata u povijesti i u narodnoj pjesmi* / Weapons of the Ancient Croatians in History and Folk Songs (Zagreb: Matica Hrvatska, 1943).

small mallet,[31] producing a modeled quality in relief on the front of the metal. The Bosnians also engage in the arts of engraving and chasing—carving and chiseling with sharp tools, and perforating brass for delicate trim. They also granulate melted silver or gold wire, producing little beads or drops, set in a series of ornamental patterns.

A favorite craft of the Bosnians involves the technique of filigree, especially in earrings and bracelets. In this process, the metal is twisted and worked into a spiral motif, or interwoven in the form of a woolen cord, to form many kinds of delicate ornaments. We have already referred to another specialty of the Bosnians, the inlaying of metal wire in wood, notably in cigar holders and cigarette cases. Inlaying is also done in metal, by inserting filaments or small plates of precious metal, gold or silver, in the hollow of another metal. This method is used to make decorated gun shafts, dagger sheaths, and inscribed mottos and name plates. The insertion of semi-precious stones and variegated glass in metal is an art that the Bosnians employ in the making of belts, handles of knives, and yataghans (Turkish long knives). The decorative designs on these objects usually consist of rectilinear or meandering lines, geometrical figures of different combinations, flowers, foliage, birds, cypresses, mosques, watch towers, hexagrams, and representations of the human eye, which are supposedly on watch for ill omens.

Cloth

Regional Specialties

Cloth enables artisans with rich imaginations to make many things, notably articles of clothing, but also items of adornment for daily use, such as towels, bandanas, and pouches. All of the regions in Croatia are bountifully represented in this sphere. The northern section of Croatia, between the Sava and Drava Rivers, and the territory surrounding the Kupa River, are areas in which the people reveal great skill in tailoring, dying, and in the production of decorative pieces, such as veils, shoulderettes, aprons, sashes, and sox.

The best preserved central area or nucleus of the original, ancient art of dressmaking in its various forms is along the upper Posavina in the direction of Zagreb, especially in towns like Pisarevina, Orešje, and Sveta Nedjelja. In the south—in northwestern and western Bosnia, all of Hercegovina, the Dalmatian Zagora and northern Dalmatia and

[31]Gavazzi, "Obradba kovina." See also his *Hrvatska narodna umjetnost* / Croatian Folk Art (Zagreb, 1944), xvi.

Lika—the fancy work of the people is distinctive, particularly with regard to vests, shirts, sashes, aprons, veils, sox, and slippers, all of which are richly decorated. In Lika and in northern Dalmatia, richly embroidered red caps with the letter S, formed by a string of beads, are characteristic. The significance of this decorative S is obscure; some scholars believe that it is derived from the swastika.[32]

Embroidery

The members of the urban population of Bosnia-Hercegovina, especially the young women, do fine work with needles, embroidery frames, rich silk threads, and silver and gold wire. They embroider fancy handkerchiefs (in gold and silver threads), towels, shirts, bandanas, and sashes for underwear. Many of the designs which they use are of Oriental inspiration, and this is seen especially in motifs such as flowers, twigs, birds, mosques and watch towers.

Two techniques of embroidery are used in Bosnia-Hercegovina. In one, the method is to first trace the pattern on linen cloth; the second method involves the counting of stitches. Much of the Croatian embroidery is done on linen, which is woven in the home on a horizontal loom, and is often interwoven with colorful stripes. The Croatians also embroider on wool, and this is particularly true of the people in the Dinaric Zone and its neighboring regions in the making of clothing. The custom of combining embroidery with leather craft, and with leather in general, is restricted to the northern region of Croatia, and resembles the work of the Magyars and Slovaks close by.

Colors

A common characteristic of Croatian peasant dress is its especially fine color harmony. In this domain the peasants are real masters. Harmonious color combinations, achromatic black and white combined with red, yellow, and blue, create beautiful color schemes. Red plays an essential role in the peasant's costume. Among the secondary colors of violet, orange, purple, and green, violet is the Croatian favorite, and more especially that shade of violet which is most brilliant. Secondary colors are usually discreetly accompanied by one of the primary colors in Croatian dress. In every combination of colors, the most favored are the bright ones. The tertiary colors—those colors which are a combination of secondary ones—are often used in the peasant costume. From

[32]*Enciclopedia Espasa*, Vol. 58 (Madrid, 1927), 1172–1174. See also Rodney Gallop, *Los Vascos* (Madrid, 1955), 186ff.

this tertiary composition result the richest and most picturesque harmonies. In this respect the peasant reveals his very fine taste.[33]

Knitting

Both in the textile works and among individuals, knitting plays an important role in Croatian life. Numerous Croatians are adept at knitting stockings, sox, slippers, and gloves, all in the most beautiful manner of interlacing. This skill is developed and elaborated to very advanced degrees in the urban territories of Bosnia and Hercegovina, and, in the north, in the lands which border on the Alpine Zone.

Carpet-Weaving

Carpet-weaving[34] on a vertical loom is a special technique which is widespread throughout Lika, Slavonia, and right across Bosnia-Hercegovina. Among the many well-known centers of this craft are Sarajevo, Livno, Duvno, Glamoč, Prozor, and Foča. Popular decorative motifs used in Croatian carpet-weaving are geometrical designs, zig-zag lines, step motifs, and stylish plant and animal motifs—all of which reflect Oriental traits. On older tapestries one may note that the lines of the ornamental designs are smaller and more precise than on later ones. At one time the geometrical and geometricized design prevailed, but gradually it was largely supplanted by the naturalistic design, including —to some extent—the zoomorphic design. Nevertheless, geometrical patterns are still of significance in the ornamentation of Croatian tapestry.

Fabric Arts in the Life of the People

In the Croatian textile arts, the creator of an object frequently fashions his product with the aim that it serve as an embellishment that might add joy and gaiety to life. This characteristic is especially notable in the countless public celebrations at which the products of the textile arts help to enliven and to add atmosphere to the *kolo* and to gay folk tunes. The three elements of beautiful fabrics, the dance, and music, combine to form an organic whole. They are essential to the very spirit of the people and assist the Croatians in expressing themselves, especially at festival time.

This suggests a more serious reason for the spontaneous rejoicing

[33]Ljubo Babić, *Boja i skald* / Color and Harmony (Zagreb: Hrvatski izdavalački bibliografski zavod, 1943), 33–40. See also Babić, *Umjetnost kod Hrvata* (Zagreb, 1943), 27–28.

[34]Vladimir Tkalčić, *Seljačko ćilimarstvo u Jugoslaviji* / Peasant Carpet-Weaving in Yugoslavia, Etnološka Biblioteka / Ethnology Library (Zagreb, 1929).

that is revealed in the folk tunes which accompany almost all the work done with cloth. There are in many cases particular songs to accompany certain types of endeavor. In Bosnia especially, a young lady invariably sings when she does embroidery work. This is easily understood, because the many articles which the young girl embroiders with her own hands are being prepared for her future married life and home. Her thoughts are expressed in the songs which are directed to her loved one. Her singing becomes an advertisement for that home—a sign that there is a worthy young lady in the home, one who can embroider with real skill and diligence. The young woman who does not know how to weave, sew, embroider, and knit runs the risk of becoming a target for ridicule. There are even Croatian songs which mock just such a girl.

Gourd and Egg Coloring

Among the Croatian native artistic skills is numbered the art of gourd coloring, which is carried on only by the people of Slavonia. The colored gourds are used as decorative pieces and for drinking cups. Cutting is done by means of a carving knife, and the individual parts of the gourd are colored with an acid liquid which is often used to melt gold. The decoration usually consists of linear or vegetal motifs, or designs of birds.

A significant part of the Easter tradition among the Catholics of Croatia is the coloring of Easter eggs. Sometimes the eggs are used to add delight to snacks, or as gifts, or prizes, or even as stakes in games of chance. These marvels of color are so traditional at Easter that in earlier times the Moslems called this Christian feastday *Kyzyl jumurta*, that is, "red eggs."[35] In the north, the time following Easter was designated as "after the egg breaking," or, in Latin, *post concussionem ovorum.*[36] Until recently, eggs were colored with home-prepared dyes made from the bark of the alder tree or from cooked red onion peels. The lines are drawn on the egg by applying melted wax with a stylus, and then the egg is dipped in a warm dye. The wax is then removed, and on those areas where the writing was done with wax, the egg remains white. For this reason such eggs are called "designed eggs" (*pisanice*). In the villages around Žepče in Bosnia, the eggs are wrapped with pieces of variegated cotton thread, which make up

[35]Milovan Gavazzi, *Godina dana hrvatskih narodnih običaja* / Folk Customs of the Croatian People Around the Year, Part I (Zagreb, 1939), 40.
[36]*Ibid.*, 29.

various geometrical designs. Dyeing eggs red has preserved many ancient and primitive decorative motifs, such as the swastika, and the cross which is decorated at the ends with a series of fir needles. In northeastern Hercegovina and the neighboring Dalmatian territories, the wedge design, in different geometrical combinations, was once prevalent. The Northern Zone, which also used a geometrical design of a more complicated form, favored the vegetal motif, and more especially the floral pattern in varied colors—white, yellow, and amber on a chestnut brown base.

The custom of coloring and dyeing eggs has its roots in ancient times. Shells of colored eggs were found in the graves of some of the old northern European peoples.[37] Dyed eggs of the Ukrainians and Poles resemble those of the Croatians both in technique and decorative motifs. These resemblances are found to a lesser degree among other southern Slavs (or they do not have them at all). Here we should emphasize that the Moslems took much pleasure in receiving these colored eggs, especially the red ones. It is known that their young women liked to wash in water into which a red egg had been dipped, so that they would then have rosy cheeks. This was done on certain days of the year, notably on the feast of St. George (April 23).

Tattooing

A Traditional Skill

The older types of designs on colored eggs greatly resemble the motifs used by the Croatians in the tattooing[38] of skin. Tattooing is an ancient tradition in the Balkans, and it was known even in the time of Herodotus, Plutarch, Cicero, and Strabo by the Thracians, the Illyrians, and that part of the latter group which intermingled with the Celts and were called Japudes. Today this practice is preserved among the Catholics in Bosnia. In the time of the Turks, the art was considered—especially among the women—to be a defense against conversion to Islam. This belief stemmed from the many crosses which were tattooed into the skin.

The Manner of Tattooing

The procedure which the Croatians use in tattooing has remained unchanged with the passing of time. A mixture is made from the soot

[37] *Ibid.*, 27.

[38] Mary Edith Durham, *Some Tribal Origins, Laws and Customs of the Balkans* (London, 1928), 101–106. The author has also made use of information obtained from Mr. Blaž Blažević of Korićani, near Travnik in Bosnia.

of a burned resinous wood or from pine resin. This ingredient is mixed with honey or milk in a small dish. Then the arm or chest is pierced with a needle making a series of small crosses in varied combinations of half moons and full circles with projecting rays which look like radiant suns. The cross with small hooked ends originated in ancient times, when it served as a symbol of the Solar cult. Other tattoos have a variety of representations—spikes of wheat, branches, firs, bracelets, and fences—but images of the human figure are never used. When the tattooing is finished, the tattoo is rubbed and covered with the honey-soot mixture and then wrapped in linen. In a day or two the tattoo is cleansed and thoroughly washed and thereafter remains permanent. Normally, tattooing is done in a period from the feast of St. Joseph (March 19) until just before Easter.

In conclusion, it might be emphasized that in the handicraft arts, as well as in other fields of creative art, the Croatians display fine aesthetic taste. Their feeling for art is inherited from the past and has been passed on through the centuries from generation to generation. This is the reason why Croatian handicrafts are permeated with remnants of ancient beliefs, and why they have not only artistic but also historical value.

Bibliography

Babić, Ljubo. *Boja i sklad* / Color and Harmony. Zagreb, 1943.

———. *Umjetnost kod Hrvata* / Art among the Croatians. (See particularly ch. 1: "Pučka umjetnost" / Folk Art.) Zagreb, 1943.

Gavazzi, Milovan. "Svastika i njezin ornamentalni razvoj na uskrsnim jajima sa Balkana" / Swastika and its Ornamental Development on Easter Eggs in the Balkans, *Zbornik za narodni život i običaje Juznih Slavena* / Symposium on the Folk Life and Customs of Southern Slavs. Vol. 27, 1–24. Zagreb, 1896–1957.

———. *Godina dana hrvatskih narodnih običaja* / Folk Customs of the Croatian People Around the Year. 2 vols. Zagreb: Matica Hrvatska, 1939.

———. *Pregled etnografije Hrvata* / A Survey of Ethnography Among the Croatians. 2 vols. Zagreb: ABC Club, 1940.

———. *Hrvatska narodna umjetnost* / Croatian Folk Art. Zagreb: Hrvatski Izdavalački Bibliografski Zavod, 1944.

Glasnik Zemaljskog Muzeja za Bosnu i Hercegovinu / Bulletin of the National Museum for Bosnia and Hercegovina. Sarajevo, 1889–1919.

Karaman, Ljubo. *La Dalmatie à travers les âges*. Split, 1933.

Praunsberger, Milan. *Oružje starih Hrvata u povijesti i u narodnoj pjesmi* / Weapons of the Old Croatians in History and in Folk Songs. Zagreb: Matica Hrvatska, 1943).

Tkalčić, Vladimir. *Seljačko ćilimarstvo u Jugoslaviji* / Peasant Carpet-Weaving in Yugoslavia (Ethnology Library series) Zagreb: Croatian National Ethnographic Museum in Zagreb, 1939.

Topali, Ljerka. "Drvene crkvice i seljačko drveno graditeljstvo u Turopolju" / Little Wooden Churches and Peasant Wooden Architecture in Turopolje, *Etnografska istraživanja i gradja.* Vol. 3. Zagreb, 1941.

Truhelka, Ćiro. *Studije o podrijetlu: Etnološka razmatranja iz Bosne i Hercegovine* / Studies of Origins: Ethnological Research in Bosnia and Hercegovina. Zagreb, 1941.

Zbornik za narodni život i običaje Južnih Slavena / Symposium on the Folk Life and Customs of Southern Slavs. Zagreb, 1896–1957.

8

Literature: from the Illyrian Movement to Realism (1835–1895)

K. B. K.

After the Congress of Vienna (1815), Dalmatia and Istria came under the direct rule of Austria; Croatia and Slavonia were governed from Budapest, while the Ottomans held Bosnia until 1878. Maria Theresa and her son Joseph II wanted to organize the Hapsburg Empire as a centralized state, with German as the official language. The Magyar and Croatian nobility, a united front, rejected this unconstitutional attempt on the part of the Austrians.[1] Then, strangely enough, the Magyars endeavored to impose their own tongue on the Croatians, instead of Latin, as the official language.

As could be expected, the Croatians resolutely opposed the introduction of the Magyar language into their lands. In spite of valiant Croatian resistance, Magyar was prescribed in 1830 for use in Croatian schools and public affairs; in this way the Budapest government hoped to Magyarize Croatia.[2] The stronger the pressure from the Magyar side, however, the more determined the Croatian resistance became.

The Illyrian Movement (1835–1849)

In the rank of the Croatian youth of this era there then appeared a new cultural, literary, political, and social movement known as the Illyrian Movement.[3] The younger Croatian patriots rejected the

[1]Ferdo Šišić, *Pregled povijesti hrvatskoga naroda* (Zagreb, 1916), 215–229.

[2]Ferdo Šišić, *Hrvatska povijest*, III (Zagreb, 1913), 145.

[3]The best studies of the Illyrian Movement are those by Ferdo Šišić, Antun Barac, and Franjo Fancev: Šišić, "O stogodšnjici ilirskoga pokreta," *Ljetopis Akademije* 49 (1935), 99–118; Šišić, "Genèse et caractère général du mouvement

legalistic struggle of the older, feudal-minded Croatian leaders and viewed the situation as they felt it really was. They saw in the Austrian and Hungarian governments two foreign powers who were attempting in every way to expand at the expense of the Slavs. There remained, they believed, one logical and inevitable conclusion: for the Croatians, as for the other Slavs, salvation would come only when the Slavs, who outnumbered the Germans and especially the Magyars, would become conscious of their solidarity.[4] Jan Kollár, a Slovak poet who wrote in the Czech language, was most ardent proponent of Pan-Slavism, which regarded all Slavs as a single nation speaking four dialects (Russian, Czech, Polish, and Illyrian). The South Slavs were called Illyrians because they were regarded by some scholars of the time as the descendants of this ancient race.[5]

The Illyrian Movement soon roused the whole of Croatia. As they grew aware of its significance, the Hungarian authorities tried to crush the movement. There followed a period of persecution for its members, and in 1843 the name Illyrian was forbidden, but it was impossible to stamp out the movement itself. On the contrary, the majority of the Croatian people stood united, ready to seize the first opportunity to deal a blow to Louis Kossuth (1802–1894), who boldly asserted that he "could not find Croatia on the map."[6]

The Illyrian Movement was most successful in the realm of literature. Aware that Croatian literature could not develop within the narrow orbit of the Kaykavian dialect, and that it was hampered by the several orthographies then prevailing, Ljudevit Gaj and his followers first tried to solve the problem of the literary language and orthography. They advocated that the Croatians, Serbs, and Slovenes should all recognize one literary language, the Shtokavian dialect, which was used by the

---

Illyrien," *Le Monde Slave* I (1937), 267–88; Barac, "Les études critiques sur la littérature de l'illyrisme," *Le Monde Slave* II, (1935), 353–73; Fancev, "Ilirstvo u hrvatskom preporodu," *Ljetopis* 49, 130–57; Fancev, "Hrvatski preporod kao općenarodni pokret," *Hrvatska Revija* 8 (1936), 412–27; Fancev, "Les origines autochtones du mouvement illyrien croate," *Le Monde Slave* II, 384–93; R. Warnier, "Illyrisme et nationalisme croate," *Le Monde Slave* III, (1935), 27–74. Very useful anthologies have been compiled by Slavko Ježić, *Ilirska antologija* (Zagreb, 1934), and Ilija Mamuzić, *Antologija ilirskog pokreta* (Beograd, 1953). For further bibliographical data, see Ježić, *Ilirska antologija*, 273–80, and Barac, *Književnost Ilirizma* (Zagreb, 1954), 302–7.

[4]Josip Horvat, *Stranke kod Hrvata i njihove ideologije* (Beograd, 1939), 17–25.

[5]See Hans Kohn, "Romanticism and Realism among Czechs and Slovaks," *Pan-Slavism, its History and Ideology* (Notre Dame, Indiana, 1953), 11–28.

[6]"In reality he (Lajos Kossuth) was no less reactionary than the Hapsburgs where any people but his own were concerned," writes Pavle Ostović in his *The Truth about Yugoslavia* (New York, 1952), 12.

Dubrovnik Renaissance writers, and which was also the language of the most beautiful Croatian and Serbian folk poems. Consequently, in 1836, the men of letters in Croatia accepted the Shtokavian dialect (Vuk St. Karadžić was still fighting for its recognition in Serbia) and the orthography proposed by Ljudevit Gaj, namely, a separate letter for each sound, using diacritical marks for those sounds not represented in the Latin script.

Having thus solved the important problems of language and orthography, the Illyrians went forward. They popularized the old Croatian literature of Dalmatia and Dubrovnik in order to demonstrate how ancient and brilliant their culture was; they drew attention to the beauty and originality of folk poetry; finally, they pointed to the best specimens of the most developed Slavic literatures, notably those of Russia and Poland. In doing all of this, the Illyrians hoped to give new direction and meaning to Croatian literature.

The literature of the Illyrian Movement was distinctly militant. It was the artistic expression of the sufferings and hopes of the majority of the people, of those who had neither power nor fortune, the bulk of the peasantry being still bound in serfdom. Having grown out of the struggle of the Croatian people for national, cultural, and social independence, this literature was of necessity tendentious. The writers regarded their work mostly as a national and political duty. Only the most talented among them succeeded in creating works which are cornerstones of modern Croatian literature and which set the course for the entire subsequent development of Croatian belles lettres.[7]

The most prominent member of the movement was Ljudevit Gaj (1809–72), who was born in Krapina, Croatian Zagorje, the son of a pharmacist. As a child, Gaj often heard the folk tale about Čeh, Leh, and Meh, who lived in Krapina before they set out to found the three great Slavic states (Moravia, Poland, and Russia). The myth quite captivated his imagination and led him to speculate on the Slavs and their glorious past. Gaj translated this folk tale from a Latin manuscript into German and published it in 1826 (*Die Schlösser bei Krapina*). The same year, his first Croatian poems appeared in the magazine *Luna*, all in the Kaykavian dialect.

While studying at Graz and Budapest, Gaj was influenced by the Pan-Slavic ideas of Kollár, Šafařík, and Kucharski, and eagerly read Serbian and Croatian folk poems published by Vuk Karadžić in the Shtokavian dialect. In 1830 he published his first and most important

[7]Mamuzić, *Antologija*, 24–26.

essay, *Kratka osnova horvatsko-slavenskoga pravopisanja* (The Elements of Croato-Slavonic Orthography), advocating that Croatian writers adopt a reformed orthography based on the principle of one symbol for each phoneme. Seeing clearly that Kaykavian, the dialect of a small district around Zagreb, was not suitable for a national revolution, which he and his followers hoped would eventually embrace all the speakers of Slavic languages in the Balkan Peninsula, Gaj also urged adoption of the more wide-spread Shtokavian.

The Illyrian Movement, of which Gaj was the chief ideologist and spiritual leader, began in an organized form when he started publication of a newspaper, *Novine Horvatske* (Croatian Paper) on January 6–10, 1835, and of its literary supplement, *Danica* (Morning Star). It is chiefly through these publications that Gaj earned a distinguished place in the history of this national movement, which ultimately won intellectual, linguistic, and educational, but not political, independence for Croatia.

To gain moral support and financial aid, Gaj visited Dalmatia, Russia, and Serbia. During the historic events of 1848, he again played a most important role and was the first to suggest Josip Jelačić as Ban of Croatia, during the public assembly in Zagreb. In 1848 Gaj became suspect and unpopular; from then until his death he struggled with all kinds of financial difficulties. Even today it is difficult to explain why Gaj fell so low in the esteem of his countrymen.[8] When he died, he was either forgotten or considered a traitor in the service of the Viennese court. Nevertheless, there is not a single literary historian who would not recognize that Ljudevit Gaj, who produced no truly outstanding work himself, made possible through his reforms and publications the flowering of Croatian literature. The most prominent political and literary movement in all Croatian history, the Illyrian Movement, was the structure to which Gaj sacrificed not only his

[8]Two basic reasons could be suggested. After the calamitous check of the Croatian revolution of 1848–9, his disappointed followers considered that Gaj, as their leader, was its cause. Furthermore, he was accused of having accepted money from the former Serbian prince, Miloš Obrenović. Antun Barac has attempted a rehabilitation of Gaj, explaining that the affair with Miloš was inspired by Ban Jelačić, who intended to destroy Gaj's position and so remain at the head of the Croatians. It is true that even Baron Neustadter, the biographer and friend of Jelačić, in his memoirs, states clearly that Gaj was obliged to spend his money for various national enterprises. See Barac, "Slom Ljudevita Gaja," *Ostvarenja* (1947), 227–41; cf. also Joseph Baron Neustadter, *Le ban Jellacic et les événements en Croatie depuis l'an 1848* (Zagreb: Institut français de Zagreb, I–II, 1939–42), *passim.*

brilliant talent, but also his energy, time, money, and finally his reputation.[9]

The most important writers of the Illyrian Movement were Ivan Mažuranić, Stanko Vraz, and Petar Preradović.[10] Ivan Mažuranić (1814–90) was born in Novi, in the Croatian Littoral. He graduated from the *Gymnasium* at Rijeka, earned a degree in law at Zagreb, and practiced as a lawyer at Karlovac. With the collapse of the feudal system in 1848, Mažuranić became a deputy in the Croatian Sabor. In 1873 he became Ban (civil governor) of Croatia, the first plebeian to be appointed to this high office.[11]

Mažuranić was actively engaged in literature only during his younger years, before he devoted himself to politics. He wrote his first verses while still a student in the *Gymnasium*. Mažuranić published a number of poems in Gaj's *Danica*, which are extremely varied in expression. He followed the classic authors and the poets of Dubrovnik in both language and meter, and for a time imitated the Italian poets. After ten years of vacillation among these styles, Mažuranić discovered a style which appealed to him in the simplicity of folk poems.[12] He composed excellent verses to complete the missing Cantos XIV and XV of Gundulić's epic *Osman* (1844).[13] His chief work, however, is the poem *Smrt Smail-age Čengića* (The Death of Smail-Aga Čengić), 1846.

Mažuranić wrote his most significant work in connection with an event which took place in 1840. The Montenegrins ambushed and killed one of their enemies, the Turkish Aga Smail Čengić, who had done much harm along their frontier, and this incident was widely

[9]Gaj could be compared with another Croatian, Pavao Vitezović (1652–1723), who also concerned himself with the problems of literary language and orthography, but who died expelled from his homeland. Their love for their native country was stronger than human injustice. Thanks to them and to others, the Croatian people can still chant the famous song written by Gaj in 1833: "Još Hrvatska ni propala . . ." (Croatia is still alive . . .). Cf. F. Fancev, "Postanak i historijska pozadina Gajeve pjesme," *Hrvatska Revija* (1935), 617–33; Miloš Savković, *Ogledi* (Beograd, 1952), 64–209.

[10]In my discussion of these three authors, I have relied extensively upon Barac, *Hrvatska književnost, I: Književnost Ilirizma* (Zagreb, 1954).

[11]The last words uttered by Mažuranić in the Croatian Diet were: "I am a firm believer in the past, the present, and the future of my Croatian nation!" (Ježić, *Ilirska antologija,* 197). Milutin Nehajev wrote an interesting article about Mažuranić and his public functions in *Hrvatska Revija* 10 (1930), 525–36 and *Hrvatska Revija* 12, 637–51.

[12]Barac, *Mažuranić* (Zagreb, 1945), 89–118.

[13]Ivan Gundulić, *Osman*, edited by Milan Ratković (Zagreb, 1955), 283; Barac, *Mažuranić*, 119–129.

publicized in the newspapers.[14] Mažuranić was concerned not so much with presenting the incident faithfully and in detail, but with taking the case of Smail-Aga as a pretext for describing the sufferings of his countrymen under the centuries-long Turkish yoke, their heroic behavior amid their hardships, and their faith in final victory over the tyrant.

The greatness of Mažuranić's poem lies in its plasticity and conciseness. His expression is reduced to the essential; not a single word could be omitted from the poem without weakening its clarity. The characters are clearly portrayed in a few lines that reveal all their individual qualities, propensities, and longings. The poem is a condensed history of the Croatians (*antemurale Christianitatis*) and of the other South Slavic nations in their long struggle with the Ottoman Empire. It is not so much a description of one skirmish among innumerable clashes on the Turkish frontier as it is an emphatic stressing of man's duty to fight against oppression. Mažuranić constantly underlines his basic idea: to those who believe in God and act as His children, the day of liberation will come; the power of all tyrants, past and present, is temporary.[15]

Smrt Smail-age Čengića is a distinctly Croatian work. It epitomizes all the elements of Croatian culture: the classical, the western European, and those of the Dalmatian and Dubrovnik period. Based as it is on folk poetry, all these foreign and national elements are assimilated to such a degree that the Croatian language flows in its most natural rhythm; and Mažuranić, as its poet, is at his most personal. Concerning Mažuranić, Franjo Marković, the renowned Croatian critic, wrote: "Our four centuries of struggle in the Balkans for faith and freedom has at length found its Homer," and Vuk Karadžić, the great Serbian literary reformer, declared enthusiastically: "Nobody in the world could have sung it better!"[16]

Stanko Vraz (1810–51), from Cerovec, Slovenia [Styria], after graduating from the *Gymnasium* in Maribor, went to Graz to study

[14]Ferdo Šišić, "Pogibija Smail-age Čengijića," *Hrvatsko Kolo* (1908), 164–81.

[15]J. W. Wiles, who translated *Smrt Smail-age Čengića* into English, rightly remarked: "A certain moral and spiritual elevation distinguishes this work. The reader is made to feel instinctively from the outset that divine vengeance must dog the steps of the sinner. . . . It is the conviction that the very stars in their courses are fighting against Smail-aga, the conviction also that to take up arms on behalf of Righteousness is not only an irresistible, but also a heart-searching and exacting call" (*The Death of Smail-Aga* [London, 1925], 12).

[16]Slavko Ježić collected an exhaustive bibliography of Mažuranić in his *Djela* (Zagreb, 1958), 45–63.

law, a subject which he later abandoned in order to study languages and literature. He learned all the Slavic and many other European languages, including Greek and Latin, and read widely in world literature. During his prolonged stay in Graz (1830–37), Vraz formed a very close friendship with Franz Miklosich, later a well-known philologist. Vraz first wrote a great deal of prose and poetry in his native tongue, Slovenian, but from 1835 on he also sent contributions to the Croatian journal *Danica.* After he settled down in Zagreb, in 1838, he wrote exclusively in Croatian. Vraz was the only writer of non-Croatian origin who espoused the Illyrian Movement in its full sense. While Gaj was the political leader of the movement, Vraz was its most eminent poet. Of all Gaj's collaborators, Vraz was distinguished by his purely literary interests. When misunderstandings arose between himself and Gaj, Vraz founded, with a group of friends, the literary magazine *Kolo* (1842), for which he wrote numerous articles and reviews under the nom de plume Jakob Rešetar. In 1846 he was appointed secretary of Matica Ilirska, a post which he held till his death from consumption in 1851.

Vraz was a prolific and versatile writer. Among his better works are three collections of original and translated poems: *Djulabije* (Sweet Apples), 1840; *Glasi iz dubrave žerovinske* (Echoes from the Grove of Žerovo), 1841; and *Gusle i tambura* (The Fiddle and Tambura), 1845. Vraz's literary reputation is founded chiefly on his love poems. At a time when other Croatian poets were composing patriotic poems, young Vraz was writing about the subject uppermost in his thoughts, love. Vraz describes his first meetings with his beloved (Ljubica Cantilly), his moments of happiness, their quarrel and separation, her marriage to another, his anguish, and her early death. Though some similarities with Petrarch, and especially with the Dubrovnik poets, can be detected, the feelings which Vraz portrays are his own, and each of his poems is indeed a true reflection of his inner life. His love for Ljubica gradually became sublimated into a love for Croatia; he came to feel a deep and tender attachment for Croatia and its destiny.[17]

Vraz introduced into Croatian literature two foreign poetic forms, the sonnet and the ghazel. The sonnet cycle *Sanak i istina* (Dream and Truth), the fruit of his new love, is the most perfect in form of Vraz's words; the cycle is characterized by a lyrical romanticism which reaches

[17]Vraz wrote from Maribor, in 1841, to his friend Vjekoslav Babukić as follows: "Croatia is like health, which one can only begin to appreciate when one has lost it!" Cf. Gjordje Živanović, "Mickiewicz in Serbo-Croatian Literature," *Adam Mickiewicz in World Literature*, ed. by Waclaw Lednicki (Berkeley, 1956), 513. The sentence is reminiscent of the opening verses of *Pan Tadeusz.*

moving heights. Something youthfully gay and direct emanates from them. As he advanced in years, Vraz began more and more to write satires and epigrams in which he bitterly condemned various negative aspects of the Croatian feudal society.[18]

Vraz's talent never found its full expression, for, as a Slovene, he did not gain complete mastery over the Croatian language and accent. As a result, irregularities and archaisms will be found in his poems; even his best poems are not completely free of such shortcomings.[19] Vraz constantly pointed out, in his reviews published in *Kolo*, that the purpose of Croatian literature as a whole was to create an artistic literature on the basis of folk poetry.[20] Accordingly, he discouraged the exaggerated admiration for the Dubrovnik writers that was then the vogue among the Croatians. He contended that the Dubrovnik writers imitated the Italians too much.[21] Vraz instead drew attention to the exceptional quality of *Smrt Smail-age Čengića*, of *Gorski Vijenac* (Njegoš), and of Radičević's lyrics. In the works of Mažuranić, Njegoš, and Radičević he saw his own ideal. Croatian literature of the nineteenth century followed the course indicated by this gifted, industrious, and altruistic writer; and although literary critics evaluate the intrinsic value of his poetry differently, no one can deny his exceptional contribution to Croatian letters.[22]

The third prominent member of this Illyrian group was Petar Preradović, born in the village of Grabrovnica near Bjelovar in 1818. He was admitted to the Austrian Military Academy at Wiener Neustadt, where he remained for eight years (1830–39). His education was so exclusively German that on a visit home he had difficulty speaking Croatian with his mother. Preradović served as an officer in numerous Austrian garrisons and reached the rank of general. He died in 1872, far away from his native land, at Fahrafeld, near Vöslau, Austria, but his remains were later transferred to Zagreb.

Compelled to serve mostly outside Croatia, Preradović felt like a

[18]For example, "Hrvat pred otvorenim nebom" (A Croatian at the Doorway of Paradise).

[19]Mihovil Kombol, *Antologija novije hrvatske lirike* (Beograd, 1956), 6.

[20]A. Barac, *Hrvatska književna kritika* (Zagreb, 1938), 5.

[21]It is difficult to disagree with Vraz when he stresses the point that Croatian literature would have been completely different—he means better and more national—if the Croatian Renaissance poets, instead of copying the Italians, had followed the language, the rhythm, and the spirit of folk poetry. Cf. Josip Torbarina, *Italian Influence on the Poets of the Ragusan Republic* (London, 1931).

[22]"Resta la figura del primo *homme de lettres* illirico, il quale ha intuito e sanzionato la razionalità intrinseca della letteratura illirica conciliando 'sogni' illirici e 'verità' estetiche." Cronia, *Storia della letteratura Serbo-Croata* (Milan, 1956), 208.

foreigner wherever he went. Constant transfers, the death of his first wife and of his children, together with his own illness, broke him morally and ruined him financially. During moments of despair he sought refuge in spiritualism. Preradović began to write in German while he was still a military cadet.[23] On duty in Milan, then under Austrian rule, Preradović, influenced by Ivan Kukuljević (1816–89), began to show an interest in the Croatian language and in Croatian literature. Later on, during a stay in Zadar, he began to publish in his mother tongue (1844). His poems immediately attracted attention because they were without the usual failings of the beginner. Preradović soon ranked among the most outstanding poets of the Croatian National Awakening. In 1846 he published his first collection of poems, *Prvenci* (The First Born), and in 1851 his second, *Nove pjesme* (New Poems). After the failure of the Revolution of 1848 he abandoned literature. With the restoration of constitutional government in Austria in 1860, Preradović again became a valued contributor to Croatian literary journals and continued to write until his death in 1872.

In his early patriotic poems, Preradović revealed the feelings of a man who had comprehended the meaning of his homeland only through living abroad. He extolled the beauties of his country, its greatness, and its glorious past. He emphasized the charm and extraordinary capacity for expression of the Croatian language. He glorified the function of poetry and the poet's national duty.[24] Preradović viewed Slavdom as a philosopher and prophet. According to him, the Slavs would reconcile all nations and, finally, create an era of love and happiness. His ode "Slavjanstvu" (To Slavdom) is the vision of Slavdom in all its vastness of scope and idea.[25] Preradović also wrote a number of love poems, touching and warm in their emotion and directness, but he was primarily inclined to reflections upon life and human destiny.

Living away from his people, Preradović lacked confidence in his knowledge of his native tongue. Yet, notwithstanding their linguistic failings,[26] his poems manifest a real lyricism and deep nobility. His

[23]Preradović's German poetry was collected and edited by Branko Vodnik in *Djela Petra Preradovića*, II (Zagreb, 1919), 277–406, 410–413.

[24]Cf. A. Barac, "Preradović u pismima i stihovima," *Republika* 8 (1952), 65–86.

[25]Paul Selver translated this ode into English in *Anthology of Modern Slavonic Literature*. Here are the opening lines: With gesture of obeisance I bow myself down unto thy black earth,/Having set foot on thy domain, riddle of all the world,/Glorious, mighty, renowned, omnipotent Slavdom! (London, 1919), 300.

[26]Albert Haler overemphasized these failings in his article "O poeziji Petra Preradovića," *Srpski Književni Glasnik* (July 16, 1928, 426–39 and August 1, 1928, 503–17).

poetry was not surpassed in Croatian lyric poetry until the coming of Silvije St. Kranjčević in the eighties.[27]

Romanticism (1849–80)

In Croatia, during the revolutionary year 1848, all relations with Hungary were cut off; an autonomous government within the Hapsburg Monarchy was established. The feudal system was abolished, and the first time commoners became members of the Croatian Sabor.[28] In order to consolidate her power, Austria abolished the constitution in 1852 and set up an absolutist government. German became the official language of the entire Empire. A gendarmerie was organized; spies and confidential officials were employed. Croatia was flooded with bureaucrats who were ignorant of the Croatian language and of Croatian traditions. The nine years of absolutist regime were nine years of terror, persecution, and fear.[29] As a consequence of the Austrian military defeat in Italy (1860), the absolutist regime was overthrown, and the different nations within Austria regained partial freedom. Croatia was granted a government independent of Hungary.

Meanwhile, negotiations were conducted concerning the political reorganization of Austria. The main issue was whether Austria should be a centralized or a federal monarchy. After Austria's defeat in the war with Prussia (1866), the Austrian and Hungarian statesmen reached an agreement (1867) by which the Hapsburg Monarchy was divided into two halves, one Austrian and one Hungarian. Without being consulted, Croatia and Slavonia were reincorporated into the Hungarian half. Austria, on the other hand, retained control of the Croatians in Dalmatia and Istria. All the Slovenian provinces (Carniola, Styria, and Carinthia) remained in the Austrian half. In this way the German minority ruled Austria, and the Magyar minority

[27]A detailed bibliography concerning Preradović is found in Mihovil Kombol, *Antologija novije hrvatske lirike* (Zagreb, 1934), 216–18.

[28]Horvat, *Stranke kod Hrvata*, 28–35. Much attention has been paid in postwar Yugoslavia to the events of 1848–49 in Croatia. Cf. Jaroslav Šidak, "Revolucija godine 1848–49," *Historijski Zbornik* 1–4 (1948), 25–42; Vaso Bogdanov, "Uloga podunavskih slavenskih naroda 1848–49," *Historijski Zbornik* 1–4 1948, 43–66. (The unjust verdict on the attitude of the South Slavic nations during the revolutionary years expressed here ought to be revised; they joined the counterrevolution when it became obvious that the Magyar and German revolutionaries did not recognize South Slavic national ambitions.) Bogdanov published many articles and two books on the same subject, *Hrvatska ljevica u godinama revolucije 1848–49* (Zagreb, 1949), and *Društvene i političke borbe u Hrvatskoj 1848–49* (Zagreb, 1949).

[29]Nikola Andrić, *Pod apsolutizmom* (Zagreb, 1906).

ruled Hungary; in Dalmatia and Istria almost all power was in the hands of the tiny Italian minority.[30]

Relations between Croatia and Hungary were partly settled in 1868, with the so-called Hungaro-Croatian Agreement (*Nagodba*). Although Croatia enjoyed autonomy in some affairs (administration, schools, jurisdiction), dissatisfaction was general in the country.[31] Eugen Kvaternik, in 1871, attempted an unsuccessful uprising.[32] Conditions improved somewhat when Ivan Mažuranić, the great Croatian poet, became Ban of Croatia in 1873. During his term of office (1873–80) he organized the school system and an advanced administration apparatus.[33]

In the 1860's, the only notable Croatian poet was Luka Botić (born in Split, 1830; died in Djakovo, 1863). Botić studied theology in Zadar; after being expelled from the seminary, he traveled through Bosnia and into Serbia. He unsuccessfully sought employment in Belgrade, worked for a certain period in Zagreb, and settled temporarily in Djakovo as an employee on the large landed estate of Bishop Strossmayer. After refusing to take a loyalty oath to the emperor, Botić was dismissed. Later he succeeded in being elected as a deputy to the Croatian Sabor. At the age of thirty-three, Botić died of tuberculosis.[34]

Botić was greeted as a very promising young writer in 1854, when he published, in the literary journal *Neven*, his epic poem "Pobratimstvo" (Brotherly Friendship), and the novella "Dilber Hasan." In a period when folklore dominated the literary scene, Botić was among the first writers to emphasize the neglected fact that Bosnian Christians and Moslems were brothers by blood, and that their religion should not be a dividing force among them. It was, until that time, customary to depict the Moslems as despots, bandits, or morally perverse persons. Botić portrays them as human, heroic, and as the best friends one can imagine. When, in 1861, on the basis of historical documents from the second half of the sixteenth century, Botić published his second epic work, "Bijedna Mara" (Unhappy Mary), he so captivated the heart of the public that even today it is read and often quoted. It has also been adapted as a musical and a play. In this story, set in Split, a

[30]Cf. Joseph Redlich, *Emperor Francis Joseph of Austria* (New York, 1929), 348–80; Grga Novak, *Prošlost Dalmacije*, II (Zagreb, 1944), 399–405.

[31]Horvat, *Stranke kod Hrvata*, 48–50; Vaso Bogdanov, *Historija političkih stranaka u Hrvatskoj* (Zagreb, 1958), 518–604.

[32]Milutin Nehajev, *Rakovica* (Zagreb, 1932).

[33]Milutin Nehajev, "O Ivanu Mažuraniću, kancelaru i banu," *Hrvatska Revija* 10 (1930), 525–36, and *Hrvatska Revija* 12, 637–51; Milan Marjanović, *Savremena Hrvatska* (Beograd, 1913), 134.

[34]Jakša Ravlić, "Introduction" to Botić's *Djela* (Zagreb, 1949), 5–15.

Christian beauty, Mara Vornić, falls madly in love with Adel, a Moslem merchant from the neighboring Klis; Mara is forced by her parents to enter a convent, where she soon dies.

Although he mostly wrote longer epic poems (his third epic is called "Petar Bačić," 1862), Botić was at his best as a lyricist. He wrote only when he found sufficient time and physical strength: this, perhaps, is the main reason why his works lack a coherent development. His lyrical digressions, too, may be partly responsible for the fact that Botić sometimes loses track of his main plots and the central idea. There is, nevertheless, unity in his basic outlook. He believes that good and honest people are always on the losing side, while unscrupulous individuals are successful everywhere.[35]

The most distinguished Croatian man of letters during the seventies was August Šenoa (1838–81); he studied law first in his native city of Zagreb, and then in Prague and Vienna. Šenoa began his varied literary career as a student in Prague from 1859 to 1865. In 1865 he moved to Vienna in order to assume the editorship of the literary review *Glasonoša*. After his return to Zagreb in 1866 he secured a position within the Municipal Council. For a time he was art director of the Zagreb Theater. He contributed regularly to the newspaper *Pozor* (later renamed *Obzor*), but from 1874 until his death in 1881 he published mainly in *Vijenac* (the best literary magazine of that time), of which he was editor-in-chief. At the peak of his fame and of an extremely productive career, Šenoa suddenly died at the age of forty-three, mourned by the Croatian public as no other writer before or since.

Thanks to Šenoa, who was in favor of replacing the German repertoire[36] in the Zagreb Theater with the works not only of Slavic but also, and especially, of French playwrights, this period witnessed translations of the latest works of Hugo, Scribe, Dumas, and others. It was at this time that Shakespeare was first presented on the Croatian stage.[37] As a drama critic, Šenoa touched on every problem of the

[35]Cf. A. Barac, *Veličina malenih* (Zagreb, 1947), 7–44; Ante Kadić, "San i stvarnost-slučaj Luke Botića," *Croatian Voice* Calendar (1955), 174–80.

[36]The year 1860 marked a decisive turning point in the history of the Zagreb Theater. During a performance in German, a violent demonstration broke out, after which the German language as well as German actors were eliminated from the Zagreb stage. Under the leadership of the author Dimitrije Demeter (1811–72) and the direction of Josip Freudenreich, Croatian drama began to develop more rapidly. The national repertoire grew, while the foreign repertoire still remained mostly of German origin.

[37]Ivo Hergešić disagrees with this statement in his *Shakespeare, Molière, Goethe* (Zagreb, 1957), 28–9.

Zagreb Theater. He insisted that it should rise to a higher artistic level and that its members should be more realistic in their interpretations.

Although he wrote his literary reviews without any clearly defined critical method, Šenoa nevertheless succeeded in pointing out the chief merits of the work under review; he emphasized especially its artistic, national, and social characteristics. In theory, Šenoa was a staunch supporter of realism. He constantly reminded young story-writers of the abundant material lying at hand in contemporary life. He discouraged them from giving conventional and lifeless portraits, advising them to study people continually. In his opinion, the models to be followed by Croatian literature were the Russians Gogol and Turgenev, and the French realists. In practice, however, in order to add to the interest of his stories and historical novels, Šenoa himself often had recourse to the many requisites of the romanticists: love at first sight, insurmountable difficulties, spies, intriguers and murderers.[38]

Šenoa made his start in literature by writing poems. Although he continued until the end of his life to write both epic and lyric poems, he cannot be called a true lyric poet; only occasionally does he reveal his own feelings of pain or joy.[39] The predominant note of his poetry is its descriptive character, with vivid evocation of some better known historic scenes (in the so-called *povjestica*, a kind of romantic ballad). Some of his most popular poems deal chiefly with the educational and social problems of his time. Their importance today lies in the fact that they are the best expression of what the average Croatian of Šenoa's period felt. In these poems Šenoa extols individuality, freedom, courage, social justice, and industriousness.

In many of his stories, Šenoa successfully portrayed the lower Croatian nobility, often making them appear ridiculous because of their altercations and petty disputes; he also presented the bourgeoisie as it gradually prospered or suddenly came to ruin; the slow disintegration of the peasant joint families (*zadrugas*); and the continuous struggle of the small man who attempts to climb the social ladder. As in his poems, in his stories he treated current social and educational problems. In "Ilijina oporuka" (The Will of Elias), 1876, for example, he described a factual case of a perverted woman who enjoyed ruining her

[38]Cf. Miloš Savković, *L'Influence du realisme français dans le roman serbo-croate* (Paris, 1935), 251–67; Barac, *Hrvatska književna kritika*, 25–39. This mixture of realism and romanticism is to be found even in the works of the most renowned Croatian realist writers, such as Gjalski, Kovačić, Kumičić, and some representatives of the Croatian *moderna*.

[39]Mihovil Kombol, *Novija hrvatska lirika* (Beograd, 1956), 7.

husband financially and her daughter morally; in "Prosjak Luka" (Luke the Beggar), 1879, he gave us a masterly sketch of a money-lender who mercilessly destroyed two respectable peasant families; in "Branka" (1881) he touched upon the problem of the village schoolmistress who kept her moral and national ideals high in the midst of humiliating and degrading surroundings. "Karamfil sa pjesnikova groba" (A Carnation from the Poet's Tomb), 1878, is an account of his pilgrimage to the tomb of Francè Prešeren, the greatest Slovenian poet, and of Šenoa's first tender but unhappy love for a Slovenian girl by the name of Neža. Šenoa was an ardent Croatian patriot, but one of those who believed in Slavic brotherhood.

Šenoa, however, devoted himself chiefly to the historical novel. Living at a time when Croatian patriots took an excessive interest in their past history in order to demonstrate that their rights were often violated by Magyars, Šenoa endeavored in particular to give an artistic presentation of those periods of Croatian history in which fundamental problems of national life were involved.[40] By drawing a comparison between events from the past and events of his day, he sought to exercise a guiding influence on his contemporaries. In his novels, he drew upon figures and events from the fourteenth century to the eighteenth. His best historical novels are: *Zlatarovo zlato* (The Goldsmith's Daughter), 1871, in which he vividly depicts some unforgettable characters from the old Zagreb, during the years 1574–90; *Seljačka buna* (The Peasant Rebellion), 1877, which concerns events which happened during the preceding years and which resulted in one of the bloodiest peasant rebellions in Croatia, under the leadership of the beloved national hero Matija Gubec (1573); *Diogenes* (1878), a brilliant sketch of Zagreb in the middle of the eighteenth century, based on the memoirs of Adam Krčelić (*Annuae*);[41] and *Kletva* (The Curse), his most extensive work, in which he insisted that, even at the end of the fourteenth century, the Croatian noblemen and clergymen fought against the unjustified Hungarian claims on Croatian national territory. This last work unfortunately remained unfinished. Finally, Šenoa's very popular novella, "Čuvaj se senjske ruke" (Beware of Uskoks from Senj, 1875), should be mentioned.

Šenoa knew very well how to present both the glorious and the tragic sides of Croatian history. He appealed to the reading public primarily

[40]Ferdo Šišić (1869–1940), one of the greatest Croatian historians, used to recommend Šenoa's work to his students. Savković is right when he affirms that "Šenoa prenait grand soin de reconstituer la vérité historique, grâce à une minutieuse documentation" (*L'Influence*, 256).

[41]Cf. V. Gortan, in B. Krčelić's *Annuae* (Zagreb, 1952), 625.

because of his narrative genius: he was able to alternate serious scenes with comic situations, pathos with sentimentality, the bloody events of war with pictures of domestic happiness. With his topic sentences he could attract the reader's attention and hold it until the end. Šenoa raised the historical novel to so high a level that none of his followers have been able to surpass him.[42]

The rapidity with which Šenoa wrote, along with his tendentiousness, caused him to neglect esthetic values in his works and, in some cases, he gives the impression of being a patriotic writer rather than an artist. However, it was with Šenoa that the modern period in Croatian literature really began.

Realism (1880–95)

In 1878, in accordance with the decision of the Congress of Berlin, Austria and Hungary occupied Bosnia-Hercegovina, on the pretext of establishing order and setting up European methods of administration. All control was placed in the hands of foreigners, notably of Germans and Magyars.[43] Croatians and Serbs were equally unhappy: the Croatians sincerely believed that this province should become a part of the Croatian realm, and the Serbs most emphatically proclaimed that Bosnia-Hercegovina was Serbian land. Because of these opposing political attitudes, the rivalry between Croatians and Serbs grew even greater.[44]

The political situation of the Croatian people inside Austria-Hungary was becoming worse and worse. Supported by Vienna, the Hungarian authorities sought to implement the dualistic principle without mercy. Mažuranić was forced to resign in 1880, and the Hungarians resumed their earlier attempts to Magyarize Croatia and Slavonia. They nominated Count Khuen Hederváry Ban of Croatia, a man who was Hungarian by birth and sentiment. The twenty years of his rule (1883–1903) amounted to twenty years of political, economic, and cultural oppression, the purpose of which was to crush the resistance of the Croatians and to turn Croatia into an ordinary Hungarian province.

[42]*Hrvatska proza*, Vol. I, ed. by P. Šegedin (Beograd, 1956), 491.

[43]"Extensive and controversial literature has been written concerning this expansion of the monarchy, but its sense and meaning is quite clear. The fatal decision had two chief motives. One was the old desire for conquest of the Hapsburg imperialism which, after so many humiliations, became again victorious. . . . The other cause was the growing desire to check the natural extension of the Serb state and of Jugo-Slav unity." Oscar Jaszi, *The Dissolution of the Hapsburg Monarchy* (Chicago, 1929), 411–14.

[44]Vladimir Ćorović, *Istorija Jugoslavije* (Beograd, 1933), 529–33.

Khuen Hedervåry deliberately fomented discord between Croatians and Serbs in order to enlist the Serbs in his cause. The reaction of the Croatian intelligentsia was either a withdrawal into silence, resignation, and a tacit acceptance of the present regime, or else membership in the very radical and militant Croatian Nationalistic Party, led by Ante Starčević, which refused to recognize that Croatia was under any legal obligation to Hungary or Austria.[45]

We have seen that August Šenoa was the champion of the theory of realism. As a definite movement, however, realism dominated Croatian literature only from after Šenoa's death until about the end of the century. As never before, the Croatian writers were numerous, prolific, and talented, excelling mostly in the field of the novel.[46] Only a few of the most outstanding writers will be discussed below in detail.

The first Croatian writer to defend realism, and even naturalism, in a programatic way, was Eugenij Kumičić (1850–1904), who was born on the east coast of Istria, in the small town of Berseč, at the foot of Mount Sisol (whence he derived his frequently-used pseudonym: Jenio Sisolski).[47] Three periods, associated with three different influences, are of great importance to an understanding of Kumičić's entire literary work. The first period comprises his early years spent in his native Istria. Here, in a happy family circle and under the watchful eye of his mother, he spent his childhood. It was then that he became sincerely attached to the Istrian peasants, fishermen, and sailors, and that his eye caught the beauties of the sea. All of these are reflected in Kumičić's works. He used to return repeatedly to his native town, to his people and the seacoves, first as a *Gymnasium* student at Rijeka, and later as a famous literary figure and well-known politician.

In the depths of his soul, often disillusioned by political strife in Zagreb, Kumičić always carried a bright memory of his early childhood. Hence, when he writes of his native region and of the people who inhabit it, he makes use of the brightest and most beautiful colors. The author takes us from daily life into the realm of the idyll. It seems as if he adhered to the motto which Rousseau once valued: the farther one withdraws from town and civilization and the nearer one approaches nature, the closer one is to honesty and other natural virtues.

[45]Horvat, *Stranke kod Hrvata*, 52–9; Alexander Flaker, "O pravaškom radikalizmu 80-tih godina XIX stoljeća," *Historijski Zbornik* 1–4 (1954), 85–101; Ćorović, *Istorija*, VI, 540–41.

[46]Miloš Savković, *L'Influence du realisme français dans le roman serbocroate* (Paris, 1935); Mihovil Kombol (ed.), *Hrvatski pripovjedači osamdesetih i devedesetih godina* (Zagreb: Minerva, 1935), 5–18.

[47]Ante Kadić, "Eugen Kumičić," *Croatia Press* 151 (1955), 2–4.

After finishing his university studies in Vienna (history and geography, 1873) and after teaching for a year in Split,[48] Kumičić went to Paris for further study and spent a little more than a year there (1875–77). Paris became for the young professor the symbol of all that was beautiful, noble, famous, and progressive.[49] He returned home under two significant influences: first, that of the French Parliament, manifested in the passionate love for eloquence which is present in all his works; and second, that of Zola and naturalism. *L'Assommoir* was published during his stay in Paris, and his greatest desire was to become the Croatian Zola.

As soon as his first novel, *Olga i Lina*, was published in 1881, the very successful novel *Gospodja Sabina* (1884),[50] and a hastily written article, "About the Novel" (in which he attempted to defend himself and his own novels more than Zola), followed. Kumičić became the cause and often the subject of the most bitter polemics; these were a novelty and signified progress in Croatian literary criticism. The majority of the literary critics of that time expressed themselves against Zola and naturalism, and favored moderation and realism. They examined Kumičić's pages with a microscope and denied him any literary talent.[51]

A very significant event in Kumičić's life was his resignation from the teaching profession (1883), in the hope that he would be free to devote his time to political and literary activities. As one of the leading personalities in the Nationalist Party, whose program included the attainment of freedom and independence for Croatia, he was elected a representative to the Diet on several occasions. Kumičić placed all his energy at the disposal of his party, and even his novels were written mainly in the service of politics. From this period originate two of his

[48]At Split, Kumičić had the opportunity of becoming better acquainted with the famous archaeologist Don Frane Bulić (1846–1934), and through him with the sarcophagi of the Croatian kings in Solin (near Split) and its environs.

[49]Sometimes with only a crust of bread in his pocket, Kumičić attended the opera or walked with clouded eyes along the boulevards, reliving the great past of this city from which there echoed throughout the world the phrase "Liberté, égalité, fraternité." Cf. Savković, *L'Influence*, 287–90.

[50]This novel was re-edited in 1955 with an excellent introduction by Krešimir Georgijević (Beograd), pp. 5–15.

[51]Only later, and then mostly because of his Istrian novels (*Jelkin Bosiljak*, 1881; *Začudjeni svatovi*, 1883; *Sirota*, 1885, etc.), did some praise him excessively, while others continued to attack him. Today it is generally held that Jakša Čedomil (1868–1929) was correct in regarding this non-objectivity of praise and abuse as one of the main reasons for Kumičić's literary indecision and his only partial success; he had lost his way and was wasting his talent as a writer on a public which had little taste. Cf. *Hrvatska književna kritika*, II (Zagreb, 1951), 260–82.

best and most widely read novels, *Urota Zrinsko-Frankopanska* (The Conspiracy of Zrinski and Frankopan), 1892,[52] and *Kraljica Lepa* (Queen Lepa or The Last of the Croatian Kings), 1902. The former was directed against Vienna, and the latter against papal Rome. The main idea presented in these two historical novels is that political unions were not successful in the past and, because of this, Croatia must abstain from future unions; the best solution for her, according to Kumičić, was complete independence. Attacked by political enemies, especially those in favor of union with Hungary, disillusioned by dissension in his own party, too harshly judged by younger critics, and exhausted by excessive work, Kumičić died in his fifty-fourth year.

Kumičić's present fame and reputation among readers rests on his Istrian and historical novels. The former are impressive even today because of the warmth with which the author portrays the Istrians, particularly the tender characters of the Istrian girls. His descriptions of the sea are also truly superlative. There has been no Croatian literary figure who has better or more picturesquely depicted the sea in all its daily and seasonal moods. It is said of Kumičić that without the sea he could not live, and that he always longed for it.

A writer who joined the ranks of the realists for political rather than for literary reasons was Ante Kovačić (1854–89), born at Marija Gorica, Croatian Zagorje, the son of an extremely poor peasant. Because Kovačić was an especially gifted child, his parish priest helped him to attend the *Gymnasium* in Zagreb. After quarrelling with his benefactor, Kovačić lived chiefly from grants and by tutoring. Left without any means of support, he entered a Catholic seminary, which he deserted two years later, and began to study law. Before completing his law studies, he married a schoolteacher, Milka Hajdinova, with whom he had five children.[53] Kovačić worked in law offices in Zagreb and Karlovac; he was overworked, underpaid, and worried about his sizeable family. He had only his evenings in which to dispose of his many obligations and to work on his projects. He was finally granted a license to become an independent lawyer, but in the remote Glina, where he found very few clients, and even these, if they could re-

[52]Counts Zrinski and Frankopan, the chiefs of the two leading Croatian noble families of the time, were beheaded in 1671 by the Austrians for their plans to free Croatia from the Hapsburgs. Cf. Vaso Bogdanov, "Historijsko značenje urote Zrinskih i Frankopana," in his *Likovi i pokreti* (Zagreb, 1957), 7–47.

[53]Among them should be mentioned Krešimir Kovačić (b. 1889), who has written satirical works and has published many interesting details about his father's tortured life, as well as his entire correspondence. Cf. *Gradja za povijest književnosti hrvatske*, ed. by the Yugoslav Academy of Sciences and Arts, vol. XXV, 7–128.

munerate him at all, paid him in fresh fruit or hens. Unhappy, tormented, and hopelessly alone, he suffered a sudden nervous breakdown and, a few days later, at the age of thirty-five, died in a mental hospital.

Kovačić wrote poems[54] and feuilletons, but his most important works are the stories "Ljubljanska katastrofa" (The Ljubljana Disaster), 1877, "Ladanjska sekta" (The Sect on Vacation), 1880, and the novels *Baruničina ljubav* (The Baroness' Love), 1877; *Fiškal* (The Solicitor), 1882; *Medju žabarima* (Among Provincials), 1886; and *U registraturi* (In the Records Office), 1888. Also worthy of mention is his travesty *Smrt Babe Čengićkinje* (The Death of the Coward Čengić), 1880, in which he bitterly, and to a great extent unjustly, ridicules the former Ban of Croatia, Ivan Mažuranić, because, in pursuing Croatian national interests, Mažuranić had followed a different method from that which Kovačić would have liked.

Kovačić was violent by character and perhaps for that reason had very few friends, even among those who belonged to the same nationalist party (led by Ante Starčević) as he did. It was no surprise that his death passed almost unnoticed. It seemed, indeed, as if Kovačić's name was doomed to complete oblivion. However, a decade after his death, two outstanding literary critics, Ivan Krnić and Milan Marjanović, wrote extensive studies about him, in which they easily demonstrated how the author of works such as *Medju žabarima*, and especially *U registraturi*, was endowed with a unique narrative talent. They also pointed to Kovačić's penetrating observations, his most astonishing imagination, and his very progressive ideas. They did not fail, however, to notice his almost unbelievable romanticism amid a number of crudely naturalistic episodes and not very convincing characters, who bore the marks of hasty composition.[55]

His most important work, *U registraturi*, which originally appeared in the literary journal *Vijenac*, was not published in book form until 1911.[56] Because Kovačić fought strenuously for the underprivileged classes and was intentionally ruined by a hostile government, and

[54]Matoš, in collaboration with Kovačić's son Krešimir, published Kovačić's selected poems and stories (*Izabrane pjesme*; *Sabrane pripovijesti*) in 1908 and 1910.

[55]*Hrvatska Moderna*, II (Zagreb, 1951), 98–122; *Hrvatska književna kritika*, III, 65–68; *Savremenik* (1907), 74–84; *Hrvatski esej*, 131–45.

[56]The main reasons why this unique work of Croatian prose did not appear before that date are probably that the official organ of the Zagreb archdiocese attacked Kovačić on the grounds of immorality and that one of the most renowned Catholic critics, Jakša Čedomil, expressed a low opinion of both the novel and its author. This problem is dealt with in detail by Milan Ratković in the introduction to Kovačić's *Djela*, I (1950), 17, 36.

especially because he was attacked by churchmen, his works are constantly published in Yugoslavia today, and the anniversaries of his birth and death are usually celebrated with eulogies. Moreover, Kovačić is presented in his country as if he were, in certain ways, the forerunner of the present-day political system.[57] It is no surprise that the Communists regularly "forget" to republish one of his most interesting works, *Ladanjska sekta,* in which he successfully ridiculed the social democrats and affirmed that even the most advanced economic ideas could be very dangerous if applied to agricultural countries, such as Croatia was in his time. He further held that the same economic principles could not be valid for countries such as England and Germany and also for the Balkan areas, where people had fought for bare national survival over five centuries.[58]

Kovačić was a man of firm character, an idealist who wanted to see his beloved country freed from its political, cultural, and social enslavement. Motivated by his childlike faith in higher values and his belief that every peasant should be considered as a human being with a consequent right to an individual, decent existence, Kovačić has very little in common with any totalitarian regime.

The most prolific writer among the Croatian realists was Ksaver Šandor Gjalski (1854–1935), who was born near Zabok, Croatian Zagorje. His real name was Ljubomir Babić. Gjalski studied law in Zagreb and Vienna. As a civil servant, he changed residence often and thus acquired an intimate knowledge of Croatia. He was sent into early retirement in 1919 and thereafter lived at his family estate in Gredice. Gjalski spoke several languages and was well read in the works of many foreign authors, especially Turgenev, Gogol, Sienkiewicz, Balzac, Daudet, and Zola; he also traveled widely. Gjalski studied philosophy and economics and for a longer time devoted himself to occult studies. These preoccupations left a definite imprint on his literary work.[59]

Gjalski began to write at an early age, but it was not until he was thirty years old that he succeeded in publishing his *Illustrissimus Batthorych.* After this work, he wrote a book almost yearly. His major collections of stories are *Pod starim krovovima* (Under Old Roofs), 1886, *Tri pripovijesti bez naslova* (Three Stories Without Title), 1887,

[57]Marijan Jurković, in the preface to the novel *U Registraturi* (Beograd, 1950), 9–28.

[58]Cf. A. Barac, "Kovačićeva Ladanjska sekta prema Lazarevićevoj Školskoj ikoni," *Prilozi za književnost*, ed. by Pavle Popović, vol. XIV (1934), 153–73.

[59]Dragutin Prohaska, *Pregled savremene hrvatsko-srpske književnosti* (Zagreb, 1921), 25–33; *Enciklopedija Jugoslavije*, vol. III (Zagreb, 1958), 460; *Prilozi* 27 (1961), issues 1 and 2, 122.

Bijedne priče (Tales of Misery), 1899, and *Diljem doma* (Cross Country), 1899. His best known novels are *U noći* (During the Night), 1886, *Djurdjica Agićeva*, 1889, *Osvit* (Dawn), 1892, and *Za materinsku riječ* (Fight for a Mother Tongue), 1906. He published his own complete works in 1913.[60]

Gjalski is the most comprehensive Croatian writer of the nineteenth century. His stories and novels constitute an extensive documentation of the political, social, economic, and cultural life of Croatia during the nineteenth century. Since he endeavored to introduce into Croatian literature problems which transcended the boundaries of that country, he was the first Croatian writer regarded by the critics to be European in spirit.[61] Gjalski opened new horizons for other writers and exercised a militant and progressive effect on Croatian readers. The younger generation at the end of the nineteenth century hailed him as its master. During the literary controversy which raged at the time, Gjalski placed himself on the side of the youth of the country, and contributed to its periodicals.[62] In spite of his aristocratic origin, he tried to be socially progressive and wrote stories about the poorest strata of society with understanding and affection.

The artistic value of Gjalski's works is not always sufficient to offset their defects resulting from his overuse of ideological and political matter. He wrote at a great pace, and often the propagandist elements in his works overshadow the creative. His plots frequently appear artificial, and his characters tend to lack depth. His earliest stories were his best; in them he described the patriarchal life of the Croatian gentry with great artistic vigor and the sensibility of an artist who was not so much a preacher and critic as a poet of a vanished period in which he recognized beauty.[63]

Vjenceslav Novak (1859–1905) was initially a school teacher in his native town of Senj. After studying for three years at the conservatory in Prague, he became a music instructor at the teachers' college in Zagreb. Novak had a large family and was very poorly paid; often he wrote just to increase his income. His religious and social convictions were quite liberal, but he felt obliged to mitigate them in writing, for

[60]The complete list of Gjalski's publications, prepared by Emil Štampar, can be found in *Djela* (Zagreb: Zora, 1952), I, 7–58.

[61]Gjalski's "San doktora Mišića" (The Dream of Doctor Mišić), an absorbing mystery story, written with extraordinary skill, is to be found in *Great Short Novels of the World*, ed. by B. Clark (New York, 1927), 963–87.

[62]*Hrvatska Moderna*, I–II (Zagreb, 1951), *passim*.

[63]Emil Štampar, in Ks. Š. Gjalski, *Djela*, I, 7–58; Krešimir Georgijević, in the introduction to Gjalski's *Izabrane pripovetke* (Beograd, 1956), 5–38.

otherwise he would certainly have incurred the disfavor of the then ruling class and of those conservatives at Matica Hrvatska or Društvo sv. Jeronima, to whom he submitted all his manuscripts for publication.[64]

Novak's most important longer stories and novels are: "Pavao Šegota" (1888); *Podgorske pripovijesti* (Tales from Podgorje), 1889; "Pod Nehajem" (At the Foot of Nehaj), 1892; "Nikola Baretić" (1896); *Dvije pripovijesti* (Two Tales), 1897; "Posljednji Stipančići" (The Last of the Stipančićs), 1899; "Dva svijeta" (Two Worlds), 1901; "Zapreke" (Obstacles), 1905; and "Tito Dorčić," 1906 (which was published after his death). In his numerous writings, Novak depicted various segments of Croatian life toward the beginning of the twentieth century: he presented his birthplace, Senj, with the gradual decline of its patrician families, with its clergymen, small merchants, and poor students. He described Podgorje, an extremely poor region south of Senj, where begging was considered a profession, with its own particular notions of morality. Novak also portrayed the Croatian bourgeoisie and the petty bourgeoisie, with their daily pleasures and great tragedies. With almost photographic fidelity, he sketched their everyday life, and Novak could therefore be considered one of the most accurate portrayers of Croatian society. He was, however, at the same time its poet and its bitter critic. Novak gradually became a poet of the poor, and in his work he presented the inhabitants of the slums of Zagreb and the underpaid manual and clerical workers. He always found words of forgiveness for their misdeeds and stigmatized the social order which had led them to their poverty. Novak was the first Croatian writer to introduce realistic scenes from the dreadful life of the working class, and he frequently depicted underprivileged and exploited beings, who spent most of their free time either in attics and cellars or in suffocating taverns.[65]

Novak was an extremely keen observer. In the course of his daily life he noted down incidents which he believed could be used later in his stories. In his writings he touched upon a multitude of problems. Owing to the rapidity with which he wrote, and to his illness, his stories often seem to be hardly more than sketches. He was indisputably a true artist, however, especially during his last years and when describing human misery, as in "U prosjačkoj kući" (In the Beggar's House),[66]

[64]Vlatko Pavletić, *Kako su stvarali književnici*, I (Zagreb, 1956), 118–37.

[65]A. Barac, in *Djela* Vj. Novaka, I (Zagreb, 1951), 7–23.

[66]Jean Dayre, who translated this story into French (*Anthologie des conteurs croates modernes*, Zagreb, 1933), remarks about Novak as a writer: "Il a mêné la vie d'un fonctionnaire besogneux pour qui la littérature devait, trop souvent, être

"U glib" (In the Mud), and "Iz velegradskog podzemlja" (From the City's Underground). These short stories, as well as some of his longer ones ("Posljednji Stipančići," "Tito Dorčić") are significant, not only as faithful descriptions of social conditions, but also as works of art which continue to occupy a high place in Croatian literature.[67]

Not as productive as some of the better-known Croatian realists was Josip Kozarac (1858–1906), who was born in Vinkovci. He studied forestry in Vienna, where he became acquainted with the works of Adam Smith and Charles Darwin. At home again, he became employed as a forester in various parts of Slavonia. Kozarac's first attempts in literature were verses and romantic stories. He then turned to writing comedies, using superficial plots based on the topics of love and money. Having lived for years in the Slavonian countryside, with few books at hand, he described the world as he saw it. His first realistic story, "Biser-Kata", was published in 1887. After it received very laudatory reviews, Kozarac continued to write about the same subject, in the same style and spirit. Besides short or longer stories, he also wrote two novels: *Mrtvi kapitali* (Dead Capitals), 1889, and *Medju svijetlom i tminom* (Between Light and Darkness), 1891.

Kozarac presented Slavonia as he witnessed it during one of its most decisive periods. Capitalism was penetrating rapidly into Slavonia; this province, the most prosperous of all Croatia, was suddenly flooded by foreigners, mostly Magyars and Germans, who came to exploit its wealth and the cheap labor of the Croatians.[68] Kozarac depicted not only this economic process, but also the people themselves; according to him, the inhabitants are lazy, and their women beautiful and sensual. He presents many of them as having strayed from the road of honor through weakness or extravagance. In his famous story, "Tri dana kod sina" (Three Days at My Son's) he portrays the gap existing between peasant parents and their educated children.[69] In most of his writing, Kazarac showed himself to be an economist and sociologist. His artistic abilities, nevertheless, are indisputable. Without writing for literary effect and without inventing exciting plots, he presented his observations and shaped his characters

---

un travail alimentaire. De là sa fécondité et aussi la négligence, le lâché de la forme, l'impression d'ébauche qui frappent dans certaines pages et qui font son oeuvre si inégale" (337–8).

[67]A. Barac, *Djela* Vj. Novaka, I, 23.

[68]Cf. Jozo Tomasevich, *Peasants, Politics, and Economic Change in Yugoslavia* (Stanford, 1955), 211–13.

[69]This story was also translated into French by Jean Dayre (*Anthologie des conteurs croates modernes*, 45–60).

conscientiously and succinctly. Seemingly a rationalist, at heart Kozarac was a tender man who felt the poetry of the woods—as in "Slavonska šuma" (The Slavonian Woods)—the beauty of youth and of love, and the superiority of feeling over cold reason.[70]

A representative of the period of transition, when the socio-economic realistic tendency gave way to psychological analysis, was Janko Leskovar (1861–1949), born at Valentinovo. He taught in many localities of Slavonia and Zagorje. He was often transferred because of his patriotic convictions, and in 1914 he went into retirement mostly as a result of his hypersensitivity. In one of his letters, Leskovar wrote: "Among philosophers I have read especially Schopenhauer, and among storytellers Turgenev." Leskovar's characters believe that they are expiating the sins of their past; his protagonists are usually male transgressors and innocent girls. His style is clear and simple, and because of the reliance on introspection, the action is reduced to the minimum.

In Leskovar's first story, "Misao na vječnost" (Thinking of Eternity), 1891, Martić is obsessed by the idea that he cannot love again because his first sweetheart committed suicide and now perhaps watches him from the stars above. In another story, "Poslije nesreće" (After the Disaster), 1894, Ivanović is unable to forgive his wife, who betrayed him, and he seeks solace in Schopenhauer's writing. In Leskovar's novel, *Propali dvori* (The Ruined Castle), 1896, the undecided Petrović loves the noble but poor Ljudmila; he remains, however, with his father, who appreciates only money and success. Leskovar stresses that class difference, completely independent from our willpower, governs our destinies. In "Jesenji cvijetci" (Autumn Flowers), 1897, we are told that a neurotic widower does not dare to marry a young girl because he is immersed in his memories. In Leskovar's second novel, *Sjene ljubavi* (Shadows of Love), 1898, the debauched Bušinski loses Ljerka, who is ready to forget his past, but his senses are enchained by visions of feminine bodies.

Leskovar's characters are selfish. They love and understand only themselves; they are lazy, passive, and lost in vague meditations. Though Leskovar was under the influence of Turgenev and Goncharov, his stories are more decadent than realistic. At the turn of the century he was considered by the younger generation as their leader. Probably feeling that he was repeating himself in his works, Leskovar stopped

[70]Cf. excellent studies about Kozarac written by Professors Emil Štampar, in *Djela* Josipa Kozarac (Zagreb, 1950), 7–35, and Krešimir Georgijević, *Mrtvi kapitali* (Beograd, 1947), 7–20.

writing around 1905. His stories were collected by Branko Vodnik in 1917, and his entire works were published in 1944 (*Pripovijesti*, 2 vols.).

The first among numerous Croatian writers to try his hand at poetic prose[71] was Fran Mažuranić (1859–1928), the son of Matija Mažuranić, the author of an important travelogue, *Pogled u Bosnu* (A View of Bosnia), 1842. Fran Mažuranić (his real name was Vladimir) became a captain in the Austrian cavalry. His hatred for Emperor Francis Joseph (1848–1916) and for Austrian military and governmental officials, who insolently ignored the just demands of the Slavic peoples, involved him in various incidents, which culminated, in 1900, in his dismissal from the army. For some thirty years nothing was known of his whereabouts, and fantastic legends circulated about him. In actual fact, Mažuranić went off to fight with the Boers against the British, and later with the Russians against the Japanese. After traveling throughout all the continents except Australia, he settled down in Berlin. There he earned his livelihood by writing in German, but always under different pseudonyms. In 1928, when everything was prepared for a long-delayed return to his native countryside, he suddenly died; the circumstances of his death remain a mystery.

Mažuranić's literary creativity can be divided into two periods, separated by an interval of forty years. The first period begins in 1885, when, under the influence of Turgenev's *Poems in Prose* (*Senilia*), Mažuranić wrote short prose fragments, which D. S. Mirsky described as "comparable in construction to the objectified lyrics of the French Parnassians, who used visual symbols to express their subjective experience; sometimes they verge on the fable and the apologue."[72] The result was a small book of not more than forty fragments, entitled *Lišće* (Leaves), 1887. This book's simplicity of style, pregnancy of expression, maturity of thought, and unusual lyricism set it refreshingly apart from the works of other writers of Croatian realism.

His second book, *Od zore do mraka* (From Dawn to Dark), 1927, consists largely of autobiographical reminiscences. Exceptionally moving and interesting are those pages in which Mažuranić describes the earliest years of childhood in Novi Vinodol, near Senj.[73] In general,

[71]Cf. *Antologija hrvatskih pjesama u prozi*, edited by Tadijanović and Tomičić (Zagreb, 1958), 6, 11–25.

[72]D. S. Mirsky, *A History of Russian Literature*, edited by Francis Whitfield (New York, 1958), 206. He speaks about Turgenev's poems in prose.

[73]Re-edited by Tadijanović, *Mladost-Radost* (Zagreb, 1950), with an excellent sketch of Mažuranić's life. This book also contains bibliographical data reprinted from *Republika* (1950), 241–44.

one can say that Mažuranić's second book contains the most intriguing experiences, which, unfortunately, are left as uncut diamonds. Only here and there does one discover "poems" which could be considered among the best Croatian prose poems. One cannot but agree, therefore, with the observation of Vladimir Nazor, who expressed disappointment that such a magnificent mine should not have been exploited by its discoverer.[74] Nazor was, nevertheless, incorrect, when he asserted that Mažuranić was not concerned about the deeper meanings and the fundamental problems of existence; on the contrary, all of his life was spent in a constant search for the key to the profound anguish of his excessively tormented soul.[75]

During this period (1880–1895), many poets were active, but unfortunately most of them were mediocre versifiers,[76] although some are still prominently mentioned in textbooks or in surveys of Croatian literature.[77] The most outstanding bard of this non-poetic and highly declamatory generation—the real bridge between the unforgettable August Šenoa and Silvije S. Kranjčević—was August Harambašić (1861–1911). In his collection of patriotic poems, *Slobodarke* (Songs of Freedom), 1883, Harambašić sang about his enslaved country and its never-ending struggle against German and Magyar oppression. His fiery utterances reflected a bitterness which had been aroused by the deteriorated position of the Croatian nation in the Austro-Hungarian Empire. Like his predecessor Šenoa, he was convinced that a man of letters has a higher mission than simply to amuse the public; according to him the writer is a kind of cultural missionary, whose duty is to enlighten the masses. Harambašić helped make Croatian verse lighter, more supple and appealing, but as he became more and more involved in politics, his lyrics gradually declined to the level of journalism. His numerous collections of poems are deficient in depth, and in the majority of his poems one can seldom find really perfect verses among the many commonplaces and platitudes.[78]

The other representative of this declamatory generation, a man of

[74]Cf. A. Barac, "Vladimir Nazor i Fran Mažuranić," *Letopis Matice srpske* (April-May, 1931), 69–88.

[75]His anti-Austrian pamphlet, *Strijele i strelice*, was recently published in *Gradja za povijest književnosti hrvatske*, ed. by the Yugoslav Academy of Sciences and Arts, vol. 16 (1948), 247–69. Its value is only historical, since his intense hatred for Francis Joseph served only to make the work verbose and repetitious.

[76]M. Kombol, *Antologija novije hrvatske lirike* (Zagreb, 1934), 10, and *Novija hrvatska lirika*, I (Beograd, 1956), 7.

[77]Cf. Bogdan Svilokos, *Hrvatska poezija od preporoda do Kranjčevića* (Zagreb, 1957).

[78]A. Barac, *Veličina malenih* (Zagreb, 1947), 165–240.

completely different education, orientation, and stamina than Harambašić, was Ante Tresić-Pavičić (1867–1949). Tresić was extremely ambitious, but he was renowned for his wide literary erudition, and was very productive in his various roles of poet, playwright, storyteller, novelist, and editor of a literary journal.[79] All his works were keyed to a high pitch. Like Franjo Ciraki ("The Florentine Elegies"), Franjo Marković, and many other Croatian neo-classicists before him, Tresić-Pavičić did not even try to be understood by the masses (*odi profanum vulgus et arceo*). In classical meter, he sang of the downfall of the Roman Republic (*Finis rei publicae*, a tetralogy, 1902–11).[80] Even when he wrote patriotic verses, personal feelings were totally absent, and his varying political views were their inspiring force. He wrote plays, based on the Croatian past, that contained an obvious political tendentiousness (*Ljutovid Posavski*, 1894; *Katarina Zrinska*, 1899).[81]

The greatest Croatian poet of the second half of the nineteenth century, and one of the greatest names in Croatian literature as a whole, was Silvije Strahimir Kranjčević (1865–1908), born at Senj. His father was a municipal clerk; his mother, a fine and delicate person who delighted her son with tales of the heroic deeds of his *Uskok* ancestors (deserters and refugees fighting against the Turks and Venice), died when Silvije was still attending the *Gymnasium*. Because he had received a poor grade "for his obstinacy and rudeness," Kranjčević was not admitted to the final examination (*Matura*). Thus, unable to attend university, and wishing to please his father, Kranjčević took up the study of theology, for which he had, however, no inclination. His ecclesiastical superiors sent him to the "Collegium Germanico-Hungaricum" in Rome; there he remained only six months. A moment of decision in Kranjčević's life occurred when he visited the catacombs in Rome and noticed a young couple there, who were displaying their love for one another amid the dust and gloom of the ancient bones. Kranjčević suddenly realized that a woman's love meant more to him

[79]Cf. Prohaska, *Pregled*, 88–93.

[80]"Molti sono gli episodi ingombranti, molti i quadri storici inanimi e i personaggi cartacei. C'è troppo verismo storico e filosofico perchè l'azione possa fluire calda e naturale. C'è troppa erudizione perchè la passione non illanguidisca nel suo nascere. Sono drammi fatti più per un' attenta lettura che per une riuscita rappresentazione. Da un poeta erudito e cerebrale come il Tresić altra opera non poteva sgorgare." Cronia, *Storia della letteratura serbo-croata*, 462.

[81]Following events and changing political ideologies closely, from an extreme Pan-Croatian he became an "integral" Yugoslav; only in 1941 did he return to ultra-Croatian ideas.

than all the glories of martyrdom ("U katakombama," 1886).[82] It happened that the great bishop, J. J. Strossmayer, was then visiting Rome, and Kranjčević poured out his troubled heart to him. The renowned bishop promised to give him his support. On his return home, Kranjčević went straight to Zagreb, where he already enjoyed high esteem for his patriotic contributions to the foremost Croatian literary journals. Two years later, in 1886, Kranjčević obtained teaching credentials.

Kranjčević was sent to Bosnia-Hercegovina, then a newly occupied province, where there was a great need for teachers. He taught first in Mostar, but soon, because he had come under the suspicion of both civil and church authorities, Kranjčević was transferred to Livno, then to Bijeljina, and four years later, back to Livno. Finally, in 1893, he came to the Bosnian capital, Sarajevo. The following year he was appointed editor of the semi-official literary paper *Nada* and, for the first time, held a position which enabled him to devote much of his time to literary creativity. In 1898 Kranjčević married Ela Kašaj, a teacher of French and part-time writer. Kranjčević, with a mind preoccupied with the insoluble problems concerning man's origin and destiny, and with a heart always ready to revolt in the cause of oppressed nations or individuals, nevertheless experienced in his marriage a few years of personal happiness, during which he wrote several sensuous love poems (e.g. "U želji ljubavi," 1898). In this period he also composed one of his most moving patriotic songs ("Moj dom," 1897). The journal *Nada* ceased publication at the end of 1903, and Kranjčević then became the headmaster of a commercial school in Sarajevo. Always hypersensitive and of delicate health, Kranjčević fell victim to painful kidney stones. In vain he sought to improve his health by spending several months in a Viennese hospital and at various spas.

When he was only twenty years old, Kranjčević published his first collection of poems, *Bugarkinje* (Plaintive Songs) at Senj in 1885. Though some of his poems were even then permeated with social tendencies, Kranjčević still swam largely in the wake of his predecessors, such as Harambašić and Šenoa, to whom he dedicated this collection. During his lifetime, two more collections of his poems were published: *Izabrane pjesme* (Selected Poems, Zagreb, 1898) and *Trzaji* (Spasms, Tuzla, 1902). His poetry was of such extraordinary

[82] "Nelle catacombe non sentiva che la polvere soffocante e il bisogno della luce solare," writes Ljubomir Maraković in *Croazia Sacra* (Roma, 1943), 133.

novelty and created such fascination that at the turn of the century he was considered the greatest living Croatian poet. This reputation endured after his last collection of poems, *Pjesme* (Poems, Zagreb, 1908), the publication of which he did not live to see. Kranjčević also wrote prose, and the best of it was collected after his death by Milan Marjanović, in a book entitled *Pjesnička proza* (Poetic Prose, Zagreb, 1912).[83]

As soon as *Izabrane pjesme*, and especially *Trzaji*, were printed, Kranjčević was hailed by liberals and socialists alike, but attacked by "clericals," who accused him of atheism. Nevertheless, some of the most cultured members of the clergy came to his defense (e.g. Jakša Čedomil). Two of the most brilliant Croatian literary critics, Matoš and Marjanović, devoted a number of penetrating studies to Kranjčević and his poetry. Marjanović admired him for his liberal tendencies and outspoken anti-clericalism, and Matoš extolled the musicality of his lapidary style.[84]

Kranjčević, it is reported,[85] died after receiving the last sacraments, and was thus reconciled with the Church for which, during his lifetime, he had never had a kind word. He was sincerely convinced that the established church had strayed far from the spirit of the Gospels. Kranjčević was heart and soul for the working man, as is seen in "Radniku" (To the Laborer), in its two different versions, and the Catholic Church appeared to him always on the side of the oppressors and exploiters; furthermore, he could not understand why those who claimed to represent Jesus lived in luxurious palaces, surrounded by affluence, and enjoyed the power of tyrants.

From Kranjčević's rather extensive religious poetry—he also wrote an oratorio, entitled *Prvi Grijeh* (First Sin), 1893—it is not absolutely

[83]It is unanimously accepted that the most comprehensive selection of his poetry was published by Matica Hrvatska in 1926, with an excellent introduction by a well-known critic, Branimir Livadić (pp. iii–lxxx). Since World War II Kranjčević's reputation has been steadily growing, though always not for literary reasons. Some critics see in him a protagonist of the proletarian or even Marxist ideology. Cf. Miroslav Krleža, in his article "Književnost danas," published in the sixth volume of the collection *Hrvatska književna kritika*, 214. Krleža also wrote "O Kranjčevićevoj lirici," *Hrvatska Revija* 3 (1931), 137–58. On the contrary, Kranjčević was a bard of Croatia, not as an embodiment of historic rights or carefully preserved parchments, but of the native land for which one feels an uncontrollable attachment. See, for example, his last and magnificent poem "Portret," 1908.

[84]*Hrvatska književna kritika*, III, 74–77; IV, 144–57. Ilija Kecmanović collected these and many other reviews in S. S. *Kranjčević, čovjek i pjesnik, ogledi i uspomene* (Sarajevo, 1955).

[85]Bishop Ivan Ev. Šarić, *Osoba i duh*, III–IV (Madrid, 1953), 87–91.

clear whether he preserved his faith in a Christian, personal God; there are strong indications that he espoused a pantheistic point of view. It was difficult for Kranjčević to reconcile the idea of an Almighty Father with the chaos and blatant injustice that has prevailed in the world from its very beginning. Nevertheless, Kranjčević believed in Jesus. Some of his best poems, even when they glorify the French Revolution or urge a child to leave the Church and go out into nature, are powerful glorifications of Jesus, as he saw Him and carried Him in the depths of his heart. One might mention, among others, "Eli! Eli! lama azavtani?," 1896; "Dva barjaka" (Two Standards) and "Resurrectio," 1897; "Hrist djetetu u crkvi" (Christ to the Child in the Church), 1900; "Hristova slika" (Christ's Image), 1908.[86]

There were some critics, among them Albert Haler,[87] who tried, on the basis of certain aesthetic principles, to prove that Kranjčević often wrote verses of poor quality and sometimes reworked forgotten platitudes. Haler also insisted that in two of Kranjčević's most renowned poems, "Mojsije" (Moses), 1893;[88] and "Zadnji Adam," (The Last Adam), 1896, Kranjčević did not compare favorably with Alfred de Vigny and

[86]But, if one asked the poet the question: If God does not exist, does that mean that Jesus was nothing but one of the many imposters who have appeared in the course of human history?, Kranjčević would probably answer: Yes, you could be right according to your own logic, but my heart is guided by principles which completely defy any human logic. I need Jesus, because without Him this chaotic world would be complete darkness for me. How could I accept Him differently than I imagined and loved Him from my early childhood? Do not ask me who created the universe, I do not know, I could guess. I know for certain that my own life, and, I suppose, yours, would be unbearable without Jesus' love and His encouraging example.

[87]In "O poeziji Silvija Str. Kranjčevića," *Srpski književni glasnik* (June-July, 1929), 265–74, 356–61, 434–443.

[88]Mr. Irwin Titunik, a former student of mine, now an instructor at the University of Michigan, has translated the beginning of this long poem as follows:

. . . Lead my people out, O Lord, / Lead them out of doleful bondage, / And cast off from drowsy lids / Scales encrusted still, scales direful, / That now shackle up their eyes! / Call to mind how cheerless bondage, / Like that ponderous tombstone there, / Weighed upon my brothers' shoulders; / How our torturers condemned / In our women's wombs our children! / Mighty Jehovah! Be kind! / Cast a curse on torturer tyrants / And my people save, O Lord!" /

—Mad wish! But how like a man! / Cast a curse on torturer tyrants? / This folk slay for that folk's sake? / O my creature! Why should I / For one another creature crush? / See where West lies, East arises, / There the North and here South loom: / All, all this have I replenished / With the spawn of life; each thing / Drawing equal breath, holds life dear. / Now you bid that I transgress / This my greatest law in nature! / Could you but take here your stand / Whence for me the vista opens; / Then would you see how minute / Your petty, bloody man's wish is. / Down from my heights, human wretch, / Jutting pyramids lie as low / As the nameless mole's dug burrow. / Vain and feckless is your toil!—

Giosuè Carducci, who wrote similar poems. Antun Barac successfully demonstrated that not only was the content of Kranjčević's poems almost completely unlike that of these writers, but also that he produced works of art that he felt were equal to the famous poems ("Moïse," and "Su Monte Mario") of these two great poets.[89]

No one before Kranjčević was capable of exploiting the powers of the Croatian language to the extent he did. In his poetry, tender feeling skillfully alternates with strong cries of protest. His poetry, mostly permeated with bitter sarcasm and hopeless anguish, also conveys the idyllic happiness which one finds on the rocky shores of his birthplace, the cheerful moods of the spring season, and the mystery of lonely winter evenings. Kranjčević always expressed his emotions with rapture and warmth, with tears and supplications, almost in prayer.[90]

Bibliography

I. Books, Essays, and Articles

Andrić, Nikola. *Pod apsolutizmom.* Zagreb: Matica Hrvatska, 1906.

Barac, Antun. Les études critiques sur la littérature de l'illyrisme," *Le Monde slave* II (1935), 353–373.

——. *Hrvatska književna kritika.* Zagreb, 1938.

——. "La culture littéraire des écrivains croates avant Šenoa," *Annales de l'Institut français de Zagreb* (Zagreb, 1941).

——. *Mažuranić.* Zagreb: Matica Hrvatska, 1945.

——. "Hrvatska novela do Šenoine smrti," *Rad,* vol. 290. Zagreb: Jugoslavenska Akademija, 1952.

——. "Preradović u pismima i stihovima," *Republika* VIII (1952), 65–86.

Bogdanov, Vaso. *Društvene i političke borbe u Hrvatskoj 1848–49.* Zagreb: Jugoslavenska Akademija, 1949.

——. *Hrvatska ljevica u godinama revolucije 1848–49.* Zagreb: Matica Hrvatska, 1949.

——. *Historija političkih stranaka u Hrvatskoj.* Zagreb, 1958.

Cronia, Arturo. *Storia della letteratura serbo-croata.* Milan, 1956.

Deželić, Velimir. *Iz njemačkog Zagreba.* Zagreb, 1902.

Fancev, Franjo, "Dokumenti za naše podrijetlo hrvatskoga preporoda 1790–1832," *Gradja* XII (Zagreb: Jugoslavenska Akademija, 1933).

[89] A. Barac, "De Vigny, Carducci, Kranjčević," *Hrvatsko Kolo* X (1929), 194–223, reprinted in "Poglavlje o Kranjčeviću," *Veličina malenih* (Zagreb, 1947), 273–309.

[90] Ivo Lendić, "Suvremenost Kranjčevića," *Hrvatska Revija* 3–4 (Buenos Aires, 1958) 213–36; *Hrvatska Revija* 1 (1959), 45–72. Ilija Kecmanović's monograph about Kranjčević was published in Sarajevo (1959); though tendentious, it contains most complete bio-bibliographical information and should be consulted as a first-rate work of reference.

——. "Ilirstvo u hrvatskom preporodu," *Ljetopis Akademije*, Vol. 49 (1935), 130–157.

——. "Les origines autochtones du mouvement illyrien croate," *Le Monde slave* III (1935), 27–74.

——. "Hrvatski preporod kao općenarodni pokret," *Hrvatska Revija* VIII (1936), 412–427.

Herceg, Jakša. *Ilirizam* (Beograd, 1935).

Horvat, Josip. *Stranke kod Hrvata i njihove ideologije*. Beograd: Biblioteka Politike, 1939 (In Cyrillic).

Kulakovskij, Platon. *Illirizm*. Warsaw, 1894 (In Russian).

Neustädter, Joseph Baron, *Le ban Jellacic et les événements en Croatie depuis l'an 1848*. I–II. Zagreb, 1939–1942.

Ostović, Pavle. *The Truth about Yugoslavia*. New York, 1952.

Prelog, Milan. *Slavenska renesansa*. Zagreb, 1924.

Prohaska, Dragutin. *Pregled savremene hrvatsko-srpske književnosti*. Zagreb: Matica Hrvatska, 1921.

Savković, Miloš. *L'Influence du réalisme français dans le roman serbo-croate*. Paris: H. Champion, 1935 (Bibliothèque de la Revue de littérature comparée, Tome 107).

Šišić, Ferdo. *Hrvatska povijest*. Zagreb: Matica Hrvatska, 1913. *Pregled povijesti hrvatskoga naroda*. Zagreb: Matica Hrvatska, 1916.

——. "O stogodišnjici ilirskoga pokreta," *Ljetopis Akademije*, Vol. 49 (1935), 99–130.

——. "Genèse et caractère général du mouvement Illyrien," *Le Monde slave* I (1937), 267–288.

Smičiklas, Tadija. "Obrana i razvitak hrvatske narodne ideje od 1790 do 1835 godine," *Rad*, Vol. 80 (Zagreb: Jugoslavenska Akademija, 1885).

Šurmin, Djuro. *Hrvatski preporod*. Vols. I and II. Zagreb, 1903–1904.

II. Anthologies

Dayre, Jean. *Anthologie des conteurs croates modernes* (1880–1930). Zagreb: Matica Hrvatska, 1933.

Gorjan, Zlatko. *Kroatische Dichtung*. Zagreb: Matica Hrvatska, 1933.

Hille, Franz. *Kroatische Novellen*. Vienna: Wiener Verlagsgesellschaft, 1942.

Ježić, Slavko. *Ilirska antologija*. Zagreb: Minerva, 1934.

——. *Prvi hrvatski pripovjedači iza preporoda 1850–1880*. Zagreb, 1935.

Kombol, Mihovil. *Antologija novije hrvatske lirike*. Zagreb: Minerva, 1934; Belgrade: Nolit, 1956.

——. *Hrvatski pripovjedači osamdesetih i devedesetih godina*. Zagreb: Minerva, 1935.

Mamuzić, Ilija. *Antologija ilirskog pokreta*. Belgrade, 1952 (Školska biblioteka 37–38, Znanje).

Maraković, Ljubomir. *Moderni hrvatski pripovjedači*. Zagreb: Minerva, 1934.

Salvini, Luigi. *Poeti croati moderni*. Milano: Garzanti, 1942.

Šegedin, Pavle. *Hrvatska proza*. Belgrade, 1956.

Tadijanović (Dragutin), and Delorko (Olinko). *Hrvatska moderna lirika*. Zagreb, 1933.

For a more complete bibliography, see the works by Barac and Ježić which are given as source for the list of Croatian authors.

Croatian Authors, 1835–1895*

SOURCES

Barac, Antun. *Hrvatska književnost od Preporoda do stvaranja Jugoslavije* / Croatian Literature from the National Awakening to the Founding of Yugoslavia. Book I: *Književnost Ilirizma* / Literature of the Illyrian Movement. Zagreb, 1954; Book II: *Književnost pedesetih i šesdesetih godina* / Literature of the Fifties and Sixties. Zagreb, 1960. Both books were published by the Yugoslav Academy of Sciences and Arts in Zagreb. Unfortunately the death of the author has halted work on this very worthwhile project.

Ježić, Slavko. *Hrvatska književnost od početka do danas 1100–1941* / Croatian Literature From Its Beginnings to the Present Day, 1100–1941. Zagreb: A. Velzek, 1944.

I. The Illyrian Movement, 1835–1849

Babukić, Vjekoslav (1812–1875). Philologist and first professor of the Croatian language at the Academy of Zagreb. Wrote several philological works, for example, *Ilirska slovnica* (1854) and *Misli o pravopisu* (1860).

Blažek, Tomo (1807–1846). Political poet. See *Političke pjesme Tome Blažeka* (1848), edited by Antun Nemčić.

Demeter, Dimitrija (1811–1872). Poet, playwright, stage manager of the Croatian National Theater in Zagreb. Epic poem: *Grobničko Polje* (1842); tragedy: *Teuta* (1844); librettos for the two operas composed by Vatroslav Lisinski: *Ljubav i zloba* (1845) and *Porin* (1846).

Drašković, Janko (1770–1856). Political ideologist of the Illyrian Movement. His political ideas are presented in his study, *Disertacija iliti razgovor darovan gospodi poklisarom*, Karlovac, 1832. This work contains the Croatian political program, written to serve as a guide for the Croatian delegates to the Hungarian-Croatian Diet in Pressburg, 1832–1836.

Gaj, Ljudevit (1809–1872). Ideological leader of the Illyrian Movement. His most important essay, written in Croatian and German, is *Kratka osnova horvatsko-slavenskoga pravopisanja / Kurzer Entwurf einer kroatisch-slavischen Orthographie* (1830). Gaj founded the Croatian newspaper *Novine Horvatske* and its weekly literary supplement *Danica Horvatska, Slavonska i Dalmatinska* (1835).

Kukuljević, Ivan (1816–1889). Poet, dramatist, literary critic, author of travelogues. Drama: *Juran i Sofija* (1839); poems: *Slavjanke* (1848); collection: *Različita djela* (1842–7).

Kundek, Josip (1809–1857). Occasional poet. Elegy: *Reč jezika narodnoga* (1832). Died as a Catholic missionary in the United States.

Mažuranić, Antun (1805–1888). Editor of *Danica* and a linguist. Croatian grammar: *Slovnica hrvatska* (1859); Short history of Old Croatian literature: *Kratak pregled stare literature hrvatske* (1855).

*Those authors whose principal or exclusive domain is literary criticism are not included here and will be treated in a separate article in a future volume.

Mažuranić, Ivan (1814–1890). Poet; chief work is the epic poem *Smrt Smail-age Čengića* (1846).

Mažuranić, Matija (1817–1881). Author of a significant travelogue about Bosnia: *Pogled u Bosnu* (1842).

Mihanović, Antun (1796–1861). Author of the Croatian national anthem "Lijepa naša domovino." Wrote a moving appeal to his countrymen to start using the Croatian language instead of Latin in science and literature: *Reč domovini od hasnovitosti pisanja vu domorodnom jeziku* (1815).

Nemčić, Antun (1813–1849). Travelogue writer, poet, and humorist. Travelogue: *Putositnice* (1845); poems: *Pjesme* (1851); comedy: *Kvas bez kruha ili Tko će biti veliki sudac* (1854). The two latter works were published by Mirko Bogović in the literary journal *Neven.*

Preradović, Petar (1818–1872). Poet. Two collections of patriotic poems: *Prvenci* (1846) and *Nove pjesme* (1851). Preradović wrote a number of love poems, as well as the ode "Slavjanstvu."

Rakovac, Dragutin (1813–1854). Poet, author of essays, editor. Poem: *Duh* (1832); essay: *Mali katekizam za velike ljude* (1842).

Šporer, Djuro (1795–1884). Editor of *Almanah ilirski za godinu 1823.*

Štoos, Pavao (1806–1862). Occasional poet. Elegy: *Kip domovine vu početku leta 1831*; epic poem: *Soko hrvatski i Slavska mati (1849)*, in honor of Ban Josip Jelačić.

Šulek, Bogoslav (1816–1895). Political writer, editor, textbook compiler. Commented on the political program of the Illyrian Movement in his pamphlet *Šta namjeravaju Iliri?* (1844). Essay: *Naše pravice* (1868); political study: *Hrvatski ustav* (1883).

Utješenović, Ognjoslav (1817–1890). Poet. Collection of poems: *Vila Ostrožinska* (1848 and 1871).

Vraz, Stanko (1810–1851). Poet and literary critic. Founded, with a group of friends, the literary magazine *Kolo* (1842). Four collections of his lyric poems are worthy of mention: *Djulabije* (1840), *Glasi iz dubrave žerovinske* (1841), *Gusle i tambura* (1845), *Sanak i istina* (1845).

Vukotinović-Farkaš, Ljudevit (1813–1893). Poet, author of short stories, editor. In his collection of poems *Ruže i trnje* (1842) is contained his *Zimske misli,* a series of feuilletons.

II. Romanticism 1849–1880

Ban, Matija (1818–1903). Poet and editor. Drama: *Mejrima* (1849).

Becić, Ferdo (1844–1916). Also known under the pseudonym Fedor Brestov. Novelist and feuilletonist. Novels: *Kletva nevjere* (1875), *Zavjet* (1882), *Errata corrige* (1908), *Sic itur ad astra* (1909).

Bogović, Mirko (1816–1893). Poet, short story writer, and dramatist. Historical dramas: *Frankopan* (1856), *Stjepan, posljednji kralj bosanski* (1857), *Matija Gubec, kralj seljački* (1859).

Botić, Luka (1830–1863). Poet and short story writer. Three epic poems: *Pobratimstvo* (1854), *Bijedna Mara* (1861), *Petar Bačić* (1862); story: *Dilber Hasan* (1854).

Jarnević, Dragojla (1812–1875). Poet and author of short stories. Short stories: *Prevareni zaručnici* (1853), *Prijateljice* (1854), *Ljepota djevojka* (1858); novel: *Dva pira* (1864).

Jorgovanović-Flieder, Rikard (1853–1880). Poet and author of short stories. Short stories: *Ženske suze* (1875), *Za jedan časak radosti* (1879), *Gavan* (1880).

Jukić, Franjo Ivan (1818–1857). Editor of the literary yearbook *Bosanski prijatelj* (1850, 1853, 1861).

Jurković, Janko (1827–1889). Short story writer, humorist, dramatist, editor, and literary critic. Humorous stories: *Izabrana djela*, Volume I, *Šaljivi spisi* (1862); stories: *Sabrane pripovijesti* (1880–81); comedy: *Izorani šaran ili što žena može* (1872); dramatic works: *Dramatična djela* (1878–79).

Kazali, Antun (1815–1894). Poet: *Zlata* (1856), *Trista Vica udovica* (1857).

Korajac, Vilim (1839–1899). Humorist and philosopher. Satire: *Auvergnanski senatori* (1877); Philosophical work: *Filozofija hrvatsko-srpskih poslovica*, Vol. I (1876). Two further volumes of the latter were never published.

Kurelac, Fran (1811–1874). Philologist, leader of the "School of Rijeka," which pleaded for an etymological Croatian orthography and favored archaic words. Studies: *Fluminensia* (1862); sketches: *Runje i pahuljice* (1866–68).

Marković, Franjo (1845–1914). Literary critic, philosopher, dramatist, and novelist. Idyllic epic poem: *Dom i svijet* (1865); romantic epic poem: *Kohan i Vlasta* (1868); tragedy: *Karlo Drački* (1872); lyric poetry: *Iz mladjih dana* (1883); literary criticism: *"Estetička ocjena Gundulićeva Osmana," Rad* 46, 47, 50, 52 (1879–1880).

Martić, Grga (1822–1905). Epic poet: *Osvetnici*, Volumes I, 1861; II, 1862; III, 1862; IV, 1876; V, 1881; VI, 1882; VII, 1883. *Posvetnici*: seven cantos describing Saint Francis of Assisi and the founding of the Franciscan Order (1895).

Nikolić, Vladimir (1829–1866). Poet and short story writer. Poems: *Bršljani* (1863); stories: *Pripovijetke* (1864).

Okrugić, Ilija (1827–1897) Playwright. Plays: *Sućurica i šubara* (1880); *Šokica* (1884).

Palmović, Andrija (1847–1882). Poet; poems published by Fran Folnegović under the title *Pjesme Andrije Palmovića* (1883).

Perkovac, Ivan (1826–1871). Editor and short story writer. Social novel: *Župnikova sestra* (1869); sketches: *Crtice iz bojnoga odsjeka* (1869); short story: *Stankovačka učiteljica* (1871).

Pucić, Medo (1821–1882). Poet and editor. Poems: *Talijanke* (1849); epic poem: *Cvijeta* (1864); editor of the literary yearbook *Dubrovnik* (1849, 1853).

Šenoa, August (1838–1881). Poet, editor, literary critic, playwright, short story writer, and novelist. His historical novels deserve particular mention: *Zlatarovo Zlato* (1871), *Čuvaj se senjske ruke* (1875), *Seljačka buna* (1877), *Diogenes* (1878), *Kletva* (1881).

Starčević, Ante (1823–1896). Political leader and ideological forerunner of modern Croatian nationalism. Poet, dramatist, philosophical and polemical writer. Many of his writings are lost. Starčević authored all the contributions to *Hrvatski kalendar za godinu* (1858), including his four hundred aphorisms, most of which pertain to ethics.

Tombor, Janko (1825–1911). Short story writer: *Odmetnik* (1854), *Hajdukova zaručnica* (1854), *Kula na Dunavu* (1855).

Tomić, Eugen Josip (1843–1906). Humorist, poet, dramatist, and short story writer. Poems: *Leljinke* (1885); comedies: *Komedije*, Vol. I (1878), Vol. II. (1882); historical play: *Franjo barun Trenk* (1880); novels: *Zmaj od Bosne* (1879), *Kapitanova kći* (1884), *Melita* (1899).

Trnski, Ivan (1819–1910). Lyric poet. Published most of his poems in *Svakolika djela*, I–II (1881–1882).

Veber, Adolf (1825–1889). Author of travelogues and short stories; literary critic and philologist. Leader of the "School of Zagreb," which pleaded for a phonetic Croatian orthography. Published his collected works in nine volumes (twenty copies only): *Djela Adolfa Vebera, zagrebačkoga kanonika* I–IX (Zagreb, 1885–1890). Pp. 3900.

Vodopić, Mato (1816–1893). Short story writer and folklorist. Stories: *Tužna Jele* (1870), *Marija Konavoka* (1875); poetic story: *Robinjica* (1875); historical novel: *Pod doborskijem razvalinama* (1881).

Vukelić, Lavoslav (1840–1879). Poet and short story writer. Stories: *Hajduk Rade* (1871), *Krvava dioba* (1871); poem: *Kod Solferina* (1879).

III. Realism and Naturalism 1880–1895

Alaupović, Tugomir (1870–1958). Poet. Epic Poem: *Naše Rane* (1898); lyric poems: *Probrane pjesme* (1902).

Arnold, Djuro (1854–1941). Poet and philosopher. Poems: *Domovina* (1888), *Izabrane pjesme* (1899), *Čeznuća i maštanja* (1908), *S visina i dubina* (1918), *Izabrane pjesme* (1923).

Badalić, Hugo (1851–1900). Poet. Ballads: *Panem et circenses* (1874); anthology: *Hrvatska antologija. Umjetno pjesništvo starijega i novijega doba* (1892). Libretto for Zajc's opera *Zrinski* (1876).

Bašagić, Safvet (1870–1934). Poet, dramatist, literary critic. Known under the nom de plume Mirza Safvet. Lyric poems: *Trofanda* (1896), *Misli i čuvstva* (1906).

Benešić, Ante (1864–1916). Poet, humorist, dramatist. Tragedy: *Damjan Juda* (1905); dramas: *Kraljević Marko* (1907), *Petronij* (1907); poems: *Anakreontika* (*1913*).

Car-Emin, Viktor (1870–1963). Novelist and dramatist. Novels: *Pusto ognjište* (1900), *Usahlo vrelo* (1904), *Kontesa Nina* (1906), *Neznatni ljudi* (1906); dramas: *Zimsko sunce* (1903), *U mraku* (1907), *Iza plime* (1913), *Starci* (1917), *Pod sumnjom* (1918), *Mrtva straža* (1924), *Nove borbe* (1926).

Derenčin, Marijan (1836–1908). Author of comedies: *Ladanjska opozicija* (1896).

Deželić, Velimir (1864–1941). Poet, novelist, and literary critic. Poems: *Pjesme* (1889), *Kopnom i morem* (1900), *Zvuci iz katakomba* (1902); stories: *U buri i oluji* (1902), *Prvi kralj* (1903), *U službi kalifa* (1908); studies: *Maksimiljan Vrhovac* (1904), *Ljudevit Gaj* (1909).

Draženović, Josip (1863–1942). Short story writer. Sketches: *Crtice iz hrvatskog života* (1884), *Iskrice* (1887), *Crtice iz primorskog života* (1893); short story: *Povijest jednog vjenčanja* (1901).

Gjalski, Ksaver Šandor. Nom de plume of Ljubo Babić (1854–1935).

Novelist and short story writer: *Illustrissimus Battorych* (1884), *Pod starim krovovima* (1886), *Tri pripovijesti bez naslova* (1887), *Bijedne priče* (1888), *Diljem doma* (1899), *U noći* (1886), *Djurdjica Agićeva* (1889), *Osvit* (1892).

Harambašić, August (1861–1911). Poet, author of short stories, literary critic, and editor. Patriotic poems: *Ružmarinke* (1883), *Slobodarke* (1883), *Rob* (1892); love poems: *Sitne pjesme* (1884), *Izabrane pjesme* (1895).

Hranilović, Jovan (1855–1924). Poet and literary critic: *Žumberačke elegije* (1886), *Pjesme svakidanke* (1890), *Izabrabe pjesme* (1893).

Ilijić, Stjepko (1863–1933). Poet, literary critic, and translator.

Katalinić-Jeretov, Rikard (1869–1954). Poet and short story writer. Poems: *Pozdrav istarskog Hrvata* (1890), *Primorkinje* (1896), *S moje lire* (1904); short stories: *Našim morem i našim krajem* (1911).

Kovačić, Ante (1854–1889). Novelist, short story writer, and poet. Stories: *Ljubljanska katastrofa* (1877), *Ladanjska sekta* (1880); novels: *Fiškal* (1882), *Medju žabarima* (1886), *U registraturi* (1888).

Kozarac, Josip (1858–1906). Short story writer and novelist. Stories: *Biser-Kata* (1884), *Slavonska šuma* (1888), *Tri dana kod sina* (1897); novels: *Mrtvi kapitali* (1889), *Medju svijetlom i tminom* (1891).

Kranjčević, Strahimir Silvije (1865–1908). Poet and editor. Poet: *Bugarkinje* (1885), *Izabrane pjesme* (1898), *Trzaji* (1902), *Pjesme* (1908), *Prvi grijeh* (1893), *Pjesnička proza* (1912).

Kumičić, Eugen (1850–1904). Novelist. Nom de plume Jenio Sisolski. Novels about Istrian life: *Začudjeni svatovi* (1883), *Sirota* (1885); social novels: *Olga i Lina* (1881), *Gospodja Sabina* (1884), *Pobijeljeni grobovi* (1896); historical novels: *Urota Zrinsko-Frankopanska* (1892), *Kraljica Lepa* (1902).

Leskovar, Janko (1861–1949). Short story writer. Stories: *Misao na vječnost* (1891), *Poslije nesreće* (1894), *Propali dvori* (1896), *Jesenji cvijetci* (1897), *Sjene ljubavi* (1898), *Kraljica zemlje* (1905).

Mažuranić, Fran (1859–1928). Short story writer: *Lišće* (1887), *Od zore do mraka* (1927–28).

Milaković, Josip (1861–1921). Poet: *Hrvaćanke* (1883), *Naša pjesma* (anthology) I (1903), II (1905).

Miličević, Ivan (1868–1950). Novelist and short story writer. Together with Osman Nuri-Hadžić, Miličević wrote under the nom de plume Osman Aziz. Novels: *Bez nade* (1895), *Bez svrhe* (1896); stories: *Na pragu novoga doba* (1896), *Pripovijesti iz bosanskoga života* (1898).

Mulabdić, Edhem (1864–1954). Novelist, short story writer, and editor. Novels: *Zeleno busenje* (1900), *Na obali Bosne* (1900); stories: *Nova vremena* (1914).

Novak, Vjenceslav (1859–1905). Short story writer and novelist. Stories: *Podgorske pripovijetke* (1889), *Dvije pripovijesti* (1897), *Iz velegradskog podzemlja* (1905); novels: *Pavao Šegota* (1888), *Pod Nehajem* (1892), *Posljednji Stipančići* (1899), *Dva svijeta* (1901), *Zapreke* (1905), *Tito Dorčić* (1906).

Nuri-Hadžić, Osman (1869–1937). Novelist and short story writer. See Miličević, Ivan.

Ostojić, Mato (1862–1929). Poet: *Iskre i plamovi* (1894).

Pavletić, Krsto (1865–1919). Poet, dramatist, and literary critic. Epic poem: *Vjerne sluge* (1898); historical dramas: *Kobna oklada* (1908), *Bratski inat* (1911); study: *Život i pjesnička djela Franje Markovića* (1917).

Rorauer, Julije (1859–1912). Dramatist: *Maja* (1883), *Olynta* (1884), *Sirena* (1896), *Naši ljudi* (1889).

Sabić, Marin (1860–1923). Poet: *Trenutci* (1901).

Šenoa, Milan (1869–1961). Dramatist and novelist. Dramas: *Kako vam drago* (1893), *Kneginja Dora* (1896), *Ban Pavao* (1903); novels: *Exodus* (1904), *Kvarnerske pripovijesti* (1912), *Iz kobnih dana* (1914).

Tordinac, Nikola (1858–1888). Short story writer: *Seoske bajke i bajalice* (1885), *Odabrane critice* (1890).

Tresić-Pavičić, Ante (1867–1949). Poet, playwright, and novelist. Poems: *Glasovi s mora jadranskoga* (1891), *Valovi misli i čuvstava* (1903), *Sutonski soneti* (1904); dramas in verse: *Ljutovid Posavski* (1894), *Katarina Zrinska* (1899); dramas in prose: *Finis rei publicae,* a tetralogy (1902–1911); novels: *Izgubljeni ljudi* (1894), *Pobjeda kreposti* (1897), *Moć ljepote* (1901).

Treščec-Branjski, Vladimir (1870–1932). Nom de plume Borotha. Short story writer and novelist. Stories: *Dva naraštaja* (1892), *Šemsudin* (1892), *Listak romana* (1893), *Ksenija* (1900); novels: *Ljetne noći* (1895), *U malome svijetu* (1901).

Truhelka, Jagoda (1864–1958). Novelist and short story writer. Historical novel: *Vojača* (1899); stories for children: *Zlatni danci* (1918).

Turić, Djuro (1861–1944). Short story writer: *Igra životom* (1909).

Velikanović, Iso (1869–1940). Poet, short story writer, and translator. Humorous epic poem: *Otmica* (1901); stories: *Srijemske priče* (1915); translator of Tolstoy, Cervantes, Goethe, and others.

9

Music

FEDOR KABALIN

THIS SURVEY is limited in scope and size to only brief mention of the highlights of the historical development of Croatian artistic music from its earliest recorded manifestations to the present day. The rich and varied folkloric music of the Croatians lies outside the range of the article, and there is unfortunately no opportunity to provide a detailed study of church music. Croatian musical activity is discussed with reference to composition, performance, organizations, and institutions. Where appropriate and pertinent to the study, reference is made to the science of musicology and to musicologists. None of the contributions to music criticism have been of sufficient importance and influence to alter the course of the development of music in Croatia, and for this reason, as well as for reasons of space, no survey of this aspect of Croatian musical life is included.

EARLY HISTORY

There is every probability that early manifestations of artistic music in the various Croatian provinces were as scarce, sporadic, and unsystematic as are the documents that serve as direct or indirect evidence of such activities. While the rest of Europe from the time of the Renaissance was uncovering and rediscovering many ideas that were to become cornerstones of our modern world, the Croatian lands were for almost four hundred years, from the fifteenth to the nineteenth centuries, leading a "frontier" life, partitioned by the iron curtain of the period which was dividing the Christian and Moslem worlds. More favorable conditions for cultural life existed in towns along the Dalmatian coast and on the islands, some dominated by Venice, others

Croatian authors. *Upper left*: Ante Kovačić (1854–89). *Upper right*: Josip Kozarac (1858–1906). *Lower left*: Silvije Strahimir Kranjčević (1865–1908). *Lower right*: August Harambašić (1861–1911).

Croatian authors. *Upper left*: Ljudevit Gaj (1809–72). *Upper right*: Ivan Mažuranić (1814–90). *Lower left*: August Šenoa (1838–81). *Lower right*: Luka Botić (1830–63).

Croatian authors. *Upper left*: Franjo Marković (1845–1914). *Upper right*: Vjenceslav Novak (1859–1905). *Lower left*: Ksaver Šandor Gjalski (1854–1935). *Lower right*: Janko Leskovar (1861–1949).

Croatian National Theater, Zagreb.

Left: Vatroslav Lisinski (1819–54), composer of the first Croatian opera.
Right: Zinka Milanov (1906–   ), renowned Metropolitan Opera soprano.

Upper: Gazi Husref bey Mosque (sixteenth century), Sarajevo.
Lower: Zagreb Cathedral (thirteenth century).

Cloister of the Franciscan Monastery, Dubrovnik (fourteenth century).

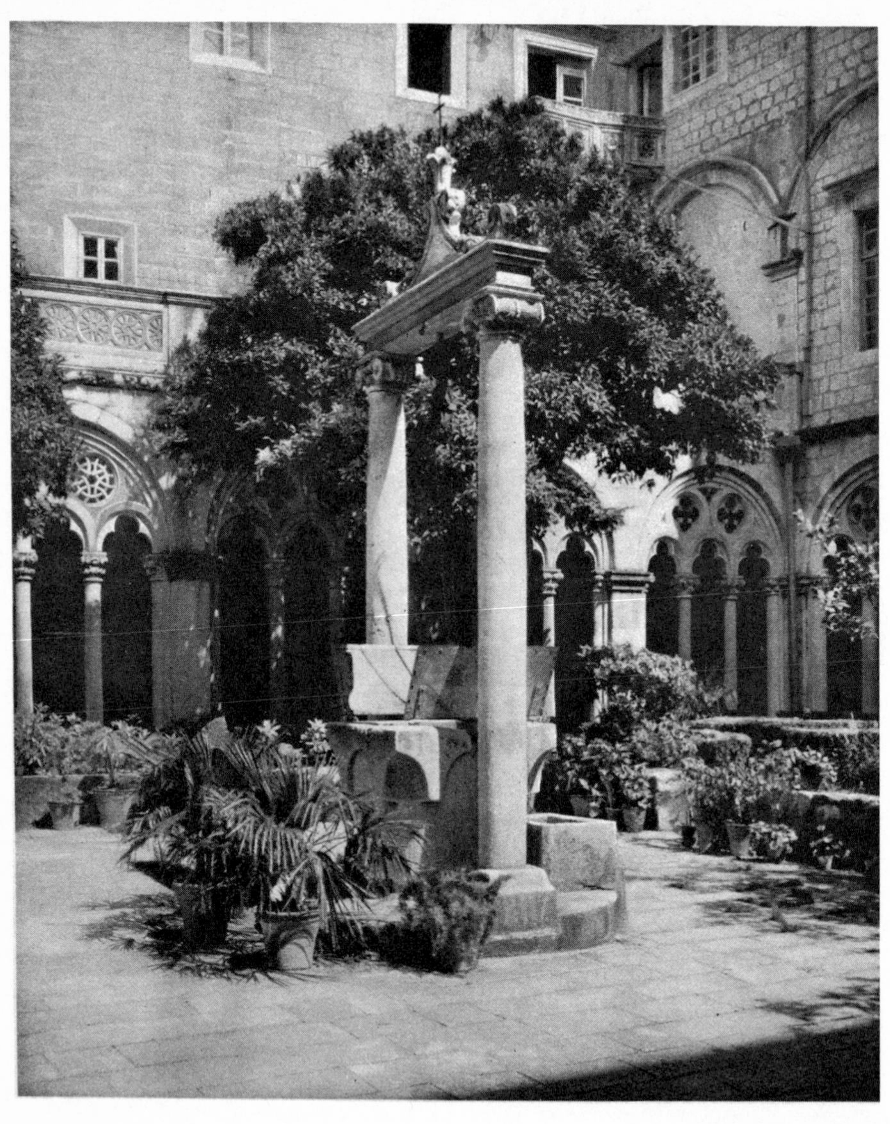

Cloister of the Dominican Monastery, Dubrovnik (fifteenth century).

united with the Croatian mainland, and in Dubrovnik, which remained an independent city-republic until the Napoleonic invasion and occupation (1808). Dubrovnik thus was not harassed by the almost continuous warfare which was the fate of the hinterland. Its inhabitants found the calm waters of sea trade a convenient medium of exchange in artistic and scientific matters as well.

In Croatia, as elsewhere, the Church was the main repository of endeavors in the field of artistic music, particularly in earlier times. A codex, presumably from the tenth century and with neumatic notation very similar to the antiphonaria of St. Gall, is preserved in Šibenik, and similar codices are to be found in some other Dalmatian cities. A twelfth century chronicle relates that Pope Alexander III was serenaded, on the occasion of his visit to Croatia, by people singing hymns in his honor "in the vernacular." Mystery plays and other types of church plays enjoyed their share of popularity. The oldest discovered manuscript of such a play, at Tkon on the island of Pašman, dates from the fifteenth century. The latest recorded performance of this type of play took place in 1837, in Starigrad on the island of Hvar.

Petar Hektorović (1487–1572), a nobleman and poet, also from Starigrad, left us the first record of two Croatian folk tunes and their texts in his *Ribanje i ribarsko prigovaranje* (Fishermen and Their Tales, 1556. Printed in Venice, 1568.) In the sixteenth century, F. Bossinensis had his tablatures for voice and lute, and A. Patricij and J. Schiavetti their motets and madrigals, published in Venice. A. de Antiquis, a sixteenth-century Istrian composer, active as a music publisher and printer in Venice, introduced Petrucci's method of printing music into Rome. A Franciscan friar from Dubrovnik, Gavro Temparičić, was a music teacher at the court in Vienna in the household of the then archduke, and later emperor, Matthias (1608–1619).

As part of the activities of the Counter-Reformation, the first Croatian songbook containing both words and musical notation was published by A. Grgičević in Vienna in 1635. A native of Rijeka, Vinko Jelić, was active in Alsace in the first half of the seventeenth century as the composer of vocal motets and instrumental ricercari. In his partly-preserved collection of spiritual concerti, he reveals himself an adherent of the monody and then incipient concertante style. Dominik Ivan Šibenčanin, also known as Rota-Kolunić, was the musical director at the Savoy court toward the end of the same century, and the composer of the very popular Italian opera of the period *Oppresso sollevato* (1692). Reversing the trend of native talent exported abroad, Toma Cecchini, a Veronese by birth, came to occupy the positions of organist and choirmaster in the cathedrals of Hvar and Split in the first half of the seventeenth century. Cecchini was a prolific and significant composer, an exponent of the new monodic style.

Perhaps the most significant among the musicians of that period was Ivan Lukačić, a Franciscan friar born in Šibenik and trained in Italy, who for some thirty years discharged the duties of organist and choirmaster at the Split cathedral and was very active as a composer of church music. He was an exponent of expressive monody, a style which gave birth to the opera, and which made itself felt at that time in sacred music as well. A collection of his motets, *Sacrae cantiones,* was published in Venice in 1620. An anthology of his works for practical use was published in Zagreb in 1935. The only extant copy of Lukačić's *Sacrae cantiones*, in the State Library of Berlin, as well as vast research material, including a transcription of it assembled by Dr. Dragan Plamenac being readied at the time for publication by the Yugoslav Academy of Zagreb, were destroyed during the last war.

In continental, or Upper, Croatia, with Zagreb as its focal point, several manuscript collections of sacred tunes have been discovered. The most important of these, and the first to be printed, was published in 1701 under the title *Cithara octochorda*, so named because of its eight divisions related to the corresponding periods of the church year. The tunes contained in this collection have been further disseminated and popularized by their subsequent harmonizations at the hands of contemporary composers of church music.

Several Croatian expatriates made names for themselves in various fields of musical endeavor during the eighteenth century. Petar Nakić-Nanchini earned a reputation as one of the best organ builders of the period in Italy. Paolo Serra, of Novi, was a singer at the Pope's chapel in Rome in 1753 and the author of a pedagogic work. Stjepan Spadina signed himself "A Dalmatian nobleman," the only clue to his identity, and must have achieved some recognition as a violin composer, since two of his compositions are included in the important collection compiled by J. B. Cartier under the title *L'art du violon* in 1798. Ivan Mane Jarnović, probably from Dubrovnik, was acclaimed as a violin virtuoso at the Paris "concerts spirituels" in 1770, and toured extensively from London to St. Petersburg, and in Scandinavia. Several of his many compositions for solo violin and string quartet were the object of a revival in the repertory of various Croatian performers in recent years. Because of his quick temper, Jarnović must have been a most interesting personality, as attested by the novel *Jarnowick* by G. Desnoiresterres-Le Brisoys (1844), and two short stories, "Une leçon de

Jarnovich," in the collection *Scènes de la vie d'artiste* by P. Smith (1844), and E. T. A. Hoffman's "Der Schüler Tartinis." Jarnović collaborated with Grétry and others in composing the opera *Abroad and at Home* in 1796 in London.

The first Croatian symphonic works of a non-concertizing nature were the fruit of the labor of an amateur composer, Luka Sorkočević, a native of Dubrovnik, whose eight symphonies were patterned after the Italian type of opera overture. Luka's son Antun was the last envoy of the Dubrovnik Republic to Paris, where he continued to live after his home government ceased to exist. He was a historian who published a number of scholarly works in French, but he also continued in his father's footsteps and composed several orchestral overtures and chamber music pieces.

Two of the traveling virtuoso-expatriates of the nineteenth century should also be mentioned here. Ivan Padovec, the "Paganini of the guitar," inventor of a ten-string instrument, author of a guitar method, and composer of many works for that instrument that were published by Diabelli in Vienna, is the first. Franjo Krežma, also a fertile composer of works for his instrument, was already a brilliant violinist of international reputation before his tragically premature death in Berlin, the last center of his activities, at the age of twenty-one.

The National Awakening

In the days of the patriotic fervor generated by the early nineteenth century Illyrian Movement, numerous Croatian musicians considered it their patriotic duty to compose articles or poems; some versifiers created their own tunes and then found someone to "put it down in notes," in the fashion of some modern "Tin Pan Alley" composers. Ferdo Wiesner-Livadić performed just such a task for the leader of the Illyrian Movement, Dr. Ljudevit Gaj, writing out the score of one of the most popular Croatian patriotic songs, *Još Hrvatska nij' propala* (Croatia Has Not Yet Perished). Livadić was a landowner from Samobor, near Zagreb; he was active in the circle of the Illyrians and the author of many small-scale compositions, especially of songs. An accomplished musician and a successful composer of the same period was the Franciscan priest Fortunat Pintarić. In the piano composition *Pastorellae*, consisting of several short movements, he consciously contrived his melodies in the folk vein or tried to evoke the sound of bagpipes, as, for example, in those called *The Bagpiper*.

It would be idle to speculate whether, all fervor and enthusiasm notwithstanding, the lack of talent evident in this period was the reason for the absence of more or better achievements, or whether the available talent could not be adequately developed because of a lack of appropriate conditions. When a man of genius, such as Ignatz Fuchs, did come along, however, the artist's musical talent asserted itself against all adversities. Fuchs, following the Illyrian trend and custom, Slavicized his name to Vatroslav Lisinski. Extremely shy and retiring by nature, perhaps because of a lame foot, the consequence of an early childhood accident, Lisinski was beset by all kinds of personal misfortune. Who knows whether he would have accomplished as much as he did, were it not for his discoverer, friend, advisor, promotor, and self-appointed honorary manager, Ognjan-Albert Štriga. Štriga was extremely active and very personable. Possessing a beautiful baritone voice, he served the Illyrian cause by his own singing, by organizing others to participate in singing, and by promoting Lisinski's work. Later, he toured many European stages as an operatic and concert singer.

After the initial success of some patriotic songs which Lisinski composed, Štriga persuaded him to write an opera, arranged for the libretto, and organized its first performance, in which he himself took the baritone lead, in the spring of 1846. *Ljubav i zloba* (Love and Malice) was received enthusiastically, and was performed several times in that and subsequent seasons. One suspects that patriotic considerations were as much responsible for the work's success as was genuine music appreciation. This first large-scale work from Lisinski's pen was not entirely his own creation, inasmuch as the orchestration was done by Karl Wisner-Morgenstern, a German musician and organist of the Zagreb Cathedral, with whom Lisinski had studied music privately.

Encouraged by this success, it was again Štriga who arranged for Lisinski to go to Prague for further studies of composition. Lisinski remained in Prague, with interruptions, from 1847 to 1850. Even if he was unable to realize his ambition of obtaining a degree from Prague Conservatory, since he was over the age limit of twenty for enrollment in the Conservatory, he returned with a more substantial accomplishment, the almost-finished score of another opera, *Porin.* Conceived on a larger scale than his first work in this medium, it was entirely his own creation—without outside technical help from more skilled hands, as in the case of his first opera—and he came closer to his ambition to create music which would incorporate melodic, rhythmic, and harmonic characteristics, present or immanent in Croatian folk music, which was and has been the credo of the Croatian nationalistic school of composition almost until the present day.

The Advent of Professionalism

At the age of thirty-five, Lisinski died in extreme penury, literally forgotten. His masterwork, *Porin*, was not to be performed in its entirety again for almost half a century after his death, until 1897. The patriotic fervor and enthusiasm of the Illyrian period gave way to gloom under the political oppression of the "Bach system," the regime of Alexander von Bach, who sought to repress the awakened nationalism throughout the Hapsburg empire with political centralization and national Germanization in the decade between 1849 and 1859.

After ten years of stagnation, a revival of musical activity was marked by a wave of choral societies founded in Croatia in the early sixties. The first among them, "Zora," was already established in 1858 in Karlovac, then an important commercial center. This choral movement represented a local synthesis of the German *Liedertafel* tradition, with its patriotic-political connotations, and a rich tradition of group singing, developed in the performance of folk music in the villages.

A national repertory theater was formed in 1860, giving dramatic performances in the vernacular. Operetta was added to the theater in 1866. The addition of an opera wing in 1870 coincided with the arrival in Zagreb of Ivan Zajc to head it, thereby opening a new chapter in Croatian musical life. Zajc was born in Rijeka (Fiume) in 1832, the son of a military bandmaster. He studied music in Milan and gained a considerable professional reputation in Vienna as a successful composer of operettas. He forsook the glamour and rewards of such a career to take up residence in Zagreb at the insistence of his Croatian friends, with whom he had kept in touch personally and through correspondence.

Zajc was extremely prolific as a composer and created some 1,200 opus-numbered compositions of every kind. Of this output, only his historical opera *Nikola Šubić Zrinski* survives in the current repertory of the Croatian opera houses, and this more for patriotic reasons than for intrinsic musical value. In his prodigious productivity, which left hardly a form or medium untouched, there is evident a marked preference for vocal compositions, to the almost total neglect of absolute music, particularly chamber and symphonic works. It may be said that Zajc composed right up until his death in 1914. He retired as active head of the Croatian Music Institute's music school only six years earlier, and for the first two decades of his sojourn in Zagreb he was also administrative head and chief conductor of the opera. Beside his administrative duties in school, Zajc also taught theory and voice. In the Zagreb Opera he had not only to coach and conduct, but also to orchestrate from vocal scores for whatever combination of musicians he happened to have at his disposal in the orchestra pit in a given season. He managed nevertheless to produce many operas only a few seasons after their world premieres in France or Italy. When original scores of works arranged earlier by Zajc were used, it was found that more often than not he had anticipated exactly the composer's own orchestration.

During Zajc's long reign in the Croatian musical life, he placed emphasis on raising the standards of proficiency and performance. This makes him, in a way, the founder of musical professionalism in Croatia. Stress on the "how" of quality and performance meant that the "what" of content and style had almost necessarily to be neglected. While performance standards—particularly in opera—were constantly being raised, the creative efforts of the period remain without special interest or historical significance. The work of Zajc and his contemporaries is distinguished as much by able craftsmanship as it is by lack of originality in style or expression. A certain epigonism of differently-tinted hues of basic romantic flavor, and provincialism of approach and esthetics are apparent.

This period, which marked the advent of the professional performer on the Croatian musical scene, is also the one in which musicology in Croatia performed its most urgent and logical function there: that of serving as the recorder and preserver of the wealth of Croatian music folklore. These pioneering melographic efforts were carried out almost single-handed by Franjo Ksaver Kuhač. Because he changed his German family name of Koch to a Croatian version by translating its meaning, and because of a certain dilletantism in his approach to music, both characteristic of the Illyrian period, Kuhač may be considered a latter-day Illyrian.

It appears that neither the scientific foundation of his work nor the musical talent of Kuhač were on a par with the magnificence of the projects that he undertook. Thus, he appears more a reporter than a scientist, and while his work has to be accepted with caution, reserve, and criticism, no reproach can be made for his boundless enthusiasm. Forgoing every comfort, and subjecting himself to the greatest sacrifices of all kinds, he traveled year after year throughout the lands inhabited by the Southern Slavs and their neighbors, collecting songs, tunes, folk instruments, and all else pertaining to musical folklore. Of a total of 2,000 collected melodies, 1,600 were published in four volumes during his lifetime, with additions of his own hackneyed harmonizations. A final volume was published without harmonizations in 1941. In his enthusiasm and patriotic zeal, Kuhač attempted to prove that such well-known international music figures as Liszt and Tartini were actually Croatians, basing his arguments mostly on the etymology of their names. He was most successful in making a Croatian out of Haydn, and his theories found currency in some English circles.

Modern Trends

The turn of the century marks the advent of the modern age in Croatia with regard to its social, economic, and political institutions. Some of the younger musicians went to study abroad at this time and returned with new ideas; others stayed abroad to exploit their consumate technical skill. Such was the case of Blagoje Bersa, a composer of note who had many of his orchestral poems and operas performed in Central Europe, where he worked for a long time as an orchestrator for various music publishers. He is also reputed to have orchestrated some of D'Albert's operas. In later years he came to Zagreb to impart his great skill and experience as an orchestrator to other musicians.

A somewhat younger member of the same generation, Antun Dobronić, made a late start in music after working for several years as an elementary school teacher. This may account for the fact that he never felt quite at home with certain technical aspects of his craft, although it did not impede him from returning from his studies in Prague full of revolutionary zeal for national expression and modernistic style that led him to pioneer in such innovations as polytonalism. He was often more persuasive as a proselytizer and polemicist than as a composer. Perhaps because he was a very prolific composer, however, and did not neglect any form—whether operatic stage, symphonic podium or chamber music—only a minor portion of his output was performed. In some of his works the freshness and sweep of his ideas transcended the insufficiency of his technical equipment.

It was not so much the proselytism of men like Dobronić that brought forward a generation of young and significant talents in the field of musical creation in Croatia as it was a series of circumstances which were not necessarily interdependent. Politically and nationally speaking, there was the fact of freedom from the bondage of the Hapsburg Empire after World War I, thus stimulating for the first time in centuries a cultural life generated from within, without foreign tutorship or emulation. Another factor was the almost chaotic variety of currents on the international musical scene, not lessened by the introduction of extreme theories of destruction of tonality, and even of the traditional sonorities, by means of atonalism or microtonalism. Among the hues of this international music spectrum which evoked the most sympathetic response in Croatia were the influences exerted by some towering giants of the newly-established Slavic music, particularly the Russian and, to a lesser degree, the Czech: the richness of the orchestral palette as epitomized in theory and practice by Rimsky-Korsakov's work, and by the impressionists and post-impressionists; the freeing of the rhythmic and metric patterns of Stravinsky's first period; and finally, those tonal methods and techniques that lent themselves best to enhancing the natural richness of materials taken from or patterned after folklore, which most Croatian composers took as their natural raw material.

Josip Slavenski was one of the most radical and most original of the post-World War I generation of composers. He studied with Kodaly and Viteszlav Novak, was greatly influenced by Bartok's research on Danubian folklore, and attempted a similar synthesis of the folklore of the Balkans in his own compositions. After attracting early attention with his first string quartet, performed at the International Festival for Contemporary Music in Donaueschingen in 1924, several of his compositions were published by Schott. One of his last large works, *Sinfonia Orienta*, also proved to be his most remarkable. Originally intended to be called "Religiophonia," it attempted an artistic synthesis of different religions throughout the cultural regions and the historic periods that they represent; the originality and sweep of the content of Slavenski's music is matched by that of its form.

Božidar Širola was a personage who embodied the qualities of both the artist and the scientist. This was partly the result of his training and long career as a teacher of mathematics and physics and his serious interest at the same time in the field of folk music and musical instruments. He was particularly attracted to musicological work by the music "dialects" of different regions. This also influenced his work as a composer, particularly with regard to his operas, in which he tried to evoke the atmosphere of the particular region in which the work was set by emulating the characteristics and style of its folklore. A deeply religious man, Širola composed many large-scale sacred compositions. His *a capella* oratorio entitled the *Life and Memory of Sts. Cyril and Methodius* was performed with considerable success at the International Society for Contemporary Music festival in Frankfurt, Germany, in 1927.

Another composer who combined an interest in folklore with creative work was Ivan Matetić-Ronjgov. He was particularly interested in his native region, the Istrian peninsula, the music of which is based on the exotic and archaic-sounding non-tempered scale, closest to the Locrian mode. In his limited output, most of it for solo voice or chorus, he tried to recreate the flavor of Istrian folk music without the use of direct quotations.

In attempting to make use of elements of folkloric music in composing, perhaps no one has gone farther than Krsto Odak, who composed an entire opera, *Dorica pleše* (Dorothy A-Dancing), while striving not to use any musical motive or phrase which was not part of the original folk music thesaurus. Although interesting as a tour de force and an experiment, this is not Odak's normal method of composition. He is more noted for the solid contrapuntal structure of his works, often quite "cosmopolitan," and not at all based on folklore.

Fran Lhotka is an interesting example of a Croatian composer by naturalization. Czech by birth and education, he was a French horn virtuoso and the director of a conservatory in Russia before coming to Zagreb. He occupied the position of the president of the State Music Academy in Zagreb on several occasions. As a composer he was a consumate technician and a steady worker. He "found himself" relatively late, when, in collaboration with the choreographers and ballet dancers Pio and Pina Mlakar, he composed several ballets. Their first composition, the complete ballet *The Devil in the Village*, has been widely performed and recorded since its premiere in Zurich and its early success in Munich, as well as being part of the repertory of the Royal Winnipeg Ballet Company in Canada.

The most successful among the Croatian composers of the "pre-1900" generation has been Jakov Gotovac. In the formal schemes of his works, he has seldom ventured beyond the three-part form, and has confined his writing almost exclusively to vocal and orchestral music, resembling in his preferences for medium those of Zajc. Although unsophisticated in his approach, Gotovac has brought to it a positive inclination and facility for singable and easily-assimilated melodies, for well-sounding if old-fashioned harmony, and for a particularly rich orchestral palette. The author of many operas and several symphonic poems, he has not yet surpassed the success of his first purely orchestral work, "Symphonic Kolo," a stylization of a popular dance of the Southern Slavs, performed in Paris and Tokyo, as well as in Chicago's Grant Park

(1957) and New York's Lewisohn Stadium (1962), and, during the 1963–64 season, in Hartford and Detroit. A similar success was enjoyed by his second opera, *Ero the Joker*, which, since its premiere in the mid-thirties, has been performed in eight languages on more than forty European opera stages, including those of the State Operas in Berlin, Munich, and Vienna, and by the Zagreb Opera ensemble in London, Rome, and Naples.

Born at the turn of the century, Zlatko Grgošević has so far shown more promise than fulfillment in his limited production as a composer. A thoroughly cultured musician, he has exerted considerable influence through his work as a teacher, and also partly as an essayist, a pamphleteer and a critic. Such activities have also been to some extent responsible for his limited activity as a composer. The two most significant compositions among his works are a choral suite and a cantata, both on the subject of harvest festivities.

Two somewhat younger composers, Rudolf Matz and Božidar Kunc, have divided their interests between composing and other activities. Matz is active as a teacher of violoncello and piano methods and as an author of theory textbooks. He was also a prime mover in the rejuvenated Croatian Choral Federation between the world wars. Intent on raising artistic and programing standards, Matz, on the invitation of the American affiliate of the Federation, came to the United States to act as director of the Croatian Choral Festival in Chicago's Orchestra Hall in 1956. On his return to Zagreb, he organized a youth orchestra that he has conducted in many successful appearances abroad.

Božidar Kunc, until his recent death, was a recital pianist of renown. Especially notable were his appearances as soloist, playing his own piano concerto in Germany, and also with the Philadelphia and Detroit Orchestras. As Zinka Milanov's accompanist, Kunc toured the world. He incorporated impressionistic elements into his personal style of composing.

One might well speak of a "generation of 1906," since that year proved a vintage one with regard to three important personages among contemporary Croatian composers. The first to emerge was Boris Papandopulo, the son of the renowned opera and concert singer Maja Strozzi-Pečić. An extremely methodical and disciplined worker, and a consumate craftsman, he is very prolific and has left hardly any musical form or medium untouched. As might be expected from one who writes with great rapidity, his output sometimes lacks inspiration or warmth of expression. But his three-movement *Symphonietta For*

Strings, published by Schott, is one of the most significant contributions to Croatian orchestral literature. Of the other two coetaneous composers mentioned, Milo Cipra prefers a contrapuntal texture, an instrumental medium, and chamber proportions. He has made significant contributions in these fields, without completely eschewing larger forms. Ivan Brkanović is more at home in works of larger scope for orchestra, often with a chorus and stage, such as his opera *Equinox* and the several symphonies that he has thus far composed.

Post-War Developments

The mainstream of Croatian musical creativity between the world wars subscribed to the nationalistic or folkloristic school. It regarded the rich resources of the, in some instances, centuries-old Croatian music folklore—which was often preserved almost untouched from outside influences—as the raw material on which to build a specifically Croatian musical idiom. The contrary is true of the two generations of composers that have emerged since the last war, and which are gradually assuming the center-stage position, and the third generation that is now following in their wake.

A surprise event of the immediate post-war years was the emergence of Stjepan Šulek as a composer. Well-known before the war as a concert violinist, chamber musician, and concertmaster, Šulek leaped instantly into the forefront among Croatian creative figures with his several scores, among them a number of symphonies and concerti. He is a consummate craftsman and a highly-regarded teacher of composition at the Zagreb Music Academy. It might develop that he is a man of transition in more than merely his chronological position in Croatian musical history. Today he is the upholder of the conservative academic tradition that is inveighing against the radical extremism of the experimental trends that are rearing their heads everywhere, Croatia not excepted. In addition to absolute music, he has also written an opera, *Coriolan* (1958), and has recently been turning more and more to conducting.

Among the standardbearers of the movement to align Croatian composition with international avant-garde trends, are Šulek's pupil Milko Kelemen and Ivan Malec. Kelemen received early recognition in the mid-fifties as the winner of several prizes, before he turned his interest to the more radical tendencies of post-Webern serialism. He is the founder and principal organizer of the Zagreb Biennale (spring, 1961, 1963) that serves as an international showcase and clearing-place for international and Croatian contemporary musical creations. Kelemen visited America in 1961 on an exchange program. Ivan Malec is a resident of Paris and an anti-romantic in his approach to composition. He is definitely oriented to the avant-garde, notably in his use of *musique concrète.*

In this context we should also mention Branimir Sakač, whose most important work to date is *Symphony of a Dead Soldier,* based on his incidental music for N. Corwin's radio drama "Without Title." This composition, dating from 1951, was adapted successfully as a ballet in 1959, and taken on tour to Naples by the Zagreb ensemble. Sakač is also interested in experimentation with concrete and electronic music, and has founded experimental studios to explore these media in Zagreb and Opatija. Another experimentalist who deserves mention at this point, rather than with other musicians of his age group, is Krešimir Fribec. Mostly self-taught, he has moved away from an early fascination with the more experimental aspects of Mussorgsky's and Janaček's styles, to a close affinity for the pointilism of the post-war atonalists. This latter tendency has induced him to write two operas, among other works.

PERFORMERS

A substantial number of Croatian performers earned widespread international recognition when the creative efforts of Croatian composers were still much confined within the limits of their own country and its audiences. The famed Croatian soprano Milka Ternina made only passing appearances in Zagreb as a young singer; beyond these, both her studies and her career were carried on entirely abroad. She was equally well-known for her Wagnerian interpretations at Bayreuth in Germany and for her performances in *Tosca* in America at Puccini's request, after her success in that opera at London's Covent Garden. She was a member of the Metropolitan Opera Company from 1893–1904.

Another brilliant career of a Croatian singer was that of the tenor Tino Pattiera, who attained world fame by his appearances as a member of the Dresden State Opera and of the German Opera of Prague, as well as in Chicago. Even though he regularly returned to his home to spend vacations there between seasons, he never performed in Croatia. He now lives in partial retirement in Vienna, remaining active as a voice teacher.

A career somewhat similar to Ternina's is that of the Metropolitan Opera's *prima donna* for more than a quarter of a century, and Ternina's former pupil, Zinka Milanov. After a decade or so as first dramatic soprano of the Zagreb Opera, a routine guest engagement in Graz in *Aïda* brought her invitations in rapid succession to sing at the German Opera and the National Theater in Prague, from Bruno Walter to appear at Vienna State Opera, and from Toscanini to sing the soprano solo in Verdi's *Requiem* at the Salzburg Festival. The way was thus paved for her engagement at the Metropolitan in 1937.

It is almost impossible at present to turn to any important opera stage or opera season without finding Croatian singers prominently represented. The entire ensemble of the Zagreb Opera has traveled, since the last war, to make many successful appearances abroad in London, Berlin, Rome, and Naples. Soprano Sena Jurinac, noted for her interpretations of music by composers such as Mozart, Beethoven, Puccini, and Strauss, is a member of the Vienna State Opera, a regular visitor to the Glyndebourne Festival, and has had considerable success at Covent Garden, with the San Francisco Opera (1959), and with the Chicago Lyric Opera in 1963. Dragica (Carla) Martinis appeared at the New York City Center Opera in 1950, and at the San Francisco Opera in 1954. She was especially noted for her interpretation of the title role in Puccini's *Turandot*. Biserka Cvejić, a mezzosoprano and a member of the Belgrade Opera, made her debut at the Metropolitan in New York in 1961 and has subsequently appeared regularly with the company. Another mezzo, Nada Puttar-Gold, left Zagreb in 1957 for an engagement with the Berlin Municipal Opera; since 1961 she has been a member of the State Opera in Frankfurt. Marijana Radev, also a mezzo, has been a frequent guest in Italy, Israel, and Germany, has appeared on operatic and concert stages, and is a noted recording artist. Georgine Milinković, a contralto, was for years a member of the opera companies in Zurich and Munich, and also sang at Bayreuth.

Baritone Vladimir Ruždjak, winner of the first prize in the Geneva International competition after World War II, and presently a member of the Hamburg State Opera, made his debut with the San Francisco Opera in 1961, and with the Metropolitan Opera in 1962. Tomislav Neralić, a bass formerly with the Vienna State Opera, is now engaged in Berlin; he sang at Chicago's Lyric Opera in 1959, and at the Teatro Colon in Buenos Aires. Dragutin Šoštarko, a singer acclaimed in guest appearances in Central Europe, toured Spain and South America as the baritone lead opposite Beniamino Gigli. Aron Marko Rothmüller made his debut in Zagreb in 1932 and later appeared there from time to time as a guest. Almost immediately after his debut, he obtained an engagement with the Zurich Opera, where he remained throughout the war. After the war, he appeared at the Vienna State Opera as Prince Igor, at Covent Garden as Wozzeck, as well as with the New York City Center and the Metropolitan Operas. Rothmüller is presently on the faculty of Indiana University. In addition to being a singer, he is also a composer and author. In his creative work, he stresses themes stemming more from his Jewish background than from his Croatian, although he has written three songs based upon the poems of the Croatian poet Vladimir Nazor.

The reason why singers should dominate the picture of performing artists "exported" from a country so well endowed with good voices and a fine musical and particularly vocal tradition, which ranges from folk singing to numerous and well-trained choral groups, is a clear and simple one. For the instrumental performers to attain a level of excellence comparable to that of the vocal performers in Croatia, a tradition of accomplished teachers and pupils, of adequate instruments, qualitative performances, and generally high standards of musical life would be necessary. Not all of these factors were present in Croatia before the onset of this century. In 1903, Vaclav Huml, a Czech and a pupil of Ševčik, came to Zagreb as a violin teacher. A few years later, Svetislav Stančić, a student of Busoni, joined him on the faculty of what is today the State Music Academy in Zagreb. Both Huml and Stančić gave up their public performances, and in Stančić's case also a promising career in composition, to devote themselves entirely to instruction. Each has raised a whole generation of pupils who have successfully continued their teacher's pedagogic work in studios, have occupied first desk chairs in renowned orchestras, or have made names for themselves as concert artists. Huml's stress on the virtuoso aspects of violin technique has produced several notable virtuosos, such as Zlatko Baloković, who came to live in the United States and is an American citizen; Zlatko Topolski, now concertmaster of the Vienna Symphony Orchestra, after a sojourn in the same capacity and as a conductor in Cordoba, Argentina; and Ljerko Spiller, who took up residence in Buenos Aires, and is active as teacher, performer and conductor.

Stančić's school produced well-rounded musical personalities, in addition to accomplished masters of the keyboard. Some of his students have embarked on full-time concert careers, while others combine such careers with teaching. Before and since the war, Branka Musulin established Germany as the center of her extensive activities as a touring and recording pianist. Melita Lorković, considered by many the outstanding Yugoslavian pianist at present, has toured with great success in Scandinavia, western Europe, and South America, and lives in Cairo, Egypt, as a pianist-in-residence. Dora Gušić spearheaded the emphasis on concertizing by Croatians, with her successful tours abroad between the wars. Of the younger generation of pianists, Jurica Murai achieved considerable acclaim abroad after the war, while Ladislav Šaban followed his teacher's footsteps in forsaking the bench of the performing pianist for the professorial chair. The renowned Italian violoncello virtuoso Antonio Janigro has made his home in Zagreb since 1939, and has raised the standards of teaching and performance with respect to his instrument to the levels already enjoyed by the piano and the violin. He is the founder of the virtuoso chamber orchestra, the Zagreb Soloists (I Solisti di Zagreb), that gained international reputation through recordings and international tours, including several in North America.

Ever since the time of Zajc, Zagreb has enjoyed the leadership of good musicians at the helm of its opera, artists who also doubled as symphony conductors for the occasional concerts of the theater orchestra, before the founding of the Zagreb Philharmonic after World War I. Zajc's immediate successor was Nikola Faller, a student of Bruckner and Massenet, who was the opera director at the turn of the century. Some of his successors were Felix Albini, the composer of the internationally successful operetta *Baron Trenk* (1908), Frederik Rukavina, the opera director in the twenties and later a frequent guest conductor with the Prague National Theatre, and the present dean of the Zagreb conductors, Milan Sachs, a Czech by birth and a great perfectionist and disciplinarian, who is presently retired but who still conducts occasionally.

The longest tenure of a director after Zajc was that of Krešimir Baranović, who presided over the Zagreb Opera, with interruptions, for more than a decade between the two world wars, with time off for a tour with Anna Pavlova's Ballet Company in 1927–28. In the 1940's he spent several years in the Slovak capital of Bratislava, and now conducts the Belgrade Opera and Philharmonic Orchestra. In addition to his outstanding work as a conductor, he is also a very distinguished composer of works for orchestra and for the stage. Since the last war, with the development of domestic film production in Yugoslavia, he has also achieved marked distinction as a composer for the cinema.

Recently the international reputations of some Croatian conductors have grown to the point where they rival those of the Croatian singers. Lovro Matačić was the first Croatian to conduct at Bayreuth (1959), and is presently the general music director of the Frankfurt Opera. He also conducted Chicago's Lyric Opera in 1959 and 1960, and was a guest conductor of the Detroit Symphony Orchestra in 1960. His student and erstwhile protégé Berislav Klobučar, is the director of the Graz Opera and made his debut with the Teatro Colon in Buenos Aires in 1963. Mladen Bašić, a post-war director of the Zagreb Opera, now heads the opera in Salzburg, Austria.

The present musical director of the Zagreb Philharmonic, which he has led in many successful tours ranging from western and central Europe to Asia and the Far East, Milan Horvat, has also had an international career of his own. He served for several seasons as the permanent conductor of the Radio Eireann Symphony Orchestra in Dublin, and enjoyed many successful guest appearances abroad, ranging from Russia to America, appearing with the Cincinnati Symphony Orchestra in 1961. Igor Gjadrov was the recipient of the first prize at the International Conductors' Competition in Besançon (1954), and has had much success as a guest conductor in western Europe. Klaro Mizerit, a former conductor of the Dubrovnik Municipal Orchestra, now conducts the Rhenish Philharmonic in Koblenz; he was a guest conductor with the Baton Rouge Symphony Orchestra during the 1963–64 season. Vladimir Benić, the director of the Rijeka Opera, was an apprentice conductor with the Cleveland Symphony Orchestra during the 1960–61 season, under a Kulas Foundation grant. Krešimir Šipuš, a resident of Paris, has composed several instrumental works, an opera and a ballet, and has appeared successfully as an opera and a symphonic conductor in Europe and in Argentina. Ante Kopitović now lives in Buenos Aires and is widening the scope of his activities as the conductor of orchestra and instrumental ensembles at the State Radio Station.

The musicologist Dr. Dragan Plamenac, who has edited works by Lukačić, has had a lifetime interest in the works of the Flemish composer Johannes Ockeghem, on whom he wrote his doctoral dissertation at the University of Vienna (1924), and for the publication of whose complete works he served as the editor. He is at the present on the faculty of the University of Illinois, and before coming to the United States in 1939 he held the chair of musicology at Zagreb University for over ten years. For two years (1950–52) he was also chairman of the New York Chapter of the American Musicological Society.

Musical Institutions

The oldest Croatian musical institution that has enjoyed uninterrupted existence to the present day is the Croatian Music Institute, formed in 1827 as a *Musikverein* with the purpose of promoting music and maintaining a music school. From an initial faculty of three, this school has grown into a state-operated, degree-granting music college, under the name of the State Academy of Music. It is now the mother institution of a network of municipal music schools on the preparatory level throughout the country. The Croatian Music Institute continues its independent existence as a civic group active in many phases of musical life.

Opera in Zagreb has always been a branch of the National Theater, which also includes a drama wing. The opera wing is in charge of all musical stage activities, comprising a ballet company that once boasted Mia Slavenska, also a Croatian, as its prima ballerina, as well as great deal of light opera. This pattern of organization is followed by the theaters in the provinces that have been organized in more recent times, for example, in Osijek, Varaždin, Rijeka, Split, and Dubrovnik. The theaters are, as is customary in Central Europe, state subsidized, with the personnel under permanent contract for a ten- or eleven-month season. A postwar development has been the addition of summer festivals of opera performances in the Roman arena in Pula on the Istrian Peninsula, in Diocletian's peristyle in Split, and of drama, opera, and concerts in Dubrovnik. Another postwar development is the creation of professional companies devoted to the presentation of folk dances, songs, and instrumental music as nearly genuine and unaltered as possible in a stage performance. The Croatian folkloric group "Lado" has been very successful in its performances at home and abroad.

Shortly before and during World War I, symphonic concerts in Zagreb were improvised by complementing the theatre orchestra with musicians from army bands or other sources for occasional performances. Of those sporadic enterprises, one should be singled out: a program conducted in 1916 by Frederik Rukavina and devoted entirely to the works of young Croatian composers, all in first performances. It proved to be a trail-blazing event that not only benefited the composers represented on the program—Baranović, Dobronić, Dugan, Pejačević, Stančić, Širola—but also marked the coming of age of the Croatian composers and their music. In 1920, opera orchestra musicians organized the Zagreb Philharmonic on a cooperative basis. They performed on nights that they were not engaged at the theater, and, generally, when it suited their fancy, without a plan or an organized subscription series. This situation was changed when the orchestra, which operated temporarily under different names, was organized as an entity completely separate from the opera orchestra, in the early forties. Such is its present organization, and once more under its original name.

Between the wars there was sporadic symphonic activity in the provinces, based mostly on the combination of interested amateurs and army band musicians, under the leadership of some enterprising conductor. At that time only Osijek, of all the Croatian towns outside of Zagreb, had permanent drama and sporadic operatic activity, with more regular symphony concerts. All musical performances were under the leadership of Lav Mirski. During the war he conducted in Palestine, returning to Osijek after the war as the head of the opera and general manager of the theater.

Until 1941, when Osijek received its radio station, Zagreb had the only broadcasting facilities in Croatia. Now each town that has its own theater, as well as some which do not, has its radio station, with the whole system operating as a network, owned and operated by the state, following the European custom. The larger stations have quite complete music staffs, and many opera performances and symphony concerts are broadcast live. A recently-added television branch has its studios in Zagreb and follows the pattern of organization established by the broadcasting system.

The choral activities in Croatia, which have spread to all the social strata and to the smallest towns and even to many villages, are amateur in nature. Many of the larger of these organizations reach high levels of perfection and artistry. The first professional organization was the Zagreb Madrigalists, founded in 1931 by Mladen Pozajić. This group gave regular concerts with a repertory covering the range of *a cappella* music suitable for a chamber music group, without limiting itself to a narrow historic period. In time this group grew into the Radio Zagreb Chamber Chorus, and then became simply the Radio Zagreb Chorus, first led by Mladen Pozajić, considered one of the finest Croatian choral conductors, and now by Slavko Zlatić, a composer and former conductor of the Sušak Philharmonic Society.

Before World War II, there was no regular music publishing activity in Croatia, with the exception of publications by the Croatian Music Institute. What was sporadically published under other auspices was often set or printed abroad. After the war, the Music Publishing House (Muzička naklada), was established. It publishes not only original works by Croatian composers, including full orchestra scores, but also standard instructional and repertory works that were formerly available only as imports from foreign publishers. The domestic commercial recordings of the Jugoton Company are devoted almost exclusively to the popular genre. Quite complete recordings of Croatian serious music literature, made by the radio network and for their use in broadcasts, are not commercially available. An important work among publications about music is the outgrowth of the activities of the Lexicographic Institute in Zagreb that publishes, in addition to a general encyclopedia, a series of specialized reference works in various fields. The *Music Encyclopedia*, under the editorship of Josip Andreis is being published in two volumes. The first volume appeared in 1958, and comprises the letters *A* to *J*. It contains 760 pages and combines serious and reliable scholarship with a high level of graphic execution.

Bibliography

The sources listed in this section and in the sections "Scores and Collections" and "Discography" should be considered introductory, rather than final or complete. The intrinsic interest of various entries, and their availability or accessibility on the North American continent were often important or deciding factors in the compilation.

I. Before 1800

Alberti, Juraj (Giorgio). *Dialogo per imparare con brevità a cantar canto figurato.* Venice: Antonio Turrino, 1619.

Banjalučanin, Mate. *Regulae cantus plani pro incipientibus.* 1687.

Bossinensis, Franciscus. *Tenori e contrabassi intabulati col sopran in canto figurato per cantar e sonar col lauto.* 2 vols., Venice, 1509–11.

Kovačević, Toma. *Brevis cantus gregoriani notitia.* Vienna, 1701

Šilobod-Bolšić, Mihajlo. *Fundamentum cantus gregoriani seu choralis.* Zagreb, 1760.

II. After 1800

Andreis, Josip. *Povijest glazbe*/History of Music. Zagreb: Matica Hrvatska, 1942.

——. *Uvod u glazbenu estetiku*/Introduction to the Esthetics of Music. Zagreb, 1944.

——. *Historija muzike*/History of Music. 3 vols. Zagreb, 1951–52–54.

——. *Hrvatski glazbeni zavod kroz 125 godina svog postojanja*/The Croatian Music Institute through 125 Years of Its Existence. Zagreb, 1952.

——. *Jakov Gotovac.* Split, 1957.

——. (ed.). *Muzička enciklopedija*/Music Encyclopedia. Vol. I, *A–J.* Zagreb: Lexicographic Institute, 1958.

Andreis, J. Cvetko, D., and Djurić-Klajn, S. *Historijski razvoj muzičke kulture u Jugoslaviji*/Historic Development of the Music Culture in Yugoslavia. Zagreb: Školska knjiga, 1962.

Andreis, J., and Zlatić, S. (eds.). *Yugoslav Music.* Belgrade, 1959.

Andrić, Josip. *Slovačka glasba.* 1944.

Goglia, Antun. *Hrvatski glazbeni zavod 1827–1927*/Croatian Music Institute, 1827–1927. Zagreb, 1927.

———. *Komorna muzika u Zagrebu*/Chamber Music in Zagreb. Zagreb, 1934.

———. *Orkestralna muzika u Zagrebu*/Orchestral Music in Zagreb. Zagreb, 1935.

Ivakić, Branimir. *Razvoj hrvatske muzike*/The Development of the Croatian Music. Zagreb, 1930.

Kassowitz-Cvijić, Antonija. *Vatroslav Lisinski u kolu Ilira*/Vatroslav Lisinski in the Circle of Illyrians. Zagreb: Matica Hrvatska, 1919.

Klobučar, A. "Franjo Dugan, Život i rad"/Franjo Dugan, Life and Work. Thesis, Zagreb Music Academy, 1955.

Kovačević, Krešimir. *Hrvatski kompozitori i njihova djela*/Croatian Composers and Their Works. Zagreb: Naprijed, 1960.

Kuhač, Franjo Ksaver. *Vatroslav Lisinski i njegovo doba*/Vatroslav Lisinski and His Time. 2nd ed. Zagreb: Matica Hrvatska, 1904.

Kukuljević-Sakcinski, Ivan. *Slovnik umjetnikah jugoslavenskih*/A Dictionary of Yugoslav Artists. Zagreb, 1858.

Ljubić, Šime, *Dizionario biografico degli uomini illustri della Dalmazia.* Vienna, 1856.

Milčetić, I. *Dr. Julije Bajamonti.* Zagreb, 1912.

Ogrizović, Milan. *Hrvatska opera* (1870–1920)/Croatian Opera (1870–1920). Zagreb, 1920.

Plamenac, Dragan. "Vatroslav Lisinski," *Književni Jug* (Zagreb, 1919).

———. "O hrvatskoj muzici u vrijeme renesanse" / About Croatian Music in the Renaissance Period, *Hrvatska revija* (Zagreb, 1936).

———. "Toma Cecchini, kapelnik stolnih crkava u Splitu i Hvaru u prvoj polovini XVII stoljeća"/Toma Cecchini, Choirmaster of the Split and Hvar Cathedrals in the First Half of the Seventeenth Century, *Rad* (Zagreb: Yugoslav Academy of Arts and Sciences, 1938), Vol. 262, 77.

———. "Music of the 16th and 17th Centuries in Dalmatia," *Proceedings of the American Musicological Society for 1939.* Published in 1944. Also condensed in G. Reese, *Music in the Renaissance* (New York: W. W. Norton, 1954), 757–762.

Schneider, Artur. *Ivan Mane Jarnović, hrvatski guslač i skladatelj 18. stoljeća*/Ivan Mane Jarnović, Croatian Violinist and Composer in the 18th Century. Zagreb, 1944.

Širola, Božidar. *Pregled povijesti hrvatske muzike*/Survey of Croatian Music History. Zagreb, 1922.

———. "Stara hrvatska muzička nastojanja"/Old Croatian Musical Efforts, *Narodna starina,* 10 (Zagreb, 1925).

———. *Hrvatska umjetnička glazba*/Croatian Artistic Music. Zagreb, 1942.

———. "Crkvena glazba u Hrvatskoj"/Church Music in Croatia, *Croatia Sacra* 20–21 (Zagreb, 1943).

Šram, Franjo. *Crtice iz hrvatske glazbene kulture*/Notes about Croatian Music Culture. Zagreb, 1940.

Urukalo, A. "Dr. Julije Bajamonti i njegov rad na području muzičke umjetnosti"/Dr. Julije Bajamonti and His Work in the Field of Music. Thesis, Zagreb Music Academy, 1954.

Vidaković, Albe. *Crkvena glazba u zagrebačkoj stolnoj crkvi u XIX vijeku/*

Church Music in the Zagreb Cathedral During the 19th Century. Zagreb, 1945.

——. *Vinko Jelić (1596–1636?) i njegova zbirka duhovnih koncerata i ricercara "Parnassia militia" 1622*/Vinko Jelić and His Collection of Spiritual Concerts and Ricercari "Parnassia militia" 1622. Zagreb: Yugoslav Academy, 1957.

Zjalić, M. *Crkvena muzika*/Church Music. Samobor, 1925.

Scores and Collections

I. Before 1800

Cecchino, Veronese Tomaso. *Amorosi concetti*, bk. I, 1612; *Canti spirituali*, op. 3, 1613; *Motetti concertati*, op. 4, 1613; *Amorosi concetti*, bk. III, op. 7 ("il terzo libro de' madrigali a una, e due voci"), G. Vincenti, Venice, 1616; *Madrigali e canzonette*, op. 12, 1617; *Madrigali a 5*, op. 15; *Otto messe brevi, facili et ariose*, op. 11, 1617; *Psalmi, missa et alia cantica*, op. 14, 1619; *Missarum 3 et 4 vocum cum motetta 4 et 5*, bk. II, op. 17; *Messe ariose*, bk. III, op. 19, 1624; *Corona sacra connexa ex flosculis musicalibus praestantissimorum autorum*, 1626; *Missae*, bk. IV, op. 22, 1627; A collection of 5 masses, 22 motets, and 8 instrumental sonatas, op. 23, 1628; One-voiced accompanied motets, op. 27, 1635.

Grgičević, Atanazije. *Pisni za naypoglavitye, naysvetye i nayveselye dni svega godischia sloxene: i kako se u organe s' yednim glasom mogu spivati, napravgliene.* Po Atanasiu Georgiceu u Becu. Iz Pritiskopisa Matea Formike, MDCXXXV/Songs for All Holidays of the Year, Arranged for One Voice and Organ. By A. Georgiceu, Vienna, M. Formica, 1635.

Ielich, Vincentius. *Parnassia militia*, op. I, P. Ledertz, Strassburg, 1622; *Arion primus, op. II*, P. Ledertz, Strassburg, 1628; *Arion secundus, op. III*, P. Ledertz, Strassburg, 1628.

Lucacich de Sebenico, Ioannis. *Sacrae Cantiones Singulis Binis Ternis Quaternis Quinisque Concinendae*, Gardani, Venetiis MDCXX.

Patricij, (Petris) Andrija. Four 4-part madrigals in A. Barges, *Il primo libro da Villotte*, A. Gardano, Venice, 1550.

Schiavetto, Julije. *Madrigals*, G. Scotto, Venice, 1563; *Motets*, G. Scotto, Venice, 1564.

II. Folksongs

Bersa, Vladoje. *Zbirka narodnih popjevaka iz Dalmacije*/A Collection of Folksongs from Dalmatia (ed. B. Širola, V. Dukat), Yugoslav Academy, Zagreb, 1944.

Kuhač, Franjo Saver. *Južno-slovjenske narodne popievke* / Chansons nationales des Slaves du Sud, 4 vols., C. Albrecht, Zagreb, 1878–81, vol. V, Yugoslav Academy, Zagreb, 1941.

III. Modern Scores

Albini, Felix. *Baron Trenck*, operetta in 3 acts, vocal score, J. H. Remick, New York, 1911; *Madame Troubadour*, operetta in 3 acts, vocal score, J. W. Stern, New York, 1910.

Bersa, Blagoje (Benito). *Der Eisenhammer*, opera in 3 acts, vocal score, L. Doblinger, Leipzig, 1911; *Sunčana Polja*/The Sunny Fields, symphonic poem, Nakladni zavod Hrvatske, Zagreb, 1950.

Brkanović, Ivan. *Symphony No. 2*, full score, Nakladni zavod Hrvatske, Zagreb.

Gotovac, Jakov. *Ero s onoga svijeta/Ero der Schelm*, comic opera in 3 acts, op. 17, vocal score (Croatian and German texts). Universal Edition No. 12261, Vienna, 1955.

Grgošević, Zlatko. *Okolo žnjačkoga venca*/Around the Harvest Wreath, suite for mixed chorus a cappella, Muzička naklada No. 692, Zagreb.

Hirschler, Žiga. *Sonatina*, piano solo, *Jugoslawisches Album*, Universal Edition No. 10250, Vienna, 1935.

Jelich, Vincentius. *Sechs Motetten* aus Arion primus (1628), ed. A. Vidaković, Graz, 1957.

Kabalin, Fedor. *Divertimento* for wind septet, op. 7, score and parts, Tritone Press, 1962; *Poem and Rhymes*, viola or 'cello and piano, op. 18, Tritone Press, 1962.

Kelemen, Milko. *Concertino*, double bass and orchestra, score, H. Litolff No. 30109, Frankfurt, 1960; *Kleine Streichermusik*, string orchestra, score, Schott's, No. 5095, Mainz, 1960; *Equilibres* for 2 orchestras, score, Peters No. 5814, H. Litolff, Frankfurt, 1962; *Skolion* for orchestra, score, Ars Viva, Mainz, 1962; *Transfigurationen*, piano and orchestra, score, H. Litolff, Frankfurt, 1962.

Kunc, Božidar. *Improvisation über ein Volkslied*, piano solo, *Jugoslawisches Album*, Universal Edition No. 10250, Vienna, 1935; *Strepnja*/Quivering, op. 30 (1) Songs for voice and piano, *Čežnja*/Longing, p. 30, (2) and *The World is Empty*, op. 52: G. Ricordi and Co., New York, 1955.

Lisinski, Vatroslav. *Porin*, heroic opera in 5 acts, vocal score, Zagreb, 1919.

Lukačić, Ivan. *Odabrani moteti*/Selected Motets, ed. D. Plamenac, Hrvatski glazbeni zavod, Zagreb, 1935.

Odak, Krsto. *String Quartet No. 2*, op. 7, B. Schott's Söhne No. 3495, Mainz.

Papandopulo, Boris. *Kolo* (Reigen), piano solo, *Jugoslawisches Album*, Universal Edition No. 10250, Vienna, 1935; *Sinfonietta*, string orchestra, full score, B. Schott's Söhne, Mainz; *Concerto da camera*, op. 11, soprano vocalist and 9 instruments, score, Universal Edition, Vienna, 1941.

Pintarić, Fortunat. *Kompozicije za klavir*/[Selected] Piano Compositions, edited by S. Stančić, Hrvatski glazbeni zavod, Zagreb, 1927.

Rothmüller, Aron Marko. *Divertimento*, trombone solo, timpani, and string orchestra, Hawkes and Son, London, 1955.

Shlik, Miroslav. *Slavonic Songs* for 2 violins, E. C. Schirmer, Boston, 1940.

Slavenski, Josip. *Gebet zu den guten Augen*, mixed chorus *a cappella*, B. Schott's Söhne, Mainz; *Zwei Liebeslieder*, mixed chorus *a cappella*, Schott's; *Zwölf Volkslieder*, mixed chorus *a cappella*, Schott's; *Vöglein spricht*, 4–part women's chorus with piano, Schott's; *Scherzlied*, 3-part women's or men's chorus (or 6-part mixed), Schott's; *Spottlied*, 3-part women's or men's chorus (or 6-part mixed), Schott's; *Tänze und Lieder aus dem Balkan*, piano solo, 2 vols., Schott's No. 1413/1417; *Aus dem Balkan*, piano solo, Schott's No. 1817; *Aus Südslawien*, piano solo, Schott's No. 1818; *Südslawischer Gesang und Tanz*, violin and piano, Schott's No. 1951; *Südslawische Suite*, piano solo, op. 2, Schott's No. 1819;

Streichquartett, op. 3, Schott's No. 3461/3127; *Sonate*, piano solo, op. 4, Schott's No. 1820; *Slawische Sonate*, violin and piano, op. 5, Schott's No. 1952; *Aus Dem Dorfe* (fl, cl, vn, vla, cb), op. 6, Schott's No. 3139/3140; *Sonata religiosa*, violin and organ, op. 7, Schott's No. 1966; *Balkanophonia*, orchestra, op. 10, Schott's No. 3377; *Lyrisches Streichquartett*, op. 11, Schott's No. 3490/3149.

Šulek, Stjepan, *Symphony No. 1* (in A), full score, Nakladni zavod Hrvatske, Zagreb, 1950; *Symphony No. 2* (in D) "Eroica," full score, Nakladni zavod Hrvatske, Zagreb, 1951; *Symphony No. 3* (in E) full score, Nakladni zavod Hrvatske, Zagreb, 1951.

Croatian Musicians

Alberti, Juraj (Giorgio). Author of *Dialogo per imparare con brevità a cantar canto figurato*, printed by Antonio Turrino, Venice, 1619.

Albini, Srećko (Felix) (1869–1933). Composer and conductor; director of the Zagreb Opera.

Alesani, Jerolim (1778–1823). Zadar organist and church music composer.

Andreis, Josip (1909–). Professor of music history at the Zagreb Music Academy.

Andrić, Josip (1894–). Folklorist, composer for the tamburitza, author of the first history of Slovak music (1944).

Antiquis (Antico), Andrea de (first half of 16th c.). Composer and music printer.

Bajamonti, Julije (1744–1800). Physician, composer, and encyclopedist; after 1790 organist of the Split Cathedral.

Baloković, Zlatko (1895–). Violin virtuoso; since 1924 a resident of the United States; now in semi-retirement in Maine.

Banjalučanin, Mate. Franciscan friar from Banjaluka; author of *Regulae cantus plani pro incipientibus* (1687).

Baranović, Krešimir (1894–). Composer and conductor in Belgrade; director of the Zagreb Opera 1929–40.

Bašić, Mladen (1917–). Opera director in Salzburg, Austria; former director of the Zagreb Opera.

Benić, Vladimir (1922–). Conductor (since 1950) and director (since 1963) of the Rijeka Opera; in Cleveland 1960–61.

Berdović, Vladimir (1906–). Composer, violoncellist, and conductor from Dubrovnik.

Bernardić, Dragutin (1912–). Leading bass, Zagreb Opera.

Bersa, Blagoje (Benito) (1873–1934). Composer and orchestrator; 1911–19, arranger for Doblinger music publishers, Vienna; after 1922, professor of orchestration at the Zagreb Music Academy.

Bersa, Vladimir (Vladoje) (1864–1927). Blagoje Bersa's brother; attorney and composer. Collector of folk tunes in Dalmatia, published posthumously (1944).

Bjelinski, Bruno (1909–). Professor of counterpoint and polyphonic composition at the Zagreb Music Academy. Primarily a composer of instrumental and chamber works.

Bombardelli, Silvije (1916–). Composer and conductor, former general manager and opera director of the Split Theater; founder of the Split Summer Festival.

Bossinensis, Franciscus. Author of *Tenori e contrabassi intabulati col sopran in canto figurato per cantar e sonar col lauto,* two volumes of tablatures for voice and lute, published in Venice, 1509, 1511.

Bradić, Zvonimir (1904–). Student of B. Bersa. Completed some of Bersa's works and edited his orchestration lectures.

Brajša-Rašan, Matko (1859–1934). Attorney, self-taught musician, collector of Istrian folk tunes and original compositions mostly for chorus.

Brkanović, Ivan (1906–). Composer of many long vocal-instrumental works; wrote five symphonies. Among most significant active exponents of national-folkloristic orientation in composition; strong individual style.

Burić, Marijan (1913–). Composer and theorist; since 1946 a teacher at the State Music School, Zagreb.

Cecchini (Cecchino), Toma (b. 1580, Verona; d. 1644, Hvar). From 1606, choirmaster at Split Cathedral; after 1614, choirmaster and later organist at Hvar Cathedral.

Cipra, Milo (1906–). Professor at the Zagreb Music Academy since 1941. Composer chiefly of absolute, chamber, and orchestra music, with a developed sense for the polyphonic voice leading.

Ciprin, Vladimir. (1903–). Music critic of leading Zagreb newspapers in 1930's and 1940's. Now in Buenos Aires.

Cossetto, Emil (1918–). Noted choral conductor; composer mainly of choral music.

Cvejić, Biserka (1923–). Mezzosoprano, Belgrade Opera. Since 1961 at the Metropolitan Opera, New York.

Degrel, Ivo (1909–). Composer and chorus conductor, now in Argentina. His *Pastoral Overture* premiered by the Orquesta Sinfonica, Radio Nacional, Buenos Aires.

Dešpalj, Pavle (1934–). Composer and conductor; student of S. Šulek.

Devčić, Natko (1914–). Professor at the Zagreb Music Academy; pianist; has composed in most media; one opera.

Dobronić, Antun (1878–1955). Pioneer of contemporary trends and national-folkloristic orientations in music composition.

Dugan, Franjo (1874–1948). Long time organist of the Zagreb Cathedral and professor of counterpoint and composition at the Zagreb Music Academy.

Dugan, Franjo Jr. (1901–1934). Shipbuilding engineer and outstanding compositional talent. Many smaller works and a choral Mass in Ancient Slav.

Dumičić, Petar (1901–). Concert pianist and composer; composes mostly for piano.

Eisenhuth, Djuro (1841–1891). Violinist, concert master, and theater conductor. His choruses, patriotic for the most part, are still very popular.

Erdödy-Rubido, Sidonija (1819–1884). Member of the aristocracy, but an ardent Illyrian. A trained singer; created the female lead in Lisinski's "Love and Malice."

Faller, Nikola (1862–1938). Director of the Zagreb Opera, 1896–1902; president, Croatian Choral Federation (since 1924).

Feller, Marijan (1903–). Pianist; since 1958 professor at Sarajevo Music Academy.

Filjak, Ranko (1927–). Pianist.

Flögl, Ivo (1890–). Composer of vocal works and shorter orchestra pieces, using in his compositions folkloric material from Medjimurje. Lives in Buenos Aires.

Fribec, Krešimir (1908–). Composer with atonal leanings.

Gagić, Bogdan (1931–). Student of M. Kelemen. Composed for the most part instrumental works, including film music.

Geiger-Eichhorn, Antonija (1893–). Concert pianist, professor at Zagreb Music Academy.

Gjadrov, Igor (1929–). First prize at international competition for conductors, Besançon, 1954.

Gjungjenac, Zlata (1898–). Leading lyric soprano at three main opera houses in Yugoslavia until her retirement in 1947. Now professor at the Belgrade Music Academy.

Goglia, Antun (1867–1958). Attorney, amateur cellist, author of numerous historic and biographical articles in the field of Croatian musical history.

Gotovac, Jakov (1895–). One of the leading living Croatian composers.

Grančarić, Slavomir (1878–1941). Composer, choral conductor, and teacher; studied with Dvorak and Faure.

Grgičević, Atanazije (c. 1590–1640). Author of both words and music for twelve sacred songs in a songbook published in Vienna, 1635.

Grgošević, Zlatko (1900–). Composer, critic, professor at the Zagreb Music Academy and at the Zagreb Teachers' College before his retirement.

Gušić, Dora (1908–). Concert pianist with international successes; professor at the Zagreb Music Academy.

Hanich, Stephen V. (1919–). Former secondary school music teacher and military bandmaster in Croatia; now an American citizen, active as a choral conductor in San Francisco and Cleveland.

Hatze, Josip (1879–1959). Studied with Mascagni in Pesaro. Wrote almost exclusively for voices: solo songs, choruses, cantatas, operas. Traditionalist in his stylistic leanings.

Hercigonja, Nikola (1911–). Since 1950 professor of music history at the Belgrade Music Academy. Chief work to date is the opera-oratorio *The Mountain Wreath* (1957), after the epic poem of the Montenegro poet P. P. Njegoš.

Horvat, Milan (1919–). Most prominent Croatian conductor of the younger generation; music director of the Zagreb Philharmonic since 1957.

Hržić, Drago (1896–). Lyric baritone of the Zagreb Opera, 1919–45; now teaching.

Huml, Vaclav (1880–1953). Violin teacher; Czech by birth; student of Ševčik. From 1903 until his death a professor at the Zagreb Music Academy.

Ivellio, Rade (1902–1947). Opera conductor in Zagreb and Osijek.

Ivšić, Matija (1894–). Priest and composer of sacred music (masses, motets).

Jagušt, Mladen (1924–). One of the younger generation of conductors.

Janigro, Antonio (1918–). Italian violoncello virtuoso, domiciled in Zagreb; professor at Zagreb Music Academy 1939–55; 1954 founded the *Zagreb Soloists.*

Jarnović, Ivan Mane (1745–1804). Violinist of international fame; composer of orchestral and chamber works; foremost exponent of French violin concerto in the second half of the 18th century.

Jelačić, Anka (1909–). Contralto with the Zagreb Opera and the Vienna Volksoper; guest appearances in Central Europe.

Jelić (Ielich, Jeličić), Vinko (1596–1636?). Native of Rijeka; boy chorister of the court chapel in Graz, then member of the court orchestras there and in Zabern, Alsatia.

Jozefović, Oskar (1890–1941). Opera conductor in Zagreb and, until his death, director of the Split Opera.

Jurinac, Sena (Srebrenka) (1921–). Leading soprano of the Vienna State Opera since 1944; recordings and guest appearances on major stages of Europe and America.

Kabalin, Fedor (1920–). Composer and conductor in Chile, 1947–50, and then in the United States; since 1961 on the faculty of State College, Indiana, Pa.

Kaplan, Josip (1910–). Composer of chamber music and vocal works, and of several compositions for children, including a children's opera.

Karas, Vjekoslav (1821–1858). Painter with an active interest in music (flute, voice); a limited opus of 30 odd vocal compositions.

Kelemen, Milko (1924–). One of the most important composers of the younger generation. In 1954 started writing in a neo-baroque manner; following a longer stay in Paris became interested in the more radical contemporary tendencies.

Kirigin, Ivo (1914–). Composer and critic, active in the field of film music; music director of Croatian folkloric group "Lado."

Klaić, Vjekoslav (1849–1928). Professor of history at Zagreb University with intense interest in music. Author of many articles on music; organizer and director of music groups, and an occasional composer.

Klepač, Rudolf (1913–). Bassoon soloist of international reputation; professor at Salzburg's Mozarteum.

Klobučar, Andjelko (1931–). Composer of the recent generation.

Klobučar, Berislav (1924–). Opera director, Graz, Austria; formerly a conductor at the Vienna State Opera and in Zagreb; guest appearances in Barcelona, Buenos Aires, and elsewhere.

Kokot, Ivo (1905–). Priest and composer of sacred music; presently a resident of California.

Kokša, Ana (1919–). Pianist and piano teacher, now active in Buenos Aires.

Kolander, Vatroslav (1848–1912). From 1875 until his death the organist of the Zagreb Cathedral; composed mainly for organ.

Kolarić, Mirko (1910–). Mainly a composer of choral compositions.

Kolb, Kamilo (1887–). Priest and composer of masses and sacred songs; skilled harmonizer.

Kopitović, Ante (1913–). Studied at Zagreb Music Academy and at Sta. Cecilia Academy in Rome. Now active in Buenos Aires as a composer and a choral and orchestral conductor.

Kovačec, Mirko (1909–). Priest, concert organist, and composer of sacred works; now resident of Buenos Aires.

Kovačević, Krešimir (1913–). Critic, music essayist, and author.

Kovačević, Toma (1663–1724). Canon of the Zagreb diocese, author of *Brevis cantus gregoriani notitia*, Vienna, 1701. Possibly also the compiler of the collection of unison sacred songs *Cithara octochorda*.

Kozinović, Sister Lujza (1897–). Nun and composer of church music.

Krežma, Franjo (1860–1881). Brilliant violinist of international reputation and a fertile composer of music for his instrument.

Križaj, Josip (1887–). Slovenian bass and long a prominent member of the Zagreb Opera.

Krnic, Boris (1900–). For the most part a composer of vocal works.

Kuhač, Franjo (1834–1911). Pioneer investigator of Croatian music folklore; also published in the fields of Croatian music history and of music theory. Original compositions few and of limited interest.

Kunc, Božidar (1903–1964). Pianist and composer; since 1950 a resident of New York City.

Lang, Ivana (1912–). Composer and conductor. Interested in Istrian music folklore, with its characteristic features noticeable in her compositions.

Lhotka, Fran (1883–1962). Czech by birth; came to Zagreb in 1909 to teach the French horn, and later harmony and conducting, at the Music Academy.

Lhotka-Kalinski, Ivo (1913–). Son of Fran Lhotka; composer, concert singer, and voice teacher. Wrote several operas and long instrumental works. Author of two books on the technique and art of singing.

Lisinski, Vatroslav (1819–1854). Composer of the first Croatian opera.

Lorković, Melita (1907–). One of the foremost contemporary Croatian pianists.

Lučić, Franjo (1889–). Composer, organist, teacher of theory, and textbook author. His *Symphony in F* (1917) is the first complete Croatian symphony after some attempts in the eighteenth century.

Lukačić (Lucacich), Ivan (1587–1648). Franciscan friar; motets printed in Venice, 1620.

Lukić, Darko (1922–). Contemporary concert pianist.

Maček, Ivo (1914–). Pianist; abandoned concertizing and composing in favor of teaching and a growing interest in philosophy.

Magdalenić, Miroslav (1906–). Composer and teacher; has written shorter instrumental and vocal works, but also a symphony (1939).

Majer, Milan (1895–). Music critic, piano accompanist, chamber musician, and lawyer. Came late to composing; has written several larger works for orchestra and piano, as well as some chamber music.

Malec, Ivan (1925–). Composer of anti-romantic and avant-garde tendencies; lives in Paris; also active in music journalism.

Mallinger, Matilda (1847–1920). Zagreb Opera member during Zajc's era; created the part of Eva at the world premiere of Wagner's *Meistersinger* in Munich, 1868.

Mandić, Josip (1883–1959). Music journalist; resident of Prague for 40 years; composer of three operas and other works.

Markantun. Organist at Hvar in 1558.

Markovac, Pavao (1903–1941). Musicologist; his doctoral dissertation at Vienna University was on Mussorgsky's harmony. Music critic, editor of music magazines, and organizer and conductor of workers' choral groups.

Marković, Vilim (1902–). Military bandmaster; original compositions for orchestra; arranged works of other Croatian composers for band.

Martinis, Dragica (Carla). Dramatic soprano; member of Vienna State Opera; sang in New York and San Francisco.

Matačić, Lovro von (1899–). Since 1961 general director of Frankfurt Opera; conducted at Bayreuth, and in Vienna, Paris, Italy, Chicago, and Detroit.

Matetić-Ronjgov, Ivan (1880–1960). Integrated tonal vocabulary of Istrian folk music into his compositions. Best known composition is the choral lament "Ćaće moj" (My Father).

Mattei, Djordje (1675–1728). A priest and poet from Dubrovnik; one of the first collectors of folk poetry and folk tunes.

Matz, Rudolf (1901–). Composer, conductor, teacher, and very active organizer and leader of many musical institutions and performing groups.

Milanov, Zinka (1906–). Renowned dramatic soprano; member of the Metropolitan Opera in New York since 1937.

Milinković, Georgine (1913–). Mezzo-soprano; appeared at Bayreuth; member of opera companies in Zagreb, Zurich, Munich, and Vienna.

Mirski, Lav (1893–). Conductor and music teacher in Osijek.

Mitrović, Ančica (1894–). Mezzo-soprano; between the wars a long-time member of opera companies in Zagreb and Germany.

Mitrović, Andro (1879–1940). Critic and opera conductor. Composed vocal works and one opera to his own libretto.

Mizerit, Klaro M. Conductor of the Rhenish Philharmonic, Koblenz; appeared as guest conductor in Baton Rouge, Louisiana, 1963–64.

Muhvić, Ivan (1876–1942). Military bandmaster in Zagreb since 1901; composer of works for voice, orchestra, and band.

Murai, Jurica (1927–). Concert pianist; toured extensively in Europe with notable success.

Musulin, Branka (1917–). A long-time resident of Germany; concert and recording pianist of great renown in central and western Europe.

Nakić (Nachini, Nanchini), Petar (1700–1770). Born in the Knin region in Dalmatia; became a priest and well-known organ builder in Venice. Rebuilt the organ of St. Justina's church in Padua, Italy, in 1735, then the best in the Apenines. Inventor of the "tiratutti"—a device to open all the stops of an organ at once.

Neralić, Tomislav (1917–). Renowned operatic bass, especially in Wagnerian portrayals. Presently in Berlin; appeared at Buenos Aires' Colon, and sang Wagner's Flying Dutchman at Chicago's Lyric Opera in 1959.

Nicolaus de Zagabria. "Tubicen" in Dubrovnik, 1411–14; possibly the earliest known Croatian musician.

Njirić, Nikša (1927–). Composer of instrumental, chamber, and vocal works, and compositions for children.

Novak, Vilko (1865–1918). Composer of very popular choral compositions; conductor of Zagreb's leading chorus, "Kolo," 1903–10.

Novak, Vjenceslav (1859–1905). Important writer of fiction; since 1887 professor of music at Zagreb Normal School; author of textbooks; harmonizer of sacred tunes. A few organ compositions and solo songs preserved.

Nožinić, Vilma (1897–). Leading lyric soprano of the Zagreb Opera between the wars.

Obuljen, Milan. A native of Split; founded the "Edition Slave" in Vienna (1918), dedicated to publications of composers from Yugoslavia.

Odak, Krsto (1888–). Until his retirement in 1961 was for almost 40 years a professor at Zagreb Music Academy. Propensity for the use of modality and polyphonic textures in his works.

Padovec, Ivan (1800–1873). Guitar virtuoso, teacher, composer, and inventor.

Papandopulo, Boris (1906–). Composer, conductor, pianist, and sometime music critic.

Parač, Ivo (1892–1954). Composer and poet of Italian verses; studied with Perosi and Pizzetti; until late 1920's considered himself an Italian. Basically a lyricist; adopted a late romantic style.

Patricij (Petris), Andrija (16th century). Native of the island of Cres; had four of his 4-part madrigals—one on Petrarca's verses—published in *Il primo libro da Villotte*, by Antonino Barges, Venice, 1550.

Pattiera, Tino (1890–). Renowned dramatic tenor; sang in Dresden, Prague, and Chicago.

Pejačević, Dora (1885–1923). Among the first of Croatian composers to devote her attention mostly to instrumental music; she wrote for the piano, chamber groups, and orchestra, including a symphony.

Pervizović, Toma. Compiler of *Muka i smrt Kristuševa* (The Passion and Death of Christ) in 1764, in which is recorded the traditional singing of the passion at the Zagreb cathedral.

Pettan, Hubert (1912–). Composer and author; now teaching at the State Music School in Zagreb. His solo song cycles are among his most successful compositions.

Pibernik, Zlatko (1926–). Composer of several symphonic and chamber works.

Pinkava, Ivan (1912–). Concert and orchestra violinist; concertmaster of the Zagreb Soloists on their first two American tours (1956, 1957).

Pintarić, Fortunat (1798–1867). Franciscan friar and secondary school teacher; follower of the Illyrian movement, composer of sacred and secular vocal works, and of piano and organ pieces.

Plamenac, Dragan (1895–). Since 1954 professor at the University of Illinois. Ph.D. from Vienna University under G. Adler in 1924. Expert on Western European music of the 14th and 15th centuries, among the first to study Croatian music history of the 16th and 17th centuries.

Pokorni, Franjo, Jr. (1825–1859). Theater conductor and music teacher in Zagreb; best known composition is his incidental music for the popular play *Graničari* (The Frontiersmen), by J. Freudenreich (1857).

Pospišil-Griff, Marta (1892–). Prominent contralto; member of the Zagreb Opera in the 1920's and early 1930's.

Pozajić, Mladen (1905–). Since 1947 professor of the Music Academy and opera conductor in Sarajevo. Has composed mostly smaller vocal and chamber works.

Prejac, Gjuro (1870–1936). Actor, librettist, and composer of operettas and popular solo songs.

Preprek, Stanislav (1900–). An elementary school teacher, musically self-taught. A well-informed, eclectic, prolific composer; has written three symphonies, five string quartets, and other works; few of these performed.

Puttar-Gold, Nada (1923–). Mezzo-soprano with the Frankfurt Opera; formerly in Berlin and Zagreb.

Radev, Marijana (1915–). Mezzo-soprano of international renown; opera, concerts, and recordings.

Radica, Ruben (1931–). Student of Kelemen and Leibowitz; composed mainly instrumental music.

Radić, Stjepan Jr. (1928–). A noted concert pianist of the younger generation.

Rafaelli, Josip (1767–1843). Priest; studied music in Italy, 1804–9; choirmaster in Split, then at the cathedral of his native Hvar. Mostly composer of sacred songs.

Razmilović, Bono (1636–1686?). A Split resident; author of a collection of "chorales," i.e. church chants.

Rihtman, Cvjetko (1902–). The first president of the Sarajevo Music Academy (founded after World War II). Collector and arranger of Croatian music folklore and author of several studies in that field; composer of solo songs and choruses.

Rosenberg-Ružić, Vjekoslav (1870–1954). Since 1910 director of the music school of the Croatian Music Institute; after 1935, member of the preparatory department of the Music Academy. Author of piano and violin methods; compositions of various merit, some semi-popular, but also four piano sonatas representing the first serious attempts of that form in Croatia (Sonata I, 1891; Sonata IV, 1920).

Rota-Kolunić. See Šibenčanin.

Rothmüller, Aron Marko (1908–). Voice professor at Indiana University; writer and composer.

Rukavina, Frederik (1880–1941). Director of the Zagreb Opera in the late 1920's; later guest-conductor with the Prague National Theater.

Runjanin, Josip (1821–1878). Army officer and amateur composer; writer of music for the Croatian national anthem "Lijepa naša domovino" (O Thou Beautiful Country of Ours!).

Ruždjak, Vladimir (1922–). Operatic and concert baritone; composer.

Šaban, Ladislav (1918–). Professor of piano at the Zagreb Music Academy.

Sachs, Milan (1884–). Czech by birth, he came to Belgrade early in the century as a concertmaster; then went to Zagreb where he stayed, except for about six years in the 1930's as a director in Brno. As conductor and sometime director of opera he has contributed considerably to the raising of performing standards.

Šafranek-Kavić, Lujo (1882–1940). General manager of the Zagreb Fair; active as a music critic and composer of shorter forms of music or music for the stage, including two operas and two ballets.

Sakač, Branimir (1918–). Composer, interested in achievements and further experimentation with concrete and electronic music.

Savin, Dragutin (1915–). Opera conductor in Osijek. Composed orchestra works and radio operas, the latter in a pleasingly attractive style for less sophisticated audiences.

Schiavetti (Schiavetto, Skjavetić), Julije. In the 1650's in the service of the Šibenik diocese. Collections of madrigals and motets in the polyphonic style of the Netherlands published by G. Scotto, Venice, 1563–64.

Schneider, Artur (1879–1946). Art historian and long time secretary of the Croatian Music Institute. Author of the most complete biography of Ivan Mane Jarnović (1944).

Serra, Paolo (born *c.* 1730, Novi). Singer in the Pope's chapel in Rome, 1753; author of "Introduzione armonica sopra la nuova serie de' suoni modulati in oggidì, e modo di rettamente e più facilmente intuonarla."

Šestak, Tomo (1852–1921). Organist and conductor from Koprivnica. Composer of instrumental and choral works.

Šibenčanin, Dominik Ivan (Sebenico, Domenico Giovanni, also known as Rota-Kolunić). Savoy court musical director at the end of the 17th century.

Šilobod-Bolšić, Mihajlo (1724–1787). Author of the first arithmetic in Croatian, and of *Fundamentum cantus gregoriani seu choralis* (1760), written in dialogue form.

Šipuš, Krešimir (1930–). Resident of Paris; composer of instrumental works, an opera and a ballet. Successful as opera and symphonic conductor in Europe and Argentina.

Širola, Božidar (1889–1956). The first Croatian Ph.D. in musicology; dissertation on Istrian folk music at the Vienna University (1921); author of numerous works about historic and ethnographic aspects of Croatian music, and prolific composer.

Slavenski, Josip (Family name Štolcer, 1896–1955). Student of Kodaly and Novak, one of the most original and remarkable Croatian composers of the first half of the century.

Slavković, Milan (d. 1832). Native of Zagreb; violin virtuoso and pedagogue; died in Odessa, Russia, where he spent the last seven years of his life. Called by some critics "another Paganini," he composed mostly for his instrument.

Šlik (Shlik), Miroslav (1898–). Concert violinist and violin teacher; before the war, resident of England and British subject; presently lives in Prague. Turned to composition rather late, subscribing to the national folkloristic manner.

Sokol, Bernardin (1888–1945). Priest, composer of sacred compositions and secular choruses; good contrapuntist; writer of music essays.

Sorkočević, Antun (1775–1841). Diplomat, historian, and amateur composer.

Sorkočević, Luka (1734–1789). Father of Antun. Composer of first Croatian symphonies.

Šoštarko, Dragutin (1907–). Operatic baritone, former member of the Zagreb Opera.

Spadina, Stjepan N. 18th century composer for violin.

Špiler, Miroslav (1906–). Piano accompanist and chamber musician;

for a long time on the Radio Zagreb staff; now with Radio Sarajevo. Composed for orchestra and chorus.

Spiller, Ljerko (1908–). Concert violinist, violin teacher, and conductor. Resident of Buenos Aires for some thirty years.

Špoljar, Zlatko (1892–). Melographer, composer of choruses, and arranger of folk tunes from Podravina.

Stahuljak, Dubravko (1920–). Faculty member of the Osijek music school, composer of an opera, various vocal, and several instrumental works.

Stahuljak, Juraj (1901–). Composer, mostly of chamber music.

Stahuljak, Mladen (1914–). Concert organist, now in Sarajevo. Composed for his own instrument, for orchestra and numerous chamber music.

Stančić, Svetislav (1895–). Concert pianist and composer, who, in the early 1920's, turned exclusively to teaching.

Stefanović, Franjo (1878–1924). Pioneer of children's music theater in Croatia; wrote several children's operas with piano accompaniment, basing his music on folk tunes.

Stöger-Stazić, Franjo (1824–1911). The tenor lead in the first performances of Lisinski's "Love and Malice" (1846); enjoyed considerable success on the first operatic stages in Central Europe and Russia, before his retirement in 1874.

Stöhr, Ante (1847–1923). Pianist, violinist and voice teacher. After 1877 in Varaždin, where he founded a private music school. Composed mostly potpourri-phantasies for piano in "salon" style.

Štoos, Pavao (1806–1862). Priest, patriot, writer, and amateur composer. Set to music some of his own poems and published a sacred songbook for organ in 1858.

Štriga, Alberto Ognjan (1821–1897). A self-taught baritone and ardent patriot associated with Lisinski. Studied voice in Vienna; appeared in opera in Prague and Russia; final appearance in a "Trovatore" performance in Croatian that he organized in Zagreb, 1869.

Strmić, Nikola (1839 or 1840–1896). A native of Zadar and graduate of the Milan Conservatory. Violinist and composer of operas and instrumental works. Culturally, and by political orientation, an Italian who did not speak Croatian; showed some interest in the budding Croatian nationalism. His opera "La madre slava" was performed in Zagreb (1866).

Strozzi-Pečić, Maja (1886–). Opera and concert soprano of international renown. Stravinsky dedicated compositions to her. Mentioned in Thomas Mann's novel *Doktor Faustus*.

Šulek, Stjepan (1914–). Professor of composition at Zagreb Music Academy since 1947; one of the most important contemporary Croatian composers.

Supičić, Ivo (1928–). Studied in Paris; author in the field of esthetics and sociology of music.

Suppé, Franz von (1820–1895). Native of Split; popular composer of operettas in Vienna.

Taclik, Rudolf (1894–1942). Composer of vocal music, secular and sacred.

Tempari̇čić (Tamparica, Temparricius) Gavro. A 16th century Franciscan friar from Dubrovnik; music teacher at the court in Vienna.

Left: The Cathedral in Šibenik (fifteenth century).
Right: Portal of the Cathedral of Trogir, sculpted by Radovan.

Ivan Meštrović, "Pietà."

Ivan Meštrović, "Croatian History."

Upper: Jozo Kljaković, "The Oath of King Zvonimir."
Lower: Maksimiljan Vanka, "Croatian Death in Pennsylvania."

Ternina, Milka (1863–1941). First Croatian to sing at Bayreuth, Covent Garden, and the Metropolitan Opera.

Tijardović, Ivo (1895–). All-round theatre personality: composer, conductor, librettist, stage director, scenographer. Best known for the popular operetta about his native Split, *The Little Floramy* (1926), which received an amateur performance in Cleveland. After the war, he was general manager of the Zagreb Theater. Wrote two operas and the first Croatian musical, "Catherine the Great" (1960).

Tkalčić, Juro (1887–). Concert violoncellist, long-time resident of Belgrade.

Tončić, Nada (1909–). Since late 1930's, leading lyric soprano of the Zagreb Opera.

Topolski, Zlatko. (1914–). Concertmaster of Vienna Symphony Orchestra; served in the same capacity, and as concert violinist and conductor, in Yugoslavia, Argentina, and Germany.

Turanyi, Dragutin (1806–1872). Born in Osijek; studied in Vienna. Excellent pianist; since 1832 conductor of amateur theater orchestra in Zagreb; since 1842, conductor in Aachen, where he also composed instrumental music.

Turkali, Nenad (1923–). Music critic and author of several books on music.

Vancaš, Antun (1867–1888). Showed great promise; studied in Vienna, and in Paris with Massenet. Wrote several works for orchestra, string quartet and chorus.

Vidaković, Albe (1914–). Student of Casimiri and Refice in Rome; the most important exponent of the contemporary sacred music in Croatia, and a composer of masses, motets and organ works. Musicologist of note; editor of the works of Vinko Jelić, and author of many monographs on the early Croatian music.

Vidošić, Tihomil (1902–). Former military bandmaster and later a secondary school music teacher; uses folkloric motives of his native Istria in his works. Wrote operas, instrumental and vocal music.

Vilhar-Kalski, Franjo S. (1852–1928). Slovenian by birth. After almost a decade in Rumania, came to Croatia in 1881; moved to Zagreb in 1891, where he was choir director at St. Mark's Church. Wrote mostly for voice, solo or chorus; very popular composer around the turn of the century.

Vraz, Stanko (1810–1851). A Slovenian who wrote Croatian poetry. Good amateur musician, proficient on the flute and guitar; collected many folk tunes.

Vrhovski, Josip (1902–). Uses elements of folklore in his numerous instrumental and vocal compositions, mostly of chamber dimensions.

Vušković, Marko (1877–1960). A noted baritone who enjoyed international successes in the first quarter of the century.

Wiesner-Livadić, Ferdo (1799–1878). Illyrian composer of shorter works, mostly for solo voice or piano.

Wisner-Morgenstern, Juraj Karlo (1783–1855). Born in Arad, Hungary; since 1819 chorister of Zagreb Cathedral, one of the founders of the *Musikverein* (1827). Extremely versatile; was in his time the best trained musician in Zagreb.

Zajc, Ivan (1832–1914). Between his arrival in Zagreb in 1870 and his retirement in 1908 as the head of Croatian Music Institute's conservatory, and, for the first nineteen years, of the opera as well, was the main force of Zagreb and of Croatian music life.

Žganec, Vinko (1890–). Director of the Ethnographic Institute in Zagreb. Composer of choral works; melographer of folk tunes, particularly of Medjimurje.

Zlatić, Slavko (1910–). Conductor of the Radio Zagreb chorus; professor at the Zagreb Music Academy. In his vocal and instrumental compositions, mostly in shorter forms, uses elements of Istrian folklore.

Županiović, Lovro (1925–). Numerous works of chamber music proportions, following the national folkloristic trend; also two elementary school songbooks.

Discography

ABBREVIATIONS: *bsn.*, bassoon; *btn.*, baritone; *cdr.*, conductor; *comp.*, composer; *conc.*, concerto; *fl.*, flute; *hpsd.*, harpsichord; *mzs.*, mezzo-soprano; *ob.*, oboe; *pia.*, piano; *sopr.*, soprano; *str.*, strings; *ten.*, tenor; *vn.*, violin.

I. Ensemble Performances

"Dalmatian Singers," Monitor 349.

"Lado," Croatian Song and Dance Ensemble, Monitor 344.

Zagreb Joža Vlahović Society: "Robeson Favorites," vol. 2 (Robeson; cdr. Cossetto), Monitor 581.

Zagreb Soloists (Solisti di Zagreb), cdr. Janigro:

- Bach, Brandenburg Conc. 5 (Rampal, Stanic, Veyron-Lacroix); Suite 2 (Rampal), RCA Victor LM2460; LSC2460.
- Bach, Chorales; Corelli, Christmas Conc.; Haydn, Toy Symphony; Torelli, Pastoral Conc., Bach Guild 569; S:5006.
- Bach, Chorales; Corelli, Conc. Grosso, op. 6, no. 8; Haydn, Toy Symphony; Torelli, Conc., Bach Guild 589; S:5014.
- Bach, Conc. vn. ob. str. (Klima, Lardrot); Conc. in A, fl., vn., hpsd., str. (Tripp, "Pinkava," A. Heiller), Bach Guild 562.
- Barber, Adagio for Str.; Mozart, Serenade K 525; Pergolesi?, Concertino in G; Respighi, Ancient Airs and Dances, suite 3; Sibelius, Valse triste; Vaughan Williams, Greensleeves, Vanguard 1095; S:2126.
- Boccherini, Cello Conc.; Vivaldi, Cello Conc. (Janigro), RCA Victor LM2365; LSC2365.
- Couperin, Pièces en concert (Janigro); Britten, Simple Symphony; Corelli, Conc. grosso, op. 6, no. 4; Mozart, Divertimento K 136, RCA Victor LM2653; LSC2653.
- Mozart, Fl.-harp Conc. K 299 (Baker, Jelinek); Telemann, Suite in A, fl., str. (Baker), Bach Guild 636; S:5048.
- Rossini, 4 Sonatas, Vanguard 488.
- Telemann, Oboe Conc. in D, E (Lardrot); Viola Conc. (Passaggio); Violin Conc. (Krek); Sonata a Quattro in A, Bach Guild 575; S:5028.
- Virtuoso Trumpet (Wobisch, Holler, Hell, Conrath), Bach Guild 617; S:5041.

Vivaldi, Conc. for Orch. P 143; Oboe Conc. P 259, 309; Bsn. Conc. P 137; Sinfonias 1, 2, Bach Guild 560.

Vivaldi, Four Seasons (Tomasow), Bach Guild 564; S:5001.

Zagreb National Opera Orchestra:

K. Baranović, Gingerbread Heart, ballet suite; F. Lhotka, Devil in the Village, ballet suite, London LL-1235.

II. Individual Performances

Baranović (Baranovich), Krešimir (comp.). Gingerbread Heart, ballet suite, Zagreb National Opera Orchestra, London LL-1235.

——. (cdr.) Belgrade National Opera: Mussorgsky, Boris Godunov, 3 London A4317.

Cossetto Emil. See above, Zagreb Joža Vlahović Society.

Cvejić (Tzveych), Biserka (mzs.). Tschaikovsky, Eugen Onegin; Belgrade Opera, 3 London A4324.

Gotovac, Jakov (comp.). Symphonic Kolo, Vienna Philharmonia, cdr. Kempe, Angel 35975; S-35975.

Horvat, Milan (cdr.), Radio Eireann Symphony Orchestra

Boydell, Megalithic Ritual Dances; Bodley, Music for Strings; May, Suite of Irish Airs, Decca 9843.

Potter, Variations on a Popular Tune; Larchet, Dirge of Ossian; MacAnanty's Reel; Kelly, 3 Pieces for Strings; Duff, Irish Suite for Strings, Decca 9844.

——. Vienna State Opera Orchestra.

Mendelssohn, Piano Conc. I, II (Gianoli), Westminster 18043.

Mozart, Piano Conc. 20, 23 (Badura-Skoda), Westminster 18225.

Jurinac, Sena (sopr.)

Beethoven, Fidelio; Bavarian State Opera, 3 Westminster 3318; S:318.

Beethoven, Fidelio; Vienna Philh., 3 Electrola 90071/3; excerpts: Electrola 80038.

Kodaly, Te Deum; Vienna Symph. Orch., Westminster 18455.

Mozart, Don Giovanni; Berlin Radio Symph. Orch., 3 Deutsche Grammoph. 18580/2; S:138050/2; excerpts, Deutsch Grammoph. 19224; S:136224.

Mozart, Don Giovanni; Vienna Symph. Orch., 3 Epic SC-6010.

Mozart, Idomeneo; Glyndebourne Fest., 3 Angel 3574C/L.

Mozart, Marriage of Figaro; Vienna Philh., 3 Elektra 90292/4; excerpts: Angel 35326

Mozart, Marriage of Figaro; Vienna Symph. Orch., 3 Epic SC-6022.

Mozart, Requiem; Vienna State Opera Orch., 2 Westminster 2230; S:205.

R. Strauss, Ariadne auf Naxos; Vienna Philh., 3 RCA Victor LD-6152; LDS-6152.

R. Strauss, Rosenkavalier; Vienna Philh., 4 London A-4404; excerpts London 5615.

Kelemen, Milko (comp.). Etudes contrapuntiques; Travis, Hamburger Kammersolisten, Time 58006; S:8006.

Klepač, Rudolf (bsn.) Vivaldi, Conc. in E; Lucerne Festival Strings, Deutsche Grammoph., Arch. 3116.

Klobučar, Berislav (cdr.), Berlin Comic Opera
Thomas, Mignon (excerpts—Elektra 80639; S-80639).
Puccini, Madame Butterfly (excerpts), Elektra 80632; S-80632.
——, Berlin Municipal Opera
Lortzing, Zar und Zimmermann (excerpts), Elektra 80568; S-80568.
——, Berlin State Opera
Flotow, Martha (excerpts), Elektra 80593; S-80593.

Lhotka, Fran (comp., cdr.). Devil in the Village, ballet suite, London LL-1235

Matačić, Lovro von (cdr.), London Symphony Orchestra
Bruch, Violin Conc. I;
Prokofiev, Violin Conc. I (Oistrakh), Angel 35243.
——. Philharmonia Orchestra
Glazounov, Violin Conc.; Paganini, Violin Conc. I (Rabin), Angel 35259.
Rimsky-Korsakov, Sheherazade, Angel 35767; S-35767.
——, La Scala.
Leoncavallo, Pagliacci; Verdi, Choruses, 2 Angel 3618B/L; S-3618B/L.
Puccini, Fanciulla del West, 3 Angel 3593C/L; S-3593C/L.

Milanov, Zinka (sopr.)
Great Love Duets, RCA Victor LM-2628.
Great Moments in Opera, 2 RCA Victor LM-6061.
Opera for People Who Hate Opera, RCA Victor LM-2391; LSC-2391.
Operatic Arias, RCA Victor LM-2303; LSC-2303.
Ponchielli, Gioconda; Accademia Sta. Cecilia, 3 RCA Victor LM-6139; 4 LSC-6139; arias 3 RCA Victor LM-6138; 4 LSC-6138.
Puccini, Tosca; Rome Opera, 2 RCA Victor LM-6052; 3 LSC-6052.
Verdi, Aida; Rome Opera, 3 RCA Victor LM-6122; excerpts RCA Victor LM-2046.
Verdi, Forza del destino; Accademia Sta. Cecilia, 4 RCA Victor LM-6406; LSC-6406; excerpts: RCA Italiana LM-20043; LSC-20043.
Verdi, Rigoletto, Act IV; NBC Symph. Orch., 2 RCA Victor LM-6041.
Verdi, Trovatore, RCA Victor Symph. Orch., 2 RCA Victor LM-6008; excerpts RCA Victor LM-1827.

Musulin, Branka (pia.). Chopin, Conc. I, II; Süddeutscher Rundfunk Orch., Period SHO-306.

Neralić, Tomislav (btn.). Beethoven, Fidelio; Vienna State Opera, 3 Vox VBX-250.

Pattiera, Tino (ten.). Giordano, Andrea Chenier (excerpts), Eterna 755.
Mamma mia, Eterna 728.
Verdi, Otello (excerpts), Eterna 747.
Verdi, Trovatore: Di quella pira, Tap 333.

Pinkava, Ivan (vn.). Bach, Concerto in A (fl., vn., hpsd., str.); Zagreb Soloists, Bach Guild 562.

Rothmüller, Marko (btn.).
Bartok, Cantata Profana; New Symph. Orch., Bartok 312
Bloch, Sacred Service; London Philh., London 5006.

Slavenski, Josip (comp.). Sinfonia Orienta, solos, chorus, orch., London LL-1216

Soljanich, Ante (ten.). Songs, Music Library 7036.

10

Architecture, Sculpture, and Painting

RUŽA BAJURIN

WHEN THE Croatians arrived at the shores of the Adriatic from their original land between the Baltic Sea and the Ural Mountains, they already possessed their own culture. They brought with them not only their own language, religion, legends, and music, but also the ability to express themselves and their individual spirit in wood, clay, textiles, and leather. At the time of the Croatian arrival, the Roman Illyricum was already a graveyard of the civilizations which had disappeared in the conflagrations of the centuries. The Croatians brought fresh blood and primitive, raw forces to the anæmic remnants of the ancient world. They began to settle, and by the turn of the eighth century they proved successful not only in the realm of politics, but also in that of the arts.

ARCHITECTURE

As the oldest mode of artistic expression, architecture is the basis for the development of all other branches of art. When a group of people come to rest and build permanent homes, spiritual and material energies previously dormant are enabled to come alive. The first permanent habitations of man had as their purpose to grant him protection and security. They were initially fortifications difficult to reach, but gradually man came to lay stress on making them more comfortable and beautiful.

The first Croatian homes were built of wood, because the Croatians' new territory was as rich in forests as their former one. Herodotus describes Slavic settlements between the Volga and the Don, recording that the houses, palaces, temples, and fortresses were built of wood. These settlements were usually constructed with only one entrance, in a form of a circle, with a fountain in the center. The new Croatian fatherland was endowed with an ample supply of lumber. The Dalmatian oak for centuries provided the best material for the Roman galleys, and so it was that the first homes were made of wood. These original structures have long since disappeared,[1] and the present-day peasants throughout Croatia build their houses, adorned with many archaic forms—ornaments, geometrical and floral designs—out of stone. Dalmatian stone buildings and the stone remnants of Roman ruins were not destroyed by the passing centuries. Rural architecture in the coastal villages still includes the type of primitive one-room house (*bunja*), consisting of a round base, an open fireplace, with a crude slab of granite as a roof, that has been passed down through the ages.

In spite of incessant wars, plagues, earthquakes, and invasions, the oldest Croatian architectural achievements were formidable. Under the rule of the medieval nobility, the master architects built churches, palaces, monasteries, walls, and gates. In Nin, seat of the Croatian kings and bishops, an unknown master built the Church of the Holy Cross (Sveti Križ) around the year 800.[2] This "smallest cathedral of Christianity," with its base in the shape of a simple cross, was, according to an inscription, erected for the purpose of saving the soul of Count Godežav. Such miniature churches, with bases in the shape of a cross, three-, four-, six-, and eight-foiled clovers, and with cupolas above, belong to the Old Croatian or Preromanesque period (*c.* 700–1000), and were usually richly endowed by kings, queens, and noblemen. St. Krševan and St. Donatus on the island of Krk, St. Michael in Ston, and Holy Trinity in Poljud, a suburb of Split, are but a few of the numerous churches built in this style. The dome-shaped structures were typically Slavic and were brought from the old country, as the European churches of this time had only wooden roofs. The different foundations and shallow engraved decorations were a continuation of old forms expressed in the new medium of stone. St. Donatus at Zadar is the largest church representative of this period. In solitary splendor, this huge place of worship rests on the paving stones of a Roman forum. This church was built in 805, and during World War II everything around it was destroyed by bombs, while it remained.

The names of the architects of the earliest Croatian period are unknown today, but their work is an imposing document that records

[1]Some carvings on Bosnian tombstones (*stećci*) portray wooden houses featuring logs in a horizontal or vertical position.

[2]Ljubo Karaman, an historian of Old Croatian Art, believes, however, that this church dates from the eleventh century. See his work *Pregled umjetnosti u Dalmaciji* / A Survey of Art in Dalmatia (Zagreb, 1952).

the struggle of medieval Croatia to attain recognition and salvation through its churches. The eleventh century brought with it closer contact with the Western civilization, and from that time on, the Croatian architecture developed parallel with that of the rest of Western Europe.

The Romanesque basilica—simple, massive and archaic, with a square base, a three-decked nave, and rows of pillars along the sides—is typical of the architectural style so often duplicated in Croatian churches. One finds the oldest basilicas of this kind in Kotor (St. Trifun: ninth century), on the island of Rab (St. Peter at Draga), and in Zadar (St. Krševan). The cathedrals located in Rab, Zadar, Trogir, and Split represent the most beautiful creations of this structural pattern. The monastery of the Franciscan friars in Dubrovnik was built by the architect Miha of Bar in 1317 in this same style. A school of architects was founded in Miha's native town, and many of its members were active in neighboring places. Although the Romanesque style was widespread and became recognized throughout Europe, Croatian architects succeeded in introducing their own characteristics into this design. Braided ornaments were common decorations used by them, and massive belfries gave their churches the appearance of fortresses rather than of temples. They also used this style in Istria and Northern Croatia, and it dominated in the latter after the founding of the archdiocese of Zagreb (1094). The tower of the Church of St. George in Belec, parts of the Church of the Holy Cross in Budinšćina, of the monastery of the Templars in Glogovnica, and of churches in Irig, Šid, and Ilok are representative of this style—of which one now finds only ruins or perhaps renovations in some later form. Typical is the example of the cathedral at Zagreb, the oldest Romanesque monument in Northern Croatia. This church was consecrated in 1227; it was demolished shortly thereafter, during the Tatar attacks, and restored in 1280. After the earthquake of 1881 it was renovated, mostly in Gothic style.

The Croatian architects of the thirteenth and fourteenth centuries were primarily concerned with the building of fortresses, walls and military units. The population of the fortified cities grew, and houses, because of limited space, became two and even more floors high. The few streets were winding and narrow. According to information gleaned from various archives, the builders often followed blueprints and strict city regulations in erecting buildings; a board was usually elected to supervise the construction of projects. Under the ordinances of Dubrovnik, every master architect and stonecutter was supposed to keep at least two apprentices and to teach them his trade, so that the city would always have a sufficient number of competent masters. Many cities rose in this period, and one may admire their architectural beauty even today. The city of Dubrovnik—first mentioned in 670, in connection with the destruction of Epidaurus, a Greco-Roman settlement, by the Avars and Slavs—is the best-preserved medieval architectural ensemble in Europe, a unique monument of stone, permeated by contrasts and yet conceived with the harmony of the finest craftsmanship. In the interval from the fourteenth to the sixteenth centuries, Dubrovnik acquired the shape that nowadays makes it such a perfect setting for Shakespearean and other plays. This was the prosperous period when new stone buildings replaced old wooden houses, and when the towers, fountains, harbor, and many public and private structures were erected. Stone buildings were constructed throughout the city of Dubrovnik, preserving the past for the generations to come. Hvar, with its oldest theatre and its many churches, should be mentioned as another architectural jewel in which the past is charmingly blended with the modern age. Ston, Korčula, and many other cities, were begun at this time with similarly planned structures, on a smaller scale, illustrating the fact that the Dalmatian cities were in a close touch with one another.

The massive Romanesque style gave way to the more gracious and less weighty Gothic style. More light came in through the higher windows that characterized this style, and balconies lent a new elegance to palaces and summer homes. The Croatian master Nikola Tvrdoje built the pride of Split, the St. Domnius belfry, in this style. *Gotico Fiorito,* the Venetian version of the same style, was very popular in Dalmatia, then under the rule of Venice. This variation of the Gothic style was stressed in the education of Juraj Dalmatinac (Georgius Dalmaticus or Giorgio da Sebenico), the greatest Croatian architect and sculptor of the fifteenth century. He became very famous in Italy, where he built many masterpieces, but he was even more prolific in his own country. The monumental cathedral in Šibenik is his creation, as are the well-known Minčeta tower in Dubrovnik, the chapel and tomb of St. Anastasius (Staš) in the cathedral of Split, and the blueprint of the city of Pag. Many Croatian artists worked under Dalmatinac's supervision, and they helped to spread *Gotico Fiorito* throughout Croatia. Andrej Aleši built the portal and baptistry in the cathedral of Trogir, as well as the dividing columns in the cathedral of Rab. Many churches were erected in Istria in the same style, such as St. Mary's in Beram, the parish church in Pazin and that in Butoniga, and the names of their builders are recorded; among them are Nikola of Piran, Matej of Pula, and Nikola of Rovinj.

The Gothic style from France and Germany, as well as from the Dalmatian coast, spread widely in Upper Croatia. St. Mary's in Jajce showed a definite influence from the Dalmatian masters. The blending of Romanesque and Gothic styles is evident in many medieval cities between the Sava and Drava Rivers. More than one hundred cities had a special royal charter that insured their independence inside their gates. The picturesque Upper Town in Zagreb developed from just such a chartered royal city. Grič and its towers, walls, and gates has also preserved the spirit of the Middle Ages to the present day.

Many a Croatian architect of the Gothic period went on to work in Italy and in other countries, after receiving his early schooling at home. Ivan Splićanin participated in the building of the Palazzo Ducale in Venice; the master Sebastijan Schiavone da Rovigno was responsible for woodcarvings found in many churches in Venice; Lucijan Vranjanin (Luciano da Laurana) was the chief architect for Count Federigo da Urbino and was a builder of palaces, hospitals, and bridges in Urbino and Pesaro. His younger brother, Franjo Laurana, built palaces and water systems in Italy and France.

Juraj Dalmatinac and his students and successors prepared the way for the Renaissance which spread rapidly throughout Dalmatia. Gothic and Renaissance architectural styles blended very successfully to produce the harmony of form, structure, and function of Dubrovnik's Sponza custom house, called Divona, built by Paskoje Miličević and the brothers Andrijić, between 1516 and 1521. On the ground floor are Renaissance arcades, while the first floor provides an example of interlaced Gothic triforas. The second floor has simple Renaissance windows, and the roof the graceful Gothic acroterium. Also in Dubrovnik, one finds another excellent example of the blending of styles, with decorative elements of Gothic style prevailing, in the patio of the Dominican monastery. The well-known architects Antun Nogulović and Pavao Gospodnetić built many simple and beautiful structures in the Renaissance style. The summerhouse of the poet Hanibal Lucić, and Tvrdalj, the fortified palace of the poet Petar Hektorović, were the most important Renaissance buildings on the island of Hvar; both were constructed in the first half of the sixteenth century.

The later Renaissance did not result in many outstanding architectural achievements in Croatia. In that period the Dalmatian cities were losing their independence, and most of the country was a bloody battlefield as a result of the efforts against the Turkish invasions. The age of great buildings was over. The many and constant wars illustrated the truth of the saying *Inter arma silent musae*. Many workshops of the Croatian architects and stonecutters remained deserted while their masters and students became soldiers or left for another country in search of peace and prosperity.

A special style of architecture developed in the Croatian regions which were under Turkish domination. A strong oriental influence became evident in Croatian mosques, fountains, konaks, amams, markets, and cemeteries. Minarets pointed their spear-like tips to the sky, lending a foreign touch and a strange beauty to the Croatian land. Some of these buildings revealed themselves partially influenced by the Christian belfries. The most complete example of the Turkish style of architecture is the city of Sarajevo. In Roman times Sarajevo was a military camp, and during the Middle Ages it became a Christian settlement (Vrhbosna). Gazi Husref Bey developed this settlement into a new Turkish city, one in which Eugene of Savoy was able to count more than 120 mosques in 1697. The Turkish urbanistic architecture differed in many ways from the Western style. The main characteristics of the Turkish architecture were the absence of geometrical planning, crooked streets, and picturesque houses, the latter usually turned to the well-kept gardens and almost unnoticeable from streets. The outsides of the Turkish buildings were usually simple, severe, squat, and built of heavy stones. The interiors, by contrast, were rich, comfortable, and colorful, with huge transparent ceilings, mosaics, and the gracious rhythm of arabesques. The Turks also built fine roads and bridges, some of which are still in use today, for example, the one-span bridge over Neretva, built in 1566 by the architect Hajrudin.

The wars against the Turks and their domination in parts of Croatia continued during the seventeenth and eighteenth centuries, while the Austrian influence prevailed in the rest of the country. From the West there came the new architectural style, the Baroque, introduced by the Jesuits, and its influence was felt in almost every corner of the country. This style of architecture was especially popular in Hrvatsko Zagorje and Medjimurje. In some parts, the Baroque style even became a form of expression in peasant architecture. The church in Belec, near Zlatar, is considered the most worthy example of Baroque architecture among the peasants at that time. The new style also appealed greatly to the city dwellers. Many churches, palaces, and summer residences were built in Zagreb—for example, St. Catherine's church; the palaces of Counts Ivan Drašković, Oršić, and Rauch; and in Varaždin the palaces of Counts Patačić, Drašković, and Keglević. The Baroque also penetrated into Dalmatia, and many churches and private homes followed this highly decorative pattern. The most successful creations here are the churches of St. Blasius and St. Ignatius in Dubrovnik, and the attractive church in Nerežišće, on the island of Brač. The cathedral church in Dubrovnik was rebuilt in the Baroque style in 1713. To a greater extent than in large architectural structures, the Baroque was used in interior decoration, and there is hardly a region in Croatia into which this ornate style did not penetrate.

During the same period, the Austrian government was responsible for building numerous army centers in Vojna Krajina, the fighting line against the Turks. Many of these centers, such as Koprivnica, Bjelovar, Glina, Nova Gradiška, Brod, and Petrinja, were influenced by Karlovac, built at the end of the sixteenth century by the architect Matija Gambor. Strategy and military need principally dictated the plan of the city. A central square was the focus of a geometrical net of streets in all four directions. The Catholic and Orthodox churches were usually in the middle, and close by were the arsenal, barracks, and governmental buildings. Like lines of soldiers, trees were planted around the square and along the main street. All but devoid of ornament, these cities and buildings remain as illustrations of the power of rules and regulations.

The strengthening of the middle class had a decisive influence on the architecture of the nineteenth century. The feudal nobility declined, their castles were no longer the lively centers of entertainment that they formerly were, and everybody with money and desire for social life moved to the cities. The prosperous middle class craved luxuries, and the architects found a clientele eager for their work. Many foreign architects discovered a favorable market for their abilities in Croatia, and quite a few stayed to become an organic part of the country. One of these was Bartol Felbinger, who particularly influenced the development of modern architecture in Zagreb. His creations were the beautiful residences in the Upper Town and Narodni Dom, in Opatička Street. He originated parks and promenades that brought fresh beauty to the city. Tuškanac, Zelengaj, Rokov Park, Zrinjevac—all attractive places of recreation for the citizens of Zagreb —were begun or influenced by Felbinger. His greatest success was the bishop's summer residence in Maksimir. The buildings he created were symmetrical and peaceful in their classical beauty, with columns, balconies, and entrances characteristic of this form. The calm harmony of Felbinger's realization did not exist in the buildings that his contemporary, the architect Perišić, erected under the influence of Italian

Neoclassicism; buildings such as the City Hall in Split (Procuratura), and Bonda's Theatre in Dubrovnik.

After the successful Felbinger period, which gave the Croatian capital its architectural outline, the desire to embellish the homes of wealthy citizens led to the development of a mixture of all possible styles, an era which could be called an epoch without any style of its own. The architect responsible for this period was the Austrian Hermann Bollé, along with his students and followers. They flooded the country with richly decorated structures that incorporated domes, pillars, belfries, angels, and floral and geometrical designs. The interior of these buildings was most impractical, including dark, narrow hallways, steep stairways, and unusually high ceilings in small rooms. Ugly and expensive, these architectural monsters could be found in almost every corner of central Europe.

During this time of imitation and formalism, Viktor Kovačić, a truly great architect, became active in Zagreb. It was Kovačić who pointed out the road of modern Croatian architecture. In his theory and practice he emphasized the view that every style is the product of its time, and his theory that architecture must serve and satisfy the practical and artistic needs of men. St. Blasius' Church in Zagreb, the best of Kovačić's works, was built on a simple cross base, as was the miniature church in Nin many centuries before. The Stock Exchange (Burza) is another masterpiece that revealed, especially inside, the simple, noble, harmonious lines that appealed to Kovačić. His ideas that Croatian architecture should satisfy the needs of its people and express the characteristics of the Croatian soil were accepted by many of his successors in the period between the two world wars, by men such as Drago Ibler, Stjepan Planić, Lavoslav Horvat, Edo Schoen, Alfred Albini, Frane Cota, Aleksandar Freudenreich, Hugo Ehrlich, Stjepan Hribar, and Bruno Bauer. Kovačić's convictions remain modern and valid even in our times.

The sculptor Ivan Meštrović demonstrated a deep interest in architecture in the period before World War II. His home, centered in a beautiful park in Split, harmonizes perfectly with his various sculptures and symbolizes the unity between sculpture and architecture in a striking fashion. He also built the impressive round Art Pavilion in Zagreb, a building of simplicity and great nobility. Three minarets were added to this building during the last war, without the consent of the artist, and thereby the art gallery was transformed into the largest mosque in Croatia. After the war, the rotunda was restored to its original form, and it now houses the Museum of National Liberation. The strong influence of functionalism and constructivism was also felt at this time. Many Croatian architects tried to imitate the creations of the outstanding representatives of the new schools, such as those inspired by Le Corbusier, Gropius, and Frank Lloyd Wright.

At the present time, architecture is flourishing in Croatia, especially in the attempt of the architects to provide comfortable and pleasant structures for the life, work, and leisure of modern man. The architects had, first of all, to restore and replace the buildings destroyed during World War II. Changes in the country, and in modern life in general, created many new needs. Whole new cities were planned, and new schools, factories, hospitals, and atomic institutes were built, and numerous city and national parks and recreational centers were also founded.

Among the modern Croatian architects, one can discern two different groups. The larger of the two groups continues the tradition of Felbinger and Kovačić. Neven Šegvić is active in housing projects; Marijan Haberle designs most of the blueprints for the annual fair in Zagreb; Mladen Kauzlarić, Stjepan Gomboš, and Vladimir Juranović built the Rade Končar Factory in Zagreb and participated in many other industrial projects, such as the designing of a wagon factory in Slavonski Brod, of the Ferolegura concern in Šibenik, of oil refineries in Rijeka and Split, and of an iron works in Sisak. Ivo Vitić and Josip Seissel erected, in beautiful harmony with the hills and woods in the vicinity of Zagreb, the City of Pioneers, a Croatian version of Disneyland. Djuro Neidhardt made use of autochthonous Bosnian architecture in the building of many projects, as for instance in the development of Zenica.

The second group of architects mentioned tends to ignore the national tradition and to emphasize international patterns and trends in contemporary architecture. The builders in this group belong mostly to the younger generation and have, for the most part, been educated abroad. Some of them work in different parts of the world, either in the framework of the United Nations, or as experts sent to a foreign land by their own government. Vladimir Turina, who built Dinamo Stadium in Maksimir (Zagreb), and Zvonimir Požgaj are well-known architects of sports arenas and have been the winners of many prizes. Vlado Antolić, Vido Vrbanić, and others are engaged in various projects in Asia and Africa.

The increased building activity after the war provided much opportunity in the areas of planning cities, expanding industrial facilities, and designing housing units. These developments have offered to both the old and the new generation of Croatian architects wide possibilities to employ their creativeness and ingenuity. Croatian architects are now engaged in an over-all architectural reconstruction of their country, and they continue to express their individuality in this task with ambition and determination, while satisfying the needs of their society.

Sculpture

For a long time Croatian architecture and sculpture were closely related, in that they used the same kinds of materials and tried to achieve the same lasting values. Many remains of ancient Croatian churches and monasteries have different designs, ornaments, and inscriptions that were probably executed by the same masters who built the buildings themselves.

The Croatian braided ornament on the baptistry in Nin, *c.* 800, is the oldest such relief that has been found. In later years, artists expanded and enriched this simple type of ornament by adding to it crosses, stars, flowers, animals, and finally even human figures. The rigid figure of an unknown Croatian king with a crown and globe in one hand and a cross in the other, looks down at the visitor from his throne in the Diocletian Palace at Split. Prostrate in front of him is one of his subjects, and standing close to him, a nobleman. Who is this king? Who is the sculptor of this relief, which dates back to the eleventh century, and which still forms a part of the baptistry of the cathedral in the Diocletian Palace? Thus far it has been impossible to answer these significant questions, but in spite of this the relief is one of the most valuable documents of Croatian history. Similar anonymous sculptures with precious old Croatian inscriptions can be dated back as far as the eleventh and twelfth centuries, and these provide important evidence of history and literacy, as well as of art among the early Croatians. The ivory cover of a diptych, considered to belong to the eleventh century, is kept in the treasury of the cathedral in Zagreb; it presents scenes of the Annunciation, the birth of Christ, His Resurrection, and His Ascension.

The thirteenth century brought to light two powerful artists who broke the tradition of anonymity among artists and engraved their own names on their sculptures. The works of these masters, Buvina and Radovan, have evoked the enthusiasm of the best authorities on the works of their period. In 1214, Andrija Buvina carved scenes of the life and death of Christ into the walnut portal of the cathedral in

Split in twenty-eight simple Romanesque rectangles. With a skillful hand and a rich imagination he expanded the biblical story and added various animals and decorations, interwoven with leaves and little boys eating grapes.

The second great sculptor of this century is Radovan, who created the portal of the cathedral in Trogir in 1240. The cathedral was built by the people of Trogir during the reign of Count Stipko Šubić-Bribirski, who successfully defeated the Turks and defended the city. The massive entrance door is a superb piece of carving, showing biblical scenes, saints, animals, grotesque shapes—flanked by two heraldic lions supporting giant figures of Adam and Eve. The carvings resemble enlargements of precious miniatures from old missals, especially with regard to the representation of sin and redemption. Sin is symbolized in the portrayal of Adam and Eve in a framework of the allegorical representation of different months. Redemption is represented by Christ, whom the artist depicts from His birth to His death. Radovan proved that he had completely mastered the ornamental and plastic art of portraying the human form, and he united both in the harmony of his composition. His sculptures of Adam and Eve are perhaps the earliest portrayals of the nude figure in medieval art and demonstrate not only the technical skill but also the courage of the sculptor. Radovan's portal radiates a love for nature and life and is so realistic in parts that even today the landscape of Trogir and its surroundings can be easily recognized. Radovan's depiction of the months of the year is permeated with the astrology and the superstition of the Middle Ages, but when it is a question of portraits, those of peasants performing their everyday chores are so full of life that one is immediately able to recognize people at the same tasks today. Radovan established his own art school, and many of his students carved and engraved church towers, pulpits, choirs, and pews in the cathedrals of Split and Trogir in the style of their teacher.

In the thirteenth, fourteenth, and fifteenth centuries, there flourished a unique art in the midst of the almost inaccessible forests of Bosnia and Hercegovina, and partially in Dalmatia. The almost unknown masters of these regions created a type of mysterious tombstone (*stećak*) that is fully as enigmatic as the huge sculptures of Easter Island. Some of these granite tombstones weigh as much as twenty-nine tons, and more than 30,000 have been discovered in the territory included in Radimlja, Donja Zgošća, and Visoko. These heavy stones take the shape of the sarcophagus, slab, and obelisk. On some of them are recorded the names of the artists—for example, Grubač, Petko,

Zelija, Dragoje, and Radić—and on some of the stones are also inscribed the names of the dead. The dead were the Manichean heretics (Bogomils), who were in conflict with Rome because they did not recognize the authority of the Church. A few hundred of these tombstones show signs of original artistic expression. Beside widely-known Croatian ornamental motives and inscriptions of great historical value, the most wonderful of these stones are those which depict scenes from life. In spite of the passing of so many centuries, one may still admire the peaceful pastures, slim towers in the moonlight, boys and girls dancing the *kolo*, the hunting scenes, and the tournaments represented in stone. These *stećci* were made for the dead, but they glorify life, joy, and pleasure, and provide an outlook on life quite different from that of other medieval art. On many of these tombstones there is portrayed the figure of a knight with a large raised hand. What was the meaning of this gesture? One common interpretation is that the knight's gesture symbolized the efforts to stop the crusaders send by the Pope, or the Turkish invader, who was coming closer every day, and who eventually conquered Bosnia in 1463.

A great part of Croatia was for many centuries a battlefield on which the Croatians fought against the Turks. Only the Republic of Dubrovnik, as a result of adroit diplomacy, enjoyed relative security and prosperity. In Dubrovnik, as in the rest of Europe in the fifteenth century, the humanistic schools prospered, and the arts were greatly appreciated; the rest of Dalmatia fell under Venetian domination. The influence of Italian art became more and more evident through Venetian channels, but Croatia nevertheless succeeded in preserving her original form of artistic expression.

Stone from Brač and Korčula was considered the finest type of material by Croatian architects and sculptors, and it was transported to all parts of the country. The archives of Dubrovnik often mention transactions involving this kind of stone, and it was the material used for the monument of Orlando, by Antun Dubrovčanin in 1417. The monument of this young hero, with a typically Gothic smile—the symbol of the judicial power of the markets in medieval cities—was the only public one in Dubrovnik at the time. The goldsmiths of Dubrovnik were widely recognized and much in demand in that period. The golden cross in the cathedral of the city of Korčula by Ivan Progonović fashioned in 1471, is considered a masterpiece.

Juraj Dalmatinac (Giorgio da Sebenico) was an architect and sculptor of the fifteenth century, who, together with his students, left a powerful imprint on the whole Dalmatian domain. His sculptural masterpiece is the apse of the cathedral in Šibenik—a row of seventy-four human heads, molded in stone in life-size dimensions. Each one is strikingly individual in age, profession, and facial expression, so that we may still read in this series of faces the hopes and the achievements, the defeats and the disappointments of the human race. It is evident that the artist sculpted the people of his own time, whom he knew well, and thereby expressed in his work the spirit of the Renaissance, the new style that emphasized individuality.

Many Croatian sculptors won fame abroad during this period. Ivan Duknović (Giovanni Dalmata 1440–1509) sculpted an exquisite statue of St. John in the cathedral of his native Trogir. He later became well-known at the royal and papal courts. In Rome, in cooperation with Mino da Fiesole, Duknović created a sculpture of Pope Paul II. Later he portrayed the Hungarian-Croatian king Matthias Korvin and his wife Beatrice of Aragon in stone. One of the courtisans of King Matthias in Budim was the sculptor Lucijan Vranjanin (Laurana, d. 1479), who was well-known in Italy and France. His brother Franjo (1425–1502), also a sculptor, fashioned a noteworthy monument to Charles IV in the cathedral of Le Mans in France. Nikola Lazanić (Nicolaus Lasaneus Dalmata) of Brač was a sculptor of reputation in Italy. In Dubrovnik, in 1590, he created excellent sculptures of St. Jerome and St. Blasius, captivating in the way that they express life and motion.

The centuries that followed did not result in many significant Croatian artistic achievements. The country was torn by many conflicting powers, and new wars were everyday experiences. Very few members of the nobility could take the time or spend the money to have artists embellish their castles or to have sculptures brought from foreign countries. The Baroque style, however, brought with it new life and interest. This artistic style was for the most part imported from Austria. The first representative of the Baroque in Croatia was the Jesuit Andrija Fabijanić, who carved wooden statues of saints. The Paulists Toma Jurjević and Pavao Belina made use of stone in their sculptures. At the same time, laymen concentrated on sculpturing tombstones and decorative pieces, but most of this work remained more in the realm of the crafts than of art. "Watery," mediocre Baroque sculptures were still prevalent until the beginning of the nineteenth century, but an atmosphere of change was everywhere evident. Zagreb became the political and cultural center of Croatia, and many schools and institutions were founded, such as the Yugoslav Academy of Sciences and Arts, the School of Applied Arts, and the Croatian Art Society, which heralded a new era in sculpture.

Dalmatia was the source of the best Croatian sculptors in the earlier period, and again in the modern age it was to be the Dalmatians who dominated Croatian sculture, even though artists from other parts of the country also were active. The father of modern Croatian sculpture was Ivan Rendić, who, in his father's quarry on the island of Brač, discovered the beauty and the value of stone. After studying in Venice and Florence, he created more than two-hundred monuments in various cities—chiefly decorative allegories, fountains, and portrait-busts. A skillful master, Rendić was at his best as a realist (for example, in the statue of Kačić-Miošić in Zagreb), and weaker when giving free rein to his imagination or when composing sculptures of groups of persons. Rendić's talent, his technical skill, love for his profession, and will-power, blazed the trail for the generation that continued his work. His successors were to Croatian sculpture what the members of the Painters School of Zagreb were to Croatian painting. Decorative figures, monuments, memorial plates, and reliefs in many cities date from this period, and Mirogoj, the beautifully situated cemetery of Zagreb, owes many of its outstanding monuments to that era.

Among Rendić's students, many outstanding names are to be found. Robert Frangeš-Mihanović, who was at his best in the creation of small bronze statues ("Annunciation," "Flight to Egypt") became world-famous as a result of the many medals and plaques which he won. In his youth he worked in Paris under Rodin, and his later works express some of the massive dynamics characteristic of Rodin. The equestrian statue of the first Croatian king, Tomislav, in front of the railway station in Zagreb, is a good example of this. Rudolf Valdec created works noted for their precise attention to anatomy, as in the busts of Rački and Bishop Strossmajer. Ivo Kerdić, a goldsmith and maker of medals, carved the small statue called "The Goldsmith's Daughter" (*Zlatarovo zlato*) with warmth and feeling; it simply and unobtrusively decorates the medieval Stone Gate (Kamenita Vrata) in Zagreb. The talented sculptor Branislav Dešković was able to grasp and express motion in stone and bronze, and he added strength to the type of animal carvings already introduced by Frangeš. Dešković sought to capture the rhythm of motion, and he succeeded to a great extent, especially in his sculpture of a dog, "On the Track."

All of these sculptors possessed excellent technique and fashioned accomplished, well-rounded sculptures; they were accepted and recognized by the public—but none of them produced a work that was monumental or revolutionary. This was left to a group of younger artists from Dalmatia, organized under the name "Medulić." The members of this group sought to break away from foreign influences; they strove to produce powerful sculptures inspired by the Croatian national epics and by history. The slogan of this organization was "In spite of the non-heroic times" (*Nejunačkom vremenu u prkos*). The leader of the Medulić group was Ivan Meštrović, a sculptor of phenomenal talent, who succeeded in attaining world recognition before he reached the age of twenty-five. Employing all the artistic materials and techniques, Meštrović's dynamic personality ignored the traditions of his time and milieu, and created a style and a form of its own. His themes are manifold: religious, allegorical, classical, and national. He is renowned for his sculptures of American Indians,[3] his portraits of famous personages of the past and present, for his self-portraits, and for works depicting members of a family. In many variations he has approached the problem of portraying a mother, including his own mother, his wife with child, the Virgin Mary, and working finally toward an expression of timeless maternity, simple and great in love and sacrifice. His portraits, from his Moses on, have the stamp of the philosophy of an artist who is struggling for the rights, freedom, and dignity of man. Meštrović's sculptures radiate peace and harmony, as well as his own personal love for his fellow man.

Meštrović died in South Bend, Indiana, where he worked and taught at the University of Notre Dame, adding yearly to the number of his outstanding sculptures. Of Meštrović's works, Norman Rice has written: "The major works of Meštrović have a quality of timelessness which does not depend on either a past style or a current fashion for their artistic strength,"[4] and this harmony in his works is perhaps best expressed in his home in Split, the gift of the artist to his native country. This house, built by the sculptor himself, reminds one of ancient times, with its park, containing many sculptures in wood, stone, and bronze, of which each represents a different glimpse of human life. Especially interesting are the powerful figures of Adam and Eve, which are carved in living trees. In this park one may also note and admire many smaller sculptures, some of them first sketches of ideas that Meštrović later developed into larger works.

[3]See especially his sculpture at the Congress Street entrance to Grant Park in Chicago.

[4]Norman Rice, *The Sculpture of Ivan Meštrović* (Syracuse University Press, 1948), Introduction.

The powerful personality of Ivan Meštrović attracted many Croatian sculptors and painters, but it was extremely difficult for the latter to approach in their own creations the excellence of his achievements. Meštrović endeavored to develop in his students perfection of technique and the aspiration to solve in their works their own philosophical problems. Among his students in the United States, Josip Turkalj and Teodor Golubić were represented in a significant art exhibit in New York in 1958. Also prominent in the United States is the sculptor-portraitist Paul Kufrin, who shows classical inspiration in his work.[5] A young sculptor, Augustin Filipović, is active in Canada and has exhibited his works in Toronto, where he has his own art school.

In Croatia many sculptors—a large number of them educated under Meštrović—are active today. Toma Rosandić worked in the same workshops and studios as Meštrović, and his talent was formally recognized in an exhibition in Rome in 1911. The urge to create never leaves Rosandić, and he is always completely absorbed in his work. In his sculptures the classical tradition and a modern feeling of form blend with great integrity. He has attained a high degree of mastery of his art form, and this is united with deep feeling and a humane spirituality. Where Meštrović is more the master of the broad stroke, Rosandić excells at detail. His composition of Christ laid in the tomb, located in the mausoleum of the Petrinović family on the island of Brač, is one of his most successful expressions of the eternal theme of sacrifice and the sorrow of a parting from loved ones. Frane Kršinić also passed through the Meštrović school. His sculpture is the creation of a dreamer who is motivated by an intense inner life. The pure and perfect lines of his sculpture reveal Kršinić's relationship to the classic period. His nudes are slender, warm, and completely feminine.[6] His reliefs express the mood of the life of peasants and fishermen and capture the motion and rhythm of life. His monuments are easily assimilated into their surroundings, as illustrated by his statues of Bulić and Kumičić in Zagreb.

Antun Augustinčić is the most significant sculptor in Yugoslavia today. Born in 1900 in Hrvatsko Zagorje, he was a student of Frangeš and Meštrović. His sculpture "Peace," a woman on horseback holding a globe and an olive branch, stands in front of the United Nations Building in New York. Augustinčić has received many prizes for his

[5]Antun Bonifačić, in his article "Pavao Kufrin," *Osoba i Duh* (1955) 68 (372) n. 3, says about Kufrin: ". . . to him the truth in art is a necessary condition of artistic activity."

[6]Kršinić himself defined his art as follows: "I do not look for naturalism, but for the poetry expressed in the plastic material." *Jugoslavija* X (1955), 12.

work in Yugoslavia and abroad, and even before World War II he was internationally recognized. One of his most successful sculptures before 1945 is his "Miner," executed for the International Organization of Labor in Geneva, Switzerland, a representation of the typical miner of his native country. From his statue of Christ in the church in Tuhelj to the many monuments that grew out of the Partisan War, in which he participated, Augustinčić has successfully depicted subjects from his own time. As a sculptor, he does not look favorably on today's abstract art, and he has posed this artistic question, one most characteristic of him: "How could a man who has learned how to model and to give life to stone be satisfied with simply making egg- or shell-shaped creations? To devote oneself to abstraction, to form as a goal, is equivalent to limiting oneself to only five hundred words when one knows many thousands."[7] Augustinčić's sculpture achieves an artistic balance between form and motion. He is interested in the full scale of the emotions of human life and this is what he tries to express. At the present time, Augustinčić is considered the foremost sculptor in Yugoslavia, and he is not only prolific in his creations, but he is also an excellent educator, engaged in training new generations of sculptors.

Vanja Radauš also made his debut between the world wars. From the very outset he has striven to reveal the psychology of the characters whom he has depicted. His goal is not merely to record a realistic portrait, or to express motion, but also to duplicate in clay, stone, and bronze the dynamics of human feelings. His creations, such as "Prisoner," "Beggar," "François Villon," and "Shaggy-Haired Peter," illustrate this intense striving, which was so evident in his individual art show held in 1958. Powerfully reflected in this exhibition was Radauš' condemnation of war.

Among other contemporary sculptors in Croatia today, one may point to Marin Studin, who at first stressed religious motifs in his primitively naive and powerful sculptures. Now he tends to simplify and stylize the figures of people and animals, and to emphasize the dynamics of masses. His relief "Dark Days," which one can relate to the recent period of war, was purchased by the Tate Gallery in London. Grga Antunac expresses himself in simple and precise busts that remind one of ancient Roman art. Ivan Lozica, killed during the last war, admirably succeeded in representing in his work his love and understanding of the people of his native Dalmatia. The figures of simple, warm, and patient peasants, fishermen, hard-working women, and children were impressed in his memory from earliest childhood,

[7] *Jugoslavija* X (1955), 15.

and they served as a rich source for his art. Primitivism has its place in sculpture as it does in painting, and many talented peasants, who might be totally without a formal education, make use of a few idle days on the farm to carve and model. One of the most productive of these persons is the Dalmatian peasant Petar Smajić. His excellent works are closer to the ancient epochs and the Middle Ages than to any of the work of his contemporaries.

For a short period after World War II, sculpture in Yugoslavia was almost exclusively of a propagandistic nature. Many monuments and reliefs were erected in honor of the Red Army, Stalin, hostages, war heroes, and especially Tito. Some of these works, scattered throughout the country, are not only propagandistic but also of very poor quality. But even during this period the sculptures of a few talented young artists aroused attention. Vojin Bakić, Kosta Angeli-Radovani, Vjekoslav Rukljač, and Andro Krstulović are worthy of mention here. Today quality is emphasized above all in Yugoslavian sculpture, and works of art are widely recognized that would have been condemned only ten years ago as "decadent creations."

Painting

The names of Croatian painters before the fourteenth century remain unknown, mostly because it was not customary for these artists to affix their signatures to their works. Some information about early Croatian paintings is, however, available from various religious and secular documents, as from an eleventh century codex, which mentions portraits of the Croatian national dynasty located in the Church of St. George in Ravna, near Obrovac on the Zrmanja River in Dalmatia. These portraits are said to be of Mislav, Trpimir and Mutimir.[8] If the codex statement is indeed true, it would be evidence of Croatian paintings dating from as early as the ninth century; but so far these pictures have not come to light. The oldest extant Croatian picture dates from the eleventh century and hangs on the wall of the little Church of St. Michael, near Ston. This mural, whose colors are still bright and vivid, portrays St. Michael with an unidentified Croatian king, who holds a model of the church, which he quite probably donated with a view toward the salvation of his soul. The Latin inscriptions and the costume of the king as depicted on the mural reveal Western influence. The portrait is painted in the oldest known

[8]This document was published by Dr. F. C. Arens, *Hrvatska Revija* (1940), 595.

technique, the "al fresco," with primary water colors applied on wet plaster.

Not long ago, pictures of Christ's life and scenes from His passion were discovered in the belfry of St. Mary's Church in Zadar, which could be dated from as far back as the beginning of the twelfth century. The sacristy of the cathedral in Zagreb is another location of very valuable frescoes from the thirteenth century. The most recently discovered frescoes are at Grohote, on the island of Šolta. One can trace back to the thirteenth and fourteenth centuries many such wall paintings in different churches, monasteries, chapels, and castles along the Croatian coast. All of these paintings are an integral part of the architectural structures designed by unknown artists. In some of these murals one can identify various influences: those of Byzantine ikon painters, Italian masters, or—as in Istria—the peasant style characteristic of the Tirol and of the Alpine regions in general. In their own period, these medieval pictures had a very practical purpose: they helped the faithful who could neither read nor write to interpret biblical stories. The few precious handwritten books of the time were far from the reach of the common people. The anonymous painters were probably talented members of the Christian communities, and they therefore depicted religious scenes and the teachings of the Church.

From the fourteenth century one begins to determine the names of individual masters. The archives of the Republic of Dubrovnik are especially helpful in this regard, revealing even the characters of some of the painters, the location of their workshops, the number and ages of their apprentices, as well as the prices and terms of delivery of their paintings. Many murals of this period have been well preserved down to the present day and they offer interesting insights into the creative process behind the often naive presentations. Frequently one can discern an attempt by a painter to breathe life into his stiff figures and to paint the familiar landscapes realistically. The most popular paintings of this time were triptychs and polyptychs, altar pictures that could be folded. The most renowned painters of these were Blaž Jurjev Trogiranin, Živan Ugrinović, Matej Junčić, Lovro Marinov, Mihajlo Hamzić, Vicko Lovrin, and the foremost painter of this period, Nikola Božidarević (Nicolaus Ragusinus). Three of the latter's paintings have been identified: the "Mother of Christ with Her Child, Angels and Saints," in the Dominican church in Dubrovnik; the "Annunciation," in the monastery adjoining the Dominican church in Dubrovnik; and the triptych in the Church of St. Mary, at Danče, near Dubrovnik.

Božidarević's works still retain freshness and beauty and express the dreams of the human soul in the frame of the Gothic style. With his own scale of colors, he solved the problem of the landscape by adding perspective.

Gothic painting also flourished in Istria, as is seen from the discovery in the last century of more than ninety paintings dating from this period. The majority of the paintings are anonymous, but some names are mentioned, such as Klerigin of Kopar, the Master of Trviž, Antun of Kašćerga, and Benko of Šočerga. The greatest of those named, Vincent of Kastav, dated his murals in 1474 at St. Mary's Church in Škriljine, near Beram. His themes were biblical and depicted the lives of Christ, Mary, and St. Martin, together with those favorite Gothic motifs, the dance of the dead and the wheel of fortune. The influence of folklore is evident in Vincent's work, and he successfully portrayed the life of the common people and local atmosphere at the same time as religious themes. One feels that the more frivolous world of the Renaissance is already peeking through Vincent's medieval form.

The mastery of the medieval painter is evident in the many handwritten missals and breviaries that were profusely decorated with initial letters and ornamental and figural miniatures. The Glagolitic missal of Duke Hrvoje Vukčić-Hrvatinić, illustrated in 1405 by the priest Butko of Omiš, is the most famous Croatian example of this art form. Among the miniaturists, the Croatians produced one world-famous artist, Juraj Klović (Julius Clovius, or Giulio Clovio Cravata), who, aside from his work in the field of miniatures, was a well-known medal cutter in Italy, and an illustrator of the works of Dante and Petrarca. His miniatures of Latin religious writings are considered the best of that epoch, and today most of them are in the Sloane Museum in England and in the Pierpont Morgan Library in New York.

Many Croatian painters of the fifteenth and sixteenth centuries worked in foreign countries, and at present their paintings may be seen in almost all of the major galleries in the world. Most of the Croatian artists of this period were called Cravates, Slavs, Slavonians, Dalmatas, and other local variations, because their work represented the characteristics of their native country and of their cultural heritage. Juraj Ćulinović (Giorgio Schiavone) of Skradin encircled his Madonnas with Glagolitic inscriptions and signed his name in Croatian. He presented, in one of his Renaissance portraits, what was considered the ideal woman. Andrija Medulić (Andrea Meldolla Schiavone) painted religious, mythological, and allegorical scenes and devoted more attention to landscapes than his Croatian contemporaries. His composition and the harmony of the colors he used are at the same time a masterly imitation of the formulas initiated by Correggio and a continuation of the style of Croatian artists from the Middle Ages down to his time. Medulić's engravings show him to have been a master of precision, and he knew how to extract the most from his material and from the technique of copper-engraving. In the sixteenth century, a great lithographer, Martin Kolunić Rota of Šibenik, was prominent, and his etchings spread the works of Michelangelo, Titian, and Dürer throughout Europe. He also engraved many portraits and pictures of cities, which bear his characteristic signature, "Martin Rota Sebenzanin fecit."

At the turn of the seventeenth century, the traveling artist Federiko Benković came to prominence. Born in Dalmatia, educated in the Venice and Bologna cultural milieus, he worked and wandered with his students from Zagreb to Brussels, and from Venice to Kraków. His special technique of painting diffused light reached its fullest expression in his painting "The Sacrifice of Abraham." Distinctive traits of his style were simplicity of composition and moderation in color. Through these means he achieved the portrayal of an intensified facial expression which added conviction to the composition as a whole. Tripo Kokolja, a painter who worked in churches in Perast, Bol, on the islands of Brač and Korčula, was one of the best local talents at this time.

During the Baroque period, Zagreb became the Croatian cultural center. Bernardo Bobić of Zagreb was not only a goldsmith but also the most famous painter of this period. The exceptional detail of his pictures adds to the perfection of his design. His paintings for the Church of St. Catherine in Zagreb, and his portrait of King Ladislaus in the Cathedral of Zagreb acquire a sheen as a result of the ornaments, gold, and jewels portrayed in them. The other important Baroque painters were members of various religious orders, as for instance the Paulist Franjo Bobić, a noteworthy interior decorator and painter of the monastery in Lepoglava.

In general, however, the Baroque style produced only mediocre painters who spent their time and effort working on ornaments and precise details. Croatia was a favorite stopping-place for many wandering artists who often painted altar pictures and people's portraits in exchange for board and room.

Amateur artists were very prolific in Croatia in the first half of the nineteenth century, because the arts—especially painting—were considered a necessary part of a good education. One may still see depicted in many residential houses various still lifes, portraits, and landscapes, the result of this period of activity. Often, in the mass of mediocre work produced in this period, one may recognize a modest sparkle of a true talent.

The beginnings of modern Croatian painting can be linked with the tragic career of Vjekoslav Karas, whose life and paintings possessed many of the characteristics of the development of Croatian painting in general. Fate was not kind to most of the talented Croatian artists who were unable to develop freely and fully because of poverty and a lack of understanding on the part of their society. Many young artists became despondent, and Karas was one of these. He committed suicide to put an end to a life of misery, to his unfinished studies in Italy, and to a dreary teaching position in a vocational school. In spite of his short life, Karas left behind a few portraits that are notable for the way in which he succeeded in combining realistic representation and an acute psychoanalysis of the characters he portrayed. During his studies in Italy, this gift was already visible, in his painting "Roman Lady with Lute," for instance, and later he became even more adept in this field with his paintings "Little Boy" and "The Krešić Family."

With the founding of the Croatian Art Society,[9] artistic life in Zagreb began to flourish. The first group of professional painters, the School of Zagreb (Zagrebačka Škola), operated within the framework of this organization. This group did not have a special program, but it was important because of its aspiration to link modern art with the great creations of the past and to emphasize the continuity of Croatian painting. The leader of the School of Zagreb was the Dalmatian Vlaho Bukovac, who, after much traveling and many different occupations, came to Paris to study under Cabanel, in whom he recognized a noteworthy and admirable style.[10] Bukovac stayed in Paris for fifteen years, studying and striving for recognition. He painted portraits of his creditors and tried to arouse interest by depicting Croatian national costumes and historical scenes. He attained success in the French Salon in 1882 with his "La Grande Iza," based on the main character of a popular novel. This portrait was striking, with its rather dark colors, its realistic details, and Bukovac's characteristic embellishments. After this triumph in Paris, Bukovac came to Zagreb as a recognized artist and an accepted judge of Croatian painting. He had a great talent for details and the ability to perceive and portray on canvas the important

[9] *Hrvatsko Društvo Umjetnosti*, founded in 1878 by Iso Kršnjavi (1845–1926).

[10] Alexandre Cabanel (1823–1889), the French classicist and painter of mythological scenes.

characteristics of his objects—and these skills made him a very successful portrait painter. In spite of the great speed with which he worked, and his high fees, he was unable to continually satisfy his vast clientele, even though he created some 400 portraits and more than 200 larger works in a relatively short time. The people wanted their portraits done by Bukovac not only on account of his popularity, but also because he presented his subjects in a very favorable light. Bukovac is the first Croatian modern painter who successfully tackled the problem of large composition. "The Dream of the Poet Gundulić" (Gundulićev San) and "The Croatian National Awakening" (Hrvatski Narodni Preporod) are two of his more widely reproduced pictures. The latter is painted on the gala curtain in the Theater of Zagreb and adds a festive touch to its theatrical surrounding. Gradually Bukovac made more abundant use of color and often painted his portraits with the range of colors found in landscapes. This quality influenced a number of Croatian painters, who earned, with Bukovac, the name of the "Colorful School of Zagreb" (Šarena Zagrebačka Škola) at foreign exhibitions.

In close contact with Bukovac were many of his disciples who had been educated in Zagreb, Vienna, and Munich. Their aspiration was to revive Croatian folklore and history. Their themes were varied and included portraits, countrysides, still lifes, and folklore studies, as well as large compositions of figures associated with motifs taken from the history and life of the Croatians. All strongly emphasized their Croatian national identity. Nikola Mašić expressed the character of his native soil and depicted the Croatian people. Ferdo Kovačević painted the countryside close to the Sava River. Klement Crnčić-Menci portrayed the charm of the Adriatic, and Bela Csikos-Sessia legendary and symbolic themes. Ferdo Quiquerez and Oton Iveković concentrated on important historical episodes and personalities, such as Kings Tomislav, Zvonimir, and Petar Svačić, Matija Gubec, the leader of the Croatian peasants' revolt, and the members of the Zrinski family who fought against the Turks and Hapsburgs. The priest Celestin Medović is one of the most talented and the most individual in this group. With his darker colors and his religious motifs, he strove to emphasize the inner life of his subjects. Some of his portraits successfully express a spirit of ecstasy and a psychological insight that was not to be found in Bukovac's portraits. Two talented women painters of this period were Slava Raškaj and Nasta Rojc. The former, in spite of a short and tragic life, portrayed excellent spring landscapes and peasants' homes around Ozalj; the latter successfully exhibited her portraits in Croatia and in foreign countries. The work of all of these painters has been the subject of discussion at art exhibits in Paris, Saint Petersburg, Rome, and Copenhagen.

At the beginning of the twentieth century two groups of artists in Croatia clashed with the School of Zagreb, which had monopolized Croatian painting for more than two decades. The first of these was the Medulić Club, whose leader was Ivan Meštrović. This group, mostly composed of young sculptors and painters from Dalmatia, was enthusiastically patriotic. Its members were influenced by the Secession, the German Neo-romantic movement. At the end of the nineteenth century, this latter idealistic movement was formulated and expressed itself in the magazine *Jugend* in Munich. Its followers decided to fight academism and the current taste of the bourgeosie. The Secessionists were dynamic and emotional, and they emphasized content above all. The ideas of the Secessionists were accepted by young artists in Berlin and Vienna, and through these channels the Secession penetrated into Croatian painting, sculpture, and literature. Among those influenced by this movement was Mirko Rački, who depicted Kraljević Marko, the powerful hero of folklore, in one of his works. Jozo Kljaković was another whom it influenced, especially in his frescoes that have religious and legendary motives as their subject matter. He also illustrated the epic poem *Death of Smail-Aga Čengić*, by Ivan Mažuranić. The lithographer Tomislav Krizman shows the Secessionist influence in his etchings of famous Croatian men and of the countryside.

The other group, the "Pure Painters," consisted of Josip Račić and Miroslav Kraljević, painters who were far from the academism, embellished realism, the Secession influence, and the romantic nationalism of the Medulić group. Ljubo Babić, himself a painter and the best historian of the development of Croatian painting, characterizes the role of these two painters as follows:

> Račić and Kraljević are in the first place the necessary artistic link with the best tradition of our old masters. They represent the connection with the contemporary West, which was the decisive leader throughout the nineteenth and the beginning of the twentieth centuries. They made the break with mediocre influences and attached themselves to the strongest focus. Although this attachment could have been dangerous, it was precisely the element that led to our artistic progress. Finally, and the most important fact, these artists represented the turning point in and the antidote to all nebulous ideologies, because they took a firm stand on a realistic basis. In our country, and for all future generations, they signified the starting point.[11]

[11]Ljubo Babić, *Umjetnost kod Hrvata u XIX stoljeću* / Art Among Croatians in the Nineteenth Century (Zagreb: Matica Hrvatska, 1934), 142–143.

The first-named artist of this group, Josip Račić, began as a child to draw in charcoal on the walls of his father's inn in Horvati, a suburb of Zagreb. After his schooling in professional workshops and art studios in Zagreb, Vienna, and Paris, he broke with the traditions of his time and developed his own style. His style of painting is influenced by a life filled with poverty and struggle. Račić is a master of the clear, peaceful, and complete brush stroke, a quality which lends life to his portraits and landscapes. His self-portrait, dark and simple, in the style of Manet, whom he respected, represents what many feel is the most expressive picture in Croatian art. His "Pont des Arts" is a perfect impressionistic paysage and an excellent example of his talent. The well-proportioned soft tones and silvery colors of his work make one sensitive to the pure pleasure of this painting for its own sake, completely free from any moral, national, or intellectual preoccupations.

Miroslav Kraljević was to Croatian painting what his friend Matoš was to Croatian literature. Both were educated in Western Europe and were enthusiastic about Paris. Temperamental, sometimes frivolously superficial and ironic, they were always permeated with love for their native country. In his best works, Kraljević was the unmistakable impressionist, for whom the play of light, shadow, and color was more important than any psychology. His "Self-portrait With Pipe" is one of the most powerful Croatian pictures of this epoch, and "The Little Girl With A Doll" is a portrait of rare liveliness.

The sound impressionism of Manet was also the basis for the works of Vladimir Becić, and his painting style is characterized by a deep feeling for proportions and monofigurism, as well as by a peaceful simplicity. He is at his most successful in his landscapes of Bosnia. For a long time, Becić represented the contact between his colleagues Račić and Kraljević, who died young, and the new generation of artists which accepted and continued their ideas.

After World War I, artistic activity in Croatia was full of life and variety. The Academy of Plastic Arts[12] provided a solid education for young artists. Most of them traveled abroad often and studied new ideas, methods, and techniques, either as students or as tourists. They absorbed the experiences of Western Europe that helped them to build up their own artistic creeds. Their bold individual experiences penetrated into the Croatian milieu, causing new activity and fresh approaches. Many of these painters exhibited either as individuals or in groups in Croatia and abroad. The Spring Salon, a professional

[12]The first works of the Academy are now in a private school of painting founded in 1905 by the painters Csikos and Crnčić, and turned into School of Arts and Crafts in 1907.

organization of painters in Zagreb, organized most of the exhibitions between 1915 and 1923. The important members of the Spring Salon were Vilko Gecan, a representative of Croatian Expressionism, and Milivoj Uzelac, a painter and illustrator who at present is working in Paris.

One of the most important years for Croatian painting was 1929, when two groups were founded which exerted strong influence in the period between the world wars. The first of these was the Group of Three (Grupa Trojice), consisting of Becić, Babić, and Miše. This group aspired to emphasize quality without regard for the type of content. Its members played an important role in educating the public through well-organized exhibits, articles, and lectures, and it was extremely helpful toward young talent, giving it the opportunity to exhibit within the frame of the Group of Three. Among these younger talents the following are worthy of mention: Antun Motika, Bruno Bulić, Slavko Šohaj, Ivo Šeremet, Mladen Veža, and Slavko Kopač. The organizer and leader of the group was Ljubo Babić, from Hrvatsko Zagorje, the respected painter, historian, art critic, lecturer, and writer. His work is a synthesis of sound erudition, deep knowledge of techniques, and a refined artistic feeling. A student of Crnčić's school of painting and the academies of Munich and Paris, Babić was attracted to Gustave Courbet's passionate contrasts of light and shadow. Babić's flowers especially show the characteristics of these contrasts. A master of color, he sought to portray the beauty of his native Croatian landscapes. In his studies of national costumes, Babić tried to express the essence of the autochthonous folk art, and in his religious motifs to present the philosophy of modern man. As a set designer, Babić prepared the scenery for many pieces in the repertoire of the Opera house in Zagreb.

Jerolim Miše was the third member of the Group of Three. A student of the Croatian, German, and French academies, he has succeeded in expressing the inner life of his subjects, especially that of young girls. In his large number of oils, watercolors, and drawings, Miše attempted to record life in all its aspects, and this was evident at his Retrospective Exhibition (1914–1954) in Zagreb. The ideas of the Group of Three influenced many other painters, such as Milivoj Uzelac, Juraj Plančić, Marijan Trepše (a painter, decorator, and set designer), and Marin Tartaglia, who developed his style by studying expressionism, cubism, and the works of his favorite painter, Cézanne. In a wide range of colors, Tartaglia strove to depict the rhythm of the inner laws of nature in his portraits and landscapes.

Another group that presented itself to the public at the same time as the Group of Three was called Earth (Zemlja) and was founded by the painter Krsto Hegedušić. It was joined by many painters and architects of distinctly progressive convictions. The exhibitions of the Earth group depicted the social conditions of Croatian peasants; the members support their creations with crushing statistics. For the artists in this group, ideology and content are of prime importance, and their art is a grotesque-naive illustration of the conditions of the poor and of life in the villages. The members differ in their artistic methods of solving these problems. Some of the painters work in the tradition of folklore and continue the technique of the peasant painters, a tendency especially evident in their votive pictures in churches. Others in this school search for their inspiration in the works of the old masters, notably in the paintings of Pieter Brueghel, the Flemish painter of peasant scenes in the sixteenth century. The most modern of this group accept primitivism and expressionism in an effort to return to the type of art expressed in the caves of the Stone Age, or in medieval frescoes.

Krsto Hegedušić has painted the epic struggle of the Croatian peasant with nature and the government, together with his miseries and his joys, in his paintings "Flood," "Funeral," and "The Fair in Podravina." Hegedušić founded the School of Hlebine in the small village of Hlebine in Podravina, whose members are peasants who paint during the rainy season or on their holidays. Their chief theme is the life of the peasant, and their technique is that of oil on glass or wood, or that of fresco murals. The central figure in this regard at present is Ivan Generalić, and among the many members of the school, one should mention the talented peasants Franjo Mraz, Slavko Stolnik, Dragan Gaži, and Franjo Filipović. Since 1949, these peasant painters have exhibited their paintings yearly, under the name of the Painters' School of Hlebine (Hlebinska Slikarska Škola), and many foreign galleries now purchase their creations. Other members of the Earth school of painting include the painter and lithographer Djuro Tiljak, Oton Postružnik, and Vilim Svečnjak. Among the architects in this school are Stjepan Planić and Drago Ibler. Many members of this organization participated in World War II as Partisans, and some, like Mirko Virius, lost their lives. After the war they depicted war themes almost exclusively. The painters of this school tried, in realistic and figural composition, to express what they had seen. Some, in their attempt to present a synthesis of the war years turned to abstraction, as, for instance, Edo Murtić.

The war was also the theme chosen by many other painters, some of whom are now members of the ULUH (*Udruženje Likovnih Umjetnika Hrvatske* / Association of Plastic Artists of Croatia), founded after 1945 and the ULUBH (Association of Plastic Artists of Bosnia and Hercegovina). Marijan Detoni, Zlatko Prica, and Petar Šimaga are only a few of the artists interested in the same subject. Not all the painters of these groups chose the theme of war, however, even if most of them provided some contribution to this topic. The tendency to express their own individuality became especially noticeable among artists after 1948. Frano Šimunović, formerly a painter of war horrors and of Partisan heroism, now paints the mountainous landscapes of Dalmatia. Oton Gliha has been working for years on poetic pictures of the rocky terrain of the island of Krk, with such a success that the Guggenheim Museum in New York bought his "The White Rocks" in 1958. Vjekoslav Parač paints women from Kaštel and their husbands who till the land. Ivan Lovrenčić expresses, in his sensitive etchings, the loneliness of peasant children whose parents work their small pieces of land from dawn to dusk. Mila Kumbatović produces warm coastal landscapes, and Vladimir Kirin and Zdenka Sertić continue to popularize Croatian costumes and folklore.

Some modern Croatian painters lean toward surrealism and try to interpret the subconscious mind, as, for instance, Omer Mujadžić, Leo Junek, and Miljenko Stančić. Here one should also mention Antun Motika, a very successful painter of interiors, whose surrealistic scenes—especially in glass—are widely recognized as positive innovations. Before World War II, Motika held three one-man exhibitions in Zagreb. White was the dominant color he employed, and he was the first Croatian artist interested in collage and other similar experiments. His seemingly effortless art, permeated with a spirit of joy, stresses poetry and imagination. Another painter who held one-man exhibits was Emanuel Vidović, who never belonged to a professional organization, but who was recognized as a painter of interiors in a lyric style, and of warm and glittering Dalmatian landscapes.

Today most of the exhibits in Croatia take place within the framework of the ULUH, and in Bosnia-Hercegovina the ULUBH, and they represent the achievements of both groups and individuals. Another association, EXAT 51, a group of young painters,[13] held its first exhibit in Zagreb in 1952. Its best representatives are Ivan Picelj, Josip Vaništa, and Aleksandar Srnec, men who are trying to achieve pure abstract form in their work. Exhibitions of artistic creations are very popular,

[13]EXAT is the abbreviation for "Experimental Atelier."

not only in Zagreb, Split, Rijeka, and Sarajevo, but in almost every large city in Yugoslavia. The ULUH and ULUBH help young artists, build studios, popularize art, and succeed in selling many pictures at fair prices. Croatian artists participate in many exhibits abroad, at the Biennale, the Triennale, and in Unesco, for example, especially since Tito's break with the Stalinist philosophy. Before that time, Yugoslav artists were limited almost exclusively to exhibitions held in Communist countries.

The contemporary Croatian painter does not confine the subject matter of his work to his native country. Many painters fled Croatia after World War II, and some left it even before that time, but the majority still express in their works their adherence to the Croatian tradition. Some of the artists who left Yugoslavia had to struggle desparately for recognition, while some of them were renowned artists and were easily accepted in their new lands. Maksimilijan Vanka came to the United States as a respected painter of the countryside of his native Hrvatsko Zagorje. The warmth of his work had been compared in Croatia to the poems of Ljubo Wiesner. He came to New York during the depression and attracted the attention of the American public with his portraits of workers and tramps. In the Church of St. Nicholas near Pittsburgh, Vanka depicted in frescoes Croatian life, as well as the Croatian emigration. In his religious motifs, he has even portrayed Croatians in their national costumes. Jozo Kljaković came to South America as a painter with a world-wide reputation; he now lives and works in Rome. Kristian Kreković attained recognition in Peru. His monumental paintings, dynamic and powerful, present in vivid colors the past and present of Peru. His Incas and his Andean landscapes have been enthusiastically accepted in both Americas, and even in Europe, where he accompanied one of his exhibitions. Gustav Likan, Josip Crnobori, Zdravko Dučmelić, Žarko Šimat, Anka Jakšić-Brown, and Ivan Galantić, are but a few of the promising Croatian *émigré* painters from whom much might be expected in the future.

Bibliography

The beautiful illustrated magazine *Jugoslavija*, published quarterly in Belgrade in various languages, frequently contains interesting articles on Croatian artists. The magazine *Čovjek i prostor* / Man and Space (Zagreb, 1954–59) has, from time to time, also reviewed recent achievements in the arts.

Babić, Ljubo. *Obzor Spomen Knjiga* 1860–1935 / Obzor Memorial Book 1860–1935. Zagreb, 1935, 149–153.

———. *Umjetnost Hrvata u XIX stoljeću* / Art Among Croatians in the Nineteenth Century. Zagreb: Matica Hrvatska, 1934.

———. *Boja i sklad* / Color and Harmony. Zagreb, 1943.

———. *Umjetnost kod Hrvata* / Art Among Croatians. Zagreb, 1943.

Bach, Ivan. "Srednjevjekovna umjetnička baština naroda Jugoslavije" / The Medieval Art Heritage of the Peoples of Yugoslavia, *Arhitektura* 5–6 (1960).

Bašićević, Mića. "Ivan Generalić," *Jugoslavija* XI, 59.

Batušić, Slavko. "Slikarstvo Zagrebačkog Središta" / Painting of the Zagreb Center, *Pola vijeka jugoslavenskog slikarstva 1900–1950* / A Half-Century of Yugoslav Painting, 1900–1950. Zagreb, 1953.

———. *Umjetnost u slici: Pregled povijesti umjetnosti* / Art in Pictures: A Survey of the History of the Arts. Zagreb: Matica Hrvatska, 1957. Pp. 726; 712 illus. Second revised ed. 1961. This work contains a survey of the arts throughout the world. It also proves helpful for a study in the history of Croatian art, however, since it devotes a relatively large amount of space to the Croatian scene. This is particularly true of recent developments in Croatian art, which the author considers on pages 513–78.

Bihalji-Merin, Oto. "Jugoslovenska skulptura dvadesetog vijeka" / Yugoslav Sculpture of the Twentieth Century. *Jugoslavija* X, 1955.

Bošković, Djordje. *Arhitektura srednjeg veka* / Architecture of the Middle Ages. Beograd, 1957.

Bulat-Šimić, Anka. *Vjekoslav Karas*. Zagreb, 1958.

Depolo, Josip. "Još jednom o našim primitivcima" / Once More About Our Primitives, *Republika* (September, 1957), 28.

Digović, Pero. "L'Art en Croatie Dalmate," *La Dalmatie* (Lausanne, 1944).

Dobrovnić, Nikola. *Urbanizam kroz vekove* / Urbanism Throughout the Centuries. Beograd, 1950.

———. *Dubrovački dvorci* / The Castles of Dubrovnik. Beograd: Urbanistički Zavod. Book no. 3.

Enciklopedija likovnih umjetnosti / Encyclopedia of the Plastic Arts. Zagreb: Lexicographical Institute of PFRY, 1960. Editor-in-Chief: Dr. France Stelé.

Fisković, Cvito. *Naši graditelji i kipari XV. i XVI. stoljeća u Dubrovniku* / Our Architects and Sculptors in Dubrovnik in the Fifteenth and Sixteenth Centuries. Zagreb: Matica Hrvatska, 1947.

———. "Radovan," *Republika* 3 (1951), 245–259.

Frajtić, August. *Kroatien*. Wien, 1944.

Gomboš, Stjepan. "Moderna arhitektura u Hrvatskoj" / Modern Architecture in Croatia, *Jugoslavija* XI, 102.

Jackson, T. G. *Dalmatia, the Quarnero and Istria*. Oxford, 1887.

Jiroušek, A. "Martin-Rota Kolunić," *Vijenac* 25 (1923), 497.

Jiroušek, Vesna. "Jerolim Miše," *Naprijed* (Zagreb, 1958).

Jiroušek, Željko. *Umjetnost u Hrvatskoj*/Art in Croatia. (Zagreb, 1938).

Karaman, Ljubo. "Kroatische Kunst an der Ostkueste der Adria," *Croatia* VI, 8–20.

———. *Umjetnost u Dalmaciji u XV. i XVI. vieku*/Art in Dalmatia in the Fifteenth and Sixteenth Centuries. Zagreb, 1943.

———. *Pregled umjetnosti u Dalmaciji*/A Survey of Art in Dalmatia. Zagreb, **1952.**

Kastelić, Joža. "Dva lika Berama"/Two Figures of Beram, *Jugoslavija* XI, 117.
Krleža, Miroslav. *Izložba srednjevjekovne umjetnosti naroda Jugoslavije: Uvod*/Exhibition of the Medieval Art of the Peoples of Yugoslavia: Introduction. Zagreb, 1951.
———. "O smrti slikara Račića," *Jugoslavija* XI, 25.
Peić, Matko. *Slava Raškaj*. Beograd, 1957.
Perc, Aleksandar. "Srednjevjekovno zidno slikarstvo Istre"/Medieval Frescoes in Istria, *Osoba i Duh* I (1954), 60–69.
Prijatelj, Kruno. "Umjetnički spomenici naših otoka"/Art Monuments of Our Islands, *Jugoslavija* (1958), 113.
Prpić, Jure. "Maksimilijan Vanka," *Hrvatska Revija* VIII, vol. 3, 275.
Radaić, Ante. "Slikarstvo Kristiana Krekovića"/Painting of Kristian Kreković, *Hrvatska Revija* VIII, vol. 1, 58.
Rakovac, Milan. "Gustav Likan," *Hrvatska Revija* II, vol. 1, 180.
———. "Dvije izložbe Zdravka Dučmelića" / Two Art Exhibits of Zdravko Dučmelić, *Hrvatska Revija* VI, vol. 3, 275.
Rice, Norman (ed.), *The Sculpture of Ivan Meštrović*. Syracuse, New York: Syracuse University Press, 1948.
Salmi, Mario. *Italian Miniatures*. New York, 1954.
Schmeckebier, Laurence. *Ivan Meštrović Sculptor and Patriot*. Syracuse, New York: Syracuse University Press, 1959.
Šegvić, Neven. "Dubrovačka arhitektura," *Jugoslavija* (1951), 38.
Šepić, Dragovan. "Antun Motika," *Kultura* (Zagreb, 1957).
Šrepel, Ivo. *Hrvatska umjetnost: Predgovor*/Croatian Art: Foreword. Zagreb, 1943.
Vučetić, Šime. "Crteži i grafika NOB"/Drawings and Graphics of the National Liberation Movement, *Republika* 11–12 (1955), 1003.

Croatian Artists

Albini, Alfred (1896–). Architect: "Croatian Home in Osijek."

Aleši, Andrej. Sculptor and architect of the fifteenth century. Worked with Juraj Dalmatinac.

Andrijić, Marko. Architect and sculptor of the fifteenth century.

Angeli-Radovani, Kosta (1916–). Sculptor of war heroes: "Nada Dimić," "Ivo Lola Ribar."

Antolić, Vlado (1913–). Architect.

Antun Of Kašćerga. Medieval painter from Istria.

Antunac, Grga (1906–). Sculptor: "Actress"; "My Family."

Augustinčić, Antun (1900–). Sculptor: "Miner"; "Peace"; "Tito."

Babić, Ljubo (1890–). Painter, set designer, art critic: "My Native Land"; "Figs."

Bakić, Vojin (1915–). Sculptor: "Worker"; "Ivan Goran Kovačić."

Bartolić, Ivan (1911–). Architect.

Bauer, Bruno (1884–). Architect.

Becić, Vladimir (1886–1954). Painter of Bosnian landscapes: Oak, "Blažuj" (near Sarajevo).

Belina, Pavao. Baroque sculptor.

Benko Of Sočerga. Fifteenth-century sculptor and architect from Istria.
Benković, Federico (Fridrik) (1677–1753). Painter: "Sacrifice of Abraham."
Bobić, Bernardo (d. 1693–1698?). Baroque painter and goldsmith: 1683, painting for St. Catherine's Church in Zagreb; 1691, painting of St. Ladislaus for the Cathedral of Zagreb. Both paintings are today in the Gallery of the Yugoslav Academy in Zagreb.
Bobić, Franjo (1677–1728). Painter and interior decorator of the monastery in Lepoglava.
Bollé, Hermann (1845–1926). Architect in Zagreb.
Božidarević, Nikola (Nicolaus Ragusinus). Painter in Dubrovnik in the fifteenth century. Triptychs in the Dominican church and in the church at Danče.
Bukovac, Vlaho (1855–1922). Painter: "La Grande Iza"; "Croatian National Awakening"; "Dream of Gundulić"; "Poet."
Bulić, Bruno (1903–). Painter: "Self-Portrait With A Glass"; "Frying Pan With Eggs."
Butko. Priest who, in 1405, illustrated the Glagolitic missal of Duke Hrvoje Vukčić.
Buvina, Andrija. Sculptor: carved the wooden portal of the cathedral in Split in 1214.
Cota, Frane (1899–1951). Sculptor and architect: "Woman Reading."
Crnčić-Menci, Klement (1865–1930). Painter and lithographer: "Kaptol"; "Dolac."
Crnobori, Josip (1907–). Painter: "Maksimir"; "Portrait of a Lady."
Crnota, Stjepan (Stephanus de Cernota pictor, Stefano Cernotto, Stephano discipolo di Titiano). Painter in the sixteenth century. Worked in Venice. Paintings: St. Peter, St. Paul, Jesus Driving Merchants from the Temple.
Csikos-Sessia, Bela (1864–1931). Painter: "Penelope"; "The Christening of the Croatians."
Ćulinović, Juraj (Giorgio Schiavone) (1435–1505). Painter of Renaissance madonnas.
Dalmatinac, Juraj (Juraj Matejević, Georgius Dalmaticus, Giorgio Orsini, Giorgio da Sevenico). Sculptor and architect of the fifteenth century: apse of the cathedral in Šibenik; Minčeta Tower in Dubrovnik, 1463.
Dešković, Branislav (1885–1939). Sculptor: "Donkey"; "On the Track."
Detoni, Marijan (1905–). Painter: "Crossing Neretva River."
Dragoje. Bogomil sculptor.
Dubrovčanin, Antun. Sculptor: The Orlando monument in Dubrovnik, 1417.
Dučmelić, Zdravko. Painter: "Girl Friends"; self-portrait.
Duknović, Ivan (Giovanni Dalmata) (1440–1509). Sculptor: St. John in the Cathedral of Trogir.
Ehrlich, Hugo (1879–1935). Architect: the New School of Technology in Zagreb.
Fabijanić, Andrija. Baroque sculptor: statues of saints in wood.
Felbinger, Bartol (1785–1871). Architect: Narodni Dom in Zagreb.
Filipović, Augustin (1931–). Sculptor: "Stepinac"; "Death of Matija Gubec."
Filipović, Franjo (1930–). Peasant-painter: "Winter"; self-portrait.
Frangeš-Mihanović, Robert (1872–1940). Sculptor: "Flight into Egypt"; "King Tomislav."

Freudenreich, Aleksandar (1892–). Architect: Mother House of Croatian Artisans, Zagreb.
Galantić, Ivan (1921–). Painter in the United States: "Procession."
Gambor, Matija. Sixteenth-century architect; active builder in the city of Karlovac.
Gaži, Dragan (1930–). Peasant-painter: "The Old Woman"; "Wedding."
Gecan, Vilko (1894–). A representative of Croatian expressionism.
Generalić, Ivan (1914–). Peasant-painter: "Funeral of Štef Halaček"; "Rebellion in Djelekovec."
Gliha, Oton (1914–). Painter: "Building the Road"; "White Rocks."
Golubić, Theodore. Sculptor in the United States: "Beatitudes."
Gomboš, Stjepan (1897–). Industrial architect.
Gospodnetić, Pavao. Renaissance architect.
Grubač. Bogomil sculptor.
Haberle, Marijan (1908–). Architect.
Hajrudin. Architect (1566) of the one-span bridge in Mostar.
Hamzić, Mihajlo. Painter in Dubrovnik: triptych in the Dominican church in 1512.
Hegedušić, Krsto (1901–). Painter: "Flood"; "Fair"; "Tempest."
Herman, Oskar (1886–). Painter: "Old Man"; "Landscape With Red Mountain."
Horvat, Lavoslav (1901–). Architect: *Gymnasium* in Bol (Brač island).
Hribar, Stjepan (1890–). Architect: Yugoslav Pavilion in Paris, 1925.
Ibler, Drago (1893–). Architect: new Opera House in Belgrade.
Ivan Splićanin (John of Split; Dalmata). Architect of the fifteenth century.
Iveković, Oton (1869–1939). Painter: "Coronation of King Tomislav."
Jakšic-Brown, Anka. Primitive painter of the Slavonian countryside; now in England.
Juhn, Hinko (1891–1940). Ceramist.
Jurčić, Matej. Painter of the polyptych on the island of Lopud, 1452.
Junek, Leo (1899-). Painter: "Gladiolas"; "Maternité de Port Royal."
Juranović, Vladimir (1900–). Architect.
Jurjev-Trogiranin, Blaž. Painter of the fifteenth century.
Jurjević, Toma. Baroque sculptor of the seventeenth century.
Karas, Vjekoslav (1821–1858). Painter: "Roman Lady with Lute"; "Little Boy"; "The Krešić Family."
Kastelančić, Ante (1911–). Modern painter of landscapes.
Kauzlarić, Mladen (1896–). Architect.
Kerdić, Ivo (1881–1953). Goldsmith and sculptor: "The Goldsmith's Daughter"; "Gjalski."
Kinert, Albert (1919–). Lithographer and painter: "Bloody Wedding"; "Road."
Kirin, Vladimir (1894–1963). Illustrator and lithographer: Old Zagreb; Split.
Klerigin Of Kopar. Istrian medieval painter.
Klajaković, Jozo (1889–). Painter: "Return of the Fishermen"; "Resurrection."
Klović, Juraj (Giulio Clovio, Julius Clovius) (1498–1578). Miniaturist: "Book of Hours," 1546.

Kokolja, Tripo (1661–1713). Painter for churches in Perast, Bol (on the island of Brač), and the city of Korčula.

Kolunić-Rota, Martin. Sixteenth-century lithographer: etchings of Michelangelo, Titian.

Kopač, Slavko (1913–). Painter.

Kovačević, Branko (1911–). Painter of landscapes.

Kovačević, Ferdo (1870–1927). Painter of landscapes around the Sava River.

Kovačić, Viktor (1874–1924). Architect: St. Blasius' Church in Zagreb; Stock Exchange (Burza) in Zagreb.

Kraljević, Miroslav (1885–1913). Painter: "Self-Portrait With Pipe"; "Little Girl With A Doll."

Kreković, Kristian (1901–). Painter of Peruvian landscapes and Indians.

Krizman, Tomislav (1882–1955). Painter, lithographer, and set designer.

Krstulović, Andro (1912–). Sculptor.

Kršinić, Frane (1897–). Sculptor: "Awakening"; "Mother's Play."

Kršnjavi, Iso (1845–1926). Art critic and founder of many art institutions.

Kufrin, Pavao (1887–). Portraitist and sculptor: "Clarence Darrow"; "Cardinal Mundelein"; "David Lloyd George." Works in the United States.

Kulmer, Ferdo, (1925–). Painter: "Rest."

Kumbatović, Mila (1915–). Painter of coastal landscapes: Vrbnik; Mali Lošinj.

Lazanić, Nikola (Nicolaus Lasaneus Dalmata). Sculptor: St. Jerome and St. Blasius, carved in Dubrovnik, 1589.

Likan, Gustav (1910–). Painter: "Mother With Child"; "Young Man With A Dog"; "Ivan Meštrović."

Lovrenčić, Ivan. Painter: theme of the loneliness of children.

Lovrin, Vicko. Fifteenth-century painter: polyptych in the Franciscan church in Cavtat, near Dubrovnik.

Lozica, Ivan (1910–1943). Sculptor: "My Brother"; "Girl With A Winebag."

Marinov, Lovro. Painter of the fifteenth century: madonna in the church at Danče in Dubrovnik.

Master Of Trviž. Istrian painter of the fifteenth century.

Mašić, Nikola (1852–1902). Painter: "Posavina"; "The Man from Lika."

Matej Of Pula. Medieval Istrian architect.

Medović, Mato Celestin (1857–1919). Painter: "Arrival of Croatians on the Adriatic"; "Council of Split."

Medulić, Andrija (Andreas Meldolla Schiavone) (1503–1563). Painter: "Orpheus"; "Narcissus."

Meštrović, Ivan (1883–1962). Sculptor and architect: "Fountain of life"; "Croatian History"; "American Indian."

Miha Of Bar, Fourteenth-century architect: the convent of the Franciscan Friars in Dubrovnik (1317).

Miličević, Paskoje. Sixteenth-century architect.

Miše, Jerolim (1890–). Painter: "Little Girl"; "Under the Olive Trees."

Motika, Antun (1902–). Painter: "Moslem Woman"; "Flowers on the Windowsill."

Mraz, Franjo (1910–). Peasant-painter: "Winter"; "Plowing."

Mujadžić, Omer (1903–). Painter: "Harvest."

Murtić, Edo (1921–). Painter of Partisan themes.

Neidhardt, Djuro (1901–). Architect: urban projects in Zenica and Sarajevo.
Nikola Of Piran. Medieval Istrian architect.
Nikola Of Rovinj. Medieval Istrian architect.
Nogulović, Antun. Renaissance architect.
Ostrogović, Kazimir. Architect: Rudjer Bošković Institute in Zagreb.
Parač, Vjekoslav (1904–). Painter: "Café de la Coupole"; "Milkwomen."
Perić, Pavao (1907–). Medalist and lithographer.
Perišić. Architect: builder of the Bonda theater in Dubrovnik, 1862.
Petko. Bogomil sculptor.
Picelj, Ivan (1924–). Painter: "Compositions."
Plančić, Juraj (1899–1930). Painter: "Return From Fishing"; "Sardines."
Planić, Stjepan (1900–). Architect: Building at 1 Bogovićeva Street, Zagreb.
Postružnik, Oton (1900–). Painter: "Wine and Flowers"; "Fish."
Potočnjak, Vladimir (1904–1952). Architect: remodeled the interior of the Croatian Diet Building in Zagreb.
Požgaj, Zvonimir (1907–). Architect: new beach in Zadar.
Prica, Zlatko (1918–). Painter: "Danće"; "Flower Girl."
Progonović, Ivan. Goldsmith: carved the famous golden cross in Korčula, 1471.
Quiquerez, Ferdo (1845–1893). Painter: Matija Gubec, Zrinski, and Frankopan.
Račić, Josip (1885–1908). Painter: self-portrait; "Lady in Black"; "Pont des Arts."
Rački, Mirko (1879–). Painter: "Kraljević Marko"; "The Mother of the Jugovićs."
Radauš, Vanja (1906–). Sculptor: "Radovan"; "Petrica Kerempuh."
Radić. Bogomil sculptor.
Radovan. Sculptor of the apse of the cathedral in Trogir, 1240.
Rašica, Boško (1912–). Architect and painter: remodeled the Drama Theater in Zagreb.
Raškaj, Slava (1877–1906). Painter: "The Tree in Snow"; "Early Spring."
Rendić, Ivan (1849–1932). Sculptor: Kačić-Miošić; Gundulić.
Rojc, Nasta (1883–). Painter: "Traveler"; self-portrait.
Rosandić, Toma (1878–1958). Sculptor: "Pietà"; "Tired Warrior."
Rukljač, Vjekoslav (1916–). Sculptor.
Schoen, Edo (1877–1949). Architect: Building of the Yugoslav Academy in Zagreb.
Sebastian (Schiavone da Rovigno). Renaissance sculptor.
Sertić, Zdenka. Painter of national costumes and customs: "Moreška"; "Harvest."
Seissel, Josip (1904–). Architect: the Pavilion of Yugoslavia in Paris 1937.
Smajić, Petar (1910–). Peasant-sculptor: "Horsemen"; "Widows."
Stančić, Miljenko (1926–). Painter: "Love Song"; "Dead Child."
Steiner, Milan (1894–1918). Painter: "Spring"; "Rain"; "Street in Petrinja."
Stolnik, Slavko (1929–). Peasant-painter: "Wedding"; "Funeral."
Strižić, Zdenko (1902–). Architect: Hotel Excelsior in Dubrovnik.
Studin, Marin (1895–1960). Sculptor: "Dark Days."

Svečnjak, Vilim (1906–). Painter: "Wounded"; "Harvest."
Šegvić, Neven. Architect.
Šerement, Ivo (1900–). Painter.
Šimaga, Petar (1912–). Painter: "In His Destroyed Home."
Šimat, Žarko. Painter: "Memories"; Papal Poor Man's Dining Room, Rome.
Šimunović, Frano (1907–). Painter: "Olive Trees"; Stone Houses, Dalmatia.
Šohaj, Slavko (1908–). Painter: "In the Studio"; "Boy."
Tartaglia, Marin (1894–). Painter: "My Wife"; "Intérieur."
Tiljak, Djuro (1895–). Painter: "Gračani."
Trepše, Marijan (1897–). Painter and set designer.
Turina, Vladimir (1913–). Architect.
Turkalj, Josip (1924–). Sculptor: "Violin"; "Young Woman." Works in the United States.
Turkalj, Joža (1890–1943). Portraitist.
Tvrdoje, Nikola. Architect of the fifteenth century.
Ugrinović, Živan. Painter of the fifteenth century.
Urlich, Antun (1902–). Architect; urbanist.
Uzelac, Milivoj (1897–). Painter: "Lady in Red"; "Street in Versailles."
Valdec, Rudolf (1872–1929). Sculptor: Rački, Strossmayer.
Vaništa, Josip (1924–). Painter: "Laterna Magica."
Vanka, Maksimilijan (1890–1963). Painter: Murals in the Church of St. Nicolas in Millvale, Pittsburgh.
Veža, Mladen (1916–). Painter.
Vidović, Emanuel (1872–1953). Painter: "Interior of a Church"; "Old Doll."
Vincent of Kastav. Painted murals in a church close to Beram, 1474.
Virius, Mirko (1889–1943). Peasant-painter: "Bride and Groom"; "Procession."
Vitić, Ivo. Architect: the City of Pioneers, Zagreb.
Vranjanin, Franjo (Francesco Laurana) (1425–1502), Sculptor: saints and madonnas.
Vranjanin, Lucijan (Luciano da Laurana) (d. 1479), Architect: Palazzo Ducale, Urbino.
Vrbanić, Vidov (1910–). Architect.
Zelija. Bogomil sculptor.

APPENDIXES

APPENDIX A

Biographies of the Authors

Ivan Meštrović

Ivan Meštrović was born on August 15, 1883, at Vrpolje, in the district of Slavonski Brod, Croatia. When still a child, he returned with his parents to their native village of Otavice, near Drniš, in Dalmatian Zagora. His mother was a deeply religious woman, and his father, the only literate man in his village, spent long hours reading the Bible and epic folk poetry to young Ivan.

In 1900 Meštrović left home to spend a year as an apprentice to a stone cutter, Pavle Bilinić, in Split. He then went on to Vienna, where, after a series of struggles and disappointments, he was admitted to the Vienna Academy of Art. Meštrović proved to be a brilliant student who quickly achieved independence from the established standards of art. He soon became a member of and a regular exhibitor for the "Secession," a group of young non-conforming artists.

Five years later, Meštrović moved to Paris, where he attracted the attention of August Rodin, the great French sculptor. The two artists remained close friends until Rodin's death. Rodin is reported to have called Meštrović "the greatest phenomenon among sculptors." Meštrović's main work in Paris was the Kosovo Plain monument, a pantheon dedicated to the fallen heroes of the battle that took place in 1389; this sculpture was executed in pieces and was never assembled as a whole. Meštrović first received universal acclaim in 1911 for his exhibits of the figures from the projected Kosovo pantheon in the Serbian pavilion at the International Exhibition held in Rome.

Forced to flee from Croatia at the outbreak of World War I in 1914, he lived in Rome for a year and worked on sculptures with religious themes, while studying art in the Vatican. The following year numerous exhibitions of his creative work were held in Great Britain. Meštrović never wished to be a politician, but during World War I he helped to organize the Yugoslav Committee in London. This group fought for the liberation of the Croatian people from the Austro-Hungarian Empire and for union with the Serbs, Montenegrins, Slovenes, and Macedonians in a confederative state. After World War I, the new state, the Kingdom of the Serbs, Croatians, and Slovenes (named Yugoslavia by the king-dictator Alexander Karadjordjević in 1929) was created. Meštrović lived in his native country, but took no part in political life; he dedicated himself entirely to his art. For some twenty-five years he taught his technique to the students of sculpture who came from all over the world to his studio and to the Academy of Art in Zagreb.

In the period between the world wars, Meštrović was represented in many international exhibitions in the capitals of most of the European nations. His sculptures, of which we can mention only a few here—are to be found today in museums throughout the world. Among his most famous works are three chapels for which he designed both the architectural plan and the sculptural decorations. These are the memorial chapel of the Račić family at Cavtat, near Dubrovnik, Meštrović's personal chapel in Split, and his family chapel in Otavice. Among his best known sculptures are the bronze statue of Bishop Gregory of Nin, a chancellor of the first Croatian king, Tomislav (910–928); the statue of the artist's mother "My Mother at Prayer"; the symbolic statue, "Croatian History"; and two sculptures called "Pietà," one in the National Gallery in London, and the other in Sacred Heart Church of Notre Dame University in South Bend, Indiana. In 1928 Meštrović sculpted two equestrian Indians in bronze for Grant Park, in the city of Chicago. In this striking work, the Indians face each other, the one with a spear and the other with a bow. Among the numerous portraits by Meštrović are those of Herbert Hoover, Pope Pius XII, and Aloysius Cardinal Stepinac, the Croatian hero of the resistance to both Nazism and Communism, and a close friend of the artist. One of the greatest achievements of Meštrović's art is a series of thirty reliefs carved in walnut, which depict the life of Christ. These are kept in his chapel in Split, which is now a museum. The artist has given this chapel and the reliefs contained in it to the Croatian people as a gift.

During World War II, Meštrović spent a short time in Rome before moving to Switzerland with his family. When the Communists took control of Yugoslavia in 1945, the artist chose to go into exile. From the year 1946, Meštrović lived in the United States, where he taught sculpture at Syracuse University until 1955, and subsequently at the University of Notre Dame until his death in 1962. In 1947 he was accorded the rare privilege of a one-man show in the Metropolitan Museum of Art in New York City.

Meštrović's prodigious creativity was not diminished during his stay in the United States, and many American cities now possess examples of his art. Representative of these are in "Man and Freedom," a twenty-four-foot bronze figure high above the entrance of the New Mayo Clinic in Rochester, Minnesota; two compositions for the National Shrine of the Immaculate Conception in Washington, D.C.; and two monuments in Florida. Meštrović frequently sent sculptures to his native Croatia, in the firm belief that the silent but persistent language of carved stone would help inspire in his countrymen the ideals of the freedom and dignity of man, which he held so dear.

Awards of merit were presented to Meštrović by the American Academy of Arts and Letters, the American Institute of Architects, and Assumption University, in Windsor, Ontario. He received honorary degrees from many universities, among them Columbia University, the University of Notre Dame, and Marquette University. He was a member of many Academies of Arts and Sciences, including those of the cities of Zagreb, Belgrade, Prague, Vienna, Munich, Brussels, Paris, and Edinburgh, and those of Canada and the United States.

Meštrović was not only an exceptional sculptor and one of the great Croatian thinkers, he was also a writer who possessed a beautiful style. His study *Michelangelo* appeared in Croatian in *Nova Evropa* (November 1926), and his *Dialogues with Michelangelo* were published in German in

Kunst im Volk (Vols. viii, ix, Vienna, 1957–58), and in Croatian in *Hrvatska Revija* (Buenos Aires, Argentina: I, 3, 1951, pp. 205–9; III, 1, 1953, pp. 43–49; X, 4, 1960, pp. 503–7). His *Christmas Dialogue,* written in Croatian, has been published in German under the title, *Dennoch will ich hoffen* (Zürich, 1945), and in Croatian in the *Hrvatska Revija.* His memoirs were published shortly before his death, under the title *Uspomene na političke ljude i dogodjaje* / Remembrances of Political Men and Events (Buenos Aires: Knjižnica *Hrvatske Revije, 1961*). Meštrović died on January 16, 1962, at the age of 78, at work to the very last in his studio at the University of Notre Dame. His remains were flown to Croatia and buried in his family chapel in the village of Otavice.

For a more detailed biographical sketch of the life of this great sculptor, the reader is referred to two excellent monographs published by Syracuse University Press, which provide an extensive biography of Meštrović, and illustrations of most of his works: Harry Hilberry, *Ivan Meštrović* (1948), and Laurence Schmeckebier, *Ivan Meštrović, Sculptor and Patriot* (1959). A third illustrated volume that is of interest was written in English and published in Croatia: Željko Grum, *Ivan Meštrović* (Zagreb: Matica Hrvatska, 1962. Photographs by Tošo Dabac).

Francis H. Eterovich

Francis H. Eterovich was born in Pučišća, on the Island of Brač. He is a member of the Dominican order and studied theology and philosophy at the Dominican Institute in Louvain, Belgium, from 1937 until 1939. In 1944 he obtained his M.A. in Classical Languages from the University of Zagreb. He holds a licentiate in theology from the State University of Olomouc, Czechoslovakia (1948), and earned his Ph.D. in theology at the Dominican University in Etiolles, France (1949). Professor Eterovich has taught at several universities since 1945, and came to the United States in 1952. Since that time he has taught theology, philosophy, and sociology at various universities in the American Middle West. At present he teaches philosophy at De Paul University in Chicago.

Dr. Eterovich was the originator and editor of the quarterly journal for contemporary problems *Osoba i Duh* / Person and Spirit, founded in Madrid, Spain, in 1949. He continued to publish the journal in America at Albuquerque, New Mexico, until 1955. At that time he began work on *Croatia: Land, People, Culture*, and soon afterward he was joined in this project by Professor Christopher Spalatin of Marquette University.

Besides numerous editorials, studies on ethical problems, and book reviews which he has written for *Osoba i Duh*, Father Eterovich has contributed to many magazines and journals, especially to those published by Croatian émigrés in various countries after World War II. Several of his studies have appeared in *Hrvatska Revija* / The Croatian Review, which is published in Buenos Aires, Argentina. Of particular interest is his article "Subjective Demands of Human Action," published in Spanish in *Revista de Filosofia* (Vol. XI, No. 41, 1952), a journal of the Philosophical Institute of the University of Madrid.

Christopher Spalatin

Christopher Spalatin was born in Ston, Croatia, on October 15, 1909. He attended the *Gymnasium* in Šibenik, graduating in 1927. He studied French and Latin Language and Literature, as well as Croatian and Serbian Literature, at the University of Zagreb, obtaining his M.A. degree in 1931. He obtained his doctorate at the University of Zagreb in 1934. His doctoral thesis, on Saint Evremond, was written in French and published in Zagreb in 1934. He continued his graduate studies at various universities in Paris, Rome, and Chicago. Dr. Spalatin has taught French Language and Literature at the University of Zagreb, Croatian Language at the University of Rome, Croatian and Serbian Literature at the Naples Oriental Institute, and French, German, and Latin at Wesleyan College in Mount Pleasant, Iowa. At present he teaches French at Marquette University, Milwaukee, Wisconsin.

Among his published works are the Croatian translations of two books from the French, *Communism and Christians* / Komunizam i Kršćani (1937) and *Sexual Problems* / Seksualni Problemi (1939), both printed in Zagreb. Dr. Spalatin's articles have been published in French, Italian, English, and Croatian, and he has contributed a number of studies to the *Hrvatska Revija*. Especially noteworthy is his work in the field of informing and educating the Croatian people about trends, ideas, theories, and systems in other European countries. Professor Spalatin is currently writing a book on the subject of rendering Croatian foreign terms into English, French, Italian and German, and frequently contributes articles in English about the Croatian language to various journals and periodicals.

Vladimir Markotić

Vladimir Markotić is an anthropologist who specializes in the study of Old World archaeology. He was born in Banjaluka, Bosnia, and studied at various universities in Europe and the United States. In 1955 he received his M.A. degree from Indiana University; the title of his thesis was "Glotochronology as the Method and the Slavic Languages." He was Thaw Fellow at Harvard University during the academic year 1961–62, and received his Ph.D. from Harvard in 1963. His doctoral thesis, "Starčevo and Vinča" was concerned with two of the Neolithic cultures of Southeast Europe.

Professor Markotić has conducted field work on the prehistoric sites of New England and Kansas, as well as at Thomas Jefferson's Monticello in Virginia. He is currently studying an Archaic culture in a cave in Missouri. He is the editor of "European Part of the Soviet Union" for the Council of Old World Archaeology (COWA). At present Dr. Markotić is Assistant Professor of Anthropology at Illinois State Normal University, Normal, Illinois, where he founded the Central Illinois Archaeological Society, whose purpose is the exploration and reconstruction of the prehistory of this region.

Stanko Guldescu

Stanko Guldescu was born in Trieste (then Austro-Hungary), in 1908. He studied the history of Central and Eastern Europe at the universities of

Zagreb, Madrid, and Chicago. At the University of Chicago, he obtained both his M.A. and his Ph.D. degrees in history. Dr. Guldescu has taught at St. John's University, Shanghai (1945–6), New Mexico State Teachers College (1947–8), Indiana University, Extension Division (1954), Washington and Lee University (1956), South Dakota State Teachers College (1957), and is at present on the faculty of Central Methodist College, Fayette, Missouri.

Among Professor Guldescu's numerous studies are: "The Kossuth Tradition and Hungary's Delusion of Grandeur," "The Background of the Croatian Nationalist Movement," and "Austria's Economic Future," all in the *South Atlantic Quarterly;* "Spain and Totalitarianism," *Thought* (Fordham Univ.); "The Habsburg Hysteria," *Social Science Quarterly*; "The Slovenes," *Social Studies*; "Austrian Attitudes Towards the Anschluss From October 1918 to September 1919," *Journal of Modern History*; "The Rumanians of Istria," *New Pioneer*; "Submarine Warfare in the Adriatic: the Otranto Barrage, 1915–1918," *U.S. Naval Institute Proceedings*; and "Titos Kärntner Aspirationen," *Austria.* Other important articles and reviews by Dr. Guldescu have appeared in the *Hungarian Quarterly*, the *Danubian Review*, and the *China Press* (Shanghai).

In recent years, Professor Guldescu has devoted his time almost exclusively to the study of Croatian history. His book, *History of Medieval Croatia* (The Hague: Mouton and Company), was published in 1964, and Dr. Guldescu is currently working on a manuscript on the subject of Croatia, Slavonia, and Dalmatia, 1526–1814.

Ivan Babić

Ivan Babić, a former lieutenant-colonel on the General Staff of the Yugoslav and Croatian Armies, was born on December 19, 1904. After graduating from the *Gymnasium*, he went on to the Military Academy in Belgrade, where he attained the rank of lieutenant in the artillery in 1924.

In 1928, he entered the Officers Training School in Belgrade, and in 1929, following a special examination, he was sent to the Ecole Supérieure de Guerre in Paris, from which he graduated in 1931.

Lieutenant-Colonel Babić passed the final examinations for Officers of the General Staff of the Yugoslav Army in 1935, and was assigned to the Operative and Organizing Department of the General Staff in Belgrade. At the same time, he served as Instructor of Tactics in the Military Academy until 1938. From 1938 until 1941, he served as Divisional Chief of Staff—at first on the Albanian frontier (during Mussolini's invasion of Albania), and afterwards on the Italian and German frontier.

After the collapse of Yugoslavia, Lieutenant Colonel Babić entered the newly-formed Croatian Regular Army (*Domobranstvo*), and served in the War Ministry. Because of divergencies with the leading circles in matters of general and military policy, he was removed from his post and sent to the Croatian Legion on the Russian front as a military observer, where he was appointed Commanding Officer of the Croatian Legion. Babić led the Legion in its operations against the Bolsheviks in the Donetz basin until the end of May 1942. Recalled to Croatia, he was assigned to organize a Croatian Military School.

In January, 1944, following an invitation by the British, Lieutenant-Colonel Babić was elected a special emissary of the Croatian Army. He then flew on a secret mission to the Allies in Italy, the purpose of which was to arrange for the co-operation of the Croatian armed forces with the Allied forces. This mission failed when, at the conference in Tehran, the Allies put all their trust and hopes upon the Communist Tito. Babić is presently occupied with writing articles and studies on Croatian military history for various European military journals.

Drago Matković

Drago Matković was born in Vodice, Croatia, in 1909. He studied political economy, business, law, international law, history, and geography at universities in Zagreb, Cologne, Berlin, and Leipzig. Dr. Matković specialized in the field of trade and marketing, and for a time was a professor of economics at the Academy of Trade in Split, Croatia. He served with the Croatian diplomatic corps in Berlin, Budapest, and Vienna, and was a department head for the economic and consular department of the Croatian Foreign Office during World War II.

Dr. Matković lectures frequently at many economic institutes; he is also a producer of radio programs broadcast to Yugoslavia within the Voice of the Federal Republic of Germany, the West German government-sponsored radio station. He often writes articles for journals and yearbooks in Germany, Switzerland, and the Netherlands. Dr. Matković has made significant contributions to the study of economic problems not only in Southeastern Europe, but also in the Asiatic and African countries, in which he has taken a great interest in recent years. He has also published many articles in various German, Swiss, Dutch, and Croatian scholarly journals and yearbooks.

Tomo Marković

Born in Livno, Bosnia, on February 26, 1894, Tomo Marković has been a member of the Jesuit order since 1910. He attended the *Gymnasium* in Travnik (Bosnia), studied scholastic philosophy in Innsbruck, Austria (1915–1918), theology in Enghien, Belgium (1922–1926), and ethnography and ethnology at the University of Zagreb, Croatia (1928–1932). At the University of Zagreb, Father Marković earned his M.A. in anthropology. He taught in the *Gymnasium* in Travnik from 1932 to 1942. He became a *custos* in the State Ethnographic Museum in Sarajevo, in 1942, and occupied that position until the end of the war in 1945. Father Marković has been studying and collecting examples of the folklore of Bosnia and Hercegovina ever since he completed his studies at the University of Zagreb.

In 1940, the Croatian National Ethnographic Museum in Zagreb began to publish Father Marković's contributions to the study of folk customs. His study, *Božićni običaji Hrvata u Bosni i Hercegovini* / Christmas Customs Among Croatians in Bosnia and Hercegovina, is the second volume of the Museum's series *Ethnografska istraživanja i gradja* / Ethnographic Research and Materials (pp. 5–86). The remaining volumes in this series remained in manuscript because of the political changes in Yugoslavia at the end of World War II. Since 1945 Father Marković has been active in popularizing Croatian folklore among émigré Croatians. He now lives in Venezuela, where he is engaged in research on the Guaraos and Grajiros Indian cultures.

Fedor Kabalin

Fedor Kabalin is presently on the music faculty of the State College, Indiana, Pennsylvania. He was formerly chairman of the music theory department of the Music and Arts Institute in San Francisco, and was on the staff of the San Francisco and Chicago Lyric Opera Companies.

His academic training includes M.M. degrees from the Vienna Music Academy and from Northwestern University, with advanced work at the Eastman School of Music in Rochester, New York, and studies at the International Summer Academy at the *Mozarteum* in Salzburg, Austria. Mr. Kabalin wrote and conducted the original background music for the Chile Films feature-length production *El Paso Maldito.* His "Divertimento" for wind septet was commissioned and first performed on the occasion of the hundredth anniversary celebration of the Chilean National Conservatory of Music, Santiago, and has had several performances in this country. His "Reflections For Orchestra" won an award and were performed by the Louisville Orchestra, and by the Chicago Little Symphony on tour. Mr. Kabalin's works have been performed at the University of Kansas and at the San Jose (California) State College symposia, and at the University Composers Exchange Festival.

As a conductor, he has been guest conductor of the Chilean Symphony Orchestra in Santiago, and the conductor of orchestral concerts at the Music and Arts Institute in San Francisco. Recently he presented the first North American performance in English of Lortzing's *Tsar and Carpenter* with the College Opera Workshop at Indiana, Pennsylvania.

Mr. Kabalin has also been a music critic in Zagreb, and on the staff of the Chilean weekly magazine *Pro Arte.* He has contributed articles to the *Research Bulletin,* State College, Indiana, Pennsylvania, to *Musical America,* and to a number of other journals, magazines, and newspapers in North and South America.

Ruža Bajurin

Ruža Bajurin (nee Starchl) was born on October 2, 1918, in Zenica, Bosnia. She attended the *Gymnasium* and the State University in Zagreb. At the State University, from which she graduated in 1940, she specialized in Croatian literature and in the French and Russian languages. She served for five years as a teacher in the Peoples' Republic of Croatia. Since 1952 she has been teaching in San Francisco, California.

Professor Bajurin's numerous studies, essays, and articles have appeared in *Annales de l'Institut Français* (Zagreb), *Hrvatska Revija,* and *Hrvatski Glas* / Croatian Voice (Winnipeg, Canada), as well as in other periodicals and journals.

APPENDIX B

General Reference Works on Croatian Life and Culture

The following list of reference works has been compiled to aid those engaged in research on the various aspects of Croatian life and culture and all others who are interested in reading further on these topics.

I. BIBLIOGRAPHIES

Bibliografija knjiga i periodičnih izdanja štampanih u Hercegovini 1873–1941 / Bibliography of Books and Periodical Publications Printed in Hercegovina from 1873 to 1941. Compiled by Lina Štitić and Hamid Dizdar. Mostar, 1958.

Bibliografija rasprava, članaka i književnih radova / Bibliography of Treatises, Articles, and Literary Works. Zagreb, 1956. Editor-in-chief: Dr. Mate Ujević. Published by the Lexicographical Institute of FPRY, this work contains a list of scientific and literary articles dating from the beginnings of scientific literature in the nineteenth century. It is a monumental achievement, one which provides a systematic bibliography for various scientific branches, and it is of great assistance to the researcher. The six volumes which have been published to date have fulfilled all expectations.

Hrvatska bibliografija / Croatian Bibliography. Zagreb, 1948– .

Group A: *Bibliografija knjiga tiskanih u Narodnoj Republici Hrvatskoj* (1945–) / Bibliography of Books Printed in the People's Republic of Croatia (1945–).

Group B: *Bibliografija rasprava, članaka i književnih radova u časopisima Narodne Republike Hrvatske* (1945–) / Bibliography of Treatises, Articles, and Literary Works Published in the Periodicals of the P.R. of Croatia (1945–).

Group C: *Special Bibliographies.* To date the bibliographies of the city of Zadar, Dubrovnik, and Rijeka, as well as those of various cultural programs, such as Croatian drama and health sciences, have been published.

Jugoslavenska bibliografija / Yugoslav Bibliography:

Popis svih knjiga i časopisa koji izlaze u Jugoslaviji / List of All Books and Journals Published in Yugoslavia. Belgrade: Monthly Review, 1934–35. Superseded by *Prilog jugoslavenskoj bibliografiji* / Supplement to Yugoslav Bibliography. Belgrade, 1935–39.

Pejanović, Djordje. *Bosansko-hercegovačka bibliografija. Knjige i brošure 1945–1951* / Bibliography of Bosnia and Hercegovina. Books and Pamphlets 1945–1951. Sarajevo, 1953. Lists 1747 items.

Štampa Bosne i Hercegovine 1850–1941 / Books and Periodicals in Bosnia and Hercegovina 1850–1941. Sarajevo, 1949. Pp. xviii + 136. An historical survey with a bibliography listing 405 items. Index. Printed in Cyrillic letters.

Yugoslav Bibliographical Institute. The following three reviews of Yugoslav bibliography are published by the Institute in Belgrade:

Članci i prilozi u časopisima, novinama i zbirnim delima / Articles and Contributions Published in Journals, Newspapers, and Symposia. Belgrade: 1950, Monthly Review, 1950. This bibliography is published in three sections—Section A: Social Sciences; Section B: Natural and Applied Sciences; Section C: Philology, Arts, Sports, and Literature.

Knjige, brošure i muzikalije / Books, Pamphlets, and Musical Works. Belgrade: Published monthly between 1950 and 1954, and bi-monthly since 1954. Each annual volume contains an index of authors and one of subjects.

Spisak listova i časopisa štampanih na teritoriji FNRJ / List of Periodicals and Journals Published in the Territory of the FPRY. Belgrade: Quarterly Review. This publication ends each year with a special issue containing an alphabetical list of all periodicals classified according to subject.

A summary of the activities of the Yugoslav Bibliographical Institute has been written by Mate Baće, Librarian of the Institute, published in the *UNESCO Bulletin for Libraries*, Vol. XIII, No. 10 (Paris, October, 1959), Item 425, pp. 228–30. See also the Institute's volume: *Bibliografija jugoslovenskih bibliografija* 1945–1955 / Bibliography of Yugoslav Bibliographies 1945–1955. Belgrade, 1958. Pp. ix + 270. Lists 1141 bibliographies. Indexes.

II. DICTIONARIES

Drvodelić, Milan (ed.). *Hrvatskosrpsko-engleski rječnik* / Croatoserbian-English Dictionary. Zagreb, 1961. Pp. 912.

Filipović, Rudolf *et al.* (eds.). *Englesko-Hrvatski Rječnik* / English-Croatian Dictionary. Zagreb, 1955. Pp. xviii + 1430.

Imenik Mesta / Register of Places. *Pregled svih mesta, opština, i srezova u Jugoslaviji sa poštama i teritorijalno nadležnim sudovima i javnim tužioštvima* / Survey of All Places, Communes, and Districts in Yugoslavia with Post Offices and Corresponding Territorial Courts and State Prosecutor's Offices. Beograd, 1960. Second revised and enlarged edition.

Iveković, Franjo, and Broz, Ivan (eds.). *Rječnik hrvatskoga jezika* / Dictionary of the Croatian Language. Zagreb, 1901. 2 vols. Pp. viii + 952; 884.

Ko je ko u Jugoslaviji / Who's Who in Yugoslavia. *Biografski podaci o jugoslovenskim savremenicima* / Biographical Data about the Contemporary Yugoslavs. Beograd, 1957. Pp. 810.

Laszowski, Emilij (ed.). *Znameniti i zaslužni Hrvati te pomena vrijedna lica u hrvatskoj povijesti od 925–1925* / Famous and Credit-Deserving Croatians, as well as Persons Worthy of Mention in Croatian History from 925 to 1925. Zagreb, 1925. Published on the occasion of the millennial anniversary of the Croatian Kingdom. Contains a survey of the history of Croatia, Bosnia, and Istria; a history of Croatian language and literature; and a list of Croatian rulers, dukes, bans, and bishops.

Mažuranić, Vladimir. *Prinosi za hrvatski pravno-povjestni rječnik* / Contributions to an Historical Dictionary of Croatian Law. Zagreb: Yugoslav Academy, 1908–22. Pp. 1756.

———. *Dodatci uz Prinose za hrvatski pravno-povjestni rječnik* / Supplement to the "Contributions. . . ." Zagreb, 1923. Pp. xv + 74.

Rječnik hrvatskoga ili srpskoga jezika / Dictionary of the Croatian or Serbian Language. Zagreb: Yugoslav Academy, 1880– . This is a monumental comparative and etymological dictionary of the Croatian language. The first volumes, however, are now partially outdated. The last volume (XVI), published in 1956–8, reached the entry "Sunce."

Šamšalović, Gustav (ed.). *Leksikon Minerva, praktični priručnik za modernog čovjeka* / Minerva Lexicon, a Practical Handbook for Modern Man. Zagreb, 1936. Pp. 792.

III. ENCYCLOPEDIAS

Krleža, Miroslav, *et al.* (eds.). *Enciklopedija Jugoslavije* / Encyclopedia of Yugoslavia. Zagreb, 1955. 4 vols. Miroslav Krleža, Editor-in-Chief, and Dr. Zvonko Tkalec and Dr. Mate Ujević, Associate Editors. Over 1,000 contributors; magnificently planned and well-executed work. Main defect is frequent omission of names and works proscribed by the present political regime in Yugoslavia.

Lexicographical Institute of Zagreb. The following encyclopedias are excellent sources of specific information in their respective fields. The contributors to these reference works are for the most part professors at the University of Zagreb and members of the Yugoslav Academy of Sciences and Arts.

Enciklopedija Leksikografskog Zavoda—Opća Enciklopedija / Encyclopedia of the Lexicographical Institute—General Encyclopedia. Zagreb, 1956– .

Enciklopedija likovnih umjetnosti / Encyclopedia of the Plastic Arts. Zagreb, 1960– . Editor-in-Chief: Dr. France Stelé.

Medicinska enciklopedija / Encyclopedia of Medicine. Zagreb, 1957– . Editor-in-Chief: Dr. Ante Šercer.

Muzička enciklopedija / The Music Encyclopedia. Zagreb, 1958– . Editor-in-Chief: Josip Andreis.

Pomorska enciklopedija / The Maritime Encyclopedia. Zagreb, 1955– . Editor-in-Chief: Dr. Mate Ujević.

Stanojević, Stanoje (ed.). *Narodna enciklopedija srpsko-hrvatsko-slovenačka* / Serbian-Croatian-Slovenian People's Encyclopedia. 4 vols. Zagreb, 1925–1929.

Ujević, Mate (ed.). *Hrvatska Enciklopedija* / Croatian Encyclopedia. Zagreb: Croatian Bibliographical Institute, 1941–5. 5 vols. This is an unfinished general encyclopedia. It is skillfully illustrated and contains the work of over 500 contributors in various branches of human knowledge. I: A–Automobil (1941, pp. xv + 808); II: Autonomaši–Boito (1941, pp. viii + 728); III; Boja–Cleveland (1942, pp. viii + 800); IV: Cliachit–Diktis (1942, pp. viii + 776); V: Dilatacija–Elektrika (1945, pp. viii + 738).

IV. SURVEYS, MEMORIAL BOOKS, AND SYMPOSIA

Horvat, Josip: *Kultura Hrvata kroz 1000 godina* / A Thousand Years of Croatian Culture. Vol. 1. Zagreb, 1939. Pp. xv + 462. Numerous illustrations.

———. *Kultura Hrvata kroz 1000 godina*; *Gospodarski i društvovni razvitak u 18. i 19. stoljeću* / Economic and Social Development in the Eighteenth and Nineteenth Centuries. Vol. 2. Zagreb, 1942. Numerous illustrations.

Naša Domovina / Our Country.

Vol. I: *Hrvatska Zemlja, Hrvatski Narod, Hrvatska Poviest, Hrvatska Znanost* / Croatian Land, People, History, Science. Zagreb, 1943. Pp. 624.

Vol. II: *Hrvatska književnost, Hrvatska umjetnost, Nastava i školstvo, Suvremeni kulturni život Hrvata; Politička povijest Hrvata* / Croatian Literature, Arts, School System, Contemporary Cultural Life, and Croatian Political History. Zagreb, 1944. Pp. 1174. Prof. Filip Lukas, Editor-in-Chief, and Dr. Vladimir Bazala and Dr. Nikola Peršić, Associate Editors. This is the only attempt in the Croatian language to present a comprehensive survey of Croatian culture. The war prevented the editors from carrying this project to a conclusion in the way in which they had planned.

Obzor Spomen-knjiga 1890–1935 / Memorial Book of "Obzor" (Daily newspaper) 1890–1935. Zagreb, 1935. Pp. 326. Edited by Dr. Milivoj Dežman and Dr. Rudolf Maixner.

Povijest hrvatskih zemalja Bosne i Hercegovine od najstarijih vremena do godine 1463 / A History of the Croatian Lands Bosnia and Hercegovina from the Most Ancient Times to the Year 1463. Book I: edited by Dr. Krunoslav Draganović. Sarajevo: Hrvatsko Kulturno Društvo "Napredak," 1942. Pp. vii + 853. No further books of this series have been published.

Spomenica Matice Hrvatske prigodom 1.000 godišnjice hrvatskoga kraljevstva / Memorial Book of Matica Hrvatska on the Occasion of the Millennial Anniversary of the Croatian Kingdom. Zagreb, 1925.

Sveslavenski Zbornik. Spomenica o tisućugodišnjici hrvatskoga kraljevstva / All-Slavic Symposium. A Memorial Book on the Occasion of the Millennial Anniversary of the Croatian Kingdom. Zagreb: Zajednica Slavenskih Društava, 1930.

Zbornik kralja Tomislava u spomen tisućugodišnjice hrvatskoga kraljevstva / The King Tomislav Symposium on the Occasion of the Millennial Anniversary of the Croatian Kingdom. Zagreb: Yugoslav Academy, 1925. Pp. cix + 681.

V. PUBLICATIONS OF THE YUGOSLAV ACADEMY OF SCIENCES AND ARTS

The publications of the Yugoslav Academy of Sciences and Arts in Zagreb are indispensable for all who wish to study the culture, history, language, and literature of the Croatian people, and to some extent of the other South Slavic peoples. The Yugoslav Academy and the University of Zagreb are the scientific research and publishing centers of Croatia. The Academy's research is developed primarily through eight departments, which are closely associated with fifteen institutes. The departments and institutes publish their research papers and findings periodically in collaborative works. The institutes and departments of the University of Zagreb publish their studies in their own *Zborniks* (Yearbooks of Scientific Contributions).

A list of all the publications of the Yugoslav Academy is found in *Popis izdanja Jugoslavenske Akademije Znanosti i Umjetnosti 1867–1950* / Catalogue of the Publications of the Yugoslav Academy, 1867–1950 (Zagreb, 1951, 521 pages). A new edition of this catalogue, which will include the ten years from 1950 to 1960 has not as yet been published. The Publishing Institute of the Yugoslav Academy sends out periodic catalogues, and the latest one, printed in Zagreb in 1960, contains all of the publications of the post-war period, 1945–1960.

A summary of the studies published in the periodicals of the Yugoslav Academy appears in French, German, and English in the *Bulletin international de l'Académie Yugoslave des Sciences et des Beaux-Arts* (Zagreb, 1882–). This publication also provides a summary of all contributions published in *Rad Jugoslavenske Akademije Znanosti i Umjetnosti.*

The following section lists first the publications of the Academy that are of general interest, and then the periodicals in which the contributions of each of the departments appear.

1. *General Reference Works*

Ljetopis Jugoslavenske Akademije Znanosti i Umjetnosti / A Chronicle of the Yugoslav Academy of Sciences and Arts. Zagreb, 1877– . This publication contains a report on events connected with the life of the YA, a list of its new members and their biographies, as well as necrologues of deceased members. It also publishes scientific contributions of its members who have been assisted by the YA.

Rad Jugoslavenske Akademije Znanosti i Umjetnosti / Work of the Yugoslav Academy of Sciences and Arts. Zagreb, 1867– .

Zbornik jugoslavenskih narodnih popjevaka / Collected Yugoslav Peoples' Melodies. Zagreb, 1924– . Franjo Kuhač and Dr. Vinko Žganec are engaged in collecting and publishing folk melodies from various Croatian regions.

Zbornik sadašnjih pravnih običaja u Južnih Slavena / Collected Present Customary Laws Among the South Slavs. Zagreb, 1874– . Baltazar Bogišić has collected worthwhile materials for the student of private and public law as it is found among the people.

Zbornik za narodni život i običaje Južnih Slavena / A Symposium on the Life and Customs of the South Slav People. Zagreb, 1896– . This publication contains papers on the folklore, ethnography, and ethnology of the Croatian people, and, in part, of other South Slavic peoples.

2. *Department of Literature, History of Literature, and Philology*

Dokumenti o piscima XX. stoljeća / Documentary Sources on Authors of the Twentieth Century. Zagreb, 1960– .

Filologija / Philology. Zagreb, 1957– . Contains excellent studies in linguistics and literary criticism, not only of Croatian language and literature, but of the other principal Western languages and literatures as well.

Gradja za povijest književnosti hrvatske / Source Materials for the History of Croatian Literature. Zagreb, 1897– .

Hrvatski latinisti / Croatian Latin Writers. Zagreb, 1951– .

Noviji pisci hrvatski / Modern Croatian Authors. Zagreb, 1949– . This publication lists works of nineteenth-century Croatian writers.

Stari pisci hrvatski / Early Croatian Writers. Zagreb, 1869– . The works of all Croatian writers preceding the Illyrian Movement are being published in this collection.

3. *Department of Mathematical, Physical, and Technical Sciences*

Rasprave Odjela za matematičke, fizičke i tehničke nauke / Studies of the Department of Mathematical, Physical and Technical Sciences. Zagreb, 1952– .

4. *Department of Medical Sciences, Medical Research, and Hygiene*

Arhiv za higijenu rada i toksikologiju / Archive for the Hygiene of Work and Toxicology. Zagreb, 1950– .

5. *Department of Music*

Djela suvremenih hrvatskih autora / Works of Contemporary Croatian Composers. Zagreb, 1959– .

Spomenici hrvatske muzičke prošlosti / Monuments of Croatian Musical History. Zagreb, 1957– .

6. *Department of Natural Sciences*

Palaeontologia jugoslavica. Zagreb, 1958– .

Prirodoslovna istraživanja / Natural Science Research. Zagreb, 1913– . This publication contains studies in geology, mineralogy, physical geography, biology, and related sciences.

7. *Department of Philosophy and Social Sciences (History, Archaeology, Law, Economics, Maritime Affairs)*

Codex Diplomaticus regni Croatiae, Dalmatiae et Slavoniae. Vol. 2. Zagreb, 1904– . First volume was never published. Historical documents of importance for the study of Croatian history are being published in this collection.

Gradja za gospodarsku povijest Hrvatske / Source Materials for the Economic History of Croatia. Zagreb, 1951– .

Gradja za noviju povijest Hrvatske / Source Materials for the Modern History of Croatia. Zagreb, 1950– .

Gradja za pomorsku povijest Dubrovnika / Source Materials for the Maritime History of Dubrovnik. Dubrovnik, 1954– . This is the publication of the Maritime Museum of the YA in Dubrovnik.

Jadranske monografije / Adriatic Monographs. Zagreb, 1955– . This publication contains research papers on various maritime affairs pertinent to the Croatian Adriatic coast.

Monumenta Catarensia–Kotorski Spomenici / Historical Monuments of the City of Kotor. Zagreb, 1951– .

Monumenta historica ragusina–Dubrovački Spomenici / Historical Documents of the City of Dubrovnik. Zagreb, 1951– .

Monumenta historico-juridica Slavorum meridionalium. Zagreb, 1868– . Important documents for Croatian legal history are being published in this collection.

Monumenta spectantia historiam Slavorum Meridionalium. Zagreb, 1868– . This is a collection of important Croatian historical documents.

Pomorsko Pravo / Maritime Law. Zagreb, 1951– . This is the publication of the Adriatic Institute of the YA in Zagreb. It contains not only studies on maritime law pertinent to the Adriatic Croatian coast, but many studies in international maritime law as well.

Prilozi novijoj jugoslavenskoj historiji / Contributions to Recent Yugoslav History. Zagreb, 1956– .

Prinosi proučavanju ekonomike ribarstva i ribarstvenog prava / Contributions to the Study of Economic and Legal Aspects of Fishing. Zagreb, 1955– .

Starine / Antiquities. Zagreb, 1869– . Studies in early Croatian history.

Starohrvatska Prosvjeta / Early Croatian Civilization. Zagreb, Series I: 1895–1904; Series II: 1926–1928; Series III: 1948– . The latest series is published by the Museum of Croatian Antiquities in Split. It contains research papers on the Croatian past, especially on its early period.

8. *Department of Plastic Arts*

Bulletin Instituta za Likovne Umjetnosti / Bulletin of the Institute for Plastic Arts. Zagreb, 1953– . This publication changed its name in 1959 to *Bulletin Odjela VII. za likovne umjetnosti* / Bulletin of Department VII for the Plastic Arts.

VI. MATICA HRVATSKA

A cultural institution that is widely known and cherished among the Croatians is Matica Hrvatska, which has devoted itself for over one hundred years to publishing the works of Croatian authors. Recently the comprehensive history and all-inclusive bibliography of Matica Hrvatska was published in one extremely useful volume: *Matica Hrvatska 1842–1962*, by Jakša Ravlić and Marin Somborac (Zagreb: Matica Hrvatska, 1963).

VII. ZEMALJSKI MUZEJ, SARAJEVO

This National Museum began publishing its yearbook, *Glasnik Zemaljskog Muzeja*, in 1889. For a bibliography of the articles published in this yearbook, see Rudolf Zaplata, *Inhaltsverzeichnis der wissenschaftlichen Mitteilungen*, Vols. I–XIII (Sarajevo: Državna štamparija, 1935). The book covers the years 1893–97, 1899, 1900, 1902, 1904, 1907, 1909, 1912, and 1914. The following two volumes continue this bibliography: Rudolf Zaplata, *Pregled Sadržaja Glasnika Zemaljskog muzeja u Sarajevu od 1889–1937 godine* (I–XLIX) / Survey of the Contents of the Bulletin of the National Museum in Sarajevo from 1889 to 1937 (Sarajevo: Državna štamparija, 1938); Vukosava Popović, *Pregled Sadržaja Glasnika Zemaljskog muzeja od 1938–1952* / Survey of the Contents of the Bulletin of the National Museum from 1938 to 1952 (Sarajevo: Državna štamparija, 1953).

APPENDIX C

GEOGRAPHICAL NAMES

Since a number of cultures have left traces on the lands today inhabited by the Croatians, it is helpful to know the most frequently used variant forms of Croatian place names. The Croatian names are followed in the list by any Croatian variants (*Cr.*), and by the appropriate ancient (*anc.*), English (*Eng.*), French (*Fr.*), German (*Ger.*), Greek (*Gr.*), Hungarian (*Hung.*), Italian (*It.*), Latin (*Lat.*), or other equivalents. The Croatian forms of some non-Croatian place names are also given. The abbreviation *obs.* is used to indicate a variant form that is now obsolete.

ADIDŽA; *see* Adige

ADIGE (river), *Cr.* Adidža, *Ger.* Etsch

ADRIATIC SEA, *Cr.* Jadransko More or Jadran

AEGEAN SEA, *Cr.* Egejsko More, *Serbian* Jegejsko More

AKVILEJA; *see* Aquileia

ALSACE (region of France), *anc.* Alsatia, *Cr.* Elzas, *Ger.* Elsass

ANCONA (Italy), *Cr.* Jakin (*obs.*)

AQUILEIA (Italy), *anc.* Aquileia, *medieval* Aglar, *Cr.* Oglaj (*obs.*) or Akvileja

ATENA; *see* Athenai

ATHENAI (Greece), *Cr.* Atena, *Serbian* Atina, *Eng.* Athens

BAKAR, *Lat.* Volcera, *It.* Buccari

BANOVIĆ; *see* Banovići

BANOVIĆI or Banović

BAR (Montenegro), *Gr.* Antibaris, *Lat.* Antibarum, *Albanian* Tìvari or Tivari, *It.* Antivari

BAŠKA (on the Island of Krk) or Baškanova, *It.* Besca (nuova)

BENKOVAC, *It.* Bencovazzo, *Ger.* Benkovatz

BEOGRAD (Serbia), *Lat.* Singidunum, *Fr.* and *Eng.* Belgrade, *It.* Belgrado

BERAM (near Pazin), *It.* Vermo

BIHAĆI; *see* Bijaći

BIJAĆI (near Trogir) a popular form of Bihaći

BIOGRAD or Biograd na moru (White City on the Sea), *It.* Zaravecchia

BIOKOVO (mountain), *It.* Monte Biloco or Monti Albii

BITOLA (Macedonia), *Cr.* Bitolj

BITOLJ; *see* Bitola

BJELOVAR, *Hung.* Belovár

BLATO (on the Island of Korčula), *It.* Blatta (di Curzola)

BOHEMIA (part of Czechoslovakia), *Cr.* Češka, *Czech* Čechy, *Ger.* Böhmen

BOKA KOTORSKA, *It.* Bocche di Cattaro, *Eng.* Gulf of Kotor

BOSANSKA GRADIŠKA, *Lat.* Servitium

BRAČ (island), *Lat.* Brattia, *It.* Brazza

BRATISLAVA (Czechoslovakia), *Cr.* Požun, *Ger.* Pressburg, *Hung.* Pozsony

BRIJUNI or Brioni (islands), *Lat.* Insulae Pullariae, *It.* Isole Brioni

BRIONI; *see* Brijuni

BROD, Brod na Savi, or Slavonski Brod, *Lat.* Marsonia

BROD NA SAVI; *see* Brod

BUCARESTI (Rumania), *Cr.* Bukurešt, *Eng.* Bucharest

BUDAPEST (Hungary), *Cr.* Budimpešta, Budim, or Pešta

BUDIM; *see* Budapest

BUDIMPEŠTA; *see* Budapest

BUDVA, *It.* Budua

BUKUREŠT; *see* Bucaresti

BURGENLAND (Austria), *Cr.* Gradišće

ČAKOVEC, *Ger.* Csakathurn, *Hung.* Csáktornya

CARIGRAD; *see* Istanbul

CARINTHIA (region in Central Europe), *Cr.* Koruška, *Ger.* Kärnten

CARNIOLA (region in Yugoslavia), *Cr.* Kranjska, *Ger.* Krain

CAUCASUS, *Cr.* Kavkaz

CAVTAT, *anc.* Epidaurus, *Lat.* Civitas Vetus, *It.* Ragusavecchia
CELJE (Slovenia), *anc.* Claudia Celeia, *It.* Cilli
CELOVAC; *see* Klagenfurt
ČEŠKA; *see* Bohemia
CETINA (river), *anc.* Tilurius
CHINA, *Cr.* Kina or Kitaj (*obs.*)
ĆIĆARIJA (region), *It.* Cicceria
ČIOVO (island), *Lat.* and *It.* Bua
CIPAR; *see* Cyprus
ČITLUK (near Sinj), *Lat.* Aequum
CRES (island), *Lat.* Crepsa; Cres and Lošinj had a common name in antiquity, Apsyrtides; *It.* Cherso
CRETE, *anc.* Creta or Candia, *Cr.* Kreta or Kandija (*obs.*), *Serbian* Krit
CRNA GORA, *Eng.* and *It.* Montenegro
CYPRUS, *Cr.* Cipar, *Serbian* Kipar
DALJ (near Osijek), *Lat.* Teutoburgium
DANSKA; *see* Denmark
DANUBE (river), *Cr.* Dunav; Danube River Basin, *Cr.* Podunavlje
DARUVAR, *Lat.* Aquae Balissae
DENMARK, *Cr.* Danska
DINARA (mountains), *It.* Alpi Dinariche
DJAKOVO, *Hung.* Diakovár
DJURDJEVAC or Gjurgjevac, *Ger.* Sankt Georgen
DRAČ; *see* Durrës
DRAGONJA (river), *It.* Dragogna
DRAVA (river), *Ger.* Drau, *Hung.* Dráva; Drava River Basin, *Cr.* Podravina
DRAŽDJANI; *see* Dresden
DRENOPOLJE; *see* Edirne
DRESDEN (Germany), *Cr.* Draždjani (*obs.*)
DRVENIK (island), *It.* Zirona
DUBROVNIK, *Gr.* Rausion, *Lat.* Rhagusium or Racusa, *It.* Ragusa
DUGI OTOK (island), *It.* Isola Lunga or Isola Grossa
DUNAV; *see* Danube
DURRËS (Albania), *Lat.* Dyrrachium, *Cr.* Drač, *It.* and *Eng.* Durazzo, *Turkish* Dradj, Draj, or Draç
DUVNO or Tomislav-Grad, *Lat.* Delminium
EDIRNE (Turkey), *anc.* Adrianopolis or Hadrianopolis, formerly Adrianople, *Cr.* Jedrene or Drenopolje
EGEJSKO MORE; *see* Aegean Sea
EGYPT, *Cr.* Egipat or Misir (biblical)
EISENSTADT (town in Burgenland, Austria), *Cr.* Železno (*obs.*), *Hung.* Kismarton
ELBE (river), *Cr.* Laba
ELZAS; *see* Alsace
ERDELJ; *see* Transylvania
FALAČKA; *see* Palatinate
FILIPJAKOV, *It.* Santi Filippo e Giacomo
FIRENCA; *see* Firenze
FIRENZE, *Cr.* Firenca, *Eng.* and *Fr.* Florence
GALIPOLJE; *see* Gallipoli
GALLIPOLI (Turkey), *Cr.* Galipolje
GENÈVE, *Cr.* Ženeva, *Eng.* Geneva; Lake of Geneva, *Cr.* Ženevsko Jezero
GERMANY, *Cr.* Njemačka
GJURGJEVAC; *see* Djurdjevac
GORNJI GRAD; *see* Grič
GRADAC; *see* Graz
GRADEŽ; *see* Grado
GRADIŠĆE; *see* Burgenland
GRADO (on the Adriatic, near Aquileia, Italy), *Cr.* Gradež (*obs.*)
GRAZ (Austria), *Cr.* (Štajerski) Gradac (*obs.*)
GRIČ or Gornji Grad, part of the city of Zagreb
GRUŽ, *It.* Gravosa
HAVAJI; *see* Hawaii
HAWAII, *Cr.* Havaji
HERCEG-NOVI, *It.* Castelnuovo (di Cattaro)
HUNGARY, *Cr.* Madjarska, Madžarska, or Ugarska
HVAR (island), *Gr.* Pharos, *Lat.* Pharia or Pharus, *It.* Lesina
IMOTSKI, *It.* Imoschi
IST (island), *It.* Isto
ISTANBUL (Turkey), *anc.* Byzantium, *Cr.* Carigrad, Stambol (*obs.*) or Stambul (*obs.*), *Fr.* and *Eng.* Constantinople
IŽ (island), *Lat.* Esum, *It.* Eso
JABUKA (island), *It.* Pomo

JADRAN; *see* Adriatic Sea
JADRANSKO MORE; *see* Adriatic Sea
JAKIN; *see* Ancona
JEDRENE; *see* Edirne
KALAMOTA; *see* Koločep
KANDIJA; *see* Crete
KARLOVAC, *Ger.* Karlstadt, *Hung.* Károlyváros
KASTAV, *It.* Castua
KAŠTEL-SUĆURAC, *see* Sućurac
KAŠTELA KOD SPLITA, *It.* Castelli di Spalato
KAVKAZ; *see* Caucasus
KERKYRA (Greece), *anc.* Corcyra, *Cr.* Krf, *Eng.* Corfu
KINA; *see* China
KITAJ; *see* China
KLAGENFURT (Austria), *Cr.* Celovac, *Slovenian* Celovec
KLIS, *It.* Clissa
KNIN, *It.* Tenin
KOLOČEP (island) or Kalamota, *It.* Calamotta
KOPAR, *It.* Capodistria
KOPRIVNICA, *Ger.* Kopreinitz, *Hung.* Kapronca
KORČULA, *Lat.* Corcyra Nigra, *It.* Curzola
KORUŠKA; *see* Carinthia
KOTOR, *Gr.* Dekatera, *Lat.* Catharum, *It.* Cattaro
KRALJEVICA, *It.* Porto Re
KRANJSKA; *see* Carniola
KREMLIN, *Cr.* Kremlj
KREMLJ; *see* Kremlin
KRETA; *see* Crete
KRF; *see* Kerkyra
KRIŽEVCI, *Ger.* Kreuz, *Hung.* Kőrös
KRK (island), *Lat.* Curicum or Curicta, *It.* Veglia
KRKA (river), *Lat.* Titius, *It.* Cherca
KVARNER, *It.* Quarnaro or Carnaro
LABA; *see* Elbe
LANGOBARDIJA; *see* Lombardy
LASTOVO (island), *Lat.* Ladesta, *It.* Lágosta
LAVOV; *see* Lwiw
LEIPZIG, *Cr.* Lipsko (*obs.*)
LIPSKO; *see* Leipzig
LISABON; *see* Lisboa
LISBOA, *anc.* Olisipo, later Felicitas Julia; *Cr.* Lisabon, *Eng.* Lisbon
LOMBARDY, *Cr.* Langobardija, *It.* Lombardia
LORRAINE, *Cr.* Lotaringija, *Ger.* Lothringen
LOŠINJ MALI (*see* Cres), *It.* Lussinpiccolo
LOŠINJ VELI, *It.* Lussingrande
LOTARINGIJA; *see* Lorraine
LOURDES, *Cr.* Lurd
LOVĆEN (mountain), *It.* Monte Leone
LOVRAN, *It.* Laurana
LURD; *see* Lourdes
LUSATIA (region in Germany), *Cr.* Lužica, *Ger.* Lausitz
LUŽICA; *see* Lusatia
LWIW (Ukraine), *Cr.* Lavov, *Eng.* Lvov, *Polish* Lwow
MADJARSKA; *see* Hungary
MADŽARSKA; *see* Hungary
MAIN (river), *Cr.* Majna
MAJNA; *see* Main
MAKARSKA, *It.* Macarsca
MARIBOR (Slovenia), *Ger.* Marburg
MARMARA, Sea of, *Cr.* Mramorno More
MARTINŠĆICA, *It.* San Martino in Valle
MAUN (island), *It.* Maon or Maoni
MEDITERRANEAN SEA, *Cr.* Sredozemlje or Sredozemno More
MEDJIMURJE or Medjumurje (region)
MEDJUMURJE; *see* Medjimurje
METKOVIĆ, *It.* Metcovich
MISIR; *see* Egypt
MITROVICA; *see* Srijemska Mitrovica
MLECI; *see* Venezia
MLETAKA; *see* Venezia
MLJET (island), *It.* Meleda
MOHAĆ; *see* Mohács
MOHÁCS (Hungary), *Cr.* Mohać
MOLAT (island), *It.* Melada
MONAKOV; *see* München
MRAMORNO MORE; *see* Marmara
MUĆ (near Split), *It.* Mucci
MÜNCHEN (Germany), *Fr.* and *Eng.* Munich, *It.* Monaco di Baviera *Cr.* Monakov (*obs.*)
MURA (river), *Ger.* Mur

MURTER (island), *It.* Morter
NAPOLI, *anc.* Neapolis, *Cr.* Napulj, *Ger.* Neapel, *Fr.* and *Eng.* Naples
NAPULJ; *see* Napoli
NERETVA (river), *Lat.* Naro, *It.* Narenta
NEREŽIŠĆE (on the Island of Brač), *It.* Neresi
NETHERLANDS, *Cr.* Nizozemska
NIN, *It.* Nona
NIZOZEMSKA; *see* Netherlands
NJEMAČKA; *see* Germany
NOVI, Novi Vindolski or Vinodol
NOVI VINDOLSKI; *see* Novi
ODER (river), *Cr.* Odra
ODRA; *see* Oder
OGLAJ; *see* Aquileia
OLIB (island), *It.* Ulbo
OLOVO (a mine), *Lat.* Plumbum
OMIŠ, *Lat.* Almissium, *It.* Almissa
OPATIJA, *It.* Abazzia
ORMOŽ (Slovenia), *Ger.* Friedau
OSIJEK, *Lat.* Mursa, *Ger.* Esseg, *Hung.* Eszek
OŠLJE (near Ston), *It.* Oseglie
PAD; *see* Po
PAG (island), *It.* Pago
PALATINATE (region in Germany), *Cr.* Falačka, *Ger.* Pfalz
PARIS, *Lat.* Lutetia (Parisiorum), *Cr.* Pariz, *Ger.* and *Eng.* Paris
PARIZ; *see* Paris
PAŠMAN (island), *Lat.* Postumiana, *It.* Pasman
PAZIN, *It.* Pisino
PEČ; *see* Pécs
PÉCS (Hungary), *Cr.* Pečuh (*obs.*) or Peč, *Serbian* Pečuj (*obs.*)
PEČUH; *see* Pécs
PELJEŠAC (peninsula) or Stonski Rat, *It.* Sabbioncello
PERAST, *It.* Perasto
PEŠTA; *see* Budapest
PETROVARADIN, *Ger.* Peterwardein, *Hung.* Pétervárad
PIRINEJI; *see* Pyrenees
PLANINSKI KANAL; *see* Velebit Channel
PLITVICE; *see* Plitvička Jezera
PLITVIČKA JEZERA or Plitvice, English Plitvice Lakes
PO (river, Italy), *Cr.* Pad
PODGORSKI KANAL; *see* Velebit Channel
PODRAVINA; *see* Drava
PODUNAVLJE; *see* Danube
PORAJNJE; *see* Rhine
POREČ, *Lat.* Parentium, *It.* Parenzo
POSAVINA; *see* Sava
POŽUN; *see* Bratislava
PRAG; *see* Praha
PRAHA (Czechoslovakia), *Ger.* and *Cr.* Prag, *Fr.* and *Eng.* Prague
PROVANSA; *see* Provence
PROVENCE (region in France), *Cr.* Provansa
PRVIĆ (island), *It.* Pervicchio
PTUJ (Slovenia), *Lat.* Petovia
PULA, *Lat.* Pietas Iulia, *Slovenian* Pulj, *It.* Pola
PYRENEES (mountains), *Cr.* Pirineji, *Spanish* Pirineos, *Serbian* Pireneji
RAB (island), *Lat.* Arva, *It.* Arbe
RAJNA; *see* Rhine
RAŠA (river), *It.* Arsa
RHINE (river), *Cr.* Rajna; Rhine River Basin, *Cr.* Porajnje
RIJEKA, *It.* Fiume
RIM; *see* Roma
ROMA, *Cr.* Rim, *Fr.* and *Eng.* Rome, *Ger.* Rom
ROVINJ, *It.* Rovigno (d'Istria)
SAD; *see* USA
SASKA; *see* Saxony
SAVA (river), *Lat.* Savus, *Ger.* Sau, *Hung.* Száva; Sava River Basin, *Cr.* Posavina
SAVINJA (river), *Ger.* Sann
SAXONY, *Cr.* Saska, *Ger.* Sachsen
SĆEDRO (island), *It.* Torcola
SEDMOGRADSKA; *see* Transylvania
SELCA (on the Island of Brač), *It.* Selza
SENJ, *Lat.* Senia, *It.* Segna, *Ger.* Zengg
SESTRUNJ (island), *It.* Sestrugno or Sestro
SHKODËR or Shkodra (Albania), *anc.* Scodra, *Cr.* Skadar, *Turkish* Iskenderiye, *It.* and *Eng.* Scutari
ŠIBENIK, *It.* Sebenico

SIGET; *see* Szigetvár
SILBA (island), *It.* Selve
SINJ, *It.* Signo
ŠIPAN (island), *It.* Giuppana
SISAK, *Lat.* Siscia or Segestica
SKADAR; *see* Shkodër
SKOPJE (Macedonia), *anc.* Scupi, *Cr.* Skoplje, *Turkish* Üsküb
SKOPLJE; *see* Skopje
SKRADIN, *It.* Scardona
SLOVONSKI BROD; *see* Brod
SMRDELJE (near Skradin), *It.* Lentischeto
SNJEŽNIK (mountain), *Slovenian* Snežnik, *It.* Monte Nevoso, *Ger.* Schneeberg
SOLIN, *Lat.* Salona, *It.* Salona
ŠOLTA; *see* Sulet
SOLUN; *see* Thessalonike
SPIČ, *It.* Santa Maria degli Ospizi
SPLIT, *Gr.* Aspalathos, *Lat.* Spalatum, *It.* Spalato
SPREE (river), *Cr.* Spreva (*obs.*)
SPREVA; *see* Spree
SREBRENICA or Srebrnica, *Lat.* Domavia
SRBRNICA; *see* Srebrenica
SREDOZEMLJE; *see* Mediterranean
SREDOZEMNO MORE; *see* Mediterranean
SRIJEM (region), *Serbian* Srem, *Ger.* Syrmien, *Hung.* Szerém
SRIJEMSKA MITROVICA or Mitrovica, *Serbian* Sremska Mitrovica, *Lat.* Sirmium
SRIJEMSKI KARLOVCI or Karlovci, *Serbian* Sremski Karlovci, *Ger.* Karlowitz
ŠTAJERSKA; *see* Styria
STAMBOL; *see* Istanbul
STAMBUL; *see* Istanbul
STARIGRAD (on the Island of Hvar), *It.* Cittavecchia
STON, *Lat.* Stagnum, *It.* Stagno
STONSKI RAT; *see* Pelješac
STYRIA (region in Austria), *Cr.* Štajerska, *Ger.* Steiermark
SUĆURAC or Kaštel-Sućurac, *It.* Castel San Giorgio
SUĆURAJ (on the Island of Hvar), *It.* San Giorgio (di Lesina)
SULET or Šolta, *Lat.* Solentia, *It.* Solta
SUPETAR (on the Island of Brač), *It.* San Pietro (di Brazza)
SUPETARSKA DRAGA (on the Island of Rab), *It.* San Pietro in Valle or Valle di San Pietro
SUŠAK, *It.* sometimes Porto Baross
SUTOMORE, *Lat.* Sancta Maria, *It.* Santa Maria
ŠVAJCARSKA; *see* Switzerland
SVETI VID; *see* Vidova Gora
ŠVICARSKA; *see* Switzerland
SWITZERLAND, *Cr.* Švicarska or Švajcarska
SZIGETVÁR, formerly Sziget (Hungary), *Cr.* Siget
TARANTO (Italy), *anc.* Tarentum, *Cr.* Tarent
TARENT; *see* Taranto
TEMZA; *see* Thames
THAMES (river), *Cr.* Temza
THESSALONIKE (Greece), *Cr.* Solun, *Eng.* Salonica, Salonika, or Saloniki
TKON (on the Island of Pašman), *It.* Tuconio
TRANSYLVANIA or Ardeal (Rumania), *Cr.* Transilvanija, Erdelj (*obs.*), or Sedmogradska (*obs.*), *Hung.* Erdely, *Ger.* Siebenbürgen
TRENTO (Italy), *anc.* Tridentum, *Cr.* Trident, *Eng.* Trent
TRIDENT; *see* Trento
TRIESTE (Italy), *anc.* Tergeste, *Slovenian* and *Cr.* Trst, *Ger.* Triest
TRILJ (near Sinj), *It.* Treglia
TROGIR, *Gr.* Tragurion, *Lat.* Tragurium, *It.* Traù
TRSAT, *Lat.* Tarsatica, *It.* Tersatto
TRST; *see* Trieste
TRVIŽ, *It.* Terviso
UČKA (mountain), *It.* Monte Maggiore
UGARSKA; *see* Hungary
ULCINJ, *Lat.* Ulcinium, *It.* Dulcigno
UNIJE (island), *It.* Unie
USA, *Cr.* SAD (Sjedinjene Američke Države) or USA
VANDEJA; *see* Vendée
VARAŽDIN, *Lat.* Aqua Viva, *Ger.* Warasdin, *Hung.* Varasd
VARSAVA; *see* Warszawa

VELEBIT (mountain), *It.* Alpi Bebie
VELEBIT CHANNEL, *Cr.* Velebitski Kanal, Podgorski Kanal, or Planinski Kanal, *It.* Canal della Morlacca
VELEBITSKI KANAL; *see* Velebit Channel
VENDÉE (region in France), *Cr.* Vandeja
VENEZIA, *Lat.* Venetia, *Cr. Mleci* (Genitive: Mletaka), *Eng.* Venice
VIDOVA GORA (mountain on the Island of Brač), Vidovica, or Sveti Vid, *It.* San Vito
VIDOVICA; *see* Vidova Gora
VINODOL; *see* Novi
VIR (island), *It.* Puntadura
VIS (island), *Lat.* Issa, *It.* Lissa
VISLA; *see* Vistula
VISTULA (river), *Cr.* Visla
VOGEZI; *see* Vosges
VOLOSKO (suburb of Opatija), *It.* Volosca
VOSGES (mountain), *Cr.* Vogezi
VUKOVAR, *Lat.* Valdasus, *Hung.* Vukovár
WARSZAWA, *Cr.* Varšava, *Eng.* Warsaw
WIEN, *Lat.* Vindobona, *Cr.* Beč, *It.* and *Eng.* Vienna
WROCLAW (Poland), *Cr.* Breslava (*obs.*), *Ger.* Breslau
ZADAR, *Gr.* Diadora, *Lat.* Jadera, *It.* Zara
ZAGORA (Dalmatian hinterland), *It.* Il Montano
ZAGREB, *Lat.* Zagrabia, *Ger.* Agram, *It.* Zagabria
ŽELEZNO; *see* Eisenstadt
ZEMUN, *Ger.* Semlin, *Hung.* Zimony
ŽENEVA; *see* Genève
ŽENEVSKO JEZERO; *see* Genève
ZENICA, *Lat.* Bistue Nova
ZIDANI MOST (Slovenia), *Ger.* Steinbrück
ŽIRJE (island), *It.* Zuri
ZLARIN (island), *It.* Slarino
ZRMANJA (river), *Lat.* Tedanium, *It.* Zermagna
ŽUT (Island), *It.* Zut

APPENDIX D

Pronunciation of Croatian Letters

In the Croatian language, a Latin alphabet, consisting of thirty letters, is used. Five of these letters correspond to vowel sounds, and the rest to consonant sounds. With four exceptions, which are indicated below, each letter represents one definite speech sound, and each sound corresponds to one definite letter.

CONSONANTS

Croatian	*English*	*English Pronunciation*
c	ts	ca*ts*—always, even before *a*, *o*, and *u*.
č	ch	*ch*ur*ch*
ć	sh	as in hi*t you*.
š	t(+y)	*sh*oe
ž	z (+y)	vi*si*on, plea*su*re
dj, gj	j	as in di*d you*.
dž	d(+y)	*j*udge
g	g	go, even before *e* and *i*
j	y	*y*outh, *y*ell
lj	ll (+y)	mi*lli*on
nj	n (+y)	ca*ny*on, o*ni*on
r	r	*r*oom

The remaining consonant sounds (b, d, f, h, k, l, m, n, p, s, t, v, z) correspond closely to the English pronunciation of the same letters.

VOWELS

a	a	f*a*ther
e	e	b*e*st
i	ee	k*ee*n
o	au	c*au*ght
u	oo	sm*oo*th
r (syllabic)	—	no equivalent

APPENDIX E

Sponsors and Assistants

The editors owe a special debt of gratitude to the following six sponsors for their exceptionally generous support toward the publication of this book: Dr. Ivan Tuskan and his wife, Dr. Maria Tuskan, Cincinnati, Ohio; Mr. George Bubany, Mr. Ray Kauzlarich, and Mr. Joseph Plese, all of Gallup, New Mexico; and Rev. Innocent M. Bojanic, O.P., Chicago, Illinois. The editors also wish to express their thanks to the following individuals and institutions who helped in the preparation of this volume, either by giving generously of their time and talents or by making financial contributions as sponsors.

ADVERTISERS

Croatian Radio-Hour Producers:
Birek, John, Cleveland, Ohio
Glavanić, Charles, London, Ontario
Ivanus, Theodore B., Cleveland, Ohio
Mehes, Mirko, Sudbury, Ontario
Prepolec, John, Detroit, Michigan

Croatian Papers and Journals:
Croatia Press, News Bulletin and Comment, New York, N.Y.
Croatian Courier, Detroit, Michigan
Danica (Morning Star), Chicago, Illinois
Hrvatska Revija (Croatian Review: cultural and literary quarterly journal), Buenos Aires, Argentina
Hrvatski Glas (Croatian newspaper), Winnipeg, Manitoba
Naša Nada, Newspaper of the Croatian Catholic Union, Gary, Indiana
Nova Hrvatska (New Croatia), London, England
Zajedničar (Newspaper of the Croatian Fraternal Union), Pittsburgh, Pennsylvania

American Dailies:
Cleveland Plain Dealer, August 2, 1958
Cleveland Press, July 31, 1958
The Detroit News, January 4, 1958
Farrell Press, August 15, 1958

COPYREADERS

Bittner, Miss Frances, St. Louis, Missouri
Giletti, Mrs. Bruno J., Providence, Rhode Island
Hren, Rev. Innocent, Oak Park, Illinois
La Du, Robert R., Milwaukee, Wisconsin
Lane, Ronald, Collegeville, Minnesota
Zrims, Rudolf, Columbus, Ohio

DONORS OF ILLUSTRATIONS

Gal, Miro, New York, N.Y.
Paulin, Philip, Milwaukee, Wisconsin
Pintar, John, New York, N.Y.
Reichercer, Lucijan, New York, N.Y.
Stromar-Mirenić, Vitomir, Vienna, Austria

SUPPORTERS

Croatian Board of Trade, Detroit, Michigan
Kamber, Rev. Charles, Toronto, Ontario
Marr, Very Reverend John E., Chicago, Illinois
Meštrović, Ivan
Ostović, Pavle, Montreal, P.Q.
Prepolec, John, Detroit, Michigan
Simčić, Rev. Milan, Rome, Italy
Sullivan, Msgr. John A., Charlottetown, P.E.I.

TRANSLATORS

Izzo, John, Albuquerque, New Mexico
Labash, Miss Betty, Toronto, Ontario
Malenica, Mira, Chicago, Illinois
Mueller, Miss Mechthild, St. Paul, Minnesota
Verbanac, Sister Anthony Marie, Kettle Falls, Washington
Whiton, Mrs. J. N., St. Paul, Minnesota
Zečević, Rev. Serafin, Regina, Sask.

TYPISTS

Bartels, Mrs. Gloria, Minneapolis, Minnesota
Bozivich, Mrs. Jeanette, St. Paul, Minnesota
Breimhurst, Miss Rose, St. Paul, Minnesota
Dominican Mission Sisters, Chicago, Illinois
Dorfer, Mrs. Maria, Santa Rosa, California
Pavlich, Miss Ann, St. Paul, Minnesota
Plinski, Mrs. Eileen, Winona, Minnesota
Verbanac, Sister Anthony Marie, Kettle Falls, Washington
Winze, Miss Jeri, Milwaukee, Wisconsin

SPONSORS

Individuals

Budrovich, Rev. Stephen V., Chicago, Illinois
Chukman, Louis, Chicago, Illinois
Derpich, Nicholas, Watsonville, California
Drazenovich, Paul, Fairbanks, Alaska
Dubičanac, Stjepan, Montreal, P.Q.
Goggins, Rev. Ralph, Winona, Minnesota
Golik, Rev. Stanley, North Bend, Nebraska
Gračanin, Vlado, Cincinnati, Ohio
Hatić, Osman, Cincinnati, Ohio
Hraščanec, Rev. Rudolf, Kenmore, Pennsylvania
Ivandich, Rev. Louis, Windsor, Ontario
Juricek, Msgr. John, Omaha, Nebraska
Kamber, Rev. Charles, Toronto, Ontario
Kisić, Ivo, Caracas, Venezuela
Koenig, Georgia, Cincinnati, Ohio
Kolega, Bruno, Washington, D.C.
Koludrovich, Viktor, Cleveland, Ohio
Kufrin, Paul, Chicago, Illinois
Livajušić, Rev. Anthony, Canton, Ohio
Majnarich, George J.
Meštrović, Ivan
Oreskovich, Mr. and Mrs. Stephen, Butte, Montana
Poduje, Jozo, New York, N.Y.
Rusko, Marko, Montreal, P.Q.
Savinovich, Mrs. Maria, Guayaquil, Ecuador
Šikić, Ante, Cincinnati, Ohio
Šimić, Petar, Caracas, Venezuela
Starcevich, Stephen, San Francisco, California
Torbar, Esteban, Caracas, Venezuela
Unger, Mr. and Mrs. Paul, Cleveland, Ohio
Vodarich, Mrs. Domenika, San Francisco, California

Organizations

Canadian Croatian Club, Ottawa, Ontario
Croatian Association of Venezuela, Caracas, Venezuela
Croatian Board of Trade, Detroit, Michigan
Croatian Catholic Union, Gary, Indiana
Croatian Dominican Sisters, Windsor Mills, P.Q.
Jami 'at el Islam, San Francisco, California

FUND RAISERS

Individuals

Verbanac, Sister Anthony Marie, Kettle Falls, Washington
Kolak, Nicholas, St. Paul, Minnesota
Spraitz, Anthony, St. Paul, Minnesota

Organizations

American Croatian Academic Club, Cleveland, Ohio
Canadian Croatian Club, Sudbury, Ont.
Croatian Central Committee, Milwaukee, Wisconsin

Index

1918–41